THE OKLAHOMA CITY BOMBING
and the POLITICS OF TERROR

David Hoffman

FERAL HOUSE

The Oklahoma City Bombing and the Politics of Terror © 1998 David Hoffman

ISBN 0-922915-49-0

Feral House
2532 Lincoln Blvd. Suite 359
Venice, CA 90291

Design by Linda Hayashi

10 9 8 7 6 5 4 3 2 1

"You shall know

the truth and

the truth shall

make you mad."

—Aldous Huxley

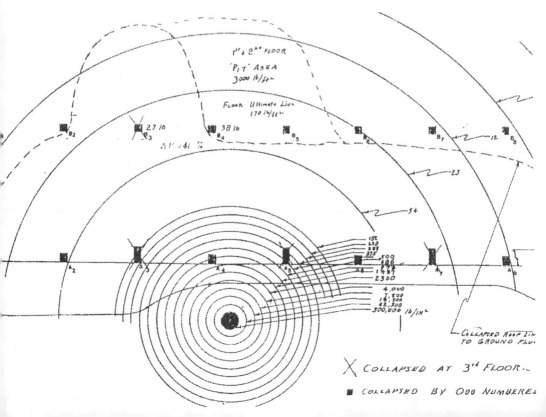

This book is dedicated to Ace Hayes,

my friend and primary mentor, who passed

away as this book went to press. As a

speaker, and through his small newspaper,

the *Portland Free Press*, Ace hammered away

at the establishment with a loquacious

cynicism and wit. Ace fought the battle

with both pen and sword, dodging the law

on the front lines of the trenches. He was

both inspirational and instrumental in

bringing this book to light. His friendship

and counsel will be sorely missed.

Note: The names of certain individuals have been changed and noted in the text. Libel law does not make generous allowances for the use of real names in the case of a person who has not been officially indicted, or who has not gone public (i.e., been previously interviewed in print or TV), or who is not a public figure.

ACKNOWLEDGEMENTS

The author would like to gratefully acknowledge the help and assistance of the following people, without whose help this story could not have been told: Melissa Klinzing and Brad Edwards, KFOR-TV, Nolan Clay, *Daily Oklahoman*, Rodney Bowers, *Arkansas Democrat Gazette*, Larry Myers and Rich Azar at *Media Bypass*, Juval Aviv of Interfor, Don Browning, Jon Rappaport, author of *Oklahoma bombing: The Supressed Truth*, Michele Moore, author of *Oklahoma City: Day One*, former DEA agent Mike Levine, Jesse Clear, Mark Sanford, Paul Friend, *Idaho News Observer*, video producer Chuck Allen, *Oklahoma City: What Really Happened?*, J. D. Cash and Jeff Holladay of *The McCurtain County Gazette*, Britt Anderson and the writers at *Mother Jones*, *The Village Voice*, Frances McMorris, *The Wall Street Journal*, Mike Whitely, Mike Vanderbeough, Mike Kemp, Ted Gunderson, Steve Wilmsen and Mark Eddy of the *Denver Post*, Mark Schafer, *Arizona Republic*, Ambrose Evans-Pritchard, *London Sunday Telegraph*, Clayton Douglas, *The Free American*, Charlie Hatfield, *Ellis County Press*, Brian Redman, *Conspiracy Nation*, Ben Partin, Tony Sgarlatti, The folks at the BBC, Sarah McClendon, Bob Hall, *Conspiracy Nation*, Ken Armstrong, Rita Cosby, Fox News, John Mattes, Julian Share, CBC, Louis Champon, Roger Bunn, Rick Sherrow, Audrey Cummings, Moshe Tal, Stu Webb, Glenn Wilburn, Pat Briley, Monte Cooley, *Idaho Observer*, *The Free American*, Hoppy Heidelberg, Eric Lighter, Bill Key, Martin Keating, Linda Thompson, Ramona McDonald, Anthony J. Hilder, Robert Bickel, Tony Scarlatti, Dr. Rick Nelson, Robert Jerlow, Robert Peterson, Jason at CBS archives, David Parker, Billy at the *Daily Oklahoman* library, and the librarians at the *Washington Post*, *New York Times*, *Dallas Morning News*, *Los Angeles Times*, *Miami Herald*, *Toronto Star*, *Covert Action Quarterly*, and others, Joe Taylor at Newstrack in Tulsa, Oklahoma, Ann Bradley and Christie, and others in Stephen Jones' office, D'Ferdinand Carone, the clerks in the Oklahoma county and federal courts, and scores of others who have selflessly provide information from their own research and investigations into this and other scandals.

My publisher, Adam Parfrey, who instinctively understood the significance of this crime, and, took a chance on me when none of the big publishers would.

State Representative Charles Key, who became a good friend. A man whose humor, faith, and courage to stand up and publicly question the governments' official line, putting his life and his career on the line, became an anchor for us all.

Jayna Davis of KFOR, the original lead investigator on the Middle Eastern angle, eventhough the New York Times Broadcasting Company shut down her investigation and took away her helicopter and cell phone.

David Hall of KPOC-TV, who gave me leads I wouldn't have gotten anywhere else. Last I heard, the IRS was screwing with Hall because of his courageous work on the Waco case.

Craig Roberts, whose humor, patience and generosity proved invaluable. Craig was a staunch ally whose tenacity and good humor proved an inspiration when I became frustrated (which was pretty often).

Craig's cop friend Randy, who sneaked into the NCIC now and then when we needed it.

Leslie Jorgensen, (*Newsweek* and *U.S. News & World Report*) a great gal with a marvelous sense of humor, who kept me up to date on the latest gossip and straightened me out about certain lawyers.

Gene Wheaton, who took me for a circuitous ride through the desert to talk to me in a scene reminiscent of Mr. "X" in the movie JFK, then regaled me mostly with personal stories about his interesting life.

Bill McCoy, who provided humorous translations for Wheaton's conspiracy theory theories, and was instrumental in keeping "scribblers" like me on the path. May he rest in peace.

Sherman Skolnick, my other mentor, who never let me forget how many years he's been in the business, and reminded me that I have a long way to go,

Will Northrop, "Matzo-Ball Charlie," who claimed to work for every Israeli intelligence agency *except* the Mossad, then took me for $1600 to sip Margaritas in Florida.

Mike Johnston, who accused me of stealing his book, *Abu-Nidal: A Gun For Hire,* when he knows full well that it was stolen by Chinese cleaning ladies and used as Won Ton wrappers.

James "Jimmy" Rothstein, whose openness, patience, and selflessness proved to be a guiding light in the murky and confusing world of spooks and criminals.

Mien Furher, Al Martin, Iran-Contra "insider extraodinaire," whose still waiting for his $100,000 retainer fee.

Bill Jasper of the John Birch Society, who is convinced it really is all a Communist plot.

George Wallace who introduced me to Jasper and kept the Commie hunters off my back.

Roger Cravens, Dave Rydel, Claire Wolfe, and other Patriots who posted important and much-needed information on the state of our nation on the

Patriots' Information Mailing List (PIML); and Ian Goddard, Bob Hall, and others who did the same on the OKBOMB mailing list.

Laurie Mylroie of the Foreign Policy Institute, for her in-depth analysis of the Iraqis and the World Trade Center bombing.

Terry Cook, for his videos and books, and his excellent and comprehensive research on the staggering new technology that is taking control over our lives.

Jim Levine, and Terry and Kelly, who handled our account and especially Jim's mother, who made me Chicken soup when I was sick.

And finally, Mr. "M," without out who's generous financial support, none of this would have been possible.

And I can't leave out all those people who, although aware of the efforts of the authors and others in attempting to bring this information to the public, were either indifferent, or actually obstructed these efforts. The first of these honors goes to the so-called "Justice" Department and the FBI. And to the state Attorney General, Drew Edmondson, and the local District Attorney in Oklahoma City, Bob Macy, who has an annoying tendency to talk out of both sides of his mouth. Oh, Bob, what *is* that stench?!

And the supervisors of the business office of Southwestern Bell and specifically Mr. Edwards and Mr. Dave Lopez, President of SWB, whose cold, callous, indifference and lack of empathy when I became behind on my phone bill resulted in the termination of my phone service for three weeks, my poor old mother thinking I was dead, and the interruption of our investigation, which they were fully aware of.

And the kind and generous folks of M.C.I. Communications, who not only refused to sponsor our investigation, they never even sent a reply to my inquiry. May they and the principals of SWB rot in Hell.

And ultimately, all my friends who have kept me [partially] same throughout the years, eventhough conspiracies have a way of making one come unglued: Ron Ulfohn, Joe Williams, John Flores, David Wills, Jon and Lisa, and all those helpful souls I've undoubtedly missed, including my parents (although I'm not sure they've helped me keep sane).

FOREWORD

On April 19, 1995 when I heard the news (and literally heard the explosion) of the Murrah building, I was dumbfounded. As the realization sunk in that so many people and children were killed, I, along with millions of others watching the news coverage, felt that indescribable, overwhelming sensation in the pit of my stomach.

Yet as the "story" unfolded, my spirits were lifted as I saw example after example of sheer human compassion and an outpouring of unblemished, unconditional love flow forth in a far greater degree than I had ever seen in any venue of life, including and especially in political circles.

However, during the intense media coverage that followed, inconsistencies began emerging. Stories kept changing and although I couldn't see the emerging political angle, I could sense it. Those who dared oppose the revisionist news accounts were ostracized, mocked, discredited, dark-cornered, etc. I know. I was one who dared to be politically incorrect.

At some point it became painfully apparent that there was more wrong than right with the federal investigation. That is when I had a very tough decision to make. Should I sit and do nothing and remain in my comfort zone simply "playing the part" of the caring politician for the photo ops? Or should I really do the right thing even if it meant giving the phrase "politically incorrect" a whole new dimension?

It didn't take long after discussing it with my wife to determine that I had to do the right thing—no matter what the consequences were to be. Having come to that conclusion, I decided to go forward to search out the truth and tell it to a waiting world. Journalists, concerned citizens, and a few ex-law enforcement officers, have made many personal sacrifices to bring this truth to the American people.

In response, the major media launched unheard of attacks against our desire to conduct constitutionally sound and proper investigations. *The Daily Oklahoman* and the *Tulsa World* have published nine separate editorials viciously attacking me, Glenn Wilburn and all those who have stood up and demanded all of the truth about this terrible crime.

An editorial from the *Daily Oklahoman* entitled, "Drop It, Mr. Key" even had the audacity to say:

As we argued when Key first set out on this course, the Legislature and its staff had no business investigating the bombing. It was, and is, poorly equipped to do so. The same can be said of a panel of local citizens.

People in powerful positions have repeatedly attacked those of us who have scrutinized the federal investigation. Oklahoma Attorney General Drew Edmondson issued a personal attack saying that I was proposing a "wasteful witch hunt" and was pushing "the worst kind of paranoid conspiracy pandering."

Oklahoma Governor Frank Keating, a former FBI agent himself, went so far as to say that "raising questions would not bring one whit of intelligence to the process." He later escalated his attacks saying those of us who were raising serious questions were "howling at the moon" and "off the reservation."

All of these people are literally robbing the victims, family members and survivors—and all of us—of their right to know the truth.

All of us have had to fight the formidable disinformation and smear campaign waged by "faceless forces" that appear to have pockets of unending depth and the mass media at their beck and call.

Glenn Wilburn, who lost two grand children in the tragedy, and I filed a petition in November, 1995, to have a local County Grand Jury impaneled to investigate the bombing. This independent Grand Jury would be fully autonomous of the federal investigation, and would double in the capacity of a watchdog of the federal investigation.

Here in Oklahoma, we are very fortunate to be one of only two states that have a constitutional guarantee that the people of a county can cause a Grand Jury to be impaneled whenever they feel there is a need simply by circulating a petition. It is and always has been a common occurrence in our state.

Nevertheless, the Presiding State District Judge, Dan Owens, tried to stop us from petitioning to impanel the Grand Jury, and we were forced to appeal his actions to a higher court. That is where the latest and some of the most intense criticism has come from recently. One year after our appeal, we finally got a written opinion from the Court of Appeals in the Tulsa district. On December 24, 1996 the court ruled not only in our favor, but they did so unanimously.

Not only was it unanimous, but the court issued the decision "For Publication." That means that it was such a clear-cut case in regard to the state constitution, statutes, and previous case law, that it constituted a precedent-setting case to be used in lawbooks, most likely for many years to come.

Yet, why is there such extreme opposition to keep this independent Grand Jury from being allowed to assemble? As you will learn by reading this book, that is because some in our federal law enforcement agencies (i.e. ATF and FBI) had prior knowledge that certain individuals were planning to bomb the Murrah Federal Building!

Prior knowledge on the part of some individuals in the Federal Government may also be why the federal prosecutors barred every single witness to John Doe(s) from the Federal Grand Jury. Of the more than 20 witnesses to one or more John Doe(s), none—not even one—were allowed to tell the Grand Jury what they saw.

Additionally, when the prosecution's list of witnesses was unsealed, we found that the one witness allowed to testify in the trial to McVeigh being in the company of a John Doe can't describe in any way who he saw. Indeed, the best witnesses who can positively place McVeigh in downtown Oklahoma City that morning, saw him with one or more individuals and are able to describe to some degree what that person or persons looked like. Those witnesses were not even allowed to testify at McVeigh's trial.

As bizarre as that sounds, Federal Prosecutors were not allowing any of those witnesses to be seen or heard by the Federal Grand Jury. This gives "blind justice" a whole new meaning.

To make this even more clear, the Federal Grand Jury wanted to interview both the eyewitnesses and the sketch artist who drew the John Doe composites but were flatly refused by the federal "authorities." Clearly, they were blatantly deprived of their basic Constitutional rights as grand jurors. Why?

Just what is it that they are trying to accomplish? Or, perhaps more pointedly, just who are they trying to protect? And what are they trying to hide?

Let's not forget, elected officials are supposed to be the servants of the people and not the other way around. Just what's going on? And how are they getting away with it?

Our efforts to reinvestigate the case before a County Grand Jury are important for numerous reasons. One of the reasons that concerns me most is that I fear that the record of McVeigh's trial will comprise the "official story" of what happened. If the evidence of prior knowledge and other perpetrators is not presented in this case, I fear that the government will be successful in shaping the official story to permanently exclude that evidence.

Another reason that I feel that the OKC bombing case is important and directly affects you is that the government has reached a new level of operating out of the bounds of the law and is becoming more and more arrogant.

I don't know about you, but that kind of arrogance sickens me and leaves me with a eerie feeling. The government must not be allowed to get away with yet another botched job! The government must be held accountable.

In spite of the seemingly impenetrable and insurmountable forces acting against us, on February 18, 1997 the Oklahoma State Supreme Court miraculously ruled in favor of allowing the independent County Grand Jury and against the Federal Government's attempt to quash the rights of the people. That Grand Jury is investigating the case as this book goes to press.

Based on two years of intense research and investigation, this book gives the public an insight into the evidence which the Grand Jury will confront. Hopefully now, the forgotten families, survivors, and victims who died from the blast will have their right to a full, open and truthful investigation of the events of April 19, 1995.

Sincerely,

Charles Key

Rep. Charles Key
State Capitol Bldg., Rm 508
Oklahoma City, OK 73105
(405) 521-2711

Publisher's note: The preceding Foreword was adapted for publication from an appeal letter sent by Representative Key to "concerned citizens" on 12 March 1997. Its publication in this book does not necessarily imply Rep. Key's endorsement of the author's conclusions. Both Rep. Key and David Hoffman spent long hours together investigating leads and sharing information regarding the Oklahoma City bombing.

Author's note: While Representative Key and the people of Oklahoma have succeeded in impaneling their Grand Jury, they are without the necessary funds to proceed with the investigation. Any contributions towards this effort may be sent to:

Oklahoma County Grand Jury & Bombing Investigation Fund
Post Office Box 75669
Oklahoma City, OK 73147

> *"All governments
> are run by liars
> and nothing they
> say should be
> believed."*
> —I.F. Stone

INTRODUCTION

The images are forever etched in our minds. Scorched, burning cars and charred, twisted metal. Piles of rubble, screaming sirens and battered, bloody bodies. And the babies. Frail, lifeless figures—tiny, silent witnesses of death and destruction.

In the early morning hours of April 19th, the Oklahoma City Federal Building had, in one long, horrible moment exploded with the force of a volcano, spewing forth the contents of its human carnage onto the streets below. What had a few moments earlier been the Alfred P. Murrah building was now a huge, gaping tomb. The entire facade of the nine-story superstructure had been ripped away, exposing its innards—dangling chunks of concrete, tangled strands of cables and bent pieces of rebar—into the choking, blackened sky. Now it stood smoking and eerily silent, except for the muffled cries of its few remaining inhabitants and the wailing of sirens off in the distance.

One man, an ex-Marine, likened it to carnage he had witnessed in war-torn Lebanon. Another veteran, Thu Nguyen, who had his five-year-old son Christopher in the day care center, said, "I've seen war ... I've seen soldiers I fought with in Vietnam cut this way, cut in half, heads cut off. That was war. These are children. This is not a war. This is a crime."

The scene was surreal—almost too horrific to bear. There were bodies—and pieces of bodies—strewn about, along with childrens' toys and workers' personal effects—tragic reminders of what had moments before been the meaningful mementos of someone's life. One passerby had been wrapped around a telephone pole, her head blown off. Workers who had been sitting at their desks were still sitting there ... lifeless, morbid, like eerie figures out of a wax museum of horrors.

Police detective Jay Einhorn remembers one scene: "There was a guy—a black guy—on the second floor, just sitting there. I knew he was dead. He's looking at me, and I'm looking at him ... if you don't think that's fucking scary. We just said, man we gotta go up there and cover that guy up." [1]

Daina Bradley, who was trapped under a slab of fallen concrete, was still conscious. With no way to remove her without upsetting the huge piece of concrete, doctors were forced to amputate her leg. As Bradley lay screaming in a pool of water, surgeons, using scalpels and saws, and without anesthesia, amputated her leg below the knee.

The federal office building, home to over 550 workers, had also housed a day care center. Nearby, a makeshift morgue had been set up in what had once been the childrens' playground. Refrigeration trucks lined up to haul away the dead bodies. Sheriff Clint Boehler, from nearby Canadian County, recalls, "We went flying down there at about 110 miles an hour ... you never saw so many services running over each other." As hundreds of volunteers poured in from all over the country, fireman, police and medical personnel began laying out the victims for identification. Shirley Moser, a nurse, began tagging dead children. "Their faces had been blown off," recalls Moser. "They found a child without a head."

Those who were lucky enough to escape the carnage were wandering about, dazed and confused. One man, his face bloodied, wandered down the street, saying he was headed home, except that he couldn't remember his name or where his home was. Another man who was entering the building had his arm blown off, but was in such a state of shock that he didn't notice it as he went about trying to help others.[2]

People who lived or worked nearby had been rocked out of their chairs. Trent Smith, 240 pounds, was tossed seven feet into the air and through the window of his hotel room. Several blocks away, a bus filled with people was nearly blown on its side. The force of the blast extended for nearly 30 blocks, blowing out windows and heavily damaging a dozen buildings, and causing damage to almost 400 more.[3]

When it was all over, more than 169 people, including 19 children, lay dead, and more than 500 were injured. The damage was estimated in the hundreds of millions.

Federal authorities were calling the bombing the single largest terrorist attack in the history of the United States. Yet it was difficult to discern whether the bombing was some ominous precursor to some as yet undeclared war, or the result of some criminal plot gone horribly awry. Just who had caused it wasn't clear.

As rescue workers continued the difficult task of searching for bodies, and hospital workers began attending to victims, law enforcement agents began searching for clues. What was clear as law enforcement personnel descended upon the scene, was that the blast had left a thirty feet wide, six feet deep crater in front of the building. Fortunately, an ATF agent who had recently attended a course on the identification of car and truck-bombs just happened to be in the federal courthouse. The agent was able to identify the cause of the blast immediately. He telephoned his superiors in Dallas and told them that an ammonium-nitrate truck-bomb had just blown up the Murrah Building.

Sixty miles away, near Perry Oklahoma, Highway Patrolman Charles Hanger was making his usual rounds. Around 10:30 A.M., Officer Hanger noticed a battered 1977 yellow Mercury, without a license plate, speeding along at 81 miles an hour. Pulling the vehicle over, Hanger cited the driver, 26-year-old Timothy James McVeigh, for driving without a license plate. As he was about to let McVeigh go, Hanger noticed a distinct bulge under McVeigh's windbreaker.

When he asked McVeigh what he had under his jacket, McVeigh casually informed the cop that he had a gun—a 9mm Glock semi-automatic pistol. Hanger subsequently arrested McVeigh for carrying a concealed weapon, driving without tags, and driving without insurance.[4]

Back in Oklahoma City, investigators were busily searching the wreckage for clues that could lead them to the perpetrators. It didn't take long for investigators to find what they were looking for—a piece of axle and a license plate—believed to have been part of the truck used in the bombing. After FBI agents ran the VIN (vehicle identification number) and the plate through their Rapid Start computer system, they discovered the vehicle belonged to a Ryder rental agency in Florida. A check with the agency revealed that the truck, a 1993 Ford, was rented out of Elliott's Body Shop in Junction City, Kansas. Elliott's said that they had rented the 20-foot truck to a Bob Kling on April 17th, and gave the FBI artist a description of two men who had rented the truck, known as Unsub #1 and Unsub #2.

Kling, Unsub #1, had listed his address as 3616 North Van Dyke Road in Decker, Michigan. The address was the home of James Douglas Nichols and Terry Lynn Nichols. A quick check of that address with the Michigan Department of Motor Vehicles revealed a license in the name of Timothy James McVeigh.

FBI agents interviewing James Nichols and relatives in Decker quickly learned that Timothy McVeigh, a friend of Nichols, possessed large quantities of fuel oil and fertilizer. Armed with a search warrant, agents found 28 50-pound bags of fertilizer containing ammonium-nitrate, a 55 gallon drum containing fuel oil, blasting caps, and safety fuse.

Interviews with neighbors revealed that the Nichols brothers and McVeigh had experimented with explosives, using household items to produce small bombs using bottles and cardboard cartons, which they would detonate on their property for fun. Witnesses also claimed that in December of 1993, McVeigh and one of the Nichols brothers visited Thumb Hobbies, Etc. to inquire about purchasing 100% liquid nitro model airplane fuel. One of these witnesses had reported that James Nichols had repeatedly blamed the U.S. government for all the problems in the world.

Federal agents then decided they had enough evidence to arrest James Nichols, and to put out a warrant on his brother Terry, who was living in Herrington, Kansas. On April 22, Terry Nichols, wondering why his name was being broadcast on television, walked into the local police station in Herrington.

In the meantime, witnesses at the scene of the bombing had given FBI agents a description of possible suspects. While interviewing people in Junction City, agents spoke to the manager of the Dreamland Motel who recognized the composite sketch of the suspect the FBI called Unsub #1. The man had registered at the Dreamland from April 14 to April 18 under the name of Tim McVeigh, had driven a yellow Mercury, and provided an address on North Van Dyke Road in Decker, Michigan.

On April 21, Carl E. Lebron, a former co-worker of McVeigh's, recognized the composite sketch of Unsub #1 on TV and called the FBI. He said that the man was named Timothy McVeigh, and that he was possessed of extreme right-wing views, was a military veteran, and was particularly agitated over the deaths of the Branch Davidians in Waco, Texas in April 1993. The man told the FBI that McVeigh expressed extreme anger towards the Federal Government. The man gave the FBI the last known address he had for McVeigh: 1711 Stockton Hill Road, #206, Kingman, Arizona.

Back in Perry, Oklahoma, McVeigh was still sitting in a cell at the Noble County Courthouse, waiting for his arraignment. After feeding McVeigh's name into the National Crime Information Center, the FBI discovered their suspect sitting quietly in the Noble County jail on a traffic and weapons charge. Just as McVeigh was about to be set free, District Attorney John Maddox received a call from the FBI telling him to hold on to the prisoner, that he was a prime suspect in the bombing of the Federal Building in Oklahoma City.

So, by good luck, diligent work, and an amazing series of coincidences, federal law enforcement authorities solved the most heinous crime in the history of the United States—all within 48 hours.

Or did they?

Chapter One

THE MANNLICHER-CARCANNO BOMB

"It had to have been mined," said the gruff, gnarly voice on the other end of the line. "It's real simple. You cannot bring down a building like that without cutting charges set on the support pillars."

Bud, an ex-Green Beret who saw heavy combat in Vietnam, should know what he's talking about. Bud had military demolitions training—the kind taught to men who need to know how to blow up hardened targets.

"It couldn't have been done externally like that," added Bud. "Without cutting charges, there's just no way to do it."

Bud didn't want me to use his full name. He was worried about his VA benefits.

One man who wasn't worried about government reprisals is General Benton K. Partin. A retired U.S. Air Force Brigadier General, Partin was responsibile for the design and testing of almost every non-nuclear weapon device used in the Air Force, including precision-guided weapons designed to destroy hardened targets like the Alfred P. Murrah Building. Partin exhaustively researched the bombing and the resulting pattern of damage.

In a letter dated May 17, 1995, hand-delivered to each member of the Congress and Senate, Partin stated:

> When I first saw the pictures of the truck-bomb's asymmetrical damage to the Federal Building, my immediate reaction was that the pattern of damage would have been technically impossible without supplementing demolition charges at some of the reinforcing concrete column bases .... For a simplistic blast truck-bomb, of the size and composition reported, to be able to reach out on the order of 60 feet and collapse a reinforced column base the size of column A-7 is beyond credulity.

The full text of Partin's report, reproduced in the appendix, too complex to elaborate here, says a truck filled with ammonium-nitrate could not have caused the degree of damage done to the Alfred P. Murrah building. Not when parked at least 20 feet away from that building. Without direct contact, the fall-off from the blast would be too great to do any serious structural damage.

Another man who knows a thing or two about bombs is Samuel Cohen, inventor of the Neutron Bomb. Cohen began his career on the Manhattan Project at

Los Alamos, where he was charged with studying the effects of the atomic bombs that destroyed Hiroshima and Nagasaki. During his 40 year career, Cohen worked with every application of nuclear weapons design and testing.

Cohen stated his position in a letter to Oklahoma State Representative Charles Key:

> It would have been absolutely impossible and against the laws of nature for a truck full of fertilizer and fuel oil ... no matter how much was used ... to bring the building down.[5]

The Ryder truck-bomb has earned the nickname the "Mannlicher-Carcanno Bomb" in reference to the cheap Italian-made rifle with a defective scope allegedly used to kill President Kennedy. District Attorney Jim Garrison joked during the Clay Shaw conspiracy trial that the government's nuclear physics lab could explain how a single bullet could travel through President Kennedy and Governor Connally five times while making several u-turns, then land in pristine condition on the President's gurney.

In the Oklahoma bombing case, it appears the government is attempting to perform a similar feat of light and magic. A non-directional, low-veolocity fertilizer bomb parked 20 to 30 feet from a modern, steel-reinforced super-structure could not have caused the pattern and degree of damage it did. But the government expects the public to believe that two disgruntled amateurs blew up the Oklahoma City Federal Building with a homemade fertilizer bomb.

Dr. Roger Raubach doesn't believe the government story. Raubach, who received his Ph.D. in physical chemistry and served on the research faculty at Stanford University, says, "General Partin's assessment is absolutely correct. I don't care if they pulled up a semi-trailer truck with 20 tons of ammonium-nitrate; it wouldn't do the damage we saw there."

Raubach, technical director of a chemical company, explained in an interview with *The New American* magazine:

> "The detonation velocity of the shock wave from an ANFO (ammonium-nitrate/fuel-oil) explosion is on the order of 3,500 meters per second. In comparison, military explosives generally have detonation velocities that hit 7,000 to 8,000-plus meters per second. The most energetic single-component explosive of this type, C-4—which is also known as Cyclonite or RDX—is about 8,000 meters per second and above. You don't start doing big-time damage to heavy structures until you get into those ranges, which is why the military uses those explosives."[6]

The government is not happy about people like Dr. Roger Raubach. They don't want you to know what Dr. Raubach knows. Sam Gronning, a licensed, professional blaster in Casper, Wyoming with 30 years experience in explosives, told *The New American:*

"The Partin letter states in very precise technical terms what everyone in this business knows: No truck-bomb of ANFO out in the open is going to cause the kind of damage we had there in Oklahoma City. In 30 years of blasting, using everything from 100 percent nitrogel to ANFO, I've not seen anything to support that story." [7]

In an interview with the author, Gronning said, "I set off a 5,000 lb ANFO charge. I was standing 1,000 feet from it, and all it did was muss my hair, take out the mud in the creek that we were trying to get rid of, and it shattered a few leaves off the trees around it. It didn't cause any collateral damage to any of the deeply set trees that were within 20 feet of it."

The FBI has a different story to tell.

The FBI claims that Timothy McVeigh and Terry Nichols bought several thousand pounds of ammonium-nitrate at a farm supply store in Manhattan, Kansas, then drove to Geary State Park where they mixed a bomb. The FBI then claims the suspects hauled their magic bomb over 500 miles, where, nearly 24 hours later, they blew up the Federal Building in Oklahoma City.

Yet what the FBI—those bastions of truth and justice—don't want you to know, is that fertilizer-grade ammonium-nitrate isn't a very good blasting agent. As a publication from the Atlas Powder company states:

Agricultural fertilizer prills when made into ANFO had very poor explosive characteristics. They would not detonate efficiently because of their high density, lack of porosity and heavy inert coatings of anti-setting agents ... The ability of an oiled prill to be detonated depends greatly upon the density of the prill. Dense prills, such as agricultural grade, often are not detonable at all; or if initiated, perform at a very low rate of detonation and may die out in the bore hole performing no useful work.

U.S. Army Technical Manual TM 9-1910 states:

The grade of ammonium-nitrate used in the manufacture of binary explosives is required to be at least 99 percent pure, contain not more than 1.15 percent of moisture, and have maximum ether-soluble, water-insoluble acidity, sulfate, and chloride contents of 0.10, 0.18, 0.02, 0.05, and 0.50 percent, respectively.

Moreover, a bomb like that is not easy to mix. According to Gronning, "You'd have to stir and stir and stir to get just the right mixture for proper combustibility. And then, if it isn't used immediately, the oil settles to the bottom and the bomb doesn't go off."

"ANFO is easy to make if you know how to do it," adds Jeffrey Dean, Executive Director of the International Society of Explosives Engineers, "but it takes years of experience to work with safely." According to Dean, "It is almost impossible for amateurs to properly mix the ammonium-nitrate with the fuel oil. Clumps of ANFO would inevitably fail to detonate."[8]

The scenario of two men mixing huge barrels of fertilizer and fuel-oil in a public park is also beyond absurdity. Such a spectacle would surely have been seen by anyone passing by: hikers, picnickers, fishermen.

"That would have drawn so much attention," says Rick Sherrow, a former ATF (Bureau of Alcohol, Tobacco and Firearms) agent with 25 years experience in explosives. "It would have required an area twice the size of a truck just to walk around … that would have not have gone okay."[9]

Naturally, the expert who testified for the government disagrees. Linda Jones, an explosives specialist who has studied IRA bombings in Great Britain, concluded that "there was one device … in the rear cargo compartment of a Ryder truck…." Jones adds that it wouldn't be difficult to build such a large bomb "provided they had a basic knowledge of explosives and access to the materials—it would be fairly simple. One person could do it on their own, but more people could do it quicker."[10]

While the government built its case on witness accounts of the single Ryder truck, numerous witnesses, uncalled to testify by the prosecution for the McVeigh trial, recall seeing *two* trucks. Could two trucks—one rented by McVeigh, and one rented by the suspect known as John Doe 2—have been used to transport the huge quantities of material necessary to build such a bomb?

"I would buy two trucks simply for logistics," said former ATF agent Sherrow. "One truck full of barrels of ammonium-nitrate, and you still got to put the fuel into it. Because you don't want to put the fuel in and let it settle for days at a time. They would have to have something to bring everything together and mix it, and that's going to take more then one truck."

Two days prior to the Murrah Building bombing—on April 17—David King, staying at Dreamland Motel in Junction City, Kansas, where McVeigh and John Doe 2 spent time, remembered seeing the Ryder truck with a trailer attached to it. Inside the trailer was a large object wrapped in white canvas. "It was a squarish shape, and it came to a point on top," said King. "It was about three or four feet high." King said that later in the day, the trailer was gone, but the truck was still in the lot.[11]

Was this witness describing some sophisticated explosive device? Or was he describing a Lely farm mixer? A Lely farm mixer is about four feet high with a pointed top. What happened to this trailer? Why did we never hear any more about it?

Then around 2 A.M. on **April 19**, a Ryder truck pulled into the Save-A-Trip convenience store in **Kingman, Kansas**, followed by a light-colored car and a brown pick-up. Assistant manager Richard Sinnett clearly recalls three men, including McVeigh and a man resembling John Doe 2 enter the store. Yet Sinnett was particularly struck by the odd contraption they were towing—a large, plastic, semi-transparent tank full of clear liquid.[12] Was this diesel fuel that the bombers intended to add to their ammonium-nitrate mixture at the last minute?

Despite a mountain of evidence against the ANFO theory, the government has gone to great lengths to convince the juries and the public that the Murrah Building was destroyed by a single ANFO bomb delivered by a pair of disgruntled right-wing extremists. In fact, the ATF televised a demonstration of an ANFO truck-bomb detonating in an effort to prove their contention. "They fired the thing off," says Gronning. "We saw it—it was on CNN—so what? All it did was set off an explosion and wiggle the trees behind it. It didn't even knock them over.

"My knowledge comes from practical handling of explosives," adds Gronning. "And my belief is that 4800 lbs of ANFO wouldn't have scuffed the paint on the building!"

The FBI changed the size of the bomb numerous times, originally claiming that it weighed 1,200 pounds, upgrading the figure to 2,000 pounds, then to 4,000 pounds, and finally, issuing a press release stating that the bomb weighed 4,800 pounds.

"It appears the government kept upgrading the size of the vehicle and the 'fertilizer' bomb to coincide with the damage," claims retired FBI SAC (Senior Agent-in-Charge) Ted Gunderson.

The government originally stated the bomb cost less than $1,000 to build. Just before the start of McVeigh's trial, that figure was upgraded to $5,000. Their rationale was based on "discovery" almost two years after the fact that the suspects had constructed their magic bomb with racing fuel, not diesel fuel, which is far less expensive.

To maintain a semblance of credibility in light of increasingly publicized reports of General Partin and others, the government also conceded—right before the start of McVeigh's trial—that the suspects probably hadn't built their bomb at Geary State Park after all.*

If Timothy McVeigh or anyone else with military training wanted to destroy the Alfred P. Murrah Building, it is unlikely they would use ANFO. Army demolition manuals clearly state ANFO is not good for destroying concrete or steel. McVeigh, the consummate soldier who studied every conceivable Army manual in his spare time—including Army Manual TM 31-210: Improvised Munitions Handbook—certainly would have known this.[13]

---

* They claimed they didn't know where it was built.

The FBI insists that amateur bomb-makers Timothy McVeigh and Terry Nichols built this remarkable ANFO bomb that killed 169 people and destroyed a modern nine-story steel-reinforced concrete building before the government's damage-control apparatus went into effect. Before it did, even the usual government talking-heads insisted that no amateurs could have done this.

Vince Cannistraro, ABC News corespondent and former CIA intelligence advisor to the National Security Council stated, "This is something professional and it really implies that the person who constructed the explosive device has experience, was trained in the use of explosives, and knew what they were doing." [14]

Before he began attacking critics of the government's case, Oklahoma Governor and former FBI agent Frank Keating stated, "Obviously, whatever did the damage to the Murrah Building was a tremendous, very sophisticated explosive device." [15]

The very next day, the government insisted that a homemade ANFO bomb, made with agricultural-grade ammonium-nitrate, did the job. FBI Special Agent John Hersley contends that traces of a military-type detonation cord known as PDTN (pentadirythri-tetranitrate), commonly known as Primadet, were found on McVeigh's clothing at the time of his arrest (in another report it was PETN, or pentaerythritol-tetranitrate). PDTN was allegedly used to wire the barrels of ANFO. [16]

Senior FBI chemist Frederick Whitehurst conducted a test on McVeigh's clothing but found no residue there, or in in McVeigh's car either. [17]

Whitehurst came forward with allegations that the FBI was slanting results of forensic tests for years. Collected in a 30-page memorandum, Whitehurst criticized FBI laboratory personnel for incompetence. As a Justice Department memorandum states: "Dr. Whitehurst contends that the Explosives Unit and the Chemistry and Toxicology Unit inappropriately structure their conclusions to favor the prosecution." [18]

According to the *Wall Street Journal*, "[Whitehurst's] accusations of bias and even manufacturing evidence have called into question several high-profile government cases, including the Oklahoma City and World Trade Center bombings." [19]

Whitehurst's allegations were further elaborated on in a highly revealing report issued by the DoJ Inspector General's Office, which concluded that "[SSA David] Williams repeatedly reached conclusions that incriminated the defendants without a scientific basis and that were not explained in the body of the report."

Indeed. It appears Williams reached his conclusions based, not on empirical evidence, but on the fact that Terry Nichols allegedly purchased large quantities of ANFO. As the OIG (Office of Inspector General) report states:

Without the evidence of these purchases, Williams admitted he would have been unable to conclude that ANFO was used. Indeed, Williams stated that based on the post-blast scene alone it could have been dynamite....

Williams claimed "that the initiator for the booster(s) was either a detonator from a Primadet Delay system or sensitized detonating cord." Yet as the OIG report states, "No evidence of a Primadet system or sensitized detonating cord was found at the crime scene."*

Controversial scientist and bomb expert Michael Riconoscuito told former FBI agent Ted Gunderson that the theory of drums of ANFO being detonated by PDTN-soaked loops of rope or "det" cord is highly improbable, if not impossible. "The only way to obtain blast control is with volumetric initiation," explained Riconoscuito. "This takes electronic circuits of similar sophistication as would be required in nuclear weapons. This sophistication is not available to the average person," he added, stating that the resultant blast would have been "confused and uncontrolled," and the energy would have ultimately "canceled itself out."[20]

Finally, the OIG report states: "Whitehurst questions Williams' conclusion that none of the structural damage evident within the Murrah building was caused by secondary explosive devices or explosions."[21]

Why is the government going to such great lengths, in spite of evidence to the contrary, to make us believe that the Alfred P. Murrah Building was destroyed by an ANFO bomb? Because the government's case is built upon the premise that Timothy McVeigh and Terry Nichols built their alleged bomb with ammonium-nitrate. The calls allegedly made by McVeigh were to stores that sell racing fuel and ammonium-nitrate. McVeigh's fingerprint is allegedly on a receipt for ammonium-nitrate. And a small trace of ammonium-nitrate was allegedly found at the scene. The government's case must proceed along those lines. Any evidence that proves the bomb was made of anything other than ANFO would not only destroy the government's case, it would open up inquiries about who actually bombed the Murrah Building ... and why.

---

* Williams' report also states that the initiator for the Primadet or the detonating cord was a non-electric detonator; non-electric, burning type fuse of either hobby fuse or a commercial safety fuse was used as a safe separation and time delay system; and the time delay for the burning fuse was approximately two minutes and 15 seconds. ... No evidence of a non-electric detonator or the named fuses, however, were found at the crime scene.... Williams also stated in his report that [a] fertilizer base explosive, such as ANFO ... among other commercial and improvised explosives, has an approximate VOD of 13,000 fps. The statement of the VOD of ANFO, however, is incomplete because ANFO has a broad VOD range. For example, the Dupont Blasters' Handbook shows commercial ANFO products with VODs in the 7,000–15,600 feet-per-second range. When Williams wrote his Oklahoma City report, he was aware of this range.

The government also stuck with the ANFO theory because Michael and Lori Fortier agreed to testify in a plea-bargain that their friend McVeigh arranged soup cans in their kitchen to demonstrate how to make a "shaped charge." Yet as bomb experts explained, there is no way to make a shaped charge out of a collection of ANFO barrels.

But the government expects us to believe that two lone amateurs with a crude fertilizer bomb, out in the open, twenty to thirty feet away from a hardened target, destroyed eight reinforced columns and killed 169 people. As General Partin said, such a scenario is "beyond credulity." *

Former ATF man Rick Sherrow, who wrote an article for *Soldier of Fortune* magazine entitled "Bombast, Bomb Blasts & Baloney," contends that General Partin's assessment of the bombing is somehow inaccurate. Sherrow claims that the pressure wave that would have struck the building from the ANFO bomb (375 pounds per square inch according to Partin's figures) would be more than enough to destroy reinforced concrete columns, which Sherrow claimed in his article disintegrate at 30 p.s.i. (pounds per square inch).[22]

To professional blaster Sam Gronning, such a statement is preposterous: "That's bullshit!" exclaimed Gronning. "Thirty p.s.i. wouldn't take out a rubber tire!" Both Partin and Rabauch contend that at least 3,500 p.s.i. is required to destroy reinforced concrete. In a letter to Partin, Rabauch states:

> I took the liberty of checking with the leading concrete supplier in my area in order to confirm the compressive yield figure that you used, that being 3,500 p.s.i. What I was told about concrete was very interesting. A 3,500 p.s.i. figure is extremely low for structural concrete. A properly mixed and cured structure of the type dealt with in your report would probably have a yield strength of 5,600 p.s.i.[23]

Those who rush to refute the evidence presented by Partin, Raubach and others cite as evidence the 1982 destruction of the Marine bunker in Beirut by a truck-bomb driven by an Islamic terrorist. In that instance, the truck was driven directly *into* the building—a structure much smaller and lighter than the Alfred P. Murrah Building.

In August, 1970, 1,700 pounds of ANFO parked in a van exploded outside the Army Math Research Lab at the University of Wisconsin in Madison. Although parked closer than the Ryder truck was to the Murrah Building, the bomb merely blew a hole in the outer wall and took out the windows. One person was killed.

In 1989, Colombian narco-terrorists detonated a truck-bomb outside the

---

* Partin pointed out that while the truck bomb that damaged the World Trade Center was in an enclosed space, thereby creating a much higher destructive force than a bomb out in the open, it did not destroy the support column next to it.

National Security Department in Bogota, Columbia. The vehicle was parked approximately ten feet from the modern high-rise building. The bomb decimated the face of the building, but left the support columns intact. Fifteen people were killed.

In the summer of 1996, an IRA truck-bomb detonated in the heart of Manchester's financial district. The device, constructed of ANFO and 3,500 pounds of Semtex, a high-velocity, military-grade plastic explosive, caused considerable damage to the surrounding buildings, but left them relatively intact. Although the device managed to break a lot of windows and injure 206 people, no one was killed.

On June 25, 1996, a tanker-trailer packed with RDX plastic explosives blew up outside the Khobar Towers apartment complex at King Abdul Aziz Air Base in Saudi Arabia, killing 19 American servicemen and injuring hundreds more. While the blast produced a crater 35 feet deep and 85 feet across (the crater in Oklahoma was approximately six feet deep and 16 feet across, although the government claimed it was 30 feet), it didn't do the same amount of damage done to the Murrah Building—a building constructed to much more rigorous codes and specifications. Yet authorities claim that the bomb was at least the size as that which blew up the Federal Building.[24]

In an analogy offered by Partin, "It would be as irrational or as impossible as a situation in which a 150 pound man sits in a flimsy chair causing the chair to collapse, while a man weighing 1,500 pounds sits in an identical flimsy chair and it does not collapse—impossible."

"But," contends Sherrow in *Soldier of Fortune*, "the [Murrah] Building was not designed to withstand explosions or earthquakes, and it's basically a weak building."

Jim Loftis, one of the building's architects, told me they were asked to make the building bomb-resistant due to left-wing radicals who were blowing up federal facilities in the early 1970s. Loftis also said the building was designed to meet earthquake standards. "We designed it to meet the building codes and earthquakes are part of that code," said Loftis.

Loftis also said that the north side of the lower level (the area impacted by the truck-bomb) was steel-rebar reinforced concrete without windows. He also concurred with Raubach and Partin that the pressure necessary to destroy reinforced concrete is in the 2,500 to 4,000 p.s.i. range—a far cry from the 30 p.s.i. cited by Sherrow.[25]

Yet Sherrow concludes that since there was so much collateral damage (damage to the surrounding buildings) the truck-bomb must have been responsible. "The collateral damage just discounts [Partin's] material."

Two experts who seem to agree with Sherrow are Dorom Bergerbest-Eilom and Yakov Yerushalmi. The Israeli bomb experts were brought to Oklahoma at the request of ATF agent Guy Hamal. According to their report, the bomb was an ANFO bomb boosted with something more powerful ... and it had a Middle Eastern signature.*

The Athenian restaurant, which sits approximately 150 feet northwest of the Murrah Building, was almost completely destroyed. Pieces of the Murrah Building were actually blown *into* the Athenian. As video producer Jerry Longspaugh points out, only a bomb inside the Federal Building would be capable of projecting parts of the building into another building 150 feet away.

As Gronning notes in a letter to Representative Key: "Not in your wildest dreams would that much ANFO affect peripheral damage at that distance. Which leads me to suspect that another more powerful explosive was used."

According to a source quoted in the *Rocky Mountain News*, an ammonium-nitrate bomb made with a racing fuel component known as hydrazine "would create one of the largest non-nuclear blasts possible." McVeigh had allegedly attempted to procure the substance from a dealer in Topeka, Kansas, who refused. Hydrazine is extremely hazardous and difficult to obtain.[26]

While not knowledgeable about hydrazine, Gronning notes that "C-4, for example, would be capable of creating those kinds of pressure waves and destroying the local foundation of the Federal Building.

"If you had 4,000 lbs of C-4 in there," continues Gronning, "now you're talking a real high-order explosive at some serious speed. And when that goes off, you're liable to take out the thing. But I still have a problem believing even at that distance away from the building, it would create that kind of damage. All you have to do to see what I'm talking about is to see what kind of bomb damage you get from a bomb in the [WWII] attacks on London."[27]

It is precisely this analogy that Sherrow attempts to use in *Soldier of Fortune*. "For perspective," notes *SOF* "demo" expert Donovan, "consider that the German V-1 and V-2 missiles that devastated London carried only 1,650 pounds of an explosive not dissimilar in brisance and yield. In other words, would three V-2s simultaneously striking the first floor of the Murrah Building do such damage? Of course they would."

Yet the Ryder truck did not impact the Murrah Building at the speed of a rocket, nor did it impact it at all. Even to the layperson, one can see that such an analogy is ridiculous. In his article, Sherrow never speculates that C-4 or any other high-velocity military type explosive might have been used.

---

* The Israeli's host in the U.S. was Oklahoma City business leader Moshe Tal, an Israeli. According to William Northrop, another Israeli and Oklahoma City resident, Tal initially circulated the report, which was three pages and mentioned the Middle-Eastern bomb signature. After Tal was summoned to Israel, he returned denying those aspects of the report. It was suddenly, in keeping with the U.S. Government's position, no longer a Middle-Eastern bomb, and the report itself incredibly shrank from three pages to only one.

Still, the former ATF man contends that an ANFO bomb parked out in the open could have caused the pattern and degree of damage done to the Murrah Building. "Absolutely and without a shadow of a doubt, and I base that on 30 years in the business, and shooting ANFO—from a couple pounds to 630 tons in one shot." Sherrow goes on to state that Partin's conclusions were based upon mere "theoretical analysis," not hands-on experience.

Yet Partin spent 25 years in the defense research establishment, including hands-on work at the Ballistic Research Laboratories; Commander of the Air Force Armament Technology Laboratory; Air Force System Command, and the Office of the Secretary of Defense (OSD) management. Such credentials speak of a man who knows his explosives.

It is unclear why the former ATF man was trying to discredit Partin, and by association, others who disagreed with the government's theory. What is clear however is that *Soldier of Fortune,* the magazine in which Sherrow's article appeared, is owned by Paladin Press regarded a CIA proprietary. Robert K. Brown, the magazine's publisher, is an associate of General John Singlaub, a key Iran-Contra player who ran the genocidal Phoenix Program in Vietnam, and helped train death squads in Central America. Both men reportedly played an ancillary role in the 1984 La Penca bombing, which resulted in the deaths of eight journalists. Sherrow admits to working for the CIA in Africa. What he did there isn't exactly clear.[28]

If the CIA (or one of its tentacles) were involved, they would have a strong motive to cover up their involvement and redirect the investigation. The most common way of doing this is through the use of propaganda and disinformation. While Sherrow himself criticized the ATF, and wrote several articles debunking the government's theory regarding militia groups, this particular article appears to be a "hit-piece" designed to discredit any legitimate analysis of the bombing.

Some critics of the government's story have gone beyond the relatively ordinary explanations of Partin, Gronning and others to suggest that the Federal Building was destroyed by a device called an "A-Neutronic Bomb." These advocates cite as evidence the nature of the spalling (the disintegration of the concrete into tiny pieces) on the top of the building, and the extent of the damage to surrounding buildings that would be impossible for an ANFO bomb.

Larens Imanyuel, a Berkeley assistant physics professor who has studied the bombing, is one such advocate. Imanyuel's analysis, which appeared in *Veritas* newsletter, indicates that the wide extent of the collateral damage was not consistent with a conventional explosion. As Imanyuel writes:

There was some very sophisticated bomb that was capable of causing a tremendous blast atmospheric pressure wave that blew out windows in so many of the surrounding buildings. This had to be some sort of very high-tech dust explosive-like bomb—one that creates a widely dispersed explosive mixture in the very air and then detonates it with a secondary charge. This last spectacular high-tech bomb served the purpose of convincing the general public that the alleged solitary truck-bomb was powerful and "devastating" enough that it could wipe out and collapse a nearby building.[29]

Consider the comments of a local structural engineer, Bob Cornforth, "The range of this blast has really impressed me—the extent of the damage and the distance out." A mile away, window frames had been pushed back two feet. On the other hand, he inspected two buildings just a little over 200 feet. from the so-called crater, the YMCA center and the Journal Record building, which lost part of its pitched concrete roof. To his surprise, "The structural frames performed extremely well. We design for 80 mph winds," which he says seems adequate. The lack of damage to the frames, despite the massive light-structural damage showed that the shock waves were of short duration. This was consistent with a many-point explosion, but not with a single-point explosion large enough to knock out the four heavy columns that had collapsed in the Murrah Building.[30]

The A-Neutronic bomb, or "Electro-Hydrodynamic Gaseous Fuel Device," was reportedly developed by the young scientist-prodigy Michael Riconosciuto in the early 1980s while he was working for Hercules Manufacturing in Silicon Valley, CA. The first bomb test at the Pentagon's secret Area 51 in Nevada apparently resulted in the death of a technician and injured several others due to the underestimation of its power. The project was reportedly compartmentalized and classified under the "Nuclear Weapons" category by President Reagan.

According to Imanyuel, a member of a public watchdog group that monitors military and nuclear procurement activities, "The design would be particularly suitable for use as a cruise missile warhead, where a non-nuclear charge is required that can reliably destroy a hardened target despite a several-meters targeting error. Such weapons are designed as part of the Advanced Technology Warhead Program of Lawrence Livermore and Los Alamos National Laboratories."

Ted Gunderson, who independently investigated the bombing, included numerous letters and memos in his report pointing to the existence of such a device. He reported that the government contract number for the bomb was DAAA-21-90-C-0045, manufactured by Dyno-Nobel, Inc., in Salt Lake City. Dyno-Nobel was previously connected with Hercules Manufacturing, where Riconosciuto worked. The Department of the Army denies that contract DAAA-21-90-C-0045 exists. Dyno-Nobel refused to respond to inquiries from Gunderson or the author.[31]

Curiously, the bomb specialist called as the government's expert witness during the Federal Grand Jury was Robert Hopler, who recently retired from Dyno-Nobel.

Sherrow raises the issue of the Electro-Hydrodynamic Gaseous Fuel Device in his *Soldier of Fortune* article. According to Imanyuel, "Gunderson's bomb model was clearly unworkable as presented in *Soldier of Fortune*, but contained the essential information that the bomb generated an electrostatically charged cloud."[32]

One victim in the HUD office in the Murrah Building described in a National Public Radio interview on May 23, 1995 how she felt a heat wave and a static electricity charge immediately before the windows blew in.

Daina Bradley, who lost her mother and two children in the bombing, said she felt electricity running through her body right before the bomb went off.[33]

Another victim, Ramona McDonald, who was driving about block away, remembers seeing a brilliant flash and described the feeling of static electricity. "It made a real loud static electricity sound. It sounded like a big swarm of bees— you could actually hear it. The next thing was a real sharp clap, like thunder." McDonald also described gold and blue flashes of light. Riconiscuto called his device "Blue Death."[34]

Another survivor of the blast was quoted on CNN as saying, "It was just like an atomic bomb went off. "The ceiling went in and all the windows came in and there was a deafening roar."[35]

Proponents of the A-Neutronic Bomb conclude that these are all signatures of such a device.*

While both Gunderson and Riconosciuto have received ridicule for suggesting that a super-secret pineapple-sized device may have destroyed the Murrah Building, Cohen cautions: "Look, when I first came up with that concept [the Neutron Bomb, developed in the 1970s] the ridicule I took from the scientific community was something awful. And this included scientists at the Nobel Prize level." "Regarding Riconosciuto," adds Cohen, "the guy's a madman … but technically, there's no doubt in my mind that he's brilliant."[36]

Gene Wheaton, a former Pentagon CID investigator, claims that the fuel-air bomb was deployed in the Gulf War, along with other experimental weapons responsible for much of the massive devastation inflicted on Iraq.[37] The fuel-air explosive, or FAE, can cover an area 1,000 feet wide with blast pressures of 200 p.s.i. According to a CIA report on FAEs:

> [T]he pressure effects of FAEs approach those produced by low-yield nuclear weapons at short ranges. The effect of an FAE explosion within confined spaces is immense. Those near the ignition point are obliterated. Those at the fringes are likely to suffer many internal injuries, including burst eardrums and crushed inner-

---

* Other people who were working in office buildings at the time reported that sparks flew out from their computers just before the blast. The manager of the Journal Record parking garage, two blocks from the Murrah Building, reported that the electronic computers in at least half a dozen cars had malfunctioned as a result of the blast.

ear organs, severe concussions, ruptured lungs and internal organs, and possible blindness.[38]

Moreover, it seems that the German firm Messerschmitt-Bolkow-Blohm supplied Iraq with plans for a fuel-air explosive. The blueprints were allegedly passed on to the Iraqis by the Egyptians, and Iraq commenced commercial production of the weapon—the force of which is the equivalent of a small atomic explosion.[39]

A few minutes before 9:00 A.M. on April 19, a young Arabic man carrying a backpack was seen in the Murrah Building hurriedly pushing the elevator button as if trying to get off. A few minutes after he exited the building, the bomb(s) went off. The elevator doors, which were on the opposite side of the building from the truck-bomb, had their doors blown *outward*.

Another military source agreed that a device similar to the fuel-air explosive exists. "It's called a Special Atomic Demolition Munitions or SADM," said Craig Roberts, a Lt. Colonel in the Army Reserve. According to Roberts and Charles T. Harrison, a researcher for the Department of Energy and the Pentagon, this munition has been deployed with artillery units in Europe. The SADM can also be carried in a backpack.

Another source who has monitored top-secret weapons projects confirmed this information:

I do not know a lot about SADM's, but I have friends—ex-British SAS and RAF— who were trained in their use a few years ago for behind-the-lines sabotage in the event of a Russian breakthrough in Europe. They believe from their still-serving military contacts that the earlier football sized back pack weapons that they were trained on have been significantly microed such that a device would now easily fit in a grapefruit and deliver five to ten tons TNT equivalent—or less [i.e.: down to one ton TNT]. These things easily fit into a 105mm howitzer shell or a briefcase.

Exactly what components are utilized in these weapons is difficult to get as the still serving British officers are reluctant to talk about them in detail. One can assume that a mixture of Plutonium 239 (highly refined hence relatively low radioactivity emission on detonation), Lithium 6 Deuteride Tritide, Tritium, and possibly Beryllium and Uranium 238 (NOT 235) would be involved as a series of lenses in a Bi-Conical shape. I am endeavoring to get more data but this a very touchy area.[40]

An article in *The Nashville Tennessean* insists Saddam Hussein has been developing 220 pounds of Lithium 6 a year. Lithium 6 can be converted to Tritium, an essential ingredient in thermonuclear reactions.[41]

Other sources say that 6,000 to 7,000 SADMs were produced, some of which made their way to Israel and other countries.[42] Sam Cohen confirms this information in the Fall issue of *Journal of Civil Defense,* Cohen, echoing Harrison, charges that the U.S. has purposefully underestimated the number of nuclear warheads that Iran, Iraq and North Korea could produce, and deliberately discounted their capacity to produce substantially smaller warheads.

"A couple of years ago," states Cohen, "disturbing statements on advanced small, very low-yield nuclear warheads, began emanating from Russia.* Cohen adds that these articles "revealed a massive smuggling ring had emerged where the material was being sold around the world to a number of countries, some of which were terrorist nations." [43]

Had the Murrah Building been destroyed by a SADM or a backpack nuke, using the truck-bomb as a cover? British bomb experts, with extensive experience dealing with terrorist truck-bombs, told McVeigh's attorney, Stephen Jones, that the ANFO bomb could not have done all of the damage to the Murrah Building. [44]

British bomb expert Linda Jones, testifying for the prosecution in McVeigh's trial, came to the opposite conclusion, however. Nevertheless, the site was quickly demolished and covered over with concrete; the remains taken to a secure dump and buried. What was the government trying to hide? Nuclear Physicist Galen Winsor, General Partin, and KPOC manager David Hall went to the building and disposal sites with radiation measuring equipment, but were kept away. They managed to gather some fragments anyway, and when they measured them with Winsor's NaI Scintillator detector, they registered radiation levels 50 percent higher than normal.

"A new class of nuclear weapons could exist which could have an extremely disturbing terrorist potential," says Cohen. "And to admit to the possibility that the warheads might be sufficiently compact to pose a real terrorist threat was equally unacceptable [to the government]." [45]

So was the Federal Building blown up by demolition charges, a truck filled with C-4, a fuel-air explosive, a miniature nuke, or some combination of the above?

KFOR-Channel 4 reported that the mysterious severed leg clothed in military garb found in the rubble allegedly had PVC embedded it. PVC pipe is sometimes used to pack plastic explosives. It increases the shear power. Had this leg, unmatched to any of the known victims, belonged to the real bomber? **

---

* Within the last few years, articles have appeared in the U.S., European, and even Russian media dealing with an exotic new material known as "Red Mercury" which had been developed by the Russians and allegedly held properties capable of producing far more efficient nuclear fission warheads than the conventional explosives developed thus far.

** Authorities later backtracked on the leg, claiming that it belonged to Air Force recruit Lakesha Levy. They originally said the leg belonged to a light-skinned male in his 30s. They then said it belonged to a black female, in order to match it with Levy.

Then on March 20, 1996, *Strategic Investment* newsletter reported that a Pentagon study had been leaked which backed General Partin's analysis:

A classified report prepared by two independent Pentagon experts has concluded that the destruction of the federal building in Oklahoma City last April was caused by five separate bombs. The two experts reached the same conclusion for the same technical reasons. Sources close to the Pentagon study say Timothy McVeigh did play a role in the bombing but peripherally, as a "useful idiot." The multiple bombings have a Middle Eastern "signature," pointing to either Iraqi or Syrian involvement.[46]

Finally, in the Spring of 1997, explosives experts at Eglin Air Force Base's Wright Laboratory Armament Directorate released a study on the effects of explosives against a reinforced concrete building similar to the Federal Building. The Air Force's test closely matched the conditions under which the government contends the Murrah Building was destroyed.

The Eglin Blast Effects Study, or EBES, involved a three-story reinforced concrete structure 80 long, 40 feet wide, and 30 feet high. The building constructed for the test, the Eglin Test Structure (ETS), while smaller than the Murrah Building, was similar in design, with three rows of columns, and six-inch-thick concrete panels similar to those in the Murrah Building. Overall, the ETS was considerably weaker than the Murrah, which had five times the amount of steel reinforcing than the ETS, and 10 times the amount of steel in its columns and beams. As *New American* editor William Jasper noted in regards to the EBES:

If air blast could not effect catastrophic failure to the decidedly inferior Eglin structure, it becomes all the more difficult to believe that it was responsible for the destruction of the much stronger Murrah Building.

The experts at Eglin conducted three tests. They first detonated 704 pounds of Tritonal (equivalent to 830 pounds of TNT or approximately 2,200 pounds of ANFO), at a distance of 40 feet from the structure, equivalent to the distance the Ryder truck was parked from the Murrah Building. The second test utilized an Mk-82 warhead (equivalent to 180 pounds of TNT) placed within the first floor corner room approximately four feet from the exterior wall. The third test involved a 250-pound penetrating warhead (equivalent to 35 pounds TNT), placed in the corner of a second floor room approximately two and a half feet from the adjoining walls.

The first detonation demolished the six-inch-thick concrete wall panels on the first floor, but left the reinforcing steel bars intact. The 14-inch columns were unaffected by the blast—a far cry from what occurred at the Murrah Building. The damages to the second and third floors fell off proportionally, unlike that in

Oklahoma City. The 56-page report concluded:

> Due to these conditions, it is impossible to ascribe the damage that occurred on
> April 19, 1995 to a single truck-bomb containing 4,800 lbs. of ANFO. In fact, the
> maximum predicted damage to the floor panels of the Murrah Federal Building is
> equal to approximately 1% of the total floor area of the building. Furthermore, due
> to the lack of symmetrical damage pattern at the Murrah Building, it would be
> inconsistent with the results of the ETS test [number] one to state that all of the
> damage to the Murrah Building is the result of the truck-bomb. The damage to the
> Murrah Federal Building is consistent with damage resulting from mechanically
> coupled devices placed locally within the structure....
>
> It must be concluded that the damage at the Murrah Federal Building is not the
> result of the truck-bomb itself, but rather due to other factors such as locally placed
> charges within the building itself ... The procedures used to cause the damage to
> the Murrah Building are therefore more involved and complex than simply parking
> a truck and leaving.[47]

Even the Federal Emergency Management Agency (FEMA) was forced to
conclude that 4,800 pounds of ANFO could have not caused the so-called 30-
foot crater in Oklahoma City. FEMA's report, published on August 30, 1996,
inadvertently concluded that the bombers would have had to use approximately
three times the amount reportedly used in Oklahoma City.[48]

Another interesting confirmation came from FBI agent Danny Defenbaugh,
who, along with U.S. Attorney Beth Wilkinson, visited General Partin in June,
1995. Part of the team that prosecuted McVeigh and Nichols, Wilkinson interviewed Partin on the presumption that he would be called as a witness. "[Agent
Defenbaugh] was going through the report that I did," recalls Partin, "and he put
his finger on that picture I had in the report ... the designated crater, and he said,
'Suppose I told you that is not the crater?'"

Partin believes Wilkinson and Defenbaugh (who Partin described as belligerent) interviewed him as part of a ruse to find out what he knew about the blast(s),
so the government could carefully avoid those issues at trial. While they pretend-
ed to be interested in Partin's analysis, they never kept their word to follow up the
interview.

"I think what they did," said Partin, "was they looked at my credentials and
technical justification of all this stuff, and they found that what I had was based
on some pretty sound footing ... I think that's why they framed the case the way
they did."[49]

Whatever blew up the Alfred P. Murrah Building, one thing's for sure, enough
ANFO was present at the site to leave visible traces. Randy Ledger, a maintenance man who was in the building at the time of the blast, claims fellow work-

ers who rushed into the building immediately after the explosion "complained of burning eyes, heavy dust and choking lungs. That is right out of the textbook of a diesel-fertilizer bomb, because it creates nitric acid," said Ledger. "The guys I work with, they're not going to make it up that their eyes are burning." [50]

Dr. Paul Heath, a VA psychologist who was on the fifth floor of the building at the time of the blast, said, "I picked fertilizer out of my skin ... I could see the fertilizer actually exploding in the air; you could see it popping all around you."

Ramona McDonald, who also survived the blast, concurs with Heath. "There was a bright flash, and then boom! And you could see the fertilizer popping in the air."

Given this scenario, it's reasonable to conclude that the Ryder truck was filled with something more powerful, with just enough ANFO to leave a visible trace.

Cohen agrees. "The damage that resulted could not have occurred from a van parked outside ... I don't care how fancy an explosive was used. What did in that building ... was an inside job."

It would appear that experts' analysis' are not the only evidence of an inside job. In an interview with a local TV station, a man who escaped the building said, "I was sitting at my desk, and I felt a rumbling, a shaking in the building ... so I decided to get under my desk ... the glass windows blew in and knocked down the ceiling and some of the stuff above the ceiling and it all landed on top of my desk."

Another man said, "I thought it was an earthquake because I resided in California for many years, and it was almost like it was in slow motion. I felt a shake, and then it began shaking more, and I dove under my desk, and then the glass all came flying in."

A friend of Dr. Ray Brown's, who's secretary was in the building said, "She was standing by a window. The window cracked, then she got away from it and then she was blown across the room and landed in another woman's lap. Another woman I know, Judy Morse, got under her desk after feeling the building shake, and before the glass flew."

"Dr. Brian Espe, who was the sole survivor in the Department of Agriculture's fifth floor office, told the author he first "heard a rumbling noise."

According to these individuals' accounts, if the truck-bomb—the alleged sole bomb—had detonated first, how would they have felt a rumbling, had time to think about the situation, then dive under their desks? The resulting blast wave from the truck-bomb would have been immediate and total. Such an account could only be indicative of demolition charges placed inside the building.*

"The inside charges—demolition charges," said Cohen, "may have gone off

---

* David Hall, manager of KPOC-TV in Ponca City, who has done considerable investigation into the bombing, told me that two Southwestern Bell employees called him and claimed they had a surveillance tape that showed the Murrah Building shaking before the truck bomb detonated.

first, and so the columns now started to collapse. Boy, that would produce one hell of a rumble, to put it mildly." [51]

A caller to the Oklahoma Radio Network related the experiences of his friend, a Federal Government worker, who had witnessed the blast first-hand. "He was approximately five blocks from the building whenever the building went up. He claims that the top of the building went up like a missile going through it. The debris was coming back down when the side of the building blew out. He said third and last, the truck blew up on the street." [52]

Notice this witness said the building "blew out" contrary to the effect of an explosive blowing the building in from the street. Candy Avey, who was on her way to the Social Security office when the explosions occurred, was blown away from the building, struck a parking meter, and then hit her car. [53] Said Suzanne Steely, reporting live for KFOR, "We could see all the way through the building. That was just the force of the explosion—it just blew out all the walls and everything inside." Ramona McDonald saw a flash and smoke rising up from inside the building, "like a rocket had shot out the top of the building." [54]

It should be obvious to the reader that it's unlikely an ANFO bomb parked out in the street would have the force to blow all the way through a huge superstructure like the Alfred P. Murrah Building.

No matter how hard the government tried to distort the truth, evidence would come back to haunt them.

On April 19, a tape recording made during a conference at the Water Resources Board directly across from the Murrah Building indicates a succession of blast events, spaced very close together.

The tape recorder at the Water Resources Board was not the only instrument recording explosions that morning. The seismograph at the Oklahoma Geological Survey at the University of Oklahoma at Norman, 16 miles from the Murrah Building, recorded two waves, or "two events," on the morning of April 19. Another seismograph at the Omniplex Museum, four miles away from the Federal Building, also recorded two events. These seismic waves, or "spikes," spaced approximately ten seconds apart, seem to indicate two blasts.

Professor Raymond Brown, senior geophysicist at the University of Oklahoma who studied the seismograms, knew and talked to people inside the building at the time of the blast. "My first impression was, this was a demolition job," said Brown. "Somebody who went in there with equipment tried to take that building down."

Not so, according to the U.S. Geological Survey's analysis. The USGS put out a press release on June 1st, entitled "Seismic Records Support One-Blast Theory in Oklahoma City Bombing."

The bomb that destroyed the Alfred P. Murrah Building in Oklahoma City produced a train of conventional seismic waves, according to interpretations by scientists with the U.S. Geological Survey and the Oklahoma Geological Survey (OGS).

Scientists from those agencies said the seismic recordings of the May 23 demolition of the building reproduced the character of the original, April 19th seismic recording by producing two trains of seismic waves that were recorded on seismometers near Norman, Okla.

"Seismic recordings from the building's implosion indicate that there was only one bomb explosion on April 19," said Dr. Thomas Holzer, a USGS geologist in Menlo Park, Calif. Holzer is one of several USGS and OGS scientists who analyzed the shock waves created by the April 19 explosion and the May 23 implosion.[55]

Holzer added that the two distinct waves from the April 19 explosion(s) were the result of the same wave traveling at two different speeds through two separate layers of the earth's crust. The "illusion" of a double explosion was simply the result of the building's collapse, he claimed. "So the bottom line then," said Holzer, "is I think these observations are totally consistent with a single explosion. It doesn't require multiple explosions to do it."[56]

Dr. Brown has an honest difference of opinion with folks at the U.S. Geological Survey. "I will candidly say that we are having trouble finding that velocity difference," said Brown. "We have not identified a pair of layers that could account for the ten-second difference.

"Whatever the USGS saw in that data convinced them that the original blast was one bomb," he added. "I find that hard to believe ... What was uncomfortable and might be construed as pressure is that they were going to come out with a press release that says we have concluded that data indicates one bomb. It puts us in the uncomfortable stance of saying that we, too, have concluded that, and we haven't."

Yet the USGS press release said that Dr. Charles Mankin of the OGS, Brown's boss, was "pleased with the work performed by Dr. Holzer and his USGS colleagues in the analysis of the seismic records." Mankin actually urged Holzer to delay the press release. "Everybody that has looked at the signal has said a refraction [an echo] would really be strange because there's absolutely no loss of energy in the recorded seismic signal. The second event has the same amplitude as the first ... The arrival time is wrong for a refracted wave. We've ruled out reflections, refractions, and the air blast. We determined that these two records of these two events corroborate our interpretation that there were two explosions."[57]

The mainstream media, of course, jumped on the USGS's findings, with headlines like "Single Bomb Destroyed Building" and "Seismic Records Shake Murrah Multiple Bomb Theory." "The news media even reported two bomb blasts initially," said Mankin, "but later changed their story."

"The USGS's conclusions are not supported by either data or analysis," added Brown, who asked that his name be taken off the report. Although Brown cautions that his own conclusions are far from conclusive and require "more thorough investigation," the most logical explanation for the second event says Brown, is "a bomb on the inside of the building."

"Even the smallest of those detonations (from the May 23rd demolition) had a larger effect on the recording than the collapse of the building," he added, "which demonstrates that the explosives are much more efficient at exciting the ground motion than is the collapse of three-fourths of the building. So it is very unlikely that one-fourth of the building falling on April 19th could have created an energy wave similar to that caused by the large [truck-bomb] explosion." [58]

One of the problems with the two event theory is that the spikes on the seismic readings were ten seconds apart. With that much difference, most everybody in the vicinity should have heard two separate blasts. But given the traumatic nature of being in the immediate vicinity of a bombing, would witnesses necessarily have heard two explosions? Although the sound of a truck-bomb would certainly have made a loud, roaring noise, complete with lots of smoke and flying debris, experts say that the "crack" of a C-4 cutting charge is "downright disappointing" to hear.

One man working as a parking garage attendant one block north of the Murrah Building told *The New American* that he was test driving a new pickup truck near the building when the bomb went off. "It seemed like one, big, long explosion," he said, "but I can't say for sure. My ears were ringing and glass and rocks and concrete were falling all over and around me." [59]

Dr. Paul Heath, who was on the fifth floor, says he heard only one blast. But fellow VA worker Jim Guthrie stated in an interview with the *Washington Post:*

"I felt a boom and was picked up off my feet and thrown under a water fountain." He heard a second explosion and covered his ears. Diane Dooley, who was at a third floor stairwell, also believes she heard a second explosion. [60]

P. G. Wilson, who worked in the Murrah Building, told researcher Michele Moore, "A second explosion came after the first one and shards of glass began flying in the office." [61]

Hassan Muhammad, who was driving for a delivery service that day, had his ears ruptured by the explosions. Muhammad told the author he clearly recalled hearing two distinct blasts. "When I was crossing the street [at 10th and Robinson] ... the first explosion went off, and it was a loud explosion. And my friend who was coming out of the warehouse asked me what was it, because we thought it was a drive-by shooting ... and we got on the ground, and by the time we got on the ground, another one went off, and that's when all the windows came out." Muhammad recalls that it was about three to four seconds between blasts. [62]

Jane C. Graham, a HUD worker injured in the bombing, also clearly felt two distinct blasts. As Graham stated in a videotaped deposition: "I want to specify that the first bomb—the first impact—the first effect, was a waving effect, that you got when the building was moving, you might have maybe felt a little waving, perhaps an earthquake movement, and that lasted for several seconds.

"About six or seven seconds later, a bomb exploded. It was an entirely different sound and thrust. It was like it came up right from the center up. You could feel the building move a little. But there were two distinct events that occurred. The second blast not only was very, very loud, it was also very powerful. And as I said, I just felt like it was coming straight on up from the center of the building—straight up."[63]

Michael Hinton, who was on a bus near NW 5th and Robinson—one block away—also heard two explosions. "I had just sat down when I heard this violent type rumble under the bus," said Hinton. "It was a pushing type motion—it actually raised that bus up on its side. About six or seven seconds later another one which was more violent than the first picked the bus up again, and I thought that second time the bus was going to turn over."[64]

What Hinton describes is consistent with a two-bomb scenario. The first, smaller explosion being the more subdued blast of the demolition charges. The second, larger explosion being the blast of the truck-bomb—the blast pressure wave of which almost tipped the bus over.

In an interview with *Media Bypass* magazine, attorney Charles Watts, who was in the Federal Courthouse across the street, describes hearing and feeling two separate blasts:

Watts: I was up on the ninth floor, the top floor of the Bankruptcy Court, with nothing in between the two buildings. We were on the south side, out in the foyer, outside the courtroom. It was nine o'clock, or just very, very shortly thereafter. Several lawyers were standing there talking and there was a large explosion. It threw several of the people close to me to the floor. I don't think it threw me to the floor, but it did move me significantly, and I threw myself to the floor, and got down, and about that time, a huge blast, unlike anything I've ever experienced, hit.

Media Bypass: The blast wave hit?

Watts: A second blast. There were two explosions. The second blast made me think that the whole building was coming in.

Watts, a Vietnam veteran, has experienced being within 100 feet of B-52 air strikes. Watts told *Media Bypass* he never experienced anything like this before.[65]

Another veteran who heard the blast is George Wallace, a retired Air Force fighter pilot with 26 years in the service. Wallace, who lives nine miles northwest of the Federal Building described the blast as a "sustained, loud, long rumble, like several explosions." Wallace likened the noise to that of a succession of bombs being dropped by B-52s.[66]

Taken together, the evidence and witness accounts appears to indicate that there were at least two blasts on the morning of April 19.

General Partin, along with Senator Inhoffe, Representative Key and others, asked Congress that the building not be demolished until an independent forensic team could be brought in to investigate the damage.

"It is easy to determine whether a column was failed by contact demolition charges or by blast loading (such as a truck-bomb)," Partin wrote in his letter to Congress. "It is also easy to cover up crucial evidence as was apparently done in Waco. I understand that the building is to be demolished by May 23rd or 24th. Why the rush to destroy the evidence?"*

Cohen echoed Partin's sentiments: "I believe that demolition charges in the building placed at certain key concrete columns did the primary damage to the Murrah Federal Building. I concur with the opinion that an investigation by the Oklahoma State Legislature is absolutely necessary to get at the truth of what actually caused the tragedy in Oklahoma City."

Yet the Feds in fact did demolish the Murrah Building on May 23, destroying the evidence while citing the same reason as they did for quickly demolishing the Waco compound: "health hazards." In the Waco case, what was destroyed was evidence that the Feds had fired from helicopters into the roof of the building during the early part of the raid, killing several people, including a nursing mother. In the Oklahoma case, what was destroyed was evidence that the columns had been destroyed by demolition charges.**

The rubble from the Murrah Building was hauled by Midwest Wrecking to a landfill surrounded by a guarded, barbed-wire fence, sifted for evidence with the help of the National Guard, then subsequently hauled off to BFI Waste Management and buried. Along with it was buried the evidence of what really happened on the morning of April 19.

"It's a classic cover-up," said Partin, "a classic cover-up."

---

* Unfortunately, Partin shot himself in the foot in his first letter to Congress by insinuating that the bombing was the work of a Communist conspiracy (The Third Socialist International), thereby possibly portraying himself in the eyes of some as a right-wing "kook." But in spite of his politics, his technical credentials are beyond reproach.

** This is reminiscent of the cover-up of the JFK assassination, where Secret Service agents carefully washed down the president's limo immediately after the shooting with buckets of water to remove all traces of bullet fragments, and had Governor Connolly's clothes, bullet holes and all, cleaned and pressed.

"EVERYTHING SHORT OF A T-72 TANK"

If the bombing of the Murrah Building was the result of an inside job, who is responsible? Was it wired for demolition, and if so, who could have wired it?

Dr. Heath, who has worked in the Murrah Building for 22 years, was present on the day of the bombing. Although Heath personally discounts the second bomb theory, he explained that poor security in the building would have permitted access to almost anyone, anytime.

"The security was so lax in this building, that one individual or group of individuals could have had access to any of those columns," said Heath, "almost in every part of the building, before or after hours, or even during the hours of the workday, and could have planted bombs."

Guy Rubsamen, the Federal Protective Services guard on duty the night of the 18th, said that nobody had entered the building. Yet Rubsamen took off at 2:00 A.M., and said that nobody was guarding the building from 2:00 A.M. to 6:00 A.M.[67]

"It was a building you could have planted a bomb in anytime you wanted to," said Heath. "It was a building that was not secure at all. I've gone in and out of this building with a pen knife, just by slipping a knife in the south doors, slide the bolt back, and go in without a key. I've done that ever since the building was new. If you wanted into it, you could have gotten into it any time you wanted to."*

Heath also explained that visitors could drive right into the garage, anytime. "There was no guard. You could drive inside the garage—four stories—anytime you wanted to, and carry anything you wanted to inside the car."[68]

It appears that alleged bomber Timothy McVeigh (or someone driving his car) did just that. On the morning of April 19, attorney James Linehan was stopped for a light at the corner of NW 4th and Robinson at approximately 8:38 A.M. when he observed a battered yellow Mercury run the light and drive directly into the underground parking garage. Linehan said the driver had sharp facial features similar to McVeigh's, although he thought the driver may have been a woman.

Referring to the well-publized scene of McVeigh being led out of the Noble County Courthouse, Linehan said, "That's it! That's the same profile." Curiously, one month later Linehan said, "My gut feeling is that it was a female driving."[69]

Why did "McVeigh" drive into the garage? Could he have done so to plant additional bombs? Or perhaps someone in McVeigh's car made it *appear* that he was doing so? A fall-guy for the real bombers?

"If McVeigh was totally outside the law, he certainly wouldn't have snuggled

---

* Such a situation is reminiscent of JFK's visit to Dallas, where the plotters made sure the President's protective bubble was removed from his limousine, and made sure the Secret Service never bothered to check the many open windows around Dealy Plaza—a standard security procedure in such a situation.

up against them by driving into that basement that morning," said David Hall, general manager of KPOC-TV in Ponca City, Oklahoma, who has investigated the ATF's role in the bombing."

Yet Hall doesn't believe "the ATF or the FBI or anybody went around and wired columns or anything like that. What [Partin] said was that there may have been some explosives stored by some columns that went off. I don't feel that those people set out to kill 168 people in Oklahoma City intentionally. But I think that because of incompetence on their part that very well may have happened in two or three different ways...."

Shortly after the bombing, an unidentified witness called Representative Key and told him that she saw two men in the garage who appeared to be "sawing" on the pillars. The men were working in almost total darkness. When she asked them what they were doing, they said, "We're just putting things right again."

Were they "putting things right," or were they weakening the support columns just enough to make sure that they'd fail at the appropriate moment? [70]

Then, on the Friday before the bombing, HUD worker Jane Graham noticed three men in the garage whom she thought were telephone repairmen. As Graham stated in her deposition, the men were holding what appeared to be C-4 plastic explosives:

"It was a block, probably two by three inches or three by four, in that area, but it was a putty color—solid piece of block—I don't know what it was. But they had that and they had this wiring. When they saw me watching them, they were down there and they had plans of the building. They were discussing—they were arguing in fact—apparently there was a disagreement, because one of the men was pointing to various areas of the garage. They were talking about, I assume, plans of the building. I thought maybe they were telephone men at first.

"When they saw me watching them, they took the wiring—it looked like cord, telephone cord—it was putty colored—they took whatever else was in their hand, they put all of that back into a paper sack, they put it in the driver's side, behind the passenger seat [of a] pale green, slightly faded station wagon."

Graham later told me that one of the men was holding a one by two by three inch device that looked like "some sort of clicker, like a small TV remote-control," she said.

The men stopped working abruptly when they saw Graham. "They looked uncomfortable," she said. "They were as intent looking at me as I was at them." She also stated that the men were not wearing uniforms and were not driving a telephone or electric company truck. They were, however, very well-built. They "obviously lifted weights" said Graham.

(Graham's account is backed up by IRS worker Kathy Wilburn, who also saw the trio of men in the garage, as did a HUD employee named Joan.)

Although the FBI interviewed Graham, they never showed her any pictures or brought her before a sketch artist. "They only wanted to know if I could identify McVeigh or Nichols," she said. "I said it was neither of these two gentlemen."[71]

A call to the local electric, telephone, and natural gas companies revealed that the men were not authorized repairmen. Nor were they construction workers inspecting the premises for a proposed renovation project by the General Services Administration (GSA). The 20 or so contractors involved in that bid stated emphatically that the men were not their employees.[72]

David Hall (who stopped working on the case in late 1995 due to an IRS audit) wasn't aware of the Graham deposition, but he did drop a bombshell.

"We do know that explosives were delivered there without a doubt. We know there were six boxes of 25 to 35 pounds marked 'high explosives' delivered to the building two weeks prior to the explosion. We had contact with the truck driver who was involved in that delivery. The name of the trucking company is Tri-State, located in Joplin, Missouri."

Tri-State is an explosives carrier.

"We've talked to the driver," said Hall. "We've talked to two drivers. Nobody knows what was in them because they were boxed and marked 'high explosive.'"

Then Hall dropped another bombshell.

"We also know that the ATF had a magazine inside the building, which was illegal. But the floor was blown out of that magazine. And there's some question about what was in there too that created that damage, because that was a foot of concrete that was blown out of that magazine."[73]

While several other unexploded bombs were pulled out of the wreckage, none were widely mentioned.

One such bomb was a two by two foot box marked "High Explosives" *which had a timer on it.* This was confirmed by Oklahoma City Fire Marshal Dick Miller. The timing mechanism apparently had been set to detonate at ten minutes after nine. Apparently it had malfunctioned due to the initial blast.[74]

According to Toni Garrett, a nurse who was on the scene tagging dead bodies: "Four people—rescue workers—told us there was a bomb in the building with a timing mechanism set to go off ten minutes after nine." According to Garrett, witnesses told her it was an active bomb. "We saw the Bomb Squad take it away."[75]

This fact was confirmed by an Oklahoma City Police officer who inadvertently began to walk into the building when a fireman yelled, "Hey idiot, that's a bomb!" The stunned officer looked over and saw the two by two box surrounded by police crime tape. He then heard the fireman yell, "There's one over there and another over there! We're waiting for the Bomb Squads to come back from hauling off the others."

Investigator Phil O'Halloran has Bill Martin of the Oklahoma City Police Department (OCPD) on tape stating that one of the bombs found in the building was two to three five-gallon containers of Mercury Fulminate—a powerful explosive—one not easily obtainable, except to military sources.[76]

Citizens monitoring police radios heard the following conversation on the morning of the 19th:

First voice: "Boy, you're not gonna believe this!"
Second voice: "Believe what?"
First voice: "I can't believe it … this is a military bomb!"[77]

Apparently, the containers, with "Milspec" (military specification) markings clearly visible, were found in the basement. Could this explain what McVeigh's car was doing in the underground parking garage? Mercury Fulminate is a highly volatile booster material. Volatile enough to create a very powerful explosion.*

Shortly thereafter, a fireman up on the third floor of the building noticed two military ambulances pull up to the building, and saw several men in dark fatigues carrying stretchers from the building to the waiting ambulances. What were on the stretchers were not bodies, but boxes, which appeared to contain documents. One of the stretchers had on it what appeared to be a missile launch tube. The missile, apparently part of the Army recruiting office's display, was confirmed the 61st EOD to be inert.[78]**

What is also interesting is that General Partin stated the building's support structures failed primarily at the third floor level. In speculating who would have access at that juncture, it may be relevant to note that the Department of Defense (DoD) was on the third floor, adjoining column B-3, which Partin believes contained the main detonation charge.†

Partin was also informed by an acquaintance in the CIA that several of their personnel who examined the site discovered Mercury Fulminate residue on several rooftops near the building.[79]

---

* According to an Army technical manual on military explosives, Mercury Fulminate is only safe to handle if it is "dead-pressed."

** It was the presence of military ordinance that brought the 61st EOD (Explosive Ordinance Demolition) team from Fort Sill in to examine and defuse the bombs.

† The Army had a recruiting office in the building, which would have made the presence of military personnel inconspicuous. The Department of Agriculture also had an office in the building. The Department of Agriculture has been used as a front for IRS intelligence, and also the 113th M.I.G. (Military Intelligence Group) in Chicago in 1970. Given the easy access to military personnel in the building, it would have been easy for military personnel to go through the building unnoticed.

Around the same time as the Eglin Air Force Base report was being made public, William Northrop, a former Israeli intelligence agent, told me that a friend in the CIA's Directorate of Operations informed him that there was plastic explosive residue on the building's columns.

Adding more fuel to the theory of an inside job was the dismembered military leg found in the wreckage—a leg not belonging to any of the known victims. (Authorities would later attempt to attribute the leg to Airman Lakesha Levy.)

Nor was the local media attributing the bombing to the work of amateurs. "Right now, they are saying that this is the work of a sophisticated group," stated a KFOR-TV newscaster. "This is the work of a sophisticated device, and it had to have been done by an explosives expert, obviously, with this type of explosion." [80]

Even Governor Frank Keating told local news stations: "The reports I have is that one device was deactivated, and there's another device, and obviously whatever did the damage to the Murrah Building was a tremendous, very sophisticated explosive device."

Newscasters live on the scene could be heard throughout the day announcing, "We have reports of two other bombs pulled out of the building," and "The second two devices were larger than the first," and so on:

KFOR Channel 4: The FBI has confirmed there is another bomb in the Federal Building. It's in the East side of the building. They've moved everybody back several blocks, obviously to, uh, unplug it so it wont go off. They're moving everybody back. It's a … it's a weird scene because at first everybody was running when they gave the word to get everybody away from the scene, but now people are just standing around kind of staring. It's a very surreal, very strange scene.

Now, we want to get some information out to people, to people who are in the downtown area. You don't want to stand on the sidewalk, and the reason for that is there are gas mains underneath and if there's a second explosion, that those gas mains could blow. But, again, we do have confirmation. There is a second bomb in the Federal Building. We know it's on the east side. We're not sure what floor, what level, but there is definitely danger of a major second explosion. They're warning everybody to get as far back as they can. They're trying to get the bomb defused right now. They are in the process of doing it, but this could take some time. They're telling people that this is something to take very seriously, and not to slip forward to get a look at this, because this thing could definitely go off.

KWTV Channel 9: All right, we just saw, if you were watching, there, there was a white pickup truck backing a trailer into the scene here. They are trying to get people out of the way so that they can get it in. Appears to be the Oklahoma Bomb Squad. It's their Bomb Disposal Unit, is what it is, and it is what they would use if, if, the report that we gave you just a few minutes ago is correct, that a second explosive device of some kind is inside the building. They'll back that trailer in there, and the Bomb Squad folks will go in and they'll use that trailer. You see the bucket on the back? This is how they would transport the Explosive Device away from this populated area. They would try to do something.

Finally, KFOR announced:

The second explosive was found and defused. The third explosive was found—and they are working on it right now as we speak. I understand that both the second and the third explosives were larger than the first.*

When Channel 4 interviewed terrorism expert Dr. Randall Heather at approximately 1:00 P.M., he stated: "We should find out an awful lot, when these bombs are taken apart ... We got lucky today, if you can consider anything about this tragedy lucky. It's actually a great stroke of luck, that we've got defused bombs. It's through the bomb material that we'll be able to track down who committed this atrocity." [81]

It is uncertain whether or not the bombs were taken apart and examined. As stated in a report prepared by the National Fire Protection Association: "The device was removed in the Sheriff's bomb trailer and exploded in a remote location." [82]

The additional bombs inside the building then became a car-bomb outside the building, then a van containing 2,000 pounds of ANFO, and finally a truck containing 4,800 pounds.

Governor Keating, who himself reported a second device, later reversed his position, proclaiming that Representative Key and others investigating additional bombs and suspects were "howling at the moon," and "off the reservation."

When J.D. Cash, a journalist writing for the *McCurtain County Gazette*, tried to interview members of the Bomb Squad, Fire Department and Police, he was told by potential interviewees, "I saw a lot that day, I wish I hadn't. I have a wife, a job, a family ... I've been threatened, we've been told not to talk about the devices." [83]

When I attempted to interview two members of the Sheriff's Bomb Squad who were first on the scene, they told me there were *no* additional bombs taken away or detonated. When questioned further they became visibly uptight and referred me to their superior.

Oklahoma City FBI SAC Bob Ricks, of Waco fame, coolly stated to the press, "We never did find another device ... we confirmed that no other device existed." [84]

The ATF, who initially denied even having any explosives in the building, eventually recanted their statements and told reporters that the two by two foot

---

* According to the September, 1995 edition of *Firehouse* magazine, there were three bomb scares: one at 10:22, one at 10:45, and one at 1:51.

box was a "training bomb." I asked General Partin if there could be such a thing as an ATF "training bomb."

"I would certainly not think so," said Partin. "Look, when you have an EOD team—EOD teams are very well-trained people. And any training device would have to be so labeled—so labeled. And the EOD people who were there were claiming it was explosives."[85]

Former ATF man Rick Sherrow had his own thoughts on the issue of training bombs. "All the field offices have that material [training bombs]. It's 100 percent on the outside—weighs the same, looks the same, but it has no fill—no inert markings or anything else. I can't say absolutely that's what was found in the building, but it's more than likely. They had stun grenades too, which are live. They can't contribute anything [to the damage], but they lied about it, and that jams up their credibility."[86]

Cash interviewed GSA workers who helped the ATF unload their arsenal room two weeks after the blast, describing, in a series of *Gazette* articles beginning May 4, 1995, how the ATF had stored weapons, explosives and ammunition in the Murrah Building, contravening the very laws they were supposed to enforce:

Both the Alcohol, Tobacco and Firearms Bureau (ATF) and the Drug Enforcement Bureau (DEA) had explosives and weapons—including an anti-tank missile—illegally stored in the building when it blew up April 19, the *McCurtain Gazette* has learned. An eyewitness observer told the *Gazette* recently of assisting federal agents to remove weapons and explosive devices from a partially-damaged arsenal inside the Federal Building after the explosion.*

Lester Martz, ATF Special Agent in Charge for the region told *The Dallas Morning News* and the author, "That locker was intact." Martz went on to say that the blasted-out area between columns B-2 and B-4 was the result of DEA ordnance. Yet the DEA offices were on the west side of the building on the seventh floor, nowhere near that area. The ATF offices, however, were in close proximity to blasted area, located in the top rear east corner of the building.

ATF officials adamantly denied that no explosives were stored in the building. But OCPD Officer Don Browning, who viewed video footage taken by Sheriff Melvin Sumter, says C-4 was "definitely" carried out of the building. Browning, a Vietnam veteran, described the explosives he saw: "It was in wide blocks, about 3/4" thick, around 10" long, and about 2" wide, wrapped in cellophane."[87]

Cash interviewed at least one unnamed witness who described helping ATF agents remove ordnance from their storage locker:

---

* The TOW missile, inspected by the 61st EOD team out of Ft. Sill was inert, as reported on the Oklahoma County Sheriff's Evidence/Ordinance Acceptance Form, dated 4/19/95.

"One night, up on the ninth floor, where the ATF offices [were], I helped some of their agents load onto an elevator small arms, machine guns, several cases of ammunition and even some boxes marked 'Explosives.'"[88]

The *Gazette* interviewed two more witnesses who assisted in the post bombing clean-up. One, a civilian contractor hired by the GSA, told the *Gazette* July 30:

"They had everything! ... home-made zip guns, AK-47s, sawed-off shotguns, AR-15s, M-16s—literally hundreds of guns. You name it, they had it all ... any kind of weapon you could ever want." He also said he recalls seeing an ATF agent with a five-gallon bucket of hand-grenades.

"They carried out every conceivable type of firearm known to man," Cash told video producer Chuck Allen, "including hundreds of thousands of rounds of ammunition, boxes marked explosives, hand grenades, everything short of a Russian T-72 tank." Finally, a witness told the *Gazette:*

"What was left of that [ATF magazine] room is in the far southeast end of the ninth floor, but much of it was blown away and [apparently] disappeared into the rubble right on top of the America's Kids Day Care Center."

The area just below the ATF's arsenal room—the coned-in area on the far left (southeast) side of the building seen in aerial photographs—is where most of the casualties occurred. This area extends one to two stories below the street level.

This is not the first time such a "mishap" occurred. Approximately 10 years ago, some captured Soviet ordnance, including rockets with high-explosive warheads, wound up stored at FBI headquarters in Washington, D.C. A fire exploded the ordnance, causing more than a little consternation among firefighters, especially when one rocket took off and blasted a two-foot diameter hole in a cinder block wall. When the story leaked out, the ATF reacted by removing more than 30 pounds of explosives from their own offices down the street.[89]

In Allen's video, Cash makes the assertion that the massive internal damage to the building was the result of secondary explosions caused by illegally stored explosives. The ordnance, which included percussion caps for C-4 (and C-4 itself), had fallen from their ninth floor storage area after the initial truck blast, Cash suggests, to one of the lower floors, where it detonated, causing massive internal damage. Although C-4 is relatively safe to handle, according to Cash's experts, it can be set off with 3500 p.s.i. of pressure.

General Partin disagrees with Cash's analysis, explaining: "For anything to have tumbled down from up there and done the increased damage is technically impossible ... if something had fallen after that section had collapsed and caused an explosion that brought down [column] B-3, the thing would not have cropped the way it did. If you look up there at the top left hand side, you don't see anything up there that would indicate that you had a big blowout at the top. If it had, it wouldn't of had anything to do with the column collapsing down below—they're too far away."

I asked Partin if C-4 could explode due to the increased air pressure resulting from the truck blast, from the weight of falling debris, or simply by falling eight or nine stories.

"Look," said Partin, "C-4 is kinda tough to get to go; ammonium-nitrate is even tougher. It takes a real intense shock wave to get that kind of explosive to go." Partin added, "I thought I explained it to Cash, but I guess he's persisting with his story."

Why Cash persists with his story while largely sidestepping Partin's analysis is curious. Yet if the ATF were responsible for the secondary explosion, they would have reason to lie.

Was the ATF in fact responsible, knowingly or unknowingly, for the explosion that destroyed the Murrah Building? Consider the following article which appeared in the June 5, 1995 issue of *Newsweek:*

> For the past year, the ATF and the Army Corps of Engineers have been blowing up car bombs at the White Sands Proving Ground in New Mexico. The project, code-named Dipole Might, is designed to create a computer model to unravel terrorist car- and truck-bomb attacks. By coincidence, an ATF agent assigned to Dipole Might, happened to be in Oklahoma City on April 19th, working at the Federal Courthouse, which stands across the street from the Murrah Building. He saw the devastation and called the ATF office in Dallas. The Murrah Building had just been hit by 'ANFO' (ammonium material) bomb of at least several thousand pounds, he reported. Within minutes, explosives agents trained under Dipole Might were dispatched to the scene. They identified the type and size of the bomb almost immediately.

Just how this agent (Harry Eberhardt) was able to immediately ascertain the building had been blown up by an ANFO bomb, when no forensic analysis had yet been conducted, is unclear. When Phil O'Halloran, a freelance journalist, attempted to ask the ATF Public Relations Bureau why a Dipole Might expert just happened to be in the courthouse at that moment, and how he could immediately have known the exact nature of the bomb, O'Halloran, rather than given a rational explanation, was accused of attacking the agency and was promised a fax of agency views on right-wing conspiracists (which never arrived).[90]

It's also unclear why the Sheriff's Bomb Squad was in the parking lot between the Murrah Building and the Federal Courthouse at 7:45 that morning. The Bomb Squad denies being there. But Norma Smith and other Federal

Courthouse employees recall seeing the Bomb Squad's distinctive white truck. "We did wonder what it was doing in our parking lot," recalled Smith. "Jokingly, I said, 'Well, I guess we'll find out soon enough.'"[91]

Oklahoma City attorney Daniel J. Adomitis told the *Fort Worth Star-Telegram* he also saw the Bomb Squad there that morning. "As I was passing the back side of the County Courthouse, I noticed a truck with a trailer and the truck said 'Bomb Disposal.' I remember thinking as I passed that, 'Gee, I wonder if they had a bomb threat at the County Courthouse?'"[92]

Was the Bomb Squad alerted something was in the works? "I have not come across any information that any kind of bomb unit was at the building prior to the bombing," announced Lester Martz at the same time he lauded the heroism of Luke Franey, the ATF agent who supposedly "karate-kicked" his way through three walls.*

What is certain is that the Murrah Building had a bomb threat one week prior to the 19th. Michael Hinton remembers looking out the window of his YMCA room around the 12th and saw 200-300 people gathered outside. The incident didn't jog his memory until the local TV networks announced on the morning of the blast that the Federal Building had received a threat just a week before.[93]

Nurse Toni Garret recalled talking to several people who said there had been bomb threats two weeks prior to the bombing. "The FBI and the ATF knew that these bomb threats were real, and they did nothing about it."

Terrorism expert Dr. Randall Heather confirmed these reports, adding, "I know that there had been a threat phoned in to the FBI last week, but I don't know what the nature of that was."[94]

According to the Oklahoma City Fire Department, the FBI phoned in a warning on April 14, almost a week before the bombing. Assistant Fire Chief Charles Gaines told Glenn Wilburn, who lost two grandsons in the blast, that there was never any warning. The grieving grandfather then walked down the hall to Assistant Chief Dispatcher Harvey Weathers' office. Weathers told Wilburn in no uncertain terms that the Fire Department had indeed received a warning on April 14. Relating Gaines' apparent loss of memory to Weathers, he replied, "Well, you asked me and I told you. I'm not going to lie for anybody...."[95]

When asked during a press conference if the FBI had received a warning, FBI SAC Bob Ricks said, "The FBI in Oklahoma City has not received any threats to indicate that a bombing was about to take place."

The transparent stories told by the ATF and FBI are familiar to those pro-pounded in the wake of the 1993 World Trade Center bombing. In that case, the FBI had one of its own informants—former Egyptian Army Colonel Emad Eli

---

* This author interviewed a retired Army criminal investigator who complained about Lester Martz's stonewalling a similar investigation he was involved in.

Salem—inside the group responsible for the bombing. According to Salem, who made secret tapes of his conversations with his FBI handler, Nancy Floyd, her supervisor refused to let Salem substitute a harmless powder for the real explosive. The agent then pulled Salem off the case. Soon afterwards, the bomb blew up, killing six people and injuring almost 1,000 more.

The ATF's Dipole Might tests are uncannily similar to the May 24, 1990 bombing of Earth First! activist Judi Bari. The FBI claimed that Bari and her companion Daryl Cherney, who were on their way to a peaceful protest rally, had inadvertently blown themselves up with their own pipe-bomb. After Bari sued the FBI for false arrest and civil rights violations, she found out though discovery that the FBI ran a "bomb school" at Eureka College of the Redwoods in April of 1990 for both FBI and local police. The classes included blowing up cars with pipe bombs, ostensibly to demonstrate the tactics used by terrorists (the same reason cited in the ATF's case). The instructor for this "school of terrorism" was none other than Frank Doyle Jr., the FBI Bomb Squad expert who showed up at the scene of Bari's car bombing one month later.

According to Freedom of Information Act records, Project Dipole Might was initiated under the authorization of Clinton's National Security Council. One of the stated purposes of the project was to produce computer models of bombings to "be displayed in a courtroom to aid in the prosecution of defendants." The Justice Department used the videotapes shot at White Sands during McVeigh's trial to "prove" that an ANFO bomb blew up the building. As Lawrence Myers, writing in *Media Bypass* magazine, asked:

> Why the National Security Council would fund such an ATF project, despite the absolute rarity of the crime, has not been explained.... Nor has it been explained as to what specific threat assessment information the government had when it decided to engage in such a project, just a few months before a Ryder Truck laden with ammonium-nitrate fertilizer exploded in front of the Murrah Building.[96]

As Myers points out, the last-known case of a truck-bomb exploding in the U.S. was in 1970, when an ANFO bomb exploded in front of the Army Math lab at the University of Wisconsin in Madison. Why then, would the National Security Council suddenly feel the need for detailed information regarding ANFO truck-bomb attacks?

Was the ATF expecting such a bombing? Were they in fact responsible for blast or the secondary damage to the building? Or was the building wired for demolition as part of a larger plot?

"Before the

Government tries

to convict someone,

they try first to

demonize him."

—Gerry Spence

On May 1st, 1995, a stunned America was introduced to "The Face of Terror." The steely-eyed mug of Timothy James McVeigh, superimposed over the limp, bloody body of a tiny dead child, stared coldly out at us from the cover of *Time* magazine.

Suddenly, there was no longer any doubt who had bombed the Murrah Building. As John Doe No. 1 was led from the Noble County Courthouse in handcuffs and leg irons, the scene was akin to a medieval script. "Baby killer!" the crowd screamed. "Burn him! Burn him!"

In the pages that followed, *Time* and others would set out to "reveal the paranoid life and times of accused bomber Timothy McVeigh and his right-wing associates." [97] With the ink barely dry on the indictments, the national news media quickly began pumping out story after story focusing on the trivial banalities of McVeigh's life, attempting to reinforce the official allegations of his guilt. While the *New York Times* set the overall tone based on "leaks" from federal law enforcement sources, self-styled experts came crawling out of the woodwork:

"In deeply disturbing ways, his is a portrait of his generation," quipped Dale Russak and Serge Kovaleski, two sociologists moonlighting for the *Washington Post.*[98]

"His tortured path—is a psychological portrait of his deterioration," John Kifner of the *New York Times* announced with Freudian authority. "First there was McVeigh's own stunted personality and immediate frustrations. He was never able to overcome a sense of abandonment by his mother." [99]

"Not making the Special Forces was something that was very hard for him to deal with," said an FBI agent training for his Ph.D. in psychology. "In his mind, much of his life has been one of thinking that he is a kind of Special Forces of his own." [100]

Finally: "He was the quiet one," said McVeigh's former 10th grade English

36 OKLAHOMA CITY BOMBING

teacher Colleen Conner. "A lot of the quiet ones are the ones who have ended up doing scary things."[101]

There it was—trial by media. Timothy McVeigh must be guilty. After all, his face glared at us on the cover of *Time* magazine.* Fortunately, in the avalanche of articles that followed, small hints of reality occasionally seeped through the mire.

"That just doesn't ring true to me, as to the person I knew," said Sheffield Anderson, a correctional officer who had gone through basic training with McVeigh and served with him in the Gulf. "In that picture of him coming out of the courthouse, he looks like a real mean guy. But I didn't sense anything out of the ordinary. McVeigh was a rational type guy, a thinking type person. The bombing thing is totally contrary to the person I knew."[102]

"The Timothy McVeigh I talked with didn't seem like a baby killer," said former Army Colonel David Hackworth about his *Newsweek* interview with McVeigh.**

During an interview on Prime Time Live, Lana Padilla, Terry Nichols' ex-wife told Diane Sawyer, "It's not the same person. I mean, you know."

Sawyer: "The stony face."
Padilla: "No."[103]

"It became obvious during the hour-long discussion that Timothy McVeigh is neither a monster nor a madman," wrote Lawrence Myers, who interviewed McVeigh for *Media Bypass* magazine. "He left the impression that he is a man with strong convictions and a sense of honor."[104]

So just who is Timothy James McVeigh? Is he a hardened killer as the press and federal authorities have made him out to be? Or is he an ordinary man who became caught up in a complicated web of intrigue and deception?

"TIMMY"

Timothy James McVeigh was born in Pendelton, New York April 23, 1968, a small working class town of 5,000 people just outside of Buffalo. Tim was the second child of Bill McVeigh, an auto worker, and Mildred, a travel agent. The elder McVeigh, 55, coached Little League and ran bingo night at the local Catholic church, spending his free time golfing, or putzing in his garden. A heavily wood-

---

* Lori Fortier originally told the press, "It truly sickens me when I see my friend's face, yes my friend's face, portrayed on the cover of *Time* magazine as the face of evil."

** Noble County Assistant Attorney Mark Gibson, who has prosecuted many killers, said, "You could just feel the evil in them." Yet he said of McVeigh, "I looked at him and realized I felt no repulsion or fear."

ed rural area, young Tim spent his time hiking or playing sports with the neighborhood boys.

"He lived a few house down from me, said boyhood friend Keith Maurer. "We played hockey, baseball and just about every other sport in the neighborhood. He wasn't the best athlete in the bunch, but he showed up to play every day and he always played hard."

The bright and inventive youngster also spent his time engaging in novel activities such as setting up a haunted house in his basement, where he charged admission, or holding weekend casino fairs, where he acted as the dealer.

"He was very advanced for our age, "Maurer said. "I remember saying to myself: I wouldn't have thought of that."

Pat Waugh, a neighbor, said "I used to think to myself, that kid is going to go somewhere just because he's such a mover and shaker. I pictured him growing up to be a salesman, sort of a shyster."

When Tim's mom moved out in June of 1984, the outgoing young McVeigh became more reserved, as he and his sisters, Patty and Jennifer, attempted to deal with the trauma of the breakup. Reverend Paul Belzer of the Good Shepherd Roman Catholic Church in Pendelton knew the family for 20 years. "People asked me, wasn't Tim crushed? But he didn't seem to be. He lived in the same house, had the same friends. Yeah, he'd have to miss his mother, but so many of the anchors were there."

Yanya Panepento, a classmate of Tim's recalled, "He was a quiet boy. He kept to himself. He didn't seem like he was a troublemaker or anything like that."

Yet, nine months after the bombing, the *Times* John Kifner would write, "As commonplace as this seems, criminologists say, these traits are often the stuff of serial killers, terrorists and other solitary murders."

To the armchair mainstream/tabloid media psychoanalysts, the breakup would be the first of two major events; the second being his initial failure to make the Special Forces that profoundedly and adversely affected young McVeigh's personality. The first indications came when reporters discovered in his high school yearbook that Tim had been voted "most talkative" by his senior class.

"The only thing I can remember is that he was very quiet and polite," recalls Cecelia Matyjas, who taught 10th grade geometry. "He didn't cause any problems in class. He seemed to be cooperative and attentive. He was on the track team and the cross-country team, so he was able to get along with others."

Brandon Stickney, a journalist contracted to produce an unauthorized biography of McVeigh for Prometheus Books, said, "Tim was not the most talkative out of his class of 194 students, but he was by no means introverted. He was certainly an outgoing young man who had many friends and acquaintances."

None of these easy-to-check facts were ever mentioned in the voluminous articles appearing in the *Times*. Kifner, the *Times* "resident analyst," proclaimed with surety, "He was never able to overcome a sense of abandonment by his mother, who left the family when he was a boy; nor could he find a home outside the Army."

Backing up Kifner was John Douglas of the FBI's Psychological Profile Unit, who claimed McVeigh was "asocial, asexual, a loner, withdrawn, from a family with problems, strong feelings of inadequacy from early in life, an underachiever."

"I think it's a bunch of psychobabble if you ask me, if you want to know the truth," says Jennifer, Tim's younger sister. "We were free to live with who we wanted. We could visit the other parent whenever we wanted. There was no bitterness between my parents."

"There's nothing there," says Timothy McVeigh, responding to the media's analysis of him in a July 3, 1995 interview with *Newsweek*.

Apparently, Douglas and the *New York Times* journalists never bothered to check on the fact that Tim had many friends, including several girlfriends later in life, was close to his Father and his sister Jennifer, and was a Regents Scholar.

Not to be hamstrung by such minor details, the *Times* and the *Washington Post* quickly jumped on Tim's interest in firearms. "In a region of hunting enthusiasts, it caused little stir when Tim, at 10, became interested in guns. But a close relative said that the family saw this as a bid for attention by a boy who didn't know how else to ask for it."

"He had a semiautomatic BB gun that could fire 15 rounds with the pull of a trigger," added the *Post*. "Other boys had only single-shot varieties. Tim used to show them at school how he held it, posing police-style with hands clasped together. During boring classes, when other students doodled, he drew guns."

Tim's father did buy him a .22-caliber rifle, which young McVeigh used for target practice in woods behind his home. Yet apparently Tim was not the young bloodthirsty adventurer the media made him out to be. "I remember starting to hunt at age 11," said his friend Keith Maurer, "and Tim never had any interest in this,"

McVeigh was later able to indulge in his interests in firearms as a security guard for Burke Armored, where he worked for a year or so in 1987. Jeff Camp, McVeigh's co-worker, noted that he had a keen interest in guns, although he didn't find it unusual since most full-time security guards and law enforcement personnel owned an assortment of firearms.

One story eagerly circulated amongst the press is that McVeigh showed up at Burke one day with a huge Desert Eagle pistol and bandoleers slung in an "X" across his chest. "He came to work looking like Rambo," recalled Camp. "It looked like World War III."

McVeigh laughs off the tale, stating that he and some other employees were simply playing a joke on their supervisor, who was sending them on a high profile assignment for the day. Apparently, their supervisor was not amused.

According to the *Post*, McVeigh also worked as a gun salesman at a sporting goods store in Lockport.

"Guns were the entire focal point of the 27-year-old Mr. McVeigh's life," wrote the *Times'* Kifner.

"This obsession with weapons—a form of power—is an overcompensation for deep-rooted feelings of inadequacy," added the FBI's Douglas, attempting to drive another nail into McVeigh's coffin.

One must wonder if an interest in stamp collecting or bird watching—other legitimate hobbies—could be construed as a "bid for attention." The author—much more of a "troublemaker" in his formative years than Timothy McVeigh—personally remembers his own interest in guns, and even military armor. Like motorcycles, fast cars or other macho symbols, such interests pass as one matures. Yet federal authorities, with the backing of the media, attempted to make this a cornerstone of their psuedo-psychological case against McVeigh. He was "obsessed with guns," ergo, he is a mad bomber. I doubt that gun enthusiasts in the country would be pleased to know they are, by association, being implicated as mad bombers.

Not to be deterred, *Washington Post* reporters discovered that young Tim had stockpiled food, camping equipment and weapons in case of a "… nuclear attack or the Communists took over the country," said an anonymous neighbor in the *Post*. "Perhaps it made sense that a young boy often forced to fend for himself would fantasize about fighting the world all alone," mused the *Post*. Fighting the world? Or developing common sense at a young age? In his *Media Bypass* interview, McVeigh recalled that one of his most vivid memories was the winter blizzard of 1977, which dumped 15 feet of snow on Pendelton, stranding his mother miles away, and knocking out power and phone lines for days. The young, inventive McVeigh responded by helping his father store necessities, even recommending that the older McVeigh purchase a generator.

Apparently the armchair psychoanalysts of the mainstream press felt this indicative of early creeping paranoia, rather than the natural combination of the active imagination and common sense inherent in a remarkable nine-year old boy. If the youngster was concerned about Communists, one only need ask where such fears were incubated.

The *Post*, keeping with the propaganda of Timothy McVeigh as underachiever, was quoted as saying "Tim's high-school yearbook entry in 1986 listed no organized activities (he omitted the track team), rather: 'staying away from school, losing sleep, finding it in school.'"

Yet even the *Post* admitted that Tim's guidance counselor, Harold Smith, said that he had not missed a day of classes from seventh through twelfth grade. Far from being an underachiever, his record indicates a young man with remarkable discipline.

Justin Gertner, who knew McVeigh since second grade, recalls, "he hung around with the intelligently elite at Starpoint. Tim was in the Regent's program in our school for advanced placement students who planned on attending college. He also created and ran our computer bulletin board system."

In fact, McVeigh excelled in computers, taking every available computer class in high school. He even designed his own computer program. "That was the age when there was no software to speak of, and it wasn't user friendly," said a teacher who asked to remain anonymous, "But Tim and some other kids went out and did this.... In a way, that was fairly advanced. This demonstrates his bright mind and his ability."

This bright mind and ability led McVeigh to Bryant & Stratton Business College in Williamsville, N.Y. to study advanced COBOL and FORTRAN programming languages. In spite of his abilities, opportunities for decent employment were uncertain in Buffalo in the mid-1980s. Buffalo, like the rest of the Rust Belt, was experiencing the worst of economic trends. Several steel and auto plants had shut down, and two major banks failed, throwing thousands of white-collar workers out of jobs and causing downturns in real-estate, advertising, law and other fields.[105]

"There are no jobs around here unless you want to work for $6 an hour or less at a McDonald's or Wendy's," said Bill McVeigh. "It's rough for anybody looking for work."

McVeigh apparently did not feel comfortable that his auto-worker father was paying for most of his college tuition. So in December 1987, he took a job with Burke Armored Truck (now known as Armored Services of America) in Cheektowaga, near Buffalo.

"He was a very alert guard." said Jeff Camp, McVeigh's co-worker. "He worked a lot of overtime and was polite with our customers." McVeigh was also moody, ranging from intense to quiet. "If someone was driving badly, cutting us off or interfering with our schedule, he could get pretty mad," added Camp. "His face would turn red and he would yell and scream inside the truck, although he calmed down pretty fast." (Similar to the way the author drives.) Camp also described an incident where a woman had hit their truck. Although the woman was upset, McVeigh calmed her down and told her not to worry, that there was no damage to the truck, and that he would even report it as their fault, which it wasn't.[106]

McVeigh worked at Burke from April of 1987 till May of 1988. By the time he was 19, McVeigh had built up a substantial savings account and he and a friend, David Darlak, acquired 10 acres of land for $7,000 at a hunting and camping retreat north of Olean, N.Y. The two young men bought the land as an investment, and to use for camping and for target practice.* Reported the *Post:*

---

* Real estate agent Anne Marie Fitzpatrick said McVeigh was "very dynamic" and had "a twinkle in his eye and a smile." (*Washington Post,* 7/2/95.)

"Robert Morgan, who lives nearby, said his father Charlie once called the state police to complain about all the gunfire. 'My dad turned him in,' he said. 'One day it sounded like a war out there. Sometimes he'd come down during the week, sometimes the weekend. He had on hunting clothes. Camouflage.'" [107]

While the press made much out of the fact that McVeigh and his friends used the land for target practice, it should be noted that McVeigh was law-abiding and did not have a criminal record.

By the Spring of 1988, the young security guard felt he was going nowhere. He was working in a relatively low-wage job while listening to the fate of those who had been laid-off while working other jobs. Tim's father listened with concern as his son vented frustration, complaining that he was unemployable except at jobs that paid "no money." One night Bill McVeigh and a friend from the auto plant suggested that the younger McVeigh enter the service.

"Bill and I had both been in the service," the friend said, "and one night we said to Tim, 'That's what you ought to do: go in the service.' A week later, he had joined."

"It happened in a split second," said Tim's co-worker Jeff Camp. "He didn't tell anyone he was joining. He just came to work one day and said he was going in the Army.[108] I never saw a guy who wanted to go in the Army that bad. I asked him why the Army, and he said 'You get to shoot.' He always wanted to carry an M-16." [109]

Keith Maurer said, "I couldn't see him joining the military. He had a lot of options. He was very smart. I didn't see the military as the one he needed to take." McVeigh saw the Army made perfect sense among his career options in economically depressed upstate New York. The Army held the possibility of travel and adventure for a boy from a small town. In the Army, he could choose his specialty, indulging his interest in firearms or computers.

On May 24, McVeigh drove the 25 miles to the Army recruiting office in Buffalo, and signed up for a three-year hitch. "In a couple of days he was gone," said Camp.

SERGEANT MAC

McVeigh arrived at Fort Benning, Georgia on May 30, and was assigned to Echo Company, 4th Battalion, 36th Infantry Regiment, 2nd Training Brigade. The unit was a COHORT unit, an acronym for "Cohesion Operational Readiness and Training." In a COHORT unit, soldiers were supposed to stay together for their entire three-year enlistment period. The COHORT concept originated in 1980, in an attempt to correct the problem of sending in raw green recruits for those who had been killed in battle. The Army discovered that many new replacements had difficulty adjusting to a new unit in the heat of battle, resulting in a higher number of casualties. Moreover, Pentagon studies from the Vietnam War era suggested that soldiers who had developed bonds of friendship were more likely to perform courageously. Unfortunately, the Army soon developed a new problem: many of the soldiers became sick of each other after three years, resulting in soldiers committing suicide or going AWOL.

Although McVeigh originally wanted to try out for Army Ranger School, he didn't want to wait for an available opening, and decided to join the infantry immediately. As he soon found out, he had been misled by the Army recruiter. Once in the COHORT unit, it was not possible for him to enter Army Ranger School. Yet the disappointed young recruit quickly made the best of the situation, scoring a high 126 points on his General Technical test score, putting him in the top 10 percentile among new recruits.

"McVeigh was really motivated to be a good soldier and performed well at everything expected of him," said assistant platoon leader Glen "Tex" Edwards. "You could load that boy up with 140 pounds of gear and he would carry it all day on the march without complaining. He was thin as a rail but he never fell out of formation," said Edwards, recalling the hot Georgia summer of 1988. "It was the worst time of the year to go through the course, but it did not seem to bother McVeigh one bit."

Although McVeigh didn't have many friendships during basic training, he would develop one with Terry Nichols. Nichols, 13 years McVeigh's senior, was promoted to platoon leader due to his age and maturity. Despite their age difference, the two men bonded, sharing similar interests. "Terry and Tim in boot camp went together like magnets," said Robin Littleton.

By the end of basic training, McVeigh was promoted to private E-2, having managed to score higher than anyone in his battalion on mid-cycle and end-of-cycle testing. "Any test, he'd ace it," said David Dilly. "He knew exactly what the Army wanted. It was going to be an easy life for him."

On August 25, 1988, McVeigh was awarded a certificate by his commanding officer, then in September the unit was shipped out to Fort Riley, Kansas, where McVeigh was assigned to the 2nd Battalion, First Infantry Division, part of the "Dagger Brigade" of the famous "Big Red One" that made the assault on Normandy during WWII. While McVeigh was assigned to Charlie Company, Nichols went to Bravo Company.

A mechanized infantry unit, 2nd Battalion was equipped with M-2 Bradley Armored vehicles, a more sophisticated version of the famous M-113 Armored Personnel Carrier used during the Vietnam War. In addition to ferrying troops, the aluminum Bradley has a turret-mounted 25mm cannon, a 7.62mm machine gun and anti-tank missiles. McVeigh was the gunner on one of four Bradleys attached to Charlie Company's First Platoon. Naturally, he scored higher than anyone else in the battalion. In 1989, his commander selected him as gunner on the "Division Display Vehicle," used to demonstrate the M-2 system for Pentagon officials and visiting dignitaries.

"He was without a doubt the best soldier I have ever trained with," said Staff Sergeant Albert Warnement, McVeigh's supervisor at Fort Riley. He was motivated and very interested in learning everything he could about being a professional soldier."[110]

"As far as soldiering, he never did anything wrong," recalled Todd Reiger, assigned to McVeigh's Bradley. "He was always on time. He never got into trouble. He was perfect. I thought he would stay in the Army all his life. He was always volunteering for stuff that the rest of us wouldn't want to do, guard duties, classes on the weekend."[111]

McVeigh studied every conceivable Army manual, including the Ranger Handbook, the Special Forces Handbook, and the Improvised Munitions Handbook. But press reports reported McVeigh as a mad bomber:

> McVeigh's love of guns and explosives stood out even in the Army, where gun lovers abound. In the first weeks of basic training, when soldiers learn to make explosives, recalled platoon mate Fritz Curnutte, McVeigh boasted to fellow soldiers that he already knew how to make a powerful bomb using a bottle, then told them how to make a Molotov cocktail.[112]

According to Warnement, such knowledge is not unusual for the serious soldiers, who routinely studied manuals on survival, evasion, resistance, escape, and improvised munitions. "You have to remember," said Warnement, "at that time, we were training to fight the Russians in Western Europe and it was expected the Red Army would probably break through our lines almost immediately. We were encouraged to learn how to improvise. Our survivability on the battlefield would likely depend on our skills in unconventional warfare."[113]

Although McVeigh's military record makes no mention of formal demolitions training, in her book, *By Blood Betrayed,* Lana Padilla calls McVeigh a "former Army demolitions expert."[114] But Sheffield Anderson, who served with McVeigh since basic training says, "He had the same training that the rest of the outfit had."*

The only thing that differentiated McVeigh from the rest of the outfit was his dedication and commitment to the military. "He played the military 24 hours a day, seven days a week," said Curnutte. "All of us thought it was silly. When they'd call for down time, we'd rest, and he'd throw on a rucksack sack and walk around the post with it."

---

* Padilla later told me that information about McVeigh's "demolitions expertise" was provided by co-writer Ron Delpit.

This "silliness" led to McVeigh making sergeant ahead of the rest of his unit. "It was unusual to have sergeant stripes so soon," said Reiger. "The rest of us in the Cohort [unit] were specialists," a non-supervisory rank similar to corporal.

In fact, after the bombing, when McVeigh's records and test scores were shown to a master sergeant without revealing his identity, he stated that the subject "would make a great infantry officer, tanker, artillery officer or combat engineer." His electronic aptitude, said another official, qualified him for "repairing satellite communications." [115] "He has a very high IQ," said a federal source familiar with the suspect's military record.[116] McVeigh was, in fact, rated among the top five percent in combat arms.

McVeigh rented a three-bedroom house in the spring of 1991 in Herrington with Corporal John Kelso and Sergeant Rick Cerney. But the arrangement was not a comfortable one for McVeigh, and he soon moved into another house he shared with Sgt. Royal Wilcher, who served with McVeigh in the Bradley.

The *Times* quoted members of the McVeigh's unit claiming that he had no close friends. "He kept to himself," said Robert Handa. "He was a dedicated soldier. He loved being a soldier. I didn't. So after duty hours he'd stay in the barracks while everybody else took off, go out to town. I never saw him go anywhere. He always had a highly pressed uniform." Reiger recalls that McVeigh had a TV and a VCR and stayed in and watched movies, or occasionally went bowling.

"The whole thing is," said John Kelso, who shared a house off-base with McVeigh and fellow soldier Richard Cerney, "he couldn't have a good time."

"He was very shy of women—almost embarrassed," remembers Anderson. "It didn't seem he was gay. He was just awkward." McVeigh disputed this analysis in his April 15th *Time* interview, stating:

> "I don't think there is any way to narrow my personality down and label it as one thing or another. I'm just like anyone else. Movies I enjoy, comedies, sci fi. The big misconception is that I'm a loner. Well, I believe in having my own space. But that in no way means I'm a loner. I like women, social life."

McVeigh became friends with bombing suspect Michael Fortier while stationed at Fort Riley; occasionally they would go shooting together at a friend's farm near Tuttle Creek Lake, and stop by and visit Terry Nichols at his house near the base.

The press was quick to pick up on McVeigh owning lots of guns he kept hidden around his house. According to Sgt. Wilcher, "He had a couple in the kitchen, a couple in the living room under the couch. I think there was one in the bathroom, behind the towels. As you go up the steps there was a little ledge and he kept one in there too, a .38 revolver." "I don't know if he was paranoid or what," added Wilcher. "Or maybe he had some friends that were after him. I don't know." [117]

According to an account in *USA Today* and the *Times*, McVeigh and Nichols, who by now were pretty far along in their "anti-government" beliefs, attempted to recruit other military personnel for a militia Nichols was purportedly starting. Nichols reportedly told at least one fellow soldier that he'd be back to Fort Riley after his discharge to recruit new men, and McVeigh's co-worker at Burns Security, Carl Lebron, would later tell the FBI that McVeigh was always trying to "recruit him into an undescribed group." [118]

According to his roommate Dave Dilly, McVeigh rented a storage locker in Junction City stocked with weapons, military meals (MREs), and a 100-gallon jug of water—in case of disaster or a Communist attack. [119]

"He was halfway there when I knew him," said Dilly, referring to McVeigh's Patriot beliefs. During McVeigh's tenure at Burns Security, McVeigh would inundate his co-workers with Patriot literature, such as *Spotlight* articles and videos on Ruby Ridge and Waco, and books such as *Detaxing America.*

For his part, McVeigh says, "If you had to label what I think, then I would say I am closest to the views of the Patriot movement," McVeigh told the *London Sunday Times.* "For a long time, I thought it was best not to talk about my political views, he added, "but millions share them, and I believe it is gravely wrong that I should allow the government to try and crucify me just for believing what I do."

Another issue the media focused on were race problems in Charlie Company, and with McVeigh in particular. Regier told the *Post* that McVeigh was criticized for assigning undesirable work to black soldiers, making black specialists sweep out the motor pool, work that would have ordinarily gone to privates. Other soldiers said he made derogatory remarks about blacks. "It was pretty well known, pretty much throughout the platoon, that he was making the black specialists do that work," said Reiger. "He was a racist. When he talked he'd mention those words, like nigger. You pretty much knew he was a racist." The black soldiers complained to a company commander and McVeigh was reprimanded, the only time he ever got into trouble according to Regier. [120]

Said Dilly, "Race was an issue, like everywhere in America, but not one that affected anyone's promotion. McVeigh picked the best man for the job."

Yet the *McCurtain Gazette* discovered that McVeigh held membership in the Ku Klux Klan, personally approved by Thom Robb, the KKK's national chaplain. "He was a very racist person," said Wilcher.

"Charlie Company as a whole had a problem with race," said Captain Terry Guild, who served briefly as McVeigh's platoon commander after the Gulf War. "There was graffiti on the walls of the barracks' bathroom: 'Nigger' or 'Honky, Get Out.' They were mild incidents. If a problem was identified, a leader in Charlie Company wouldn't let it happen again if he saw it. But it was definitely a problem in the company. And his platoon had some of the most serious race problems. It was pretty bad."

In spite of such interpersonal or racial difficulties, most of the platoon held McVeigh in high esteem for his soldiering abilities. "He could command soldiers of his own rank and they respected him," said Barner. "When it came to soldiering, McVeigh knew what he was doing."

"If we ever went to war," said Edwards, "every one of us wanted to go to war with McVeigh." [121]

During the summer of 1989, after returning from a week-long orientation session in Heidelberg with the West German Army, or Bundeswehr, McVeigh decided to try out for the Army Special Forces. To the young sergeant who had long desired to be a member of the Army's elite, the Special Forces provided the chance. It also provided McVeigh an opportunity to graduate from the COHORT unit. Yet the physical requirements to even qualify for the Special Forces are among the toughest in the military. Requirements include swimming 50 meters with full gear; 42 push-ups in two minutes; 52 sit-ups in two minutes; and running two miles in less than 15 minutes, 54 seconds. To pass the grueling tests, McVeigh vigorously trained in the summer of 1989, forcing himself to march 10 miles with 100 pound packs. By the summer of 1990, he had passed the Special Forces physical fitness test, and was ordered to report to Fort Bragg, NC on November 17 to begin the Special Forces Assessment and Selection Course (SFAS). Towards the end of 1990, McVeigh reinlisted for another four years. [122]

McVeigh's dream of becoming a Green Beret would have to wait. On November 8, with the conflict in the Persian Gulf coming to a head, the Pentagon canceled all leaves and training assignments. McVeigh's unit was activated for deployment. Although he was a consummate military man and a gung-ho soldier, McVeigh opposed going to war. "McVeigh did not think the United States had any business or interest in Kuwait," said Warnement, "but he was a good soldier. He knew it was his duty to go where he was told, and he went." He was promoted to sergeant on February 1, 1991. [123]

Unlike the steely-eyed killer the press painted him to be, McVeigh was as scared as the rest of the platoon. "The night before the ground war kicked off, he was saying he was scared because we were going to be part of the first wave," Anderson recalled. "He was scared we weren't going to come out of it. Maybe we would get shot, blown up. It wasn't cowardly. He was just concerned. I was feeling the same way, but most people didn't express it." [124]

On February 24, 1990, the 2nd Battalion was ordered across the southern Iraqi desert to punch a hole in Iraqi defenses—a line of dug-in infantry supported by tanks and artillery. McVeigh's platoon was attached to the "Ironhorse" tank company, and McVeigh's Bradley was the lead track in the platoon. McVeigh, the "top gun," took out an enemy tank on the first day with a TOW missile.

The "Ironhorse" protected units clearing trenches. Using tanks and trucks equipped with plows, the U.S. forces would follow behind the Bradleys, burying the Iraqis dead or alive to create a smooth crossing point for the infantry and avoid engaging the enemy in hand-to-hand combat.

McVeigh's moment of glory came when his platoon encountered a dug-in enemy machine-gun emplacement and came under fire. McVeigh took the head off an enemy soldier 1,000 yards away with a 25mm cannon. His next shot induced the raising of more than 60 hands into the air.

For his role in the battle, McVeigh was awarded an Army Commendation Medal which read in part: "He inspired other members of his squad and platoon by destroying an enemy machine-gun emplacement, killing two Iraqi soldiers and forcing the surrender of 30 others from dug-in positions." McVeigh also earned a Commendation medal with an upgrade for valor, two Army Achievement medals, and the Bronze Star "for flawless devotion to duty."

This "flawless devotion to duty" resulted in McVeigh's unit being invited to provide personal security for General "Stormin' Norman" Schwarzkopf.

A much-hackneyed phrase attributed to Sergeant James Ives, which the media like to play over and over again was, "If he was given a mission and a target, it's gone." Yet Roger Barnett, who served in McVeigh's Bradley, told the *Times* that McVeigh never expressed any desire to kill troops who were surrendering and never seemed bloodthirsty in any way.[125]

One story appearing in *Media Bypass* recounts how McVeigh saved an accident victim's life on a lonely stretch of highway. The man was ejected from his over-turned car, laying semi-conscious and bleeding. McVeigh, on the way to his home town of Pendelton, recently finished a 46-hour medical aid course at Fort Riley. Against regulations, he had taken his Combat Lifesaver Pack with him on the 1200-mile drive. As he came upon the scene, McVeigh saw that an EMS (Emergency Medical Service) crew had not yet arrived. Trained in night vision techniques, McVeigh the soldier quickly spotted the injured motorist in the grass along the median strip.

The victim recalls that the soldier was confident, quiet and efficient. To centralize his circulation, he elevated the man's undamaged limbs and warned him to be calm to avoid going into shock. He checked his pulse and flashed a small penlight across his pupils. The man, who only moments earlier was convinced he was going to die, shivered in the dark and started laughing. He told the tall young stranger he was never going to buy another Chevy Blazer again.

The soldier smiled as he rolled up the victim's right sleeve and inserted the needle to start a saline IV into his veins. "You've lost a lot of blood and you risk going into shock. This is an IV to help stabilize you and keep your fluids going. Relax. You'll be fine," he told him. He placed the clear plastic IV bag under the man's hip and checked his pulse again.

In the distance, an ambulance siren screamed over the sound of the truck engines as Timothy James McVeigh quickly packed up his Army issue trauma kit and disappeared into the night. The responding EMS crew told the state police officer who arrived at the accident minutes later that they had never come upon such a potentially deadly crash to find a severely injured man relaxed and laughing, neatly bandaged with an IV dangling from his arm.[126]

In a flurry of articles, mainstream media painted McVeigh as a psychotic, attention-seeking loner with a grudge against the government and a hatred of humanity—"a stunted personality" who led a "tortured path" "obsessed with weapons" with "deep-rooted feelings of inadequacy." When the press couldn't find evidence of overt violence or hostility, his noted politeness and manners suddenly became evidence his of his psychosis. "It is a personality that a Seattle forensic psychiatrist, Kenneth Muscatel, has described as the 'Smerdyakov Syndrome,' announced the *Times,* "after the scorned half-brother in Dostoyevsky's *Brothers Karamazov* who listens to the other brothers inveigh against their father until, finally, he commits patricide."[127]

McVeigh was painted as a sociopath by Lana Padilla in *By Blood Betrayed,* hinting that McVeigh may have been responsible for the death of 26-month-old Jason Torres Nichols—Terry and Marife's son—who accidentally suffocated to death in a plastic bag in November, 1993.[128] In her book, Padilla included a photo of McVeigh laughing and playing with the little boy. According to Terry Nichols, McVeigh tried to revive the infant for nearly half-an-hour, and had called the paramedics—a response apparently out-of-character with the actions of a deranged sociopathic killer.[129]

Captain Jesus Rodriguez, who commanded McVeigh during Desert Storm, described him as a friend who was "really compassionate" and "really cared" when Rodriguez's brother-in-law died in an accident.[130]

Further evidence of McVeigh's humanity can be found in a letter he wrote to the *Lockport Union-Sun & Journal* on March 10, 1992.

To buy your meat in a store seems so innocent, but have you ever seen or thought how it comes to be wrapped up so neatly in cellophane?

First, cattle live their entire lives penned up in cramped quarters, never allowed to roam freely, bred for one purpose when their time has come.

The technique that I have personally seen is to take cattle, line them up side by side with their heads and necks protruding over a low fence, and walk from one end to the other, slitting their throats with either machete or power saw. Unable to run or move, they are left there until they bleed to death, standing up.

Would you rather die while living happily or die while leading a miserable life? You tell me which is more "humane."

Does a "growing percentage of the public" have any pity or respect for any of the animals which are butchered and then sold in the store? Or is it just so conveniently "clean" that a double standard is allowed?

The mainstream press twisted the context of McVeigh's letter. In *A Force Upon the Plain,* author Kenneth Stern writes: "McVeigh said he thought a human being was, by nature, 'a hunter, a predator.' He also asked: 'Is civil war imminent? Do we have to shed blood to reform the current system?'"[131] Stern combines two unrelated letters written by McVeigh to suggest the humane killing of animals is part and parcel of McVeigh's bloodthirsty desire to kill human beings.

Reality paints a much different picture of Timothy James McVeigh. In February, 1996, Ron Rice and Carol Moore of the American Board of Forensic Examiners were asked to produce a profile of McVeigh's personality based on a handwriting analysis.* Both Rice and Moore characterized McVeigh as an introverted person—what they term an "Apollonian" personality—"a steady, unemotional, organized individual who [is] not devoid of emotion/passion, but more apt to value reason over passion." Like Sheffield Anderson, who described McVeigh as a "thinking type person," the examiners stated that McVeigh was "head-oriented." "They tend to be distrustful of feeling in the belief that following one's feelings can lead to trouble," the report stated. "Rarely, will he allow his emotional expressions to be directed at another person out of fear of hurting them."

The report concluded with the observation that Timothy McVeigh "is a military man ... his heart and soul belongs to the military of the U.S. Government. In a non-military environment, McVeigh will not undertake any form of overt hostility that will be harmful to others or dangerous to himself.... It is not logical that he would undertake any action against our government in which others would be hurt or killed. To do so would violate everything he stands for."[132]

In April of 1991, McVeigh put his heart and soul into his long-awaited dream of becoming a Green Beret. On March 28 he reported to Camp McCall, the Special Forces Assessment and Selection (SFAS) training facility west of Fort Bragg for the grueling 21-day assessment course. McVeigh, who kept himself in top shape by doing 400 push-ups a day and marching around the post with a 100 pound pack, was now out of shape and he knew it. The Bradley gunner who had served in the Persian Gulf for four months was also drained from the stress of combat.

As the recruits stood at attention, the instructor asked several of the recently returned war veterans if they wanted to return to their unit to get back in shape. One of the soldiers yelled that they were ready, so out of a sense of gung-ho pride, nobody backed out.

The first day of testing was devoted to psychological screening. McVeigh

---

* Rice is president of New England Investigations. He teaches the only accredited course in the subject of profiling, and has testified in state and federal court in regards to handwriting analysis, and Moore runs an executive assessment firm in Washington, D.C. that specializes in assessing personality traits of applicants based on their handwriting samples.

claims he had no problem with the psychological tests, which included the Adult Personality Inventory, the Minnesota Multiple Phase Personality Test, and a sentence completion exam designed by Army psychologists.

The second day tests began with an obstacle course which McVeigh passed with ease. After lunch, the recruits were led on a high-speed march with 50 pound rucksacks. Yet new boots tore into McVeigh's feet during the five mile march, and with the worst yet to come, he and another recruit, David Whitmyer, decided to drop out. McVeigh signed a Voluntary/Involuntary Withdrawal from the SFAS school. His single sentence explanation read: "I am not physically ready, and the rucksack march hurt more than it should." [133]

The mainstream press jumped on his initial failure to make Special Forces. He was "unable to face the failure" stated the *New York Times.*

"He washed out on the second day." [134] "There were no second chances," claimed the *Washington Post.* "His spirit was broken." [135]

These reports also suggested that McVeigh failed the psychological screening tests. "Military officials said that preliminary psychological screening had shown him to be unfit," reported the *New York Times.* "[He] saw his cherished hope of becoming a Green Beret shattered by psychological tests." [136] "It was apparently a blow so crushing that he quit the Army and went into a psychic tailspin." [137] Pundits backed up their armchair analyses with statements from several of McVeigh's former buddies.

"Anyone who puts all that effort into something and doesn't get it would be mentally crushed," said Roger Barnett, the driver of McVeigh's Bradley. "He wasn't the same McVeigh. He didn't go at things the way he normally did ... He didn't have the same drive. He didn't have his heart in the military anymore." [138]

"He always wanted to do better than everyone," said Captain Terry Guild, "and that [Green Berets] was his way of trying to do it. He took a lot of flak. He was really down on himself." [139]

"That's a bunch of bunk," claimed McVeigh in response to the allegations. "Any realist knows that if you develop blisters on the second day ... you're not going to make it." [140]

According to McVeigh's attorney Stephen Jones, his Army records indicate that his SFAS psychological tests weren't graded until April, 1995. The "military official" who leaked the story about McVeigh's "psychological test failure" turned out to be none other than FBI Agent John R. Hersley, who testified to this repeatedly during the Federal Grand Jury hearings. Apparently, Hersley never told the grand jurors that he was moonlighting as an Army psychologist.

Although McVeigh may have been genuinely disappointed by his initial failure, the school's commander invited the decorated war veteran to try out again whenever he felt ready. McVeigh was not too disappointed to score a perfect 1,000 points during a Bradley gunner competition six months later at Fort Riley, earning him another Army commendation and the honor of the division's "Top Gun"—a rare achievement. Army evaluation also rated him "among the best" in leadership potential and an "inspiration to young soldiers." [141]

In spite of McVeigh's achievements, "a bit of doubt started to surface" in his mind about a potential for a career in the military.[142] Although a friend said "I swear to God he could have been Sergeant Major of the Army—he was that good of a soldier," McVeigh was having second thoughts. Most of these, his Army buddies said, stemmed from military downsizing. He also confided to his friend Dave Dilly that without being a Green Beret, the Army wouldn't be worth the effort. "I think he felt he got a raw deal, and wanted out," said Littleton.

Given McVeigh's achievements—quick rise to sergeant, medals of commendation, distinction of "Top Gun," and the extremely high praise of his superiors—one has to wonder about his real motives. McVeigh was a spit and polish soldier with a top notch record, totally devoted to the military. He served in combat earning several medals. If anything, he was due for promotion. The commander of the Special Forces school even invited him to try out again in a few months. As Sheffield Anderson said, "He seemed destined for a brilliant career in the military."

These observations are backed by McVeigh's sister, Jennifer. "I thought it was going to be his career. He was definitely a career military type. That was his life, you know. His life revolved around that."

It seems unlikely that an ambitious soldier who recently signed on for another four year hitch would opt out so easily. Yet, on December 31, 1991, Sergeant McVeigh took an early discharge from the Army, and went back to his home town of Pendleton, NY.

THE MANCHURIAN CANDIDATE

To fulfill his military obligation, McVeigh signed with the Army National Guard in Buffalo, landing a job as a security guard with Burns International Security. McVeigh was assigned to the night shift, guarding the grounds of Calspan Research, a defense contractor that conducts classified research in advanced aerospace rocketry and electronic warfare.

In a manner mirroring his conduct in the service, McVeigh became the consummate security guard. Calspan spokesman Al Salandra told reporters that McVeigh was "a model employee." Yet, according to media accounts, McVeigh had lost his confidence ... and his cool.

"Timmy was a good guard," said former Burns supervisor Linda Haner-Mele. "He was "always there prompt, clean and neat. His only quirk," according to Mele, "was that he couldn't deal with people. If someone didn't cooperate with him, he would start yelling at them, become verbally aggressive. He could be set off easily. Co-workers at a Niagara Falls convention center where McVeigh was assigned described him as "emotionally spent, veering from passivity to volcanic anger." An old friend said he looked "like things were really weighing on him."[143]

"Timmy just wasn't the type of person who could initiate action," said Mele. "He was very good if you said, 'Tim watch this door—don't let anyone through.' The Tim I knew couldn't have masterminded something like this and carried it out himself. It would have had to have been someone who said: 'Tim, this is what you do. You drive the truck.'"

Mele's account directly contradicts the testimony of Sergeant Chris Barner and former Private Ray Jimboy, both of whom served with McVeigh at Fort Riley, claiming he was a natural leader.[144] Backing up Jimboy was McVeigh's friend and Calspan co-worker, Carl Lebron, who described McVeigh as "intelligent and engaging; the sort of person who could be a leader."[145]

Mele's testimony also contradicts McVeigh's service record, which rated him "among the best" in leadership potential and an "inspiration to young soldiers."[146] "He had a lot of leadership ability inside himself," said Barner. "He had a lot of self confidence."

Apparently, "Something happened to Tim McVeigh between the time he left the Army and now," said Captain Terry Guild.

"He didn't really carry himself like he came out of the military," said Mele. "He didn't stand tall with his shoulders back. He kind of slumped over." She recalled him as silent, expressionless, and subject to explosive fits of temper. "That guy didn't have an expression 99 percent of the time," she added. "He was cold."[147]

Colonel David Hackworth, an Army veteran who interviewed McVeigh for *Newsweek,* concluded that McVeigh was suffering from a "postwar hangover." "I've seen countless veterans, including myself, stumble home after the high-noon excitement of the killing fields, missing their battle buddies and the unique dangers and sense of purpose," wrote Hackworth. "Many lose themselves forever."*

Although such symptoms may be seen as a delayed reaction syndrome resulting from the stress of battle, they are also common symptoms of mind control. The subject of mind control or hypnosis often seems emotionally spent, as though he had been through a harrowing ordeal.

While visiting friends in Decker, Michigan, McVeigh complained that the Army had implanted him with a miniature subcutaneous transmitter, so that they could keep track of him.[148] He complained that it left an unexplained scar on his buttocks and was painful to sit on.**

---

* McVeigh himself admitted that the postwar hangover "was delayed in my case."

** This was confirmed to me by Terry Nichols' ex-wife, Lana Padilla: "Terry told me that. Terry just said that when he was in the Gulf War, they had implanted that to keep track of him."

To the public unfamiliar with the bewildering lexicon of government mind control research, such a claim may appear as the obvious rantings of a paranoiac. But is it?

Miniaturized telemetrics have been part of an ongoing project by the military and various intelligence agencies to test the effectiveness of tracking soldiers on the battlefield. The miniature implantable telemetric device was declassified long ago. As far back as 1968, Dr. Stuart Mackay, in his textbook entitled *Bio-Medical Telemetry*, reported, "Among the many telemetry instruments being used today, are miniature radio transmitters that can be swallowed, carried externally, or surgically implanted in man or animal. They permit the simultaneous study of behavior and physiological functioning."[149]

Dr. Carl Sanders, one of the developers of the Intelligence Manned Interface (IMI) biochip, maintains, "We used this with military personnel in the Iraq War where they were actually tracked using this particular type of device."[150]

It is also interesting to note that the Calspan Advanced Technology Center in Buffalo where McVeigh worked is engaged in microscopic electronic engineering applicable to telemetrics.* Calspan was founded in 1946 as Cornell Aeronautical Laboratory, which included the "Fund for the Study of Human Ecology," a CIA conduit for mind control experiments by émigré Nazi scientists.

According to mind control researcher Alex Constantine, "Calspan places much research emphasis on bioengineering and artificial intelligence (Calspan pioneered the field in the 1950s)." In his article, "The Good Soldier," Constantine states:

> Human tracking and monitoring technology are well within Calspan's sphere of pursuits. The company is instrumental in REDCAP, an Air Force electronic warfare system that winds through every Department of Defense facility in the country. A Pentagon release explains that REDCAP "is used to evaluate the effectiveness of electronic-combat hardware, techniques, tactics and concepts." The system "includes closed-loop radar and data links at RF manned data fusion and weapons control posts." One Patriot computer news board reported that a disembodied, rumbling, low-frequency hum had been heard across the country the week of the bombing. Past hums in Taos, NM, Eugene and Medford, OR, Timmons, Ontario

---

* The firm does classified research for both NASA and the Air Force, and is a ranking subcontractor for Sentar, Inc., an advanced science and engineering firm capable, according to company literature, of creating artificial intelligence systems. Sentar's customers include the U.S. Army Space and Strategic Defense Command, the Advanced Research Projects Agency (see discussion of ARPA later in this chapter), Rockwell International, Teledyne, Nichols Research Corp. and TRW. Their sales literature boasts a large energy shock tunnel, radar facilities "a radio-frequency (RF) simulator facility for evaluating electronic warfare techniques." (Constantine)

and Bristol, UK were most definitely (despite specious official denials) attuned to the brain's auditory pathways....

The Air Force is among Calspan's leading clients, and Eglin AFB has farmed key personnel to the company. The grating irony—recalling McVeigh's contention he'd been implanted with a telemetry chip—is that the Instrumentation Technology Branch of Eglin Air Force Base is currently engaged in the tracking of mammals with subminiature telemetry devices. According to an Air Force press release, the biotelemetry chip transmits on the upper S-band (2318 to 2398 MHz), with up to 120 digital channels.

There is nothing secret about the biotelemetry chip. Ads for commercial (albeit somewhat simpler) versions of the device have appeared in national publications. *Time* magazine ran an ad for an implantable pet transceiver in its June 26, 1995 issue opposite an article about a militia leader who was warning about the coming New World Order. While monitoring animals has been an unclassified scientific pursuit for decades, the monitoring of humans has been a highly classified project which is but a subset of the Pentagon's "nonlethal" arsenal. As Constantine notes, "the dystopian implications were explored by *Defense News* for March 20, 1995":

NAVAL RESEARCH LAB ATTEMPTS TO MELD NEURONS AND CHIPS: STUDIES MAY PRODUCE ARMY OF "ZOMBIES."

Future battles could be waged with genetically engineered organisms, such as rodents, whose minds are controlled by computer chips engineered with living brain cells.... The research, called Hippo-campal Neuron Patterning, grows live neurons on computer chips. "This technology that alters neurons could potentially be used on people to create zombie armies," Lawrence Korb, a senior fellow at the Brookings Institution, said.

It's conceivable, given the current state of the electronic mind control art, a bio-cybernetic Oz over the black budget rainbow, that McVeigh had been drawn into an experimental project, that the device was the real McCoy....[151]

The Defense Department newsletter may have been discussing the successor to the "Stimoceiver," developed in the late 1950s by Dr. Joseph Delgado and funded by the CIA and the Office of Naval Research. The Stimoceiver is a tiny transceiver implanted in the head of a control subject, which can then be used to modify emotions and control behavior.

According to Delgado, "Radio stimulation of different points in the amygdala and hippocampus in the four patients produced a variety of effects, including pleasant sensations, elation, deep, thoughtful concentration, odd feelings, super relaxation, colored visions, and other responses.... One of the possibilities with brain transmitters is to influence people so that they confirm with the political system. Autonomic and somatic functions, individual and social behavior, emotional and mental reactions may be invoked, maintained, modified, or inhibited, both in animals and in man, by stimulation of specific cerebral structures. Physical control of many brain functions is a demonstrated fact. It is even possible to follow intentions, the development of thought and visual experiences."[152]

The military has a long and sordid history of using enlisted men and unwitting civilians for nefarious experiments ranging from radiation, poison gas, drugs and mind control, to spraying entire U.S. cities with bacteriological viruses to test their effectiveness. The most recent example involves the use of experimental vaccines tested on Gulf War veterans who are currently experiencing bizarre symptoms, not least of which is death. Attorneys, representing former soldiers, requested military medical files, and discovered no record of the vaccines ever being administered.[153]

Is it possible that Timothy McVeigh was an Army/CIA guinea pig involved in a classified telemetric/mind-control project—a "Manchurian Candidate?"

Recent history is replete with cases of individuals who calmly walk into a restaurant, schoolyard, or post office and inexplicably begin shooting large numbers of people as though they were in a trance. What appear like gruesome but happenstance events to the casual observer raises red flags to those familiar with CIA "sleeper" mind control experiments. Such cases may be indicative of mind control experiments gone horribly wrong.

A recent case occurred in Tasmania, where Martin Bryant calmly walked to a tourist site in May, 1996, methodically shooting and killing over 35 people. Bryant was in possession of an assault rifle that had been handed to Victoria police as part of a gun amnesty program but mysteriously wound up in Bryant's hands before the massacre.*

As in Bryant's case, many bizarre killers meekly surrendered to authorities after their sprees. When stopped by State Trooper Charles Hanger for a missing license plate, McVeigh was carrying a loaded Glock 9mm pistol. Although he could have easily shot and killed the officer, McVeigh informed him that he was carrying a concealed weapon, then meekly handed himself over for arrest. Why does a man who allegedly killed 169 innocent people balk at killing a cop on a lonely stretch of highway?

After McVeigh's arrest in Noble County, Assistant Attorney General Mark Gibson stated, "There stood a polite young man who gave polite, cooperative answers to every question. It was like the dutiful soldier," Gibson said. Emotions

---

* After his arrest, Bryant said that he had been "gotten to," and "had been programmed."
"Sleepers" such as Bryant were most likely programmed to kill their victims in order to precipitate law and order crackdowns, such as occurred in the aftermath of the Australian melee, where the government recently outlawed almost all types of guns.

don't come into play, right and wrong don't come into play. What happens next doesn't come into play ... his mood was so level, it was unnatural. I looked at him and realized I felt no repulsion or fear. It was like there was an absence of feeling. He exuded nothing."

Trooper Hanger told *The Times* , "And when he grabbed his gun and there was no reaction, no shock, that didn't seem right, either." [154]

An "absence of feeling" among a man who committed a heinous crime—or is thought to—may well have been indicative of a psychologically controlled "sleeper" agent, a person trained to carry out a preconceived order upon command. Such an individual could conceivably carry out a horrendous crime, then have no recollection of the event. Far from the stuff of spy novels or conspiracy theories, sleeper agents have been developed and used by intelligence agencies for decades.

The CIA's interest in mind control originally dates back to WWII when the Office of Strategic Services (OSS), under Stanley Lovell, developed the idea of hypnotizing German prisoners to re-infiltrate the Third Reich and assassinate Adolf Hitler. After the war, the OSS, re-formed as the CIA, brought Nazi doctors and scientists to work for them under the cover of Operation PAPERCLIP. Some of these included war criminals spirited away through Nazi-Vatican "Ratlines" under the aegis of Operation OMEGA, conveniently missing their day in court at the Nuremberg War Crimes Tribunal. Their colleagues wound up in Central and South America, drained from the best of Nazi blood under Operation VAMPIRE.

By the late 1950s, the military was well on its way to investigating potential for "brainwashing," a term coined by the CIA's Edward Hunter to explain the experience of American POWs in Korea. In 1958 the Rand Corporation produced a report for the Air Force entitled "The Use of Hypnosis in Intelligence and Related Military Situations," stating that "In defense applications, subjects can be specifically selected by a criterion of hypnotizability, and subsequently trained in accord with their anticipated military function."[155] The CIA's plunge into the mind control netherworld got underway in 1950 with Project BLUEBIRD, renamed Operation ARTICHOKE in 1952, coordinated by CIA Security Officer Shefield Edwards under the authority of Deputy CIA Director Richard Helms.

Taking the Hippocratic Oath for ARTICHOKE was Dr. Sidney Gottlieb, mind-control emeritus of the CIA's Technical Services Division (TSS), the real-life counterpart to the mythical "Q-Branch" of Ian Fleming fame. TSS was engaged developing the usual James Bond spy toys—miniature cameras, shooting fountain pens, and, under the tutelage of Dr. Gottlieb, poisons that could kill in seconds, leaving no trace. With Operation ARTICHOKE, the CIA broadened its horizons into the realm of psychological warfare. ARTICHOKE was one of the CIA's latter-day attempts to create an electronically-controlled Manchurian Candidate.

In the 1950s, under the code name MKULTRA, the CIA set up safe houses in San Francisco and other cities experimenting on unwitting subjects using LSD and other drugs. In 1960, Edwards recruited ex-FBI agent Robert Maheu to approach Mob bosses Sam Giancana and John Rosselli to create CIA foreign leader assassin teams using techniques acquired by Gottlieb's TSS.

By 1963, reported the Senate Intelligence Committee, the number of operations and subjects increased substantially. As far back as 1960, TSS officials, working along with the Counterintelligence staff, expanded their hypnosis programs to coincide with MKULTRA experiments. According to John Marks' *The Search for the Manchurian Candidate*, "the Counterintelligence program had three goals: (1) to induce hypnosis very rapidly in unwitting subjects; (2) to create durable amnesia; and (3) to implant durable and operationally useful posthypnotic suggestion."

By 1966, MKULTRA spawned Operation MKSEARCH, and then Operations OFTEN and CHICKWIT, using biological, chemical and radiological substances to induce psychological and physiological changes. Operations THIRD CHANCE and DERBY HAT surreptitiously dosed victims in Europe and the Far East. MKDELTA, an offshoot of MKULTRA, sprayed massive doses of LSD and other drugs by the Army over areas inhabited by Viet Cong.[156]

CIA psychiatrist Dr. Ewen Cameron is the noted progenitor of "psychic driving," the technique where the controller repeatedly plays back selected words or phrases to break down psychological barriers and open up the victim's unconscious.[157] Such techniques would be eagerly incorporated into the program for creating Manchurian Candidates unleashed at the behest of the Agency to kill upon command. A discussion surrounding the creation of a Manchurian Candidate is revealed by JFK researcher Dick Russell in his book *The Man Who Knew Too Much*:

In 1968, Dr. Joseph L. Bern of Virginia Polytechnic Institute questioned authorities on hypnosis about whether the creation of a "Manchurian Candidate" was really feasible. As Author [Walter] Bowart recounted one expert's response to Dr. Bern: "I would say that a highly skilled hypnotist, working with a highly susceptible subject, could possibly persuade the subject to kill another human." Another believed it was even possible, through posthypnotic suggestion, to make a subject unable to recall such an act: "There could be a conspiracy, but a conspiracy of which the principal was unaware."[158]

"Psychic driving" impacted Sirhan Sirhan believes Charles McQuiston, a former Army intelligence officer who performed a Psychological Stress Evaluation on Sirhan's voice recordings. Says McQuiston, "I believe Sirhan was brainwashed under hypnosis by the constant repetition of words like, 'You are nobody, you're nothing, the American dream is gone' ... Somebody implanted an idea, kill RFK, and under hypnosis the brainwashed Sirhan accepted it."[159] The accused assassin couldn't even recall the murder.

Contract agent Colonel William Bishop explains some of the rudiments of CIA mind control operations:

"There were any number of psychological or emotional factors involved in peoples' selection. Antisocial behavior patterns, paranoia or the rudiments of paranoia, and so on. But when they are successful with this programming—or, for lack of a better term, indoctrination—they could take John Doe and get this man to kill George and Jane Smith. He will be given all the pertinent information as to their location, daily habits, etc. Then there is a mental block put on this mission in his mind. He remembers nothing about it." [160]

On March 3, 1964, CIA Director John McCone sent a memo to Secret Service chief James Rowley stating that after his surgery at the hospital in Minsk, Oswald might have been "chemically or electronically 'controlled' ... a sleeper agent. Subject spent 11 days hospitalized for a minor ailment which should have required no more than three days hospitalization at best." [161]

Even J. Edgar Hoover told the Warren Commission, "Information came to me indicating that there is an espionage training school outside of Minsk—I don't know whether it is true—that [Oswald] was trained at that school to come back to this country to become what they call a 'sleeper,' that is, a man who will remain dormant for three or four years and in case of international hostilities rise up and be used."[162]

The CIA's interest in producing the perfect programmed assassin took a new bent, when in 1965, the Agency, in cooperation with the DoD, set up a secret program for studying the effects of electromagnetic radiation or microwave (EM) weapons at the Army's Advanced Research Projects Agency (ARPA) at Walter Reed Army Institute of Research. The project was inspired by the Soviets, who had been dousing the American Embassy in Moscow with a lethal dose of microwave radiation, causing many of its personnel to die from cancer.

Causing degenerative disease was not the main goal of the DoD/CIA EM weapons research, code named PANDORA. Spooks were interested in microwaves for controlling behavior. By 1973, both the Americans and the Soviets were far along in their mind control applications, using pulsed microwave audiograms and acoustical telemetry to create voices in a subject's mind, or erase his mind completely.[163] With the advent of EM technology, scientists bypassed the need for electrodes implanted in the brain, and controlled subjects directly. Author Lincoln Lawrence describes a technology called RHIC-EDOM, or "Radio Hypnotic Intracerebral Control and Electronic Dissolution of Memory":

It is the ultra-sophisticated application of post-hypnotic suggestion triggered at will by radio transmission. It is a recurring state, re-induced automatically at intervals by the same radio control. An individual is brought under hypnosis. This can be done either with his knowledge—or without it—by use of narco-hypnosis, which can be brought into play under many guises. He is then programmed to perform certain actions and maintain certain attitudes upon radio signal.

Lawrence goes on to state, "Use of radio-waves and ultra-sonic signal tones … in effect blocks memory of the moment."[164] "Such a device has obvious applications in covert operations designed to drive a target crazy with 'voices' or deliver undetected instructions to a programmed assassin," believes Dr. Robert Becker.[165]

Thane Eugene Cesar, believed to be an accomplice in the murder of Robert Kennedy, held a vaguely-defined job at Lockheed, a CIA/PANDORA contractor. Retired Lockheed engineer Jim Yoder told former FBI agent William Turner that Cesar worked floating assignments in an "off-limits" area operated by the CIA.[166] The parallel is strikingly similar to that of Timothy McVeigh, who worked at Calspan, another high-tech military contractor engaged in top-secret telemetric work.

The preeminent don of CIA's psychological warfare program (MKULTRA), Dr. Louis Jolyon (Jolly) West, sent an Oklahoma City Zoo elephant careening on a massive LSD trip, triggering its death hours later. Studying the use of drugs as "adjuncts to interpersonal manipulation or assault," Jolly West was among the pioneers of remote electronic brain experimentation on unwitting subjects. His good friend Aldous Huxley passed on the idea to West that he hypnotize subjects before administering LSD, orienting drug-induced experience toward a "desired direction."

West was given the job of examining Jack Ruby, Lee Harvey Oswald's killer. Ruby's refusal to admit insanity, and his belief that a right-wing cabal was responsible for JFK's murder, led West to conclude Ruby was mentally ill, the proper candidate for anti-depressants. Ruby died of cancer two years after the exam, claiming to have been injected with malignant biological material. West also examined Sirhan Sirhan, a hypno-patsy jailed for murdering Robert Kennedy.

Chairman of UCLA's Neuropsychiatric Institute, Jolly West headed the American Psychological Association (APA) trauma response team that rushed to Oklahoma City in wake of the disaster. Confirming that he had indeed traveled to Oklahoma City with his team, Dr. West made a curious Freudian slip when asked if he examined McVeigh: "No, I haven't been asked to do that. I think his lawyer wouldn't want someone he didn't trust … pick." (According to ex-FBI Ted Gunderson, West did indeed examine McVeigh.[167]) The FBI's Behavioral Sciences unit inherited the role of interviewing McVeigh. John Douglas of the FBI's Psychological Profile Unit was quoted in the *Times* as saying, "This is an easily controlled and manipulated personality," unwittingly confirming that

McVeigh is perfect material for the CIA's psychological mind control program.

McVeigh was subjected to psychological torture while in prison.[168] Placed in a cell with a guard—with whom he was not allowed to speak—McVeigh was watched around the clock. The lights in his cell were kept on 24-hours-a-day, depriving him of sleep—a standard technique designed to break down a subject's psychological barriers. Eventually, McVeigh called in a psychiatrist to help treat anxiety.

Less than three weeks before the bombing, McVeigh appeared at the Imperial Motel in Kingman on March 31 and rented a room. For the next 12 days, according to owner Helmut Hofer, he just sat there, emerging only for meals or to pay his bill. He had no visitors, made few phone calls, and barely disturbed the furnishings. No one ever heard his television, and his car never moved from its spot outside.*

"That's the funny thing," said Hofer. "He didn't go out. He didn't make phone calls. He didn't do anything. He just sat up there and brooded."

Earline Roberts, housekeeper at Oak Cliff rooming house where Oswald stayed just prior to JFK's murder remarked that the famous lone assassin seemed like a brooder, too, staying in his room, having no visitors and never socializing.

Perhaps McVeigh simply rented a room at Imperial Motel for 12 days to brood. Or maybe he was told to wait somewhere until contacted, or simply put on ice, waiting to be activated by some sort of signal. It is possible McVeigh's anger at the Federal Government was stoked by a more mysterious enemy, one he didn't see or feel … but heard.

One of the most famous documented cases of "hearing voices" was that of Dennis Sweeny, the student activist who shot and killed his mentor Allard Lowenstein. Lowenstein, who marched in the 1964 Freedom Summer in Mississippi, campaigned for Robert Kennedy and Adlai Stevenson and ran the National Student Association before the CIA took over. Lowenstein, who was also friends with CIA propagandist William F. Buckley, attempted to prove that a conspiracy was responsible for the deaths of Martin Luther King and the Kennedys. (At the time he was of his murder, he was assisting Ted Kennedy in the 1980 presidential election.) [169]

Sweeny calmly walked into Rockefeller Center and pumped seven bullets into his mentor. He then sat down, lit a cigarette, and waited for the police to arrive. "Sweeny claimed that the CIA, with Lowenstein's help, had implanted a telemetric chip in his head 15 years earlier, and had made his life an unbearable torment. Voices were transmitted through his dental work, he said, and he attempted to silence them by filing down his false teeth. Sweeny blamed CIA 'controllers' for his uncle's heart

---

* McVeigh was not there the entire time. Phone records indicate he made steady calls until the 7th of April, when he was seen at a bar in Tulsa, Oklahoma. Phone calls resume April 11.

attack and the assassination of San Francisco mayor George Moscone."[170]

Those who believe that electronically-manipulated scenarios are stuff of fantasy should take note that no less than three support groups currently deal with the trauma of military and intelligence agency brainwashing.

An ex-CIA agent interviewed by Jim Keith claimed to have knowledge of biological warfare testing and special medical and Psy-op facilities at Fort Riley—where Timothy McVeigh took a Psy-op course. The agent stated that experimentation was conducted "in collaboration with the whole range of intelligence agencies, FBI, CIA, NSA, the works." The agent also said he witnessed psychological operations performed on the crew of the Pueblo naval vessel at Fort Riley, and at Fort Benning, Georgia prior to the ship's capture under mysterious circumstances by the North Koreans. Fort Benning is also home to the notorious School of the Americas, where CIA and Special Forces trained Latin American Death squad leaders for over three decades.

Fort Riley was home to a mysterious plague of murders and shootings around the time of the Oklahoma City bombing. On March 2, 1995, PFC Maurice Wilford shot three officers with a 12-gauge shotgun before turning the gun on himself. On April 6, Brian Soutenburg was found dead in his quarters after an apparent suicide.[171]

After his arrest, Timothy McVeigh was taken to Tinker Air Force Base. Why he was taken to a military installation remains unclear. Was McVeigh manipulated through the use of a subcutaneous transponder? Was he a "sleeper agent," programmed to do a dirty deed and have no memory of it afterward? Interestingly, Richard Condon's classic play, *The Manchurian Candidate,* made its debut in Oklahoma City exactly one year after the actual Manchurian candidate potentially made his debut.

It's also possible that someone working for the government convinced McVeigh of a cover story—that he was on an important, top secret mission. McVeigh's indifference to his arrest may have simply been indicative of his understanding that he was working for a government agency, delivered a truck as he was told, and, had not killed anyone.

McVeigh was concerned about military cutbacks when resigning the Army in December, 1991. It is possible that he was offered a more lucrative career—one that promised more excitement, adventure and money than the National Guard, which he quit in June, 1992.

Timothy McVeigh would have been what the intelligence community were looking for—a top-notch, gung-ho but impressionable young soldier, a taciturn individual who followed orders without hesitation and who knew when to keep his mouth shut, a prerequisite of any good intelligence operative.

According to former CIA agent Victor Marchetti, intelligence agencies regularly recruit from the military, and military files are routinely reviewed for potential candidates—those who have proven their willingness and ability to kill on command and without hesitation. Those whose combat training and proficiency with weapons make them excellent candidates for field operations. Having taken the PSYOPS course at Fort Riley, McVeigh was well on his was way to a career in covert intelligence. His above-average military record and his tryout for Special Forces, created as the covert military arm of the CIA, would have made him a natural choice. According to Lt. Colonel Daniel Marvin (Ret.), "almost all of the independent operations within the Green Berets were run by the CIA." [172]

McVeigh's racism and espousal of militia-type views would have made him a perfect operative to infiltrate any far right-wing or white supremacist group. Likewise it would have made him the perfect patsy to implicate in connection with any right-wing group, possessing all the qualities that would have made him an excellent undercover operative and a perfect fall-guy.

In May, 1992, McVeigh was promoted to lieutenant at Burns Security, informing his National Guard commander by mail that his civilian job required his presence. "The letter was real vague," said his commander. "It didn't say just what this new job was." Approximately nine months later, when McVeigh was going to be promoted to supervisor at Burns, he suddenly quit, saying that he had "more pressing matters to attend to."

What these "pressing matters" were is not exactly clear. Burns co-worker Carl Lebron says McVeigh told him he was leaving to take a civilian position with the Army in Kentucky painting trucks. He later told Lebron that he became privy to a top-secret project at Calspan called "Project Norstar," which, according to McVeigh, involved bringing drugs into the country via miniature submarine. He told his friend that he was afraid that those responsible for Project Norstar were "coming after him" and that he had to leave.

While this explanation may strike one as bizarre, McVeigh wrote his sister Jennifer that he was picked by the Army for a highly specialized Special Forces Covert Tactical Unit (CTU) involved in illegal activities. The letter was introduced to the Federal Grand Jury. According to former grand juror Hoppy Heidelberg, these illegal activities included "protecting drug shipments, eliminating the competition, and population control." While all the details of the letter aren't clear, Heidelberg said that there were five to six duties in all, and that the group was comprised of 10 men.

Such units are nothing new. During the Vietnam War, CIA Director William Colby and Ted Shackley—who also ran a massive heroin smuggling operation—created what they called Provincial Reconnaissance Units (PRUs), which would capture, torture, and kill suspected Viet Cong leaders.*

---

* Former intelligence operative Gene "Chip" Tatum described a recent massive heroin and cocaine smuggling operation being run by rogue elements of the U.S. Government

Former Army CID investigator Gene Wheaton also described a covert unit created by the highly secretive NRO (National Reconnaissance Office), which used assassination and torture to eliminate "enemies of the state." In 1985, Wheaton was approached by security consultants to Vice President Bush's "Task Force on Combating Terrorism" who were working for USMC Lt. Colonel Oliver North and Associate Deputy FBI Director Oliver "Buck" Revell. "They wanted me to help create a 'death squad' that would have White House deniability to assassinate people they would identify as terrorists," said Wheaton.

Code-named "Zeta Diogenes" in the USAF subset, this secret project, according to Wheaton, "was created in a rage by the covert intelligence leadership after the failed Bay of Pigs operation against Cuba in 1961." Wheaton claims the program continues to the present day.[173]

Anyone who prefers to think that agencies of the U.S. Government and Special Forces are above assassinating U.S. citizens, not to mention senior U.S. officials when expedient, may wish to consider testimony given by Colonel Daniel Marvin, a highly decorated Special Forces Vietnam veteran. While going through Special Forces training at Fort Bragg in 1964, Marvin's group was asked if any members would like to volunteer to take special assassination training on behalf of the CIA, eliminating Americans overseas who posed "national security risks." About six people, himself included, volunteered.

"The CIA had agents there all the time at Fort Bragg, in the Special Warfare Center Headquarters," recalls Marvin. "My commanding officer, Colonel C.W. Patton, called me up to his office one day in the first week … and he said, "Dan, go out and meet the 'Company' man standing there underneath the pine trees, waiting to talk to you."

Ironically, Marvin had been motivated to join the Special Forces by the death of President Kennedy, who had conferred upon the unit their distinctive and coveted green berets. Marvin began his assassination training in the Spring of 1964. "During one of the coffee breaks, I overheard one of the [CIA] instructors say to the other one, 'Well, it went pretty well in Dallas. Didn't it?'"

Marvin says his group was shown "16 millimeter moving pictures that we assumed were taken by the CIA of the assassination, on the ground there at Dallas … We were told that there were actually four shooters. There was one on the roof of the lower part of the Book Depository, and there was one shooter who was in front of and to the right of the vehicle. And I'm not sure whether it was on the Grassy Knoll area that they were speaking of, or, as some people have

---

across the Canadian border into Montana with the complicity of local officials. "These officials were recruited to assist in the smuggling operations, thinking they were part of a government-sanctioned covert operation." Excerpt of a letter from Tatum to the Montana Senate Judiciary Committee, 3/22/97.

reported, [a shooter firing] out of a manhole to the right-front of the vehicle."

He added that two additional snipers with spotters were stationed on the routes that the motorcade would have used to travel to the hospital. If the spotter determined Kennedy had survived, he was to finish him off.

Marvin claims his assassination training was reserved solely for citizens outside the United States, not on U.S. soil. "The Mafia lists were the ones being used [to kill Americans] in the continental United States," says Marvin. "We were being used overseas." That was, until he was asked to kill an American Naval officer—Lt. Commander William Bruce Pitzer, the X-ray technician who filmed the Kennedy autopsy, "as he was, supposedly, a traitor, about to give secrets to the enemy. It turned out that these 'secrets' were the photos of the *real* autopsy of President John F. Kennedy. And the 'enemy' was us!"

When he found out that his assignment was to be conducted in the U.S., he refused. "That wasn't my mission," says Marvin. "When I took my training, I volunteered to do this kind of thing overseas where it could be covered, as far as the family goes. I had a wife and three children. If I were to accept that mission to kill Commander Pitzer right here in the United States, I would have been dropped from the rolls immediately as a deserter so that it would cover me for taking off and taking care of that mission." [174]

Such a "cover" tactic appears to closely parallel that of Timothy McVeigh, who "dropped out" of Special Forces training before embarking on his bewildering and mysterious journey prior to the bombing.

Still another, more well-documented reference to similar illegal operations is made by *Wall Street Journal* reporter Jonathan Kwitny in his best-selling book, *The Crimes of Patriots.* Kwitny describes in how rogue CIA agents Edwin Wilson (who reported to Shackley) and Frank Terpil were not only illegally selling huge quantities of C-4 plastic explosives and sophisticated assassination gear to the Libyans, but were actually hiring anti-Castro Cubans from Shackley's old JM/WAVE program, and U.S. Green Berets to assassinate Qaddafi's political opponents abroad.

> Some U.S. Army men were literally lured away from the doorway of Fort Bragg, their North Carolina training post. The GIs were given every reason to believe that the operation summoning them was being carried out with the full backing of the CIA. [175]

Could this be the same group McVeigh claims to have been recruited for? Considering the allegations of the Federal Government against McVeigh, being chosen for such a clandestine and blatantly illegal government-sponsored operation seems highly revealing.

According to Heidelberg's account of the letter, McVeigh turned the government down. "They picked him because he was gung-ho," said Heidelberg. "But they mis-judged him. He was gung-ho, but in a sincere way. He really loved his country." [176]

In another version of the story reported by Ted Gunderson, an intelligence informant indicated McVeigh was "trained to work for the CIA in their illegal drug operations," then "became disenchanted with the government, and voiced his displeasure." At that point he was sent to Fort Riley for discharge, at which point John Doe 2 "was planted on him" and "orchestrated the bombing." [177]

Whether McVeigh turned down this illegal covert operations group, or worked for them for a short time, he likely worked for the government in some fashion. There is simply no logical explanation for McVeigh to give up a hard-earned and brilliant military career, and subsequently quit his security guard job on the eve of his promotion to take a job painting old army trucks, or go tooling around the country in a beat-up car hawking used firearms and militia paraphernalia.

If McVeigh was recruited, his "opting out" of the military was most likely a cover story for that recruitment. Former Pentagon counter-intelligence officer Robert Gambert told of the mysterious activities of his cousin Richard Case Nagell, "Dick played the role of a disgruntled ex-Army officer … he was really still operational, in an undercover capacity, for the Army Intelligence…. They're not gonna' trust anybody who's active military or a friendly retiree. They're gonna trust somebody who's going around griping against the military, against the intelligence operations, against the government." [178]

After McVeigh's mysterious departure from the Army, his friend Robin Littleton received a strange letter from him, illustrating a cartoon depicting a skull and crossbones with the caption "so many victims, so little time." [179] Whether he meant it as a joke, or intended a hidden message, is unclear. But considering the letter he wrote to Jennifer regarding the Covert Tactical Unit (CTU), its implications are unsettling.

A patriotic soldier like Timothy McVeigh wasn't the type to gripe against the government. But, said the *Post:* "McVeigh was by now railing at virtually every aspect of American government, and at least beginning to consider a violent solution, as reflected in letters he wrote to the *Lockport Union-Sun & Journal* in February and March 1992, (entitled 'America Faces Problems.')" [180]

Crime is out of control. Criminals have no fear of punishment. Prisons are overcrowded so they know they will not be imprisoned long. This breeds more crime, in an escalating cyclic pattern.

Taxes are a joke. Regardless of what a political candidate "promises," they will increase. More taxes are always the answer to government mismanagement. They mess up, we suffer. Taxes are reaching cataclysmic levels, with no slowdown in sight.

The "American Dream" of the middle class has all but disappeared, substituted with people struggling just to buy next week's groceries. Heaven forbid the car breaks down!

Politicians are further eroding the "American Dream" by passing laws which are supposed to be a "quick fix," when all they are really designed for is to get the official re-elected. These laws tend to "dilute" a problem for a while, until the problem comes roaring back in a worsened form (much like a strain of bacteria will alter itself to defeat a known medication).

Politicians are out of control. Their yearly salaries are more than an average person will see in a lifetime. They have been entrusted with the power to regulate their own salaries and have grossly violated that trust to live in their own luxury.

Racism on the rise? You had better believe it! Is this America's frustrations venting themselves? Is it a valid frustration? Who is to blame for the mess? At a point when the world has seen Communism falter as an imperfect system to manage people; democracy seems to be headed down the same road. No one is seeing the "big" picture.

Maybe we have to combine ideologies to achieve the perfect utopian government. Remember, government-sponsored health care was a Communist idea. Should only the rich be allowed to live long? Does that say that because a person is poor, he is a lesser human being; and doesn't deserve to live as long, because he doesn't wear a tie to work?

What is it going to take to open up the eyes of our elected officials? America is in serious decline!

We have no proverbial tea to dump; should we instead sink a ship full of Japanese imports? Is a Civil War imminent? Do we have to shed blood to reform the current system? I hope it doesn't come to that! But it might.

An ordinary gripe letter written by an individual with above-average intelligence was turned into a manifestation of suppressed frustration and violent overtones by psychojournalists of the mainstream press. If McVeigh was under the influence of mind control, it's possible the letter, and the one to Littleton, might have been the beginnings of a plan to "sheep-dip" McVeigh as a disgruntled ex-military man.*

It is also possible that McVeigh, tasked with the responsibility of infiltrating the Militia movement, became genuinely enamored with its ideals and precepts.

---

* The term "sheep-dipped" is best clarified by former CIA-Department of Defense liaison L. Fletcher Prouty, in his classic work on the CIA, *The Secret Team* (Prentice Hall). "It is an intricate Army-devised process by which a man who is in the service as a full career soldier or officer agrees to go through all the legal and official motions of resigning from the service. Then, rather than actually being released, his records are pulled from the Army personnel files and transferred to a special Army intelligence file. Substitute but nonetheless real-appearing records are then processed, and the man 'leaves' the service."

Whether or not this is true, McVeigh's letter to the *Lockport Union-Sun & Journal* and to Robin Littleton were two more nails the government and the press would use to drive into McVeigh's coffin.

The major nails in McVeigh's coffin were yet to come.

THE MAN WHO DIDN'T EXIST

In September, 1992, McVeigh sold his property in Olean, NY, and in early 1993 traveled to Kingman, Arizona to visit his old Army friend Michael Fortier. McVeigh's father didn't approve of Tim's letters in the local paper. A friend of McVeigh's father told the *Post* that one of the reasons McVeigh left was because "he wanted to be somewhere he could talk about what he really believed."

In Kingman, a rugged high-desert town where anti-government sentiments run strong, McVeigh would find like-minded souls. "Arizona is still gun-on-the-hip territory, rugged individuals who don't like the government in their business," said Marilyn Hart, manager of the Canyon West Mobile Park.

After spending a brief time living with Fortier at his trailer home on East McVicar Road, McVeigh rented a trailer at Canyon West where he lived from June to September, 1993, for $250-a-month.

The *Times*, the *Post*, *Time* and *Newsweek* all reported that McVeigh was a belligerent beer-drinking, loud music-playing slob who stayed at the Canyon West Mobile Park and was subsequently evicted. According to the *Times:*

> Residents of the Canyon West Mobile Park drew a picture of an arrogant loner who worked as a security guard for a now-defunct trucking company, lived with his pregnant girlfriend, expressed deep anger against the Federal Government and often caused trouble for his neighbors. "He drank a lot of beer and threw out the cans, and I always had to pick them up," Bob Rangin, owner of the park, was quoted as saying. He said he had frequent fights with Mr. McVeigh, who often wore Army fatigues, over such things as loud rock music coming from his trailer and a dog he kept in violation of his lease.[181]

> "Just about any free time, he'd be walking down there, or across the railroad tracks and firing his guns," said Marilyn Hart, nodding at the landscape of canyons and mesas around the Canyon West trailer park here that is one of the last known addresses of the man arrested for bombing the Oklahoma City Federal Building. "He just plain didn't care. Didn't matter the time of day or night, he'd be out there shooting."

> "Basically he just had a poor attitude, a chip on the shoulder kind of thing," said Rob Rangin, the owner of the trailer park. "He was very cocky. He looked like he was ready to get in a fight pretty easy. I'll tell you, I was a little afraid of him and

I'm not afraid of too many people.

Mr. McVeigh brought in a big brown dog in defiance of the camp regulations and left a wrecked car parked by his trailer, Mr. Rangin said, and even a nearly totally deaf neighbor, Clyde Smith, complained about the music. Finally, said Mr. Rangin, "he piled up so many violations, I asked him to leave."

"When he did, the trailer was a disaster," he said. "It was trashed." [182]

These accounts of McVeigh in the *Times* on April 23 and 24 are totally contrary to accounts on May 4 and December 31, describing him as compulsively neat, disciplined, respectful of his elders, and courteous to a fault. Friends and acquaintances interviewed also claimed that McVeigh was extremely quiet, never drank, and never had a date, much less a pregnant girlfriend.

Yet on April 23, the *Post* described how McVeigh played loud music, terrorized his neighbors, and was evicted from the park. Then on July 2, the *Post* wrote:

When he moved into the Canyon West trailer park outside Kingman in 1993, his first act was to wash the dirty curtains and dust, vacuum and scrub the entire trailer spotless, said owner Bob Rangin, who so liked McVeigh that he offered to lower the rent to keep the ex-soldier from moving.

The *Post* also ran an interview with neighbor Jack Gohn, who said McVeigh was so "quiet, polite and neat and clean" that "if I had a daughter in that age bracket, I would have introduced them." [183]

Said Marilyn Hart of Timothy McVeigh: "He was very quiet, very polite, very courteous, very neat, very clean, quiet, obeyed all the park rules. He worked on the trailer, did some painting, he did some cleaning on it, he bought new furniture, things like that." [184]

The *Times* was not reporting on Timothy McVeigh at all, but a completely different man! According to Hart, the mix-up came when reporters from the *Times* were given information about Dave Heiden, who also was just out of the service, and had lived in trailer #19 (McVeigh lived in trailer #11). "They thought it was the man who lived down below," said Hart. "He *was* a slob. But he was not Tim McVeigh. The other guy took his guns out across the way and fired them all the time, he got drunk and got up on top of the trailer and did all kinds of noisy things."

According to Hart, after the man's girlfriend gave birth he sobered up. "Now they're married, the baby was born, he's straightened up his life," said Hart. "He straightened up his act, and he doesn't act that way any more at all."

Rangin called authors Kifner and McFadden of the *Times* to correct them. "I tried to tell them that wasn't McVeigh," said Rangin. "I called that fellow at the *Times* who came down here, and told him they got the wrong guy." [185]

For days the *Times* painted McVeigh as a pathological, asexual neat freak who was extremely polite. These traits, the *Times'* psychobabblists claimed, were indicators of a mass killer. The *Times* then claimed on the very next day that McVeigh was a belligerent slob with a pregnant girlfriend, and all of a sudden, *these* were the characteristics of a mass killer. Obviously, to the *New York Times,* it didn't matter what McVeigh's actual personality really was.

While in Kingman, McVeigh worked at different jobs through an agency called Allied Forces. "He did a number of jobs that way," said Hart. "He was a security guard, he did a number of different jobs. But he always went to his job, did them well ... any of the people who worked with him said he didn't act odd, you know, it was totally out of character." [186]

McVeigh worked for a time at True Value Hardware, on Stockton Hill Road, a job that Fortier helped him get. Paul Shuffler, the store owner, said McVeigh "was a young and clean looking person so I gave him a job." According to Shuffler, "If he was a radical around here, I would have noticed it pretty quick and I would have fired him. Radicals don't last long around here because they just make a mess of things." [187]

McVeigh also worked for a spell at State Security. The *Times* interview with co-worker Fred Burkett took a slightly different slant, painting his co-worker McVeigh as an arrogant, gun-toting loner. "He had a very dry personality," Burkett told the *Times.* "He was not very outgoing, not talkative and not really that friendly. He wasn't a person that mingled. He was a kind of by yourself kind of person, a loner."

> Once, Burkett went with McVeigh on a target-shooting course in the desert, where McVeigh "pretty much went crazy," Burkett said. After running through the course, picking off targets with a Glock .45, McVeigh began "emptying clips on pretty much anything—trees, rocks, whatever happened to be there." [188]

"Other than that," Mr. Burkett said, "he seemed pretty much normal. The only thing he ever indicated was that he didn't care much for the United States Government and how they ran things. He didn't care much for authority and especially when it concerned the government."

Authorities speculated that McVeigh's interests went beyond mere dissatisfaction with the Federal Government. According to Carl Lebron, McVeigh once brought him a newsletter from the Ku Klux Klan. [189] McVeigh was also fond of a book called the *Turner Diaries.* Written by former physics professor and neo-Nazi William Pierce, the *Turner Diaries* was a fictionalized account of a white supremacist uprising against ZOG (Zionist Occupational Government). The book, exceedingly violent and racist in tone, is a fictionalized account of the overthrow of the Federal Government—which by that time had become the "Jewish-liberal-democratic-equalitarian plague"—by a right-wing paramilitary group called the "Organization," which then goes on to murder and segregate Jews and other "non-whites." The protagonists also blow up FBI headquarters with a truck-bomb. The *Turner Diaries* was found on Timothy McVeigh upon his arrest.

The book became the blueprint for a neo-Nazi group called The Order, which terrorized the Midwest in the early to mid '80s with a string of murders and bank robberies. Authorities have speculated that McVeigh, who carried the book with him constantly and sold it at gun shows, was inspired by its screed to commit his terrible act of violence. Yet McVeigh dismisses such suggestions as gibberish. "I bought the book out of the publication that advertised the book as a gun-rights book. That's why I bought it; that's why I read it." [190]

In Kingman, McVeigh made friends with an ex-Marine named Walter "Mac" McCarty. McVeigh apparently sought out the 72-year-old McCarty for discussions in which he tried to make sense of the actions of the Federal Government at Ruby Ridge and Waco, and such issues as the United Nations, the Second Amendment, and the "New World Order."

"I gathered that he was following the right-wing, survivalist, paramilitary-type philosophy," McCarty said. "I also got the sense that he was searching for meaning and acceptance." [191]

McVeigh and Fortier also took handgun classes from McCarty during the summer of 1994, which is odd considering that the two men, McVeigh especially, were extremely proficient in the use of firearms. "Believe me, the one thing he did not need was firearms training," said Fred Burkett, McVeigh's co-worker at State Security. "He was very good and we were impressed with his actions." [192]

McCarty himself was suspicious of McVeigh's motives. "They wanted to hear certain things from me to see if they could get me involved," said McCarty. "They definitely liked what they heard. We were on the same page about the problems of America."

Why would McVeigh, a consummate firearms expert, bother taking a course in handguns? Perhaps to be around like-minded individuals or as a harmless diversion. It is also possible, like the Lee Harvey Oswald impostor seen at the Texas rifle range, McVeigh was being sheep-dipped. "I know brainwashing when I see it, McCarty said. "Those two boys had really gotten a good case of it." Perhaps McCarty was being more literal than he realized. [193]

After the August 1994 passage of the Omnibus Crime Bill outlawing certain types of semi-automatic weapons, "McVeigh's demons finally became unbearable," claimed the *Times*. "What will it take?" wrote McVeigh to Fortier, expressing his exasperation. [194]

It's possible that McVeigh had some contact with a local militia while in Kingman. According to reporter Mark Schafer of the *Arizona Republic*, Fortier, who worked at True Value, knew Jack Oliphant, the elderly patron of the Arizona Patriots, an extreme right-wing paramilitary group. Oliphant had been caught in

1986 planning to blow up the Hoover Dam, the IRS and a local Synagogue. After the FBI raid, Oliphant was sentenced to four years in jail, and the Arizona Patriots went underground. It is reported that Fortier, who sported a "Don't Tread on Me" flag outside his trailer-home, was friendly with some of the Arizona Patriots, including Oliphant.

According to federal authorities, McVeigh also left a note addressed to "S.C." on a utility pole near Kingman seeking "fighters not talkers." It has been speculated that "S.C." is actually Steven Colbern, who lived in the nearby town of Oatman, and was friends with McVeigh.

Federal authorities became very interested when they learned that a small explosion, related to a home-made bomb, had slightly damaged a house down the road from the trailer park. That house was owned by Frosty McPeak, a friend of McVeigh's who had hired him in 1993 to do security work at a local shelter. When McPeak's girlfriend was arrested in Las Vegas on a bad credit charge, Clark Vollmer, a paraplegic drug dealer in Kingman, helped bail her out. In February, '95, Vollmer asked McPeak to ferry some drugs. He refused. On February 21, a bomb exploded outside McPeak's home. When he went to Vollmer's house to confront him, he found Timothy McVeigh, along with another man he didn't recognize.[195]

According to Mohave County Sheriff Joe Cook, the explosion "wasn't really a big deal" and probably wasn't related to the explosion in Oklahoma City.[196]

What does Marilyn Hart think about McVeigh's connection to the local militias? "I probably do know several people who are militia," said Hart. "But they don't advertise it, and they're not kooks. To me, McVeigh didn't have the money. The two other guys, Rosencrans and Fortier, went to school with our children, and neither of them have money either."

"OBSESSED WITH WACO"

Whether or not McVeigh's "demons" became "unbearable" after the passage of the Omnibus Crime Bill, his anger, along with that of millions of others, would be justified by the government's massacre of 86 innocent men, women and children at the Branch Davidian Seventh Day Adventist Church near Waco the following April. The ostensible purpose of the ATF's raid was to inspect the premises for illegal weapons. The Davidians were licensed gun dealers who invited the ATF to inspect their weapons, but the agency declined, obviously more interested in staging a show raid to impress the public to help increase their budgetary allowance. The raid was in fact code-named "Show Time."

On February 28, 1993, without a proper warrant and without identifying themselves, over 100 agents stormed the Church compound. Residents who answered the door were immediately fired upon. At least one ATF helicopter began strafing the building, firing into the roof. For the next hour, ATF agents fired thousands of rounds into the compound. Many church members, including women, children and the elderly, were killed by gunfire as they lay huddled in fear, the women attempting to cover the children with their bodies. Church members repeatedly begged the 911 operator to stop the raid. In the ensuing battle, four ATF agents were killed, although there is evidence that indicates they were killed by "friendly fire."

Several days later, the FBI took over. Almost immediately, they began psychologically harassing the Church members with loud noise. For over a month and a half, the Davidians were tormented by the sounds of dying animals, religious chants, loud music, and their own voices. Their electricity was cut off, and milk and other supplies necessary for young chidden was not allowed into the compound. Bright lights were shined on residents 24 hours-a-day, and armored vehicles began circling the compound, while flash-bang grenades were thrown into the courtyard.

The media was kept at bay, fed stories by FBI spokesmen that painted the Davidians as crazed cultists with desires for apocalyptic self-destruction—dangerous wackos who stockpiled machine-guns and who abused their children. The mass media happily fed these images to a gullible public.*

After a 51-day standoff, newly appointed Attorney General Janet Reno, approved an FBI plan to assault the compound with a highly volatile form of tear gas, proven deadly to children, who she was ostensibly trying to protect from "abuse." On April 19, tanks from the Texas National Guard and the Army's Joint Task Force Six, in violation of the Posse Comitatus Act forbidding the use of military force against private citizens, stormed the compound, firing hundreds of CS gas ferret rounds into the buildings. The tanks also rammed the buildings repeatedly, knocking holes in them, the official explanation being so that the residents could more easily escape. Instead, what it did was cause the buildings to collapse, killing dozens as they lay crouched in fear. Kerosene lanterns knocked over by the tank ramming ignited the highly flammable CS gas, and the holes created a flue effect through the buildings, caused by 30 mile-an-hour winds. Immediately the compound became a fiery inferno.

While some residents managed to escape, most were trapped inside, aphyxiated by gas, crushed by falling debris, or burned alive. Some who tried to escape were shot by FBI snipers. One unarmed man who tried to enter the compound to be with his family was shot six times, then left lying in a field where prairie dogs picked at his bones. During the final siege, which lasted for six hours, fire

---

* Child Protective Services went to the compound, knocked on the door, walked in, and interviewed the children. They found no evidence of abuse and left.

trucks were purposefully kept away. Bradley M-2 armored vehicles fitted with plows pushed in the still standing walls, burying people still trapped inside. A concrete vault where approximately 30 people had sought refuge was blasted open with demolition charges, killing most of the people inside.

When it was all over, the fire department was allowed inside the compound to pump water on smoldering debris. Out of approximately 100 Church members, 86 perished, including 27 children. No FBI agent was injured. The remaining 11 church members were put on trial for attempted murder of federal agents. During the trial, government prosecutors repeatedly withheld, altered, and destroyed evidence. The government even cut off electricity to the morgue, preventing autopsies on the bodies.

The judge, recently under scrutiny by the Justice Department, also refused to allow the testimony of critical witnesses. Although the jury found all 11 innocent, the judge reversed the verdict. Nine Davidians were imprisoned for attempting to defend their families. Some received sentences up to 40 years.

In a symbolic gesture of public reconciliation, Reno took "full responsibility" for the actions of the FBI, but never resigned or served time. Larry Potts, who led the raid on behalf of the FBI, was promoted.

The assault was compared to the massacre of the Jews in Warsaw by the Nazis during WWII. A bunch of religious fanatics. Who'd complain? Who'd care? Yet the government didn't count on the fact that a lot of people would care. Millions, in fact. The murder of the Branch Davidians would indeed become a wake-up call for a citizenry concerned about an increasingly tyrannical, lawless government. A government that murders its own citizens with zeal and impunity. A government that lies to its citizens, and held accountable to no one.

In March, 1993, Timothy McVeigh traveled from Kingman to Waco to observe the 51-day standoff. He was photographed by the FBI along with others protesting the siege on the road outside the compound, selling bumper stickers out of his car. Like Lee Harvey Oswald, who was photographed at the Cuban embassy in Mexico (a claim made by the government, but never substantiated), the photo of McVeigh would be added proof of his far-right associations.

A day and a half later, McVeigh drove to Decker, Michigan to be with his old Army buddy, Terry Nichols. The Nichols family sat with McVeigh in their living room as they watched M-2 Bradley assault vehicles storm the compound. On April 19, they watched as the Branch Davidian Church burned to the ground. "Tim did not say a word," said James Nichols, who watched the compound burn to the ground along with Tim and his brother. "We stood there and watched the live television footage as the church burned and crumbled ... we couldn't believe it."[197]

McVeigh could see Green Berets from the Army's Joint Task Force Six advising the FBI, and had watched while Bradley armored vehicles—the same vehicles he had served in—gassed and bulldozed the citizens of a country he had sworn to defend.

The Federal Building was blown up on April 19, the two year anniversary of the Waco conflagration. Like millions of other citizens, McVeigh was angry about the deadly raid. He was particularly incensed about the participation of the Army's Joint Task Force Six, and about the deployment of the Seventh Light Infantry during the Los Angeles riots in 1992, and the United Nations command over American soldiers in Somalia. His former Army friend Staff Sergeant Albert Warnement told the *Times.* "He thought the Federal Government was getting too much power. He thought the ATF was out of control." [198]

"I saw a localized police state," McVeigh told the *London Sunday Times,* "[and] was angry at how this had come about." [199] "Their [the FBI's] actions in Waco, Texas were wrong. And I'm not fixated on it," he told *Newsweek.*

"It disturbed him," said Burkett. "It was wrong, and he was mad about it. He was flat out mad. He said the government wasn't worth the powder to blow it to hell." [200]

McVeigh's sister Jennifer said that during her brother's November, '94 visit to the McVeigh family home in Lockport, he confided that he had been driving around with 1,000 pounds of explosives. During his trial Prosecutor Beth Wilkinson asked Jennifer if she had questioned her brother about why he was carrying so much. "I don't think I wanted to know," she said. [201]

Just what was McVeigh doing driving around with explosives, and where did he acquire them? Were these explosives part of the batch of ammonium-nitrate Terry Nichols allegedly purchased from the Mid-Kansas Co-op on October 20, or perhaps the Dynamite and Tovex the government alleged Nichols stole from the Martin Marietta rock quarry in September?

Obviously, this, and McVeigh's expression of anger at the Federal Government, would become the foundation of their case against him. In a letter Tim wrote to Jennifer, he was highly critical of the ATF. The anonymous letter, which was sent to the federal agency, was accompanied by a note that read: "All you tyrannical motherfuckers will swing in the wind one day for your treasonous actions against the Constitution and the United States." It concluded with the words, "Die, you spineless cowardice bastards." [202]

"He was very angry," recalled Jennifer during her brother's trial. "He thought the government gassed and murdered the people there."

Jennifer also claimed her brother wrote a letter to the American Legion saying that ATF agents "are a bunch of fascist tyrants." He identified himself in the letter as a member of the "citizens' militia." He also sent his sister literature on the standoff at Ruby Ridge, the Constitution, and even a copy of *The Turner Diaries.* [203]

By the Spring of 1995, he told Jennifer not to send any more letters to him after May 1 because "G-men might get them." Then he sent her a letter saying, "Something big is going to happen in the month of the Bull." He did not explain what that meant, but Jennifer looked in her astrology book and saw that the "month of the Bull" (Taurus) begins in late April. McVeigh also advised her to extend her Spring break—which began on April 8—a bit longer than the planned two weeks, and instructed her to burn the letter.[204]

For McVeigh's part, he wrote that this "expression of rage" the government claimed was so key, was nothing more than "part of my contribution to defense of freedom, this call to arms … I intend to become more active in the future. I would rather fight with pencil lead than bullet lead. We can win this war in the voting booth. If we have to fight in the streets, I would not be so sure…. All too often in the past, we gutsy gun owners have lost the battle because we have failed to fight. The Brady Bill could have been defeated in Congress if gun owners had become more involved in electing officials and communicating to those officials what was expected to them…. Start your defense today. Stamps are cheaper than bullets and can be more effective."

This letter, found by authorities in McVeigh's car, speaks of a man committed to fighting for freedom in the "voting booth" and with pen and paper. Yet lead prosecutor Joseph Hartzler would read this letter, along with quotes such as this one: "My whole mindset has shifted … from the intellectual to the animal," into evidence at McVeigh's trial, in an attempt to prove that Timothy McVeigh was committed to violence.

Like Lee Harvey Oswald, who was upset about the Cuban Bay of Pigs invasion and American foreign policy in general—a view expressed to friends in Dallas—McVeigh was upset about the government's foreign policy, a view he expressed to his friends here. "He wasn't happy about Somalia," that if we could put the United States under basically UN command and send them to Somalia to disarm their citizens, then why couldn't they come do the same thing in the United States?" Sergeant Warnement said.

McVeigh was also reportedly angry over the killings of Sammy and Vicki Weaver, who were killed by federal agents at their cabin in Ruby Ridge, Idaho in August, 1992. Randy Weaver had become a fugitive wanted on a minor weapons violation. During the stand-off, U.S. Marshals had shot 14-year-old Sammy Weaver in the back, and had shot Vicki Weaver, Randy's wife, in the face, as she stood at the cabin door holding her infant daughter. McVeigh also traveled to Ruby Ridge and came back convinced that federal agents intentionally killed the Weavers.

Although his anger over Waco and Ruby Ridge hardly implicates McVeigh in the destruction of the Federal Building, the government would make this one of the cornerstones of its case. The press naturally jumped on the bandwagon. When Jane Pauley of NBC's Dateline interviewed Jennifer McVeigh about her thoughts on Waco, she said, "The way I saw it, the Davidians were just a group of people who had their own way of living, perhaps different from the mainstream. But they were never really harming anybody. And to bring in all those tanks and things like that to people who are just minding their own business, not harming anybody, I just—I don't think that's right."

But the dead, burned children at Waco were not what the producers at Dateline wanted the public to see. Immediately after Jennifer's statement, they cut to an image of the bombed-out day care center inside the Murrah Building. "We've been hoping this wouldn't be the case," said the live voice of an unidentified rescue worker, "but it is the case, there was a day-care inside the building."

Time ran a page dedicated to the Waco theory, stating, "The date of last week's bombing and the anniversary of the apocalyptic fire [notice they don't say government massacre] at the Branch Davidian compound in Waco—has only gained in infamy, intricately bound as it is to the mythologies of homegrown zealots like McVeigh." [205]

Sheep-Dipped

It would appear that the seed that gave root to McVeigh's "homegrown zeal" was incubated in a U.S. government hothouse and fertilized by a heaping dose of intelligence agency fanaticism.

After Waco, with the emergence of the Militia movement, the stage would be set, the die would be cast—for Timothy McVeigh to be poured into like a miniature lead soldier. While the FBI and the press admitted that McVeigh didn't actually belong to any organized militia organization, "there was considerable evidence that he sympathized with and espoused their beliefs," wrote the *Times*.

> He voiced their ideas in conversations, he wrote letters expressing them, he read their literature and attended their meetings. And he lived, worked and traded weapons in areas where the paramilitary groups enjoy considerable support. [206]

Like Lee Harvey Oswald, who appeared to be an avid Communist, distributing leaflets on behalf of the Fair Play for Cuba Committee, McVeigh would play the part of a militant right-winger, distributing literature about taxes, Waco and Ruby Ridge. Like Oswald, who left behind a diary widely believed to be a CIA forgery, McVeigh was purported to have similarly documented his own extremist position. According to the *Times:*

> Law enforcement officials say McVeigh left behind a large body of writings about his ideological leanings, including extensive tracts in letters to friends and relatives, that describe his belief in the constitutional principles that he adamantly maintained allowed him to carry firearms and live without any restraints from the government. Prosecutors are likely to use such documents to establish his motive at a trial. [207]

Like Oswald, McVeigh departed the military under mysterious circumstances. And like Oswald, an ex-Marine with top-secret security clearance who appeared to "defect" to the Soviet Union, McVeigh would appear to be a "disgruntled" ex-Army sergeant who happened to "drift" into the fringes of the far-right. Yet, like Oswald, who lived and worked amongst the bastions of the far-right in Dallas while purporting to be a Marxist, McVeigh was not the ultimate right-wing fanatic he was made out to be. In a letter to his hometown newspaper in February, 1992, he wrote:

> At a point when the world has seen Communism falter as an imperfect system to manage people; democracy seems to be headed down the same road. Maybe we have to combine ideologies to achieve the perfect utopian government. Remember, government-sponsored health care was a Communist idea.

Obviously, such views are anathema to the far-right, who see any attempt to socialize society as a major step towards a great one-world Communist conspiracy. It is possible that McVeigh was more progressive than his right-wing associates. It is also possible that McVeigh was being sheep-dipped as a militant right-winger.

After Waco, McVeigh traveled to Michigan, staying for a time with Terry Nichols. He worked on Nichols' farm, and went hunting and target practicing. Neighbors recall how McVeigh and Nichols made and detonated small homemade bombs. Paul Izydorek, a neighbor, recalls, "When they were around, they'd get different guns and play and shoot and stuff." On at least one occasion, Izydorek heard blasts at the farm and noticed Terry Nichols and a man he thought was McVeigh. "I'd seen them playing around with different household items that you can make blow up. Just small stuff. Just outside in the yard, blowing away." [208]

Nichols' brother James also admitted to the FBI that McVeigh and Terry made and exploded "bottle bombs" at his farm, using brake fluid, gasoline, and diesel fuel, and that he sometimes participated. [209]

In his interview with *Newsweek*, McVeigh dispelled the myth that his bomb making was a precursor to more deadly acts. "It would amount to firecrackers. It was like popping a paper bag," said McVeigh, who had also experimented with small explosives on his land in Olean, NY prior to entering the Army.

Yet a relative also told the FBI that James Nichols kept a large supply of ammonium-nitrate fertilizer on the farm—the very substance federal authorities accused the suspects of using to manufacture their alleged truck-bomb, a fact that would become yet another linchpin in the government's case against the two men.

While in Michigan, McVeigh also started working the gun shows. From April, 1993 to March, 1995, McVeigh would travel from Kingman, Arizona to Decker,

Michigan, and across the U.S., attending militia meetings and working the gun show circuit. A gun collector interviewed by the *Times* said that he had encountered McVeigh in gun shows ranging from Florida to Oklahoma to Nevada. "At the S.O.F. (Soldier of Fortune) convention he was kind of wandering around," said the gun collector, who requested anonymity, "like he was trying to meet people, maybe make converts. He could make ten friends at a show, just by his manner and demeanor. He's polite, he doesn't interrupt."

"McVeigh traveled around the country in a rattletrap car," wrote the *Times*' Kifner, "his camouflage fatigues clean and pressed, his only companion a well-thumbed copy of the venomous apocalyptic novel, *The Turner Diaries.*"

Yet it would seem McVeigh is not the asexual, sociopathic loner that the press made him out to be. Had Kifner read the May 5th edition of *Newsweek,* he would have discovered that McVeigh had more than an old book for a companion. *Newsweek* reported that a Kansas private investigator had tracked down an old [platonic] girlfriend of McVeigh's—most likely Catina Lawson of Herrington, Kansas—attempting to convince her to sell her story to a news agency.[210]

Robert Jerlow, an Oklahoma City private investigator, was also tracking down a girlfriend of McVeigh's in Las Vegas.[211] And CNN indicated that authorities had discovered a letter in the glove compartment to an old girlfriend.*

Yet McVeigh's gypsy-like travels across the country in an old beat-up car were slightly more then unusual. He traveled widely with no visible means of support, other than trading and selling guns and military paraphernalia. Yet acquaintances and other witnesses recall he always had wads of cash on him. Upon his arrest, McVeigh was holding $2,000. Reportedly, he had thousands more stashed away. He also traveled without luggage, making his car and occasional cheap motels his only home.

"He lived in his car," said the gun dealer quoted in the *Times*. "Whatever he owned it was in that car."[212]

According to his sister Jennifer, his closest confidant, "Half the time we didn't know where he was. Half the time he wouldn't even tell us where he was living."[213]

Again, one has to ask why McVeigh would voluntarily give up a promising military career to go careening around the country hawking used military surplus in an old car.

McVeigh used the name "Tim Tuttle" while working gun shows, claiming an alias was necessary to protect him from people who didn't share his political views.[214] There is another possible reason McVeigh may have used an alias.

At one gun show in Phoenix, an undercover detective reported that McVeigh had been attempting to sell a flare gun which he claimed could be converted into

---

* The letter to the girlfriend apparently was indicative of plans to bomb other locations. Interesting that the suspect would leave such a curiously incriminating trail of evidence.

a rocket launcher. According to Bill Fitzgerald of the Maricopa County Attorney's office in Phoenix, McVeigh "took a shell apart and showed that the interior could be removed and another package put in that could shoot down an ATF helicopter." He was also handing out copies of the name and address of Lon Horiuchi, the FBI sniper who shot and killed Vicki Weaver, and selling caps with the letters "ATF" surrounded by bulletholes.[215]

"He had come to see himself as a soldier in his own strange war against the United States," wrote the *Times*. McVeigh's mother told an acquaintance after visiting with him in her home state of Florida that he was "totally changed," observing, "it was like he traded one Army for another one." [216]

While highly possible that McVeigh, like many people, genuinely disliked the ATF and FBI, it is also possible he used such high-profile anti-government tactics as a ruse for working undercover. Such behavior is a classic agent provocateur technique. The ATF routinely works undercover at gun shows, searching for people selling illegal firearms. Who better to lure and entrap unwary victims than a gun dealer claiming to be virulently anti-ATF? It is also possible that McVeigh was working undercover for another agency.

In an illuminating series of phone calls to Representative Charles Key, an anonymous source stated that McVeigh was present at several meetings with ATF and DEA agents in the days immediately preceding the bombing. The meetings took place in Oklahoma City at different locations. The ostensible purpose of the meetings were to provide McVeigh with further instructions, and to facilitate a payoff.

David Hall of KPOC-TV uncovered information that McVeigh met local ATF agent Alex McCauley in a McDonalds the night before the bombing. The ATF agent was seen handing McVeigh an envelope.

CNN would cast a pale over this [largely unknown] information by reporting in June of 1995 that McVeigh had been under surveillance by an undercover operative at an Arizona gun show two years prior to the bombing.

This fact was reinforced when the Anti-Defamation League of B'nai B'rith (ADL) reported that McVeigh ran an ad for a "rocket launcher" (actually a flare gun) in the far-right *Spotlight* newspaper on August 9, 1993. In fact, the ad didn't appear until the following week, August 16. McVeigh had originally paid to have the advertisement run on the 9th. Not being aware of the *Spotlight's* impending scheduling conflict, however, the ADL reported that the ad had run one week before it actually did. This subsumes that the ADL, long known for its spying and intelligence-gathering activities, had McVeigh under surveillance as well.[217]

Interestingly, McVeigh's young friend, Catina Lawson, recalled a strange man who occasionally showed up at summer parties the high-schoolers threw. The soldiers from nearby Ft. Riley would attend the gatherings looking to meet girls, and McVeigh and his friends Michael Brescia and Andy Strassmeir (who lived at the white separatist compound in Southeast Oklahoma known as Elohim City), would often attend.

Yet the man Catina described was neither a high-schooler nor a soldier. This strange character, who often wore a suit and a tie and was in his late 30s to mid-40s, was apparently not there to pick up girls. As Connie Smith, Catina's mother told me, "The man did not interact with anyone else ... he stayed off ... he never interacted with anybody else," only McVeigh.

Barbara Whittenberg, who owned the Sante Fe Trail Diner in Herrington, Kansas, also remembered the man. The restaurant owner recalled that he would come in with McVeigh and Terry Nichols, who lived nearby. She didn't know where he was from, and had never seen him before.

Was McVeigh an informant? Was he working for two different agencies? Numerous Kennedy researchers have uncovered evidence that Oswald was an FBI informant at the same time he was being sheep-dipped by the CIA for his role in the JFK assassination. According to Jim Garrison:

Oswald appears to have been extensively manipulated by the CIA for a long time prior to the assassination and may well have believed he was working for the government. Oswald was also a confidential informant, a job that provided additional control over him and may have given him a reason to believe he was actually penetrating a plot to assassinate the president.[218]

In a rather prophetic statement, Michael Fortier's mother was heard to remark that McVeigh led "a double life." But it is uncommon for a man like McVeigh to give up a promising military career to hawk used duffel bags from an old car. But then again, in the twilight netherworld of intelligence operations, things aren't always what they seem.

While in Michigan, McVeigh also began tuning in to the Voice of America and Radio Free America on his shortwave. He was drawn to personalities like Chuck Harder, Jack McLamb, and Mark Koernke, all conveying an anti-federalist, anti-New World Order message. "He sent me a lot of newsletters and stuff from those groups he was involved in," said Warnement, then stationed in Germany. "There were newsletters from Bo Gritz's group, some other odd newsletters, some from the Patriots; then he sent that videotape 'The Big Lie' about Waco."[219]

McVeigh also began attending militia meetings. According to Michigan Militia member Eric Maloney, McVeigh was present at a truck-stop near Detroit for a January 25, 1995 meeting of approximately 70 members of the Oakland County Six Brigade. Members had obtained photographs of T-72 tanks and other Russian vehicles en route via railway flatcars to Camp Grayling, an Air National Guard base in northern Michigan. Although the captured Iraqi tanks were for target practice, the militiamen interpreted the equipment as proof positive of a UN plan to disarm American citizens and declare martial law.

According to Maloney and militia member Joseph Ditzhazy, a plot was hatched to attack the base by Mark Koernke, a high-profile militia spokesman known to his radio listeners as "Mark from Michigan." According to Maloney, Koernke said, "We can either take them out now while we're still able to, or wait until the sons of bitches are rolling down the street." Three days later, about 20 members met at a farm near Leonard to discuss plans for the attack. According to Maloney, McVeigh was one of 13 who volunteered for the assault. "McVeigh was there," recalled Maloney on ABC's Prime Time Live. "My wife sat next to him. He was very attentive, very interested in being involved in that operation, volunteered his services."

The plan never came off. Ditzhazy and Maloney alerted State Police, who then contacted federal authorities. When the plot was made public, the Michigan Militia issued a press release stating that the plan was the brainchild of Koernke, working alongside a group of renegade members. Others who attended the meetings said that it was actually Maloney who pushed the plan, and had to be dissuaded from going through with it. Interestingly, Maloney was to provide weapons training for several of the attackers, and Ditzhazy, who made audiotapes of the meetings, is a former military intelligence officer. When the FBI was contacted about Ditzhazy's claim that the plot was hatched by McVeigh and others, the FBI refused comment.[220]

Koernke is a former Army intelligence officer. A veteran of the 70th Army Reserve Division in Livonia, Michigan, Koernke refers to himself as an "intelligence analyst" and "counterintelligence coordinator" with a "top-secret clearance." He also purports to have trained two "special-warfare" brigades that trained Army personnel in "foreign warfare and tactics." While his claims may be exaggerated, Koernke did attend the Army's intelligence school at Fort Huachuca, Arizona. He returned to Michigan an E-5 specialist with a G-2 (security) section of a peacetime Reserve unit.[221]

Koernke quickly rose to become one of the most sought-after speakers on the Patriot circuit, leading off seminars in over 40 states. His video, *America in Peril*, sounds apocalyptic warnings of the coming New World Order, including plans by the Council of Foreign Relations, the Trilateral Commission, and the Bilderbergers to dominate and enslave America—with of course, a little help from Russian troops, Nepalese Gurkhas, and L.A. street gangs. It seems that Koernke was employing a time-tested technique of intelligence PSYOP disinformation. While purporting to rail against what may be genuine plans of a New World Order cabal, Koernke slips in just enough ridiculous disinformation to discredit his thesis, and by association, anyone who supports it.

Though Koernke boasted freely that he was once employed as a "provocateur," he didn't say for whom. In his tape, Koernke holds an AK-47 and a cord of rope, stating: "Now, I did some basic math the other day, not New World Order math, and I found that using the old-style math you can get about four politicians for about 120 feet of rope. And, by the way, DuPont made this. It is very fitting that one of the New World Order crowd should provide us with the resources to liberate our nation."

Koernke's rant smacks of the classic art of propaganda—that of the agent provocateur. Many in the Militia movement have accused him of just that.

On September 8, 1994, Fowerville, Michigan police stopped a car that contained three men in camouflage and black face paint, armed with three 9mm semiautomatics, a .357 Magnum, an assortment of assault rifles, and 7,000 rounds of ammunition. The men claimed to be Koernke's bodyguards.

Ken Kirkland, an official of the St. Lucia County, Florida Militia said that McVeigh was acting as Koernke's bodyguard at a March, 1994 meeting. Kirkland recalled a bodyguard in Army camouflage clothes resembling McVeigh who introduced himself as "Tim" and was "really upset about Waco." [222]

Koernke and McVeigh both deny this. As McVeigh told *Newsweek* "I was never to one of their meetings, either." [223]

Was Koernke's "bodyguard" actually Tim McVeigh? In the September, 1995 issue of *Soldier of Fortune,* an ATF agent—the spitting image of Tim McVeigh—is seen accompanying ATF Agent Robert Rodriguez to the trial of the Branch Davidians. Was this in fact the "McVeigh" who accompanied Koernke?

Given both mens' mysterious backgrounds, their curious intersections in Florida and Michigan, and the Camp Grayling and Fowerville incidents, it is highly likely that we are looking at two agent provocateurs. Evidence of McVeigh's own potential employment as an agent provocateur would surface later. In a statement he made to *Newsweek* in response to a question about Reno and Clinton asking for the death penalty, McVeigh said: "I thought it was awfully hypocritical, especially because in some ways the government was responsible for doing it. I thought she was playing both sides of the fence." One must wonder just how McVeigh knows that "in some ways" the government was "responsible for doing it."

McVeigh's own insurrectionist tendencies began coming to fruition towards the end of 1993, according to authorities, when McVeigh informed his sister that he was part of an anti-government group that was robbing banks. This startling revelation came in the form of three $100 bills he sent Jennifer in a letter dated December 24, 1993. The money was part of the proceeds from a bank heist. As Jennifer told the FBI on May 2, 1995:

"He had been involved in a bank robbery but did not provide any further details concerning the robbery. He advised me that he had not actually participated in the robbery itself, but was somehow involved in the planning or setting up of this robbery. Although he did not identify the participants by name, he stated that 'they' had committed the robbery. His purpose for relating this information to me was to request that I exchange some of my own money for what I recall to be approximately three (3) $100.00 bills.

"He explained that this money was from the bank robbery and he wished to circulate this money through me. To the best of my recollection, I then gave my brother what I recall to be approximately $300.00 of my personal cash, in exchange for 3 $100.00 bills, which I deposited within the next several days in an account at the Unit No. 1 Federal credit Union, Lockport, New York."

Jennifer recalled Tim stating, "Persons who rob banks may not be criminals at all. He implied Jews are running the country and a large degree of control is exercised by the Free Masons. Banks are the real thieves and the income tax is illegal." *

Was Timothy McVeigh in fact a bankrobber? If so, he may have been inspired by the *Turner Diaries*. The protagonists in that novel finance their overthrow of the "Zionist Occupational Government" by robbing banks and armored cars. As previously discussed, the book became a real life inspiration for Robert Mathews' Order, also known as "The Silent Brotherhood," which engaged in heists of banks and armored cars throughout the Midwest during the 1980s. The Order was part of the white Aryan supremacist community that sought to establish an all-white homeland in the Northwest.

In December of 1984, Mathews was killed in a flammable war with the FBI and police, and the Order disintegrated. Yet the white supremacist movement lived on, in such guises as the Aryan Nations, White Aryan Resistance (WAR), and a new, as yet unheard of group—the Aryan Republican Army, whose members are believed to be direct descendants of the Order.

It was to this last group that Timothy McVeigh would be drawn, at a rural white separatist religious community in southeast Oklahoma called Elohim City. It was there that McVeigh would meet such self-styled revolutionaries as Peter "Commander Pedro" Langan, who, along with Scott Stedeford, Kevin McCarthy, and the late Richard Guthrie, would go on to rob over 22 banks across the Midwest, collecting a total of $250,000.

In a recruitment video obtained by the *McCurtain Gazette*, Langan appears in a disguise, explaining the goals of the ARA—the overthrow of the Federal Government, and the subsequent execution of all Jews and the deportation of all non-whites from the U.S.

In the tape, made only a few months before the Oklahoma City bombing,

---

* Interestingly, Jennifer was found burning papers on an outdoor grill when the FBI showed up on April 23.

Langan says, "Federal buildings may have to be bombed and civilian loss of life is regrettable but expected." [224]

According to ATF informant Carol Howe, interviewed by *Gazette* reporter J.D. Cash, both McVeigh and Fortier visited Elohim City, as did Langan, Guthrie, Stedeford and McCarthy. A secret recording made by the informant apparently reveals discussions between Andreas Strassmeir, Elohim City's chief of security (also suspected of being an informant), and various ARA members, discussing plans to blow up federal buildings. While it is not known if McVeigh was intimately involved with the ARA bank robbers, he was seen with Strassmeir and ARA associate Michael Brescia at parties in Kansas, and at a bar in Tulsa shortly before the bombing. McVeigh had also called Elohim City looking for Strassmeir the day after he reserved the Ryder truck allegedly used in the bombing.

In Fall, 1994, McVeigh and Terry Nichols allegedly began hoarding ammonium-nitrate and diesel fuel. By mid-October, the pair had, according to official accounts, managed to stockpile approximately 4,000 pounds of fertilizer, which they stashed in storage lockers from Kansas to Arizona.*

Like Mohammed Salemeh, a World Trade Center bombing suspect arrested when he attempted to retrieve his truck rental deposit, McVeigh was linked to the bombing by the first in a chain of damning evidence—his thumbprint on a fertilizer receipt found in Terry Nichols' home, inquires about bomb-making materials made on his calling-card, and the paperwork used to rent the Ryder truck itself.

Like Salemeh's rental receipt which had traces of ANFO on it, McVeigh's clothes would allegedly contain traces of a detonator cord known as PDTN.** Like the World Trade Center bombers who stockpiled bomb-making equipment in rented storage lockers in New Jersey, McVeigh and Nichols would store their ammonium-nitrate in rented lockers in Kansas and Arizona. And like the World Trade Center bombers who called commercial chemical companies requesting bomb-making materials, McVeigh would implicate himself by using a traceable phone card to make his purchases.

The most damning evidence linking McVeigh to the crime would be the witness sightings placing him at the Murrah Building just before the bombing, following the Ryder truck, then speeding away in his yellow Mercury several minutes before the blast.

Yet the most curious evidence implicating McVeigh in the bombing came from witnesses who say he cased the building on December 16, when he and Michael Fortier drove through Oklahoma City en route to Kansas, then again approximately one and a half weeks before the bombing.

---

* Interestingly, authorities wouldn't find any traces of ammonium-nitrate in these lockers.

** FBI chief chemist Frederick Whitehurst, who tested McVeigh's clothes, said no explosive residue was found.

Danielle Wise Hunt, who operated the Stars and Stripes Child Development Center in the Murrah Building, told the FBI that on December 16, a clean-cut man wearing camouflage fatigues approached her, seeking to place his two children in the day care center. Hunt told agents that the man didn't ask typical parent-type questions, but instead wanted to know about the day-care center's security. Hunt thought he might be a potential kidnapper. Later, after seeing his face on TV, she recognized the man as Timothy McVeigh.[225]

If the man was indeed Timothy McVeigh, it is curious that he later claimed ignorance of the day-care center in the building. If McVeigh was so upset about the deaths of innocent children at Waco, why would he knowingly bomb a building containing innocent children as an act of revenge?

Yet this "act of revenge" is precisely what the government claims motived him. Such an act could only be the result of a deranged man. Yet McVeigh is anything but deranged. In his July 3rd *Newsweek* interview, he said, "For two days, in the cell, we could hear news reports; and of course everyone, including myself, was horrified at the deaths of the children. And you know, that was the No. 1 focal point of the media at the time, too, obviously—the deaths of the children. It's a very tragic thing."

Perhaps "deranged" isn't the proper word; perhaps "controlled" would be more appropriate. After his arrest, McVeigh was shown photographs of the dead children. He claimed to have no emotional reaction. Again, this could very well be indicative of a psychologically-controlled individual.

There is another strong possibility. The man whom witnesses say is Timothy McVeigh may not have been Timothy McVeigh at all.

"LEE HARVEY" MCVEIGH

"It may be the case of an innocent person turned into a scapegoat in a well prepared plan, by people who know how to prepare such plans."
—Fidel Castro on Lee Harvey Oswald

As previously discussed, McVeigh, along with his friends Andreas Strassmeir, Mike Fortier, and Michael Brescia attended parties in Herrington, Kansas in the Summer of '92. Catina Lawson was actually good friends with McVeigh, and her roommate, Lindsey Johnson, dated Michael Brescia. Lawson's accounts are well documented.[226]

Yet calling card records obtained by the *Rocky Mountain News* indicate that each call charged to the card during 1992 originated within western New York, where McVeigh was working as a security guard for Burns International Security. There appears to be little time he could have gone to Kansas to party with teenagers.

Dr. Paul Heath, the VA psychologist who worked in the Murrah Building and survived the blast, spoke to an individual named "McVeigh" late one Friday afternoon, a week and a half before the bombing. In an interview with the author, he described in vivid detail his encounter with "McVeigh" and two other men, one of whom appears to be one of the elusive John Doe 2s.

"I've narrowed this to probably a Friday [April 7], at around three o'clock," recalls Heath. "A bell rang in the outer office of room 522. No one answered, so I went out to the waiting room … A man came in with two others to apply for a job. One other was American-Indian looking, the other was Caucasian. A male individual was standing there, and I introduced myself as Dr. Heath, 'How can I help you?' and this individual said, 'My name is something' and I don't remember what his first name was, but he told me his last name was McVeigh.

"So I said, 'Can I help you?' and he said, 'Well, we're here looking for work.' and I said 'what kind of work are we looking for?' He said 'we are looking for construction work.' And I said, 'well Mr. Birmbaum, the gentleman who is the job counselor for the state jobs office, is not here.' And this individual—I asked him if I could go back and get the job openings from the job counselor's desk—and he said, 'No, that won't be necessary.' So I said, 'Well, I'm very familiar with the area, and I could give you some job leads,' and I began to tell him about job leads, and began to give him some names and some different projects, and I said, 'Would you like me to get you the phone book; I could get you the state jobs offices.' He said, 'No, that won't be necessary.'

"And about somewhere along in this conversation, the man who was sitting on the east wall, directly behind the man who named himself as McVeigh, came up behind the man, and said 'Can I use your phone?' I would describe him as vanilla, 5' 7" or 5' 9", mid-30s. [Then] the third party who was in the office, looked directly at me, made eye contact with me, and … I got the impression that this individual's nationality was Native American, or half-Native American or half-Mexican American or a foreign national. He was handsome—at one time my mind said maybe he was from South America.

"I continued to talk to Mr. McVeigh and I said, 'Mr. McVeigh, did you take anything in high school that would be beneficial for me to know about so I could refer you to a different type of job?' And he said, 'Well, probably not.' And I said, 'Well, where did you go to high school?' And he either said up north or New York. And then I said, 'Where are you living?' And he said, 'Well, I've been living in Kansas.' So then I said, 'Do you happen to be a member of the McVay family from Cussing, Oklahoma?' He said, 'Well Dr. Heath, how do they spell their name?' 'Well I assume, M-c-V-a-y.' And he took his finger, and he kind of put it in my face and said, 'Well Dr. Heath,' in kind of a boisterous way, 'Dr. Heath, you remember this. My name is McVeigh, but you don't spell it M-c-V-a-y.'"[227]

What Dr. Heath was describing appears to have been Timothy McVeigh and his co-conspirators casing the Murrah Building. As the press reported, the men went floor-to-floor, asking job-related questions and picking up applications. Yet if McVeigh had already cased the building on December 16, as reported by Danielle Hunt, why would he need to case it again?

Moreover, if McVeigh wanted to case the building, why would he do it in such a conspicuous manner? Why would he go from floor-to-floor asking about job openings, then pretend not to be interested in following them up? And if McVeigh was planning on committing such a horrific crime, why would he make it a point to tell people his name, saying to Dr. Heath, "You remember this ... *My name is McVeigh.*"

Former federal grand juror Hoppy Heidelberg concurs. "Why would McVeigh walk around the building before the blast telling people his name?" [228]

If McVeigh was keen on informing people of his identity before committing a heinous crime, he was on a roll. On Saturday, April 8, McVeigh and friends Andreas Strassmeir and Michael Brescia—both living at Elohim City at the time—were seen at Lady Godiva's topless bar in Tulsa, Oklahoma. According to a security camera videotape obtained by J.D. Cash of the *McCurtain Gazette*, and Trish Wood of CBC, McVeigh's boasts were the topic of discussion among the dancers that night. In the tape, one of the girls named Tara is overheard relating the conversation to another girl in the dressing room:

> "He goes, 'I'm a very smart man.' I said, you are? And he goes, 'Yes, you're going to find an (inaudible) and they're going to hurt you real bad.' I was, like, 'Oh really?' And he goes, 'Yes, and you're going to remember me on April 19, 1995. You're going to remember me for the rest of your life.'
>
> Laughing, she replies, "Oh, really?"
>
> "Yes you will," McVeigh says. [229]

The sighting of McVeigh in Tulsa on April 8th, along with an older, pale yellow Ryder truck that appeared to be privately owned, directly contradicts the testimony of the maid at the Imperial Motel who says McVeigh was there each day.

Phone records indicate McVeigh made a steady series of calls up until April 7, suddenly resuming them again on the 11th. Could McVeigh have flown to Oklahoma to pick up the old Ryder truck, then have flown back to Kingman several days later? As J.D. Cash notes in the September 25, 1996 *McCurtain Gazette:*

> It is not merely idle speculation that McVeigh flew to eastern Oklahoma or western Arkansas to pick up the second truck. Records subpoenaed by the government indicate McVeigh may have made such a trip to Fort Smith, Ark., between March 31 and April 14, 1995. Curiously, an employee of the airport taxi service in Fort Smith could not elaborate on why the taxi firm's records for that period were seized

by federal agents working on what the government calls the "OKBOMB" case.

If McVeigh actually did fly from Arizona to Arkansas, then drive the truck to Kansas, then fly back to Arizona again, he apparently was a very busy man. Witness accounts and phone records put him in Oklahoma City on the 7th, in Tulsa on the 8th, in Kansas from the 10th to the 14th (although he's supposed to be in Kingman on the 11th and 12th), then back in Oklahoma City on the 14th, 15th and 16th (when he's supposedly in Kansas) then in Kansas on the 17th and 18th (when he's also seen in Oklahoma City), and finally in Oklahoma City on the 19th, the day of the bombing.

While McVeigh was supposedly seen at Terry Nichols' house in Herrington, Kansas on the 13th, witness David Snider saw his car in Oklahoma City. A Bricktown warehouse worker, Snider remembers seeing McVeigh's distinctive yellow Mercury whiz past around 2:30 P.M., not far from downtown. Snider is certain it was the same battered yellow Mercury driven by McVeigh. "I was standing there with my friend, who does auto bodywork," said Snider, "when the car went past. I turned to him and said, 'My Mom used to have a car just like that ... It looks like homeboy needs a primer job.'" Snider said the car had an Oklahoma tag, as witness Gary Lewis later reported, not an Arizona tag as the FBI claims.

On Thursday, April 13, a federal employee in the Murrah Building saw two men, one of whom she later identified as McVeigh. She was riding the elevator when it stopped at the second floor. When the doors opened, there were two men in janitorial smocks waiting to get on. She didn't recognize the men as any of the regular janitors, and thought it odd that they turned away when she looked in their direction.

On Monday, April 17, janitors Katherine Woodly and Martin Johnson, who were working the 5-9 P.M. shift, saw McVeigh and his companion again. Martin said McVeigh spoke to him about a job, and the man who resembled John Doe 2 nodded to Woodly.[230]

That same day, or possibly the following day, Debbie Nakanashi, an employee at the Post Office across from the Murrah Building, saw the pair when they stopped by and asked where they might find federal job applications. It was Nakanashi who provided the description for the well-known profile sketch of John Doe 2 in the baseball cap.

Craig Freeman, a retired Air Force Master Sergeant who works in the same office as Dr. Heath, was one of the people who saw McVeigh in Oklahoma when he was supposedly in Kansas. Freeman recalls sharing the elevator with a man who resembled McVeigh on Friday, April 14. "The guy was tall ... What struck me is his hair was cut real low. I thought he was a skinhead." Freeman, who is black, said 'Hey man, how's it going?' "And he looked at me like he was just disgusted with me being there. Most people in the building speak to each other, you know, so I spoke to this guy, and he looked at me like ... pure hate."

About a week and a half before the bombing, a HUD employee named Joan was riding the elevator with a man she described as Timothy McVeigh. What struck her was the man's strict military demeanor. He stared straight ahead making no eye-contact or conversation. "He won't last long in this building," Joan thought to herself.[231]

The Friday before the bombing, when Craig Freeman walked out of the building to mail his taxes, he saw an individual he believes to have been Terry Nichols, "because he looked just like the picture of him," said Freeman. "He was standing there, he had a blue plaid shirt on. He was standing in the front of the building—he was just standing there, looking kind of confused. You know, how somebody looks when they're nervous."

Was the man in the elevator Freeman was describing actually Timothy McVeigh? According to phone records obtained from the Dreamland Motel, McVeigh made several phone calls from his room on the morning of Friday, April 14. Is it still possible that McVeigh drove down to Oklahoma City in the afternoon?

If he did, he would had to have been back in Kansas by early next morning. Barbara Whittenberg, owner of the Santa Fe Trail Diner in Herrington, remembers serving breakfast to Nichols, McVeigh, and John Doe 2 around 6 A.M. on Saturday.

"I asked them why they had a Ryder truck outside," said Whittenberg. "I wasn't being nosy, I just wondered if Terry Nichols was moving. My sister was moving here, and she needed to find a place. Well, the guy who they haven't arrested yet—John Doe #2—he blurted out that they were going to Oklahoma. When that happened, it was like someone threw ice water on the conversation. McVeigh and Nichols just stared at the guy."[232]

A dancer in Junction City, Kansas had the same experience as Whittenberg, when four of the suspects stopped by the Hollywood Supper Club around 10:30 that evening. The dancer, who we'll call Sherrie, definitely recognized two of the men as McVeigh and Nichols.

"The only reason I really remember it," said Sherrie, "is just because I had a conversation with one of them about Oklahoma, and my husband's family is from Oklahoma. He said they were planing a trip down there, and he said—I think it was for hunting or something ... then one of them kind of gave him a look, and they changed the subject."

Sherrie also said one of the men, who was quiet and sat in the corner, appeared Middle-Eastern. The other was Hispanic or part Hispanic, and was friendly. When he mentioned Oklahoma, Nichols shot him a hard look.[233]

Additionally, while the records at Elliott's Body Shop indicate that "Bob Kling" rented his truck on April 17, Barbara Whittenberg saw the truck outside her restaurant on the 15th. Later that day she saw it at Geary State Fishing Lake, along with three people and a light-colored car, possibly a Thunderbird, with Arizona tags.*

Backing up Whittenberg is Lee McGowan, owner of the Dreamland Motel in Junction City, where McVeigh stayed from April 14 to April 17. McGowan told the FBI that McVeigh was in possession of his truck the day *before* "Kling" allegedly rented his. She remembered the day clearly because it was Easter Sunday.

McGowan's son, Eric, as well as motel resident David King and his mother, also stated that they saw McVeigh driving an older faded yellow Ryder truck at the motel around 4 P.M. on April 16.[234]

Yet McGowan's testimony contradicts that of Phyliss Kingsley and Linda Kuhlman, who worked at the Hi-Way Grill in Newcastle, just south of Oklahoma City. The two women saw McVeigh and three companions around 6 P.M. April 16, when they stopped in the restaurant and ordered hamburgers and fries to go. The two women distinctly recall the Ryder truck pulling into the restaurant at SW 104th and Portland, accompanied by a white Chevy long-bed pick-up, and an older, darker, possibly blue pick-up, which may have belonged to Terry Nichols. Accompanying McVeigh was a short, stocky, handsome man, of either Mexican or American Indian descent. The man closely resembled the FBI sketch of John Doe 2, they said.[235]

According to the FBI, this was the same day that McVeigh called Nichols from a pay phone at Tim's Amoco in Herrington, Kansas at 3:08 P.M., and asked him to drive him to Oklahoma City. It would have been impossible for McVeigh and Nichols to drive from Junction City to Oklahoma City in less than four hours.

Reports soon surfaced that "McVeigh" had stayed at a motel south of downtown Oklahoma City on the night of the 18th. Witnesses recall seeing a yellow Ryder truck, and two companions. They recall that "McVeigh" gave them a "go to hell look" as he pulled away.

Later that morning, at 8:35 A.M., Tulsa banker Kyle Hunt was driving to an appointment when he came upon the Ryder truck at Main and Broadway, trailed by a yellow Mercury. "For some reason I thought they were out of state, moving and lost in downtown Oklahoma City," said Hunt. "I felt sorry for them and then when I pulled up beside them, I got that cold icy stare from a guy that had a real short GI haircut."[236]

Hunt described the driver of the Mercury as Timothy McVeigh. "He gave me

---

* She saw the truck at 6 a.m. at the diner, then it left before 7 a.m. She then saw it at Geary Lake in the afternoon on her way to Junction City, then saw it there on return trip around 3-4 p.m. The mainstream-press originally said Whittenberg saw the truck on Tuesday, parroting the FBI's line that McVeigh had rented the truck on the 17th.

that icy, go-to-hell look," said Hunt. "It kind of unnerved me." While Hunt didn't see the occupants of the truck, he did recall two passengers in the Mercury. The rear occupant, said Hunt, had long hair, similar to the suspect Phyllis Kingsley and Linda Kuhlman saw on Sunday at the Hi-Way Grill South of the city.

Around the same time as Hunt saw this convoy, David Snider, a warehouse worker in Bricktown, a few blocks southeast of downtown, saw a heavily loaded Ryder truck with two men inside, slowly making its way towards him. Snider had been expecting a delivery that morning, and explained that people sometimes get lost because the loading dock is on a different street than the warehouse. The time was 8:35 A.M. Thinking the truck was his delivery, Snider waved them down. Snider, who by now was gesticulating wildly, became frustrated as the two men, staring at him, continued on their way.

While he never received his delivery, Snider did get a good look at the two men and the truck, which appeared to be an older model with a cab overhang, not the newer version the FBI claimed was destroyed in the bombing.

Snider described the driver as barrel-chested and dark-skinned with long, straight black hair, parted in the middle, wearing a thin small mustache. The man, who was also wearing tear-drop style sunglasses and a dark shirt, was of American Indian or Hispanic decent. "I lived in New Mexico for years," said Snider; "I know the look." The passenger, wearing a white T-shirt, Snider said, was Timothy McVeigh.

"He looked at me like 'who the hell are you?'—real attitude," recalls Snider, and began yelling profanities at the loading-dock worker. Snider, who was not in a great mood that morning to begin with, yelled back, "Fuck you, you skinhead motherfucker!"

Snider and Hunt weren't the only individuals who saw McVeigh and the Ryder truck that morning. At 8:40 A.M., Mike Moroz and Brian Marshall were busy at work at Johnny's Tire Store on 10th and Hudson, when a yellow Ryder truck pulled in looking for directions to the Murrah Building. The driver, who Moroz later identified as Timothy McVeigh, was wearing a white T-shirt and a black ball cap on backwards. Moroz caught a glimpse of the passenger—a stocky man with dark curly hair, a tattoo on his upper left arm, and a ball cap worn similar to McVeigh's. The passenger, said Moroz, stared straight ahead, never turning to look in his direction.*

Moroz then proceeded to give directions to McVeigh, whom he described as polite, friendly, and relaxed—quite interesting considering that McVeigh is supposedly minutes away from murdering 169 people. After thanking Moroz,

---

* It is interesting that McVeigh would choose to hang around the scene of the crime, along with his easily identifiable yellow Mercury Marquis, minutes after it occurred. Johnston described the John Doe 2 as shorter and darker than McVeigh.

McVeigh got back in the truck, sat there for a few minutes, then took off in the direction of the Federal Building.

At approximately the same time as McVeigh was seen driving the Mercury by Kyle Hunt, and seen as a passenger in the Ryder truck by David Snider, and seen driving the Ryder truck by Mike Moroz, he was then seen driving the Mercury by attorney James Linehan.

As previously discussed, Linehan, a Midwest city attorney, was stopped at a red light at the northwest corner of 4th and Robinson, one block from the Murrah Building. Late for an appointment, Linehan looked at his watch. It read 8:38 A.M. When he looked back up, he noticed a pale yellow Mercury stopped beside him. While he could not positively I.D. the driver, he described him as having sharp, pointed features, and smooth pale skin.

A second later, the Mercury driver gunned his engine, ran the red light, and disappeared into the underground parking garage of the Murrah Building.

Is it possible these witnesses are describing two different people? In Snider's account, the driver is American Indian or Hispanic with long, straight black hair, wearing sunglasses. The passenger is McVeigh. Neither one is wearing a ball cap. The time is 8:35 A.M. In Moroz's account, the driver is McVeigh, while the passenger is a stocky man with short curly hair. Both men are wearing ball caps on backwards. The time is 8:40 A.M.

Snider and Moroz both saw a Ryder truck containing Timothy McVeigh, yet with completely different companions. While Snider was yelling at McVeigh in the Ryder truck in Bricktown, Hunt was watching the truck being trailed by McVeigh in the Mercury several blocks away. A few minutes later, Linehan watched as the Mercury drove into the Murrah Building garage.

Each witness saw these convoys at approximately the same time. It's possible that the heavily loaded truck seen by Snider could have made it from 25 East California in Bricktown to 10th and Hudson in five minutes. But in order to do so, they would have had to drop off one man, pick up another, exchange places in the truck, and put on ball caps. Then they would have to drive a distance of approximately 25 blocks—during morning rush hour traffic. Possible, but not too likely.

Is it possible one of these witnesses has his story wrong? Well, if he does, he has it quite wrong. How could apparently credible witnesses mistake a short-curly-haired man with a black ball cap for a long straight-haired man with teardrop sunglasses? One who is clearly the passenger, the other who is clearly the driver? In numerous interviews with the author and other journalists, Snider went into great detail about his encounter, and never wavered.

Mike Moroz struck me as a sincere, sober, young man in a taped interview. Both Linehan and Hunt are solid, professional people. It is not likely that these witnesses are relaying inaccurate information.

"Their stories really seem to check out," says video producer Chuck Allen, who interviewed many witnesses. "They go into great depth and detail about all this. If you ever meet these guys, you'll know their stories are very strong—very believable." [237]

Researchers have also questioned why McVeigh, who had supposedly been to the Murrah Building at least three times—once on December 16, again a week and a half before the bombing, then again on April 14—would need to ask directions to it when he was only six blocks away. But according to Moroz, who has helped more than a few lost travelers, the number of one-way streets in the downtown area often confuses people. "A lot of people get lost down here, even people who live here, he said." [238]

Finally, HUD employee Germaine Johnston was walking through an alley approximately two blocks from the Murrah Building about 15 minutes after the blast when she ran into McVeigh and another man. "They were just standing there watching," said Johnston.

McVeigh then asked the dazed passerby, "Was anyone killed?" When Johnston answered that numerous people had been killed, including many children, McVeigh's expression suddenly turned sad. He and his companion then got up and left. [239]

Mike Moroz was eventually called in to identify McVeigh in a photo line-up. Yet he was never called to testify before the Federal Grand Jury. Snider was initially interviewed by two FBI agents, including Weldon Kennedy and Rob Ricks, but was never brought in to a line-up or called to testify before the Federal Grand Jury.

Considering he had close and sustained contact with "McVeigh" and several of his associates, Dr. Heath should have been a key prosecution witness. Yet the FBI never called Dr. Heath in to identify McVeigh in a line-up. Nor was Dr. Heath ever called before the Federal Grand Jury. Nor was Freeman ever called in to see a line-up, or before the Grand Jury. Linehan, Hunt, Johnston, and numerous other witnesses were likewise never called.

On May 10, the *Los Angeles Times* reported, "Investigators said authorities theorize that John Doe 2 could be two people, and that McVeigh and his alleged conspirators could have used different men to accompany him in order to serve as 'decoys' and confuse investigators trying to trace his movements." [240]

The *Los Angeles Times* report, which would tend to account for the two different trucks, only gives half the story. What they aren't saying is that not only were there at least two John Doe 2s—there apparently were two "Timothy McVeighs." One was probably a double.

THE USE OF DOUBLES

The use of doubles in espionage work is not new. In fact, the use of impostors, look-alikes and doubles was well-documented in the JFK and Martin Luther King assassinations.

Like the "Lee Harvey Oswald" who was seen filing out numerous job applications in New Orleans, "McVeigh" was seen going floor-to-floor in the Federal Building in Oklahoma. Except that the "Oswald," who filled out job applications listed his height as 5′ 9″, while the real Oswald's height was 5′ 11″.

According to employees at Elliott's Body Shop in Junction City, the "McVeigh" (alias "Kling") who rented the truck on April 17 was of medium build, 5′ 10″ to 5′ 11″ and weighed 180-185 pounds. Elliott's employee Tom Kessinger stated on his FBI FD-383 report that the man had a "rough" complexion with "acne."[241]

The only problem is, Timothy McVeigh is 6′ 2″, weighs 160 pounds, and has a totally clear complexion. Another shop employee, Vicki Beemer, said the man had a deformed chin, unlike the real McVeigh.[242]

Nevertheless, federal prosecutors would claim that a "little curlicue" on the "K" in "Kling's" signature was indicative of McVeigh's handwriting. Yet if McVeigh was the same person who rented the truck at Elliott's on the 17th, why didn't he also use an alias while signing the motel register? While the "McVeigh" who rented the truck listed his name as "Bob Kling," 428 Malt Drive, Redfield, SD, the "McVeigh" who checked into the Dreamland, right down the street, signed his name as "Tim McVeigh," and listed his address as 3616 North Van Dyke Road, Decker, Michigan, the home of James Nichols.[243]

If McVeigh was planning on committing such a heinous crime, certainly he would not leave such a blatantly incriminating trail of evidence. This makes about as much sense as McVeigh going from floor to floor in the Murrah Building filling out job applications and announcing his name. Or telling a dancer in Tulsa, "You're going to remember me on April 19th."

These preposterous scenes were practically identical to those of all-time patsy, Lee Harvey Oswald. In early November, 1963, a "Lee Harvey Oswald" applied for a job as a parking lot attendant at the Southland Hotel. During his interview with the manager, he asked if there was a good view of downtown Dallas from the hotel.[244]

On January 20, 1961, two men, one representing himself as "Lee Harvey Oswald," walked into the Bolton Ford dealership in New Orleans and requested a bid for 10 pick-up trucks, ostensibly for the Friends of Democratic Cuba Committee. Lee Harvey Oswald was in Russia at the time.[245]

Then in September of 1963, a man purporting to be "Lee Harvey Oswald" showed up at the Mexican Consulate in New Orleans. According to Mrs. Fenella

Farrington, "Oswald" said, "What do you have to do to take firearms or a gun into Mexico?"

A "Lee Harvey Oswald" subsequently phoned, then showed up at the Soviet embassy in Mexico City, speaking with a trade consultant who was allegedly a member of the KGB's "liquid affairs" bureau (hit squad). The CIA later turned over to the Warren Commission a surveillance snapshot of a man they claimed was Oswald at the Soviet embassy. The man looked nothing like Oswald.

On April 17, 1995, a "Bob Kling" showed up at Elliott's Body Shop in Junction City, Kansas and rented a Ryder truck. Yet according to surveillance footage taken from a nearby McDonalds, McVeigh was sitting in the restaurant eating a hamburger at the time. He was wearing completely different clothes than those ascribed to "Kling."

Yet the FBI contends that McVeigh left the restaurant 20 minutes before the truck was rented, walked the 1.3 miles to Elliott's—a 15-minute walk—in a light rain, then showed up at Elliott's nice and dry, wearing completely different clothes.

In November of 1963, a "Lee Oswald" walked into the downtown Lincoln Mercury dealership in Dallas announcing his intention to buy a Mercury Comet. According to the salesman, Albert Bogard, "Mr. Oswald" took him on a wild test drive, speeding along at 60 to 70 miles an hour. After he was told the amount of the down payment, another salesman, Eugene Wilson heard "Oswald" say, "Maybe I'm going to have to go back to Russia to buy a car."

During the Warren Commission hearings, salesman Frank Pizzo described the customer as 5' 8" tall. When the Warren Commission showed Pizzo a photo of Oswald taken after his arrest, he said, "I have to say that he is not the one." [246]

After the bombing in Oklahoma City, ATF informant Carol Howe told the FBI that she recognized the two men on the FBI's original wanted posters as Peter Ward and Michael Brescia—two Elohim City residents. She said that neither man was Tim McVeigh. [247]

In early November of 1963, Mrs. Lovell Penn of Dallas found three men firing a rifle on her property. After they left, she found a spent cartridge bearing the name "Mannlicher-Carcanno," the rife that the Warren Commission claimed Oswald used to perform his historic feat of marksmanship in Dealy Plaza.

As District Attorney Jim Garrison later noted, "These scenes were about as subtle as roaches trying to sneak across a white rug."

No less subtle were the scenes and events leading up to the Oklahoma City bombing. It is highly possible that the man Dr. Heath saw in the Murrah Building a week and a half before the bombing was not Timothy McVeigh at all, but a double. The scenario of McVeigh—the alleged "lone nut" bomber—going from floor to floor in the target building announcing his name while leaving a paper trail is beyond credulity.

Like Oswald, who repeatedly telephoned, then appeared at the Soviet embassy in Mexico, McVeigh would telephone Elohim City—a white separatist compound—just before the bombing, asking to speak to Andy Strassmeir.

Like Oswald, who left behind a diary of his "left-leaning" writings, McVeigh purportedly left intentions of his plans to bomb other targets in the glove compartment of his car—a car which could be easily recognized and traced to him.

Like Oswald who, after purportedly killing the president of the United States, walked into a movie house without paying, purposely attracting the attention of the police, McVeigh would speed down the highway at 80 miles an hour without a license plate, purposely attracting the attention of the Highway Patrol. He would then meekly hand himself over for arrest, not even attempting to draw his Glock 9mm pistol on the approaching cop, whom he could have easily shot and killed.

Like the Mannlicher-Carcanno rifle which Oswald purportedly bought from a mail-order supply house, and the Mannlicher-Carcanno cartridge found by Mrs. Penn, McVeigh would leave a business card from Paulsen's Military Surplus with a notation to pick up more TNT in the police cruiser after his arrest.[248]

As Jim Garrison noted, "Some of these scenes were so preposterous only the most gullible could swallow them."

Like Oswald, who was led out of the Dallas Police Department and immediately shot by Jack Ruby, McVeigh would be led out of the Noble County Courthouse in a bright orange jumpsuit, without a bulletproof vest, paraded before an angry crowd on the verge of violence.

Finally, like James Earl Ray, who was accused of killing Martin Luther King, Jr., we are left pondering the significance of two similar vehicles, both apparently tied to the crime. Ray had owned a white Ford Mustang, which was seen speeding away after the assassination. Yet another white Mustang was seen parked in front of Jim's Grill in Memphis, near where Ray had his car parked. The two cars were almost identical, except for two things: While Ray was wearing a suit on April 4, 1968, the driver of the other Mustang was wearing a dark blue windbreaker; while Ray's car had Alabama plates, the other car had Arkansas plates.[249]

One is reminded of the contradictory testimony of David Snider and Mike Moroz, who saw two Ryder trucks on the morning of April 19, but with different occupants.

Another interesting parallel is that while McVeigh's Mercury reportedly had Arizona tags, a white Oklahoma tag was seen by Gary Lewis dangling from one bolt as the car sped away from the scene.

In spite of the numerous discrepancies, it seemed that by a convenient string of associations, a carefully placed trail of evidence, and a carefully planned and executed operation, Timothy McVeigh was implicated as prime suspect number one in the plot to blow up the Alfred P. Murrah Building.

Like Lee Harvey Oswald, who was declared the "lone assassin" within weeks, Timothy McVeigh would be declared—along with Terry Nichols—the "lone bomber" within days. On the indictments, the Justice Department would gratuitously add, "with others unknown." Yet these "others unknown" would fade from official memory as the so-called "Justice" Department withdrew the John Doe 2 sketch and the subsequent reward offer.

After his arrest, Lee Harvey Oswald announced to the television cameras, "I'm a patsy!"

After his arrest, Timothy McVeigh told the *London Sunday Times* he was "set up" for the bombing by the FBI because of his extreme political views.[250]

Never since the frame-up of Lee Harvey Oswald has the media gone out of its way to portray a suspect as dangerous and malignant. While the mainstream press took their cues from the FBI, they contradicted their own journalistic common sense. The government and the mainstream media have based their theories of Timothy McVeigh upon the flimsiest of pretenses, while ignoring the more obvious facts. Willing to take the Federal Government's word as gospel, the mainstream press succumbed, and perpetrated, the most obvious propaganda. In so doing, they have violated every principle of thorough and honest journalism, and have become nothing but a willing tool of the corporate/intelligence establishment.

As Stephen Jones said, "Before this investigation is all over with, the government will have Tim McVeigh standing next to Lee Harvey Oswald."[251]

Chapter Three

TERRY NICHOLS: "NON-RESIDENT ALIEN"

The image of Timothy McVeigh—the stoneface killer—would fade in the wake of court appearances and media interviews, as Stephen Jones sought to portray his smiling and chiding client as the simple boy next door.

The enigmatic figure of Terry Nichols, however, would haunt public perception, as his attorney jealously guarded the mysterious, brooding figure from prying eyes.

It was the older, quiet, bespectacled Nichols, some theorized, who was the "brains" behind the bombing, guiding his young friend in the sinister and deadly plot.

Nichols' ex-wife, Lana Padilla, doesn't agree. "I believe that Terry bought his home, brought his family there … truly, truly … wanted to have a family and just get on with his life. I just don't think this man could have done this. I just don't think with any knowledge he could have done this." [252]

Neighbors Bob and Sandy Papovich, long-time friends, wrote the press that Terry Nichols is a "kind, gentle, generous man absolutely incapable of violence." As Papovich told the author, "I've known Terry for over 15 years, and I've never heard this man utter the word "hell" or "damn." Terry doesn't want to hurt anybody … and all these people want me to believe that this man is capable of murdering hundreds of innocent people. It ain't possible." [253]

Terry Nichols told Federal Public Defender Steve Gradert, "Heck, I've got kids, too," in response to the bombing. [254] A peaceful person, Nichols reportedly loved children, including his son Josh, with whom he maintained a close relationship. One day, the astute 13-year-old told his mother he had to call the FBI. He was frantic. "I've got to tell them!"

"What do you got to tell them, Padilla asked?"

"I've got to tell them that my dad wouldn't do that. He loves children. He wouldn't do that to those children." [255]

Yet the press painted Terry Nichols with the same broad brush they used to paint Timothy McVeigh—focusing on the fact Nichols came from a broken home, dropped out of college, worked a series of odd jobs, and was anti-government. Like McVeigh, the media, anti-militia activists, and scores of pseudo-experts would do their best to cast Nichols in the same extremist mold—a man, authorities claimed—capable of killing 169 innocent people.

The third of four children, Terry Nichols grew up on a farm near Lapeer, Michigan. His father, Robert—quiet and soft-spoken—labored hard on the family's 160-acre farm. Like his son, he also worked a series of odd jobs, doing construction, selling encyclopedias, and putting in shifts at the Pontiac and Buick plants in an effort to keep the family afloat in a county where farming had become less and less prosperous.

His mother Joyce was a sharp contrast. Hard-drinking, often violent with explosive fits of temper, she had once rammed Robert's tractor with her car, and had threatened the local sheriff with a chainsaw. After 24 years of difficult marriage, the couple finally divorced. Padilla said Terry took it hard.[256]

Nichols dreamed of going to medical school but his grades weren't good enough for most pre-med programs. He enrolled at Central Michigan University, but after his parents' divorce in 1974, he dropped out at the request of his mother, who needed help on the family farm in Decker. But Nichols told friends he would never be a farmer.[257]

Yet, like McVeigh, Nichols was an intelligent man. He passed a difficult test for a securities license with a minimum of study and preparation, but told friends he was bored with college, which he found no more challenging than high school.

While in Decker, Nichols met his first wife, Lana Padilla, and they married in 1981. Two years later, they had a baby boy, Joshua. Shortly thereafter, Padilla's sister Kelli married Terry's brother James, and the four lived together at James's Decker, Michigan farmhouse.

Not satisfied with farm life, Nichols tried a number of different occupations. He delved into penny stocks, went on to sell insurance and real estate, managed a grain elevator, and worked occasionally as a carpenter. Nothing held his interest.

"No matter what he tried to do, every time he tried to break away, he ended up back on the farm trying to help his mother and James," said Padilla.[258]

While Padilla devoted time to building her real estate career, Nichols cooked, cleaned house, and cared for the kids, but grew increasingly restless and depressed. "Terry got real down on life," said his father. "He didn't care what he had done. He lost his vitality."[259]

One afternoon Padilla brought home pamphlets from the local Army recruiting office, and laid them out on the table. When she came back, the pamphlets were gone. Like many men uncertain about their future, Nichols decided to try a career in the military.

"He was just searching for a career, something he enjoyed," Nichols' friend Sandy Papovich told the *Dallas Morning News*. "He thought he would like it."[260]

It was an unusual career move for a 32-year-old man with children. Yet Nichols hoped he would be able to rise quickly through the ranks, and Padilla thought the experience would strengthen Terry and save their marriage.

On May 24, 1988, Nichols was assigned to Fort Benning, Georgia for basic training. "He said the government had made it impossible for him to make a living as a farmer," recalled assistant platoon leader Glen "Tex" Edwards. He hated the United States government. I thought it strange that a 32-year-old man would be complaining about the government, yet was now employed by the government. Nichols told me he signed up to pull his 20 years and get a retirement pension."[261]

Because of his age and maturity, Nichols was quickly made platoon leader. The obvious discrepancy in years earned him the nickname "Old Man."

"The drill sergeant said that because Nichols was older than the rest of us, he would hopefully be more mature and able to lead the younger guys in the unit. He also had some college background and came into the Army as a PFC," said Edwards.[262]

It was at Fort Benning that Nichols would meet Timothy McVeigh. The two men had enlisted on the same day. According to an account in the *Post:*

William "Dave" Dilly, who was McVeigh's roommate for about a year in the service, said McVeigh and Nichols "hit it off from the start, like Terry was his big brother. Tim was real frail and unsure of himself. Terry was the oldest guy and real sure of himself."

But the two men found they had a lot in common. McVeigh too came from a broken, blue-collar home and had an abiding interest in firearms and far-right politics. Both men fancied themselves as survivalists, and both loved to spend time on the rifle range. Both were looking for lifetime careers in the service. They quickly became friends.[263]

Another one of their friends was Michael Fortier, who joined Nichols and McVeigh at Fort Riley. The three would spend free time together, going fishing, shooting, and sharing their political beliefs.

Yet while McVeigh would rise quickly through the ranks, Nichols' Army career stalled. It seemed his platoon leadership status had been rescinded due to a prank he and McVeigh had pulled.

Around the same time, Padilla filed for divorce, and made plans to move her real estate business to Las Vegas. On May 15, 1989, after 11 months in the service, Nichols put in for a hardship discharge due to a "family emergency" that was never publicly explained. Yet it apparently had nothing to do with his divorce. He told Padilla it was to take care of his son Josh. As Padilla later wrote, Nichols already had Josh with him at Fort Riley, where the pair lived in a house off-base. As Padilla wrote in her book, *By Blood Betrayed:*

I've always wondered just why he was released, less than a year after enlisting, and have always been told it was because he had to take care of Josh. But this theory never washed with me because he'd had Josh with him all along. I really believe that Josh was just a convenient excuse and that Terry had become disillusioned with the Army because he believed he would never rise through the ranks.[264]

Perhaps Nichols' "hardship discharge" was similar to Lee Harvey Oswald's "hardship discharge" from the Marines that never was explained. And that of Thomas Martinez, the FBI infiltrator into the Silent Brotherhood (The Order), who was given an honorable discharge during basic training, which was never explained.[265]

Even more interesting is the parallel to McVeigh's discharge after "failing" his Special Forces try-out in April of 1991. McVeigh's sudden and mysterious departure from the Army, like Nichols', was never fully explained. As suggested previously, McVeigh's sudden decision leave a brilliant military career behind may have resulted from his being "sheep-dipped" as an intelligence operative. Yet mainstream media psychojournalists insisted that Nichols' departure from the Army was nothing more than the inevitable result of a consistent string of life-long failures.

Glen "Tex" Edwards put a slightly different spin on the matter. Edwards said that shortly before he left the Army, Nichols invited him to be part of a "private army" he said he was creating. "He told me he would be coming back to Fort Riley to start his own military organization," recalled Edwards. "He said he could get any kind of weapon and any equipment he wanted."

Nichols also said he intended to recruit McVeigh, Fortier, and others. "I can't remember the name of his organization, but he seemed pretty serious about it," Edwards said, adding that he reported Nichols' offer to the FBI shortly after the bombing.

In spite of flamboyant tales about recruiting a private army, Nichols returned to his old life in Michigan, working for a time as a carpenter, then moving back to the farmhouse in Decker. In spite of his short career in the Army, or perhaps because of it, Nichols developed a deep distrust of the Federal Government.

It was a feeling that was shared by his brother James, who, as a farmer, suffered through floods in the late '70s and early '80s, blaming the Federal Government for failing to provide adequate disaster relief. Nichols, along with his Sanilac country neighbors, witnessed dozens of farm foreclosures as a result. It was the Federal Government's policies that led to the rise of such far-right groups as the American Agricultural Movement and the anti-tax Posse Comitatus. As the *Post* writes:

Many residents around Decker said they share Terry and James's angry politics, but are less vocal because they fear government retribution. "Much of what the Nichols brothers believe is not that different or radical from what lots of people around here think," said local truck driver Jack Bean. "We feel our liberties and freedoms are being chipped away at and we want all this authority off our backs. The difference between the Nichols and others in this community is that they are just not afraid to say what they think, to challenge what is wrong."[266]

In spite of their differences, Terry and James had a lot in common. Both were fathers, had married sisters, and had suffered through difficult divorces. Both shared an ideological distrust of the Federal Government.

James Nichols studied the Constitution, Black's Law Dictionary and the Uniform Commercial Codes. He read the works of Jefferson and Paine and was particularly inspired by Jefferson's maxim, "The tree of liberty must be refreshed from time to time with the blood of patriots and tyrants." Perhaps not coincidentally, this passage was discovered in McVeigh's car upon his arrest. It would later be read into evidence at his trial.

Both Terry and James held a view shared by many beleaguered farmers: that the Federal Reserve was not empowered to coin money, and that U.S. currency printed after 1930—when the nation went into debt—was valueless. Following the advice of financial books that warned of an imminent crash, the brothers put their money into precious metals such as silver and gold.

Yet their activities took still more dramatic turns. In 1990 James tried to renounce his citizenship, and plastered his car with anti-government and Second Amendment bumper stickers.

Terry purchased a pick-up truck and decided not to register it, instead, making his own tag and placing it on front. Both men renounced their driver's licenses.

In March of 1994, Terry sent a dramatic affidavit to the Evergreen Township claiming himself to be a "Non-Resident Alien" private citizen not bound by the laws of the U.S. government. He also renounced his voting rights due to "Total corruption in the entire political system from the local government on up through and including the president of the United States of America, George Bush."* These activities were not condoned by the local authorities. In 1992, Chase Manhattan Bank went after Nichols for racking up $17,860 in unpaid credit card debts. The largely out-of-work farmer had spent over $35,000, using Chase and First Deposit National Bank cards, on farm equipment, personal effects, and airline tickets. He attempted to pay off the debts with his own "Certified Fractional Reserve Check," a bogus check distributed widely among farmers by a group called Family Farm Preservation. He signed the check, "Explicitly reserving all my rights, Terry L. Nichols." He then sent the bank a letter retroactively revoking his signature from the credit card contract.

---

* In October, 1959, Lee Harvey Oswald appeared suddenly at the American Embassy in Moscow, and dramatically handed over his U.S. Passport and a letter renouncing his American citizenship.

"There are two sides to that man, maybe many more," said Dennis Reid, a Sandusky, Mich., lawyer who has observed Nichols and his brother, James, during court proceedings in Michigan. "Jim to me I really expect is kind of a sissy. He was always shaking when he'd go into the courtroom and spout off," attorney Dennis Reid said. "Terry seemed to be more level-headed. He was still saying things that were strange, but he was certainly more cold and more calculating." [267]

Terry definitely didn't seem "level-headed" when he went to court to answer the lawsuit by Chase. He refused to come before the bench, shouting to Judge Donald Teeple from the back of the room that the court had no jurisdiction over him. During the hearing, the bitter and sarcastic defendant accused the bank of fraud. "They knowingly and willingly know how to make credit out of nothing and make interest on it and actually steal people's hard earned money," he told the Judge. "They gave me valueless nothing for something they want to take from me that has value. That's not right, is it?"

He claimed to have determined that the bank's business was based upon "fraud and misrepresentation, collusion, color of law, conspiracy, enticement, inducement, seduction, duress, coercion, mistake [and] bankruptcy," and he filed a counterclaim against First Deposit and its attorneys for $50,000 or 14,200 ounces of silver. Nichols charged the bank with "mental and emotional damage, loss of happiness and the unjust destroying of credit history ... by wanton acts when no probable cause existed." [268]

The judge was not impressed. He accused Nichols of playing with words and ordered him to pay the debt. Nichols didn't pay.

When FBI agents questioned Lana Padilla after Nichols' arrest, they asked a curious question: Did Nichols ever dye his hair? The Bureau had been investigating a string of bank robberies throughout the Midwest. One of the robbers had dyed his hair, and was Nichols' height and weight.

The group, known as the Midwest Bank Bandits, had robbed over a quarter-of-a-million dollars from more than 22 banks between January, 1994, and December, 1995, in a spree that took them across six states, including Kansas. The bandits were tied to a group of men who made their temporary home at Elohim City, a far-right religious compound in Southeastern Oklahoma. McVeigh and his friend Michael Fortier were known to have visited the compound. Some of the men were also seen in Kansas with the bombing defendants.

If the FBI's question came as a shock to Padilla, she would turn pale when she opened her ex-husband's storage locker on December 15, 1994, and discovered wigs, masks, and pantyhose. The Midwest Bank Bandits had worn masks.

Could Nichols have been robbing banks? "Not the Terry I knew," said Padilla.

"I was just speculating, but everything that has come out about that side of Terry was a total ... maybe I just turned my face and never noticed it, never wanted to notice it, but ... I never thought of him ... of course I never would have thought of him sleeping with a gun under him either." [269]

Yet considering Nichols' hatred of banks and his rallying cry against the monetary system, it would not be too far-fetched a scenario. Such speculation is bolstered by the fact that McVeigh sent his sister a letter in December, '93 informing her that he was part of a group that had been robbing banks. Although he himself didn't admit to taking part in any of the robberies, he asked her to "launder" three $100 bills "they" had stolen.

McVeigh returned to Decker, Michigan in the Spring of 1993 to see his old Army friend Nichols. Just back from Waco, where he had witnessed the carnage inflicted upon the Branch Davidians, McVeigh was instilled with a new sense of urgency and rage. At the Nichols farm, he would find like-minded souls who shared his frustration.

By the Fall of '93, McVeigh was living at the farmhouse, helping with the chores, and reportedly urging the Nichols brothers onto more militant activities. The men practiced target shooting and setting off small bombs on the property.

"You know how little boys like to play with things that blow up?" recalled [neighbor Phil] Morawski. "That was what they were like. And everything they mixed out there in the cornfields seemed to work."

The government would focus heavily on this activity later on.

According to Michigan Militia members, the Nichols brothers also began attending meetings, but the militia found their rhetoric too strong. Michigan Militia member John Simpson recalled: "Terry came to one of our meetings and wanted to talk about a tax revolt, having to have a drivers license and eliminating the government. We did not believe in his tactics—particularly the stuff about a revolt." [270] James reportedly talked about the "necessity" of taking on police officers, judges and lawyers. Apparently, McVeigh accompanied Nichols to some of the meetings.

According to *Time* magazine, McVeigh and the Nichols brothers went on to organize their own militia:

The three men formed their own cell of the "Patriots," a self-styled paramilitary group that James Nichols had been affiliated with since 1992 when he began attending meetings in a nearby town. The trio decided to recruit members and establish other cells around the area, but determined that for security reasons no unit should grow larger than eight members. [271]

If this account is accurate, it would tend to jibe with what Nichols told Army buddy Glen "Tex" Edwards about "recruiting" his own private army. Perhaps one of Nichols' recruits was Craig O'Shea, who lived just off Highway 77 in Herrington. A friend of Nichols who was kicked out of the service, O'Shea used to work for Barbara Whittenberg, who owns the Sante Fe Trail Diner in Herrington. Whittenberg described O'Shea as a "demolitions expert," and said she saw him occasionally with Nichols. "He's a very violent man," said Whittenberg, who said O'Shea had once threatened to kill her and her husband.[272]

In March, '94, Nichols took a job at the Donahue ranch in Marion, Kansas.

Co-worker Tim Donahue recalled that Nichols worked long hours, sometimes six days a week, without complaint and appeared to enjoy his job, which he did well. Nichols would grouse about taxes and the government conspiring to seize people's firearms. One day when Nichols and Donahue were talking about the use of fertilizer in farming, Nichols mentioned that he knew how to make a bomb.[273]

Four months later, in August of '94, Nichols gave Donahue 30 days notice. His dream of setting up a private army metamorphosized into simply supplying that army. He told Donahue he was going into the army surplus business with a friend. On September 30, that friend—Timothy McVeigh—showed up to help him pack.

It was during this period that his ex-wife began picking up strange signals from her former husband.

Earlier in the month, he had called her from Kansas. "He was very upset," she said. "He was very emphatic. He talked about Waco and that shooting at the White House (where a Colorado Springs man fired a gun toward the White House). He said, 'You know, that guy wasn't all wrong. There's going to be some civil unrest in this country.'"[274]

During one of his frequent visits to Padilla's house in Las Vegas, Nichols displayed his Glock .45. "I never knew him to carry a gun," Padilla told the *Denver Post*. "He liked guns and collected them, but this was new. He acted like he was afraid for his life. He slept with it on."[275]

Traveling the gun show circuit with McVeigh, Nichols was now a virtual nomad, living out of his pick-up. His few remaining possessions were stored in a locker in Las Vegas. He also told Padilla that he was he was switching the beneficiary of his life insurance policy from her to his new wife, Marife.

A 17-year-old Filipino mail-order bride, Marife Torres met Nichols through Paradise Shelton Tours of Scottsdale, Arizona. The young woman looked forward to leaving her life of poverty in Cebu City, Philippines, where the unemployment rate often topped 40 percent. After a year of exchanging heartfelt letters, they married on November 20, 1990 in a small restaurant in Cebu City. Yet it took over four months of bureaucratic hassles and red tape to arrange Marife's entry into the U.S.

"That one episode soured Terry on government," his father recalled. "He originally told me it would take six weeks for her to come here ... but it was red tape, red tape, red tape."

At first the newlyweds tried life on the Decker farm, where Jason, Marife's son by a former boyfriend, was born on September 21, 1991. Yet Marife found herself "working like a maid," cooking and cleaning for "three husbands"—Terry, James, and Tim, who often stayed at the house. She wrote her friend Vilma Eulenberg that she thought the place was haunted, and resented McVeigh, who she thought was a bad influence on her husband.

The couple eventually moved to warm, sunny Las Vegas, but Marife missed her Philippine home. To accommodate his new wife, Nichols moved to Cebu City. But the noise, heat and smog was too much for him, and in mid-1993, after barely a month in the Philippines, they moved back to the States, shuttling back and forth between Michigan and Nevada.

Nicole, their first common child, was born on August 1, 1993.

Two months later, on November 22, tragedy struck, when 26-month-old Jason accidentally suffocated to death in a plastic bag. While Marife wondered if Terry was capable of killing a child, Padilla assured her he was not, then hinted darkly in her book that McVeigh may have been responsible for the death. She neglected to mention the fact that McVeigh and James had tried to revive the youngster for nearly half-an-hour, then called the paramedics.

A month later, the couple moved to Las Vegas, where they rented a condominium for $550 a month. It was during this period that Marife began traveling to the Philippines to finish her physical therapy degree. According to Padilla, Terry also traveled to the Philippines about four times a year over a four year period. She wrote that he sometimes traveled to Cebu City without taking Marife, whom he occasionally left behind.

"Sometimes he went when Marife was in Kansas. It didn't make sense, but I never asked why."[276]

Padilla subsequently told me in July, '96, "I have not known him to leave her here and just go to the Philippines. If he made a trip by himself, it was because she was already there."*

Whichever account is true, Nichols did travel to Cebu City in late November to meet with "potential business partners." According to Padilla, Nichols was making arrangements to bring back "butterflies."

---

* When I questioned her about this apparent contradiction, she told me her later statement was correct, and the book's account was wrong.

"One time he brought back butterflies—little butterflies that they make over there—he brought them back here to sell." [277]

Butterflies. Curious merchandise for a man trying to set himself up in the military surplus business.*

Then on November 22, 1994 Nichols made a final visit to the Philippines to visit Marife. His parting words to Josh left the 12-year old convinced he was never going to see his dad again. As he got into the car with Padilla after dropping his father off at the airport, he started crying.

"What's the matter?" Padilla asked.

"I'm never going to see my dad again. I'm never going to see my dad again."

"Of course you will," Padilla said reassuringly. "He's gone to the Philippines a lot of times. You know he always comes back."

"This time is different," he blurted through big tears. [278]

Nichols called his ex-wife from Los Angeles several hours later. "Had a little excitement at the airport after you left," he said, laughing. He told Padilla that airport security had stopped him for trying to sneak a pair of stun guns through the metal detector. They called the cop on duty who ran Nichols' name through the computer. Although he had several outstanding traffic warrants, the police let him continue on his way.

Just why was Nichols attempting to carry stun guns on an international flight? According to Bob Papovich, Terry was afraid of the high crime rate in poverty-stricken Cebu City. He also said that Nichols was afraid of Marife's ex-boyfriend. Jason, her son by this man, had died while in Nichols' custody. The ex-boyfriend allegedly threatened to kill him should he return.

Padilla doesn't think the story is credible. "I think it's something they dreamed up," she said. Yet upon his return he told Padilla that he could get "killed down there" and he was never going back. [279]

Obviously, somebody was out to hurt Terry Nichols, possibly kill him. When he departed for Cebu City, he left a mysterious package for his ex-wife, saying, "If I'm not back in 60 days, open it and follow the instructions." At first, Padilla did as she was told. But her instincts eventually took over.

"I was uneasy about his warning, and Josh's, 'I'll never see my dad again' kept echoing in my brain." [280]

Padilla secured the package in her office safe. Now she slipped quietly into the conference room, opened the lock, and laid the mysterious brown paper bag on the table. It stared ominously back at her. As she ripped it open, nearly a dozen keys slid out onto the table. She didn't recognize any of them.

---

* Nichols became interested in selling military surplus in December, '93 to April, '94 according to Padilla.

There was Terry's life insurance policy with a note saying he had changed the beneficiary from her to Marife, and two handwritten lists saying, "Read and Do Immediately." One of the lists directed her to a storage locker in Las Vegas:

All items in storage are for Joshua. The round items are his when he turns 21, all else now....

The note also instructed her to remove a small plastic bag taped behind a utensil drawer in Nichols' kitchen:

All items in plastic bag are to be sent to Marife, for Nicole, if for any reason my life insurance doesn't pay her. Otherwise, half goes to Josh and half to Marife.

She removed a letter to McVeigh's sister, Jennifer. Inside the letter to Jennifer was another one stamped and addressed to McVeigh:

Tim:
If you should receive this letter, then clear everything out of CG 37 by 01 Feb 95 or pay to keep it longer, under Ted Parker of Decker. This letter has been written & sealed before I left (21 Nov 94) and being mailed by Lana as per my instructions to her in writing. This is all she knows. It would be a good idea to write or call her to verify things. [address redacted] Just ask for Lana (card enclosed). Your on your own. Go for it!!
Terry
Also Liquidate 40

At the bottom it read, "As far as I know, this letter would be for the purpose of my death."

"Why would he write that letter?" asked Padilla. "He has been there so many times. Never—ever, has he written a letter like that. Never—ever." [281]

Two weeks later, on December 15, Padilla and her oldest son, Barry, drove to Nichols' apartment. Following Nichols' instructions, Barry reached behind the kitchen drawer and pulled out a plastic bag. It was crammed full of twenties and hundreds—a total of $20,000 cash.

Already in a state of shock, the pair drove to the AAAABCO storage facility and nervously fumbled with the lock. They were stunned when they opened the door.

There were wigs, masks, pantyhose, freeze-dried food, and various gold coins (obviously the "round" objects for Josh), along with gold bars and silver bullion stacked neatly in boxes. There were also some small green stones that appeared to be jade. I estimated at least $60,000 street value in precious metals! [282]

There was also a large ring with what appeared to be safe deposit box keys.

Two months later, on January 16, Nichols returned from the Philippines, alive and well. "Where's the package?" he asked Padilla.

"I opened it," she stated boldly.

"Why?!" he exclaimed. "You betrayed my trust. I told you not to open it for 60 days."

"Because I was frightened. I thought something terrible had happened to you. I thought you were dead. And where did you get all that money?"

The couple then argued over finances, but Nichols wouldn't explain the mysterious letters, or where he had gotten the cash, the gold, and the safe deposit box keys. She didn't ask about the wigs, the masks, and the pantyhose, and he didn't tell her. But she was worried nonetheless.

"I think those letters were written because there is somebody bigger than any of us will ever know involved in this," said Padilla. "Why did he change his beneficiary on his life insurance? It wasn't because her boyfriend might take a potshot at him ... and then he said in that letter not to say a word to Josh until it's all taken care of ... what the hell is he talking about? It isn't the boyfriend." [283]

If the boyfriend story is untrue, perhaps Nichols' "butterfly" partners were out to get him.

Or perhaps it was someone else, someone bigger and more dangerous. Such players aren't hard to come by in Cebu City, home to a number of terrorists groups such as the Liberation Army of the Philippines, the Communist Huk, and the Abu Sayyaf, an organization with close ties to the Mujahadeen and World Trade Center bomber Ramzi Yousef.

Was Nichols meeting with terrorists in the Philippines? Incredibly, FBI 302 reports and investigations conducted by McVeigh's defense team indicate that Yousef, Abdul Hakim Murad, Wali Khan Amin Shah, and several other terrorists met in Davao, on the Island of Mindanao, in late 1992 or early 1993, to discuss the Oklahoma City bombing plot.

One of the men at the meeting, recalled an Abu Sayyaf leader, introduced himself as "a farmer." [284] When the "farmer" returned from his November, 1994 trip, and discovered that Padilla had opened the package and read the letter, he turned "white as a ghost," then immediately began making a series of desperate calls to a boarding house in Cebu City.

Curiously, Nichols would call his party, have a brief 34-second conversation, then hang up and immediately redial the number 14 consecutive times, letting it ring each time. This he repeated on January 31, with nine calls and one 14-minute conversation; then on February 14 he placed 22 calls within a 40-minute time-period, with one 23-minute conversation; then on the 28th he made 31 calls within three hours, with no conversations; then finally on March 7 and 14 he made two calls, speaking 24 minutes each. [285]

Since Nichols didn't time-out these consecutive calls (as one would tend to do if there was no answer or the line were busy), but made one call right after the other, is it possible he was sending some sort of signal or code? *

Helen Malaluan, who runs the boarding house, told me Nichols was probably trying to reach Marife, who she said was staying there at the time. Her brother Ernesto also said that boarders from the island of Mindanao often stayed at the house. The Abu Sayyaf, coincidentally, is headquartered in Mindanao. Was Nichols using Marife to send a message to someone else?

In February, '95, Terry and Marife moved to Herrington, Kansas, where Nichols purchased a modest home for $25,000.

"We all thought he was just a little bit different," Herrington real estate agent Georgia Rucker said. "We had to pry any information out of him." [286]

In Herrington, Nichols appeared to settle down. He attended army surplus auctions at nearby Fort Riley and tried to make a living selling army surplus gear.

"He spent the morning of April 19, around Herrington, picking up business cards, registering his truck with the state, and calling on a couple of local shops, asking about their interest in buying government surplus," said Padilla. "Those are not the actions of a guilty man." [287]

But are they?

On September 30, the same day that Nichols quit the Donahue ranch, someone using the name "Mike Havens" purchased 40 50-pound bags of ammonium-nitrate from the Mid-Kansas Co-op in McPhearson. Although employees never positively identified Nichols as the customer, a receipt with McVeigh's fingerprint was found in Nichols' home. The FBI asserts that the fertilizer was kept in a storage shed in nearby Herrington, rented by Nichols under the alias "Shawn Rivers." **

Then, that same weekend, 299 dynamite sticks, 544 blasting caps, detonator cord, and a quantity of an explosive called Tovex were stolen from the Martin Marietta Aggregates rock quarry just north of Marion. Marion County Sheriff Ed Davies testified at McVeigh's trial that he found metal shavings and tumblers on the ground in front of the magazines. FBI Agent James Cadigal, an FBI firearms and tool marks identification specialist, said that a drill bit in Nichols' home matched the signature of the hole drilled into the lock.

Finally, Lori Fortier, Michael Fortier's wife, testified that McVeigh told them

---

* Earlier, McVeigh had told Padilla, "I'll write to him (Nichols), but I guess I'd better do it in code, because there are a lot of nosy people."

** Nichols' attorney Michael Tigar claimed his client's use of aliases while renting the storage lockers was to prevent the credit card companies from coming after him.

that he and Nichols had broken into the quarry.*

On October 18, 1994, 40 additional 50-pound bags of ammonium-nitrate were purchased from the Mid-Kansas Co-op by "Havens." Havens was reportedly driving a dark-colored pickup with a light-colored camper top—the kind owned by Terry Nichols. (Another version of the story has a red trailer attached to the truck, which didn't appear to be Nichols'.) The FBI believed the fertilizer was stored in a locker in Council Grove—number 40—rented the previous day by "Joe Kyle." This apparently was the "liquidate 40" that Nichols referred to in his mysterious note to McVeigh.

Jennifer McVeigh later testified that when her brother visited Lockport in November, '94, he confided to her that he had been driving around with 1,000 pounds of explosives. Could these "explosives" have been the ammonium-nitrate purchased at the Mid-Kansas Co-op?

Then on November 5, 1994, several masked men robbed gun dealer Roger Moore. The 60-year-old Moore was surprised by two men carrying shotguns, wearing camouflage fatigues and black ski masks, who bound him with duct tape. They proceeded to ransack his house, making off with a large collection of weapons, plus a number of gold and silver bars, and a safe deposit box key.

Interestingly, Moore (aka Bob Anderson) knew McVeigh, who once stayed at his house. Moore had met McVeigh at a gun show in Florida in 1995.

For his part, McVeigh had a solid alibi. He was in Kent, Ohio on November 5, at a gun show. Yet after the bombing, Fortier reportedly told the FBI that McVeigh called him after the robbery and said, "Nichols got Bob!" Some of the guns were later pawned by Fortier at the behest of McVeigh, according to the FBI, which contends that the proceeds were used to finance the bombing.

Interestingly, Nichols was seen in Sedalia, Missouri on February 10 and 11, the same weekend that gun dealer William Mueller was robbed. Mueller's Tilly, Arkansas home, 150 miles south of Sedalia, was burglarized of $40,000 worth of silver coins, gun parts, survival gear, and 30 cases of ammunition.

What makes this even more interesting is that Nichols had checked into the Motel Memory the evening of February 10, after a long drive from Kansas, telling owner Phillip Shaw he was there for the gun show. Yet Nichols had missed the first day of the two-day show.

The next morning, while Nichols was apparently at the show, Shaw's wife Betty opened his room and saw dozens of boxes of ammunition scattered across the floor. The presence of such a large quantity of ammunition puzzled local

---

* McVeigh Defense attorney Christopher Tritico questioned the analysis, noting the FBI laboratory isn't accredited by any agency for such a test. Tritico also used photographs of a test hole drilled into lead by the bit to argue that grooves and scratches didn't resemble those in the hole closely enough to call them a match.

investigators, who knew there was too small a profit margin in legally-purchased ammo for gun show dealers to bother messing with it. Moreover, if Nichols *had* planned on selling the ammunition, why had he left so much of it in his room?

Tragically, Mueller, his wife, and their 8-year-old daughter, Sarah, were found murdered on June 28, 1996. Their bodies were by pulled from the Illinois Bayou after a fisherman discovered a portion of a leg. The family had been handcuffed, their heads covered with plastic bags wrapped with duct tape. They were found in 20 feet of water, tied to a heavy rock.

Unaccounted for was some $50,000 the *Arkansas Gazette* reported the Muellers were believed to have received only days before they disappeared.

While Timothy McVeigh had known Roger Moore, his friend Michael Brescia, and his friend and roommate Andy Strassmeir met Bill Mueller at a Fort Smith, Arkansas gun show earlier that year. As reported in the *McCurtain Gazette:*

> Mueller then told [Gene] Wergis that he remembered the two because he believed they might be connected with his home's burglary—or even the ATF. Wergis also reported that Mueller showed him a spiral notebook where the exhibitor had gone so far—so great was his concern—as to write down the two men's names.[288]

Both Brescia and Strassmeir, who also knew McVeigh, lived at Elohim City, the white separatist compound near Muldrow, Oklahoma. Brescia was later arrested for his alleged role in the robbery of a Madison, Wisconsin bank—part of the string of robberies committed by the Midwest Bank Bandits. As previously mentioned, some of the robbers made their temporary homes at Elohim City.

After the bombing, the FBI questioned Padilla about the items found in Nichols' home and storage lockers. Among those items were large quantities of ammunition and a safe deposit box key belonging to Roger Moore. As of this writing it is not known whether the FBI traced the ammo to Mueller.

Also found in Nichols' home, according to ATF Agent Larry Tongate, were 33 firearms, five roles of 60-foot Primadet detonator cord, non-electric blasting caps, containers of ammonium-nitrate, a fuel-meter, and four 55-gallon blue and white plastic drums.

Not exactly the everyday stuff of an ordinary guy from a small town in Kansas.

Similar items were found in James Nichols' farm, including blasting caps, safety fuses, ammonium-nitrate, and diesel fuel. Nichols, who was taken into custody the same day as his brother, denied any wrongdoing, and authorities dropped all charges. As for his brother, he commented, "My gut feeling. I didn't do anything. He didn't do anything." When asked by a reporter, "How about Timothy McVeigh? he replied, "I want to see some facts."

Yet the facts against Terry seemed to be piling up.

On April 15, 1995, Barbara Whittenberg served breakfast to three men at the Sante Fe Trail Diner: Terry Nichols, Tim McVeigh, and a third man with dark features. She also recalled seeing a Ryder truck outside, and asked the men where they were headed. Suddenly, she said, it was "as if ice water was thrown on the conversation."[289]

The men left before 7:00 A.M. Later that afternoon, as Whittenberg and her son were driving to nearby Junction City, they saw the truck parked at Geary State Fishing Lake—where authorities originally claimed the bomb was mixed. The truck was still there when they drove past around 3:00 or 4:00 P.M. Whittenberg's son recalled seeing three men along with what he described as a Thunderbird with Arizona tags.

Later that day Nichols visited a Conoco station in Manhattan, Kansas, and a Coastal Mart in Junction City, and bought over 30 gallons of diesel fuel. Nichols' pick-up has a diesel motor, according to his brother, and Nichols' had been a regular diesel customer for over two months prior to the bombing, according to Shan Woods of Klepper Oil Co., purchasing between $20 to $30 worth of diesel fuel "two or three times a week." Receipts were again found in his home.[290]

The next day, Nichols purchased an additional 21 gallons from the Junction City Conoco station.

Then, on the evening of April 17, 1995, a Ryder truck was seen parked behind Nichols Herrington home. A Ryder truck was seen that same week backed up to a storage shed that Nichols rented.

On the morning of the 18th, several witnesses again saw the Ryder truck parked at Geary Lake. Parked next to appeared to be Nichols' pick-up. When the FBI subsequently inspected the area, they allegedly recovered bits of ammonium-nitrate and strands of detonator cord, and saw signs of diesel fuel.

That same day, or possibly the day before, a convoy pulled in for gas at the Easy Mart in Newkirk, 100 miles north of Oklahoma City. It was a Ryder truck accompanied by a blue pick-up with a camper top. Manager Jerri-Lynn Backhous recalled seeing three men. The passenger in the pick-up was dark skinned with black hair, average height, and had a "real muscular build," she said. He was wearing a t-shirt and sun-glasses, and "looked just like the John Doe 2 sketch."[291]

Backhous also saw a reflection of the person in the Ryder truck. He was a short man with close cropped, dark hair and glasses, she said. Employee Dorinda J. "Wendy" Hermes waited on the third man—Terry Lynn Nichols—who came into the store and bought food for the others. Hermes particularly recalled Nichols' pick-up. "It caught me funny because it had street tires on it, but it was all muddy," she said.[292]

Perhaps most interestingly, Nichols' son Josh recalled accompanying McVeigh and his father on the ride back to Kansas that Sunday. McVeigh asserts that he called Nichols from Oklahoma City because his car had broken down, and asked

Nichols to pick him up. On the way back, according to Josh, McVeigh made his infamously cryptic remark: "Something big is going to happen."

Nichols reportedly asked him, "What, are you going to rob a bank?"

"Something big is going to happen," McVeigh stoically replied.

A curious statement. If McVeigh and Nichols had conspired to bomb the Murrah Building, wouldn't Nichols *already* know that "something big" was going to happen?

Or was the statement invented by Nichols to exculpate himself from the plot in the eyes of investigators? Given the fact that the statement was relayed to the FBI by Nichols' 12-year-old son, this seems unlikely.

And if Nichols was involved in the plot, there is evidence that in November, '94, he wanted out. Among the documents prosecutors handed over to the defense is testimony from Lori Fortier that McVeigh began to solicit help from her husband because Nichols was "expressing reluctance."

It should be noted however that the FBI and the Justice Department is infamous for framing people, and they brought enormous pressure on the Fortiers, threatening them with knowledge of a terrorist plot, weapons violations and other charges if they did not testify against Nichols and McVeigh. Federal prosecutors subsequently coached Lori Fortier heavily before McVeigh's trial, having her practice her testimony in two mock trials.

Yet if Nichols had no involvement in the plot, what was he doing with large quantities of ammonium-nitrate, blasting caps, detonator cord, and a collection of 55-gallon drums? Why the purchases of diesel fuel? Were these items planted by the FBI?

If Nichols was involved in the bombing, why didn't he make any attempt to hide or dispose of these incriminating items before April 19, or even by the 22nd? Why would a man, who had allegedly just blown up a building, killing 169 people, plainly leave a receipt for the so-called bomb ingredient in his kitchen drawer?

In fact, Nichols didn't attempt to hide any of these items before he casually walked into the local police station on April 22 after hearing his name on TV. Such do not seem like the actions of an intelligent, calculating, cold-blooded killer.

But then, there were the mysterious trips to the Phillippines. Those trips, and Nichols' clandestine meetings with some mysterious players in Las Vegas, would begin to intrigue a handful of journalists and investigators, as the Oklahoma City bombing plot took them down an even darker and more insidious road.

Chapter Four

MILLAR'S RENT-A-NAZI

Authorities have postulated that McVeigh's "obsession with Waco" and Nichols' hatred of the Federal Government were the driving forces that led them to bomb the Federal Building. Their alleged association with militias and other paramilitary groups, authorities claimed, was the key influence that guided them along their sinister path to their final, vicious act of revenge.

These numerous pseudo-experts also theorized that McVeigh himself was inspired by the *Turner Diaries*, written by former physics professor William Pierce. In this fictionalized account of white race-warriors' overthrow of the Zionist Occupational Government (ZOG), the "heroes" demolish the FBI building in Washington, D.C. with a fertilizer bomb at precisely 9:00 A.M.

The idea for bombing a federal facility is hardly new. In the mid-1970s Oklahoma resident Harawese Moore was convicted of planting an incendiary device outside both the Federal Courthouse and the Alfred P. Murrah Building— a case, coincidentally, defended by Stephen Jones.

In 1983, members of the Covenant, Sword and the Arm of the Lord (CSA), a white supremacist group based in northern Arkansas, planned to truck-bomb the Alfred P. Murrah Building. In 1988, former CSA leader James Ellison turned states' evidence and testified that CSA member Richard Wayne Snell and others had participated in the plot. Snell was bitter toward the government, Ellison claimed, because the IRS and FBI had seized his property.

Other defendants included Richard Girnt Butler, chief of the Aryan Nations; Robert E. Miles, a former Ku Klux Klansman; and Louis Beam, Jr., former Grand Dragon of the Texas Ku Klux Klan, and Aryan Nations "Ambassador at Large"— who led a campaign of terror against Vietnamese-American fisherman.*

Ellison, who fancied himself "King James," was surrounded at his CSA compound near the Missouri-Arkansas border on the prophetic date of April 19 (ten years to the day of the Oklahoma City bombing), leading to a four-day standoff against 200 heavily-armed agents. Ellison later testified at his sedition trial that at Snell's request, he had cased several buildings, including the Alfred P. Murrah Building.

---

* Butler and Snell also reportedly had connections to Jack Oliphant of Kingman, Arizona.

"He took me to some of the buildings and asked me to go in the building and check the building out," Ellison said. According to his testimony, rocket launchers were to be "placed in a trailer or a van so that it could be driven up to a given spot, parked there, and a timed detonation device could be triggered so that the driver could walk away and leave the vehicle set in position and he would have time to clear the area before any of the rockets launched." [293]

Ellison would later deny this. Yet on October 22, 1996, the Canadian Broadcasting Company (CBC) played a clip of Ellison, where the former CSA leader admitted his involvement in the plot:

Ellison: Wayne Snell ... had made a trip to Oklahoma City, and Wayne came back and told me about different buildings that he had seen, wanted to know if I would look at them with him sometime. And Steve talked to me and gave me a description of these buildings and asked me to design a rocket launcher that could be used to destroy these buildings from a distance ... heavy, large buildings.

In the CBC piece, former CSA member Kerry Noble states: "I still look at things like this and realize how close we were, and, you know, that this could have been me having done this." The reformed Noble, now a critic of the militant extreme-right, spoke openly about the plot with CBC's Trish Wood:

Noble: It was one of the targets that we had talked about at [the] CSA in '83. The day it happened, as soon as I heard it on the news, I said, the right-wing's done it— they finally took that step.

Noble explained that the Murrah Building was a target because it was a low security complex that housed many different federal agencies. He said the plotters thought it would have more effect on the country "than if you did a building, say, in New York City or something." [294]

Wood: Do you think—and I know this is a guess—that Snell or Ellison told [Reverend Robert] Millar about the early plans to blow up the Murrah Building in Oklahoma City?
Noble: ... I think that probably Millar knew that something major was going to happen. Now, whether he knew the exact details, chances are he probably did not, because he would not want to know specific details at first. But I think he knew something major was going to happen.

Ellison later settled at Elohim City at the behest of Millar, who claims to disavow the bombing. "If I knew something like that was taking place then or today," said the Christian Identity minister, "I'd do everything I could do to prevent it and, if necessary, call in government agents to help stop it."

While all 14 defendants in the original 1983 bombing plot were acquitted, Snell was executed on the ever-prophetic date of April 19, 1995, the very day the Murrah Building was bombed. Snell was convicted of killing a black state trooper in 1984, and a pawnshop owner he thought was Jewish. While under arrest, Snell called himself a "prisoner of war," precisely what authorities claimed McVeigh said.

Before his death, Snell had time to watch scenes from the bombing on his jail-room TV. Millar, who was with the 64-year-old Snell during his final hours, said he was appalled at the destruction. Yet according to Arkansas prison official Alan Ables, "Snell chuckled and laughed as he watched television coverage of the Oklahoma City disaster."

Both Millar and Snell's wife contend that the convicted murderer was saddened by the bombing. Yet Noble thinks McVeigh was in some way inspired by Snell.

> **Wood:** Did you ever think that it was a coincidence that Tim McVeigh—if, in fact, he did it—chose that building?
>
> **Noble:** No, I don't think it's any coincidence. When you bring that into account with the declaration of war that we made, the pressure that the older leaders of the groups are putting on the younger followers to do something in a major way before they die—no, it's no coincidence.
>
> **Wood:** How would McVeigh have known about the earlier plans for the Murrah Building?
>
> **Noble:** It's very feasible and likely that he would have kept in communication with certain people and said ... you know, then if somebody said, well, what would you recommend as a starting place—it's very likely he could have said, well, this is what we had picked out.

Interestingly, Ables told the *Denver Post*, "Snell repeatedly predicted that there would be a bombing or an explosion the day of his death."

> **Ables:** A few days before the execution I began to hear things from the director, the wardens, just talk in the office, that strange things were going on, Snell was talking strangely, he was, you know, making statements that were a little scary ... catastrophic events, things were going to happen. This date, April 19th, was going to be something that the governor would regret perhaps.

Snell's parting words before leaving this Earth were, "Look over your shoulder, Governor, justice is coming. I wouldn't trade places with you or any of your cronies. Hell has victory. I am at peace."

Wood: Are those the ravings of a man about to be executed or are they the comments of a man with a plan?

Noble: I think a man with a plan, I think a man who is taking the satisfaction that his death may mean something after all and that it may be the catalyst that puts somebody over the line to do what he himself didn't get the chance to do.[295]

A similar bomb plot surfaced a year after the Oklahoma City bombing, when Richard Ray Lampley, 65, his wife Cecilia, and friend John Baird were convicted of a plot to bomb the ADL office in Houston, the Southern Poverty Law Center (SPLC) in Montgomery, and various gay bars and abortion clinics. Lampley made his intentions known at one of Dennis Mahon's WAR meetings. A former Grand Imperial Dragon of the KKK, and number three man in WAR, the Tulsan was a frequent visitor to Lampley's place, and to Elohim City.

A self-proclaimed "Prophet of God," Lampley claims he was entrapped by Richard Schrum, an FBI informant. Schrum was sent by the Bureau to infiltrate the Oklahoma white separatist compound, but when he found nothing illegal there, he infiltrated Lampley's group instead.

According to defense attorneys, it was Schrum who ran the cell to which Lampley belonged, and threatened to leave when it appeared Lampley was wavering. "If anyone formed any kind of conspiracy, it was Richard Schrum," defense lawyer Mark Green said. Defense attorney Warren Gotcher backed up Green, stating "This conspiracy to build a bomb is totally on the orders of Richard Schrum." Schrum told Lampley that he had a brother in the Special Forces at Fort Bragg, NC, who would provide logistic support when the "New World Order" invasion came.[296]

The bomb, a mixture of homemade C-4, was supposed to tested at Elohim City.[297]

Whatever the reality of that case, it provides a unique insight into the characters and players of the white supremacist community of Southeastern Oklahoma—a community that drew to it like a magnet some of the key players of the Oklahoma City bombing conspiracy.

Led by the 71-year-old Millar, Elohim City (Hebrew for "City of God") is a 1,100-acre Christian Identity compound near Muldrow, Oklahoma. Founded in 1973 by the Canadian-born Mennonite, the community is home to approximately 90 residents, about half of whom are direct descendants of Millar.

Christian Identity adherents believe that white Anglo-Saxons, not Jews, are God's chosen people, being descendants of the 12 lost tribes of Israel, and that America, not Israel, is the Promised Land. This sanctified doctrine also holds that Jews are the spawn of Satan, and non-whites are "pre-Adamic," a sub-species.

Only whites are the "true sovereign citizens" of the Republic, and all others are "Fourteenth Amendment citizens"—the creation of an illegitimate "ZOG."

Believers of this odd mix of theology not only believe that the end times are near, but that a great messiah will arise to lead these "holy warriors" in a terrible final battle against the evil ZOG.

Those who monitor right-wing extremist groups say Millar is probably the most influential Christian Identity leader in the Great Plains.[298] As Millar explained it:

"We are opposed to governmental misuse of tax money.... We are opposed to some of the actions of government. We're not anti-government ... Our people are all self-employed, and we all pay taxes.... "We are racist," Millar said, "but we aren't anti-Semitic. I think it's better for races and cultures ... to have relationships within their own ethnic group. That doesn't mean isolationism, but it means separatism."[299]

Yet the group does maintain connections to white supremacist and neo-Nazi organizations, including WAR, the somewhat defunct CSA, and the violent but largely disbanded Order. The Christian Identity adherents also formed alliances with Richard Butler, Christian Identity "minister," and head of the Aryan Nations in Hayden Lake, Idaho. The Hayden Lake compound served as a nexus for white supremacist groups from all over the country, including the KKK, Posse Comitatus, William Pierce's National Alliance, and Robert Mathews' Order. It was Mathews' group, inspired by Pierce's *Turner Diaries*, that went on to commit a string of bank robberies, counterfeiting, bombings, and murder throughout the Mid- and Northwest in the 1980s.*

Amassing between $2 and $4 million from robberies and heists of armored cars, the group distributed the proceeds amongst the white supremacist movement. They also purchased land in northern Idaho for paramilitary training, but moved to northern Arkansas, linking up with the CSA when they found the harsh climate unsuitable for their purposes.

The Order's exploits came to an end in November, '84, when Mathews died in a shoot-out with police and federal agents on Whidby Island off the coast of Washington. It's members who managed to escape fled across the country, integrating themselves into different white supremacist groups, or went underground altogether.

Richard Lee Guthrie, Jr., son of a CIA employee, discharged from the Navy for painting a swastika on the side of a ship and threatening superiors, his childhood friend Peter K. Langan, and Shawn Kenny, went on to form the nucleus of a group known as the Midwest Bank Bandits. The group stole more than $250,000 from 22 banks between January, '94 and December, '95 in a spree that

---

* Mathews himself was the Northwest representative of William Pierce's National Alliance.

led them across Ohio, Wisconsin, Iowa, Nebraska, Kansas, and Missouri. The four-member group would often wear FBI jackets agents to taunt the Bureau, and create diversions to foil police, including leaving behind inert pipe-bombs to slow pursuit. The bandits even had a macabre sense of humor, wearing a Santa Claus suit during a hold-up around Christmas, and an Easter basket with a gold paint-ed pipe-bomb left inside a bank in Des Moines.

"Wild Bill" Guthrie also admitted to a West Virginia sheriff that he had helped Butler's Aryan Nations raise another quarter million dollars through fraud. Both Guthrie and Langan were regular visitors to the Hayden Lake com-pound.

The seeds for the mens' dalliance with the paramilitary extreme-right was sown in 1991, when Shawn Kenny, a friend of Langan and Guthrie, began dis-cussing their plans to further the "cause."

Interestingly, the Secret Service recruited Langan as an informant in August of 1993 to keep an eye on his friend Guthrie, who had made threats against the lives of Presidents Clinton and Bush. Langan was released from his Georgia jail cell (serving time for robbing a Pizza Hut with Guthrie) and set up in a house in Ohio, where he was to assist the Secret Service in locating his old friend. The deal soon went sour.

Secret Service Agent Dick Rathnell summed up the fiasco this way: "Our main interest was to find if there was an interest to harm the President or overthrow the government.... We didn't know they were these bank robbers."[300]

Langan went south on the Secret Service six weeks later, and soon located his old friend Guthrie. The two set themselves up in a safehouse in Pittsburg, Kansas, from which they were alleged to have launched their notorious crime spree.

In November, '94, Mark Thomas, the local Aryan Nations representative, unit-ed the two with others of their kind. Thomas' farm, located rather appropriately next to a toxic waste dump, has been the site of skinhead and neo-Nazi rallies such as White Pride Day and the annual Hitler Youth Festival, where participants enjoyed such wholesome activities as pagan rituals and cross-burnings.

Thomas introduced the pair to Pennsylvania native Scott Stedeford, a rock musician and artist, and Kevin McCarthy, bassist in a white-power band named "Day of the Sword." Thomas was instrumental in helping the men form an alliance which they would call the Aryan Republican Army (ARA).

Taking the moniker of "Commander Pedro," Langan became the group's leader. According to testimony provided by Kenny at Stedeford's trial, Langan boasted that the gang was modeled after The Order.

"Learn from Bob [Mathews]," Langan is heard saying on a home-made recruit-ment video. "Learn from his mistakes. Study your enemy. Study his methods."[301]

The Pennsylvania Posse Comitatus leader would also introduce Stedeford and McCarthy to Michael Brescia, a Philadelphia native and rock musician who would go on to form a speed metal band with McCarthy and Stedeford called "Cyanide." The rock 'n' roll bank robbers decided to recruit the 24-year-old La Salle University student after planning the heist of a large bank in Madison, Wisconsin, which the trio robbed on August 30, 1995.

The three men came to know "Grandpa Millar" at Elohim City courtesy of Thomas, and Brescia was soon engaged to Millar's granddaughter, Ester. Brescia wound up living at the reclusive compound for two years. It was there that he would meet his new roommate, Andreas Carl Strassmeir, the mysterious German who settled there in 1991. It was also at Elohim City that Brescia would meet Timothy McVeigh. As ATF informant Carol Howe recalled:

"Sometime before Christmas [of 1994] a lot of guys showed up at EC [Elohim City]. One that I recall was Tim [McVeigh], who I only knew as Tim Tuttle. He was there with a guy who used the name Fontaine, a person I now recognize as Mike Fortier."

Referring to McVeigh, she said, "I never even spoke to him. He was considered a 'good soldier' by the members of the ARA, but not a leader; he was just someone you sent out on jobs, because he was reliable." [302]

Were McVeigh and Nichols involved in bank robberies? Had the robberies financed the bombing? It was a question that has disturbed Nichols' ex-wife Lana Padilla, who discovered masks, nylon stockings, and wigs in her former spouse's storage locker. Nichols was known as a vehement critic of the banking system, had been on the losing end of a large credit card lawsuit, and had declared the Federal Reserve corrupt.

McVeigh himself sent his sister Jennifer three $100 bills, telling her they were the proceeds from a bank robbery. While there was no proof that the pair had actually participated, authorities would ponder the significance of the associations. As the *Gazette* writes:

A reliable source familiar with the investigation confirmed that admitted co-conspirator Michael Fortier told the FBI that ex-army buddy Tim McVeigh said in February 1995 that he (McVeigh) was going to Colorado to join "The Order." [303]

Interestingly, what is not known is just where McVeigh was on the days immediately before and immediately after 11 of the robberies.

It is known that Brescia, Strassmeir, and McVeigh became friends, attending gun shows, traveling the white supremacist circuit, and crashing high-school parties in Kansas, not far from Terry Nichols' house. Neighbors recalled seeing men who fit the general description of McVeigh and John Doe 2 at Nichols' Herrington home.

For his part, Strassmeir claims he'd "never been in Kansas," then admitted, "well, once, driving through." [304]

Catina Lawson's roommate, Lindsay Johnson, dated Brescia, and Lawson was close friends with McVeigh. Both she and Lawson recalled seeing Strassmeir, Brescia, McVeigh and Fortier at the Kansas parties around the Summer of '92. The young women allegedly referred to the handsome young Brescia as "Mike Breezy."

It is Brescia, some investigators claim, who is the mysterious John Doe 2 originally sought by the FBI. Bombing victim Glenn Wilburn, along with investigator J.D. Cash, learned of Brescia's relationship to Strassmeir and McVeigh after talking to people at Elohim City and others in the white supremacist underground. The family filed a $30 million lawsuit against McVeigh, which includes Strassmeir, and named Brescia as John Doe 2.

Robert Millar insists that Brescia, who is engaged to Millar's granddaughter, is not John Doe 2, but simply a "cleancut, college type boy." [305]

Yet several witnesses in Kansas claimed that Brescia closely matches the FBI's wanted sketch. Like John Doe 2, Brescia has a tattoo on his left arm. Curiously though, Brescia's tattoo is circular—a cross inside a wheel—an emblem associated with Aryan Nations. The tattoo seen by Mike Moroz and other witnesses on John Doe 2 more closely resembled a dragon, an anchor, or a snake. But then again, according to numerous witnesses, there is more than one John Doe 2.

While Brescia's connection to Elohim City centered around his relationship with Ester, it was Strassmeir who was his roommate. A German national, the 38-year-old Strassmeir is the son of Günter Strassmeir, former Parliamentary Secretary of State to German Chancellor Helmut Kohl. Strassmeir's uncle is in the German parliament, and his brother Alexander sits on the Berlin City Council. Like Langan, Strassmeir's father also reportedly has connections to the CIA.

Andreas served as a lieutenant in the German Panzer Grenadiers (the equivalent of our Special Forces), had formal military intelligence training, and did a stint as a liaison officer with the Welsh Guards. He told the *London Sunday Telegraph* that part of his work was to detect infiltration by Warsaw Pact agents, and then feed them disinformation. "If we caught a guy, we'd offer him amnesty. We'd turn him and use him to feed false information back to the Warsaw Pact." [306] While Strassmeir would not admit it, it is reported that he is an agent for the German national anti-terrorist police, the GSG-9.*

"Andy the German," as he became known, arrived in the U.S. in May of 1991, without being documented by the INS (Immigration and Naturalization

---

* It may be telling that part of Strassmeir's training involved feeding people disinformation.

Service), and lived on a credit card provided by sources unknown. He soon became Elohim City's Director of Security.[307]

According to Strassmeir, his path crossed McVeigh's at a Tulsa gun show in April, '93. Strassmeir stopped by McVeigh's table and bought a few military souvenirs and discussed events at Waco. He then gave McVeigh his card bearing the inscription "Elohim City." In an interview in *Soldier of Fortune*, Strassmeir professed never to heard of McVeigh, though he later recanted his story for the *Telegraph*. "I met the guy once at a gun show," he said. "We spoke for five minutes, that's all."[308]

It would seem the relationship goes deeper than that. Strassmeir reportedly met McVeigh again at the first anniversary of the Waco massacre in April, '94. According to journalist William Jasper, sources close to the investigation revealed that McVeigh visited Elohim City on at least 20 occasions. Traffic records show McVeigh was stopped for speeding on October 12, 1993, two miles north of Cederville, Arkansas, less than 10 miles from Elohim City, on a remote road leading to the compound. ATF informant Carol Howe also recalled seeing McVeigh and Fortier at Elohim City during the winter of '94.

Yet possibly the most revealing connection surfaced in the form of two phone calls, one placed by McVeigh from the Imperial Motel in Kingman, Arizona to Strassmeir on April 5, just two weeks before the bombing and minutes after McVeigh allegedly called Junction City to reserve the Ryder truck. According to Millar's daughter-in-law Joan, who answered the phone, the caller asked to speak to "Andy." Andy wasn't in. McVeigh left a message saying, "Tell Andy I'll be coming through."

Robert Millar, Elohim City's "spiritual leader," claimed ignorance of McVeigh or the phone call.[*] He later recanted his story.

Then one day before the bombing, McVeigh called Strassmeir's U.S. attorney, Kirk Lyons, looking for Andy. Not finding him there, he engaged Lyons's assistant, Dave Holloway, in a 15-minute conversation about Waco, Lyons claims, and the need to "send a message to the government." It seemed McVeigh also needed to send a message to Strassmeir.

For his part Strassmeir claims McVeigh never visited Elohim City. "I don't know why McVeigh was trying to contact me," he said.

Catina Lawson, who was close friends with McVeigh for two years, remembers seeing Strassmeir at the Junction City parties. "He was just someone you'd see every once in a while," said Lawson, who, along with friends, would meet and party with the soldiers from nearby Fort Riley. "He was tall, skinny and pale, with

---

* Around the same time, the caller telephoned the National Alliance office in Arizona. The National Alliance is the organization formed by William Pierce, who wrote *The Turner Diaries*.

crooked teeth and sunken eyes surrounded by dark circles. And he had this accent...." [309]

Larry Wild and his wife Kathy also recall seeing Strassmeir on one of their fishing trips to Cameron Springs Lake, near Fort Riley. The Wilds remember seeing Strassmeir with two other men with an old Ryder truck one week before the bombing. Just who those two other men were they couldn't say. Wild did recall speaking with Strassmeir though. "I said, 'Your dialect is really different. Are you a soldier?' He said, 'No.' I said, 'Do you work for the government?' He just kind of laughed."

Yet still more witnesses recall seeing the two men together. At least five dancers recall seeing McVeigh, Nichols, Brescia, and Strassmeir at Lady Godiva's, a strip joint in Tulsa, which the men visited on April 8, 1995. In an interview with CBC's Trish Wood, the dancers, who wish to remain anonymous, were "positive" of Strassmeir and McVeigh's presence just eleven days before the bombing:

Wood: You saw this man in here?
Unidentified: Yes.
Wood: And how do you remember? What makes you remember seeing him in here that night?
Unidentified: From one of the girls. I just heard her say something about a couple of guys, there were a couple of weird guys, she wanted somebody to go sit with them.

As discussed earlier, McVeigh bragged to one of the girls that "something big" was going to happen. "On April 19, 1995, you'll remember me for the rest of your life," McVeigh said.[310]

Also present that night was an old, faded Ryder truck, seen by the bouncer. The truck appeared to be privately-owned, adding further proof that at least two trucks were used in the bombing. It was this truck seen by witnesses at Geary State Park, several days before authorities allege that McVeigh rented his. J.D. Cash speculates that McVeigh flew to Fort Smith from his motel room in Kingman on April 7 to pick up the truck and meet his comrades, then the men stopped by Tulsa on their way back to Kansas.

If they stopped by Tulsa, maybe it was to check out the Indian Territory Gun Show. It also might have been to meet Dennis Mahon. The WAR official, National Socialist Alliance (NSA) leader, and former KKK Imperial Grand Dragon traveled frequently to the reclusive compound where he kept a trailer, "to visit and fellowship and do some target shooting and military maneuvers," he said. Mahon was close friends with Brescia and Strassmeir, both of whom he "loved like brothers." [311]

In what may seem like an even more bizarre twist, Mahon claims he was funded by the Iraqis during the Gulf War. Like Order leader Robert Mathews, who was reportedly offered funding by the Syrians, Mahon received $100 a month, for a total of $4,800, from the Iraqis to stir up opposition to the Bush/UN-imposed sanctions. Mahon, operator of the Dial-a-Racist hot line, also produced several videotapes which he distributed to public access stations, expressing his dissenting view on the U.S. policy.[312]

Mahon started receiving Iraqi funds shortly after he began holding anti-war rallies, he said. "It's coming from the same zip code where the Iraqi Embassy is, but they don't say it's from the Iraqi Embassy."[313]

Jeff Steinberg, an investigator for the LaRouche Foundation, says such a scenario is not at all unusual. "This kind of stuff happened all the time," says Steinberg. "In the '70s, they had people whose job it was to show up at every sort of left-wing rally."

Yet why would the Iraqis give money to an avowed white supremacist like Mahon? "Hatred of the Jews," says Steinberg. "Some low-level person at the embassy gives it out to these guys, and you'd be surprised at who they give it to—they're not that bright."[314]

In McVeigh's Petition for Writ of Mandamus, filed one week before McVeigh's trial, Stephen Jones made note of the fact that three members of the American Agricultural Movement also met with Iraqi officials. Their purpose was to work with the Iraqis to negotiate a peaceful withdraw from Kuwait. "We wanted to get a dialogue going and stop a shooting war," said one member. "As Americans, that's what we tried to do."[315]

Yet it seemed the meeting between the farmers and the Iraqi ambassador wasn't the only meeting that took place. Jones stated that Terry Nichols, who he refers to only as "Suspect I," made calls to two Kansas-based Posse Comitatus members—David Oliphant and Buddy Snead. Like Nichols, Snead is married to a Filipino woman. It is not known whether he met her through the same mail-order bride service as Nichols.*

A CIA source contacted by Jones indicated that two members of the Posse Comitatus (it is not known who) visited with an Iraqi diplomat in New York City around the same general time. While the author was unable to locate these two individuals to confirm the story, it is possible they met with the diplomat to express their horror over Bush's "Desert Massacre."

It is also possible that the Iraqis viewed the meeting as an opportunity to strengthen their ties to the white supremacist movement. As will be seen, collab-

---

* Although Jones only refers to "Suspect I," it is well-known that he is referring to Nichols, because he says he was "A subject of the FBI and Grand Jury investigation." There were only two people investigated by the Federal Grand Jury: Timothy McVeigh and Terry Nichols.

oration between Arab states, Middle-East terrorists, and neo-Nazis is a long and well-documented one.

Unfortunately for Dennis Mahon, the Iraqis severed their ties with him after the bombing. "They cut me off, a month after the bombing—bastards!"[316]

It is also likely that Mahon, who traveled to Germany to recruit young skinheads for the KKK, may have met up with Michael Kühnen. A prominent neo-Nazi, Kühnen formed the Anti-Zionist League, which preached hatred of Jews, and sought to form a common bond between Nazis and their Arab brethren. Kühnen also negotiated with the Iraqis, providing them with 200 German, American and British skinheads to fight alongside Iraqi troops. There is reportedly a videotape of these storm troopers in S.S. uniforms being greeted by Iraqi Information Minister Abdel Lateef Jassem.[317]

Kühnen's successor, a name named Hubner, has connections to Kirk Lyons, Andreas Strassmeir's North Carolina-based attorney. Lyons also spoke with Hubner at meetings of the group "Deutsche Alternative." Like Mahon, Lyons traveled the German white supremacist circuit. Strassmeir and Mahon were close friends, until Mahon and his brother Dennis reportedly called Germany with orders to kill Strassmeir.

Another friend of Mahon's is Gary Lauck of Lincoln, Nebraska. The leader of the neo-Nazi National Socialist Worker's Party, Lauck wrote a 20-page manifesto entitled, "Strategy, Propaganda and Organization," about integrating worldwide extremist groups into a tight network, and "military education with terrorist aims." Lauck has reportedly had frequent contact with Arab terrorist groups according to McVeigh's defense counsel.

Finally, there is the Libyan government, widely reported to have funded both the Irish Republican Army (IRA) and U.S. citizens, including a Chicago street gang called the El Rukns—convicted of conspiracy to commit terrorist acts throughout the U.S.

"Upon hearing that Louis Farrakhan had received $5 million from the Libyan government, the leader of the El Rukns actively sought sponsorship from Libya in exchange to an in-kind amount of money. Members of the El Rukns actually traveled to Libya to meet with military official of the Libyan government."*

Farrakhan, the leader of the Nation of Islam (NOI, or "Black Muslims"), carries forth a unique historical precedent. His predecessor, Elijah Muhammad,

---

* The El Rukn case is documented in the *Federal Reporter in Unites States v. McAnderson*, 914 F. 2d 934 (7th Cir. 1990). "The El Rukns sought to impress the Libyans and to demonstrate the depth of their commitment by discussing specific terrorist acts, among them destroying a government building, planting a bomb, blowing up an airplane, and

invited American Nazi Party leader George Lincoln Rockwell to address an NOI rally on June 25, 1961 in Washington, D.C. There is a photo of Rockwell's Nazis in full regalia (including Swastika armbands) seated in the front row, with the Black Muslims seated directly behind them.[318]

Rockwell appeared at an NOI rally in Chicago one year later, where he announced, "Elijah Muhammad is to the so-called Negro what Adolph Hitler was to the German people...."

In September, 1985, the NOI invited Tom Metzger, former Grand Dragon of the KKK and current leader of WAR to its forum in Ingelwood, California, and accepted a small financial contribution from the notorious white supremacist. Metzger declared that his alliance with the NOI was a "logical one: They want their territory and that's exactly what we want for them and for ourselves. They speak against the Jews and the oppressors in Washington."[319]

It therefore comes as no surprise that Libya funded the NOI to the tune of $5 million dollars. The motive behind Arab funding of Western racist and dissident groups was—and is—to forment revolution and destabilize the "Great Satan." Just as Libyan President Muammar al-Qaddafi serves as the inspiration behind many militant Black Muslims, so the IRA served as the spiritual inspiration behind the Aryan Republican Army, the group founded by Richard Guthrie and Peter Langan, which included Michael Brescia.

As Stephen Jones eloquently states, "These people are targeted because their ideological compass is preset against the Federal Government.... Although the white supremacist community are diametrically opposed to that of Black Muslims, it is a well known fact that both share a common hatred for the Federal Government."

When the ARA was eventually disbanded, the FBI discovered an IRA terrorist manual called the "Green Book," literature on Ireland, Gaelic language tapes, Semtex explosives, a shoulder-fired rocket launcher, and 11 pipe bombs.[320] Semtex is normally used by Mid-East terrorists, usually being supplied by Russia, China and North Korea.

It seems the connection goes even deeper. Dennis Mahon claims he advised the IRA, encouraging them to murder "top British officers and police officials" but avoid killing civilians. That statement ties-in to others Mahon has made, including the idea of blowing up the Oklahoma Federal Building at night, when no one was around, and other methods which "are legitimate to save your nation."

It seems the IRA may have returned the favor. According to Carol Howe, the outlawed Irish resistance group supplied the detonator used in the Oklahoma

---

simply committing a wanton 'killing here and a killing there' to get the Libyans' attention. Eventually, the leader of the El Rukns decided that the Libyans would only be impressed by the use of powerful explosives." (Jones, Writ of Mandamus, p. 85.)

City bombing. The author is not quite sure why the bombers would need to go to the IRA for a detonator, or exactly how such a connection would be arranged, but it seems rather dubious. Sinn Fein (the political arm of the IRA) President Gerry Adams called the claim "preposterous rubbish." *

It may seem even more preposterous in light of the fact that Adams had won the political favoritism of President Clinton, having been the guest of honor at a recent White House reception.

Yet Howe alleged that Andreas Strassmeir was the key link between the ARA and the IRA. Interestingly, the *Dublin Sunday Times* reported on July 13, 1997 that Strassmeir has indeed associated with Sinn Fein:

> Strassmeir moved to Dublin last February and is living in an apartment in the city owned by George Maybury, general secretary of the association of Garda Sergeants and Inspectors. He has been working on construction sites and has attended Sinn Fein meetings and social events.[321]

Furthermore, federal informant Cary Gagan, who met with Jones after the bombing, told the author he met with an IRA bomb expert while in Mexico City, who instructed him on the use of timers. Gagan claims to have been deeply immersed in the Middle Eastern cell involved in the bombing.

When Fox News reporter Rita Cosby asked Robert Millar if there was any Middle Eastern connection to Elohim City, he answered, "No, not that I can even dream of." Strassmeir likewise denied any Middle Eastern connection to the bombing in an interview with the author.[322] As of this writing, former ABC 20/20 invetigator Roger Charles was checking a lead that Middle Eastern individuals were indeed trained at Elohim City. It has not yet been confirmed.

Just what Andreas Strassmeir was doing in the U.S. is not altogether clear. In a five-part interview in the *Telegraph*, Strassmeir said that he came to the U.S. in 1989 to work on a "special assignment" for the Justice Department. "I discussed the job when I was in Washington. I was hoping to work for the operations section of the DEA," he explained. "It never worked out."

The former German intelligence officer was recommended for these positions by Vincent Petruskie, a retired U.S. Air Force colonel. Strassmeir told attorney Mike Johnston, who flew to Berlin to interview him, that Petruskie is "a former CIA guy who my father had known since he (Petruskie) was stationed in Berlin during the Cold War." In an interview with *New American* editor William Jasper,

---

* British officials no doubt took the implications seriously. Jones had spent considerable time consulting with British explosives experts who planned to testify on behalf of the defense, as well as officials from MI5, Britain's domestic intelligence service and even an unnamed IRA member. (Associated Press, 3/30/97.)

Petruski denied any CIA connections:

As for the CIA connection, "That's totally wrong," insisted Petruskie. "I'm a retired Air Force officer, that's all." According to Petruskie, he was a special agent for the Air Force Office of Special Investigation (OSI), and retired as a colonel after serving from 1954 to 1975. Was he a friend of Andreas' father? "I've never met his father; we've only spoken over the phone."

How had Petruskie come to know the younger Strassmeir? Andreas arrived in the late 1980s with some other German lads for the reenactment of the Battle of Gettysburg. The German visitors had authentic period uniforms, rifles, bayonets, etc. and an amazingly detailed knowledge of the battle. But they apparently had not done their homework concerning economic realities of contemporary America and so were short of cash for living accommodations and had no credit cards with which to rent a vehicle. That is when a mutual friend put them in touch with Petruskie, who put them up for a while at his home.

Strassmeir was "a mixed-up kid, a very immature 34-year-old when he came over here," recalled Petruskie. "Andy wanted to work for the U.S. government—DEA, Justice—undercover. [He] thought his background with military and German government would help. I explained he'd need a green card, education, and set him down with some people in Washington who explained that it wasn't that simple. I think he went down to South Carolina and then to Texas to go to school." [323]

In an interview with the *Oklahoma Gazette,* Petruski once again attempted to distance himself from Strassmeir. "This kid is what we would call a putz," he said. An interesting description for a former intelligence officer and lieutenant in the elite Panzer Grenadiers.[324]

Petruski also claims that Strassmeir's job with the DEA "fell through." Is one seriously supposed to accept the premise that a man with Strassmeir's background, influence, and connections came to the U.S. on the off-chance of finding a job with the DEA? That he traveled all this way to run around playing toy soldier for a couple days? And that Petruski just "happened" to meet him at a battle reenactment at Gettysburg?

More likely, Gettysburg was a necessary cover-story to infiltrate Strassmeir into the country. Appearing to be a military enthusiast makes it easier to infiltrate the extreme right. And Petruski's tale about his DEA job falling through is a "limited hang-out," just enough information revealed to satisfy nosy journalists, with enough disinformation mixed in to steer them away from "unapproved" areas. And while Petruski said that Strassmeir never got a job with the DEA, he never said he didn't get a job with the ATF, FBI, or CIA. Curiously, when the FBI queried various law-enforcement and intelligence agencies to determine if Strassmeir was a cooperating witness or confidential informant, only the CIA reported that it held any records on him. These records were turned over to prosecutors, but never made available to McVeigh's defense team despite a court order compelling their disclosure.

With his cover-story firmly in place, Strassmeir then drifted into far-right militant circles, stopping long enough to pick an ordinary job as a computer salesman to further enhance his image as an innocent drifter.

"Andy the German" was now ready to infiltrate the neo-Nazi cliques of the extreme right. With his German background and accent, it was easy to convince white supremacists of his legitimacy. In 1991 he settled in Elohim City, where he established himself as Chief of Security and weapons training.

According to a report from the Oklahoma State Bureau of Investigation (OSBI), Strassmeir trained platoon-sized groups consisting of 30 to 40 individuals from throughout the U.S. every three months at the reclusive compound. According to a law enforcement source interviewed by the *McCurtain Gazette,* they consisted primarily of members from the Aryan Nations, and included Timothy McVeigh.[325] As the *Gazette* reported:

> "Strassmeir went out and replaced all our deer rifles with assault weapons," said [resident Zara] Patterson. "Next, he wanted us to start doing illegal stuff ... a lot of illegal stuff. I kept telling Andy that we were defensive here, and we didn't want any problems from the law. During the mid-'80s, we had a standoff with the Feds. I told him to keep us out of trouble." [326]

Was Strassmeir attempting to infiltrate Elohim City? "If the agent penetrates the group," Strassmeir said in an interview with the author, "the first thing they do is try to sell them weapons." When asked if that wasn't exactly what he did, he replied, "I just advised them about weapons, as an experienced soldier. That's what I did for years and years. I was an infantry man—I just gave advice. But, I always obeyed the law." He then admitted that he "didn't know the law. I'd have to consult my lawyer."

According to information obtained by the *Telegraph,* Strassmeir infiltrated the Texas Light Infantry militia between 1988 and 1989, and set up some illegal gun purchases. They soon suspected that Strassmeir was a ATF informant. When some members followed him to a federal building one night, they observed him entering it using the building's combination key-pad.*

ATF agent Angela Finley-Graham, the agent who supervised ATF informant Carol Howe, had aerial surveillance photos of Strassmeir with an assault weapon, and photos of concrete bunkers at Elohim City. In fact, in 1992, some 960 yards

---

* Cases involving violence or planned violence by militias from around the U.S. show a recurring theme of government penetration and infiltration of militia groups. For example,

of concrete were transported to the compound, presumably for bunkers and weapons storage facilities.

Law enforcement officials also received reports that the compound was believed to be generating income through the sale of illegal drugs. A source I spoke with who is familiar with the community told me that Bruce Millar, Robert Millar's son, was supposedly "strung out" on methamphetamines. Speed is a highly popular drug among the neo-Nazi crowd, and was in fact invented by the Nazis during WWII to bolster the fighting ability of their troops.

Several weeks before the bombing, the Tulsa office of the ATF put out a BOLO (Be On The Lookout For) on Strassmeir, which was transmitted to the Oklahoma Highway Patrol (OHP).

ANDREAS STRASSMEIR, W/M, 5/17/59, heavy German accent. Black Hair/Blue Eyes. 1" scar on chin, wears cammo fatigues. Possible Tennessee driver's license. Came to USA in 5/91, passport was good until 8/91. He never left the country. INS says he does not have an extension of his VISA. Possibly in blue Chevy, late model, tag BXH 346 (not on file), usually has someone driving him. Carries a .45 auto pistol at all times. He is an illegal alien, ATF wants to be notified if he is stopped and has the gun on him. They will file the charges. Contact: Agent Angela Finley, ATF. Office: 918-581-7731 (or) Pager: 918-672-2755.

What's odd is that the BOLO was for an INS violation, not exactly the jurisdiction of the ATF. Moreover, according to a Tulsa police intelligence source, the INS was told not to make any effort to focus on visa violations due to manpower shortages.

The *McCurtain Gazette*, which uncovered the BOLO, thinks it was put out by the ATF to provide cover for Strassmeir—an aid for his extraction from Elohim City. The OHP subsequently typed up the BOLO, which was eventually "leaked" to various sources, including the residents of the rural community. According to Glenn Wilburn, the BOLO was circulated with the stipulation that Strassmeir not be arrested.*

Curiously, when Finley attempted to get a warrant for Strassmeir's arrest, she was stonewalled by the INS. A Tulsa police intelligence source told me that Finley "was out to get the whole place." This fact was confirmed by information obtained by McVeigh's defense counsel during discovery.[327] This is extremely interesting in light of the fact that the INS and ATF had planned a joint raid on

---

testimony in the Muskogee bombing case showed that the FBI was literally paying the operating expenses, including the phone bills for the Tri-State Militia.

* BATF regional director Lester Martz denies that the BOLO was put out by the BATF.

the compound—a plan which suddenly came to a halt in late February of '95.*
As one INS memo stated:

> Investigation pending—no arrest or warrent as of yet—Northeastern Oklahoma—
> requested participation. Raid—next month.

It seems the ATF and INS weren't the only ones interested in Elohim City. As
a report of Finley-Graham's dated February 28 states:

> On 22 February 1995, this agent met with OHP Trooper Ken Stafford to exchange
> certain information regarding this investigation. Trooper Stafford indicated that the
> FBI also had an ongoing investigation regarding Elhim City. On this same date,
> RAC David Roberts met with the United Sates Attorney for the Northern Judicial
> district of Oklahoma, Steve Lewis, to discuss this investigation.
> On February 23, 1995 RAC David Roberts was contacted by FBI supervisor,
> Marty Webber, who stated that FBI Special Agent in charge, Bob Ricks, would be
> available during the week of February 27 through March 3, 1995 to meet with ATF
> Special Agent in Charge, Lester Martz. RAC roberts then contacted Dallas
> Division to request SAC Martz meet with SAC Ricks to discuss the investigation
> of Elohim City.

As an interesting historical precedent, [former] FBI agent James Rodgers had
developed a massive FBI raid on Elohim city in 1988, but it was called off for reasons that have never been made clear.

One month before the bombing Howe got "fed up" with Elohim City and the
ATF's attitude towards the investigation. "Angie hadn't made any arrests either,"
Howe told the *Gazette*, "and that was frustrating, so I quit going out there ... until
after the building got blown up!"[328] (Howe's allegations of federal malfeasance
dovetailed with those of federal informant Cary Gagan, who was inside the
Middle Eastern cell tied to the bombing.)

Three days after the bombing, the ATF's Washington headquarters pulled the
Tulsa office off the case, and the FBI requested them to turn over all their files on
Elohim City.

The question is, just who was Strassmeir reporting to? The Tulsa ATF office,
which has jurisdiction over Elohim City, may not have been informed if
Strassmeir were reporting to a higher authority, a different agency, or was a confidential informant on a national level.

Strassmeir's cover-story that his Justice Department job "never worked out"

---

* Former FBI agent James Rodgers had developed a massive FBI raid on Elohim City in
  1988 but it was called off for reasons that have never been clear.

also smacks of McVeigh's story that his tryout for the Special Forces didn't work out due to a "blister." Perhaps Strassmeir—a seven-year German Army veteran— failed his indoctrination due to a nosebleed.

In spite of his vehement denials, Strassmeir practically admitted to the *Telegraph* that he was an undercover agent. "The right-wing in the U.S. is incredibly easy to penetrate if you know how to talk to them," he told the *Telegraph*. "Of course it's easier for a foreigner with an accent; nobody would ever suspect a German of working for the Federal Government."

This certainly appears to be no ordinary slip of the tongue. How would Strassmeir know the extreme-right is "incredibly easy to penetrate" unless he had penetrated them? His statement that "nobody would ever suspect a German" sounds like an admission that he was doing so.

On February 28, 1992 Strassmeir was arrested and his car impounded by the OHP for driving without a license. When the police opened his briefcase, they found a number of documents, including some in German. There were statements from foreign bank accounts, false identity papers, and a copy of *The Terrorist Handbook.*

According to the tow-truck driver, Kenny Pence, Strassmeir soon brought heavy pressure to bear. "Boy, we caught hell over that one," he said. "The phone calls came in from the State Department, the Governor's office, and someone called and said he had diplomatic immunity...." [329]

According to Strassmeir, the entirety of the story amounts to a pair of cops who were out to harass him and his friend Peter Ward (recall that Howe identified Ward as John Doe #1). Interestingly, federal prosecutors filed a motion requesting that Judge Matsch block efforts by McVeigh's defense team who was seeking government files on Strassmeir's activities. It was eventually revealed to Jones through discovery that Strassmeir held a tourist Visa with the designation "A O." Neither Jones nor Ambrose Evans-Pritchard, who reported extensively on Strassmeir, could learn what the designation meant. The INS denied any knowledge of its meaning. Curiously, the entries, which appeared on all of Strassmeir's INS files, suddenly vanished in March, 1996. Somebody had erased them.

All told, these are strange circumstances for a former German intelligence officer—the politically well-connected son to a top aide in Chancellor Helmut Kohl's government. It seems unlikely that this ordinary "computer salesman" and "neo-Nazi" with diplomatic immunity, backed up by the State Department and the Justice Department, brought federal pressure to bear in order to have a minor traffic violation cleared.

More likely, Strassmeir was in danger of having his cover blown by unsuspecting law enforcement agents. The situation had to be corrected, and quickly.

After the bombing, with the increasing attention of investigators, and his cover almost blown, Strassmeir fled to Germany, taking a circuitous route through Mexico and Paris—a route commonly used by spies. Strassmeir's attorney, Kirk Lyons, detailed his client's escape, stating that it was aided by Germany's vaunted counter-terrorism unit, GSG-9, the equivalent of our Delta Force. Curious that GSG-9 would assist in Strassmeir's retreat. Were they helping one of their own? [330]

To help maintain his cover, the Justice Department questioned Strassmeir in North Carolina at his attorney's office, then called him in Berlin to ask about his alleged ties to McVeigh. "The FBI asked where I was on the day of the bombing," he told the *Telegraph*. "They wanted to help debunk the rumors spread about me." *

Why the FBI would be in the business of debunking rumors, unless it is about them, is unclear. In this case, since any ties between Strassmeir and the Justice Department would lead directly back to the them, it seems that is exactly what they are trying to do. **

If Strassmeir had any ties to McVeigh, or to McVeigh's companions, or to those who had planned the 1983 bombing of the Murrah Building, the Justice Department should have served him with a Grand Jury subpoena or a warrant. Yet all the FBI did was call Strassmeir on the phone to "debunk the rumors" spread about him.

As one law enforcement officer told the *McCurtain Gazette*, "We found the axle from the truck that led to Junction City and McVeigh. Our Highway Patrolman arrested McVeigh. And that arrest led to Terry Nichols and Mike Fortier. Since then, nothing in this investigation has accomplished anything. But we're told by the Bureau that Strassmeir and his buddies are not important. Bullshit!" [331]

The *Gazette* also uncovered an intelligence bulletin issued by the Diplomatic Security Division, Counter Terrorism Unit, of the Department of State on March 18, 1996 concerning Strassmeir's alleged criminal activities in the U.S.

> The cable states that Strassmeir overstayed his visa in 1991 and was known to have been the militia training officer for a white separatist group called WAR.
>
> Quoting the cable, "He [Strassmeir] has been the subject of several investigations for purchasing weapons, and making the weapons fire on full automatic. Strassmeir should not be allowed to return to the U.S."

---

* The FBI didn't go to any great lengths to question Strassmeir, nor his roommate Michael Brescia. Months after the bombing, the FBI placed a leisurely call to Strassmeir's home in Berlin. They made no attempt to question or arrest Brescia.

** When Middle Eastern suspect Hussain al-Hussaini came under scrutiny by KFOR and other investigators for his role in the bombing, the FBI "debunked" the "rumors" about him, too. Was he also an agent?

Yet this cable makes it appear as though the FBI didn't know anything about Strassmeir—who was apparently under the protection of the State Department. Was this another cover ploy to protect their informant, or was Strassmeir working for the ATF, who weren't communicating with the FBI? If so, it would subsume that the ATF's Washington office didn't inform the Tulsa office about Strassmeir (or so we are led to believe).

Interestingly, the FBI would claim they weren't aware of Carol Howe's status as an informant either. During her July, 1997 trial (the result of trumped up charges by the so-called Justice Department), FBI agent Pete Rickel told the jury that he spoke to Howe in the Spring of 1996, when she requested protection, complaining that her cover had been blown. "We were interested to see if there might be any further information we could gather about activities involving people at Elohim City who may have been connected with the bombing," said Rickel. Yet the agent insisted he had no idea of who Howe really was when the FBI raided her home in December, '96.

ATF agent Angela Finley-Graham likewise claimed that she was unaware that an FBI raid was planned on Howe's home. Yet as the *McCurtain Gazette* reported, this premise was destroyed when FBI Special Agent Chris Peters took the stand:

> After explaining his role in the raid on the Howe residence, Peters was asked by defense attorney Clark Brewster during cross-examination who he was married to. "Angela [Finley] Graham," Peters replied.[332]

Strassmeir's own cover would finally be blown when the *Gazette* reported on July 14, 1996, that "a highly-placed source at the FBI has confirmed that Andreas Carl Strassmeir was a paid government informant sent by the Bureau of Alcohol, Tobacco and Firearms to infiltrate Elohim City...."[333]

For his part, Strassmeir claims he was at work repairing a fence near Elohim City on April 19. Yet Strassmeir hasn't exactly held tight to his story. According to Glenn Wilburn, who has intensively investigated the connection, Strassmeir claimed he stopped working when it started to rain, then went home and watched the bombing on TV. When Wilburn checked the weather reports for the area that day, he found that it hadn't begun to rain until much later. Strassmeir then claimed the farmer he was working for was George Eaton, a friend of the murdered Mueller family. Later, according to Wilburn, Strassmeir stated that he couldn't recall exactly what he was doing until he talked to his attorney, Kirk Lyons.

"Andy has been damaged," exclaimed Lyons, angrily refuting the allegations against his client. "Anybody who puts out the lie that he was linked to the Oklahoma bombing in any way is going to pay for it."[334]

Lyons claims his client had been dragged into the conspiracy by McVeigh's defense team—a ploy, he said, to muddy the waters by painting a vast conspiracy involving neo-Nazis in Europe and terrorists in the Mideast. "I call it the Space Alien Elvis Presley theory, and it's been fueled by nut cases and conspiracy theorists."

Lyons himself is no nut case, merely a hardcore racist and neo-Nazi. The simple "country lawyer" married the sister of a prominent member of The Order. The ceremony was performed by Aryan Nations "pastor" Richard Butler at the group's compound in Hayden Lake.

At the 1988 Aryan Nations World Congress, Lyons suggested forming an ACLU of sorts for the extreme-right, and attended the annual event in Hayden Lake as Louis Beam's representative. Not that Lyons was desperate for clients. He happily defended the Confederate Hammer Skinheads of Dallas, the National Socialist Skinheads of Houston, the White Vikings of Chicago, and WAR leader Tom Metzger, who was accused of inciting the murder of a black student from Ethiopia. Lyons also defended Holocaust revisionist Ernst Zündel, who claimed that Nazi gas cjambers were a Jewish invention, and other so-called "prisoners of conscience."[335]

Lyons was also the guest of honor at the British Nationalist Party in London, where he applauded the Party's stance on white power, and like William Pierce, predicted a future race war. The erudite, ever-socially conscious attorney was also quick to defend Louis Beam, the Texas Grand Dragon of the Ku Klux Klan. Beam fled to Mexico after being indicted for conspiracy to overthrow the government. As discussed, Beam was charged with harassing Vietnamese fishermen along the coast of Texas.[336]

Interestingly, when Terry Reed was in Guadalajara on behalf of the CIA, working with Oliver North's "Enterprise," Beam mysteriously showed up as his neighbor. With the help of Lyons, Beam was acquitted after his wife shot and killed a Mexican Federalé.

Lyons has likewise vehemently defended Strassmeir's role in the bombing, and claims he is not a government agent. Interestingly, Lyons arranged Strassmeir's stays in Knoxville, Houston, Elohim City, and even Lyons' own home in North Carolina.

One thing that can be deduced from all this is that Strassmeir and Lyons aren't very good liars.

According to Stephen Jones, Dennis Mahon made statements to the effect of, "If a person wanted to know about the bombing, then they should talk with Andy Strassmeir because he knows everything."

For his part, Strassmeir claims he's not a government agent. In his *Telegraph* interview, he states, "I've never worked for any U.S. government agency, and I've not been involved in any intelligence operation since my discharge from the German army in 1988. This family [the Wilburns] is on a fishing expedition."

Yet in the very same article, Strassmeir admits that the bombing was the result of a government sting gone bad—a sting involving agents of the ATF. Considering the revealing nature of Strassmeir's information, the article, entitled "Did Agents Bungle U.S. Terror Bomb?" might just as well have been called

"Thank You, Andy." As Strassmeir states:

> "The ATF had an informant inside this operation. They had advance warning and they
> bungled it," he said. "What they should have done is make an arrest while the bomb
> was still being made instead of waiting till the last moment for a publicity stunt."
>
> Asked if he thought the alleged informant would ever speak out, he replied with
> passion: "How can he? What happens if it was a sting operation from the very
> beginning? What happens if it comes out that the plant was a provocateur? What
> if he talked and manipulated the others into it? What then? The country couldn't
> handle it. The relatives of the victims are going to go crazy, and he's going to be held
> responsible for the murder of 168 people? Of course the informant can't come for-
> ward. He's scared shitless right now." Before and after this outburst he kept repeat-
> ing that he was not making veiled references to himself.[337]

When I interviewed Strassmeir, he insisted that he had been quoted out of
context. That statement, he claimed, was made to him by a former ATF agent.
"He made some hints that the ATF probably knew that this was coming down,"
said Strassmeir. The source, he said, was "pretty reliable," although he was quick
to qualify it by stating that he wasn't certain of the information.*

Referring to the sting, he said, "What kind of gives me a bad taste, is that all
the ATF agents were apparently not in the office during the blast, all of them."
As to just what the sting involved, Strassmeir claimed he didn't know. But regarding John Doe 2, he said, "For some reason they don't look for this guy anymore.
That, for some reason, I think is very strange."[338]

If Strassmeir was involved in a sting operation, it may have been to stop the
flow of Nazi propaganda emanating from the U.S. Such influences have made
their presence felt in an unsettling way in Germany in recent years. It is likely that
the FBI requested the assistance of the Bundeskriminalamt (BKA), the German
FBI, and the Bundesnachrichtendienst (BND), the German CIA, to help gather
intelligence on such groups as Michael Kühnen's Anti-Zionist League, and their
connections to both Arabs and American neo-Nazis.

FBI Director Louis Freeh had announced a joint U.S.-German intelligence
gathering operation on neo-Nazi groups as far back as 1993. Freeh pledged to
work alongside German law-enforcement to stem the spread of Nazism emanating from the United States.

---

* "When *The New American* asked Evans-Pritchard if he believed Strassmeir was referring to himself when speaking in the third person of the "informant," he replied, 'Of
course, there's no doubt that is exactly what he meant to convey. He was stating it as
plainly as he could without admitting criminal culpability on his own part." (William
Jasper, "Elohim, Terror and Truth," *The New American*, 3/31/97.)

On April 20, 1995, the American National Socialist Worker's Party announced that the Secret Service and ATF had been investigating Gary Lauck, leader of the domestic NSDAP/AO. Lauck, who publishes the neo-Nazi newsletter *N.S. Kampruf,* had been a major influence in Germany and was an object of concern among German authorities. (German sedition laws forbid the publication of Nazi literature.)[339]

It seems that certain information provided by Strassmeir resulted in Lauck's arrest. With Strassmeir's help, the "Farm Belt Fuhrer" was arrested in Copenhagen and extradited to Hamburg. The arrest coincided with major raids by German police of NSDAP/AO cells all over Germany.

Lauck wasn't the only one beckoning young Germans to join the white supremacist movement. Research conducted by McVeigh's defense team indicates that Dennis Mahon traveled to Germany to recruit individuals into the Ku Klux Klan. A video reportedly shows Mahon in Germany in full KKK regalia, lighting a cross. Mahon himself joked that if he was fined the usual 1,000 Deutsche Marks for every time he gave the Nazi salute, he would owe 10,000,000 Marks.[340]

Only a few weeks before the Oklahoma City bombing, Mahon received a phone call from Lauck. "Yeah, I got a call from Lauck sometime before the bombing ... He told me that he was making another trip to Europe. I told him he was too hot, and he shouldn't go." Shaking his head, Mahon says now, "He should have listened."

Did the authorities know Lauck was coming? "Well, I did tell Strassmeir about the trip," said Mahon. (Or did Mahon tell the government himself?)

With Lauck's European arrest, the NSDAP noted, "U.S. officials have been doing extensive surveillance of Lauck's contemporaries in Oklahoma, Kansas, Nebraska and north Texas. These surveillance activities were being coordinated out of the OKC offices, according to our sources."

Interestingly, the newsletter added that "the OKC office of the ATF had plans to serve search warrants 'by the beginning of Summer' on several well-known white supremacists."

It seems the warrants were never issued.[341]

Interestingly, Lyons told the German magazine *Volkstreue:* "There are many spies within [the Klan] and most of its best leaders have left the Klan to do more effective work within the movement.... The man who is mainly responsible for the success of the Klan in Germany—Dennis Mahon—has left the Klan."

Apparently, Mahon is still concerned enough about his responsibility to the white supremacist movement to have telephoned Germany with orders to kill Strassmeir. According to a conversation overheard by Cash, "[Mahon] wanted Andreas shot in both kneecaps and a confession elicited from him, then hold a

30-minute trial and then execute him."[342]

Investigator Jeff Steinberg takes this one step further, believing that Mahon himself may be an ATF operative. He says the ATF had him on a charge then dropped it. "He may have been turned," said Steinberg.

Obviously, Strassmeir wasn't the only informant at Elohim City. Mahon, who knew Guthrie, McCarthy, Stedeford, and Langan, had introduced his new-found friend Carol Howe to the white separatist community. It was there that the attractive 24-year-old daughter of a prominent Tulsa businessman would meet Strassmeir. As Howe told the *Gazette:*

> "I kinda had a relationship with him for a while. We talked about relationships once, and he said he wasn't interested in settling down with a woman. All he wanted to do was blow up federal buildings. It was also at that same meeting that he shoved his hand down my dress and I thought, well, he was doing something else, but now that I think about it, I think he was feeling for a wire."

Howe also said she overheard Mahon and Strassmeir discuss plans to bomb the Oklahoma City Federal Building. As Howe related it:

> "I started going to as many of their meetings as I could and met a lot of people who were very secretive. But sometime in November there was a meeting and Strassmeir and Mahon said it was time to quit talking and go to war, and time to start bombing federal buildings."
>
> "I reported all this to Angie."[343]

According to her attorney, Howe provided telephone numbers, license tags, names, family trees, (including the location and design of tattoos) drawings of buildings, pictures, and descriptions and lists of individuals who were involved in criminal activity.

In fact, Confidential Informant 53270-183 or CI-183 (whose neo-Nazi handle was "Freya" and "Lady MacBeth") made over 70 reports to Finley-Graham during the 1994–95 time frame. Finley-Graham paid Howe $120-a-week to provide the ATF regular updates on the activities at Elohim City, and those of Strassmeir and Mahon in particular. Finley-Graham filed her preliminatory ROI (Report of Investigation) on Carol Howe on August 30, 1994. Entitled "White Aryan Resistance, W.A.R.," it states, in part:

> On August 24, 1994, this agent met with CI-183 in the Tulsa ATF Field Office and discussed in great detail the federal firearms and conspiracy violations of the White Aryan Resistance....

W.A.R. is described briefly as being radical, paramiliatry, Neo-Nazi, anti-government and violent. W.A.R. has national and international affiliates to include the KKK and a racist following in Germany....

W.A.R. has several training sites in Oklahoma. The primary training location is called Elohim City, which is in a rural area near the border of Oklahoma and Akransas in Adair County, Oklahoma. The members of the religious organization, The Covenant, Sword and Arm of the Lord live at Elohim City. The Covenant, Sword and Arm of the Lord is a separatist organization that conjointly trains with and exchanges weapons with W.A.R....

Regarding statements by Mahon secretly videotaped by Howe, Finley-Graham writes:

Mahon has made numerous statements regarding the conversion of firearms into fully automatic weapons, the manufacture and use of silencers and the manufacture and use of explosive devices. Mahon has stated both the knowledge and ability to manufacture a range of explosive devices. Mahon intends to manufacture and use any or all of the above when he deems necessary. Mahon and his organization are preparing for a race war and war with the government in the near future and it is believed that they are rapidly stockpiling weapons.

Mahon responded to Howe's allegations in the *Village Voice:* "This woman has got some shit on me. They're lies. But it's my word against hers."

It was only after Mahon and Howe had a romantic falling-out that the 24-year-old Howe switched from being an avowed white supremacist to an ATF informant. A temporary protective order was issued against Mahon by a Tulsa court in August, '94, after Howe alleged that Mahon threatened to "take steps to neutralize me," by breaking her knees if she tried to leave the white supremacist movement.[344]

"I was contacted by Dennis Mahon after I ordered some literature from this group called White Aryan Resistance," Howe told the *McCurtain Gazette.* "He wanted to have a closer relationship than I did, and later he threatened me when I tried to get away from his group.[345]

It was after Howe sought the restraining order that Finley-Graham recruited her into the ATF. Mahon claims it was Howe-the-informant who advocated most of the violence. Depicting himself as the fall-guy in the affair, he told the press, "They want to drag me into this thing and I barely remember even meeting Tim McVeigh. It was Strassmeir who was meeting with McVeigh, not me."[346]

Curiously, Mahon later sent a videotape to McVeigh's prison cell expressing his views on the "movement." McVeigh's defense team was concerned about the video, not knowing whether the intended message "was to encourage the Defendant to 'sacrifice' himself for the eventual 'justice' of the cause or was a subtle threat intended to remind the Defendant that members of his family were vulnerable."*

While Mahon vehemently denied Howe's allegations, the ATF's ROI (Report of Investigation) January 11, 1995 (three months before the bombing) states, in part:

> During the Sabbath meeting, Millar gave a sermon soliciting violence against the US government. He brought forth his soldiers and instructed them to take whatever action necessary against the US government. It is understood that ATF is the main enemy of people at EC.... He explicity told 183 that they were preparing to fight a war against the government.

Howe reported to Finley-Graham that James Ellison also planned to reconstruct the CSA. Her report also stated that Millar planned to consolidate his compound with groups in Texas, Missouri, Arkansas and Oklahoma to prepare to fight a war with the government. Posse Comitatus members from Pennsylvania allegedly lent a hand by helping Elohim City residents convert their weapons to full automatic.

"These people have the means and the desire to start a terrible war in America," wrote Howe in a letter to her father in August of 1994. "They must be stopped, one group at a time."[347]

To precipitate that war, Strassmeir was apparently willing to procure grenades, C-4 and other explosives. (According to ATF ROI, 9/26/94.) This is hardly surprising. In 1979, ATF informant Bernard Butkovich and FBI operative Edward Dawson led a group of KKK and Nazi Party members on a shooting spree during a parade in Greensboro, North Carolina, which led to the deaths of five members of the Communist Workers Party.**

The *Washington Post* reported how Butkovich "urged members to buy equipment to convert semi-automatic guns to fully automatic weapons, and offered to procure explosives (including hand grenades)."

According to the *New York Times*, witnesses reported that Butkovich, a veteran demolitions expert, also offered "to train them in activities such as making pipe bombs and fire bombs," and that "the Nazis take weapons to the [Communist] rally in the trunks of their cars."†

---

* According to reports, it was Cash who "persuaded" Mahon to make the recording.

** Dawson was also a paid informant for the Greensboro Police Department.

† With a map of the parade route supplied by Greensboro Police Department Detective Jerry Cooper, Dawson, Butkovich, and their KKK and neo-Nazi comrades were able to select the most advantageous site for their ambush. Although Cooper and other officers surveilled the house where the killers had assembled and took down license numbers, they inexplicably decided to take a lunch break less than 45 minutes before the march.

With a map of the parade route supplied by Greensboro Police Department Detective Jerry Cooper, Dawson, Butkovich, and their KKK and neo-Nazi comrades were able to select the most advantageous site for their ambush.

According to Stephen Jones's appeal brief, Finley-Graham's handwritten notes confirmed a report from Howe that Dennis Mahon had bomb-making expertise, including allegedly exploding a 500 lb. ammonium-nitrate bomb in Michigan five years earlier. [348]

Howe also told the agents that Strassmeir and Mahon cased the Tulsa IRS building and the Oklahoma City Federal Building in November and December of 1994, and once during February of '95. Mahon told reporters that as a "revolutionary," he would indeed blow up the Federal Building, but do it at night, when no one was around.

Shockingly, much of this information was provided the ATF before the bombing.[*]

J.D. Cash, reporting for the *McCurtain Gazette,* claimed to have received information from an intermediary that a source at the headquarters of the Aryan Nations in Hayden Lake, Idaho, said that Mahon was "one of the ring leaders in the group that bombed the Federal Building." Cash, who interviewed Mahon on numerous occasions by posing as a white supremacist, wrote the following in the *Gazette:*

And he [Mahon] indicated that the results of the bombing were not as he anticipated. He felt like this would cause a coming together of radicals around the country who would begin a campaign of terrorism. In retrospect, he feels like the IRS building should have been bombed instead of the Murrah Building and probably should have been bombed at night. The day care center and the killing of the children was having a negative effect.

By the time the shooting started, the tactical squad assigned to monitor the demonstration was still out to lunch. Even more inexplicably, two officers responding to a domestic call at the Morningside projects, the site of the CWP march, noted the suspicious absence of patrol cars usually assigned to the area. One of the cops, Officer Wise, later reported receiving a bizarre call from police dispatch, advising him to "clear the area as soon as possible." The incident resulted in an ATF/FBI-led cover-up similar in most respects to the Oklahoma City whitewash, with most of the suspects being acquitted of first degree murder charges. Echoing the factitious rants of federal officials in Oklahoma, FBI Director William Webster called the charges of federal complicity "utterly absurd." Although the killers had been recruited, organized and led on their murderous rampage by ATF and FBI operatives, none ever served a day of jail time.

[*] Just as federal informant Cary Gagan provided the FBI and U.S. Marshals with warnings.

For his part, Mahon claims he has an alibi for the morning of April 19. Yet Bricktown witness David Snider is sure the driver of the Ryder truck which slowly made its way past his warehouse that morning was Dennis Mahon. Although the driver had long hair and was wearing sunglasses, Snider is adamant. Snider showed the County Grand Jury a video showing Mahon wearing the same sunglasses he was wearing on the morning of the blast. Snider's half-sister, Kay Clarke, testified that she drew the composite sketch of the man Snider saw.[349]

Mahon, who said he believes others were involved with McVeigh, told the *Daily Oklahoman,* "I have never been in downtown [Oklahoma City]. I am squeaky clean."[350]

Interestingly, Mahon also claimed himself to be a makeup artist, and described himself as "the master of all disguises." In a somewhat startling statement, Mahon told Ambrose Evans-Pritchard of the *London Sunday Telegraph:*

> "I always deliver my bombs in person, in disguise," he said mischievously. "I can look like a Hispanic or even a Negro. I'm the master of disguise."[351]

Howe, who was debriefed by the ATF and FBI after the bombing, told agents Blanchard and Finley-Graham that the sketches of the suspects who rented the Ryder truck appeared to be Elohim City residents (and Mahon and Strassmeir associates) Peter or Sonny Ward. She also reportedly told the agents, "No one in the world looks more like the sketch of John Doe 2 than Michael Brescia." Howe's report to Finley-Graham stated, in part:

> SA BLANCHARD and SA ANGIE FINDLEY, ATF, talked with SA FINDLEY's confidential source "CAROL." CAROL stated she believes in 1994, she saw an individual resembling the composite of UNSUB #1 in a white separatist paramilitary camp called "Elohm City" (phonetic) (EC). This camp is located around Stillwell, Oklahoma. CAROL knows this person as "PETE." CAROL has seen an individual named "TONY" resembling the composite of UNSUB # 2. TONY is PETE's brother, and is not well liked at EC. TONY would do as his brother directed however.
>
> When CAROL saw the television pictures of TIMOTHY JAMES MCVEIGH, she said MCVEIGH doesn't look like "PETE." CAROL recalled that she did see a person who looked like MCVEIGH in a photograph in a photo album she saw at a 1994 Klan Rally.

NBC, putting the official Justice Department spin on the story, claimed Howe's reports contained no specific information regarding the plot. Yet according to the *Gazette,* "Howe was routinely polygraphed by the government during the time she was making her monthly reports. The government's own documents indicate she passed, 'showing no deception on her part in any polygraph examination.'[352] As Finley-Graham testified during Howe's pre-trial hearing:

> Brewster: "Now, you were interested in knowing as much as you could about Mr. Strassmeir, weren't you?"
> Graham: "Yes."
> Brewster: "What kind of guns he had?"
> Graham: "Yes."
> Brewster: "And the kind of threats he made about wanting to blow up federal buildings? You were interested in that, weren't you?"
> Graham: "I was interested in anything I could find out about any violation."
> Brewster: "And Ms. Howe told you about Mr. Strassmeir's threats to blow up federal buildings, didn't she?"
> Graham: "In general, yes."
> Brewster: "And that was before the Oklahoma City bombing?"
> Graham: "Yes."

At the time of this writing, federal authorities were still insisting that Howe's reports contained no specific warnings of any plot to bomb any federal building. They also claimed that they were only alerted two days after the bombing, when they debriefed their informant.*

Yet it seems Howe's reports were specific enough to warn the ATF not to be in the office the day of the bombing. No ATF employees were among the 169 killed.

Nevertheless, federal prosecutors still insisted, after Howe went public, that the informant couldn't have had any specific information about the bombing, because she was "terminated" on March 27, three weeks before the attack.

Also "terminated," it seems, was the ATF's December, 1994 report regarding Howe's activities at Elohim City. That report, sources told *The New American*, contained specific warnings about the pending attack on the Alfred P. Murrah Building. Had this report, like so much of the ATF's evidence concerning their and the FBI's atrocities at Waco, conveniently "disappeared?"

Unfortunately for the ATF, the records which show that Howe remained an active informant until January 9, 1996, hadn't disappeared. As Finley-Graham's ROI of January 31, 1996 states:

---

* When McVeigh's defense team asked federal prosecutors for Howe's reports in pre-trial discovery, they were informed the records didn't exist. When it was shown that the records did indeed exist, an angry Judge Matsch ordered the records delivered to the defense and threatened the prosecutors with removal from the case if they lied one more time.

It is requested that CI 53270-183 be retained as an active informant. It was requested by the Dallas Division office that this informant be retained as an active informant for the duration of the Oklahoma City bombing investigation.

On April 22, Finley-Graham sent the following memo to Lester Martz, SAC
of the Dallas Field office:

This informant is involved with the OKC bomb case which is pending prosecution
in Denver and was the key in identifying individuals at Elohim City, which is tied
to the OKC bomb case.

In addition to denying her employment with the ATF, the bureau attempted
to claim that Howe was "unstable," her emotional state and her "loyalty" to the
ATF being in question. Yet once again, the official records, which describe Howe
as "stable and capable" contradict these claims. As the ATF's ROI of April 22,
1996 notes:

[The agent has] known CI 53270-183 for approximately two years and can assert
that this informant has not been overly paranoid or fearful during undercover operations.

As 24-year ATF veteran Robert Sanders told *The New American,* "Howe was
a very good informant. she is obviously intelligent, resourceful, cool and convincing under pressure, and has a good sense for the kind of detailed information that
is most helpful to law enforcement and prosecutors."

Yet the Feds would make every attempt to distance themselves from their own
informant in the aftermath of the bombing. Not suprisingly, this was the same
ruse the FBI used in the aftermath of the World Trade Center bombing—pulling
undercover operative Emad Salem off the case two weeks before the tragic attack,
then claiming he was "unreliable."

Yet the FBI reactivated Salem after the bombing, just as they did with Howe,
sending her back to Elohim City to gather additional information on Mahon,
Strassmeir, and the others. Her new contract raised her pay from $25 to $400 per
day.

Curiously, neither the ATF nor the FBI offered Howe any protection. FBI
agent Pete Rickel admitted during subsequent court testimony that Howe had
come to him in May, '96 seeking protection, but he had offered none. In fact,
Rickel said he didn't even make a note of their conversation.

Not only did the FBI fail to protect what the ATF called their "key" witness linking Elohim City to the bombing, but the FBI went one step further, leaking a confidential report to the press. As Finley-Graham wrote in her April 1, 1996 report:

On March 29, 1996 this agent received a telephone call from S/A Harry Eberhardt. S/A Eberhardt stated that the identity of CI 53270-183 had been severly compromised. S/A Eberhardt stated that a report by FBI agent James R. Blanchard II contained the formal name of CI 53270-183 and enough information to reveal the indentity of CI 53270-183 without his/her name being used. S/A Eberhardt stated that he had attempted to relay this matter to FBI ASAC Jack McCoy, however ASAC McCoy showed little concern and denied that S/A Blanchard was at fault. S/A Eberhardt state that he became irate because it was appparent that nothing was going to be done in an effort to recitfy the problem or at least provide help for the safety of CI 53270-183.

Finley-Graham "immediately telphoned CI-53270-183 and informed him/her that their name had been disclosed and that he/she should take every precaution for their safety.... This agent told the CI that anything and everything will be done to insure his/her safety." It seems the government was fully aware of the danger posed to their informant, as Finely-Graham's report of April 22, 1996 notes:

Individuals who pose immediate danger to CI 53270-183 are: (1) Dennis Mahon, (2) members of Elohim City, and (3) any sympathizer to McVeigh.... This agent believes that she could be in serious danger when associates discover his/her identity.

In fact, one of Finley-Graham's initial reports indicates that Dennis Mahon "stated that he would kill any informant." Mahon subsequently sent Howe on a "night reconnaisance mission" to a secuded area—straight into the arms of a black gang, whose members pistol-whipped her and cut her with a knife. In what looked like a deliberate attempt to rid itself of an embarrassing informant, Howe was provided no protection by the government which she had loyally and courageously served.

When public criticism to make Howe "disappear" failed, the government resorted to silencing her on phony, trumped-up charges.

The Justice Department found it expeditious to indict Howe just in time for McVeigh's trial, putting her safely behind bars. The charge? Compiling a list of bomb ingredients, acquiring photographs of federal offices in Tulsa, and using her home telephone to distribute racist information—all undercover activities committed on behalf of her employer—the ATF. Howe was unanimously acquitted.

Stephen Jones believes that Howe was indicted "for the purposes of 'leverage' against her in order to keep her mouth shut about what she knows about the activities of Mahon and Strassmeir," and her employer, the ATF. [353]

Perhaps most surprisingly, during a July, 1997 pre-trial hearing for Howe, FBI agent Peter Rickel revealed that "Grandpa" Millar was a confidential FBI informant! When asked if Millar had been a source of government information or an informant, Rickel replied, "generally, yes."

It appeared there were at least three government informants inside Elohim City—Howe, Strassmeir, and Millar, the later two inciting a war with the Federal Government. Add to that the probability of Brescia, Mahon, and McVeigh being informants, and Elohim City begins to look like one great big government-run neo-Nazi training camp.

According to a former government informant interviewed by the *Gazette,* "It is typical for agencies such as the CIA, FBI and ATF to place multiple 'moles' inside a place like Elohim City and play one resource off the other, without either one knowing the identity of the other." Federal law enforcement, even different offices of the same agency, often do not share informants' names unless the mission calls for it.

"The reasons are obvious. First, there is no way a law enforcement agency is going to risk exposing the life of one of their assets should the other 'resource' succumb to torture or decide to double-cross the agency. And, of course, the monitoring of information can best be verified if neither resource knows who the other is. That's the only way this game works, and it's the only way it succeeds."

And what of Michael Brescia? Was he also an informant? Given the close, often revealing nature of a roommate relationship, it is likely that an undercover agent would room with another agent, even if nothing more than one might overhear the other talking in his sleep.

Strassmeir himself admitted the difficulty of going "deep cover," and having to keep your guard up 24 hours-a-day. "If you were an undercover agent," said Strassmeir, "you have to keep your guard up, you can't get close."

Is that why he roomed with Brescia, so he wouldn't have to maintain his guard? Not according to Strassmeir: "I would be very surprised if he [Brescia] was an undercover agent. He's a very honest, straightforward guy."

Strassmeir, along with friends Peter and Sonny Ward, fled Elohim City in August, '95, after McVeigh defense team investigators began looking into activities at the secretive compound.

Brescia left Elohim City around the same time as Strassmeir, with his fiancé Ester, traveling to Canada, and remaining mostly underground. He subsequently returned to his parents' house in Philadelphia, where he was actively sought by the media.

Curiously, like his friend Strassmeir, Brescia was completely ignored by federal authorities for his possible role in the bombing. He was finally arrested for the Wisconsin bank heist in February of 1997. Was it a legitimate bust, or did the arrest serve to silence him for his role in the bombing as the government tried to do with Carol Howe?

Shawn Kenny gave the FBI the tip that led to the arrest of Guthrie, who was apprehended after a high-speed chase outside of Cincinnati in January of 1997. He was found dead in his cell in Covington, Kentucky six months later, on July 12, hanged with a bed sheet. Authorities quickly ruled his death a suicide. According to a note found at the scene, Guthrie was apparently feeling guilty over his turncoat attitude, and didn't want to endanger his family.

"Sometimes it takes something like a suicide to settle a problem," he'd written to his attorney. "Especially one that's like … mine." [354]

Yet Dennis Mahon told *Village Voice* reporter James Ridgeway he believes Guthrie was murdered because he had threatened to reveal information about the proceeds of the loot, which was believed to have gone to the Aryan Nations and other neo-Nazi groups. Guthrie was found dead only a few hours after telling a reporter from the *Los Angeles Times* that he intended to write a tell-all book that "would go a lot further into what we were really doing." [355] He was also just days away from appearing before a Grand Jury.

With Guthrie's help, Stedeford was arrested May 24 at the Upper Darby recording studio where he worked as a guitarist, and McCarthy was captured in the Bustleton section of Philadelphia. Thomas was eventually arrested in conjunction with several robberies as well. [356]

Langan was arrested at his rented house in Columbus, Ohio several days after Guthrie, in a fusillade of bullets fired by over-eager FBI agents. The wanted fugitive, who had fired no shots, likened the arrest to an assassination attempt. Another silencing attempt perhaps? (The FBI claimed they were warned that Langan wouldn't be taken alive.)

Ironically, during his trial, the self-styled revolutionary shouted hackneyed phrases such as "Power to the People!" and told the judge that the ARA's mission was to overthrow the government and "set free the oppressed people of North America." Except, apparently, for Blacks, Jews, and homosexuals. [357]

Yet eyebrows everywhere raised when Langan showed up in jail with pink-painted toenails and long manicured fingernails. Langan's lover, a transsexual named Cherie Roberts, appeared at the trial and exclaimed during a scene with U.S. Marshals, "I can't even talk to my wife!"

Roberts, who met Langan at a Kansas City group called "Crossdressers and Friends," called the neo-macho revolutionary bank robber by his charmed pet moniker, "Donna." [358]

In a recruitment video confiscated during a search of Langan's house, "Donna" appears in a black ski-mask, exhorting potential revolutionaries to eradicate all non-whites and non-Christians from the country, and eliminate federal "whores."

"In solidarity with our Serbian brothers we understand the meaning of ethnic cleansing. To us, it's not a dirty word." Apparently, preoperative transsexuals were not included in Langan's targeted population group.

The 107-minute propaganda film entitled "The Aryan Republican Army Presents: The Armed Struggle Underground," plays out like a bad Monty Python skit. Langan shouts orders in Spanish from behind a desk festooned with hand grenades and bank booty, while his "troops" goose-step in the background. "Our basic goal is to set up an Aryan Republic on the North American continent," states "Commander Pedro." [359]

The neo-revolutionaries also expound their philosophy and tactics, which include, not surprisingly, blowing up federal buildings. "We have endeavored to keep collateral damage and civilian casualties to a minimum," announces their leader, "but as in all wars, some innocents shall suffer. So be it."

The video was completed in January, 1995, four months before the bombing of the Alfred P. Murrah Building. Langan, for his part, says he had nothing to do with the bombing. "Most of my family, my siblings work in federal buildings," he told the *Washington Post*.[360]

Yet given Langan's connections to Brescia, Strassmeir and Mahon, and their connections to Nichols and McVeigh, and the group's ties to the violent neo-Nazi underground, it is singularly curious why the FBI hasn't seriously pursued these leads.

Then there is the CSA's 1983 plot to blow up the Oklahoma City Federal Building, and Snell's strangely fortuitous statements about April 19, 1995.

What is even more shocking is why the ATF apparently ignored warnings from its own informant, Carol Howe. Had they figured they could ensnare the bombers in a highly publicized bust?

"Elohim City is not a current subject of interest," a law enforcement official in Washington told the Associated Press, almost two years after the blast.[361]

Was Elohim City of so little interest to authorities because it was a government-infiltrated spook center, kept on hand for contingencies, much as elements of the KKK were by the FBI's J. Edgar Hoover?

And what of Iraq's connections to Dennis Mahon? Is this a subject of interest? Was it just an innocent business relationship, or, like the Syrian's offer of funding to Robert Mathews, was it something more?

C h a p t e r   F i v e

TEFLON TERRORISTS

In the wake of the bombing, the media was abuzz with reports of a Middle-Eastern connection. Reporters were reporting claims of Muslim extremists, and talking heads were talking about a familiar modus operandi. Then on April 21, less than 48 hours after the bombing, the FBI announced that they had snared their elusive quarry, an angry white guy named Timothy James McVeigh. The following day, the Bureau announced that they had captured angry white guy number two: Terry Lynn Nichols.

The mainstream media, having their information spoon-fed to them by the FBI, quickly launched into in-depth analysis of the two "prime suspects." All other information quickly became buried in the great collective memory sink hole. It was as if, with the "capture" of McVeigh and Nichols, all other information became suddenly irrelevant and obsolete. The Justice Department waved their magic wand, President Clinton winked at the Middle-Eastern community, and all the world was set right again.

What remained hidden behind the official curtain of deceit however, were scores of witness accounts, official statements, and expert opinions regarding a Middle-Eastern connection. For 48 hours after the bombing, FBI officials and terrorism experts poured forth their opinions and analyses.

Robert Heibel, a former FBI counter-terrorism expert, said the bombing looked like the work of Middle East terrorists, possibly those connected with the World Trade Center bombing.[362]

Speaking on CNN, ATF Director John Magaw said: "I think any time you have this kind of damage, this kind of explosion, you have to look there [Middle East terrorists] first."

"This was done with the attempt to inflict as many casualties as possible," said terrorism expert Steven Emerson on CBS Evening News. "That is a Middle Eastern trait and something that has been, generally, not carried out on this soil until we were rudely awakened to it in 1993."

Former United States Representative Dave McCurdy of Oklahoma (former Chairman of the House Intelligence Committee) told CBS News that there was "very clear evidence of the involvement of fundamentalist Islamic terrorist groups."[363]

Former FBI counter-terrorism chief Oliver "Buck" Revell told CBS Evening News, "I think it's most likely a Middle East terrorist. I think the modus operandi is similar. They have used this approach."

Ex-CIA counter-terrorism director Vince Cannistraro told the *Washington Times*, "Right now, it looks professional, and it's got the marks of a Middle Eastern group."

Avi Lipkin, a former Israeli Defense Intelligence specialist on the Prime Minister's staff, in Oklahoma City at the time of the bombing, told investigator Craig Roberts, "this is a typical Arab Terrorist type attack." [364]

It was also reported the Israelis gave the Americans a "general warning" concerning the bombing.*

CBS News stated that the FBI had received claims of responsibility from at least eight different organizations. Seven of the claimants were thought to have Middle Eastern connections:

> An FBI communiqué that was circulated Wednesday suggested that the attack was carried out by the Islamic Jihad, an Iranian-backed Islamic militant group, said a security professional in California who declined to be named ... the communiqué suggested the attack was made in retaliation for the prosecution of Muslim fundamentalists in the bombing of the World Trade Center in February, 1993, said the source, a non-government security professional.... 'We are currently inclined to suspect the Islamic Jihad as the likely group.' [365]

James Fox, former head of the New York FBI office, told CBS News, "We thought that we would hear from the religious zealots in the future, that they would be a thorn in our side for years to come."

On July 2nd, shortly after Sheik Omar Abdel Rahman's surrender to U.S. Immigration authorities, the Egyptian Jama a' Islamiya (the group implicated in the World Trade Center bombing) issued a statement saying that if the Sheik was prosecuted or extradited to Egypt, they would begin a world-wide terror campaign against the United States.

On April 21, 1995, the *London Telegraph* reported: "Israeli anti-terror experts believe the Oklahoma bombing and the 1993 World Trade Center explosion are linked and that American investigators should focus on Islamic extremists."

The same day, the *London Sunday Times* carried a report that suggested President Saddam Hussein of Iraq may have been involved in both the World Trade Center and the Oklahoma City bombings:

---

* Lipkin also told Roberts that Stinger missiles have been smuggled into the country. A Stinger is thought by some as responsible for the downing of TWA flight 800.

Iraq was furious with America last week at its United Nations move to foil efforts to overturn Gulf war economic sanctions. Ramzi Ahmed Yousef, the recently-captured alleged mastermind of the 1993 attack on the World Trade Center in New York, was directly funded by Baghdad, according to CIA and FBI documents—and evidence so far developed about the latest bomb indicates some similarities in the planning.[366]

If those in Baghdad were angry over the brutal and relentless attack on their country by U.S. forces during the Gulf War, they had additional reason for anger when President Clinton launched a retaliatory raid against Iraqi intelligence headquarters in Baghdad. The June 26 Cruise Missile strike was directed against the complex after an alleged plot was uncovered to assassinate former president, crook, and mass murderer George Bush during his recent visit to Kuwait.* The raid merely destroyed some of the complex, and leveled about a dozen surrounding homes, killing approximately six civilians. Syndicated columnist Charlie Reese called it "high-tech terrorism."

The *Net News Service* reported the next day that the government-backed *Al-Thawra* newspaper charged that Clinton had carried out the attack only to bolster his "eroded popularity and credibility ... domestically." Both *Al-Thawra* and General Saber Abdul-Aziz Douri, head of the Iraqi intelligence service, indicated that the Iraqi government had vowed vengeance against the United States.

Backing up Douri's claims was former head of Iraqi military intelligence, General Wafiq al-Sammara'i, who told the *London Independent* that the June, 1996 bombing of the U.S. military housing complex in Dhahran, Saudi Arabia, which killed 19 servicemen, "strongly resembled plans drawn up by a secret Iraqi committee on which he served after the invasion of Kuwait. He says operations considered by Iraq, but not carried out at that time due to shortage of reliable agents, included exploding large bombs near buildings where American soldiers were living." [367]

One month later, the *Washington Post* reported:

Early on July 6, Col. Mohammar Qaddafi of Libya issued a warning that President Clinton and the United States had "blundered" in the recent missile attack on Baghdad, and that the United States should expect "a lot more terrorism" in the near future. Qaddafi spoke of increasingly violent and spectacular acts to be perpetrated expressly for broadcast on the national and international television.[368]

Shortly after the bombing, KFOR, Channel 4 in Oklahoma City received a

---

* No evidence was produced for the so-called assassination attempt. The allegations were reminiscent of the tale of Iraqi soldiers pulling babies out of incubators, which turned out to be a lie.

call from the Nation of Islam, taking credit for the bombing. Interestingly, the NOI has been directly funded by Libya.

The *Post's* Jack Anderson added that a direct attack against the U.S. would be unlikely, and that counter-terrorist analysts feared that the only viable avenue for Hussein's revenge would be through the use of terrorism. "A preferable revenge for Iraq would involve having a 'surrogate terrorist' carry out a domestic attack that Hussein could privately take credit for."

According to Dr. Laurie Mylroie, a Middle East expert at the Center for Security Policy and an authority on the World Trade Center bombing, Iraqi agents such as Ramzi Yousef infiltrated the original World Trade Center cell, resulting in the construction of a more powerful, sophisticated bomb.

Dr. Mylroie noted that on September 27, 1994, as Iraqi troops tested American resolve by preparing a new assault against Kuwait, Saddam Hussein declared: "We will open the storehouses of the universe" against the United States. Two days later, *Babil*—a newspaper in Iraq owned by Saddam's son, Uday—amplified, saying: "Does the United States realize the meaning of opening the stores of the world with the will of Iraqi people? Does it realize the meaning of every Iraqi becoming a missile that can cross to countries and cities?" [369]

Mylroie notes that there may be other Iraqi intelligence agents at large in this country, known as "sleepers," waiting to carry out far more deadly acts of revenge against the U.S. One such cell, planted by the Abu Nidal organization, was discovered in 1986. Four of their Palestinian members were arrested eight years later after one of them murdered the daughter of an FBI agent. [370]

On January 28, 1991, the *Washington Post* reported:

If Saddam is serious about terrorizing Americans at home, there are several allies he could call on for help. The most dangerous terrorist Organization in the world, the Abu Nidal organization, now based in Baghdad, has a rudimentary infrastructure of about 50 people in the United States. All of them, according to FBI sources, are under surveillance....

"Among the terrorists who are taking or would take orders from Saddam," added the *Post*, "are Abu Ibrahim, a pioneer bomb maker who designed the barometric pressure bomb that blew up Pan Am Flight 103, and Ahmed Jibril, who masterminded the Pan Am bombing on a contract from Iran." [371]

Ironically, U.S. interventions abroad have permitted the entry into America of extremist and even terrorist organizations that have subsequently gained footholds in ethnic communities across the country. Texas and Oklahoma, in fact, are major centers of Islamic activities in the U.S.

Steven Emerson was quoted on CBS Evening News as saying, "Oklahoma City, I can tell you, is probably considered one of the largest centers of Islamic radical activity outside the Middle East."

Emerson chronicled the rise of radical Islam in America in a 1994 PBS documentary which showed how fundamentalists had launched a recruiting campaign across the midwest and southwest. An Oklahoma City meeting in 1988 was attended by members of Hamas (Islamic Resistance Movement), Islamic Jihad (Holy War) and the Muslim Brotherhood, each notorious for their sponsorship of terrorism. The meeting was held only blocks from the Federal Building.

As Stephen Jones stated in his March 25th Writ of Mandamus:

The Murrah Building was chosen either because of lack of security (i.e. it was a "soft target"), or because of available resources such as Iraqi POWs who had been admitted into the United States were located in Oklahoma City, or possibly because the location of the building was important to American neo-Nazis such as those individuals who supported Richard Snell who was executed in Arkansas on April 19, 1995.

Secret workshops have reportedly been held in the U.S., where HizbAllah and Hamas members have been taught bomb making techniques and small arms practice. HizbAllah, the Iranian-sponsored and Syrian-backed "Party of God," is believed to be behind a series of bombings in July of 1994 that took 117 lives in Argentina, Panama, and Britain. HizbAllah is the same Lebanon-based terrorist group that perpetrated the October, 1983, bombing of the U.S. Marine barracks in Beirut.[372]

The most notorious U.S. terrorist cell was in Jersey City, led by Sheik Omar Abdel-Rahman, the group responsible for plotting the destruction of the UN building and the Holland Tunnel. Three of Rahman's followers were convicted for bombing the World Trade Center. One of their leaders, El-Sayyid Nosair, spelled out his plans to terrorize the United States: "We have to thoroughly demoralize the enemies of God … by means of destroying and blowing up the towers that constitute the pillars of their civilization such as the tourist attractions they are so proud of and the high buildings they are so proud of."[373]

Another influential figure in Islamic radical circles—Sheik Mohammad al-Asi, the religious leader of the Islamic Education Center in Potomac, Maryland, was quoted on PBS as saying:

"If the Americans are placing their forces in the Persian Gulf, we should be creating another war front for the Americans in the Muslim world—and specifically where American interests are concentrated. In Egypt, in Turkey, in the Indian subcontinent, just to mention a few. Strike against American interests there."

While the Arab underground structure in the U.S. is generally based on the PLO, not all of its members are Palestinian. Many may emigrate from Iran, Iraq, Syria, Sudan, and Libya, the five nations most often connected with terrorism. According to former Israeli intelligence officer William Northrop, the original PLO structure shifted in 1991, after the PLO/Israeli peace process began. As Northrop writes:

> The Texas Cell is based in Houston and is supported by several sub-cells, one of which is based in Oklahoma City. This Texas Cell was tied into the World Trade Center bombing on 26 February 1993.
>
> The Oklahoma City sub-cell originated with the Palestinian students who were sent from various Arab countries to study Petroleum Engineering at OU in Norman. (The current Deputy Petroleum Minister of Iran is an OU graduate.) [374]

Their members may also come from a broader philosophic milieu, and unlike the PLO, have a wider range of targets, including not only Israel, but secular regimes in Muslim countries and those states that support them.

Notes Middle East analyst James Phillips: "Because they are motivated by apocalyptic zeal, and not sober political calculations, their choice of possible targets is much wider and more indiscriminate than that of other terrorists." [375]

The goal of this new breed of terrorist was not aimed at influencing U.S. or world opinion over the Palestinian issue, but to prove the strength of the Muslim fundamentalist cause. As former Dallas Special Agent in Charge Oliver "Buck" Revell said:

> "If you listen to what [the Islamic extremist terrorists] are really saying, they're not just aimed at the Israelis, they are not just aimed at the Jewish state. Their goals are completely and totally to eradicate any opposition to Hamas and to Islam and to move against the United States ultimately." [376]

Obviously, these journalists and experts hadn't developed their theories in a vacuum. The evidence was clear, and the warnings were imminent. Allan Denhan wrote in *ASP Newsletter* that a Jordanian Intelligence official had passed a "target list" to an American businessman two months prior to the bombing, and the Murrah Building was on that list. Although this information is unconfirmed, it makes perfect sense, since Jordan has a long-standing intelligence relationship with the CIA.

In March of 1995, Israel's Shin Bet (General Security Services, Israel's equivalent to the FBI), arrested approximately 10 Hamas terrorists in Jerusalem, some of whom had recently returned from a trip to Ft. Lauderdale, Florida. According to Northrop, interrogation of those suspects was thought to have revealed information concerning the plot to bomb the Murrah Building. "The Shin Bet filed a warning with the Legal Attaché (FBI) at the American Embassy in Tel Aviv as a matter of course," wrote Northrop.*

On April 20, the Israeli newspaper *Yediot Arhonot* wrote:

> Yesterday, it was made known that over the last few days, U.S. law enforcement agencies had received intelligence information originating in the Middle East, warning of a large terrorist attack on U.S. soil. No alert was sounded as a result of this information.[377]

Northrop also said that the German Bundesnachrichtendienst (BND, the equivalent of the American CIA), also sent a warning to the U.S. State Department. That was followed by a warning from the Saudis. "A Saudi Major General ... informed former CIA Counterterrorism Chief Vince Cannistraro, who in turn informed the FBI. There is a 302 (FBI report) in existence." [378]

The agent Cannistraro passed the information to was Kevin L. Foust, one of the FBI's leading counterterrorism agents. Ironically, the information was given to Foust on the same day as the bombing.

According to the information obtained by Stephen Jones, the Saudi Arabian Intelligence Service reported that Iraq had hired seven Pakistani mercenaries—Afghani War veterans known as the Mujahadeen—to bomb targets in the U.S., one of which was the Alfred P. Murrah Building. They also advised the FBI that—as is often the case—the true identity of the sponsor may not have been revealed to the bombers.[379]

Interestingly, Northrop stated that three Israelis were in Oklahoma before the April 19th attack to "keep an eye on things." Avi Lipkin and Northrop were two such individuals.**

In addition to these warnings—as well as the mighty armada of U.S. intelligence agencies, analysts, and surveillance technology which would have undoubtedly been monitoring the situation—at least one local informant tried to warn authorities in advance. His warnings went unheeded.

---

* Shimon Havitz, an Israeli General attached to the Prime Minister's office, also told McVeigh Defense Attorney Stephen Jones that the Israelis had issued a warning to the Americans.

** Jones said that Lipkin met with his U.S. "counterpart," Phil Wilcox, the U.S. State Department's coordinator for terrorism, after the bombing to "compare notes." The reader will also recall that two Israeli bomb experts traveled to Oklahoma City after the bombing to analyze the bomb signature.

THE DRUG CONNECTION

After the bombing, Cary Gagan stepped forward to tell Stephen Jones that he had been present at a meeting of bombing conspirators including Middle-Easterners, caucasians, and Hispanics which took place in Henderson, Nevada.*

In depositions and interviews with Jones and in numerous interviews with the author, the government informant and former drug courier described a number of meetings at the Soviet Embassy in Mexico City. In 1980, the Soviets asked Gagan to assist them in procuring military secrets from Dan Howard, a contact of Gagan's who worked at Martin-Marietta, a large defense contractor in Waterton, Colorado. The Soviets had been watching Howard. Gagan was a friend. He informed the FBI.**

In June, 1986, the Soviets again asked Gagan's help—this time, to assist illegal Iranian immigrants needing false IDs. The small-time hustler and counterfeiter met his contact, a man named "Hamid" who worked at Stapleton International Airport in Denver, and secretly recorded the conversation. He turned the tapes over to FBI Agent Bill Maten and Kenny Vasquez of the Denver Police Intelligence Bureau.[380]

The 51-year-old government informant supported himself by ferrying cocaine between Mexico and Colorado for Colombians posing as Mexicans, living in Denver. It was through his association with these Colombians that Gagan met "Omar" and "Ahmed," in Las Vegas in March, '94.

"They tried to first play themselves off as Colombians, " said Gagan "but I knew they were Iranians or Middle-Easterners. They were multi-lingual, with big-time funding."

It was at this meeting that the drug dealer learned he was to transport kilos of cocaine from Mexico to Denver. He informed DEA Agent Robert Todd Gregory. "I told Gregory this dude looked like a banker to me. They had heavy cash. They took care of me. They had all kinds of connections."

On May 16, 1994, Gagan met his new contacts at the Western Motel in Las Vegas, where his brother worked as a pit-boss. There were eight men at the meeting, five of whom were Middle Eastern, including Omar and Ahmed. "Two of them didn't say a word," recalled Gagan, "but they looked like Colombians to

---

* Jones originally said that the meeting took place in Kingman, AZ. According to Gagan, that was incorrect.

** Gagan had intermittent contact with the Soviets throughout the mid-'80s. In 1982, Gagan met a Soviet spy named Edward Bodenzayer while in Puerto Vallerta. Bodenzayer had been exporting classified technology to Russia through his import/export business. He was eventually arrested as a result of a joint FBI/Customs counter-intelligence sting operation known as Operation Aspen Leaf.

me—you know, Latin."

One of the Middle Easterners was from Oklahoma City. He appeared to be the leader. The eighth man was Terry Nichols. In a sworn deposition, Gagan told McVeigh's attorney:

Gagan: "I met with some Arabs, and in that group, and I did not know it at the time, but in that group was Nichols."
Jones: "Terry?"
Gagan: "Terry Nichols." [381]

Gagan first recalled seeing Nichols in the parking lot of a bingo parlor the men had stopped at. "He was wearing a plaid, short sleeve shirt and dockers.... I remember going, 'That's kind of a dirty lookin' dude.' That's all I said. I thought, you know, he didn't fit in the picture here. He looked like a scientist."*

The men snorted cocaine at the Western Motel and discussed their plans, then drove to an apartment complex in Henderson called the Player's Club. It is not known whom they met with. As far as Gagan knew, they were all there to discuss drug dealing. It wasn't exactly clear what the Colombians were doing with the Arabs.**

Gagan would soon find out though. Omar and Ahmed, who had been paying Gagan with counterfeit money (mostly counterfeit Iranian $100 bills), wanted him to take part in a plot to blow up a federal building in Denver, using a mail truck packed with explosives.

"I was going to be part of it because I could move through ... because I'm Anglo and I'm a U.S. citizen and, you know, I wouldn't draw attention. I'm in and out of that federal building every day."

The truck, purchased from a government auction, was painted to resemble a working mail truck. On January 14, 1995, Gagan picked up the truck at the Metro Bar & Grill and drove it to the Mariott Hotel, just outside of Golden, Colorado.

"Omar came out with me, showed me where the truck was, and said, 'Just get in it and drive down I-70, and here's where you park it. And as soon as you make the delivery, make this call.' And I gave the FBI the pay phone number saying it was there. And I stayed in there and had a drink—in the bar, and came walking out, and the sucker was gone."

---

* Gagan later seemed to waver on this point: "I don't care what they say—where he was supposedly—he was there." He later said: "I'm not sure, but it sure looked like him. He just didn't fit."

** Gagan recalls that Omar threw something in the trash. Gagan later fished it out. They were technical diagrams in Spanish that appeared to be bomb plans.

Gagan says he talked to the FBI duty agent from a pay phone at 9th and Logan for over 35 minutes. "I said 'Hey, I need you to tell what to do here.' And they never called back."

In the back of the truck were approximately 30 duffel bags of ammonium-nitrate marked "U.S. mail," and boxes from Sandex Explosives [in Las Vegas] marked "High Explosives."

Gagan boarded a bus and went home. He said the agents never showed up.

"Can you imagine if I'm driving this truck and it blows up in the city of Denver?" said an incredulous Gagan.

Also in the back of the truck was a Lely farm mixer. Gagan recalls that it was approximately four feet high, two feet across, and "shaped like a diamond."

Interestingly, this was the same description given by witness David King. King, who was staying at the Dreamland Motel in Junction City—where McVeigh stayed—saw a Ryder truck with a trailer attached to it in the parking lot on April 17. Inside the trailer was an object secured by a canvas tarp. "It was a squarish shape, and it came to a point on top," said King. "It was about three or four feet high."

In June, Gagan discovered plastic explosives in an athletic bag packed with cocaine he was to deliver to Denver. The bag, Omar said, was to be left at the Postal Center, a shipping and receiving facility owned by George Colombo, who also operated a Ryder truck leasing center across the street. A friend of Gagan's, Colombo would occasionally let him stay at an apartment he maintained when things got too heavy.*

Things were definitely getting heavy for Gagan. When the casual cocaine user decided to open the bag and help himself to a little "blow," he discovered plastic explosives wrapped in brown paper. "And I'm thinking, 'Jesus, how the hell did this get by the airport'? So I packed it up, and I'm thinking, 'I'm going to the Feds,' because you know … I'm a felon, this is C-4 … I'm going [down] forever."

Gagan asked Colombo to hold the bag for him. He then called the Denver Police Intelligence Bureau and met them at a Burger King in Aurora. Gagan sat in the unmarked car, as his friend Billy, a cab driver, watched from nearby.

"I said, 'Look, there's some C-4 …' I'm feeling them out … I give them some names, you know, what the deal was in Las Vegas. I tell them I'm in contact with the DEA—Robert Gregory and all that. They don't say anything. This is June, mid-June of '94. They say they'll get back to me."

Three weeks later, after contacting the FBI, the police called Gagan back. "They tell me quote, 'Since you're the source of the information Gagan, we're not going to investigate.'"

---

* According to Gagan, his Arab friends were interested in buying the postal center, and asked Gagan to propose a cash deal to Colombo. They were apparently interested in its mail and truck rental facility.

Gagan then called Gregory at the DEA. Gregory told Gagan, "Hey, we can't take you on."

The informant claims he continually challenged the police and the FBI to charge him if his information was false. "If all this was a big lie, they could have charged me with lying, but they didn't."

While the FBI and the Denver Police were debating the merits of Gagan's credibility, Omar picked up the bag from Colombo and left.

Three months later, in September, Gagan was approached by Omar and Ahmed again. "They said, 'It's going to involve terrorism, do you have a problem with that?' I said, 'No.' I asked them, 'What kind of money are we looking at?' They said, 'A quarter of a million dollars.' I said, 'Up front?' They said, 'Yes.'"

Gagan accepted the money, which he believes was paid out of the Cali Cartel. "The FBI knew it," said Gagan. "They never got back to me."

Were Latin American drug dealers conspiring with Arab terrorists to blow up the Federal Building? Said 25-year DEA veteran agent Mike Levine: "When you consider terrorist actions like TWA 800 (or Oklahoma City), and you omit any drug trafficking involvement, it's insane—it doesn't make any sense.… You know you take for example two years or three years ago the La Bianca plane that was blown out of the sky—it was attributed to drug traffickers. I can think right off the top of my head of another case in Colombia of a plane blown up with a lot of passengers to kill one person, and probably many, many more."

Levine, a highly decorated DEA agent and the DEA's former Argentine Station Chief, told me that countries such as Bolivia, Paraguay, and Colombia are full of Arabs doing business with Latinos, including drug dealing. "The first thing you have to keep in mind is that drug trafficking is now a half a trillion dollar business around the third-world," said Levine, "and it's mainly a third-world business. The top drug traffickers around the world have more power than presidents. The Mujahadeen for instance, which we supported, were always top heroin smugglers. They were rated one, two and three by DEA as a source, and they right now support every Muslim fundamentalist movement on the face of the earth.…" [382]

The parallel may be more than speculative. Shortly after the bombing, on May 8, Tulsa police veteran Craig Roberts received information from a law enforcement source in Texas that "Juan Garcia Abrego was involved in the bombing as a 'cash provider' for the event. The source said that Abrego had sent two Mexican nationals to Oklahoma City with a satchel full of cash to finance the bombing."

Abrego was a Mexican Mafia chieftain involved in the cocaine and heroin trafficking through Mexico from Guadalajara to Texas. He allegedly was the ground transportation link during the Iran-Contra/Mena affair.

This information was forwarded to both the FBI and the DEA who were asked for each to check their files and/or computers, using various spellings, to see if they had heard of such an individual. Neither replied back that they had knowledge and no further action was taken....[383]

Considering the FBI's apparent lack of knowledge, it is curious that Abrego was at the top of the FBI's "Ten Most Wanted" list since March, a month before the bombing and almost two months before Roberts' original inquiry.

It seemed the FBI's lack of interest in Robert's information was suspiciously similar to their lack of interest in Gagan's.* What is also interesting is that their first effort to discredit Gagan—a drug-runner on the periphery of the Iran-Contra drug network—coincided with the Iran-Contra affair becoming public.**

"In my opinion, people were paid massive amounts of dope to carry this thing out," said Gagan. The informant's belief that he was paid by the Cali Cartel may be significant in light of Roberts' information that Abrego funneled money to the bombing conspirators.

Was the FBI's attempt to repudiate the Middle Eastern connection tied to their refusal to look at the Abrego lead?

As Levine said: "The minute you start taking about terrorist actions, and you eliminate drug trafficking, well, then ... you're just not credible ... It's just very unrealistic to look at a situation—any terrorist situation—and not look at a drug trafficking angle anymore. In my opinion, and I think there's plenty of substantiation eventhough the government won't talk about it, you can say, this vast ocean of money traveling around the world—illegal untapped money—pays for an enormous amount of terrorist activity."

If the Cali Cartel and Gagan's Arabs were connected, and in turn tied to a tentacle of the Iran-Contra Octopus through Abrego, it's only natural that the FBI—which played its own role in covering up Iran-Contra—would tend to look the other way.

In spite of the FBI's apparent refusal to act on Gagan's information, and their subsequent attempts to discredit him, on September 14, 1994, Gagan was granted a Letter of Immunity by the U.S. Attorneys Office in Denver. The immunity was arranged through Federal Public Defender Raymond Moore.[384]

The informant was told to stay with the group and report back to the Bureau. On March 17, Gagan met with his Arab friends at the Hilton Inn South in Greenwood Village, Colorado. On the table were the construction plans for the Alfred P. Murrah Building, bearing the name J.W. Bateson Company of Dallas, Texas.

Still, Gagan alleges that federal agents didn't follow up on any of his leads.

---

* What is interesting, considering the FBI's lack of response, is that the Tulsa office of the FBI commissioned Roberts to provide a report on the bombing.

** Gagan coyly admitted to knowing Iran-Contra drug runner and pilot Barry Seal.

"I knew, when they did not contact me after the truck … when I was moving explosives, I knew something was up. I knew. I figured from that point on, without a doubt, they had a government agent in this ring. Because they cannot let me do that type of stuff.

"And then, after the March 17th meeting, I waited for them to contact me, because I just had a feeling that the dude that had come up [from Oklahoma City]—the new guy on the scene there—was an agent. The way he acted and talked … I just felt different than I did around the other dudes.… That's just my personal feeling."*

Did the Feds ignore Gagan's warnings because they had their own agent in the bombing cell and wanted to obtain more information to "sting" the bombers later on? Gagan believes this is a possibility. Yet while Gagan had the option of pulling out, he realized it would be too risky to suddenly disappear from the scene. Omar and Ahmed were watching him.

On April 4, 1995, Omar pulled up at the Western Motel in Las Vegas, where Gagan's brother worked. "Come on," said Omar to a somewhat startled Gagan, "I want you to drive with me to Kingman."

The two men then drove to Arizona, where they delivered a package to a man waiting on the corner of Northern and Sierra, wearing a cowboy hat and driving a rusty brown pick-up. Could this mystery figure have been Steven Garrett Colbern, who owned the brown pick-up seen stopped ahead of McVeigh when he was pulled by Trooper Hanger over after the bombing? The description of the man matched Colbern's height and build. But Gagan did not know who he was at the time, or what was in the package.

On the way home, Gagan recalled Omar saying, "We're taking down a building in two weeks."**

On March 27 and 28, Gagan made over five calls to the U.S. Marshals Office. None were ever returned. Agent Mark Holtslaw of the FBI's Domestic Counterterrorism Squad, told me, "I can assure you that any info was thoroughly checked out.… There are things that go on in the background that the individual is not aware of." But, Holtslaw added, "There is no statutory obligation to get back to an individual regarding our investigation and its status."[385]

Gagan doesn't buy Holtslaw's explanation. The FBI's procedures regarding

---

* Gagan was referring to a Middle Eastern man who flew in from Oklahoma City. Gagan had never seen him before.

** Gagan gave accurate and specific descriptions of street addresses he had been in Kingman, and provided receipts for his travels to the Arizona town. He also provided receipts for hotel rooms in which he claims bomb planning meetings were held. He said the original plot involved blowing up a Jewish convention center in Denver where President Clinton was speaking.

informants require that they be controlled and supervised. "How do you investigate a thing if you don't contact me?" asked Gagan. "So they either had another agent or another informant inside the group."

Gagan was getting nowhere with the Marshals, the U.S. Attorneys, and the FBI. It was now less than two weeks before the bombing. On April 6, Gagan drafted a letter and delivered it to Tina Rowe, head of the U.S. Marshals Office in Denver. While Gagan waited outside, his cab driver friend dropped it off. The letter read:

> Dear Ms. Rowe:
>
> After leaving Denver for what I thought would be for a long time, I returned here last night because I have specific information that within two weeks a federal building(s) is to be bombed in this area or nearby. The previous requests I made for you to contact me, 25th & 28th of March 1995 were ignored by you, Mr. Allison and my friends at the FBI. I would not ignore the specific request for you personally to contact me immediately regarding a plot to blow-up a federal bldg. If the information is false request Mr. Allison to charge me accordingly. If you and/or your office does not contact me as I so request herein, I will never again contact any law enforcement agency, federal or state, regarding those matters set out in the letter of immunity.[386]
>
> Cary Gagan.
>
> Call 832-4091 (Now)

Rowe did not respond. When she was confronted by KFOR-TV in Oklahoma City, she said that she had never received Gagan's letter.

Yet Gagan's friend gave *New American* editor Bill Jasper a signed affidavit showing that he personally delivered the warning to the U.S. Marshals.*

According to Rowe, the point is moot, because the college graduate and former public school teacher has a history of "psychological problems." It seems that Gagan was sent to the Colorado State Mental Hospital in September of 1986 by Dr. Erwin Levy, at the behest of the Feds.**

---

* Jayna Davis, KFOR-TV broadcast, June, 1995. U.S. Marshals Service head Tina Rowe said, regarding Cary Gagan's hand-delivered letter: "I work in a federal building and all my friends work in federal buildings, and it's not something that anyone working in that environment would ever overlook." KFOR then uncovered a copy of Gagan's envelope, on which the matching signature of a Marshals Service employee was found. The Marshals Service claimed it was suspicious, because it's office policy to sign both the first and last name, and to stamp all incoming mail.

** The Judge who sent Gagan to the mental hospital, John P. Gately, was later termed incompetent and disbarred due to brain cancer.

"That was because I wasn't cooperating with my attorney," he said, referring to a 1986 theft case in Arapahoe County. "You tell somebody you're involved in espionage with the Soviets, and that's what they do, send you down to the James Bond ward." [387]

According to Gagan, the Colorado State Mental Hospital's Dr. Green pronounced Gagan sane, and he seemed level-headed when Representative Key and I interviewed him in March, '97.

Others think the informant isn't reliable. An apparent friend of Gagan's who's known him for 30 years told me he thinks Gagan's "full of shit," and "not in touch with reality."

Another, a Federal Public Defender who represented Gagan, told me, "Cary has an encyclopedic memory, of events, places and times." She said that Gagan was "bright [and] well-intentioned," although she added, "My gut sense is that the pure facts may be right, but I sometimes questioned the legal significance of some of it." Overall, she said she "liked" the informant. [388]*

Moreover, if Rowe's allegations regarding Gagan's credibility are valid, why then did U.S. Attorney Henry Solano grant him a Letter of Immunity? If the Feds thought Gagan was incompetent, they had a full decade of experience with him [as did the Denver Police] from which to establish his credibility or lack thereof.

"If I had a history of mental illness," explained Gagan, "they couldn't take me on as an informant."

The Feds' opinions may have stemmed from a 1983 incident where the informant was blacklisted by the DEA due to allegations he provided false information to the benefit of several drug dealers. Yet Gagan claims he redeemed himself by obtaining sensitive DEA-6 files that had been stolen from their office. Gagan said the DEA noted the informant's assistance on his record.**

Then in 1986, while Gagan was in jail for insurance fraud, he was visited by Kenny Vasquez, Bill Maten, and two FBI agents: Phillip Mann and Stanley Miller. They offered to get him early release if he would work again as an informant. Gagan declined. "They wanted to take me out of jail, and bring me back at night," said Gagan. "I didn't want any part of it."

In January of 1989, Agents Miller and Mann again asked Gagan to assist them in a joint FBI/Customs counterintelligence sting operation known as Operation Aspen Leaf. Their interest centered on one Edward Bodenzayer, a

---

* A voice stress analysis the author ran on Gagan's interview tapes showed he was telling the truth.

** Reports indicating that Gagan had been of assistance to the DEA were illegally removed from his informant file in an attempt to discredit him.

Soviet spy whom Gagan had met in Puerto Vallerta in 1982. Bodenzayer had been exporting classified technology to Russia through his import/export company.

Finally, on September 14, 1994, the Justice Department granted Gagan his immunity. The agreement, printed on an official U.S. Justice Department letterhead, read (in part):

> This letter is to memorialize the agreement between you and the United States of America, by the undersigned Assistant United States Attorney. The terms of this agreement are as follows:
>
> 1. You have contacted the U.S. Marshals Service on today's date indicating that you have information concerning a conspiracy and/or attempt to destroy United States court facilities in [redacted] and possibly other cities.
>
> 2. The United States agrees that any statement and/or information that you provide relevant to this conspiracy/conspiracies or attempts will not be used against you in any criminal proceeding. Further, the United States agrees that no evidence derived from the information or statements provided by you will be used in any way against you....[389]

In spite of the sensitive nature of Gagan's information, and the Letter of Immunity, "In the period of one year, from September 14, 1994, to the first week of September, 1995," said Gagan, "not one agent recontacted me, not one U.S. official of any kind recontacted me except [FBI SAC] Dave Shepard in Vegas."

Naturally, the FBI denied any wrongdoing.

Assistant U.S. Attorney James Allison was quoted in the August 12, 1995 issue of the *Rocky Mountain News* as saying, "Why would I grant somebody immunity and then not speak with him?"

When this author contacted Allison, he said, "I'm not going to discuss who is or who isn't a federal informant."

Yet U.S. Attorney Henry Solano, Allison's boss, granted an interview with Lawrence Myers of *Media Bypass* magazine, violating an informant's confidentiality agreement, placing Gagan in danger. In the October, 1995 issue, Myers printed Gagan's letter which had been hand-delivered to U.S. Marshall Tina Rowe. When Myers reprinted the letter—which was faxed to him by Solano—"April 6" was changed to "April 1," a weekend, in an attempt to show that Gagan couldn't possibly have delivered the warning. It is not clear whether Solano or Myers changed the date.

Discharged from a mental hospital in 1980 with a personality disorder, Myers was convicted of extortion in 1985 and was later asked by FBI Agent Steve

Brannon to work as an informant. Myers denied working for the FBI.

Yet in 1991 he showed up at the trial of Leroy Moody, working as an "explosives expert" on behalf of the defense. Curiously, he then turned around and fed confidential information to the FBI and the state prosecutor.[390]

Interestingly, Myers claimed to have worked for the CIA in Central America, apparently at the behest of Wackenhut, a CIA proprietary infamous for gathering intelligence on U.S. citizens. Even more interestingly, he wrote several books on explosives for Paladin Press, a possible CIA proprietary, including *Counterbomb, Smart Bombs,* and *Improved Radio Detonation Techniques.* One Myers title, called *Spycom,* instructs readers on the "dirty tricks of the trade" regarding "covert communication techniques."

Myers also showed up at ex-spook Charles Hayes' home in London, Kentucky on the premise of writing a flattering story on the CIA agent turned whistle-blower. Hayes subsequently wound up in jail on a murder conspiracy charge—a charge he adamantly denies.

> Hayes says he thinks that Myers was working for the government when he came to Kentucky to write a flattering profile of Hayes for the magazine *Media Bypass,* then privately told FBI agents that Hayes was looking for someone to kill his son.[391]

Were Solano and Myers part of a coordinated effort to discredit Gagan? Said a private investigator and retired Army CID officer regarding Myers: "I got the impression he was probably counterintelligence ... just by knowing these parts. The people he mentioned—the people he knew—told me that he was probably in the C.I.C. (Counterintelligence Corps) at one time."[392]

Conetta Williamson, an investigator for the Tennessee Attorney General's office, described Myers in court testimony as "a professional and pathological liar."[393]

Myers also wrote a piece about Federal Grand Juror Hoppy Heidelberg, the only grand juror who dared question the government's line. In fact, Heidelberg never consented to be interviewed by Myers, who had obtained the content of a privileged attorney/client interview of Heidelberg surreptitiously. The information was then crafted into an "interview" published in *Media Bypass,* ultimately resulting in Heidelberg's dismissal from the Grand Jury.

It seemed that Myers, using *Media Bypass* as a cover, had managed to put a government whistle-blower in jail, discredit a federal informant who had embarrassing information implicating the government in the bombing, and cause the dismissal of a troublesome grand juror.

If the Feds were intent on discrediting their own informant, why did they grant him a Letter of Immunity? Not only did Solano grant Gagan immunity, but the informant retained it a full 17 months. If Gagan was actually incompetent, why didn't Solano revoke immunity instead of letting Gagan continue working with terrorists?

"It doesn't make much sense does it?" said Gagan.*

It appears that the Justice Department granted Gagan immunity so they wouldn't look bad. After all, Gagan had already informed Dave Floyd at the U.S. Marshals office in September about the meeting with Omar and Ahmed.

The cat was out of the bag.

Gagan believes he was granted the Letter of Immunity as part of a sinister scheme to allow him to proceed with the bombing plot unhindered—at which point the Letter of Immunity was revoked.

"What if at that time I was told to go in and get immunity by the terrorists, and somebody working with the terrorists ... like the U.S. Government?" said Gagan. "I can't get prosecuted, can I? [The terrorists] knew that they would give me a Letter of Immunity and they knew that the FBI would cut me loose. So what's that enable them to do? If there needs to be something moved, and I'm the one that's moving it, I can't be prosecuted. I can haul as much shit as I want, and I have immunity, as long as I call the FBI, and let them know."

A Florida police detective who's investigated connections between Arab-Americans, the PLO, and the Cali Cartel told me, "Who has the best route for getting something across? Drug dealers." [394]

Was Cary Gagan part of some sinister plot by the Feds? Or was he merely used as a "mule," allowing terrorists to move money, drugs, and explosives while another government agent monitored the situation from within? Perhaps the new man from Oklahoma City who appeared on the scene in March?

Was Cary Gagan a "throwaway?"

Recall that Gagan had transported a duffel-bag filled with C-4 and cocaine, and had driven a truck laden with explosives across the state at the behest of his terrorist friends. He claims the FBI did nothing to stop him.

"You got to understand something here," said Gagan. "Federal law prohibits me from doing what I was doing. You cannot go out as an informant—I'm not an agent—I cannot take drugs and explosives from point A to point B."

Yet it seems that permitting the informant to commit such illegal acts would focus more light on the government's role—whether it involved foreknowledge or actual conspiracy—when Gagan began to go public with his story. But Gagan, who believes he was scheduled to be "terminated" after the bombing, disagrees. The informant displayed medical records showing that he was badly

---

* Gagan says the Letter of Immunity was not filed with the court, in violation of standard procedure. He also asserts that Allison's signature was signed by his secretary, and is no good.

beaten, and claims to have been the victim of a drive-by shooting.*

Whatever the case, it is interesting to note that authorities alleged that the bombing conspiracy began in September, '94, the same month Gagan received his Letter of Immunity and began informing the FBI.

On April 10, four days after he delivered the warning letter to Tina Rowe, Gagan received a note instructing him to appear at the law library of the U.S. Courthouse.

"I just gave the U.S. Marshals a bombing warning," said Gagan. "They didn't call me back. I had to go somewhere to cover my ass. I came back, I got a note saying, 'We need to see you; come to the U.S. Law Library.' I thought it was the U.S. Marshals or the FBI."

When Gagan arrived at the law library, he met his contact: an "athletic look-ing dude, 40s, short hair," dressed in a blue Nike cap and jumpsuit. "I get there and say, 'Hey, you got the shit?' He said, 'Hey, we've got everything taken care of. We need you to do this....'"

The man was not one of Gagan's Arab friends. "He was government," said Gagan. "He was probably CIA."

The mysterious figure asked Gagan to drive a trailer to Junction City, Kansas. In the trailer was the same Lely mixer that Gagan had driven to Golden on January 14. This mixer—the one that was driven to the Mariott at the behest of an Arab terrorist—was now on its way to Junction City at the request of a gov-ernment agent!

The date was now April 11, three days before Timothy McVeigh checked into the Dreamland Motel in Junction City. As previously mentioned, David King, who was staying at the Dreamland, recalled seeing a Ryder truck with a trailer attached to it in the parking lot on April 17. The trailer contained a "squarish object about three or four feet high that came to a point on top," secured by a can-vas tarp. This was the exact description Gagan gave of the Lely mixer.**

On April 13 Gagan drove to Oklahoma City, he said, to case the Murrah Building.

Three days later, Gagan says he drove a van from Denver to Trinidad, Colorado, that was picked up by Omar and Ahmed.

According to Gagan, it wasn't until three months *after* the bombing, in July of

---

* Gagan claims that on January 15, 1997, as he was waiting for a bus at 1st and Lincoln in downtown Denver, a dark four-door Buick came careening around the corner, firing at him with a silenced automatic weapon. A check with Doug Packston at the Colorado Transit Authority revealed a bullethole in the bus shelter and glass that had been replaced.

** It is unlikely that Gagan could have known about King's story, which was not widely reported.

'95, that Las Vegas FBI Agent Dave Shepard agreed to meet him. "We're sitting in the car behind the Sahara, and Shepard tells me we're not interested in pursuing the lead."*

That lead—two Arab suspects seen running from the Murrah Building towards a late model brown Chevy pick-up minutes before the blast—were the same suspects that the FBI had issued an All Points Bulletin (APB) for on April 19:

"Middle-Eastern males 25–28 years of age, six feet tall, athletic build, Dark hair and a beard—dark hair and a beard. Break."[395]

"And these two Middle Eastern dudes that were seen running from the scene—that's the same description I had given," said Gagan. "Gray in the beard, you know—Omar and Ahmed—to the FBI ... on September 14."

Gagan had provided that information to the FBI *six months before* the bombing. After the bombing, Gagan contacted Solano and said, "Isn't that amazing. You know, these are the [same] two dudes...."

In a letter to Gagan dated February 1, 1996, Solano and Allison wrote:

Attempts by federal law enforcement officers to meaningfully corroborate information you have alleged to be true have been unsuccessful.... Therefore, the immunity granted by the letter of September 14, 1994 is hereby revoked....

You are warned that any statement you make which would incriminate you in illegal conduct, past, present or future can be used against you. You are no longer protected by the immunity granted by letter on September 14, 1994.

Recall that after ATF informant Carol Howe had revealed that her knowledge of the bombing plot was reported to federal authorities *before* April 19, the ATF tried to discredit her, claiming that she was "unstable," just as they had done with Gagan. While they revoked Gagan's Letter of Immunity, they indicted Howe on spurious charges. Howe reported a bombing plot by neo-Nazi activists, but, like Gagan's warnings both before and after the bombing, she claimed her calls weren't returned.[396]

---

* The Florida police detective I spoke with told me that the FBI and state authorities "didn't want to investigate this," referring to the connections he uncovered between Arab-Americans, the PLO, and the Cali Cartel in the mid-80s. He believes the FBI's head of counter-intelligence came to Florida disguised as an agent, found out what they were working on, and took off. As he said, "Things weren't right. It was as if someone were looking at this and saying 'stay away from it.'" His experience ties into that of an Army C.I.D. officer who investigated the brother of one of the Middle-Easterners allegedly involved in the bombing, who was involved in military espionage in Huntsville, Alabama in the mid-80s. He said the FBI "stonewalled" the case.

Howe was also told by her ATF handler, Angela Finley-Graham, not to report her informant payments, and was led to believe that her debriefings were not being taped when they were. Both are a violation of C.I. (Confidential Informant) procedures. Was this a way to discredit Howe in case they needed to distance themselves from her later, as they attempted to do with Gagan?

One year later, Gagan filed a lawsuit alleging that numerous federal officials failed to uphold their agreement with him, failed to exercise proper procedures in regards to the handling of an informant, failed to investigate a terrorist conspiracy against the American people, failed to warn the public, and failed to properly investigate the crime after it occurred.

It is not surprising that officials wouldn't take Gagan's warning seriously. On December 5, 1988, a Palestinian named Samra Mahayoun warned authorities in Helsinki that a Pan Am 747 leaving Frankfurt was to bombed within two weeks.*

Two weeks later, on December 21, Pan Am flight 103 was blown out of the sky by a terrorist's bomb. Two hundred and fifty-nine people plunged to their deaths over Lockerbie, Scotland, and 11 more died on the ground.

State Department official Frank Moss later called Mahayoun's warning a "ghoulish coincidence." Mahayoun, they claimed, was just not credible.**

Demonstrating the limits of absurdity the government will go to in order to cover up its complicity and negligence, the U.S. Marshals Service was still insisting—after 169 people lay dead in Oklahoma—that Cary Gagan was still not credible.†

This is not the first time the government ignored viable warnings. Prior to the World Trade Center bombing, the FBI's paid informant, Emad Eli Salem, had penetrated Sheik Omar Abdel-Rahman's Jama a Islamiya and had warned the FBI of their plans. The agent in charge of the case, John Anticev, dismissed the former Egyptian Army Colonel's warnings, calling him "unreliable." On February

---

* A specific warning regarding flight 103 was also passed on from a Mossad Agent working at the Frankfurt airport.

** What is interesting is that Oliver "Buck" Revell, former Counter-Terrorism chief of the FBI, pulled his son and daughter-in-law off Pan Am 103 minutes before the flight. Did Revell know something the rest of us did not? (Steven Emerson doesn't bother mentioning that little fact in his piece entitled *The Fall of Pan Am 103* , which, incidentally, leaves out the entire CIA/drug connection that many feel was linked to the bombing.)

† Was Solano pressured to ignore Gagan's warning? The Denver U.S. Attorney had earlier intended to proceed with an investigation into corruption by top U.S. officials connected with Boulder Partnerships, Ltd., Twin Cities Bank of Little Rock, and MDC Holdings of Denver, until he realized who was involved—friends of Bill Clinton and George Bush.

26, 1993, a large bomb detonated underneath the twin towers, killing six people and injuring 1,000 more.

At the same time as "unreliable" people like Cary Gagan were warning federal authorities in Denver about the pending attack, *The Star Ledger*, a Newark, New Jersey newspaper, was reporting:

U.S. law enforcement authorities have obtained information that Islamic terrorists may be planning suicide attacks against federal courthouses and government installations in the United States.

The attacks, it is feared, would be designed to attract worldwide press attention through the murder of innocent victims. The *Star Ledger* has learned that U.S. law enforcement officials have received a warning that a "fatwa," a religious ruling similar to the death sentence targeting author Salman Rushdie, has been issued against federal authorities as a result of an incident during the trial last year of four persons in the bombing on the World Trade Center in New York.

The disclosure was made in a confidential memorandum issued by the U.S. Marshals Service in Washington calling for stepped-up security at federal facilities throughout the nation....

According to the source, Iranian-supported extremists have made it clear that steps are being taken to strike at the "Great Satan," a phrase that has been used to describe the United States....

Even more strenuous security precautions are being taken in New York, where 12 persons, including the blind fundamentalist Sheik Omar Abdel-Rahman, are currently on trial on charges of conspiring to wage a war of urban terrorism against the United States by blowing up the United Nations, FBI headquarters and the tunnels between New York and New Jersey....

The memo, issued by Eduardo Gonzales, director of the *U.S. Marshals Service,* warns that attacks may be designed to "target as many victims as possible and draw as much media coverage as possible" to the fundamentalist cause....

The terrorists, possible suicide bombers, will not engage in negotiations," the memo warned, and said "once the press is on the scene, the new plans call for blowing everyone up.[397]

If that last statement is true, it could explain the presence of a box of explosives found in the Murrah Building with a timer on it set for ten minutes after nine. The initial bomb(s) blew up at *two* minutes after nine.

The U.S. Marshal's Service—the federal agency charged with the task of protecting federal facilities—had clear warning from at least two different undercover informants. Why then was there no security at the Murrah Building on April 19?

It was also reported that the Israelis, the Saudis, and the Kuwaitis all warned the U.S. about an impending attack. Whatever the U.S. Marshals Service felt about Cary Gagan's warning, Gonzales apparently felt his other sources were reliable enough to issue a nationwide alert. Perhaps that memo, like the one issued by the FBI in 1963 to its field offices warning of an attempt on the life of President Kennedy, just "disappeared."

THE TRAIL OF WITNESSES

On April 19, Abraham Ahmed, a Jordanian, was detained by authorities as a possible bombing suspect as he attempted to fly from Oklahoma City to Amman, Jordan. American Airlines personnel observed Ahmed "acting nervous," prior to his flight, and notified security personnel, who in turn notified the FBI.

Agents detained Ahmed in Chicago, where the Oklahoma City resident explained that he was on his way to his father's wedding, and was scheduled to return to the U.S. in July.

Yet, Ahmed's story changes. He told reporters alternately that he had gone back to Jordan: a) for a wedding, b) to build a house, c) to replace the youngest son who had moved out, and d) to attend to a family emergency.

After being questioned for six hours, the FBI allowed Ahmed to continue on his way. Yet he was detained in London the following day, where he was questioned for another five hours, then handcuffed and put on the next plane back to the U.S.

In the meantime, Ahmed's luggage continued on to Rome, where authorities discovered a suitcase full of electronic equipment, including two car radios, silicon, solder, shielded and unshielded wire, a small tool kit, and, incredibly enough, a photo album with pictures of weapons and missiles! Security sources at London's Heathrow Airport also said that a pair of blue jogging suits and a timing device was found in one of his bags.[398]

When asked what he was doing with these items, Ahmed explained that they were for his relatives in Jordan, who could not obtain good-quality electrical components. Ahmed also had a blue jogging suit similar to what a Middle-Eastern suspect was wearing at the Murrah Building on the morning of the blast. According to an account in the *London Telegraph*, Ahmed was reportedly in Oklahoma City on Wednesday—the day of the bombing.[399]

If Ahmed had been cleared by U.S. authorities for the worst domestic terrorist attack in U.S. history, why did British authorities refuse to allow him into the country? Did they know something the U.S. did not?

The Justice Department's Carl Stern downplayed the breakthrough saying only, "There are a number of good, solid leads in this investigation."[400]

Yet in FBI agent Henry Gibbons' affidavit, special mention was made of the items in Ahmed's suitcase, and his coincidental April 19, 10:43 A.M. departure time, and Gibbons stated he considered Ahmed's testimony in front of the Federal Grand Jury vital.

One FBI source interviewed by KFOR's Jayna Davis admitted that he didn't think Ahmed was telling the truth on a polygraph test. Yet Ahmed was simply allowed to go on his way, and like so many other suspects and witnesses, was never called before the Federal Grand Jury.

Interestingly, the Middle Eastern community was apologized to by President Clinton. This is very interesting coming from a president that failed to apologize to Randy Weaver, the Branch Davidians, and the thousands of people wrongly accused, imprisoned and murdered each year by U.S. law-enforcement personnel.

A possible explanation may be found in the bombing of Pan Am 103. In February of 1989, a prime suspect in the case, Jordanian bomb maker Marwan Kreeshat, admitted in a statement provided by Jordanian intelligence that he had manufactured at least five highly sophisticated, powerful bombs for PFLP-GC (Popular Front for the Liberation of Palestine-General Command) leader Ahmed Jibril, by cleverly concealing them in portable radios—the same type which destroyed flight 103. Jordanian intelligence officials, who have maintained a close, long-standing relationship with the CIA, admitted that the Jordanian national was actually an undercover agent, and was also an asset of U.S. intelligence.[401]

Could this explain why the FBI released Ahmed?*

Taylor Jesse Clear, a retired State Department counter-terrorism expert who has studied the case, disagrees with this analysis. Clear believes that Ahmed's conspicuously timed departure, complete with nervous act and a suitcase full of electronic gear, was a diversion. "They wanted to inoculate the media to the Arab connection," explained Clear. Letting Ahmed get caught with a suitcase full of that stuff, then discovering he was innocent, inoculated everybody to the Middle Eastern connection. Then they could come back, beat their chests, and say, 'look what you did to the Arab community.'"

Yet the brown Chevy pick-up seen speeding away from the Murrah Building was traced to an Oklahoma City business run by a Palestinian, with possible PLO ties. That man is a good friend of Abraham Ahmed's. According to a witness who worked for the Palestinian, Ahmed was seen driving the pick-up in the weeks before the bombing.

Numerous witnesses also place McVeigh in Oklahoma City in the days before the bombing with a friend of Ahmed's—an Iraqi—a man who bears a strong

---

* Ahmed's detention produced a flurry of responses from the ACLU (American Civil Liberties Union), who were notified by Ahmed's friend Sam Khalid. The ACLU has long been funded (some say taken over) by the Roger Baldwin Foundation, a CIA front. Perhaps they wanted their man Ahmed released, just as the CIA wanted Jordanian Marwan Kreeshat released.

resemblance to the mysterious, stoic passenger seen in the Ryder truck by Mike Moroz on the morning of April 19 at Johnny's Tire Store.

KFOR reporters Brad Edwards and Jayna Davis broke the story on June 7, 1995 with a series of interviews with witnesses who saw McVeigh with the Iraqi, first in a bar, then in a restaurant, then in a pawnshop.

One of the witnesses, a barmaid at the Roadrunner Tavern on South May Avenue, saw McVeigh buying beer for the man on Saturday, April 15. "He was dark, kind of muscular, he had on a ball cap," said the barmaid. "He talked like they do over in Iran or Iraq, or whatever during Desert Storm, when you would hear the way they talked on TV."

When Davis asked her how sure she was that the man they had been tracking was the man she saw with McVeigh, she replied, "I'm sure."

The tavern owner also saw the Iraqi a few days after the bombing. He picked him out from a group of photos. While the Iraqi claimed he was never in any bar on NW 10th Street, a co-worker interviewed by KFOR said he had drank with him at a bar on NW 10th and Indiana, and in fact he was arrested for driving under the influence around the corner, at NW 8th and Blackwielder in early June.[402]

In another interview, three women who worked at a pawnshop stated that McVeigh and two other men came into their shop twice: "… on April 14 and again on April 17, just two days before the bombing."

"It had to have been McVeigh," said the pawnshop owner. "If it was not McVeigh, it was his twin brother."

"They spoke in a foreign language," said one of the pawn shop employees. "They huddled together and they all three spoke secretively to one another, and it was a foreign language."

A restaurant owner down the street also remembered McVeigh and the Iraqi. "[McVeigh acted] like a contractor coming in and buying his hand lunch, that was the impression I had," recalled the proprietor.

As previously mentioned, restaurant worker Phyliss Kingsley recalled a Ryder truck pulling into the Hi Way Grill at SW 104 and Portland on April 16th. Accompanying the truck was a white long-bed Chevy pick-up, and a darker pick-up, possibly blue or brown. She recalls Timothy McVeigh strolling in and ordering two "trucker burgers" and fries to go. Accompanying McVeigh was a short, stocky man of about 5' 2", either Mexican or American Indian (or Arabic) descent, with black, curly hair. She said the man closely resembled the FBI sketch of John Doe 2, but with slightly thinner features. Kingsley recalled that the man spoke briefly with McVeigh.*

---

* What must be pointed out again is that the FBI is claiming McVeigh rented the Ryder truck the following Monday, April 17. This account indicates that two Ryder trucks were involved in the operation, not one, as the FBI claims.

Waitress Linda Kuhlman described him as having straighter hair and being slightly taller. She described him as wearing green army fatigue pants and a white t-shirt.

Kuhlman, who grew up around trucks and hot-rods, is positive that one of the trucks was a Chevy long-bed, most likely an '87 model. When shown photos, including the Iraqi and Michael Brescia, they came close to picking out the Iraqi, but could not positively identify either man. The passenger in the Ryder truck, they said, a man with longish wavy, permed-out brown or dirty blond hair and glasses, never got out.

Dennis Jackson, a VA worker, recalled seeing two or three Arabic men in the Murrah Building the following day, April 17. "There was a distinct air about them," recalls Jackson. "We were working late that day, the office had closed, and they were just kind of hanging around the Social Security office. I thought that was kind of unusual ... they might have been there for Social Security, but I hardly think so."

Jackson's co-worker Craig Freeman recalled one of the men as a short, stocky Arabic man, about 5′ 2″, 150 pounds, wearing khaki military style pants, combat boots and a white T-shirt—the same combination seen on the Middle Eastern suspect described by Linda Kuhlman.

In a bizarre twist, a white Chevy pick-up showed up at Freeman's house several days after the bombing. Freeman recalls a Caucasian-looking man in the truck, which was parked near his house on two consecutive days. "It was right before and right after the FBI and OSBI came and interviewed me," recalls Freeman. "I could tell this guy was watching me because when I walked by, he sort of turned away and hid his face. I'm a former Air Force Master Sergeant and a third degree black belt, and I'm trained to be observant." [403]

Could the man Freeman saw have been there to intimidate him?

The barmaid at the Road Runner Tavern also told KFOR's Brad Edwards that after her interview aired, the Iraqi pulled up by the open back door of the tavern and stared menacingly at her. What is interesting is that the Iraqi's Palestinian boss owns a white pick up truck—a Nissan, not a Chevy. Freeman and Linda Kuhlman are positive they saw a Chevy.

Yet another witness to a post-bombing incident involving the Palestinian claimed that he also was followed by the man, who was driving a white pick-up.

Back in Junction City, the manager of the Great Western Inn was watching TV with two reporters when the sketch of John Doe 2 flashed on the screen. The manager immediately recognized the man as the person who had stayed in room 107 on April 17. "He spoke broken English," said the manager. "[He] gave a foreign name and was driving a Ryder truck."

The man's name would never be revealed, however, because the FBI confiscated the hotel's log book. [404]

Several months later, *Newsweek* reporter Leslie Jorgensen uncovered information that several men had stayed at the Radisson Inn in Oklahoma City the day before the bombing. The men were dressed in Arab garb, but according to an employee, were not Arabs. At the same time, phone calls were placed from the Radisson to one of Timothy McVeigh's friends—a man in Idaho associated with the Aryan Republican Army.

A few days earlier, across town, two men had checked into the Plaza Inn. They told desk clerk Tiffany Harper they were Spanish visitors from Mexico. But Harper thought they were Arabs because of the way they talked.

According to employee Ruby Foos, another man checked into the motel a day or two later, went to his room, then emerged wearing flowing Arab robes. As far as Foos could tell, the man was not connected with the other two men.[405]

While it may not be unusual for Arab-garbed individuals to be in Oklahoma due to its connection with the oil industry, Douglas Boyer, the security guard at the Plaza, said a yellow Ryder truck was parked out front. All of the men checked out a day or two before the bombing.

Interestingly, two Middle Eastern men were spotted driving from Oklahoma City to Dallas immediately after the bombing. The men stopped to ask directions from an Oklahoma Highway Patrolman. When the officer ran their plate, he discovered that it didn't match the vehicle. The plate belonged to a rented blue Chevy Cavalier, which was later found at a motel in Oklahoma City. The driver of that vehicle, Asad R. Siddiqy, a cab driver from Queens, along with the other two men, Anis Siddiqy and Mohammed Chafi, were taken into custody.[406]

While the men were ultimately questioned and released, a blue Chevy Cavalier would be spotted by a witness in downtown Oklahoma City—along with a Ryder truck, a yellow Mercury, and a brown Chevy pick-up—the other vehicles in the bombing convoy.

On the morning of the blast, a woman was riding the elevator in the Murrah building, when she noticed a young Arab man wearing a backpack, hurriedly pushing the buttons as if trying to get off. As previously mentioned, she followed him outside, not suspecting anything was amiss. Moments later, she was sent sprawling to the sidewalk as the building blew up behind her.

Gary Lewis, a pressman for the *Journal Record* newspaper, had just stepped outside to smoke his pipe when he remembered he had left something in his car. As he walked down the alley, a yellow Mercury peeled away from its spot near the Murrah Building, jumped a concrete barricade, swerved to avoid hitting a dumpster, then bore down on him, forcing him up onto the curb. Lewis got a good look at the driver, describing him as Timothy James McVeigh, and his passenger as resembling the sketch of John Doe 2. He said the car had an Oklahoma tag dangling by one bolt.

Several minutes later, Lewis was thrown to the floor as the Journal Record building rocked with the impact of the blast. As he picked himself up, another, more powerful explosion sent him sprawling again. As he and his fellow workers rushed outside, he noticed a peculiar sight: an Arab man standing nearby, staring at the Federal Building, grinning from ear to ear.

"It unnerved me," said Lewis, who described how the man seemed out of place among the throng of battered and bloody people. He seemed "enraptured."

As discussed earlier, another witness saw two men running from the area of the Federal Building toward a brown Chevy truck just prior to the blast. The witness described the two men as "males, of possible Middle-Eastern descent, approximately six feet tall, with athletic builds." One of the men was described as approximately 25-28 years old, having dark hair and a beard. The second person was described as 35-38 years old, with dark hair and a dark beard with gray in it—the same description Cary Gagan gave. He was described as wearing blue jogging pants, a black shirt, and a black jogging jacket. The witness also described a third person in the pick-up.[407]

Was this the same pick-up seen by Leonard Long and his daughter? Long was driving east on 5th Street at approximately 8:00 A.M. when he was forced to swerve out of the way by a erratically-driven brown pick-up with tinted windows. As the truck pulled up alongside, the passenger, a stocky, dark-skinned, dark-haired man began hurling racial epithets at the black couple. Long said the driver was a tall, thin white man with sharp features, a description not unsimilar to that given by James Linehan. The truck took the I-35 exit and headed south.[408]

Approximately 50 minutes later, as Margaret Hohmann and her friend Ann Domin were pulling into a parking spot in front of the Murrah Building, a brown pick-up peeled away from its parking spot, burning rubber as it tore down 5th Street. "Where's the cops when you need them?" Hohmann thought to herself.[409]

A few blocks away from the Murrah Building, Debra Burdick and her daughter were on the way to the doctor's office. As she stopped for a light at 10th and Robinson, she noticed three vehicles parked on the north side of the street between a church and a garage. One was a brown pick-up, one was a blue Chevy Cavalier, and the other was a yellow Mercury.

"I looked across," said Burdick, "and there was that light blue car, it had a white interior, and there were three men in it. They were dark, but they were not black ... I would say they were Middle Easterners. There was a brown pick-up, but I couldn't see in (because of the tinted windows), and behind it was the yellow car with the cream top.

"Now, I noticed the three men in the car, that guy sitting in the middle was kind of staring out.... I said 'Huh, I wonder what they're looking at?' and as I turned around, I said 'there's nothing there but buildings.'"[410]

A few moments later, the bomb(s) went off. Hohmann and Domin, who were inside one of the Murrah Building's restrooms, were sent crashing to the floor. At the same moment, Debra Burdick and her daughter went skidding to the side of the road. When she looked back, the three vehicles were gone.

Five blocks south of the Murrah Building, at Robinson and Main, Kay H. had just raced out of her office. As she stepped on to the meridian, she was nearly run over as the brown pick-up came careening around the corner. The near miss gave her an opportunity to get a good look at the occupants.

"The driver—I made eye contact with him," recalled Kay. "He looked like he was in his twenties—late twenties. [He] had an angry look on his face. I'll never forget the look on his face. It just was full of hate and anger. It really struck me, because everyone else—people were coming out and they looked scared and confused, and he just looked full of anger."[411]

Kay recalled that two of the three people in the truck were Middle-Easterners. When she was shown photos, she picked out the Iraqi—the same one seen with McVeigh—as the driver.

David Snider, the Bricktown worker who had spotted one of the Ryder trucks that morning, ran outside after the bomb went off, and saw the brown pick-up as it flew past. "They were doing about 60 mph," recalled Snider. "They turned north and headed over the Walnut Street Bridge."[412]

An all-points-bulletin (APB) was quickly put out on the pick-up:

Dispatcher: "Be on the lookout for a late model almost new Chevrolet full-size pick-up—full size brown pick-up. Will be brown in color with tinted windows—brown in color with tinted windows. Smoke colored bug deflector on the front of pick-up. Middle-Eastern males 25-28 years of age, six feet tall, athletic build, Dark hair and a beard—dark hair and a beard. Break."
Officer: "Okay, is this good information, or do we not really know?"
Dispatcher: "Authorization FBI."[413]

Strangely, the FBI canceled the APB several hours later, refusing to say why, demanding that it not be rebroadcast. When KPOC's David Hall asked the FBI why they canceled it, they denied ever putting it out. But when Hall played back his copy for the FBI man, he suddenly had "no comment."[414]

Soon after, Brad Edwards received a tip that the pick-up had been seen several times before the bombing at "Sahara Properties" (not its real name), a real-estate business in northwest Oklahoma City. The owner of "Sahara Properties," an Israeli-born Palestinian named "Sam Khalid" (not his real name), was the Iraqi's employer.*

Not long after KFOR's reports began airing, the Iraqi sued the station, then held a press conference claiming that he was not a suspect in the bombing, and that he had a solid alibi for the morning of April 19. His name was Hussain al-

---

* Ernie Cranford and neighbors saw the brown pick-up at Sahara Properties.

Hussaini, and he was at work, he said, painting a garage on NW 31st Street. Yet Alvin Devers, a neighbor interviewed by Davis, claimed no one was working on the house that day. "I didn't see anybody," said Devers. "I'd remember...."

In addition, Hussaini's co-worker, "Ernie Cranford" (not his real name), said Hussaini's alibi for the morning of April 19—a time sheet stating he was at work at 8:08 A.M.—was patently false. "Cranford" told Davis that Hussaini was working at a different house by 10 A.M., six blocks away, but wasn't there at 8:30 A.M.

"They was out there acting like they was painting on that garage all morning," "Cranford" told me. "They didn't know I was already there before...."[415]

Moreover, according to "Cranford," Sahara Properties doesn't use time sheets: "They use a time clock. They started about five months ago—five, six months ago ... I've seem them clocking in every morning." Davis later learned that "Khalid's" daughter concocted Hussaini's "time sheet" at the request of her father.*

Hussaini also claimed that he worked a second job as at the Western Sizzlin restaurant—as a janitor, three days a week, from 10 P.M. to 8 A.M.—which would have kept him too busy to be at the Murrah Building on April 19. Yet when Davis checked with Jeff Johnston, the assistant manager, she was told Hussaini hadn't worked from April 17 through April 20.

Interestingly, Hussaini reapplied for his job in May, then quit in June, saying that he didn't need a job. Had he suddenly come into a large amount of money?

When KFOR shared their evidence with the FBI, they downplayed their findings. FBI spokesman Dan Vogel said that eyewitness accounts are "notoriously inaccurate. Their credibility must be checked out, their stories corroborated."

But KFOR was able to corroborate their story with at least eight different witnesses. They not only placed McVeigh with Hussaini in at least three different locations in Oklahoma City, they were able to trace the brown pick-up to the business where Hussaini worked—to a businessman that had been investigated by the FBI for PLO ties. They determined that Hussaini had a tattoo exactly as described by the FBI, and that his alibi for the morning of April 19 was patently false.

Strangely, the FBI decided to back up Hussaini's story, telling KFOR that it might be difficult to place Hussaini near the Murrah Building on the morning of the 19th. Apparently the government had not counted on a local TV station

---

* "Khalid's" daughter Heather also told Cranford in a secretly-taped interview that she had not been able to find any time record on Hussaini for April 19, so she made one up and gave it to Dave Balut, a reporter for KWTV. Khalid employee Terry Holliday, told a reporter at KOCO-TV that Hussaini had been painting the house at NW 31st Street on April 19, then later told "Cranfield" that Hussaini had not actually been there on the 19th. Heather claimed that she had taken some supplies to Hussaini that morning, but Holliday claimed she had never been there. "Khalid" worker Barnaby Machuca also repeatedly changed his story regarding Hussaini's whereabouts.

stumbling onto Hussaini. After KFOR's story broke, a major damage control apparatus went into motion. KWTV, KOCO, the *Daily Oklahoman*, and the *Oklahoma Gazette* all ridiculed KFOR's reporting.*

Interestingly, when Hussaini appeared before TV cameras on June 15 to dispel the "rumors" about him, it was Abraham Ahmed who appeared as his interpreter!

The *Gazette* and KOCO also both claimed that Hussaini couldn't speak English, implying that he couldn't have been talking with McVeigh. Yet KFOR learned that he spoke broken English, and a police D.U.I. report indicated that he replied in English when questioned.[416]

"The information quoted on Channel Four is not true," FBI Agent Jeffrey Jenkins told the *Daily Oklahoman*. Though Jenkins later denied saying that, he admits that he "cringed when he saw the KFOR report."

Perhaps Jenkins cringed when he saw Hussaini on TV because the news station had, quite accidentally, uncovered the FBI's confidential informant (C.I.). Why else would the FBI act so patronizing towards KFOR, who had clearly established a link between Hussaini and McVeigh?

The FBI wouldn't say if they had checked out Hussaini. Nor would they clear him. They told KFOR that they were "not in the business of clearing suspects." Yet, as Jayna Davis pointed out, they did clear Todd Bunting, the Army private who they thought might have been John Doe 2. They then used the Bunting incident to say that John Doe 2 had been a red herring all along. John Doe 2, the FBI claimed, had never existed.**

Just why would the FBI would want to clear a suspect who was seen by numerous witnesses with Timothy McVeigh, and was seen speeding away from the bombing?

For his part, Hussaini claims he was an officer in Iraq's elite Republican Guard, who was imprisoned for distributing anti-Saddam literature. According to the *Gazette's* account, he was released after serving eight years of a 13-year sentence.[417]

But the story changes. According to KWTV, he escaped during a prison uprising at the end of the war, and after searching for his family, he "ran to American soldiers and asked for help." He was then interned in a Saudi refugee camp, where he spent the next four years, until he was relocated to the U.S. in 1995.[418]

The problem with this story is that U.S. forces didn't get within 200 miles of

---

* Numerous FBI and law enforcement sources Davis contacted agreed that Hussaini resembled the sketch of John Doe 2, and believed there was a Middle Eastern connection to the bombing, possibly connected to the World Trade Center bombing. (KFOR's Response to Plaintiff's Interrogatories, Hussaini vs. KFOR.)

** FBI spokesman Steve Mullins wouldn't confirm or deny whether Hussaini was a suspect; FBI agent James Strickland, who would later investigate Khalid's alleged shooting of his secretary, Sharon Twilley, declined to comment on whether Hussaini was a suspect.

Baghdad, which means that if Hussaini "ran to American soldiers," he would have had to run across several hundred miles of open dessert.

According to his boss, Sam Khalid, Hussaini was never in the Republican Guard at all. A Shíite Muslim, he was imprisoned for anti-Saddam beliefs, and forced to serve as cannon fodder on the front lines, as the Republican Guard withdrew.[419]

Yet the story changes once again. According to William Northrop, Hussaini served in the Hammurabi Division of the Republican Guard, and "was captured by the American 24th Mechanized Infantry Division in a fight on Highway 8, west of Basra, a few days after the war ended." Northrop stated that the Iraqis encountered the U.S. force, and, thinking it was merely a probe, opened fire. The Iraqis were badly beaten in the ensuing firefight, and Hussaini was wounded. He claims Hussaini was never in an Iraqi prison.*

If Hussaini was trying to concoct a cover-story, he apparently wasn't doing a good job.** According to Northrop:

> This lad was no ordinary soldier. [He] came to the United States around November of 1991. He triggered a "watch" on the Iraqi community in Boston and shortly thereafter, moved to Oklahoma City. I understand that he is currently residing in Houston.

Northrop also states that "Ramzi Ahmed Yousef, [the 'mastermind' behind the World Trade Center bombing] served in the Hammurabi Division of the Republican Guard during the Gulf War...."†

While it is not known how accurate this information is, evidence ties Yousef—a Pakistani Baluchi born in Kuwait—to Iraqi intelligence. The Baluch, who are Sunni Moslems, oppose the clerical Shia regime of Teheran, and had forged close links with Iraqi intelligence during that country's 10-year war with Iran. According to Dr. Mylroie, Iraq used the Baluch to carry out acts of terrorism against Iran.[420]

---

* William Northrop is an ex-Israeli intelligence officer who was indicted by former U.S. Attorney Rudolph Giuliani, and testified against Israel's role in Iran-Contra. A friend of the late CIA Director William Casey, Northrop's name was reportedly found in Casey's diary upon his death.

** Khalid, speaking on behalf of Hussaini, claimed his INS records were "stolen."

† Yousef arrived in New York on September 1, 1992. Many New York law enforcement officials reportedly believe that Iraq was involved [in the Trade Center bombing], although they can not prove it. (Laurie Mylroie, "World Trade Center Bombing —The Case of Secret Cyanide," *The Wall Street Journal,* July 26, 1994, p. A16), quoted in James Phillips, "The Changing Face of Middle Eastern Terrorism," *The Heritage Foundation, Backgrounder,* #1005, 10/6/94.

Alias Abdul Basit Mahmud Abdul Karim, Yousef arrived in the United States carrying an Iraqi passport.

Both Yousef and his partner in the World Trade Center bombing, Ahmed Ajaj, worked for Edwards Pipeline Testing and Technical Welding Laboratories in Houston, whose CEO is Maunal Bhajat, a close associate of Ishan Barbouti—an international Iraqi arms dealer who built Libya's chemical weapons plant at Ràbta. Barbouti's son Haidar (like Hussaini) also lives in Houston. According to Louis Champon, who went into business with Haidar, "Haidar Barbouti is an Iraqi agent."*

It was Barbouti who financed Champon's Product Ingredient Technology through his son Haidar. Wackenhut, a company with long-standing ties to the FBI and CIA, provided the security. According to Champon, Barbouti (with perhaps a little help from the secretive and mysterious Wackenhut) secretly drained thousands of gallons of ferrocyanide—a naturally occurring Cherry extract used to make cyanide gas—from Champon's plant.

Barbouti's ability to procure U.S. weapons technology for sale to Libya and Iraq wasn't hindered by U.S. officials. While the Bush administration was publicly decrying Hussein's use of chemical weapons on the Kurds, the potassium ferrocyanide was shipped to Iraq to manufacture chemical weapons for Iraq's army, with the full knowledge and complicity of the Bush administration.

Said Champon, "Not one U.S. agent—not one official, ever questioned Haidar Barbouti—for evasion of taxes, where he got his money from, his involvement … in shipping cyanide outside the P.I.T. plant … nothing. I was told—and this is a quote from U.S. Customs [agent Martin Schram]—"This matter is highly political. Haidar Barbouti cannot be indicted, and if he were, he would never be convicted." [421]

The key that allowed the Iraqi "businessman" (Barbouti doesn't like to be called an arms dealer) to interface with the CIA was one Richard V. Secord, an integral player in the Iran-Contra arms-for-drugs network. Secord, it should be noted, was also a business partner of Vang Pao, the Laotian General who ran a heroin smuggling ring out of Long Tien Airbase during the Vietnam War, and Monzer al-Kassar, the Syrian arms and drugs dealer who was involved in the Pan Am 103 bombing—another crime successfully covered up by the CIA and the FBI. According to Richard Babayan, a former CIA contract employee, "Barbouti was placed in the hands of Secord by the CIA, and Secord called in Wackenhut to handle security and travel for Barbouti and his export plans."**

Mike Johnston, the attorney who sued Barbouti on behalf of TK-7, an Oklahoma City company, ran into the same sort of stonewalling by the Justice

---

* Hussain al-Hussaini moved to Houston after going public and suing KFOR.
** Louis Champon said he saw Barbouti meet with Secord at the Fountain Blue Hotel in Miami in 1988.

Department. As Johnston was told by the federal team investigating this little corner of Iraqgate, "Mr. Johnston, you don't understand, we have to limit the objective of the investigation so we can get on with the business of running the government."

"Going into the investigation ... was a disguised whitewash," Johnston later told me, echoing what U.S. Customs agent Martin Schram told Champon.

Former CIA asset Charles Hayes said the CIA-connected Wackenhut was helping Barbouti ship chemicals to Iraq, "Supplying Iraq was originally a good idea," he maintains, "but then it got out of hand." [422]

Said Champon, "I can assure you, that if drums of cyanide left our plant, Dr. Barbouti had his reasons, either to be used against American troops or terrorist acts against the United States at home."* Cyanide is a necessary ingredient in the development of nerve gas. One thousand grams of cyanide later wound up in the World Trade Center bomb, constructed by Iraqi agent Ramzi Yousef.

Yousef's partner, Ahmed Ajaj, a member of the Egyptian-based Al-Gama'a al-Islamiya, lived in Texas. A Texas hamburger stand was reportedly used to relay telephone calls between the World Trade Center bombers as a means of avoiding detection. It was owned by some Palestinian friends of Ajaj, and Yousef and Ajaj used the number for conference calls while Ajaj was in prison.

The records may also indicate a tie between Ajaj and Hussaini's boss, Sam Khalid. Records obtained during TK-7's civil suit against Ishan Barbouti show a phone call to one of Khalid's properties in Houston. The person who made call was Ahmed Ajaj. [423]

Barbouti wasn't just trying to procure material and technology from U.S. companies on behalf of Iraq. Barbouti also built the bunkers used to house Saddam Hussein's Mig jet fighters during Desert Storm. It was during TK-7's suit against Barbouti that the Americans learned of these bunkers. Barbouti's London head of Security, Tony Davisson, decided to sell the Americans the blueprints. It isn't clear whether Davisson had a falling out with Barbouti, or was simply being patriotic. The point may be moot, as Barbouti was apparently dead. The Iraqi arms dealer died (or faked his death) around the same time the Israeli Mossad knocked off his contemporary, Gerald Bull, the developer of the ill-fated Iraqi "Super-Gun."**

Davisson called TK-7's attorney, Mike Johnston, who flew to London, where

---

* Yet according to Champon's former head of security Peter Kawaja, and Iraqgate investigator Robert Bickel, Champon himself isn't so innocent. "Champon had to know about the cyanide leaving the plant," said Bickel. "He was there every day, while the plant was being built and operated." Nevertheless, Champon went public, and was threatened and shut down by U.S. Customs and the I.R.S.

** While Ishan Barbouti allegedly "died" of heart failure in London in July of 1990, he was reportedly seen afterwards alive and well flying between Aman, Jordan and Tripoli, Libya. Other accounts indicate that he is living safe and well in Florida.

he purchased the plans for $2,700, and promptly turned them over to the CIA. With the plans for Saddam's underground bunkers, the U.S. Air Force was able to practically wipe out Iraq's entire fleet of Mig fighter jets at the start of the war.

This didn't exactly make Saddam happy. In the parlance of the Arab world, this equated to payback time. If Hussein thought Barbouti was responsible for the destruction of his air force, he may have insisted the arms dealer cooperate in an act of revenge against the United States.

IRAQI REVENGE?

The destruction of the Hussein's air force wasn't the only motive Iraq had for seeking revenge against the U.S. While Americans were busy tying yellow ribbons on their front porches for our boys in the Gulf, these same brave boys were slaughtering enemy soldiers and helpless civilians by the thousands. As reported by Mike Erlich of the Military Counseling Network at the March-April, 1991 European Parliament hearings on the Gulf War:

> Hundreds, possibly thousands, of Iraqi soldiers began walking toward the U.S. position unarmed, with their arms raised in an attempt to surrender. However, the orders for this unit were not to take any prisoners....
>
> The commander of the unit began the firing by shooting an anti-tank missile through one of the Iraqi soldiers. This is a missile designed to destroy tanks, but it was used against one man.
>
> At that point, everybody in the unit began shooting. Quite simply, it was a slaughter.[424]

The government-controlled sanitized media campaign beamed into our living rooms, replete with scenes of high-tech "smart-bombs" whistling through the windows of enemy command centers, merely belied the terrible and deliberate carnage inflicted upon thousands of helpless civilians.

On February 13, 1991, a U.S. Air Force Stealth Bomber dropped two 1,000-pound, laser-guided bombs onto the roof of the Al-Amira air raid shelter in Baghdad. Two hundred and ninety four people—mostly women and children—died in what the U.S. military called a "military surgical strike."

According to William Blum, author of *Killing Hope: U.S. Military and CIA Interventions Since World War II*, the bombing of the Al-Amira air raid shelter wasn't accidental, it was deliberate:

> The United States said it thought that the shelter was for VIPs, which it had been at one time, and claimed that it was also being used as a military communications

center, but neighborhood residents insisted that the constant aerial surveillance overhead had to observe the daily flow of women and children into the shelter. Western reporters said they could find no signs of military use.[425]

An American journalist in Jordan who viewed unedited videotape footage of the disaster, which the American public never saw, wrote:

They showed scenes of incredible carnage. Nearly all the bodies were charred into blackness; in some cases the heat had been so great that entire limbs were burned off.... Rescue workers collapsed in grief, dropping corpses; some rescuers vomited from the stench of the still-smoldering bodies.[426]

Said White House spokesman Marlin Fitzwater after the bombing of the shelter: It was "a military target ... We don't know why civilians were at this location, but we do know that Saddam Hussein does not share our value for the sanctity of life." [427]

This so-called "value for the sanctity for life" shown by American forces and lauded by the Bush administration not only included attacks such as the one at Al-Amira, but the bombing and strafing of unarmed civilians who tried to flee to the Jordanian border.

Buses, taxis, and private cars were repeatedly assaulted, literally without mercy, by rockets, cluster bombs and machine guns; usually in broad daylight, the targets clearly civilian, with luggage piled on top, with no military vehicles or structures anywhere to be seen, surrounded by open desert, the attacking planes flying extremely close to the ground ... busloads of passengers incinerated, and when people left the vehicles and fled for their lives, planes often swooped down upon them firing away....

"You're killing us!" cried a Jordanian taxi driver to an American reporter. "You're shooting us everywhere we move! Whenever they see a car or truck, the planes dive out of the sky and chase us. They don't care who we are or what we are. They just shoot." His cry was repeated by hundreds of others....[428]

Mike Ange, a GI from North Carolina, described the carnage:

I actually went up close and examined two of the vehicles that basically looked like refugees maybe trying to get out of the area. You know, you had like a little Toyota pick-up truck that was loaded down with the furniture and the suitcases and rugs and the pet cat and that type of thing, all over the back of the this truck, and those trucks were taken out just like the military vehicles.[429]

"The U.S. military considers the murdering of our children nothing more than collateral damage," said Al Kaissy, an information officer at the Iraqi Interests section of the Algerian Embassy in Washington. "They have never apologized or even admitted their mistake." [430]

At the same time, the American public, fed a daily dose of propaganda generated in Pentagon media briefing rooms, could not understand how terrorists could bomb a civilian building in the heartland of America.

While the estimate of Iraqi forces killed runs as high as 250,000, the actual number of Iraqis killed, including civilians, runs much higher. American planes deliberately destroyed Iraq's power plants, its sewage systems, and its hospitals. The economic embargo severely compounded the situation, forcing an entire population to struggle amidst massive epidemics of starvation and disease. Their infrastructure decimated, without sanitation, food and medical supplies, hundreds of thousands of civilians suffered horrible, lingering deaths—all caused by the U.S. military, the greed of big oil, and their life-long friend, George Herbert Walker Bush.

The people of Baghdad have turned the rubble of the Al-Amira air raid shelter into a shrine, complete with mementos and pictures of the children who perished.

In Oklahoma City, victims placed mementos of their dead relatives on a chain-link fence surrounding the remains of the Alfred P. Murrah Building and asked, "Who could do such a thing? Who could kill innocent civilians?"

While the World Trade Center and Oklahoma City bombings may have been the result of Iraqi revenge, what ultimately lay behind the New York and Daharan bombings appeared to stem from a broader-based alliance of Islamic militants from Iraq, Iran, Syria, Saudi Arabia, Pakistan, and other countries committed to the expulsion of U.S. troops from the region and an all-out attack on the "Great Satan." *

It has been reported that groups ranging from the Palestinian-based Islamic Jihad, Hamas, the Sudanese National Islamic Front, the Pakistan-based al-Fuqra, and groups funded by Saudi Arabian Osama bin-Laden were involved in the World Trade Center bombing and related plots.

In fact, as early as 1990, World Trade Center conspirators El-Sayyid Nossair, Mahmud Abouhalima, and al-Fuqra member Clement Rodney Hampton-El (an American Black Muslim) met in New York City with Sheik Abd-al-Aziz Awadah, who is alleged to have been a senior commander engaged in the coordination of terrorist operations with Iranian, Palestanian, and Hizbollah leaders. [431]

Such alliances were also reflected in a major terrorist conference held in Teheran in 1993, where it was decided the terrorists' war against the U.S. would include "targeting buildings for bomb spectaculars." [432]

---

* World Trade Center bomber Mahmud Abouhalima told Egyptian intelligence that the World Trade Center bombing was approved by Iranian intelligence.

Another major terrorist conference was held in Teheran on June 20-23, 1996, during which it was announced that there would be increased attacks against U.S. interests. Two days later, on June 25, the military housing complex in Dhahran, Saudi Arabia, was bombed, claiming the lives of 19 servicemen. The Movement for Islamic Change, which had already claimed credit for the Riyadh bombing, took credit.

This was followed by another terrorist conference at the Northwest Frontier Province town of Konli, near the Afghani border in Pakistan on July 10-15, 1996. The meeting saw some of the most important militant Islamic leaders come together under one tent. They included Osama bin Ladin, a Saudi Arabian who funded the Mujahadeen, was implicated in the Riyadh and Dhahran bombings, and was a close associate of Sheik Omar Abdel Rahman, Ahmed Jibril of the PFLP-GC (who carried out the Pan Am 103 bombing on orders from Teheran), Abdul Rasul Sayyaf, a senior representative of Iranian intelligence, senior Pakistani intelligence officers, and senior commanders of Hamas, HizbAllah, and other groups. All resolved to use whatever force was necessary to oust all foreign forces stationed on Islamic holy land.[433]

One Arab observer with direct knowledge of the conference said the participants' resolution was "a virtual declaration of relentless war" on the U.S.-led West.[434] A glimpse of that conference can be seen in *Defense and Foreign Affairs*:

> Rasul Sayyaf stated that "the time to settle accounts has arrived." The senior representative of Iranian intelligence declared that "attack is the best means of defense." He urged a combined offensive, both in the Muslim world, particularly the Persian Gulf and Arabian Peninsula, and at the heart of the West. He repeated Iran's commitment to the cause and reiterated Teheran's willingness to provide the Islamists with all possible aid.
>
> Another commander concurred, adding that "there is an imperative need for an integrated plan to deal a fatal blow to the international forces of arrogance." A UK-based commander from a Persian Gulf state stressed that given the immense strategic importance of the Persian Gulf to the U.S. and its allies, the only way to compel the West to withdraw was through the infliction of so much pain on these countries, that their governments would find it impossible to tolerate the public outcry and be compelled to withdraw as the only way to stop the Islamist terrorism at home.[435]

On July 16, one day after the Konli conference, the U.S. Senate passed sanctions against Iran and Libya. With their continued sanctions against the innocent civilians of Iraq, and now Iran, the U.S. was building to a confrontation with the militant Islamic community. As Ronald W. Lewis wrote in the November, 1996 edition of *Air Forces Monthly:*

On the following day (after the Konli conference), July 17, the Movement for Islamic Change sent a chilling fax to the London-based Arab newspaper al-Hayat, warning: "The world will be astonished and amazed at the time and place chosen by the Mujahadeen. The Mujahadeen will deliver the harshest reply to the threats of the foolish American president. Everyone will be surprised by the volume, choice of place and timing of the Mujahadeen's answer, and invaders must prepare to depart alive or dead, for their time is morning and morning is near." That fax, and a warning by Israeli intelligence that Iran was likely to launch an attack against a U.S. aircraft, were ignored.

At 8:31:10 p.m. (0031:10 GMT) that evening, nobody could dismiss the horrendous explosion of TWA Flight 800 off the coast of Long Island, New York. Attack number three had just been carried out.[436]

That excerpt appeared in a U.S. military newspaper. But Lewis wasn't the only observer cognizant of these facts. As Dr. Laurie Mylroie noted regarding the July 17 attack on TWA flight 800, it occurred precisely on Iraqi national day. The day of the bombing, Saddam Hussein had made his own threats, telling the U.S. that they would be unable to avoid "the sweeping flood and flaming fire that is burning under their feet...."[437]

The bombing of the World Trade Center occurred on the second anniversary of Iraq's surrender to coalition forces in the Gulf.

While reports from the State Department and such institutions as the Heritage Foundation decry the use of Arab state-sponsored terrorism against the West, the truth is that the West—and especially the U.S.—has been exporting terrorism in the form of economic sanctions, assassinations, coups, death-squads, and covert/overt wars in almost every part of the world since the beginning of the century.

To the Muslim world, and especially terrorist groups such as the PLO, Islamic Jihad, Hizbollah, and Hamas, the U.S. assault on its ally Iraq represented a turning point in Islam's struggle against the West. The Gulf War marked the first time the United States had used an all-out, full-scale military assault on an Arab country, with devastating results.

Under the influence of religious figures such as Sheik Omar Rahman, the Mujahadeen (the Afghani freedom fighters who had been trained by the CIA) and their allies became staunch opponents of the United States. Thousands of Muslims from almost 40 countries flocked to Afghanistan and Pakistan during the war, and thousands remain there, training for the day when Islam will rise up in its final great Jihad against the West.[438]

To these groups, the Gulf War marked the signal for a new escalation in their war against the U.S. The bombing of the World Trade Center, the Federal Building in Oklahoma, the Al-Khubar military complex in Daharan, and possibly the shoot-down of TWA 800, were all expressions of this rage against the United States.

On January 25, 1993, less than one month before the World Trade Center attack, Mir Aimal Kansi, a Pakistani, vented his rage by opening fire with an AK-47 outside CIA headquarters in Langley, Virginia. Two CIA employees were killed and three others were wounded. Like Ramzi Yousef, Kansi was a native Baluchi. He was involved with the Pashtun Students Organization, the student wing of Mahmood Khan Achakzai's Pakhtoon Khwa Awami Milli Party, which claimed the CIA's sudden pull-out of Afghanistan resulted in millions of deaths at the hands of the Soviets. Kansi claimed the CIA had betrayed his father.[439]

Yousef himself spent considerable time in Baluchistan. Located in western Pakistan, Baluchistan is a nexus for the Muslim Jihad, and a major arms and drug network. Pakistan has served not only as a training center for the Mujahadeen, but a haven for Philippine terrorist groups such as Abu Sayyaf and the Moro Liberation Front, who have used free-flowing Pakistani arms and drugs to promote and finance their activities.[440]

Support in the form of arms and drugs flowed from Pakistan and Afghanistan to militant Islamic groups around the world, aided by the CIA, rogue intelligence officers, and senior U.S. officials in for their piece of the action—just as Oliver North's "Enterprise" would do with the Contras in Nicaragua. In fact, many of the same individuals were involved.

Yousef next showed up in the Philippines with a Libyan missionary named Mohaimen abu Bakr, leader of the Libyan Mullah Forces. It was there that he joined forces with an Afghani named Wali Khan Amin Shah and his old friend from Kuwait, Abdul Hakim Murad. They were there to train the Abu Sayyaf.

Headquartered on the Philippine island of Mindanao, the 400-member strong Abu Sayyaf has conducted over 10 major terrorist attacks in the last six years in its bid for autonomy, and is strongly allied with other Islamic revolutionary groups, such the Philippine-based Moro Liberation Front. Abu Sayyaf's funding and support comes from high-profile Islamic leaders such as Libyan President Muammar Qaddafi, and wealthy Islamic financiers such as Tariq Jana, a Pakistani businessman, and Osama bin Laden.

Considered by the State Department to be one of the world's preeminent sponsors of Islamic radicalism, Osama bin Laden's threats to wage Jihad on Americans in the Middle East immediately preceded the November, 1995 blast at a U.S. military facility in Riyadh, Saudi Arabia, in which five Americans and two Indians were killed. Eight months later, a massive truck-bomb killed 19 servicemen and injured 400 at Dhahran.

In a March, 1997 interview with the *London Independent* from his Afghani hideout, bin Laden warned of additional measures against U.S. forces in Saudi Arabia, and said he had obtained the support of thousands of Pakistanis.[441]

Readers will also recall that General Wafiq al-Sammara'i, the former head of Iraqi military intelligence, told the *London Independent* a year earlier that the

1996 Dhahran bombing "strongly resembled plans drawn up by a secret Iraqi committee on which he served after the invasion of Kuwait...." [442]

Not surprisingly, in February, 1995, U.S. authorities named bin Laden and his brother-in-law, Mohammad Jamal Khalifa among 172 unindicted co-conspirators in the World Trade Center bombing and related plots to blow up New York City landmarks, including the Javitz Federal Building and the United Nations. Those plots were strongly linked to Iraq.*

Khalifa also ran an Islamic center in the Philippines linked to similar organizations in countries such as Iraq and Jordan. Given Abu Sayyaf's close ties with bin Laden, Khalifa, and their connections with the Mujahadeen, it is only natural that Ramzi Yousef, a Pakistani who is considered an Iraqi agent, would be involved with the group.

Abu Sayyaf's former military strategist, Edwin Angeles, who surrendered to Philippine authorities in February, '96, admitted that the Abu Sayyaf was in fact linked to Yousef and Murad—both of whom recently went on trial in New York for their role in "Project Bojinka"—a dramatic plan to blow up 12 U.S. airliners in a single day. The plot was foiled when police raided Yousef's Manila apartment on January 6, 1995, after a fire caused by the pair mixing bomb-making chemicals in a sink. While Murad was captured, Yousef escaped, making his way to Pakistan, where he was captured by police in February. [443]

Nine of his accomplices—six of them Iraqis—were rounded up one year later along with plastic explosives, blasting caps, detonating cords, time fuses, and fake passports. The terrorists, including a Sudanese and two Saudis, were part of a plot to bomb various Western targets and assassinate Pope John Paul II during his January, 1995 Philippine visit.**

Before his capture however, Yousef, an engineering graduate of Britain's Swansea University, had time to try out his new bomb—an experimental form of nitroglycerin. The small test-bomb, taped under a seat on Philippine Air flight 434, killed one Japanese tourist and injured 10 others. Before the explosion, Yousef had safely departed the plane in Cebu City.

Another temporary resident of Cebu City was Terry Nichols. As discussed, Nichols moved to Cebu City with his new wife, Marife Torres, a mail-order bride whom he met there in November, 1989. After trying life in Michigan and

---

* Abdul Rahman Yassin, an Iraqi indicted for his part in the World Trade Center bombing fled to Baghdad. His brother, Musab Yasin, provided a safehouse for the later plots. While the New York office of the FBI wanted to arrest him, curiously, the Washington office objected.

** The nine suspects are: Yousef's brother, Adel Anonn (alias Adel Bani); Abdul Kareem Jassim Bidawi; Haleem Jassim Bidawi; Jamaal Jaloud; Ibrahim Abid; and Najim Nasser (Iraqis); Emad Almubarak (Sudanese); Saleh Al Quuwaye, and Zaid Al Amer (Saudis).

Nevada, the couple moved back to Cebu City in early 1993, where they lived for a short time.

According to Nichols' ex-wife Lana Padilla, her former husband had traveled to the Philippines about four times a year since meeting Marife. Although some of the visits were to see his new bride and make arrangements for her entry into the U.S., he occasionally traveled alone.*

"Sometimes he went when Marife was in Kansas," wrote Padilla. "It didn't make sense, but I never asked why." [444]

Nichols told Padilla he was traveling to Cebu City to meet "potential business partners." The Michigan farmer was making the multi-thousand dollar trips, he said, to bring back little paper "butterflies"—curious merchandise for a man intent on setting himself up in the military surplus business. [445]

It is also curious why Nichols carried two stun-guns on his last trip, why he left $20,000 taped behind a drawer for his son, and a note to McVeigh telling him "You're on your own," and "go for it!" in case he didn't come back, and why his son cried, "I'm never going to see my Dad again."

Perhaps Nichols had reason to worry. According to FBI 302 reports and investigations conducted by McVeigh's defense team, Abu Sayyaf leader Edwin Angeles spoke of a terrorist meeting in the vicinity of the Del Monte labeling factory in Davao, on the Island of Mindanao, in late 1992 or early '93. It was there, Angeles said, that Ramzi Yousef, Abdul Hakim Murad, Wali Khan Amin Shah, and several others discussed the Oklahoma City bombing plot.**

One of the men at the meeting, recalled Angeles, introduced himself as "a farmer." [446]

When the "farmer" returned home from his last visit to the Philippines on January 16, 1995, and discovered that Padilla had opened the mysterious package and read the contents, he turned "white as a ghost." [447]

On April 19, 1995, Abdul Hakim Murad was sitting in his New York jail cell when the word went out that the Oklahoma City Federal Building had been bombed. Murad casually admitted to a prison guard that the Liberation Army of the Philippines—a group connected to Abu Sayyaf—was responsible.

Abu Sayyaf leader Edwin Angeles later corrected Murad for the record: "It was the Palestine Liberation Army and/or the Islamic Jihad which Murad was referring to," he said. "This army is associated with Hamas and based in Lebanon."

However, given the fact that Saudi intelligence informed the FBI that Iraq had

---

* Angeles told Jones that there are links to Philippine mail-order-bride businesses and criminal/terrorist activity. It was not clear from Jones' brief exactly what this entailed.

** Referring to the place in Davao, Angeles said, "It was also the place where Muslims were taught in bomb making."

hired Pakistanis who might not have known they were operating on behalf of Iraq, it is highly possible that Murad (a Pakistani) and Angeles were unaware of their true sponsor. As the *Washington Post's* Jack Anderson reported in 1991: "A preferable revenge for Iraq would involve having a 'surrogate terrorist' carry out a domestic attack that Hussein could privately take credit for."

As Stephen Jones wrote in his March 25th Petition for Writ of Mandamus:

> This terrorist attack was "contracted out" to persons whose organization and ideology was friendly to policies of the foreign power and included dislike and hatred of the United States government itself, and possibly included was a desire for revenge against the United States, with possible anti-black and anti-Semitic overtones. Because Iraq had tried a similar approach in 1990, but had been thwarted by Syrian intelligence information given to the United States, this time the information was passed through an Iraqi intelligence base in the Philippines.[448]

The sighting of Terry Nichols with Islamic terrorists in the Philippines dovetails with Cary Gagan's sighting of Nichols with his "Iranian" friends—Omar and Ahmed—in Henderson, Nevada. Gagan recalled how Nichols looked "out-of-place" among his Arab comrades at the May '94 meeting.

Was Terry Nichols associated with World Trade Center bomber Ramzi Yousef, a reputed Iraqi agent? Was Timothy McVeigh associated with Hussain al-Hussaini, a former Iraqi soldier? Were Yousef and Hussaini part of a terrorist network set up by Iraq to infiltrate the United States?

On January 28, 1991, the *Washington Post* reported that an Iraqi terrorist network was being sponsored and planned by Saddam Hussein. The article stated in part:

> Highly classified U.S. intelligence reports say that the United States has received information that Saddam has already dispatched more than 100 terrorists, both experienced and novice, to try to infiltrate the United States. One report, quoting sources inside Iraq, cites a specific number of terrorists—160—who have been sent off with missions in America.
>
> That coincides with reports that at least two and possibly as many as four Iraqi diplomats in their embassy in Washington were monitored as they attempted to set up terrorist cells in the capital and elsewhere in the United States....
>
> A recent intelligence report says that Saddam has deposited money in several Swiss bank accounts that will automatically be paid out to terrorists no matter what happens to Saddam ... Iraqis living in the United States who support Saddam strongly enough to resort to violence would probably be used to provide bank accounts, safe houses and materials for the experts who sneak into the country.

According to Northrop, information from a London banker "Sayanin" showed that several million dollars was transferred from the Bank of Iraq, through the SWIFT international banking system in Brussels, Belgium, to a bank in Kingman, Arizona under the account name of "Nayaad." Attempts by Northrop to confirm this information were unsuccessful.*

It's also interesting that Cary Gagan claimed to have received $250,000 from his Arab friend Omar, who wanted to set up an account for him. Omar and Gagan had also traveled to Kingman. The million dollar account was to be wired from a Swiss bank and deposited into the Bank of Cherry Creek in Denver.

Part of the plan was to allow Omar and Ahmed to purchase the Postal Center, a shipping and receiving store in Denver owned by George Colombo, who also operated a Ryder truck leasing operation across the street. Omar had asked Gagan to broker a deal to buy the facility from Colombo. He believes they were interested in the mail and truck rental facility. For some reason, the deal fell through.

While Gagan claims he was paid by Omar, there is no direct evidence that McVeigh or Nichols were funded by Gagan's Arab contacts. Yet there is circumstantial evidence that the two bombing defendants met with Sam Khalid, who spent considerable time in Las Vegas. The Arab high-roller frequented Binyon's Horseshoe, the Glitter Gulch, and the MGM casino where Nichols would occasionally take his 12-year-old son Josh.**

As Northrop said, "gambling is a favorite pastime of Sunni Moslems...." Was Khalid simply there to gamble, or did he have another agenda?

According to Gagan: "Omar and Ahmed were wiring money in and out of MGM. They used to get money—huge amounts of money—they were using these wire transfers."

Former CIA operative and controversial source Gunther Russbacher told author Rodney Stich that Binyon's Horseshoe was one of the casinos used for money laundering and political payoffs. Khalid is a regular at Binyon's Horseshoe.

---

* Northrop claims that when he tried to run the information down in Kingman he came up empty. His source in the U.S. Marshals Service, who was looking into the matter, received a call from the Justice Department, and was promptly stonewalled, he said.

** Casinos have been used to launder money. A drug dealer or other criminal enters the casino with dirty money, buys large quantities of chips, gambles a bit, then cashes in the chips for clean money. Russbacher told Stich that the process also works in reverse. He explained in one case how the CIA, through Shamrock Overseas Disbursement Corporation, gave money to the casino, who in turn would give gambling chips to the recipients when they arrived, then the chips were cashed in. Russbacher named three Las Vegas casinos allegedly involved in the operation, including the Frontier, Stardust, and Binyon's Horseshoe.

Two other frequent visitors to Binyon's Horseshoe, it appears, were Terry Nichols and Timothy McVeigh. The two men attended the Claude Hall Gun Show in Las Vegas in November and January of 1994, stayed at Lana Padilla's house, and reportedly frequented Binyon's and a strip joint next door called the Glitter Gulch, where "Khalid" is also a regular.*

While no one at the casinos would cooperate in placing "Khalid" with the two bombing suspects, Padilla said that Nichols had met with "Middle Eastern" men while in Las Vegas. Interrogatory answers filed by KFOR in its defense against al-Hussaini state: "[Lana] Padilla said that her son, Josh, went to Las Vegas about once a month, where he was with Tim McVeigh, Terry Nichols, and Middle-Eastern men. Padilla expressed the opinion that there was a Middle-Eastern connection to the Oklahoma City bombing."

That information dovetails with Cary Gagan's testimony. As stated earlier, the federal informant said he met with approximately eight men—five of whom were Middle Easterners—at the Western Motel in Las Vegas on May 16, 1994. There was an Arab man from Oklahoma City who Gagan referred to as the "leader."

The eighth man was Terry Nichols.

The question remained, who was Omar, and was he connected with "Sam Khalid?" Interestingly, "Khalid's" alias is "Omar." [449]

In an attempt to track "Khalid's" whereabouts in Las Vegas, KFOR's Jayna Davis hired a security guard and part-time P.I. named Louis Crousette who worked at Glitter Gulch. In a transcript of the conversation, Davis asks Crousette if Angie (not her real name), "Khalid's" favorite stripper, recognized him:

Crousette: "She knew who he was. Her eyes … her … her … how do I want to say this? Her whole demeanor changed. She went from being a calm person to being a scared little rabbit."

Davis: "All right. And she said she didn't want to get involved."

Crousette: "Does the word getting up and running and leaving the place tell you anything?

Davis: "Okay. So …"

Crousette: "She left. She got up and left. She left her money and left. She grabbed her stuff and was out the door."

According to Crousette, Angie also described an Arab man in the Glitter Gulch acting as a "recruiter," who introduced Khalid to a pair of "skinny white guys." Were these two skinny white guys Timothy McVeigh and Terry Nichols?

Angie declined to say, telling Davis that she'd "wind up at the bottom of Lake

---

* Considering the reports from dancers at two stripper bars—one in Tulsa and one in Junction City—McVeigh and Nichols had a penchant for these types of places.

Meade" if she talked.[450] *

Who was the "recruiter" Crousette saw hobnobbing in a wealthy part of town with a man in a white BMW? Just who was in the car with him isn't clear. The information is curious in light of Gagan's report that he and his Arab friends met at the Player's Club, an upscale apartment complex in a Las Vegas suburb.

Also mentioned in Crousette's phone conversation is "Jaffer," an apparent reference to Jaffer Oshan (not his real name). Oshan, who sometimes goes by the name Ossan Jaffar, is an electrical engineer who works for "Khalid," and translates for his rusty Arabic.

Oshan was reportedly the target of FBI surveillance at the same time Khalid was being indicted for insurance fraud. Like Abraham Ahmed, Oshan disappeared just before the bombing, traveling to Jordan. And like Ahmed, he gave a similar story, telling Ernie Cranford he was going to the Middle East to attend to family matters—in this case—his own wedding. According to Cranford, he did not marry.

A native Jordanian, Oshan showed up in KFOR's surveillance photos with Khalid and Hussain al-Hussaini. Crousette showed the photos to his "intelligence" source:

Crousette: Three people that I know of that went in service—two Feds and two of them were ex-company (CIA). They know who these guys are. When I showed them these pictures they looked at me and told me, "Get the hell out of it. What the hell are you doing doing this?"
Davis: Did they tell you they were Iraqi Intelligence?
Crousette: Two of them did, yes.... The Feds know who did it.
Davis: And they're not arresting them?
Crousette: I'm not gonna' get involved.
Davis: Are they Middle Eastern?
Crousette: I'm not getting involved on this. Okay. I'm sending in my bill. I'm getting out of it now.

Crousette has since avoided all attempts to contact him. Gordon Novel, who once worked for District Attorney Jim Garrison, spent a week in Las Vegas attempting to talk with the former security guard. "He was real adamant about not wanting to be talked to," said Novel.

As a frustrated Novel was about to leave, a large goon appeared at his hotel room with an automatic tucked in his belt and some words of advice: "You betta' stay da fuck out odda Oklahoma thing," he warned. "Work on da Waco thing if ya wanna, but stay out odda Oklahoma thing. There's a lodda sand out dare where

---

* After Davis questioned several employees at the MGM, two were fired.

no one will ever find ya."

"He had a very serious big gun," said Novel, "and he wasn't a cop—I don't know what he was." [451]

Why would an apparent Mob mule be concerned about steering an investigator away from a Las Vegas connection to the Oklahoma City bombing? Was Khalid connected to the Mob?

KFOR first bumped into "Sam Khalid" when reporter Brad Edwards received a mysterious phone call from Sharon Twilley, who worked at the time for "Sahara Properties," the real-estate business "Khalid" owned with his ex-wife Carol, who died in the bombing. A three-year employee, Twilley did a variety of jobs for "Khalid," including bookkeeping and acting as rental agent for his 500-plus properties.

Twilley told Edwards and Davis that she had seen her boss in the company of Abraham Ahmed, who had been detained by the FBI as a possible suspect on April 19 as he attempted to fly from Oklahoma to Jordan.

According to Twilley and "Ernie Cranford," Ahmed was seen driving the brown Chevy pick-up speeding away from the bombing, back and forth to "Khalid's" place, days prior to the bombing. Ahmed's increasingly frequent visits coincided with the arrival of Hussain al-Hussaini and five other Iraqis in November. Twilley also said that "Khalid" began acting very secretive after the arrival of the six men, and would only speak to Ahmed in Arabic.

Perhaps most incredibly, both "Cranford" and Twilley spotted a yellow Mercury Marquis parked at "Khalid's" office; Twilley said she saw Abraham Ahmed in the passenger seat.*

Ahmed's presence wasn't the only thing that raised eyebrows at "Sahara Properties" in the days following the bombing. "Cranford" told the FBI and Edwards that he saw one of "Khalid's" Arab employees, a man named Haider al-Saiidi, acting strangely ebullient after the bombing.

"When the news reports first came about some Islamic group being responsible, well, Haider kind of laughed about that," recalled "Cranford." "I heard they found three babies that was dead from the blast, and I went and told the guys … and John Doe 2 ["Cranford's" reference to Hussaini] started crying. He went out on the porch to cover his face and he stood by the wall crying. He was upset that children got hurt. He was really upset. And Haider was laughing because he was crying." **

---

* Gagan recognized Abraham Ahmed being with "Khalid." Gagan said he saw Ahmed (by another name) in Las Vegas with "Omar-Khalid" in the Summer or Fall of 1994. He said he also saw Hussain al-Hussaini in Oklahoma City when he was here in April.

** Al Saiidi, incidentally, was the man who's wife who had a miscarriage after stones were thrown through his window. When Al Saiidi went before news cameras to complain about the incident, "Khalid" fired him.

To make things even stranger, "Khalid" decided to visit Las Vegas on the evening of April 20, the day after his ex-wife Carol was killed in the bombing. It seems "Khalid" had asked her to help him with his taxes on Monday, her regularly scheduled day at the Department of Agriculture. Consequently, she went to work on Wednesday, her day off. As news reports showed Dr. Espe, Carol's boss, being carried down a ladder by rescue workers, "Khalid's" daughter began crying. She knew her mom worked in that office.

"We was all sitting around the office watching the news," said "Cranford." "And when they showed Espe being carried down that ladder, she [Najaya, "Khalid's" current wife] just burst out laughing. ["Khalid's" daughter] was crying, and Najaya was laughing." [452]

Some might consider it odd that a girl's stepmother would burst out laughing upon learning that the girl's mother had been killed. Some might consider it stranger still for a man to be partying on the eve of his ex-wife's death.

Was there a motive? Did "Khalid" know there would be a bombing on Wednesday? Did he know Carol would go into work on Wednesday to make up for her day off?

"It was set up," said "Cranford." "I know it was set up. He got rid of her because of the taxes she filed." *

It was Carol on whom fell the responsibility of preparing the returns. "Cranford" caught a glimpse of her on Monday, two days before her death.

"She didn't look happy that morning when she was doing his taxes," recalled "Cranford." "She did not look happy at all … 'cause he was fucking the government over the taxes." **

At the time of this writing there was a case pending against "Khalid" for tax fraud. Carol most likely would have testified against him in that case.

The circumstances at "Sahara Properties" in the days after the bombing were too much for "Cranford." "I left the job site and went to the office and said 'I want my money.' I told them I didn't want to work for no terrorists. I feared that these people were involved, and them workers were involved in this. And with all the strange things that was going on, I wasn't going to take no chances. And when they found Abraham [Ahmed], that was it. That was all I needed to know. That's all I wanted to know. I wanted to get the hell out of there!"

The brown Chevy pick-up that Ahmed had been seen driving was found aban-

---

* According to "Cranford," "Khalid" reported to the IRS that his employees were subcontractors, thus avoiding having to pay benefits. "Khalid's" steady worker of nine years also told me that his boss made up business cards for the employees that purported to show their "independent" status.

** The State Tax Commission also wanted "Cranford" to testify against "Khalid." Instead, "Khalid" paid a fine. "That covered up for his ex-wife getting killed," said "Cranford."

doned the Tuesday after the bombing at the Woodscape Apartment complex on Route 66. Resident Jeannie Royer recalled a heavy-set Middle-Eastern man getting out of the truck which was left near a storage shed. The man gave Royer a hard look that said, "You'd better forget what you just saw."

The man showed up a week later and followed Royer while she was out walking her dog.* When shown a photo of a heavy-set Middle Eastern suspect by KFOR (one of "Khalid's" workers), she said, "It sure does look like him. I would sure like to see a close-up of his eyes. Those eyes of his were frightening!" [453]

The abandoned pick-up, incidentally, had been painted yellow, and the serial numbers ground off. "You could see the yellow over-spray all over the chrome fender," said Joe Royer. The FBI then towed the truck to its impound lot, and nothing has been heard about it since. [454]

What is even more interesting (or coincidental, depending on your point of view) is that "Khalid" owns the property on which a body shop is located—Route 66 Auto Collision—a nondescript, run down place on the far side of town. Route 66, curiously, is two miles directly due west of the Woodscape Apartments.

A body shop would be a very convenient place to paint a pick-up.

"Khalid" bought the property in 1994 at tax auction. The sale was disputed by the current owner, Rex Carmichael, and as of this writing, the case was in court. "I'm sure it wasn't painted there," said Carmichael. "'Khalid' hasn't hadn't had anything to do with that body shop ... he's tried to get it, he's tried to own it, he's tried to possess it from me...." [455]

Interestingly, an anonymous caller to Oklahoma State Representative Charles Key, who claimed to be a friend of the brother of a man involved in the bombing, told him that a meeting of bombing conspirators took place at a garage on Northwest 39th Street. Although he didn't state the name, Route 66 is located right on Northwest 39th Street.

After the bombing, Route 66 changed it's name to Tom's, but is not listed in the phone book or the information directory under either name. KFOR's P.I., Bob Jerlow, told me he staked the place out for five days but never saw anybody go in for an estimate. "It's probably a chop-shop," said a retired police officer. [456] If so, it may fit into what Cranford told me next: "They [Khalid and his employees] would always buy cars, then I found out that they was taking them and running them to Mexico, running trips to Mexico and selling the cars.... Within two weeks to a month, everyone of them was driving a different car. They wouldn't have it but less than a month, then they'd be rid of it, and you wouldn't see it again.

"I've seen them many times up there at this garage [Route 66]. It was the same

---

* At the same time, interestingly, two Middle Eastern residents of the Woodscape apartments skipped out without paying their rent. It should also be noted that two heavy-set Arabs work for Sam Khalid.

guys that came in [in November]. The same six that came in. Just them—them six."

One of the six was Hussain al-Hussaini.

The month November, 1994 may be prophetic. Three witnesses in Stillwater, about an hour's drive north of Oklahoma City, saw a man who closely resembles Ramzi Yousef in late October, early November, 1994. The man, who called himself Y.T., was managing Boomer's Used Auto Sales in Stillwater along with a man who resembled John Doe 2. He drove a yellow Mercury Marquis similar to Timothy McVeigh's, albeit with a vinyl roof.

"Ronnie White' (not his real name), who was working as a mechanic for Boomer's at the time, said the men ran a "shoddy" operation and were "hostile" towards customers. The business, he said, was buying used cars and shipping them overseas, possibly to Kuwait. While that is not an usual practice, "White" said he saw as much as $100,000 pass through per month, which is unusual for such a small operation.

"White" says the two men suddenly departed for Ohio the last week of October, 1994. They told him, "Don't tell anybody where we're going." They left no forwarding address and no way for the customers to pay their bills. (Coincidentally, perhaps, Timothy McVeigh was in Kent, Ohio on October 5.)

Said customer Michael Reed, "They were pretty strange people. They were supposed to be running a car lot, but they were always gone." They returned from their supposed car-buying trip the first week of November with one used Honda.

White went to the FBI when he saw Yousef's wanted poster in the local police station. Like many witnesses, the FBI appeared to show no interest.

Was the man these witnesses saw really internationally wanted fugitive Ramzi Yousef? A Washington source familiar with Yousef and the World Trade Center bombing doesn't think it likely that Yousef reentered the country after the 1993 attack. The FBI put Yousef in the Philippines in November and December of '94 just in time to launch and ill-fated attack on President Clinton during his APEC visit, but his exact timeline was never established.

Yousef himself is a chameleon. One FBI photo depicts him as a thin, haunted-looking criminal, the other a boyish-looking foreign exchange student. Yet all three witnesses in Stillwater are adamant. "I was shocked," said Michael Reed, "it looked just like him."

Had the Arab cell involved in the bombing re-enlisted the aid of expert bomb maker Ramzi Yousef for the Oklahoma City attack? A U.S. Marshal told Jayna Davis that he believed the World Trade Center and Oklahoma City bombings were linked. Other sources expressed similar opinions.

Finally, the Justice Department's Office of Inspector General report on the Oklahoma City bombing indicates that nitroglycerin was found at the scene. As previously stated, Yousef had been experimenting with a new form of nitroglycerin.

If Y.T. was Ramzi Yousef, he didn't seem too concerned to operate in the U.S. as a wanted fugitive.

"Sam Khalid," who by now was being investigated by KFOR and surveilled by Jerlow, apparently didn't seem too concerned being watched either. At one point he casually strolled up to Jerlow and Edwards, who were staking out his house, rapped on their window, and said, "What do you want with me?" Jerlow, his hand on his gun, watched in amazement. Later, "Khalid" called him on the phone. "Which country hired you to investigate me," "Khalid" demanded to know, "and how much are they paying you?"

When Hani Kamal, a Lebanese/Jordanian businessman, occasional FBI informant, and long-time acquaintance of Khalid's, was shown KFOR's surveillance photos by OCPD officer Don Browning, he reportedly became frightened and said, "You have to leave this alone. This is the Mossad. You do not know what you're messing with." After that, Kamal would no longer talk to the cop.*

Jerlow's sources also came up dry. When the P.I. asked his phone company source to pull Khalid's records, they had mysteriously "disappeared." An attorney friend of Jerlow's who had some dealings with "Khalid" told him, 'Khalid' is a dangerous motherfucker. You stay away from him." He didn't explain why.[457]

His warning may have been well-founded however. Three months after the bombing, on July 3, a man matching "Khalid's" description, and driving his truck, showed up at Sharon Twilley's house, pulled out a pistol, and fired four shots. Two of the bullets went into Twilley's bedroom, one went into her car, shattering the windshield, and another lodged under a neighbor's window.

A terrified Sharon Twilley rolled out of bed, clutching the phone in her hand, and dialed 911. She then ran over to neighbor Glenn Moore's house. "He knows where I slept!" she told Moore, who had watched the scene from his window. "He could have killed me if he had wanted to!"

Just why "Khalid" would want to scare Sharon Twilley to death is an interesting question. This excerpt from the police report may shed light on the motive:

Twilley stated she worked for the suspect until after the bombing of the Murrah building when the F.B.I. came out and questioned her about the suspect's activity. The next day she was fired. Since that time the suspect has tried to kick her out of

---

* Don Browning, interview with author. Kamal had been working with the FBI to track "Khalid" and others who were involved in insurance fraud scams. Although he definitely knew "Khalid," he disputed that he said "This is the Mossad" to Browning. Browning swears he did. Yet Jayna Davis said Browning told her that Kamal said that "Khalid" was a member of "Hamas," a far cry from the Mossad, the Israeli intelligence agency. Another possible explanation is that there were Mossad agents posing as members of Hamas, but it seems unlikely that Kamal would know that.

his rent [sic] house. He had refused to accept her check & had taken her to district court & the judge ordered him to serve a 30 day notice. Twilley stated that since that time her residence was burglarized and then this incident of the shooting took place. Twilley stated the F.B.I. had spoke [sic] with her a few times since she was fired & then it all started. Twilley stated Khalid was furious when he found out she had spoken to the F.B.I.

Just what had Twilley told the FBI? When I interviewed the OCPD detective who wrote the report, he told me that Twilley had seen "some new deal he was into," and was "nervous."

"She didn't want him to know that she had talked to the FBI," said the detective. "She was definitely afraid." [458]

FBI agents James Strickland and Dave Swanson's names also appeared on the report. Why would the FBI take an interest in a local assault case? Strickland wouldn't comment.

In spite of the bulletholes in Twilley's house and car, and Moore's eyewitness account, the OCPD did little. Assistant DA Sherry Todd declined to prosecute the case on "lack of evidence." The police report stated it as follows:

Moore stated on the morning of 7-3-95 at approx. 3:30-4:00 he heard gun shots. Moore got up & looked out the window and saw a dark skinned male running from the house. I asked him if it was Mr. "Khalid." Moore stated "I think it was him, but I'm not sure. It looked like him but I'm not positive. He was driving the same white Nissan pick-up that he drives. But I'm not sure.

Moore seemed a bit more certain when I spoke to him. "He was a short guy that smokes a cigar," said Moore. "[He] looked real aggravated. He was randomly shooting; he shot four times."

In fact, the police report previously stated Moore's identification in more positive terms:

Moore recognized the suspect as the landlord who rented the house out prior to Twilley living there & knew him as having a white Toyota pick up & he said that was him, meaning the suspect.

As if to add more grist to the mill, "Khalid" and an associate had shown up at Twilley's house the previous day and had smashed a brick through her window. Moore told me he recognized "Khalid" by his baseball cap, cigar, and white pick-up.

I began to suspect that Todd's refusal to prosecute came from DA Robert Macy, who had blindly cooperated with the Justice Department by refusing to pursue a local investigation of the bombing. Todd dismissed that notion. "It's very,

very rare when he's involved in the decline or acceptance of charges," she said, then added, "I felt there were some problems with the witnesses statements."[*]

Although initially polite, when I suggested that "Khalid" might be involved in the bombing, and that she should re-open the case, she turned suddenly hostile, and said, "I'm gonna go back to work. This case is closed," then abruptly hung up.

Some time later, Mike Johnston, a local attorney familiar with the case, ran into Assistant U.S. Attorney Ted Richardson in the courthouse. Johnston raised the issue of "Sam Khalid." "Oh you must have been talking to that guy from San Francisco," Richardson replied, referring to the author. When Johnston said he had gleaned information from other sources as well, and suggested that Richardson look into the matter, Richardson looked at his watch and said, "Well Mike, that's an interesting theory. I gotta run."[**]

As for Glenn Moore, he told me he was being followed by "Khalid" and didn't want to get involved. And Sharon Twilley? Moore said she was scared and had probably moved back to Georgia.

Was "Khalid" guilty of assault with a deadly weapon? Was he involved in the bombing? His attorney, Francis Courbois, put it eloquently when he said, "He is typical of those immigrants who work hard to achieve the opportunities America offers."

Indeed.

In 1973, "Khalid" was convicted of Grand Larceny.

In 1991, he was indicted in Federal Court on eight counts of insurance fraud, which included setting fires to some of his 500-plus properties. He served nine months out of a year at El Reno Federal Prison.[†]

Robert Kulick, a former employee of "Khalid's," told the FBI that "Khalid" had instructed him to set fires to four of his properties. When agents questioned Kulick and his wife about "Khalid's" associations, Mrs. Kulick blurted out, "We don't want to get "Sam [Khalid]" in any trouble," whereupon the agents immediately advised Kulick of his Miranda rights.

Kulick later jumped bond and fled to California after claiming he had received

---

[*] Macy and State Attorney General Drew Edmondson had also pushed certain aspects of the Anti-Terrorism Bill, using the bombing as a platform.

[**] This is doubly interesting, since Richardson was the U.S. Attorney who prosecuted "Khalid" for insurance fraud in 1990. Richardson "committed suicide" in July of 1997 over "work-related" matters.

[†] While "Khalid's" attorney claimed that only $15,000 dollars or so was involved in the scams, the U.S. Attorney's report is more incriminating. "Khalid" was also accused during his arson case of employing false Social Security numbers. One of them is registered to a woman in Oklahoma City; the other to a woman in Miami.

"threatening phone calls." He didn't say from whom.*

The FBI seemed more interested in "Khalid's" connections to the PLO than in arson. According to Northrop, the FBI investigated Khalid for alleged PLO activity in 1991. "Khalid's" attorney insisted that it would have been precisely the FBI's interest in "Khalid"—"the microscope under which he, as a Palestinian, has been monitored"—which would have revealed any wrongdoing.

For all intents and purposes, "Sam Khalid" appears to be just what his lawyer says he is, a hard-working immigrant out to achieve the opportunities America has to offer. A 56-year-old Palestinian, "Khalid" emigrated to the U.S. from Kuwait in 1968.** He received his M.A. from Oklahoma City University in 1975, his Ph.D. in psychology from O.U. in 1979, and went on to teach at public schools and at nearby Tinker Air Force base. He also did a brief stint in the Oklahoma Department of Human Services.[459]

"Khalid" claims to have relatives in Jordan, Saudi Arabia, and Iraq, who provided money for his education and real-estate investments. In 1982, "Khalid" quit teaching and devoted himself full-time to his burgeoning real-estate business. By 1995 he had acquired over 500 properties, mostly through HUD, the federal agency besieged with corruption in the late '70s and early '80s.†

Hani Kamal was surprised when I told him "Khalid" owned over 500 properties: "In the '70s this son-of-a-bitch did not have a dime to his name. He couldn't survive. He used to ask me for money. Where did he get 500 properties? Where did the money come from?"

Kamal, who claimed to have worked with the Insurance Fraud Division of the FBI (Browning said he was merely an informant), believes "Khalid" is a money launderer. "'Khalid' should be a millionaire with that much property," exclaimed Kamal, "but he lives in a dilapidated shack on 32nd Street." Sure enough, "Khalid" makes his home in a run-down, low-income part of town. It is Kamal's opinion that "Khalid" is just an errand boy, and somebody else really owns the properties.

Northrop agrees. He says the money to fund this burgeoning real estate empire comes from the PLO, which instructs him on how to live for appearance sake. Northrop also indicated that "Khalid's" claim of numerous relatives—an apparently false claim—merely provides a cover for the funneling of money to his business.

---

* One of the agents, James Strickland, would later be assigned to the Twilley assault case.

** He later told investigative journalist William Jasper he emigrated from Libya.

† According to a local HUD representative I checked with, "Khalid" paid cash for most of his properties, avoiding the scrupulous background checks and the typical paper trail which accompanies them. Additionally, none of "Khalid's" three companies, which employ numerous employees, are registered with the State or have Federal Tax I.D. numbers.

Do these largely circumstantial facts make "Sam Khalid" a terrorist? That depends on whom you talk to. According to Northrop:

> [By information and belief] "Khalid" is a long-standing participant in PLO fund-raising activities in the United States. He is most probably a sub-cell leader, part of the intellectual fringe that guide the cell, a classic Russian Nihilistic Terrorist structure. The destruction of the fringe leadership can be seen in the so-called Spook War between the Israelis and the PLO that took place in Europe and the Middle East between 1972 (the Munich Massacre) and 1986 (the death of Abu Jihad).
>
> "Khalid" fits the pattern of the well-funded, well-educated father figure who takes care of his flock, remaining *outside* the center core of sub-cell foot soldiers (the *hel* in the Nihilistic structure).

A West 57th Street documentary described how fund-raising by insurance fraud is classic PLO technique. The May, 1989 episode, entitled, "Palestinians: Dirty Business," focused mostly on insurance fraud in Miami in the early to mid-'80s. Sunrise, Florida Police detective Don Cannon said the money was "being sent back to fund the PLO or the PFLP or the *Intifida.*"

The principals of this fund-raising scheme, CBS reported, hailed from the West Bank town of Deir Dibwan. Reporter Karen Burnes received confirmation from the FBI that a number of scams were going on throughout the U.S. at the time.[460]

One method of raising money involved small store owners who would open businesses, buying merchandise on credit, then quickly close shop and vanish with the proceeds. There were other scams. California insurance lawyer Gordon Park told CBS, "What they would do is throw a brick through their front window and say, 'Gosh, I got burglarized.'"[461]

In Brooklyn, investigators discovered a phony coupon redemption center run by Mahumud Abouhalima—currently serving 240 years in prison for his role in the World Trade Center bombing.*

"Insurance scams first surfaced in the United States in the mid-1970s," wrote Northrop, "when California authorities busted a PLO cell in Los Angeles." The Israeli said that "Khalid" travels to Israel at least once a year, and avoids any contact with the PLO, but communicates through a "cut-out," a member of his family. Northrop also stated that "Khalid" had been transferring funds from the Bank of Oklahoma in Tulsa to Bank Hapolim, an Israeli bank in Jerusalem:

> The signatory on this particular account in Israel is a member of the Nashashibi clan, a prominent Palestinian family who live in Jerusalem and the surrounding area

---

* "Before the bombing, we couldn't get the U.S. Attorney's office interested," said private investigator Ben Jacobson. "After the bombing, they just wanted us to keep our mouths shut."

(West Bank). These funds have been used to help finance 'Palestinian aspirations' (and all that implies).[462]

While this information itself is largely circumstantial, it begins to look less exculpatory when combined with other evidence. In May, 1996, U.S. Customs agents in Los Angeles seized a shipment of weapons—Semtex plastic explosives and small arms—bound for Florida. The North Korean-manufactured ordnance had been shipped through Manila, and was bound for a Hamas group in Miami.

The co-founder of Islamic Jihad—a close cousin of Hamas—Fathi Shikaki, had been assassinated in Syria by the Shin Bet (Israeli Secret Service) in October, 1995. Islamic Jihad sought a new leader in Professor Ramadan Abdullah Shallah, an adjunct political science teacher at the University of South Florida in Tampa.

Shallah co-founded the World Islam Study Enterprise (WISE), linked to the Islamic Committee for Palestine, both of which have been accused by federal authorities of fronting for terrorist groups.

While Shallah vehemently denied these allegations, he suddenly appeared in Syria in November, 1995 as the new head of Islamic Jihad.

Cary Gagan claims to have seen Shallah in late 1994 and February, '95 at Caesar's Palace and The Racetrack—two Las Vegas casinos. "Who is this dude?" Gagan asked Omar about the short, fat, balding man with a mustache and beard. Gagan was simply told he was a professor from Florida.

Shallah also appeared in Teheran in June, 1996 as HizbAllah International was organizing a joint working committee to coordinate international terrorist attacks. Authorities later discovered that Shallah had been Jihad's number two man in Tampa.[463]

While the Florida group had made threats over the extradition of one of their operatives—Mousa Mohammed Abu Marzuk—to Israel, the FBI and the Jewish community hadn't taken them seriously. After the Oklahoma City bombing however, and the interception of the arms shipment in May, the scenario changed. The FBI and the Jewish community were now taking a keen interest in the Miami group.

Back in Houston, Northrop was checking into some PLO suspects. He punched up an inquiry into the Aman (Israeli military intelligence) computer on Hussain al-Hussaini. It came up empty.

But the FBI had a list of 27 PLO and Hamas operatives in Florida and Oklahoma. Ten of those individuals had previously been arrested by the Israelis in March, '96, and the FBI needed their help. When an Israeli agent in New York named Avi ran the names through the computer, he noticed Northrop's inquiry on Hussaini. He called Northrop and asked him to fly to Miami.

What Northrop discovered when he arrived was that the same group he investigated in Oklahoma and Houston had been seen in Miami. Hussain al-Hussaini, "Sam Khalid," Jaffer Oshan, and Haider al-Saadi—six to seven in all—were positively ID'd by Israeli Sayanim in Ft. Lauderdale. They were there, according to sources, meeting with members of Hamas.

It appears that the "Khalid" family's activities in the terrorist underworld date back at least to 1982. According to Army CID (Army Criminal Investigation Division) records, "Khalid's" brother Mike, (aka Ahmed Khalid, Mike Yousif, Wahid S. Yousif), was involved with a group of Iranians in Huntsville, Alabama who were romancing local female enlisted personnel in an attempt to procure military secrets.*

Yousif/"Khalid's" mission was to court a woman named Walker from Tuskumbee, AL, whom he had met in Oklahoma City in late 1982, when they worked together at Shotgun Sam's Pizza Parlor. Walker's brother, Jimmy, was the pilot for General Robert L. Moore, Commander of the Redstone Arsenal U.S. Army Missile Command in Huntsville. As commander, Moore had responsibility for the Army's missile program worldwide.**

"What he had wanted, according to her," said a retired Army criminal investigator who wishes to remain anonymous, "was all kinds of information about General Moore." [464]

Moore told me the Army had stepped up security around him during this time. Interestingly, this was around the same time that attacks on U.S. military installations were occurring in Europe.[465]

The Army investigator also recalled that "Huntsville, Alabama, at that time, was a hotbed of espionage. There were 27 known KGB agents in Huntsville. They were known. They were known to the Bureau [FBI]; they were known to military intelligence."

This espionage activity was due to the close proximity of Redstone Missile Command, NASA's Marshall Space Flight Center, and similar high-tech facilities located throughout the area. The investigator has no doubts that the Iranians and the KGB were cooperating.

This account also jibes with Gagan's story. The Soviets had asked Gagan's help in obtaining classified information from his friend at Martin-Marietta. Later, the

---

* It seems the reference to "Iranians" as used by this CID officer is a generic term meant to refer to Middle-Easterners in general, although some Iranians were definitely involved.

** According to Mike Johnston, the head of security for 777 Post Oak Corporation (a high-rise office complex in Houston affiliated with IBI, Ishan Barbouti's company) had a son in U.S. military intelligence. The father, who was later wanted for impersonating a CIA agent, would call his son at the Major Command Assignments Center at Bolling Air Force in Washington, D.C. around August 1990, just prior to the Iraq's invasion of Kuwait. Some of the calls apparently involved the use of a modem to tap into the command center's computers.

Soviets introduced the informant to a man named Hamid who needed fake documentation for illegal Iranians entering the country.

"Back at the time we had a big problem with Iranians," said the former CID investigator, "a big problem. They were always trying to infiltrate the arsenal. A number of them were attending Alabama A&M University under student visas, but most of them didn't go to school. They were involved in a lot of different criminal enterprises—drugs, stolen property, prostitution, all sorts of things."

The suspects were also linked to a string of convenience stores. Northrop believes that "Sam Khalid" is a money man for Arab immigrants wishing to open businesses—namely convenience stores. Those wishing to do so must split the profits with the "money man" 50-50. Could this be another PLO funding scam?

CID opened their case on Yousif/"Khalid" in September of 1982. "During the course of all this, to verify that the guy was real, we got his phone number … and I called the number one night, and I asked for Ahmed "Khalid," and this guy got on the phone and said, 'I don't know him.' And I said, 'Well, It's got to be you. I got to talk to you—it's important.' Twenty-four hours later that guy was in Tuskumbee, Alabama."

Like his brother Sam, Wahid was never prosecuted. "The FBI [officially] took no interest…. Another CID investigator got reprimanded by our SAC, because he went and did this [interviewed Walker]. That was the total gist of the FBI's involvement."

The Army investigator's experiences parallel those of Gagan's. "That's a pretty common thread when you deal with [the FBI]," Gagan explained. "You bring them information, and you never hear another word about it."

Florida police who investigated Arab links to insurance scams and organized crime received the same treatment from the FBI. "People didn't want to investigate this," said a police detective I spoke with. "Things weren't right. It was as if someone was looking at this and saying, 'stay away from it.'"*

In spite of the FBI's stonewalling, the Army investigator remembers the case well: "The female soldiers would go out at night to the different clubs and discos and stuff … we caught one out there, and he supposedly ran a convenience store…. And we caught him on the arsenal.

"Hassan Niakossary—he was the big leader of this gang. He was associated with a local gangster named Dewy Brazelton, who ran a club called the Plush Horse. He had a lot of Cosa Nostra connections into New York—a lot. Hassan worked for him."**

---

* This detective also said that the chief of the FBI's counter-intelligence division masqueraded as a police officer and traveled to Florida to collect data on the their investigation.

** Brazelton didn't return calls.

Middle Eastern terrorists involved in espionage with the KGB, associated with the Mob? The Army investigator said Niakossary traveled frequently to Las Vegas, a known Mob town. So does Wahid's brother, "Sam Khalid." A regular high roller, Khalid reportedly shows up with at least $10,000 in his pocket.

As Hani Kamal pointed out, the Cosa Nostra cooperated with Iranian money laundering in the past. Could this explain "Khalid's" frequent visits to Las Vegas? Were his trips part of a money laundering operation?

As Gunther Russbacher explained, several Las Vegas casinos, including Binyon's Horseshoe, are payoff points for political and judicial slush-funds. Federal judges and others are allegedly paid off through Shamrock Development Corporation in Ireland, via offshore banks and Las Vegas Casinos. The bribe recipients collect their money in the form of gambling chips, then cash them in.

Is "Khalid" receiving money this way? It's hard to say, but it is worth noting that the CEO of Shamrock, Donald Lutz, was on the management staff of Silverado Savings & Loan, the S&L case tried by Judge Matsch, who would later try McVeigh and Nichols (Neil Bush, a board member of Silverado, walked).

And what about Omar's trip(s) to Kingman? It was there that Omar and Gagan drove from Las Vegas, two weeks before the bombing. Why would a high-roller like Omar drive to the dusty, isolated desert town of Kingman? One possible reason may have been to make contact with Timothy McVeigh, who was holed up in the Imperial Motel at the time.

Another reason may have revolved around drugs. Recall that Gagan's original relationship with Omar was under the guise of drug dealing. "I brought some back from Puerto Vallerta for him," said Gagan, "using a camper with a false top ... through San Diego. At one time I saw 10-15 kilos. That's quite a bit of dope."

Recall that Gagan had delivered a bag of cocaine from Kingman to Denver (which contained plastic explosives), and he believes the $250,000 Omar paid him came from the Cali Cartel.*

As mentioned earlier, on April 4, 1995, Gagan and Omar delivered a package to a man in a cowboy hat in Kingman, driving a rusty brown pick-up. Authorities reported that a brown pick-up, belonging to Steven Garrett Colbern, was caught on Trooper Hanger's video camera as he stopped McVeigh on I-35 an hour and-a-half after the bombing.**

---

* Had it actually come from Mexican drug king-pin Juan Garcia Abrego, linked to the Cali Cartel, reportedly sending two bag-men up to Oklahoma City to finance the bombing?

** Kingman has also been called the "Golden Triangle" of speed (methamphetamine), and McVeigh had known Clark Volmer, a paraplegic drug dealer and loan shark in town. On October 19, six months to the day of the bombing, Gagan was directed by a man he describes as "Hizbollah" to take a bus from Las Vegas to Kingman, to deliver a large

A chemist who knew McVeigh under the alias of "Tim Tuttle," Colbern had been spotted with a bag of ammonium-nitrate in his truck. His roommate, Dennis Malzac, was being held on charges of arson for a small explosion that damaged a house in town owned by McVeigh friend Rocky McPeak two months earlier. Colbern, who shared a mailbox in Kingman with McVeigh, was absent from work four days prior to and ten days after the bombing. He claimed he was in California visiting his parents.*

FBI agents digging in the desert outside Kingman for evidence, found more than 150 pounds of ammonium-nitrate buried in the sand.[466]

Colbern was arrested in May of 1995, and released on April 23, 1997, after serving time in Lompoc Federal Prison on illegal weapons charges.[467]

Despite the incriminating connections, Colbern disappeared from the official radar screen almost as quickly as he had appeared. The Oklahoma Highway Patrol video showing the brown pick-up—like the numerous surveillance tapes showing the activity at the Murrah Building on the morning of April 19—was "seized" by the FBI.

Was Colbern the man to whom Omar delivered the mysterious package on April 4? Was it meant for Timothy McVeigh?

Did "Khalid" meet Terry Nichols in Las Vegas in May of 1994? Were Nichols and McVeigh the "two skinny white guys" he met at the Glitter Gulch in November?

Was McVeigh's yellow Mercury at "Sahara Properties" as "Ernie Cranford" claimed? And was McVeigh with Hussain al-Hussaini at the pawnshop and the Roadrunner Tavern in Oklahoma City as KFOR's witnesses said?

Ultimately, were McVeigh, Nichols and their friends in fact plotting with Arab extremists to blow up the Alfred P. Murrah Building?

"[McVeigh] had mentioned before that he wanted to become a mercenary in the Middle East because they paid the most," recalled former Army buddy Greg Henry, "But we just took it as a joke. But he's the kind of person that would have become that."[468]

---

bag of money—estimated to be between $200,000 and $300,000 to an individual who was "militia-looking in appearance."

* McPeak hired McVeigh in 1993 to do security work at a local shelter. When his girl-friend was arrested in Las Vegas on a bad credit charge, the drug dealer, Clark Vollmer, helped bail her out. In February, '95, McPeak claims, Vollmer asked him to ferry some drugs. He refused. Shortly thereafter, an ANFO bomb exploded under a chair outside McPeak's home. When he went to Vollmer's house to confront him, he found Timothy McVeigh, along with another man he didn't recognize.

ARAB/NAZI COLLUSION?

Was Timothy McVeigh some sort of intermediary between neo-Nazi groups and Arab terrorists? While this may sound bizarre, as previously noted, cooperation between such groups has been well documented.

The origins of Arab-Nazi collaboration pre-date WWII. The Mufti of Jerusalem, who was Hitler's guest, actually raised Muslim SS units for the Nazi war effort, culled from Bosnian Muslims and Arabs.

ODESSA, the Nazi organization formed to funnel support to ex-SS members, arranged rendezvous with representatives of various Arab organizations after the war, as part of the Dulles/McCloy/OSS ratlines. This secret CIA operation also funneled Nazis to various Latin American countries, where they set up "security services" (death squads) for their respective government employers.

One ODESSA member, former Gestapo Chief General Ernst Rhemer, settled in the Middle East, where he set up intelligence operations for several Arab countries, including Syria and Egypt. Rhemer, currently active in the "revisionist" scene, played a key role coordinating German right-wing activity with the Arab world for several decades. Alois Brunner, Adolph Eichmann's chief, who murdered 128,500 people during the Nazi Holocaust, played an early role in Arab-Nazi collusion.[469]

Also playing a role in Arab-Nazi cooperation was Hitler's "favorite commando," Otto "Scarface" Skorzeny, who helped install Gamel Abdul Nasser as Egyptian president with the assistance of an elite corps of former SS storm troopers. Skorzeny also helped train early PLO groups for commando raids into Israel. The ardent Nazi, who missed his day at the Nuremberg trials courtesy of the U.S. Government, was stationed in Egypt at the behest of the CIA.

One of Skorzeny's subordinates, a Swiss Nazi named François Genoud, served with Skorzeny's troops in Egypt. Genoud also befriended Ali Hassan Salameh, the leader of Black September, the group which murdered nine Israeli athletes during the 1972 Munich Olympics. Currently a banker in Geneva, Genoud reportedly masterminded several airplane hijackings for the PLO.

A close friend of Genoud's, French attorney Jacques Vergès, defended several members of the Popular Front for the Liberation of Palestine (PFLP), and spoke as a "character" witness on behalf of the notorious Gestapo chief Klaus Barbie (the "Butcher of Lyon"), who murdered hundreds of French resistance fighters, and deported 7,000 Jews to the death camps.

And as recently as the early 1980s, a neo-Nazi named Odifried Hepp was responsible for attacks against at least four U.S. military and NATO installations, as well as German nightclubs frequented by U.S. servicemen. Hepp worked with the PFLP, and was also financed by Yasser Arafat's Al Fatah, who in turn was supported by François Genoud.

As another example of Arab-Nazi collaboration, when members of Abu Nidal, and Abu Abass' Palestine Liberation Front (PLF) hijacked the Greek cruise ship *Achille Lauro* in 1985, they demanded Hepp's release. "I know Hepp quite well," Abass told the French daily *Liberation* in 1985. "He is a friend." [470]

The German magazine *Der Speigel* reported on a group of neo-Nazis called Kampfsportgruppe, headed by a man named Hoffmann (a Hoffmann member had blown himself up, along with 11 others, at the Oktoberfest celebration in Munich in 1981). Kampfsportgruppe, it seemed, was connected to terrorist groups in Beirut. [471] At the same time, a number of German terrorists have reportedly been trained in Palestinian camps in Jordan, South Yemen, Syria, and Iraq.

Iraqi arms dealer Ishan Barbouti met with former Nazi scientist Volker Weissheimer to recruit other former Nazis to work on Libyan and Iraqi chemical weapons projects. [472]

The Syrians—who are well-known sponsors of terrorism—offered funding to Robert Mathews, the former leader of The Order, also known as "Der Bruders Schweigen" (The Silent Brotherhood). Mathews, who was killed in a shoot-out with police in 1984, had issued a "Declaration of War" against the so-called "Zionist Occupied Government," including Jews, blacks, Hispanics, Asians and white "race traitors" who didn't agree with white supremacist goals. Mathews' Order was responsible for a string of armored car robberies and the machine-gun killing of Jewish talk show host Alan Berg in Denver.

As discussed earlier, reports of other Middle-Eastern "terrorist" states such as Libya funding or offering funding to neo-Nazi and other dissident groups such as the Black Muslims and the El Rukns has been reported. One of Libya's primary beneficiaries was the Nation of Islam (NOI), whose leader, Louis Farrakhan, received $5 million dollars from Libyan President Muammar al-Qaddafi.

As previously discussed, Farrakhan's predecessor, Elijah Muhammad, had formed a pact with the KKK and American Nazi Party in 1961. This unusual alliance stretched right up to the present day. In the fall of 1992, WAR leader Tom Metzger appeared on the Whoopi Goldberg Show preaching the benefits of young blacks joining the NOI.

In 1985, Metzger and Farrakhan spoke together in Los Angeles, and in October, 1996, David Irving, a British Nazi Holocaust Revisionist, showed up with a pair of NOI bodyguards.

Twenty-five year DEA veteran Mike Levine described to me the unique connection between Nazis and Arab terrorists: "Years ago I was undercover in the American Nazi party, and it was an odd mix of people that I ran into. First of all, I'm very dark, and my undercover I.D. said I was Italian—Mike Picano. But, what I found interesting was that members of the American Nazi party were Arabs, you know, [and] there were light-skinned Latinos. There were Arab members of the American Nazi Party going all the way back to 1968, when I was a member. The mutual hatred was the Jews and the blacks.[473]

As Levine says, the ties that bind these two seemingly disparate groups is a loathing of the U.S. and hatred of "World Jewry," which they see as the dominating force behind all world political and financial power.

In April, 1991, Ahmed Rami, European correspondent for *Al Shaab* newspaper, urged a "Western Intifada" against alleged Jewish dominance. Rami's call was duplicated in several right-wing German publications, including *Deutsche Rundschall, Remer Depesche,* and *Recht Und Wahrheit,* which wrote:

> One can say that the only winner of WWII was the organized World Jewry ... attained through Auschwitz, a never-before existing freedom to unrestricted development of power. Today, Jews control all important positions of power in the U.S.A.

Similar sentiments were echoed by the Islamic Association of Palestine, which published a communiqué urging Muslims to die in a holy war against Jews, who they call "enemies of humanity, the bloodsuckers, and the killers of prophets." The principal American support group of Hamas, is the IAP in Dallas, Texas.

According to ABC 20/20 reporter Tom Jarriel, law-enforcement sources said that Iranians emigrated to the U.S. for the purpose of "recruiting" Americans for homegrown terrorism. The January, 1996 episode focused on David Belfield (aka Daoud Salahuddin), a young black man who became disenchanted with American social and economic life and was drawn to the militant Islamic movement.

In 1980, Salahuddin assassinated a former Iranian Embassy official, Ali Tabatabai, who advocated the overthrow of the Ayatollah Khomeni. Like Cary Gagan's "Iranian" friends who planned to bomb a federal building using a postal truck packed with explosives, Salahuddin used a postal jeep to gain entry into the official's home. He then fled the U.S. and assimilated himself into the Arab terrorist underground. According to the report, Salahuddin was typical of many young black males indoctrinated into the Islamic faith by Iranian agents, who convinced them that terrorism was a legitimate means of protest.

With the help of Washington, D.C. private investigator Carl Schoffler, ABC 20/20 investigators were able to obtain police intelligence reports which established that "the Ayatollah had established a recruiting and training program within the U.S. for home-grown terrorists."

Calling themselves the Islamic Guerrillas in America (IGA), the group, originally comprised of approximately a dozen young black men, became involved in murder, bank robbery, and threats on the lives of judges and prosecutors.

Regarding the assassination of Tabatabai, Salahuddin told 20/20, "I assume that the decision came from what was the Revolutionary Council in Iran, in Teheran. That's my assumption."

Another of Salahuddin's close pals was Cleven Holt, who under his Islamic name, Isa Abdullah, fought against the Israelis in Lebanon and was seen extensively outside the Marine Corps compound in Beirut just before it was bombed in 1983. Shoffler recalls that Abdullah was once arrested while casing Air Force One, the Presidential jet....

According to Schoffler, "There are clear signs that constant recruitment's going on." [474]

Some of this recruitment was for a group known as al-Fuqua, which claims between 200 and 300 operational members. A splinter from the Da'ar al-Islam sect, al-Fuqra was founded in Brooklyn in 1980 by a Pakistani cleric named Shaykh Mubarik Ali Gilani. Al-Fuqra's international headquarters is in Lahore, Pakistan, and they maintain strong ties to both Pakistani intelligence and the Mujahadeen. [475]

The group, based on the classical terrorist cell structure, is thought to have at least five operational cells in the U.S., and is suspected of 17 bombings and assassinations throughout the country, including the murder of at least 12 people. [476]

In September, 1989, the FBI confiscated the contents of a storage locker in Colorado Springs owned by al-Fuqra members, including 30 pounds of explosives (three pipe-bombs, homemade plastic explosives, hand-grenades, mines, fuses, mercury switches and timing devices), weapons (10 handguns and silencers), military manuals, bomb-making instructions, a photo of Sheik Omar Abdel Rahman, target-practice silhouettes with such headings as "FBI Anti-Terrorist Team" and "Zionist Pig." Also included in the lot were plans to attack Colorado military installations, and Colorado utilities and aviation infrastructures. [477]

Cary Gagan was already familiar with al-Fuqra from his time in prison. Omar had asked Gagan to "take care of" an al-Fuqra member named "Eddie," should he call. Gagan believes the man was Edward Flinton, a Colorado-based al-Fuqra member charged with conspiracy to commit murder in the August 1984 firebombing of a Hare Krishna temple, and the February 1993 murder of Rashid Khalifa, an Iman of a Tucson mosque.*

In August of 1995, six months after the bombing in Oklahoma City, "Eddie" called. Gagan met the al-Fuqra member, and the two allegedly discussed plans to detonate car bombs outside the Governor's Mansion, the Attorney General's office, the Department of Labor and Employment, and the Colorado Bureau of Investigation (CBI). [478]

The plan included not only blowing up buildings—but assassinating a federal

---

* The Bureau of Prisons had "no record" of Edward Flinton, eventhough he served time in federal prison. Usually this means the individual is under the "witness protection program."

judge—Lewis Babcock. Babcock was one of several judges and federal agents on the terrorists' hit list.

"He was my guy up here," said Gagan. "I was to take him out."

The idea was to take Babcock's upstairs neighbor, John Strader, hostage, tie him up, then plant a bomb in his apartment. This time, U.S. Marshals took Gagan's warning seriously. A call to Babcock and Strader confirmed the judge had extra security around him during this time. Nevertheless, Gagan said Agent James Tafoya didn't want to follow up.[479]

On October 20, 1995, Gagan returned to Denver at the behest of his "Hizbollah" contact, where he met two Americans named "Paul" and "Daniel" at the Broadway Plaza Motel. "I had just come back from Kingman, where I dropped off money to a militia-looking dude," said Gagan. The men discussed bombing targets in Denver and Phoenix. "Daniel deals with these dudes (al-Fuqra)," said Gagan. "They were connected to Hizbollah."*

Although the agencies targeted for the attacks stepped up security at these facilities, the FBI began a concerted effort to discredit Gagan, who says he helped load approximately 300 pounds of high-grade explosives allegedly stolen from Explosives Fabricators at the Tomahawk Truck Stop in Watkins, Colorado. Also loaded into a van were anti-tank weapons stolen from the Army, electronic circuitry, and boxes of chemicals marked Ammonium Silicate. Gagan says he drove the van to Denver, whereupon he contacted Agent Matt Traver of the ATF.

Gagan said he informed FBI Agents Johnson and Holtslaw and U.S. Attorneys Allison and Solano. Gagan told Holtslaw he would take a polygraph test, requested that he confirm the status of his Immunity Letter, and meet with his family to assure them that precautions would be taken for their safety. Gagan alleges Holtslaw refused, and ceased all contact with him. The FBI claims that Gagan refused to take a polygraph, and was therefore unreliable.

Gagan's involvement with al-Fuqra is significant in light of several factors. First, Clement Rodney Hampton-El and Earl Gant, both al-Fuqra members, were indicted in the World Trade Center bombing and the subsequent plot to blow up four New York City landmarks by Sheik Omar Abdel Rahman's Jama a' Islamiya. Hampton had fought with Gulbaddin Hekmatyar's Hizb-I-Islami (Islamic Party) during the Afghan War, and assisted in the testing of explosives

---

* Gagan said he saw Daniel with Omar and Ahmed in Mexico. On November 27, Gagan says he was instructed by his "Hizbollah" contact to rent a room at the La Vista Motel in Denver in preparation for another meeting. Gagan said his attempts to have the FBI stake out the room were ignored. The informant claims he learned of plans to bomb simultaneous targets in Phoenix and Denver on or about February 8, 1996—the specific targets being the ATF office in the Mile High Center at 1700 Broadway in Denver, and the DEA/Customs office at 115 Inverness Drive in Englewood, Colorado.

for the New York City bombings, although he didn't actually take part in the final plot.[480]

Second, al-Fuqra is aligned, not only with Pakistani intelligence, which supports the Mujahadeen (World Trade Center bomber Ramzi Yousef is a Pakistani who reportedly fought alongside the Mujahadeen), but to the HizbAllah International through leaders such as Gulbaddin Hekmatyar. Al-Fuqra's contacts also include Hamas, and the Moro Liberation Front, based in the Philippines, where Terry Nichols and Ramzi Yousef allegedly rendezvoused.

Third, an individual claiming to be the brother of the friend of a man involved in the plot called Oklahoma State Representative Key to provide him with information after the bombing. According to the anonymous caller, one of the bombers was a black Muslim. He spoke of a man named "Colonel Hardin" from Arizona, whose "supposed to be deeply involved in this, along with some with some Middle Eastern and some black Muslims."

The reader should take note that this conversation occurred before any discussion of Middle Eastern involvement became public as a result of Stephen Jones' Writ or other investigations:

> **Caller:** So, according to him there was nine people that he knows of that was supposedly involved in this. Now there was ... there was two white guys and a black dude. And he said that he thought one of the white guys could possibly be a short-haired girl that she looked like she might be from the Middle East or something.
>
> But the second time that he saw the car, he said it was about ten minutes before the bombing, he said they drove up to him and told him to get the hell out, that there was gonna' be a bomb. And he said it was the same car only that it had the white guy and the black dude in it. The other person, he said thought might be a female wasn't in the car at that time. Now this about ten minutes before....
>
> And this black dude—he's a member of the Nation of Islam, but he's also prior service military. And this stupid asshole, he supposedly called Channel Four after the bombing, claiming credit for it.
>
> **Key:** Well I heard that ... I forget who called in to where but somebody called in and said, you know, it was the Nation of Islam.
>
> **Caller:** Well, he was supposed to have been the one. And another thing ... Channel Four said late last night that this leg was supposed to have had some PVC embedded it. And, you know, you use PVC pipe to pack plastic explosives in. It greatly increases the detonation of it and the shear power of it, and it's also a tidy way of handling it.*

Finally, there is the unidentified leg found in the rubble of the Murrah Building. The severed leg, allegedly belonging to a black female, was clothed in

---

* This claim was allegedly based on DNA tests and footprint matches.

combat boots, two pairs of socks, and an olive military-issue blousing strap.

Authorities eventually claimed the leg belonged to 21-year-old Air Force Airman Lakesha Levy, who was in the Social Security office at the time of the blast.*

What is strange is that there were eight bodies with missing or severed limbs. If the leg was clothed in military garb, it should have been a simple task to match it with Levy, who likewise would have been wearing a military uniform. Even though Levy was buried before this leg was found, it should have been a simple task to see which of the bodies with severed limbs belonged to military personnel wearing military uniforms. Yet authorities originally buried a different leg with Levy before finding this one on May 30.

The State Medical Examiner's Office originally claimed the leg belonged to a white or light-skinned male, most likely under 30 years of age. This finding was later recanted by the FBI, who declared that it belonged to Levy. By stating the leg belonged to Levy, the FBI conveniently removed all speculation as to whom the leg really belonged to. As Stephen Jones stated, "[Perhaps] the experts are more interested in proving the non-existence of a different bomber at the scene than validating the Oklahoma Medical Examiner." [481]

Could the unidentified leg have actually belonged to the real bomber—a black Muslim prepared to sacrifice himself or herself for the cause? Perhaps this explains why authorities allegedly recovered no bodies that matched this leg. It is possible the leg belonged to an additional bomber who was disintegrated by the blast. This could also explain the confused look Daina Bradley witnessed on John Doe 2's face after he walked to the back of the Ryder truck. Perhaps upon opening the door, he was confronted with a comrade who ordered him away, then set off the device, neatly severing himself or herself in the process.

While the Nation of Islam (NOI) are supposedly enemies of Al Fuqra, it should be pointed out that the NOI has forged links with the KKK, the American Nazi Party, and Tom Metzger's White Aryan Resistance (WAR).

The Tulsa, Oklahoma leader of WAR, Dennis Mahon, freely admitted to William Jasper and other journalists that the Iraqis paid him $100-a-month— $4800 total—between 1991 and 1995, to stir up dissent among the neo-Nazi/White Supremacist community against the Gulf War sanctions. (At least Mahon believes the money came from the Iraqi embassy.) [482]

A former Grand Dragon of the Ku Klux Klan, Mahon had visited Germany in an effort to recruit young Germans into the KKK. Also recall that during the Gulf War, the Anti-Zionist League's Michael Kühnen, working with his old mercenary friend Michel Faci, negotiated a contract to provide 200 German, American and British neo-Nazi volunteers to fight alongside Iraqi troops.

As previously discussed, Kühnen was succeeded by a man named Hubner, who

---

* This claim was allegedly based on DNA tests and footprint matches.

has spoken with Kirk Lyons at meetings of the group "Deutsche Alternative." Lyons' client was Michael Brescia's roommate Andreas Strassmeir, a good friend of Dennis Mahon's. A frequent visitor to Elohim City, Mahon was close friends with Brescia. He almost certainly knew Brescia's friend, Timothy McVeigh.

Again, the question must be asked: Were McVeigh, Nichols, and their comrades in fact plotting with Arab extremists and their black Muslims counterparts to blow up the Federal Building, and was Iraq behind it?

As Jack Anderson stated: "A preferable revenge for Iraq would involve having a 'surrogate terrorist' carry out a domestic attack that Hussein could privately take credit for."

Anderson's analysis may be rather prescient. States and their intelligence agencies have being using terrorist groups as "cut-outs" for years in order to maintain deniability. *Defense & Foreign Affairs* stated it thusly:

> Despite the important evolution in the role of the terrorist organizations and other entities through the HizbAllah International, the actual control over the operations themselves remains firmly in the hands of, and under the tight control of, the sponsoring states, being perpetrated by operatives of intelligence services....
>
> It is through these "organizations" that the sponsoring states in effect take credit for their terrorist operations and have their message clear and explicit. Given the marked escalation of international terrorism and the higher stakes involved, the importance of the front groups "speaking" for the sponsoring states—particularly Iran and the global Islamic Revolution it is running—is of growing importance and centrality to international terrorism.[483]

Another example of such methodology was the World Trade Center bombing. As Ramzi Yousef's accomplice Mahmud Abu Halima put it, "The planned act was not as big as what subsequently occurred.... Yousef showed up on the scene ... and escalated the initial plot.... Yousef used [Salameh and the others] as pawns and then immediately after the blast left the country."[484] Some terrorism experts think Yousef was working for Iraq.

Stephen Jones believes a similar plan unfolded in Oklahoma City. As he stated in his March 25th Writ of Mandamus:

> The plan was arranged for a Middle Eastern bombing engineer to engineer the bomb in such a way that it could be carefully transported and successfully detonated. There is no reported incident of neo-Nazis or extreme right-wing militants in this country exploding any bomb of any significant size, let alone one to bring down a nine (9) story federal building and kill 168 persons.... This terrorist attack was "contracted out" to persons whose organization and ideology was friendly to policies of the foreign power and included dislike and hatred of the United States gov-

ernment itself, and possibly included was a desire for revenge against the United States....[485]

In November of 1994, Cary Gagan said he made a trip to Mexico City with Omar, where he ran into a familiar face amongst the terrorist crowd—Frank Terpil. "I saw him down in Mexico City ... with Omar," recalled Gagan. "We met him in the Zona Rosa area."

A retired CIA communications specialist, Terpil had been convicted, along with rogue CIA agent Edwin Wilson, of selling 20 tons of C-4 plastic explosives and 50,000 electronic timers to the Libyan government.

Terpil also lined his pockets supplying torture devices to Ugandan Dictator Idi Amin, and sophisticated detonators and communications equipment to the Popular Front for the Liberation of Palestine. He and Wilson had also set up a terrorist training camp in Libya, and had recruited U.S. Green Berets to train Arab terrorists in bombing and assassination techniques.

After being indicted, Terpil fled the country, and was last seen hiding out in Cuba, until he showed up in Mexico City ... with Omar. "They met at the bar," said Gagan. "Terpil and Omar spoke for about fifteen minutes, alone."

"Who's that dude?" Gagan asked Omar as they left the bar.

"An ex-CIA agent named Terpil," came the answer. "He lives in Cuba."

"Frank Terpil? I thought he was dead? What's up with him?"

"He lives in Cuba. He's hands-off...."

Considering Terpil's well-documented relationship with Arab terrorists, and his "wanted" status in the U.S., it is understandable why he would choose to meet Omar in Mexico City.

Gagan himself was no stranger to Mexico City. As previously discussed, the Soviets had solicited Gagan's help in 1980 to procure military secrets from his friend at Martin-Marietta. They requested his help again in 1986 to assist illegal Iranian immigrants who needed false IDs.

While in Mexico Gagan had also met an Austrian, Eduard Bodenzayer, a Soviet spy, and had been to the Russian embassy repeatedly. As he told Stephen Jones, "My contacts there were a guy named Vallery and Elyia."

Did Omar, "Sam Khalid," or their associates have contact with the Russians? Considering "Khalid's" reported ties to the PLO and Hamas, and the long history of Soviet-Arab cooperation, it is highly likely.

Like neo-Nazis who've forged links with Arab terrorists, the Soviets have provided wide-ranging support to Arab terrorist groups throughout the years. As James Phillips of the Heritage Foundation writes:

During the 1970s the Soviet Union and its satellites greatly expanded their support for terrorist groups. Moscow often used Middle Eastern client states such as Iraq,

Libya, Syria, and the former People's Democratic Republic of South Yemen as intermediaries to mask Soviet arms, training, intelligence, and logistical support for a wide variety of terrorist groups.[486]

If the Russians were sponsoring their Arab friends in terrorism, it is likely the Arabs may have wished to maintain further deniability by engaging the assistance of American neo-Nazis. This possibility became more apparent as connections were drawn, not only between WAR's Dennis Mahon and Iraqi embassy officials, but between Terry Nichols and Iraqi terrorist Ramzi Yousef, and between Timothy McVeigh and former Iraqi soldier Hussain al-Hussaini.

This likelihood became clearer after interviewing Michele Torres, the daughter of a former Communist Party official (P.R.T. Party) in Mexico City. An intelligent young woman, Michele had been raised under the harsh regimentation of a person destined for a position in the Communist Party, but had rebelled, and at age 17, fled to the United States.

Torres recalled the numerous and strange faces that would often pass through her home and her father's office. Arab men from Jordan, Palestine, Iraq; she was not allowed to ask them their names or their business.[487]

Torres claims to have heard conversations between her father and PLO representatives some years earlier. The meetings, she said, involved discussions of a bombing plot to be carried out in the U.S.

It was the winter of 1992, and Michele's father, Hirram Torres, was working in the office of the PLO in Mexico City. He was speaking with a man from Palestine, and another from Jordan or possibly Iraq. In broken English, Torres recounts the conversation:

> **Torres:** They were saying: "What do you think about the new plan?" And the other man says: "Well, we can … the Russian officers told us we can probably blame the fascists." You know what I mean? "Americans—the American Patriots, and all the stupid stuff with the white supremacists and the neo-Nazis. So we can give two strikes at once."
>
> **Hoffman:** Did he explain what he meant by two strikes?
>
> **Torres:** They didn't explain it but I understood it.
>
> **Hoffman:** Did they say anything about the Patriot Movement or the Militia Movement?
>
> **Torres:** They don't say anything about militia. When they want to talk about militia, they say fascists or neo-Nazis. They used to speak about white supremacists … all Americans … white Americans are white supremacists. Yankees and fascists.
>
> **Hoffman:** Tell me what they meant by the two strikes at once.
>
> **Torres:** They wanted … the Arab people wanted … to make a terrorist act. They

needed to make a terrorist act. There was like, some of the Arab leaders—wanted to make—wanted to give a strike to the United States. They didn't even understand why. But at the same time, the Communist Party tells them that it was a great idea to.

Hoffman: Now are you relating the actual conversation?

Torres: Yes. They were saying that it was … all the time they were talking about … what the Russian officers told them to do. So that man who was talking was the Palestinian man—my father told him that it was very good, and that they would probably find an easy way—an easy way to blame that kind of people. That he was trying … that he had tried to contact neo-Nazi people to help him.

Hoffman: Did he say who?

Torres: Yes. He tried to contact any kind of National Socialist people (American Nazi Party). I tell you the way I heard it: "We can probably use those neo-Nazi bastards. I tried to contact them, but they refused to do it, and they don't want to get involved in that kind of stuff with Communists. And I don't think anyone can get those fucking idiots, but I don't care." He said something like, "I don't care. We are anyway going to blame them."

Hoffman: We don't want to get involved with Communists and that kind of stuff and what.

Torres: "But [we] can blame them. No matter if they want to cooperate with us or not." Then he told me … he told that guy that … he was going to hire a white man.

Hoffman: To act as a neo-Nazi? You mean to play the part of a neo-Nazi?

Torres: To play the part of a neo-Nazi. And to participate with his comrades … he spoke about his Arab comrades.

Hoffman: In what respect?

Torres: His Arab comrades … and he used to call them brothers or some kind of thing.

Hoffman: Your father spoke of them this way?

Torres: Yes. But, well, he told it in Russian, that he was—that boy who they were going to hire, was going to work together with the Tobarich (Russian for comrade). With the Tobarich.

Hoffman: Do you remember any names—any specific names of any people—anybody?

Torres: No. That time, they were just going to plan it. That was the plan.

Hoffman: This was in the winter of '92?

Torres: Yes. They were just discussing the plan. They didn't even know the names. [By] that time my father was … deciding.

Hoffman: Now why do you think so long ago? That's four years between now and then.

Torres: They always plan it in that way. They take their time, and always a very long time. They always take a very long time …

Hoffman: Is there anything else about what they discussed that you haven't told me that you think is important?

Torres: They said they were going to do it in the middle of the country. And they were going to do it in a business office.

Hoffman: Did they say how big?

Torres: Yes, big. And they wanted ... children to be victims of it. There must be children there—it must be an office where children were somehow. They had to kill children. Because it was a very important part of the emotional part of the strike....

Hoffman: Did they ever mention Pan Am 103 or the World Trade Center bombings in reference?

Torres: They talked something about ... trade centers. Anyway they spoke about trade centers—about places where business were made, because Americans regard so much their money and their business. That was the explanation my father gave to the Palestinian guy. They spoke about places where business were made, and that it was not the only strike they were going to make.

You know one of the reasons I am not scared of [this interview] is because I heard—I listen to this kind of conversation all of my life. My father—he has killed a lot of people—he has done a lot of wrong things. He was involved.

While Torres' mention of Russian intelligence seems to have all the makings of a Claire Sterling novel, it should be mentioned that Mexico City is home to one of the largest Soviet consulates in the Western hemisphere, with its attendant Soviet intelligence apparatus.

Torres was probably describing more than a loose-knit group of terrorists—a sophisticated, centrally-controlled state-sponsored terrorist apparatus. As *Defense & Foreign Affairs* stated:

Despite the unprecedented role of the HizbAllah International in the decision making process, all major terrorist operations remain state-controlled. These operations are conducted by agencies of states and in pursuit of the long-term and strategic interests of the controlling and sponsoring states. The "names" and "profiles" of the organizations and groups issuing the communiqués and claims constitute an integral component of the state sponsorship mechanism. These named entities serve a specific function: stating the identity of the interests involved in, and the outlining of the logic and objectives behind, these operations without having the sponsoring states assume formal responsibility....

Incredible as it sounds, Torres' story may be a key piece of the puzzle linking the Arab and neo-Nazi contingents. Her story is significant in light of the fact that Dennis Mahon was being paid by the Iraqis to stir up dissent amongst the white supremacist community during the Gulf War.

Her story ties into the fact that Omar allegedly met with Frank Terpil in Mexico City and Terry Nichols reportedly met with Ramzi Yousef in the Philippines.

Finally, Timothy McVeigh, an alleged white supremacist, was seen with Hussain al-Hussaini, an Iraqi.*

Within hours of the blast in Oklahoma City, *Radio Teheran* in Iraq had the answer. "The perpetrators were Christian extremist militias from Montana and Oklahoma observing the two-year anniversary of the U.S. government killing of 86 men, women, and children in the Branch Davidian Waco massacre." [488]

Was McVeigh a "neo-Nazi bastard" Michele's father talked about hiring?**

And were the Russians using Middle Eastern terrorists as proxies—who in turn were using American neo-Nazis—to destabalize the West while maintaining deniability? While the apparent demise of the Soviet Union convinced a lot of people that the long-feared Communist threat was over, many within the intelligence community disagree. A recent Reuters report quotes Raymond Mislock, Chief of the FBI's National Security Division, as saying that the Russians "still are on the scene," and continue to employ intelligence officers in this country. The FBI was investigating over 200 cases of suspected Russian espionage activity at the time of this writing. [489]

And what about Khalid's employees trips to Mexico? Was "Khalid" liaisoning with terrorists there? Ultimately, the question was, who was "Khalid" working for?

Although Louis Crousette avoided any further attempts to contact him, he left Jayna Davis with one final word of advice. Echoing Hani Kamal's words of warning regarding Israeli intelligence, Crousette said, "You know who's your best bet to talk to, if you haven't thought about it … the Mossad."

That final adage led me straight back to Northrop, who stated in his report that "Khalid" fit the role of a PLO operative, and insisted that the bombing was the work of Iraqi terrorists. But if "Khalid," Hussaini, and Oshan were simple Arab terrorists—and they had left a trail of evidence a mile long—why were they still walking around?

In spite of Gordon Novel's and Jayna Davis' unsuccessful attempts to positively I.D. "Khalid" with McVeigh or Nichols, Gagan stated that he had seen Nichols with Omar at a meeting which took place just outside of Las Vegas.

The FBI also investigated "Sam Khalid" for PLO fundraising activities, and had looked into the shooting assault of Sharon Twilley.

They had put out an APB on the brown pick-up driven by Hussain al-Hussaini, which was seen speeding away from the scene of the bombing. and Hussaini's alibi for the morning of the April 19 was patently false.

---

* Michele said she overheard her father talk about approaching neo-Nazis through the National Socialist Party. Did Hirram Torres try to contact National Socialist leader Gary Lauck? Apparently, Strassmeir was on to Lauck, as he was arrested on his way to Denmark. Strassmeir had learned about Lauck's travel plans from WAR leader Dennis Mahon.

** Torres' tapes were voice stress-analyzed, which indicated she was being truthful.

KFOR's witnesses who placed Hussaini with McVeigh seem perfectly credible, and KFOR passed on their information to the FBI.

"Khalid" had access to an auto body shop, and one of "Khalid's" employees had been seen abandoning the re-painted pick-up in a nearby apartment complex.

Then there was the mysterious disappearance of "Khalid's" phone records, and the strange comments he made to Ernie Cranford when he was asked why Abraham Ahmed had been seen hanging around "Khalid's" place in the brown pick-up.

"Khalid" had been placed by Northrop's sources with the same Hamas operative in Miami—Ramadan Shallah—that Gagan had seen in Las Vegas.

Finally, Omar (Khalid?) was seen meeting with Frank Terpil—a rogue CIA agent who had supplied Arab terrorists with several tons of C-4.

Although circumstantial, the facts were sufficient to make an incontrovertible case, and yet these people seemed to walk through walls. Could the FBI be so inept? Were their agents so compartmentalized they couldn't put two and two together? Or had the Justice Department's investigation become so politicized that bureaucratic ineptitude had become the desired and inevitable result? It would seem all of the above, and yet this still appears to be too simple an answer.

Even Northrop's report seems a bit one-dimensional. While the former Israeli intelligence agent drew a picture of Arab terrorists forged in the fire of the PLO, the image that lurked just beneath the surface, one drawn in invisible ink, was that of intelligence operatives conceived in the secret chambers of the Mossad ... or the CIA.

This was the one remaining possibility that lends credence to the seemingly irreconcilable facts which presented themselves. After all, why had the FBI ignored a veritable mountain of damming evidence? Why had they suddenly and mysteriously canceled the APB on the brown pick-up? And why, after 48 hours of reporting nothing but Middle Eastern connections, did the Justice Department and the obedient lap dogs of the mainstream press suddenly announce that no Middle Eastern connection existed?

Certainly the capture of McVeigh and Nichols did not repudiate the still-standing Middle Eastern connection. Nor could the sudden change have been the result of information from low-level agents in the field. No. It could have only been the result of one thing—a strategic decision from the Justice Department, which had as its basis, a political directive from the White House.

It was to Washington that "Khalid" traveled shortly after the bombing, according to employees, to meet with a Congressional representative. The purpose? As an emissary to discuss the problem of "Muslim bashing."

Yet KFOR's P.I., Bob Jerlow claims, he spoke to the Representative's aide who checked the Congressman's schedule and claimed she never saw the name "Khalid."

If "Sam Khalid" was a run-of-the-mill Arab terrorist who had just played a role in the biggest terrorist attack in U.S. history, why would he attract attention to himself by firing shots at Sharon Twilley? A convicted felon like "Khalid" would easily earn a stiff prison sentence for possession of a firearm and assault with a deadly weapon.

Unless he was "protected."

This would tend to explain his nonchalant behavior towards "Ernie Cranford," Bob Jerlow, Brad Edwards, and the author. It would likewise tend to explain the FBI's lack of interest in "Khalid."

If Khalid and Hussaini were Arab terrorists, why did "Khalid" allegedly meet with such high-level U.S. officials? President Clinton's publicly televised admonishment not to blame the Arab community also served as a handy excuse to cover up the Middle Eastern connection.

Why would Clinton want to cover up Middle Eastern connection to the bombing? To crack down on the Patriot/Militia community who represent a threat to the international corporate "New World Order?" Once the Justice Department announced the capture of McVeigh and Nichols, the mainstream media, with information mainly supplied by the Anti-Defamation League of the B'nai B'rith (ADL), and the Southern Poverty Law Center (SPLC), focused their anti-militia spotlights. Attacks on the Patriot/Militia movement continued for months, even without documentable proof of the suspects' connections to the militias, or the militias' connection to the bombing.

Ignoring the Middle Eastern connection also disassociated the power elite from programs to bring individuals like Hussain al-Hussaini into this country. Between 1992 and 1995, over 18,000 Iraqi refugees and their families were resettled into the U.S. under a little-known program initiated by President Bush and followed up by President Clinton. These immigrants were part of a contingent of Iraqi refugees that flooded the Saudi border during and after the Gulf War, including many former Iraqi soldiers and deserters.

According to Oklahoma Senator David Boren, approximately 950 of these former soldiers were resettled in the U.S. in 1992 and 1993. Congressional Research Service figures indicate that an additional 549 soldiers were resettled in 1994 and 219 in 1995.

A "Sense of the Congress" resolution initiated by Republicans Don Manzulla of Illinois and Clifford Stearns of Florida attempted to halt the resettlement.[490]

"We're rolling out the welcome wagon to prisoners of war, yet our own veterans who fought there are having trouble getting any help," Sterns said. Some of the refugees included Shi'ite Muslims who were oppressed by Iraqi President Saddam Hussein and in some cases rebelled against him. Others included Iraqi soldiers who Hussein vowed to execute because they didn't fight to the death. "I'm sympathetic with the idea that people who opposed Saddam Hussein should not be allowed to be massacred," said Tennessee State Republican Representative

John L. "Jimmy" Duncan Jr., "but we should give the benefit of the doubt to our own people and put the burden of proof on the people who want to come in."*

In spite of the resolutions, the White House backed the program, officially admitting approximately 18,000 Iraqi refugees into the U.S. According to Manzulla's office, the figure may well be higher. Some findings put approximately 5,000 Iraqis in Tulsa and Oklahoma City alone.

Others fear that such a resettlement would create a "blowback." The U.S. already has Muslim extremist cells, and it is difficult to gather accurate intelligence on all those admitted under the program. According to the Congressional Research Service Report, "… there has been no contact with Kuwaiti intelligence services in the effort to verify that the refugees are not Iraqi agents."[491]

If Hussain al-Hussaini, a former Iraqi officer, was resettled into the U.S., it is possible—highly possible in fact—that he was recruited by the CIA or DIA as part of a deal.

There is a precedent for such collaboration. In 1949 and 1950 the National Security Council issued NSC Intelligence Directive 13 and 14, expanding authority of the CIA to function inside the U.S. (in violation of the CIA's charter). One of their programs involved bringing "favored European exiles" into the country.

"Favored European exiles" was a euphemism for Nazi war criminals.

Given the United States' precedent in using expatriated Nazis and Cubans for covert operations, and the extremely low-key nature of the Bush/Clinton Iraqi resettlement program, one has to wonder about Hussaini's real purpose.**

As former Pentagon investigator Gene Wheaton observes: "Every major Middle-Eastern terrorist organization is under surveillance and control of the intelligence agencies in the U.S. None of these guys move around as freely as they'd like you to think."

If Hussaini was working for the Mossad, FBI, DIA, or CIA, who have been known to cooperate with each other on "special projects," he may have been a double-agent, working for Iraq at the same time. Remember that Saddam Hussein threatened revenge against the United States: "Does the United States realize the meaning of opening the stores of the world with the will of Iraqi people? Does it realize the meaning of every Iraqi becoming a missile that can cross to countries and cities?"

If an element of the United States Government played a role in the destruc-

---

* The Federal Government allocated $6,000 per refugee for resettlement purposes, at the same time that veterans who suffered from Gulf War illness were being ignored by the Veterans Administration.

** Like Andreas Strassmeir, Hussaini was unable to come up with his INS records. Khalid claimed they were stolen by KFOR, a claim Jayna Davis just laughed at.

tion of the Alfred P. Murrah Building, it may have proved easier for them to use an Arab than recruit an American citizen to do its dirty work.

Sam Khalid's ability to monitor the activities of a group of Middle Easterners with dubious connections (through hiring and renting homes to Arab immigrants), and his status as former felon, make him a likely candidate as an operative or informant.

Was he playing both sides of the fence?

Politically, the government's refusal to concede the complicity of Iraq in the World Trade Center bombing, and possibly to the Oklahoma City bombing, may stem from its desire to halt any public outcry against U.S. policies. One major example is the government's refusal to face the consequences of its brutal and devastating actions in the Gulf.

Dr. Laurie Mylroie believes the Clinton administration's failure to address the problem lies in its refusal to face the specter of state-sponsored terrorism. Instead it chooses to adopt a microcosmic "law-enforcement" approach to what she perceives as an international problem—hence the focus on "domestic terrorists."

Moreover, the White House may not want to admit the specter of state-sponsored terrorism because it might panic the populace. Such is the case of a state-sponsored biological attack which has been increasingly threatening our population.

If Iraq indeed proved to be behind the Oklahoma City bombing, it would not fare well for the Clinton administration, which followed up on President Bush's Iraqi resettlement program. It would not fare well for Bush and his business and political cronies—the same CIA/Iran-Contra coterie who armed and fueled Saddam Hussein's military machine with conventional and biological weapons.

And it would preclude this same international arms/drugs cabal from profiteering by resupplying Iraq in the future. In short, it would preclude "business as usual."

Whatever the reason, the public wasn't being told the full truth about the Oklahoma City bombing. They would never be allowed to glimpse any evidence of the Middle Eastern connection.

Yet this was only part of the picture.

Chapter Six

"No Stone Unturned"

"We will leave no stone unturned in our effort to get to the truth."
—Attorney General Janet Reno

"McVeigh and Nichols are going to hell regardless. I'm just looking forward to sending them there a little sooner."
—U.S. Attorney Joseph Hartzler

Almost from the beginning, the Justice Department and the mainstream press focused their attention on Timothy McVeigh, painting him as a spurned ex-soldier who was angry for failing to make the Special Forces; an extremist right-wing Patriot who hated the government with a passion for their atrocities at Waco. McVeigh, the angry misguided loner, it is alleged, conspired with anti-government tax protester Terry Nichols to teach the Federal Government a lesson in Oklahoma.

Like the arrest of Lee Harvey Oswald, the capture of Timothy McVeigh was an incredible stroke of timing and luck. Like Oswald, who was arrested for walking into a movie theater without paying, McVeigh would be arrested for speeding down the highway with a conspicuously missing license plate.

In both cases, the FBI was quickly notified that their suspect was in custody. With their extraordinary run of good luck, the FBI instantly traced the serial number found on the bomb truck to Ford, then to Ryder, then to Elliott's rental agency, then to a "Bob Kling," and finally to McVeigh.[492]

Like Oswald's Mannlicher-Carcanno rifle, traced from its entrance into the U.S. to an importer, to Klein's Sporting Goods, to a sale to one "A.J. Hidell," then to Oswald—all without computers and over a weekend—the FBI would quickly trace the Ryder truck to the lone bomber.

Finally, like "lone nut" Lee Harvey Oswald, "lone nut" Timothy James McVeigh would be transferred from the Noble County jail, paraded in front of onlookers and the press as the mass murderer. While there was no Jack Ruby to intervene this time, McVeigh would be led away in a bright orange jumpsuit, without a bulletproof vest, which he had specifically requested.

Ironically, his departing words were, "I might be Lee Harvey Oswald, Jr....

You remember what happened with Jack Ruby."[493]

As in the arrest of Lee Harvey Oswald, the circumstances surrounding the arrest of McVeigh and Nichols would prove highly questionable. The media widely reported that McVeigh was stopped by Highway Patrolman Charles Hanger 78 minutes after the blast(s), heading north on I-35, near Perry. McVeigh was driving without a license plate. As Trooper Hanger's affivadit states:

> "That I stopped the vehicle and the defendant was the driver and only occupant of the vehicle.... That as the defendant was getting his billfold from his right rear pocket I noticed a bulge under the left side of his jacket and I thought it could be a weapon.... That I then told the defendant to pull his jacket back and before he did he said, 'I have a gun under my jacket.' That I then grabbed a hold of the left side of his jacket and drew my own weapon and pointed it at the back of his head and instructed him to keep his hands up and I walked him over to the trunk of his car and had him put his hands on the trunk...."

Yet accounts vary. Some acticles stated that McVeigh was speeding at 81 miles per hour. Yet Hanger only cited him for no license plate, no insurance, and possession of a concealed weapon. Were these accounts meant to suggest that McVeigh was trying to make a fast get-away? If so, why would a man who had just committed such a heinous crime wish to draw attention to himself?

McVeigh supposedly just blew up a building and killed 169 innocent people—men, women, and children—including a number of federal agents. Seventy-eight minutes later he is pulled over by a state trooper. He has no tags, no insurance, and is carrying a concealed weapon without a permit. He is most likely going to jail, where his name, Social Security number, and description will be uplinked to the National Crime Information Center (NCIC) at the FBI—an FBI that is now on full alert.

McVeigh is carrying a large combat knife and a Glock model 21 automatic pistol loaded with deadly hollow-point bullets. McVeigh is a trained soldier, a top marskman, and a hardened combat veteran.

The cop is exiting his vehicle and walking over to McVeigh's car. McVeigh's life outside the electric chair is very likely about to come to an end. What does McVeigh—the hardened combat veteran and brutal killer of 169 innocent people—do? He casually informs the cop that he has a concealed weapon, and meekly hands himself over for arrest.*

Of course the mainstream press wouldn't make any attempt to analyze this

---

* McVeigh was taken over to Hanger's patrol car, where he heard radio broadcasts about the bombing, and casually chit-chated with Officer Hanger. When he arrived at the jailhouse, he simply asked, "when's chow?"

bizarre inconsistency in McVeigh's behavior, only reporting that he was "uncommunicative" (*Time*), "calls himself a 'prisoner of war'" (*New York Times*), and is "refusing to cooperate with investigators and prosecutors." (*U.S. News & World Report*)—a story repeated by numerous other papers.

Yet as McVeigh stated to *Newsweek*, "I never called myself a prisoner of war." [494] McVeigh's account is backed up by the *Los Angeles Times*, which obtained McVeigh's arrest records. As the *Times'* Richard Serrano notes:

> They reveal a McVeigh sharply different from the one sources had earlier portrayed. He was not the silent soldier who gave jailers only his name, rank and serial number. Rather, he was often polite. And smooth. [495]

With only the serial number of a truck differential and a sketch to work with, the FBI fanned out through Junction City. Upon examining the rental receipt at Elliott's Body Shop, the FBI discovered all the information on it was false. As Agent Henry Gibbons' affidavit states:

> The person who signed the rental agreement identified himself as Bob Kling, SSAN 962-42-9694, South Dakota driver's license number YF942A6, and provided a home address of 428 Maple Drive, Omaha, Nebraska, telephone 913-238-2425. The person listed the destination as 428 Maple Drive, Redfield, South Dakota. Subsequent investigation conducted by the FBI determined all that information to be false.

Yet, employees of Elliott's Body Shop did recognize the sketch of Unsub #1 as the man who rented the truck used in the bombing. The FBI then took the sketch of Unsub #1 to the Dreamland Motel, where they found that Unsub #1 had rented a room from April 14 through the April 18. As the FBI affidavit states:

> An employee of the Dreamland Motel in Junction City, Kansas, identified Timothy McVeigh as a guest at the motel from April 14, 1995, through April 18, 1995. This employee, when shown a photo lineup identified Timothy McVeigh's picture as the individual who registered at the motel under the name of Tim McVeigh, listed his automobile as a Mercury bearing an Arizona license plate, and provided a Michigan address, on North Van Dyke in Decker Michigan. [496]

On April 21, only hours before McVeigh was due to be released from the Perry County Jail, "District Attorney John Maddox received a call from the FBI telling him to hang onto the prisoner." [497]

As the *New York Times* reported, "... a routine check of his Social Security number matched one flagged by the FBI as belonging to a suspect in the bombing."[498] McVeigh's Social Security number could have only been obtained from accurate registration information at the Dreamland, not the false information at Elliott's.

Why would Tim McVeigh—bent on committing such a terrible crime—use a fake name and address at the Ryder rental agency, yet use his real name and address at a motel right down the street?* Perhaps because, as will be explained below, McVeigh never visited the rental agency.

While in custody, McVeigh listed James Nichols as a reference. Why would McVeigh list the brother of his so-called accomplice as his only reference?

On April 21, Terry Nichols was busy with chores around his new home in Herrington. Unbeknownst to him, a team of 11 FBI agents had already staked out his house.

Later that afternoon, Nichols heard his name being broadcast as a possible suspect. At 2:42 P.M. he and Marife got into their blue pick-up, and drove to the Herrington police station, with the FBI on his tail. According to Marife, Terry was frightened, and anxious to know why his name was being broadcast. Inside, Nichols asked why his name was being mentioned on the radio in connection with the bombing. The cops replied that they didn't know, but they had some questions for him. "Good," Nichols said, "because I have some questions for you."

Strangely, FBI agents then read Nichols his Miranda rights, something not normally done unless someone is under arrest, and told him three times he was free to go.

In fact, Nichols wasn't free to go. An arrest warrant had been issued five hours earlier, but Nichols wouldn't be informed of this until almost midnight. In the interim, he and Marife were questioned by the FBI for over nine hours.

Back at his house, a SWAT team had already arrived, and agents were sealing it with crime tape, checking it for booby traps. It was there agents would claim to discover 55-gallon barrels, rolls of primadet detonator cord, non-electric blasting caps, and a receipt for 40 50-pound bags of ammonium-nitrate with McVeigh's thumbprint.

If Terry Nichols was an accomplice in the bombing, why would he leave such incriminating items in his house? Wouldn't he have attempted to hide the items before driving over to the police station?

Moreover, if Nichols was a co-conspirator in the largest domestic terrorist attack in the history of the country, why would he casually stroll into the police

---

* For that matter, why would he rent an easily traceable truck, apply for jobs at the Federal Building using his real name, allow himself to be filmed by numerous security cameras, stop to ask directions minutes before the bombing, hang around two blocks from the crime scene minutes after the blast, speed away without a license plate, and fail to shoot the cop who stopped him?

station asking why his name was being broadcast on TV? This makes about as much sense as Timothy McVeigh casually pulling over for Officer Hanger and meekly handing himself over for arrest.

Several days after McVeigh's arrest, Hanger claimed to have recovered a crumpled business card from behind the front passenger seat of his patrol car, where McVeigh had been sitting. The card for Paulsen's Military Supply of Antigo, Wisconsin, contained a handwritten note: "Dave. TNT at $5 a stick. 708-288-0128. Need more. Call after 1 of May, see if I can get some more."

Had McVeigh actually left such a note in the cruiser? When McVeigh defense team investigator Marty Reed attempted to interview Hanger, he was told by OHP chief legal counsel John Lindsey, "The FBI has requested that no one interview Trooper Charlie Hanger."

And as in the Kennedy case, the evidence collected by the FBI in their case, code-named "OKBOMB," would prove just as specious. The FBI quickly claimed that they had traced the Ryder truck from a serial number—6 4 PVA26077—found on its rear differential, which had flown 575 feet through the air "like a boomerang" and landed on a Ford Fiesta. (For those confused about the FBI finding the serial number on the "axle," it was actually on the axle housing.) [499]*

Curiously, while Deputy Sheriff Melvin Sumter told me he had found the axle, an Oklahoma City Policeman, Mike McPherson, claimed that he had in fact discovered it, as did an FBI agent. These three accounts were contradicted by Governor Frank Keating, who claimed that he had actually found the axle.

The Ryder truck belonging to the axle, rented under the alias of "Bob Kling," the FBI claimed, was the instrument of the deadly destruction in Oklahoma City.

But had it actually been rented by Timothy McVeigh?

The "McVeigh" Eldon Elliott described to the Grand Jury was 5' 10" to 5' 11", with medium build, weighing between 180-185 pounds. Elliott's mechanic Tom Kessinger stated that the man had a "rough" complexion with "acne," and employee Vicki Beemer said he had a deformed chin.

Not only is McVeigh clear-skinned, he is a lanky 6', 2", and weighs only 160 pounds. He does not have a deformed chin. [500]

Readers will also recall that ATF informant Carol Howe, who had penetrated the Elohim City enclave, told ATF and FBI agents that the sketch of John Doe 1 who rented the truck appeared to be Elohim City resident and close Strassmeir friend Peter Ward. [501]

According to reporter J.D. Cash, Dennis Mahon said that Ward was "known at Elohim City as 'Andy's shadow'... Ward went everywhere Strassmeir did and is

---

* The author saw a close-up videotape of the axle taken by Deputy Sheriff Melvin Sumter, which clearly shows the serial number on the differential housing, which is part of the rear axle assembly. It was not, as some researchers claimed, on the axle itself.

dumb as dirt." Mahon also added, "you know his brother, Tony, has a pocked complexion..."[502]

Yet authorities insist that it was McVeigh who rented the truck on April 17. They introduced surveillance footage from a Junction City McDonalds, slightly over a mile from Elliott's, showing McVeigh walking towards the cashier at approximately 3:55 P.M. Yet McVeigh was not wearing military attire as was "Kling." Nevertheless, the prosecution contends that McVeigh left the restaurant, walked the 1.3 miles to Elliott's during a light drizzle, then showed up nice and dry, wearing completely different clothes.

Eldon Elliott would play along for the prosecution. In spite of his previous Grand Jury testimony, and the FBI 302 statements of his employees, Elliott testified at McVeigh's trial that Timothy McVeigh was the man who rented the truck.*

Interesting that he could make such an assertion, when the FBI hadn't brought him before a line-up even though they had questioned him just 48 hours after the bombing. In fact, the FBI didn't show Elliott a photo line-up until 48 *days* later. During McVeigh's trial, Elliott attempted to compensate for the discrepancy in McVeigh's height by stating that McVeigh had "leaned" on the counter while filling out the reservation form.

Had Elliott been coached by the prosecution?**

"From his body language, the way he acted nervous, avoided my questions, I could tell he was under some sort of pressure," said former Federal Grand Juror Hoppy Heidelberg.

When defense team investigator Richard Reyna went to interview Elliott, he was told the FBI had instructed him not to talk to anyone about the case because "they didn't want to get things distorted." He then handed Reyna the card of FBI Special Agent Scott Crabtree.

When Marty Reed and co-investigator Wilma Sparks approached Elliott a week later, he referred them to a man named Joseph Pole. Pole stated that he was "working for Ryder ... indirectly." He refused to speak with the investigators and excused himself, saying he had to make a phone call. When Sparks and Reed went outside, they noticed a government car with the license number G-10 03822, parked in front of the shop.

When they returned the next day, they were again met by the mysterious "Ryder employee" who didn't produce a business card. When they asked the body shop's employees why the government car was there, they were told it was being worked on. But the investigators saw no signs of damage. Upon returning the fol-

---

* Elliott stated in his FBI 302 that a second man accompanied "Kling" on April 17, and thought he saw "fair size" light blue sedan.

** Elliott testified that he met with the prosecution for two hours several days prior to the his appearance at trial.

lowing day, the car was parked between two campers, ostensibly in an attempt to conceal it.[503]

Was the FBI attempting to influence a key witness? A reporter who worked the case later told me, "They were very hooked in with the FBI ... the Ryder security was obtained through the FBI ... and they're in constant touch with the FBI for briefings, or they were. And I got that from the PR guy who's the Vice President of Ryder in Miami. A *Newsweek* reporter that I work with got Elliott on the phone, and somebody clicked down the phone as he was talking to her. Elliott was saying 'let me just finish, let me just finish,' and all of the sudden, the phone went dead." [504]

A symbiotic relationship between the FBI and Ryder shouldn't be surprising. According to one bombing researcher, Ryder's CEO, Anthony Mitchell, is a member of the Trilateral Commission. The researcher also uncovered that both the FBI and ATF have leasing contracts with the company.*

To rent his Ryder truck, "McVeigh" allegedly used his prepaid phone card, obtained in November of 1993 through *The Spotlight* under the name "Daryl Bridges" to call Elliott's and make the reservation. Vicki Beemer told the FBI she recalled speaking to a man named "Kling." Records supposedly indicate the call was made on April 14, from a Junction City, Kansas bus station.[505]

Yet the FBI had no way of proving that the call placed to the Ryder agency under the name "Kling" was actually made by McVeigh, or even that the *Spotlight* card was used for the call. OPUS Telecom, which runs the system used for the prepaid card, maintains no records indicating who placed a specific call.[506]

The FBI originally asserted the call was made at 8:44 A.M. from a pay phone at Fort Riley. They later decided it was made at 9:53 A.M. from a pay phone in Junction City. Beemer, who took the call, said it came at 10:30 A.M.

At the time the FBI alleged McVeigh made the 9:53 A.M. call, he was at a phone booth down the street from a Firestone store, where he had been negotiating a deal on a 1977 Mercury. The store manager who sold McVeigh the car, Thomas Manning, testified that his customer excused himself, then came back 10 or 15 minutes later. The FBI contends that McVeigh used this period to make two calls, one to Terry Nichols' house, and one to Elliott's. Yet, as the *Rocky Mountain News* noted:

> An early version of the FBI reconstruction showed two calls within two minutes from phones 25 miles apart, which implied involvement by someone other than

---

* An anonymous informant who contacted State Representative Charles Key several times stated, "The ATF regularly uses leased Ryder trucks to move ordnance. And you know it's against ICC regulation and everything but he said they secretly do it." Investigator Craig Roberts said the Army also has "open contracts" with Ryder.

McVeigh and Nichols, since neither was then in the second location.

But the location of that call later was reassigned to a place fitting the government's case.[507]

How convenient.

Moreover, as the defense pointed out, Manning hadn't bothered to mention the fact that McVeigh left the Firestone store for over a year-and-a-half despite being interviewed by defense attorneys and FBI agnets 11 different times.[508]

While rental receipts and employee testimony indicate "Kling" rented his truck on the 17th, a Ryder truck was seen days earlier by James Sargeant and other eyewitnesses. Sargeant reported seeing several unidentified men crawling in and out of the cargo area for three days, backed up to the lake so that no one ashore could see inside. "I really began to wonder about why someone would be wasting their money on a rental truck out there ... no one was ever fishing, either."[509]

Barbara Whittenberg, owner of the Sante Fe Trail Diner in Herrington, recalled seeing a Ryder truck, along with McVeigh, Nichols, and John Doe 2, on Saturday, April 15. The men had stopped by the restaurant for breakfast at 6 A.M., and Whittenberg reported seeing a large Ryder truck at Geary State Fishing Lake later that afternoon.[510]

Lea McGown, owner of the Dreamland Motel in Junction City, and her son Eric, both recall seeing McVeigh pull into the motel with his truck on the afternoon of Easter Sunday, April 16, as did residents Renda Truong, Connie Hood, David King, and King's mother, Hetta. The truck appeared to be an older, privately owned Ryder truck. McGown had just returned from Manhattan, Kansas, where he and his mother were having lunch. The time was approximately 4 P.M. Truong testified she had seen it after Easter Sunday dinner, which would have been around dusk.

Yet under examination by the prosecution during McVeigh's trial, Eric McGown would not testify as to the exact date he saw the truck. Yet his FBI 302 said: "He thinks the man came there with a truck on April 16, 1995, and that the Ryder truck sat at the motel all day on April 17, 1995."*

His mother, like both Hood and Truong, was certain it was the 16th. As she stated in her FBI 302:

She is certain that the Ryder truck she saw parked at the DREAMLAND MOTEL and in which she observed TIM MCVEIGH sitting on one occasion was driven into the motel grounds on Sunday, April 16, 1995.

She recalls that the Ryder truck that was parked at the DREAMLAND

---

* Interestingly, McGown did not state on his FBI 302 who was driving the truck on April 16, when his mother had asked him to request that the driver move it.

MOTEL on April 16, 1995, through April 18, 1995, did not have the word Ryder on the back doors as do other Ryder trucks she has seen. She recalls the back doors of the Ryder truck in which she saw TIM MCVEIGH were a plain faded yellow color, with no printing visible on them.[511]

Hetta King was also sure it was Sunday the 16th. "There's no question in my mind—it was Easter Sunday," King testified.

The reader will recall that this is the exact same day that Phyliss Kingsley and Linda Kuhlman saw the convoy, including "McVeigh," John Doe 2 and 3, and the Ryder truck at the Hi Way Grill just south of Oklahoma City at approximately 6 P.M.

The two locations are hundreds of miles apart—too far apart to drive in two hours.

This is also the same day the FBI alleged Nichols drove from Kansas to Oklahoma City to pick up McVeigh, who had left his Mercury Marquis near the YMCA as the "get-away" vehicle. Yet a witness at the Dreamland recalled seeing McVeigh's yellow Mercury at the motel the next day.

Interesting that "McVeigh" and his car could be in two places at once.

Real estate agent Georgia Rucker and her son also saw a Ryder truck at Geary Lake days before "Kling" rented his. Then on Tuesday morning, as Rucker again drove by lake, she not only saw a Ryder truck, but two other vehicles as well. She thought this was "very suspicious."[512]

On Monday, April 17, Connie Hood saw the Ryder truck again. This time, there were several men "fiddling with the back of the truck." Hood thinks one of those men was Michael Fortier; she recalls he had scraggly hair and a beard. Those who recall the photo of Fortier taken after the bombing may recall that Fortier had just shaved off his beard, leaving a clearly visible demarcation line.

While these are all blatant discrepancies in the FBI's official timeline, the Bureau was apparently interested in McGown's testimony because the Dreamland is the only place where McVeigh, or someone purporting to be McVeigh, signed his real name.

It's curious that the FBI consistently promoted the idea of only one Ryder truck involved. Yet the statements of McGown, Bricktown warehouse worker David Snider, and others indicate two Ryder trucks were involved. When a *Newsweek* reporter spoke to the security guard at Elliott's, he said "Think about two trucks."[513]

This fact was reiterated by Federal Grand Juror Hoppy Heidelberg. "A small number of people testified during the Grand Jury hearings about two trucks," said Heidelberg. "McVeigh picked his truck up on Monday. John Doe 2 had his truck the weekend before. The fact that there were two trucks I'm very comfortable with."[514]

If McVeigh rented his truck on April 17, as the FBI contends, why did witnesses report seeing a Ryder truck at Geary State Fishing Lake as early as April 10? It was at this lake, on April 18, the FBI originally asserted, that the two suspects built their magic ANFO bomb. FBI agents reported finding diesel fuel and strands of detonator cord on the ground.[515]

Yet at the time witnesses first saw the truck at the lake, neither McVeigh or Nichols were in Kansas. As the *Denver Post* reported:

> Nichols was returning from a gun show in Michigan, and McVeigh was holed up in a residence hotel in Kingman, Arizona. The government's key witness, Michael Fortier, also was not in Kansas.[516]

Interestingly, shortly before the start of McVeigh's trial, the prosecution dropped its contention that the bomb was built at Geary Lake. If the defense brought up witness sightings on the 10th, the testimony would have not only conflicted with the prosecution's carefully-constructed timeline, but would have added suspects.[517]

As will be seen, this is not the first time the government excluded witnesses whose testimony didn't fit with their carefully-crated version of events.

Nevertheless, it was the truck rented by "Kling" on April 17, authorities insisted, that was loaded with ammonium-nitrate and guided by the lone bomber to its final and fateful destination at the Alfred P. Murrah Building.

To help build their ANFO bomb case, the FBI reports that McVeigh and Nichols began searching for racing fuel and detonator cord in September, '94. Using the calling card McVeigh and Nichols obtained under the pseudonym of "Daryl Bridges," ostensibly inspired by the film *Blown Away* starring Jeff Bridges, McVeigh allegedly made over 22 calls to various companies who supply chemicals, racing fuel, and even one of the country's largest explosives manufacturers.

His first call was to Paulsen's Military Supply, just outside of Madison, Wisconsin, looking for detonators. According to authorities, McVeigh left Paulsen's business card in the patrol car upon his arrest, that read, "Dave" (presumably David Paulsen, Ed Paulsen's son, who McVeigh had met at a gun show), with the notation, "More five pound sticks of TNT by May 1."[518]

A salesman at Fatigues and Things, a military store in Junction City, said McVeigh and another man bought a book entitled *Improvised Munitions* two weeks before the bombing. The other man was not Terry Nichols.

Prosecutors called an old friend of McVeigh's, David Darlak, who allegedly received a call from him in an attempt to obtain racing fuel.

Another friend was Greg Pfaff, whom McVeigh met at gun shows. Pfaff testified that McVeigh called him seeking to buy det cord. McVeigh was so eager to obtain the cord, Pfaff said, that he offered to drive to Virginia.

Another of the calls reflected on the men's calling card was to Mid-American Chemical. Linda Juhl, an employee of the company, remembered receiving a call in the Fall of 1994 from a fellow in Kansas who wanted to purchase Anhydrous Hydrazine, a rocket fuel which can be used to boost the power of an ANFO bomb.

The FBI also reported that two individuals, one named "Terry Tuttle," visited Thumb Hobbies, Etc. in Mariette, Michigan in mid-December, 1993, looking to buy 100 percent nitromethane model airplane fuel. According to Sanilac County Sheriff Virgil Stickler, the store clerk inquired about ordering it, then told the customers several weeks later that he could not or would not do so. The clerk said that "Tuttle" replied that it was okay, that they had found another source.[519]

Another incident not made public until Key's County Grand Jury investigation was the recollection of Gary Antene, who saw McVeigh and John Doe 2 at Danny's Hobby Shop in Oklahoma City the Saturday before the bombing. The two men asked him if Danny's carried 100 percent nitromethane fuel.

"I explained that no one in the RC (remote-controlled) airplane hobby used 100 percent nitromethane as a fuel, that at most we generally used nothing over 20 percent," said Antene, who reported the incident to the FBI a couple of times. Antene was not called to testify at McVeigh's trial, probably because his account didn't fit into the FBI's "official" timeline.[520]

On October 20, the FBI alleged that McVeigh checked into a motel in Pauls Valley, Oklahoma. The next day, he drove 170 miles to the Chief Auto Parts Nationals drag race in Ennis, Texas. Timothy Chambers, an employee of VP Racing Fuels, testified at McVeigh's trial that he and co-worker Brad Horton sold a man resembling McVeigh three 54 gallon drums of Nitromethane racing fuel for $2,775. The man said the fuel was for him and his friends who race Harleys once a year in Oklahoma City. Chambers testified it didn't make sense for a few motorcycle racers to buy that much fuel, and had never seen anyone pay cash for that large a purchase.[521]

Interestingly, the FBI didn't announce this new lead until one month before the start of McVeigh's trial, as other evidence, including that from the FBI's crime lab, began falling apart. The *Rocky Mountain News* reported that Glynn Tipton had alerted the ATF to the strange purchase as far back as October of 1994.[522]

Yet this "new" evidence would coalesce perfectly with the government's emerging case, now that many Americans were convinced that a simple ANFO bomb hadn't destroyed the Murrah Building. A bomb built with volatile, highly-explosive racing fuel would make the prosecution's case much more convincing.

The startling discovery of McVeigh's racing fuel purchases, like the new revelations of Thomas Manning, or those of Eldon Elliott, were reminiscent of the sudden discoveries by Lockerbie investigators of Libyan terrorists. The 1988 bombing had originally been attributed to Iran, contracted through former Syrian army officer Ahmed Jibril of the Popular Front for the Liberation of Palestine-

General Command (PFLP-GC), in retaliation for the American downing of an Iranian passenger liner a year and-a-half earlier. When George Bush needed the cooperation of the Syrians for his Gulf War coalition, the blame was shifted to someone else.

Ten months after the bombing, Lockerbie investigators discovered new evidence. The owner of a clothing store on Malta suddenly remembered to whom he sold baby clothes found in the bomb suitcase onboard the plane. In fact, not only had he recalled the customer, he remembered the precise date of the purchase, and recalled the man clearly enough for artists to render a sketch. He was Abu Talb, a PFLP-GC member who was known to have visited Malta shortly before the bombing.*

At least that's what the FBI wanted the public to believe. In fact, owner Tony Gauci and his brother Paul made 18 different statements to authorities, most of which were vague and contradictory. They then signed statements even though they couldn't read English. Nevertheless, investigators quickly placed 24-hour guards around the shopkeepers bearing this valuable "new evidence," just as the FBI had done with Eldon Elliott.

Records show calls to chemical companies continuing in October, '94 from Kingman, around the time the suspects allegedly drove there to hide stolen explosives and are said to have begun purchasing ammonium-nitrate. The indictment states that Nichols allegedly stole dynamite and an explosive called Tovex from the Martin-Marietta quarry in Marion, Kansas, not far from where Nichols had been working as a ranch hand.

Bud Radeke, a blaster and driller for Martin-Marietta, testified at McVeigh's trial that 299 dynamite sticks, 544 blasting caps, detonator cord, and Tovex was stolen over the long Labor Day weekend. FBI agents discovered a drill bit in Nichols' home that they claim matched the hole drilled in one of the magazine's locks. The suspects allegedly made the mistake of leaving one of the five locks they had drilled into behind.

Could the FBI actually tell from a hole drilled in a lock which particular bit made the impression? The FBI hadn't discovered the bit in Nichols' toolkit until six months after the robbery. No doubt it had been used since Nichols, a handyman, recently moved into his new house. The signature of the drill bit would have undoubtedly been altered. How could the FBI be sure it was the bit that drilled the locks at the quarry?

Ed Hueske, a firearm and tool examiner at Weckerling Scientific Laboratory

---

* However, the indictment named Libyan Abdel Basset Ali al-Megrahi as the customer. Authorities' second witness, Abdu Maged Jiacha, a Libyan intelligence officer who defected to the U.S., was put into the Federal Witness Protection Program and given a $4 million dollar reward for his testimony against Megrahi.

near Dallas said a drill bit can "leave marks that are characteristic of the nose of the bit," especially "if the bit is worn or damaged." A former forensic specialist with the Tulsa Police Department, Hueske added that such a test is "not routine," but is "theoretically possible." [523]

Yet if the bit was used afterwards on metal, or if it had been sharpened, it would change the striations of the markings. If it still contained bits of metal shavings from the lock, however, then a match could be made. But agents testified that no shavings were found.

Then how did the FBI match the bit? Frank Shiller, a firearm and tool examiner at Forensic Consultant Services in Fort Worth, offered his opinion: "Some of that type of work has been done, but it's not a very frequent thing. I don't think it would be very productive."

Shiller, who has 36 years experience in forensic science, has never even been asked to conduct such a test, nor has his boss, Max Courtney, with 27 years experience.

"It would be extremely difficult to match a drill," said Shiller, "because of the random motion of the drill moving through its … moving up and down the hole. So it would be hard to track any imperfections or microscopic markings that might be present. That would be a pretty tough task." [524]

Even Hueske, who admitted the theoretical possibility of such a test, said that the two or three drill bit tests he's conducted over the years produced no results.

The quarry also had pre-mixed professional grade ANFO in stock. Why didn't Nichols steal that too, since, as the government alleges, it was the prime ingredient in the bomb? This would have certainly been easier and more discreet than buying large quantities of ammonium-nitrate, diesel, and racing fuel, then attempting to mix it into a gigantic bomb. But for some reason, our prime suspects decided to leave the professional grade ANFO behind, and go to the trouble and expense of making their own.

The two men then allegedly drove to Kingman on October 4, where McVeigh rented a storage locker to hide the goods. [525] It was in Kingman that McVeigh allegedly showed his dangerous booty to his friends, Michael and Lori Fortier. Lori testified at trial that McVeigh asked her to wrap up the blasting caps as Christmas presents for the long ride back to Michigan.

A friend of Nichols and McVeigh, Kevin Nicholas, testified that he helped McVeigh unload his car upon returning to Decker. "I was just grabbing stuff and just throwing it in the back of my truck; and Tim said, "Don't handle them. I'll take care of them two Christmas-wrapped packages there." [526]

Phone records also show that McVeigh called military surplus dealer Dave Paulsen on December 17 from Kingman, and Nicholas testified that McVeigh drove to Chicago to see Paulsen in late December to sell him the blasting caps.

On September 30, 1994, according to the FBI, McVeigh and Nichols, who used the alias "Mike Havens," purchased forty 50-pound bags of ammonium-nitrate at the Mid-Kansas Co-Op in Manhattan, Kansas. Then, on October 17, after renting a room in Salina under the name "Havens," Nichols rented storage locker No. 40 at Boots U-Store-It in Council Grove, under the alias "Joe Kyle." On October 18, the dynamic duo was back again at the Mid-Kansas Co-Op, stocking up on more fertilizer, buying another forty 50-pound bags to be stored at the locker in Council Grove.

Nichols attorney, Michael Tigar, attempted to explain his client's use of aliases by stating that Nichols wanted to hide his assets from Chase Manhattan bank, which had won a large credit card lawsuit against him. This explanation does not explain why Nichols used the alias while purchasing fertilizer.

Finally, there would be the ordnance found at Nichols' home and the farm of his brother James. The Decker, Michigan farm contained 28 fifty-pound bags of ammonium-nitrate, non-electric blasting caps, a 55-gallon drum containing fuel-oil, and large fuel tanks which appeared to contain diesel fuel. As previously mentioned, neighbors Daniel Stomber and Paul Isydorak told authorities that the Nichols brothers and McVeigh would experiment with the items to make small homemade bombs.

A search of Terry Nichols' home by the ATF and FBI allegedly turned up 33 firearms, an anti-tank launcher (which was inert), five 60-foot Primadet detonator cords, non-electric blasting caps, ammonium-nitrate, a fuel meter (which was inoperable—a fact that was never mentioned), and four 55-gallon blue plastic drums. (Nichols' son Josh, who frequently played at his dad's house, believed the barrels were white with blue tops.)

While some accounts indicate that the drums were of the type used in the bombing, the *New York Times* wrote on April 30, "… it is not clear that they match blue plastic fragments found at the blast site." [527] In fact, the FBI never stated that the fragments removed from bombing victims matched those from Nichols' home. Certainly the FBI, with the most sophisticated crime lab in the world, would have been able to determine whether the fragments were of the same type. Moreover, most of the fragments, if they came from Nichols' home, would have been white, not blue.

Nichols' attorney Michael Tigar raised this issue while cross-examining an FBI agent during a pre-trial hearing. According to Tigar, the FBI's inventory list described the barrels simply as white without blue lids. The agent replied that the FBI doesn't list the lids separately. When Tigar asked the agent whey they had inventoried a collection of five-gallon buckets with lids listed separately, he had no response.

Those blue fragments may very likely have been from the 80 or so blue trash barrels distributed throughout the building for the purposes of trash collection. As Richard Williams, a 51 year-old GSA manager testified at McVeigh's trial,

"They were placed throughout the building for pickup during the week."

One month later, Nichols would write his cryptic letter to McVeigh, instructing him to extend the lease on unit number 37, which allegedly contained stolen coins and guns, and "liquidate 40," in case Nichols failed to return from his last trip to the Philippines. It was this letter that contained the infamous phrase, "You're on your own. Go for it!"

Was this a message inspiring McVeigh to bomb a federal building, or a note encouraging him to make a success of himself in the military surplus business? According to Nichols family friend Bob Papovich, the pair was selling the fertilizer at gun shows as plant food, along with an odd assortment of other items sold at gun shows, repackaging it in smaller bags to increase their profit margin.

Yet two tons of fertilizer is an awful lot to sell at gun shows. Had McVeigh and Nichols actually purchased that much fertilizer? Mid-Kansas Co-op employees were never able to positively identify McVeigh or Nichols during their purported fertilizer buying trips. Although employee Frederick Schendler thought one of the men may have been Terry Nichols, he said during a pre-trial hearing that the second man *wasn't* McVeigh. He was driving a truck that didn't appear to be Nichols', with a red trailer attached. Papovich told me that Nichols owns no such truck.

Federal prosecutors were also counting on a receipt found in Nichols' home for the purchase of a ton of ammonium-nitrate, allegedly containing McVeigh's thumbprint. Had Nichols foolishly kept a receipt for bombing materials that could be traced back to him? Was he as stupid as Mohammed Salemeh, the World Trade Center bomber who returned to the Ryder agency after the bombing in an attempt to retrieve his rental deposit? Or was McVeigh's fingerprint actually on the receipt after all?

FBI agent Louis Hupp testified at trial that he hadn't found McVeigh's fingerprints at Elliott's, in motel rooms where McVeigh stayed, or in the storage lockers where McVeigh allegedly stored the bomb-making materials.[528]

Ramsey: Agent Hupp, you identified—or handled many documents with regard to fingerprints, didn't you, with regard to this case?
Hupp: Yes, ma'am.
Ramsey: Did you also test the Ryder rental truck reservation form?
Hupp: Yes, I did.
Ramsey: And did you find Timothy McVeigh's fingerprints on that?
Hupp: No, ma'am.
Ramsey: Did you find Timothy McVeigh's fingerprints on the Ryder rental truck form where he actually—where it was actually rented?
Hupp: No, ma'am....
Ramsey: Did you check the counter at Elliott's Body Shop for fingerprints? I don't recall if I asked you that or not.

Hupp: The countertop was removed by me and transported back to headquarters and was in fact processed for latent prints.

Ramsey: And did you find any fingerprints of Timothy McVeigh?

Hupp: No, ma'am.

Ramsey: And did you also check to see if there were any fingerprints on any of the storage units that have been discussed in this case?

Hupp: Yes, ma'am.

Ramsey: And did you find any fingerprints of Timothy McVeigh?

Hupp: No, ma'am.

Hupp also testified that he had not found McVeigh's prints on the rental paperwork, or the key belonging to the Ryder truck, found in a nearby alley. Yet Hupp explained, "There are many times a person doesn't leave prints. It's a chance impression."

What if the FBI *had* claimed it discovered prints?

On November 22, 1963, after JFK's murder, the FBI took Oswald's Mannlicher-Carcanno rifle to their Washington, D.C. crime lab. The technicians concluded that Oswald's prints were not on the weapon. The FBI then returned the rifle to the Dallas Police Department. Shortly thereafter, the DPD excitedly announced that they had "discovered" Oswald's palm print.* This "new evidence" even forced Warren Commission's chief counsel, J. Lee Rankin, to conclude, "Because of the circumstances which now exist there is a serious question in the minds of the Commission as to whether the palm impression that has been obtained from the Dallas Police Department is a legitimate palm impression removed from the rifle barrel or whether it was obtained from some other source."

The fertilizer receipt containing McVeigh's thumbprint wasn't the only ammunition in the FBI's arsenal of specious evidence. Prosecutors would rely heavily on an explosive component called PETN, allegedly found on McVeigh's clothing. A pair of earplugs found on McVeigh also reportedly tested positive for EGDN, a chemical found in dynamite. Finally, there was a piece of plywood from the Ryder truck which contained glazed ammonium-nitrate crystals.

Yet once again, this evidence was highly questionable. It seemed the crystals had disappeared before independent experts for either the prosecution or defense could confirm its existence.

Interestingly, affidavits of Frederick Whitehurst, a Special Agent in the FBI's lab division, announced to an incredulous public in September, 1995 that the Bureau had been mishandling evidence and slanting results to favor prosecutors for years.[529]

As one FBI lab technician told the *New York Times*, "You get an inadvertent

---

* The Associated Press recently reported that upstate New York police had been falsifying evidence, including fingerprints, for years.

bonding of like-minded individuals supporting each other's false conclusions."

> After federal agents searched the residence of Richard Jewell, a private security
> guard who was an early suspect in a bombing at the Atlanta Olympics ... FBI sci-
> entists and other specialists warned that "you've got the wrong guy," an FBI labora-
> tory official said. But their cautionary remarks, based on the absence of even trace
> amounts of explosive materials, went unheeded for months.[530]

In March of 1997, the *Los Angeles Times* reported the findings of the Justice
Department Inspector General's office, which concluded that the lab made "sci-
entifically unsound" conclusions that were "biased in favor of the prosecution" in
the Oklahoma City bombing case.

> The still-secret draft report, obtained by the paper, also concludes that supervisors
> approved lab reports that they "cannot support" and that FBI lab officials may have
> erred about the size of the blast, the amount of explosives involved and the type of
> explosives used in the bombing.
>
> According to the *Times,* the draft report shows that FBI examiners could not
> identify the triggering device for the truck bomb or how it was detonated. It also
> indicates that a poorly maintained lab environment could have led to contamina-
> tion of critical pieces of evidence, the *Times* said.[531]

Whitehurst also told the Inspector General that the agents who conducted the
tests in Oklahoma City, including Tom Thurman, Chief of the Explosives Unit,
and Roger Martz, Chief of the Chemistry and Toxicology Unit, were not even
qualified to do so.*

During the 1993 World Trade Center bombing investigation, Whitehurst
decided to secretly test efficiency and procedures at the lab. He mixed human urine
with fertilizer and added it to some of the bomb material being tested. Martz subsequently excitedly identified the urine-fertilizer mixture as an explosive.**

Whitehurst also contended that Martz's examining room was contaminated,
making it impossible to accurately test for explosives and other substances,
including the PETN allegedly found on McVeigh's clothes.[532]

---

* As Whitehurst stated: "Mr. Thurman, in my estimation does intentionally misrepresent
  evidence and is, absolutely, without a doubt, beyond any possible other explanation's
  grasp, result oriented. He wants the answer that will prove guilt."
** Whitehurst testified that he was told not to provide any information or evidence, such
  as alternate theories to the urea-nitrate theory, that could be used by the defense to challenge the prosecutors' hypothesis of guilt in the World Trade Center case. (Ryan Ross,
  "Blasting the FBI," *Digital City Denver,* 1997.)

During the prosecution's closing argument, Martz made an interesting Freudian slip: "The evidence shows that Mr. McVeigh's clothing was contaminated with ... excuse me, Mr. McVeigh's clothing was filled with bomb residue."

Whitehurst also claimed that Martz had perjured his testimony in prior cases. Whitehurst himself was even asked to alter his reports. Materials-analysis-unit chief Corby "had me come into his room one day and told me they—I don't know who 'they' were—wanted me to take statements out of my report.... Whitehurst refused." *

During the 1991 trial of Walter Leroy Moody, convicted of killing Federal Judge Robert Vance with a letter-bomb, both Thurman and Martz "circumvented established procedures and protocols [and] testified in areas of expertise that [they] had no qualifications in, therefore fabricating evidence in [their] testimony," Whitehurst wrote in a memorandum to the Bureau's Scientific Analysis Chief James Kearny.

Both Martz and Thurman were fully aware of the fact that they were in violation of procedures and protocols of the FBI Laboratory and did knowingly and purposely commit perjury and obstruction of justice in this matter.[533]

Interestingly, the chief prosecutor in the Moody case was none other than Louis Freeh, an Assistant U.S. Attorney at the time. According to Whitehurst, Freeh did not have a single piece of evidence tying Moody to the crime and even possessed copies of reports disproving the prosecution's allegations, but did not make them available or known to the jury. Freeh also failed to inform the jury that his chief witness, Ted Banks, failed a lie-detector test regarding his association with Moody. In 1995, Banks testified at an appeal hearing that Freeh had threatened and coerced him into testifying against the defendant.[534]

Thurman's original claim to fame was the Pan Am 103 case. He had concluded that a tiny fragment of microchip, amazingly discovered two years after the bombing, was part of a batch of timers sold to the Libyans by the Swiss firm MEBO. This "new evidence" allowed the U.S. government to point the finger of blame at Libya, conveniently letting Syria—originally implicated in the bombing—off the hook.

After the assassination of JFK, nitrate tests conducted on Lee Harvey Oswald concluded that he had not fired a rifle on November 22. Yet this fact, like the false palm print, was kept secret for 10 months, then buried deep inside the Warren Commission Report.[535]

In the World Trade Center case, Whitehurst testified that he was told not to

---

* "Mr. Williams ... rewrote my reports in an unauthorized rewriting, issued these reports, unauthorized, changes being in them, and changed the meaning of the reports I think, without realizing it," Whitehurst later testified.

provide alternate explanations to the urea-nitrate theory that could be used by the defense to challenge the prosecutors' hypothesis of guilt.[536]

In Oklahoma, Whitehurst conducted a test on McVeigh's clothes, but found nothing.

While the FBI claimed it found traces of PETN in McVeigh's pants pocket, on his shirts, and on a set of earplugs, Agent Burmeister acknowledged on cross-examination that no PETN or ammonium-nitrate was found at the blast scene.

Nor was ammonium-nitrate found in McVeigh's car, his personal effects, hotel rooms he had stayed at, the various storage sheds the suspects allegedly used to store the bomb-making components, or in Nichols' Herington, Kansas home. The Bureau also found no evidence of explosives residue in samples of McVeigh's hair, or scrapings from his fingernails.[537]

Burmeister also testified that crystals of ammonium-nitrate, which he found on a piece of wood paneling from the Ryder truck, later vanished. "That piece has gone through a lot of hands since the time that I've seen it," Burmeister testified, "and I can't speak to how they could have disappeared."[538]

As Canadian County Sheriff Deputy Clint Boehler said, "The FBI disturbed and removed evidence. They don't tell anybody else; they don't work with anybody else.... How did they know it was the truck? They never looked at so many obvious things."[539]

While the FBI's evidence procedures would be called into question, prosecutors would seek to impress the jury with evidence of the suspects' militant right-wing leanings. Prosecutors began with letters McVeigh sent to his sister Jennifer, expressing rage over events at Ruby Ridge and Waco, at the same time millions of Americans were expressing the very same rage.

> "The Federal Government was absolutely out of control," said Sarah Bain, the San Antonio school teacher who served as forewoman of the jury that acquitted the [Davidian] sect members of most of the serious crimes they were charged with. "The wrong people were on trial," Bain complained. "It should have been the ones that planned the raid and orchestrated it."[540]

But it was other evidence—more incriminating and disturbing—that would provide the critical elements needed to convince the jury of McVeigh's malicious intent. In November,'94, McVeigh visited his family in Lockport, New York, where he confided to his sister Jennifer that he had been driving around with 1,000 pounds of explosives.

In a letter sent to her in March, a month before the bombing, McVeigh wrote, "Something big is going to happen in the month of the bull."

Finally, to prove McVeigh's malevolent intentions, prosecutors introduced a letter stored on Jennifer's computer. The letter, addressed to the ATF, warned, "ATF, all you tyrannical motherfuckers will swing in the wind one day, for your treasonous actions against the Constitution and the United States. Remember the Nuremberg War Trials. But ... but ... but ... I was only following orders!...... Die, you spineless, cowardice bastards!" [541]

McVeigh also supposedly left a letter to a "girlfriend" (which media psychojournalists claimed he didn't have) in the glove compartment of his car, outlining plans to bomb additional targets.

Had McVeigh actually left such a letter in his vehicle, and dropped Paulsen's business card in the patrol car? While it is possible, such scenes are reminiscent of the doctored photograph of Lee Harvey Oswald holding a rifle and a Communist newspaper, or Earth First! activist Judi Bari holding a machine gun, which was loaned to her for the photo by an FBI informant—a photo which he took.

In Oklahoma City, as in all criminal conspiracies, the old adage, "follow the money" should apply. Certainly a pair of lone nuts with a fertilizer/fuel bomb wouldn't need much—a couple of thousand dollars at most—considering they didn't have to pay off a web of co-conspirators.

A November, '94 robbery in Arkansas would prove to be just the crime investigators needed to put the final piece of the puzzle in place. When the indictments were returned, the Grand Jury concluded the bombing was financed by the robbery of gun dealer Roger Moore (aka Bob Anderson), who had known McVeigh and let him stay at his home.

But the FBI had concluded that the bomb components were already purchased or stolen by the date of the robbery. The indictment was also incongruously worded: "McVeigh and Nichols "caused" the robbery of $60,000 worth of guns, coins and precious metals. Exactly how had they "caused" the robbery? The prosecution first presented the testimony of McVeigh's friend Kevin Nichols:

Nicholas: He said that he screwed him some way out of some money or something.
Mackey: Who is "he"?
Nicholas: That Bob did for when Tim worked for him.
Mackey: And as a result?
Nicholas: He said he—that he'd be an easy guy to rob because he lived way back in the sticks and, you know, there was woods around his house and stuff.

Yet McVeigh had a solid alibi. He was at a gun show in Kent, Ohio on November 5.

Still, the government attempted to have Michael Fortier implicate his friends at trial by testifying that McVeigh called him and said, "Nichols got Bob!" This largely hearsay testimony was not backed by further evidence.

Authorities never proved that McVeigh or Nichols actually robbed Roger

Moore, but did prove that on November 7, 1994, Nichols rented a storage lock-er—number 37—in Council Grove, under the alias "Ted Parker" to store some of the stolen items.

In his "confession" to authorities, Fortier said that McVeigh met him in Kingman on the 15th, whereupon they drove to Kansas. On the way, Fortier tes-tified, McVeigh pointed out the Murrah Building as the target of the upcoming attack. When they reached the storage locker, they loaded 25 guns into Fortier's rented car.

Back in Kingman, Fortier pawned the weapons, or sold them to friends, including his neighbor, James Rosencrans.

On November 16, Nichols rented locker Q-106 at AAAABCO Storage in Las Vegas, where ex-wife Lana Padilla discovered gold and silver bars, jade, along with wigs, masks, and pantyhose. A safety deposit box key belonging to Moore was found at Nichols' home.

The 60-year-old Moore claimed he was surprised one morning shortly after 9 A.M. when two masked men accosted him outside his kitchen door. The men, wearing woodland-style camouflage fatigues, bound him and ransacked his house, taking guns, coins, jewels, and personal effects.

What is strange is that the thieves left a number of expensive handguns and large-capacity magazines, both highly desirable items. The private gun dealer, who had enough weapons to supply a platoon, did not have an insurance rider for the guns, and most of the serial numbers weren't registered.

Moore told the author he didn't have a rider because he was afraid some insur-ance company secretary would see his large collection and tell her boyfriend, who would then come and rob him. A curious explanation for failing to insure a high-ly valuable collection. Moore claims he only got a limited settlement—approxi-mately $10,000.

Interestingly, one well-connected source I spoke to asserted that "the [Moore] robbery was staged ... that's the truth.... [Moore] used a lot of aliases, he had eight different social security numbers, eight different dates of birth, and that's only the ones that I know about...."

This source also claimed, long before defense attorney Michael Tigar's allega-tions were made public, that the motive of the "robbery" was insurance fraud, staged with the help of Nichols and McVeigh. "Nichols had simply bought weapons [from Moore]. Moore approached Nichols about the fraud originally.... Moore took payment of some odd items that winds up in Terry Nichols' [storage locker]."

This assertion was reinforced at Nichols' trial, when Tigar questioned Moore's girlfriend, Karen Anderson, about why she had included on her list—a list she claimed had been drawn up in late 1992 or early 1993—a gun that hadn't been purchased until late 1994.

When I spoke to Moore's friend and neighbor, Nora Waye, she told me Moore had complained to her that the local Sheriff who investigated the robbery "blew [Moore's] cover."

Moore ran a company next to Bahia Mar Marina in South Florida (a popular hangout for the Iran-Contra crowd), which manufactured high-speed boats. The boats—sold through Intercontinental Industries of Costa Rica (an Ollie North "cut-out")—were used to mine Nicaragua's harbors in "Operation Cordova Harbor." A retired CIA/DIA agent I spoke to in Arkansas, said, "[Moore] was an Agency contractor."

Other sources say Moore was an informant for the FBI. He allegedly tried to sell heavy weapons to the Militia of Montana (MOM) as part of an FBI sting operation. A call to MOM indicated that Moore had indeed stopped by for a friendly little chat. He told Randy Trochmann, one of MOM's leaders, that he was traveling the country meeting with militia groups in an attempt to verify black helicopter sightings and rumors of UN troop movements. This seems a peculiar pastime for a man who worked for a network of spooks devoted to bypassing and subverting the Constitution.

Could a phony robbery set-up explain the wigs, masks, and pantyhose in Terry Nichols' storage locker—the type of disguises used by robbers? Given the relationship between McVeigh and Moore, it is possible the two men made some sort of deal.

Former Federal Grand Juror Hoppy Heidelberg is another person who had doubts about Moore: "Something wasn't right about him," said Heidelberg. "It wasn't that his testimony wasn't believable. He was just cocky. He had a strange attitude for a man testifying before a Grand Jury. He was so casual about it, that was strange. He testified like a man who had done it many times before…. It wasn't anything he said, it was his attitude. You'll see the same attitude in an FBI agent who's testifying." [542]

"Moore's being protected," said my source. "No matter how this thing's going to get played out. He'll talk to you all day long and won't tell you a thing. He knows how to talk."

JOHN DOE WHO?

"We have no information showing anyone other than Mr. McVeigh and Mr. Nichols are the masterminds"

—U.S. Attorney Beth Wilkinson

On the day of the deadly attack, Attorney General Janet Reno announced, "The FBI and the law enforcement community will pursue every lead and use every possible resource to bring these people responsible to justice.... It is very important that we pursue each lead ... it is going to be very important that we leave no stone unturned...."

In fact, numerous stones were left unturned.

While the Justice Department (DoJ) focused its efforts on McVeigh and Nichols, scant attention was focused on other suspects—John Doe 2, the mysterious entity who was seen with McVeigh, and had accompanied him the morning of the bombing. Witnesses also saw him with McVeigh in the Murrah Building, in stores, at restaurants, at a bar, and at the truck rental shop before the bombing. Still others claim to have seen him speeding away from the scene. All in all, there are almost two-dozen witnesses who reported seeing John Doe 2.

The FBI made a big show of tracking down this elusive, menacing-looking suspect. "The FBI has conducted over 9,000 witness interviews and has followed every possible lead in an intensive effort to identify and bring to justice anyone who was involved in this disaster," stated U.S. Attorney Patrick Ryan in a letter to the victims' families.

The search for John Doe 2 quickly became the biggest manhunt in FBI history. What authorities weren't saying, however, was that not only was there a John Doe 2, there were least four John Does! But the issue was quickly and quietly narrowed down to just one John Doe 2.

On April 23, four days after the bombing, The *Washington Post* quoted a senior law enforcement official who said "at least four" men were involved in the terrorist act last week and "there very well could be more." [543]

The FBI then requalified its position on May 15: "Wherever we look, it's Terry and Timmy, Terry and Timmy—and nobody else," quipped an unnamed FBI official in *Time* magazine.

Yet on June 11, another FBI official was quoted in the *Post* as saying, "I think

---

* My source told me that Moore's FBI contact was Tom Ross out of Hot Springs, Arkansas, one of Ollie North's "damage control" men. "Moore's being protected. No matter how this thing's going to get played out. He'll talk to you all day long and won't tell you a thing. He knows how to talk." If these allegations are true, it would tend, at the very least, to cast doubt on Moore's credibility.

when this is over we'll have at least six or eight guys indicted and in custody. It's just too big for two guys to pull off."[544]

Then on June 15, the FBI backtracked again. "Periodically you just get something in an investigation that goes nowhere. John Doe 2 goes nowhere. It doesn't show up in associations, it doesn't show up in phone calls. It doesn't show up among the Army buddies of McVeigh."[545]

The previous day, the FBI put out a story that John Doe 2 may have actually been Todd Bunting, a soldier at Fort Riley, Kansas who had rented a truck at the same dealer McVeigh had. The FBI stated that Bunting wore clothing similar to that ascribed to John Doe 2, that he had a tattoo in the same place, and that he wore a hat similar to John Doe 2's.

Yet Elliott's employees dismissed Bunting as the person who was seen with McVeigh, and Bunting held a press conference stating that he had in fact rented a truck at Elliott's—24 hours after McVeigh allegedly rented his.

The Bunting story was officially dropped.

Then, on January 28, 1996, the prosecution switched tracks again, officially resurrecting the Todd Bunting story. In a long brief, the government disclosed that Elliott's employee Tom Kessinger was the only one who could recall John Doe 2 well enough to describe him.

Now, after a November interview with a prosecutor and two FBI agents, Kessinger was "confident that he had Todd Bunting in mind when he provided the description for the John Doe 2 composite." Kessinger, the brief continued, is "now unsure" whether anyone accompanied McVeigh. But his two co-workers "continue to believe that two men came in to rent the truck."

In that brief, the prosecution speculated that the defense might use "Kessinger's admitted confusion" to challenge his identification of McVeigh.

It seemed less "Kessinger's admitted confusion" than a deliberate fabrication by prosecutors and the FBI to cover up the existence of John Doe 2. As Kessinger told bombing victim Glenn Wilburn, who conducted his own investigation, "I don't know how they came up with that one."

Kessinger later changed his story at the urging of federal prosecutors Patrick Ryan and Joseph Hartzler. During a pretrial conference, Jones challenged Kessinger:

"How can you be so wrong 60 hours after the event and so right a year and a half later?" Jones asked him. "Could you be changing your mind because the government wants you to?"

"No," Kessinger replied.[546]

Yet on March 25 and April 5, Hartzler had written Jones, "The existence and identity of this John Doe 2, whom we are confident is not Mr. Bunting, is the subject of a continuing investigation."

In a May 1, 1996 letter written by Hartzler, the government prosecutor informed Jones that Kessinger and Beemer had been shown a picture of the cap Bunting wore when he picked up a truck on April 18. "They both stated that the cap was not the same one they saw on John Doe 2," Hartzler wrote, "and they reaffirmed that this second individual accompanied 'Kling' when he rented the truck." *

But at an April 9 hearing, federal prosecutor Beth Wilkinson stated the government "has no information showing anyone but Mr. Nichols and Mr. McVeigh were the masterminds of this bombing." [547]

"They keep telling us they're looking for John Doe No. 2, but then they turn around and give statements indicating that they don't believe there is a John Doe No. 2," said a woman whose husband was killed in the bombing. [548]

Other victims, like naive children, blindly placed their faith in the government's dubious assurances. Hartzler held one meeting with bombing victims in which he "discussed and disposed of some of the more bizarre theories."

"I just got a better feeling about what's going on," said Bud Welch, whose daughter, Julie, died in the attack. "The prosecution assured us that there was no evidence that was suppressed. We really didn't know that," added Welch.

"We know what's going on now and that they're there for us," Pamela Weber-Fore said of the prosecutors. [549]

Other victims weren't as easily fooled. "I don't think that there's any question about the fact that they're covering up who was involved in the bombing," said V.Z. Lawton, a HUD worker who was injured in the blast. "I've talked to five witnesses myself who saw McVeigh with John Doe number two in Oklahoma City that morning, within fifteen minutes of the blast ... tells me that there is something wrong." [550]

As Nichols' attorney Michael Tigar said, "It's strange that the official version has focused on Nichols and McVeigh, and that the government is now busily engaged in denying all possibility that there could be anybody else." [551]

---

* Hartzler's letter, Jones said in his brief, "indicates that the Justice Department is still searching for John Doe No. 2 and may be releasing disinformation to lessen public pressure to find [him]."

Grand Jury Bypass

"The FBI has thoroughly investigated all leads and I am confident in the investigation."
—Joseph Hartzler

While many eyewitnesses stepped forward to tell the FBI they had seen additional suspects, *not one* was ever called before the Federal Grand Jury.

Yet federal prosecutors still had one hurdle to overcome before they could make their case. They had to deal with Hoppy Heidelberg. Heidelberg, who often quoted from the grand juror's handbook, was aware that the Grand Jury was charged with the task of determining the relevance of the evidence, and asking those questions pertinent to the case. So far, all the evidence centered around Timothy McVeigh and Terry Nichols. Heidelberg wanted to know why prosecutors had not subpoenaed the many witnesses who had seen John Doe 2.

"No one who saw McVeigh with other suspects, was ever allowed to testify before the Federal Grand Jury," said Heidelberg. The obvious inference being that those who saw McVeigh would have also seen John Doe 2.

But Patrick Ryan seemed to be controlling the jury. He did not like Heidelberg's tendency to go against the flow. In a letter to the victims' families, Ryan states:

> The United States has never maintained or even suggested, that no other person or persons were involved with McVeigh and Nichols in the commission of these crimes. As stated earlier, the question of involvement of others is the subject of intensive investigation by federal investigators and prosecutors who are totally devoted and committed to identifying and prosecuting all persons involved in the planning or commission of these crimes.

Though Heidelberg attempted to question Grand Jury witnesses, he was repeatedly stonewalled by prosecutors. In an interview with journalist Jon Rappaport, Heidelberg stated, "They said I'd have to get the prosecuting attorney's okay for each question I wanted to ask. But you know, in dialog one question leads to another right away, so you can't cross-examine that way.

"They kept promising and promising to answer all my questions, but ultimately they stalled me. I was had." *

In an interview on CBS This Morning, Stephen Jones said, "What is troubling here is that the prosecutors, in effect, according to this grand juror's allegation, took away from the Grand Jury their duty to go after the *full* story, not just con-

---

* The federal prosecutors' lame excuse for confining the evidence to McVeigh and Nichols was to maintain a "deadline" set by federal guidelines on providing speedy trials.

centrating on the two people that had already been arrested."[552]

Not buying the government's story of a couple of pissed-off whackos with a fertilizer bomb, Heidelberg asked that bomb experts be called in to identify the type of explosive used. "Let's get the answer ... Let's get the architects and engineers who built the building in there and question them," Heidelberg told Rappaport.

"Did you request that?" asked Rappaport.

"Of course! I demanded bomb experts all along. And engineers and geologists. They said—do you want to know what they said? They didn't have the money! I said I'd go down to the University of Oklahoma and bring some geologists back myself for free. They wouldn't let me.

"The bomb is the key to the whole case." [553]

In order to satisfy the Grand Jury that an ANFO bomb blew up the building, prosecutors called in one bomb expert—Robert Hopler. Hopler, it turns out, recently retired from Dyno-Nobel, an explosives manufacturer in Salt Lake City. Dyno-Nobel used to be Hercules Powder Company—a reputed CIA front. "I knew he was CIA," said Heidelberg. "It was pretty obvious to me and most of the jury." [554]

Judge David Russell eventually dismissed Heidelberg from the Grand Jury for having the audacity to question the government's case. In a letter to Heidelberg dated October 24, 1995, Russell states:

Effectively immediately, you are dismissed from the Grand Jury. Your obligation of secrecy continues. Any disclosure of matters that occurred before the Grand Jury constitutes a contempt of court. Each violation of the obligation of secrecy may be punished cumulatively.

The government's excuse for dismissing Heidelberg was an anonymous interview he supposedly gave to Lawrence Myers of *Media Bypass* magazine. As previously noted, Heidelberg never consented to be interviewed by Myers, and in fact, Myers had surreptitiously obtained the content of an interview conducted by the investigator for Heidelberg's attorney, John DeCamp.

But Heidelberg claims the real reason was a letter he wrote to Judge Russell dated October 5th, in which Heidelberg states:

The families of the victims deserve to know who was involved in the bombing, and there appears to be an attempt to protect the identity of certain suspects, namely John Doe 2.

"I think they (the government) knows who John Doe 2 is, and they are protecting him," said Heidelberg in an interview in *Jubilee Magazine*. "This is because John Doe 2 is either a government agent or informant and they can't afford for that to get out." [555]

Eventually, the FBI dropped the John Doe 2 lead altogether. John Doe 2 had been a red herring, a false lead, the Justice Department claimed. John Doe 2 had never really existed.*

Dozens of credible witnesses think otherwise.

Catina Lawson, who was friends with McVeigh, remembered John Doe 2 from the Summer of '92, when she and her friends would hold parties and invite soldiers from nearby Fort Riley. McVeigh showed up with Andy Strassmeir, Mike Fortier, and Michael Brescia. In fact, Lawson's roommate, Lindsay Johnson, dated the handsome, well-built Brescia.

Two days after the bombing, Lawson called the FBI and told them that Brescia closely resembled the sketch of John Doe 2.

In spite of overturning 21,000 stones, the FBI never even bothered to follow up on her story.

Robert Gohn, who lived across the road from McVeigh in Kingman, recalled seeing one of the mysterious John Does around the early Summer of '94. According to Gohn, one day a short, stocky man who looked "like a weight lifter" arrived at McVeigh's trailer with Terry Nichols. [556]

On April 7, Dr. Paul Heath was working in his office at the Murrah Building when "McVeigh" and two of his companions stopped by for a chat. Heath recalled one of the men as "American-Indian looking" and "handsome." [557]

As the Associated Press reported on April 27, 1995:

[U.S. Attorney Randy] Rathburn said neighbors of Nichols' ... reported that Nichols spent April 12-14 with McVeigh and several unidentified men. One of the men resembled sketches of John Doe 2....[558] **

On Saturday, April 15, Barbara Whittenberg served breakfast to three men at the Sante Fe Trail Diner in Herrington, Kansas. One of the men was dark-skinned and handsome. When he told her they were on their way to Oklahoma

---

* It seemed that the John Doe 2 lead was officially dropped in early May. An FBI memo regarding a John Doe 2 lead instructs all FBI offices: "In view of the fact that the Oklahoma Command Post has directed all offices to hold unsub #2 leads in abeyance, San Francisco will conduct no further investigation regarding this lead." (174A-OC-56120 TPR: investigation was conducted by Special Agent (SA) Thomas P. Ravenelle regarding Richard Dehart, DOB 6/21/65, as a Phoenix resident and a possible look-alike for unsub #2, dated 5/3/95.)

** It should be noted that McVeigh was supposedly on the road April 12, traveling from Kingman to Junction City.

City, McVeigh shot him a hard look that said "keep quiet."[559]

Early the next day, around 1 A.M., Melba was working the deli counter at Albertson's Supermarket on South May in Oklahoma City, when "McVeigh" and John Doe 2 stopped by for sandwiches.[560]

"McVeigh," it seems, was still in town when Phyliss Kingsley and Linda Kuhlman saw three vehicles pull into the Hi-Way Grill, just south of Oklahoma City, around 6 P.M. on Sunday. McVeigh came in and ordered hamburgers and fries to go, and was accompanied by a short, stocky, handsome man, of either Mexican or American Indian descent. The man closely resembled the FBI sketch of John Doe 2.[561]

That same day, back at the Dreamland Motel in Junction City, Connie Hood was returning to her room around 12:45 A.M. when a man in room 23 quickly opened the door as if expecting a visitor, then quickly closed it when he saw Hood. The man, who startled her, was in his early 20s, about 5′ 8″ tall, 180 lbs., with dark hair brushed straight back and an olive complexion. Hood recalls he closely resembled the sketch of John Doe 2, but with slightly fuller features. She described him as a "foreigner."[562]

The following day, Hood and her husband Donald returned to the Dreamland to visit their friend David King in room 22. A Ryder truck pulled up at the same time they did, the driver strongly resembling the man Hood saw the previous day.

Shane Boyd, a helicopter mechanic who was also staying at the Dreamland, later told reporters and investigators that he saw a bushy-haired man resembling the John Doe 2 sketch in the parking lot near room 25—Timothy McVeigh's room.

One exit away from the Dreamland Motel sits the Great Western Inn. According to the manager, a Middle Eastern man stayed at the motel on the 17th. "He spoke broken English," said the manager. "[He] gave a foreign name and was driving a Ryder truck." The man closely resembled the FBI's sketch of John Doe 2.

"Sometime on Monday," recalled Connie Hood, "those two—McVeigh and the foreigner—loaded up together, in a Ryder truck, and pulled out of the Dreamland parking lot together.... That was the last I saw of them."[563]

Later that day, janitors Katherine Woodly and Martin Johnson were working the 5-9 P.M. shift in the Murrah Building when they saw "McVeigh" and John Doe 2. McVeigh spoke to Martin about a job, and John Doe 2 nodded to Woodly.[564]

At 3 P.M. on Monday, or possibly Tuesday, Jerri-Lynn Backhous and Dorinda Hermes were working at the Easy-Mart in Newkirk, 100 miles north of Oklahoma City, when a convoy pulled in. One of the vehicles—a light blue pickup with a camper top—was being driven by Terry Nichols. Backhous recalled Nichols' passenger as average height, dark-skinned, with black hair and a muscular build. "He looked just like the John Doe 2 sketch," she said.[565]

Debbie Nakanashi was working at the Post Office across the street from the Murrah Building around on Monday or Tuesday when "McVeigh" and John Doe 2 stopped in and asked where they might find federal job applications. Nakanashi helped provide the description for the well-known profile sketch of John Doe 2 in the baseball cap.

Guy Rubsamen, a security guard at the Murrah Building saw a large Ryder truck pull up to the curb in front of the building around 4 P.M. on Monday the 17th. Rubsamen later concluded it was a dress rehearsal.

"There was either two or three men, but one jumped out the driver's side, and one or two out the passenger side," Rubsamen told the *Rocky Mountain News*. "The first thing that struck me was how quickly they jumped out. Those guys were in a hurry." [566]

The Ryder truck would make its appearance the following evening at the Cattle Baron's Steakhouse in Perry, Oklahoma. Jeff Meyers and another customer recalled seeing McVeigh and a companion, who stopped by for a few beers. The man was approximately six feet tall and weighed 260 pounds—a description not befitting the John Doe 2s described by other witnesses. [567]

Richard Sinnett, the assistant manager of the Save-A-Trip convenience store in Kingman, Kansas, sold fuel to McVeigh and three other men at approximately 1:30 A.M. on April 19. Sinnett saw three vehicles in all, including a Ryder truck, a brown pick-up, and a light colored car.

Sinnett described John Doe 2 as muscular, 170 to 180 pounds, with short light brown hair and a light complexion. He recalled the Ryder truck was towing a trailer that contained a large, round tank filled with clear liquid. The store is about 175 miles north of Oklahoma City. [568]

Fred Skrdla, a cashier at a 24-hour truck stop near Billings, told the FBI he sold fuel to McVeigh between 1 and 3 A.M. on April 19. The station is about 80 miles north of Oklahoma City.

As the sun rose, McVeigh and a friend sat down for coffee at Jackie's Farmers Store in Mulhall, Oklahoma. Mulhall Postmaster Mary Hunnicutt stood right next to McVeigh as he ordered his coffee. She was "advised" not to discuss what she had seen, lest she be summoned before the Federal Grand Jury. She wasn't. [569]

Ten minutes before the blast, Leroy Brooks was sitting in his car at the Sooner Post Office across from the Murrah Building, when a Ryder truck pulled up across the street, trailed by a yellow Mercury. The drivers of both vehicles got out and walked to the back of the truck, where they spoke for a few seconds, and exchanged a small package. After Brooks came out of the Post Office, he saw that the Ryder truck, which contained a passenger, had moved in front of the Murrah Building. "McVeigh" was walking briskly across 5th Street towards the Journal Record building.

Danny Wilkerson sold "McVeigh" a pack of cigarettes (McVeigh doesn't smoke) and two soft drinks at a deli inside the Regency Towers apartments a block from the Murrah Building. Wilkerson recalled a passenger sitting in the cab of the Ryder truck, which had a cab overhang, and was shorter than the 24-foot model the FBI claimed McVeigh had rented.

Federal authorities had still more witnesses to call on had they wanted to. Mike Moroz, who was at work at Johnny's Tire Store on 10th and Hudson, on April 19, looked up to see a Ryder truck pull in at 8:40 A.M. The occupants were looking for directions to the Murrah Building. Moroz caught a glimpse of the passenger—a stocky man with dark curly hair wearing a ball cap, and a tattoo on his upper left arm.

Several minutes earlier, David Snider was waiting for a delivery in Bricktown, about 25 blocks away, when a Ryder truck passed slowly by, as if looking for an address. However, this time the driver was a dark-skinned man with long, straight black hair, wearing a thin mustache and tear-drop sunglasses. The passenger was "McVeigh." Since Snider's account of the occupants differed remarkably from the previous accounts, could this have been the second Ryder truck described by witnesses? If so, did this mean there were two "McVeighs" and two John Doe 2s? *

At approximately the same time as Snider saw the Ryder truck, Tulsa banker Kyle Hunt came upon the truck at Main and Broadway, trailed by a yellow Mercury. Hunt said the Mercury driver was Timothy McVeigh. "He gave me that icy, go-to-hell look," said Hunt. "It kind of unnerved me." [570] While Hunt didn't see the occupants of the truck, he did recall two passengers in the car. One of them, he said, had long hair, similar to the man Phyliss Kingsley saw on Sunday at the Hi-Way Grill.

Just outside the Murrah Building, Dennis "Rodney" Johnson was driving his catering truck, when he suddenly had to brake to avoid hitting two men who were running towards the parking lot across the street. [571]

The men, who were in "a fast lockstep" with each other, appeared to be Timothy McVeigh and John Doe 2. Johnson described McVeigh's companion as "Mexican or American-Indian." He was "dark-skinned ... probably about five foot eight and maybe 160 pounds," Johnson said. "He was wearing blue jogger pants with a stripe across the side. He had slicked-back hair." [572]

Then there was Gary Lewis. A pressman for the *Journal Record*, Lewis stepped outside to smoke his pipe just minutes before the blast. As he stood in the alley across from the Murrah Building, a yellow Mercury peeled away from its spot and bore down on him. The driver, whom he made brief eye-contact with, appeared to be Timothy McVeigh. And his passenger resembled the sketch of John Doe 2. The car had an Oklahoma tag (not an Arizona tag as authorities claimed) dangling by one bolt.

---

* David Snider, interview with author. Snider appeared a credible witness.

Even FBI Agent John Hersley testified before the Federal Grand Jury that "Several witnesses spotted a yellow car carrying McVeigh and another man speeding away from the parking lot near the [building] before the blast." [573]

Finally there was Daina Bradley. A young mother, Bradley was standing by the window of the Social Security office seconds before the blast, when she saw a man get out of the passenger side of the Ryder truck. Moments later, Bradley's world turned to blackness, smoke and dust as she was showered by falling concrete. Bradley, who lost her leg, her mother, and her two children in the bombing, still clearly recalls the man who got out of the truck. He looked like John Doe 2.

Of course, federal "investigators" would show as little interest in these and other discrepancies as they would in the numerous John Does. Some of these witnesses were never even contacted by the FBI, even though all of them repeatedly tried to alert the Bureau. Only after federal prosecutors had coerced Daina Bradley into changing her story, did she testify at McVeigh's trial. None of the others were ever called.

"I know I wasn't called because I would have to testify that I did see John Doe 2. I know I saw John Doe 2," said Rodney Johnson.[574]

Then in March of 1997, after changing its mind half a dozen times about the existence of John Doe 2, it was "leaked" to the press that the FBI was searching for a John Doe. His name was Robert Jaques.

This "new" John Doe 2 had appeared at the office of real estate broker William Maloney, of Cassville, Missouri, in November of '94, along with Terry Nichols and a man who looked like McVeigh. They were there to discuss purchasing a remote piece of land. Joe Lee Davidson, a salesman in Maloney's office, recalled the encounter with Jaques: "The day he was here, he seemed to be the one that was in control and in charge of what was going on," said Davidson. "Nichols never said a whole lot and McVeigh never did come in." [575]

Maloney described Jaques as muscular, with a broad, dark face, similar to, but not quite identical as, the original FBI sketch of John Doe 2. Is it possible the sudden announcement of Jaques was a diversion, to satisfy a public increasingly savvy about the existence of John Doe 2? Nevertheless, a month after this new lead was announced, the government went ahead with the trial of McVeigh, making no attempt to introduce any additional suspects. They also dropped the lead on Steven Colbern, in spite of the fact that his pick-up was seen stopped ahead of McVeigh 90 minutes after the bombing.*

---

* "Reference lead #10,220: Referenced lead #10,220, San Francisco was directed to locate and interview LESTER SCANLON concerning his knowledge of STEVEN COLBERN. In view of the fact that COLBERN has been eliminated as a suspect in this matter, San Francisco will conduct no further investigation concerning lead #10,220." (FBI memo dated 5/3/95.)

The Middle-Eastern lead was also dropped. The FBI denied putting out the APB on the brown pick-up containing the three Middle Eastern males seen speeding away from the bombing. And while the FBI knew about Sam Khalid, they did nothing but ask him some questions.

An affidavit submitted by FBI Agent John Hersley stated: "A witness to the bombing saw two, possibly three persons in a brown Chevrolet pick-up—fleeing the area of the crime—just prior to the blast." Although agents interviewed the witness who saw Hussain al-Hussaini driving the brown pick-up, she was never brought before a line-up, and never called to testify before the Federal Grand Jury. Hussaini's friend Abraham Ahmed was turned loose as well.[576]

As in the Kennedy assassination, the FBI sent thousands of agents hither and yonder to scour the country, searching out even the most obscure leads. Agents swarmed through Kingman, conducting warrantless searches, arresting innocent people, and wreaking havoc. Dozens more swooped down on Terry Nichols 12-year-old son Josh, whom they thought may have been John Doe 2. Agents were sent to the Philippines to investigate Nichols' activities there, and thousands more had detained and questioned anyone even remotely suspicious.

Yet, as in the Kennedy case, few agents actually knew just why they were following up on any given lead. Very few were ever allowed to compare notes, or catch a glimpse of the "big picture."

More importantly, those individuals who should have been prime suspects for questioning were never even detained. No agents were sent to Elohim City to interview Andreas Strassmeir or Michael Brescia, or Peter and Sonny Ward. Likewise, none of the Middle Eastern suspects previously mentioned were arrested.

Had any FBI agents actually attempted to follow up on any of these leads, like their predecessors in Dallas, they would have been quickly reassigned to other cases by Washington.

The same held true for local law-enforcement. FBI SAC Bob Ricks—who doled out a mendacious dose of propaganda during the Waco massacre—was appointed Public Safety Director after the bombing, putting him in charge of the OHP.

The OSBI were made coffee boys and drivers for the FBI. District Attorney Bob Macy, along with local police, were "advised" to stay out of the case.*

Six days before the start of McVeigh's trial, Stephen Jones filed a defense motion citing law-enforcement and defense interviews with a Filipino terrorist who admitted meeting with bombing defendant Terry Nichols.

Lead prosecutor Joseph Hartzler called Jones' carefully investigated and

---

* As *Legal Times* noted: "Within hours of landing, [Deputy A. G. Merrick] Garland was hit by a barrage of legal concerns.... In subsequent days, Garland met with Oklahoma County District Attorney Robert Macy, gently notifying him of the Justice Department's desire not to have a local investigation going on simultaneously."

researched information "pulp fiction." Apparently, the government was concerned enough about Jones' revelations to order all the witness statements sealed.

A Washington-based terrorist expert who investigated the World Trade Center bombing and is familiar with some the suspects in Jones' brief said, "The whole idea that no one but Timothy McVeigh—that there's nothing wider than this—no one would believe it if the government weren't saying it. It's so implausible a story.

"The government has the nerve to call it pulp fiction," added the highly-respected source. Their story is 'pulp fiction.'"[577]

Choirboys

"Stated simply, neither the ATF nor any other federal agency had any advance knowledge of the deadly bomb that McVeigh delivered to the Murrah Building.... The prosecution is not withholding anything that even remotely would support such an outrageous charge."

—Department of Justice

"I can assure you that there has been no government misconduct and the men and women of the FBI that we're working with are beyond reproach."

—Joseph Hartzler

The Justice Department's refusal to admit the possibility of any suspects other than McVeigh and Nichols manifested in its illegal refusal to turn over discovery documents to the defense, contradicting federal Brady requirements. In a motion filed six days before the start of McVeigh's trial, Stephen Jones alleged the prosecution not only lied about the available evidence, but distorted ATF and FBI reports on Elohim City, deliberately misspelling the names Carol Howe, Robert Millar, Andreas Strassmeir, Dennis Mahon and others, so the defense would be unable to retrieve any documents regarding these suspects during computer searches. As Jones wrote in his brief:

Defense counsel is convinced that the government has engaged in a willful and knowing cover-up of information supplied to it by its informant. The defense was unable to locate this insert using a computer because all major search terms contained in the insert were misspelled. Elohim City was misspelled or misidentified (Elohm City), as was Mahon (Mehaun), Strassmeir (Strassmeyer), the Rev. Robert Millar (Bob Lamar) and in addition, Carol Howe was not identified in the insert at all.*

---

* The Brady Rule and Federal Rule of Criminal Procedure 16(a)(1)(C) provides: "Upon request of the defendant the government shall permit the defendant to inspect and copy

Thus the defense was unable to locate important information that Carol Howe, an ATF informant, had provided critical warning that the Murrah Building was about to be bombed. As Jones wrote:

> Our patience is exhausted.... We are no longer convinced the documents drafted and furnished to us, after the fact, by bureaucracies whose very existence and credibility is challenged, can be relied upon....
>
> The government has told the District Court that it had "no information" of a possible foreign involvement when it did. The government has told the District Court that "Andreas Strassmeir was never the subject of the investigation," when he was....
>
> Statements to the court by the prosecution that it cannot connect Strassmeir and Mahon to the bombing are hardly surprising. They did not try very hard to connect them because had they been connected, and Carol Howe's previous warning disclosed, the resulting furor would have been unimaginable....
>
> The repeated practice of the government and prosecution in this case when the shoe gets binding is to make a partial disclosure, assure the District Court it understands its Brady obligations, and hold its breath, hoping the court does not order further disclosure, or will rely on the prosecution's "good faith."
>
> This is a solemn criminal case, not *Alice in Wonderland* where definitions mean only what "the Queen thinks" and what she thinks is not known to anyone else.[578]

Richard Bieder, the attorney representing a group of bombing victims in their negligence lawsuit against the government, told the *London Telegraph* that he had seen internal ATF documents which supported many of the claims made by Carol Howe. But the reports for December 1994, probably the most critical ones, have vanished from the files.[579]

On April 14, 1995, the FBI placed a call to Assistant Chief Charles Gaines at the Oklahoma City Fire Department to warn him of a potential terrorist threat within the next few days. Yet like the FBI's warnings of the threat against the life of President Kennedy, or Nixon's infamous Watergate tapes, the audio logs of the Fire Department's incoming calls were mysteriously "erased."

When asked to explain this "accidental" erasure, Assistant Chief Jon Hansen intelligently replied, "We made a boo-boo." Hansen then admitted to reporter J.D. Cash that the tapes had been erased *after* the national media requested them.[580]

On April 28th the tape of James Nichols' hearing was released by court order, and it was blank. Nothing whatsoever could be heard on the tape, the sole record of the proceedings.

---

and photograph, books, papers, documents, photographs ... which are within the possession, custody or control of the government, and which are material to the preparation of the defendant's defense."

On April 19, the seismic data monitor at the Omniplex Museum, four miles from the Murrah Building, recorded shock waves of the explosion. The seismograph readings, including one from the University of Oklahoma 16 miles away in Norman, presented evidence that the explosion that ripped through the Alfred P. Murrah building may have been several distinct blasts. The implications of this are ominous.

At a meeting of the Oklahoma Geophysical Society on November 20th, Seismologists Ray Brown of the Oklahoma Geological Survey and Tom Holzer of the U.S. Geological Survey gathered to discuss the findings. Pat Briley, a seismic programmer, who has independently investigated the bombing, attended the meeting, as did U.S. Attorney Patrick Ryan and Assistant U.S. Attorney Jerome A. Holmes.

Although the two scientists disagreed on findings regarding the number of bombs, less than a third of the way through the presentation, Ryan got up, walked to the back of the room, and began giving a private press conference.

"I was certainly satisfied that these scientists could not say that there was anything other than one bomb that caused the seismology reading," said Ryan, a statement obviously inconsistent with the discussion at the time.

"Ryan lied very heavily," said Briley. "This guy really lied."

After the meeting, Briley politely asked Ryan to give him the original seismogram in the FBI's possession. Ryan got up, angrily accused Briley of working for the defense team, then stamped out of the room.[581]

Surveillance cameras located in the parking lot across from the Murrah building, and on neighboring buildings, would have recorded the entire fateful event that morning. The tapes would have also shown the building collapsing. They would have conclusively shown whether the structure was destroyed by cutting charges, or by a truck-bomb. But like Abraham Zapruder's infamous footage of the Kennedy assassination, the tapes were quickly confiscated by the FBI.

In an interview with Jon Rappaport, Hoppy Heidelberg said, "The various surveillance videotapes of the bombing, tapes from, say, Southwestern Bell and the Journal Record Building across the street, we don't know that they showed all the details of the bombing, including the perpetrators, but it's possible. None of this material was shown to us in the Grand Jury."

Certain segments of the footage was presented by the prosecution at trial. One cut included a shot of a blue GMC pick-up with a white camper top (the kind owned by Terry Nichols) driving slowly past the Regency Towers apartments near the Murrah Building on April 16—the day Nichols allegedly drove to Oklahoma to pick up McVeigh.*

---

* Judge Matsch was not impressed with this evidence. He commented during trial that there must be half a million blue GMC pick-ups with camper tops.

The prosecution also displayed a still frame of a Ryder truck driving by the Regency Towers on the morning of the blast. The time was 8:59 A.M. They then showed a still of the truck blowing up, stamped 9:02 A.M. Curiously, the government was careful not to show the jury any footage of suspects getting out of the truck.

Surveillance footage taken by Trooper Charles Hanger upon his arrest of McVeigh had caught a brown pick-up stopped just ahead—thought to belong to Steven Colbern. When researcher Ken Armstrong questioned the OHP about the tape, he was told it had been "seized" by the FBI. The OHP would not comment further.[582]

On June 1st, KFOR reporter Brad Edwards sent the Justice Department a Freedom of Information request concerning various surveillance footage. In their reply, the FBI stated:

A search of our indices to the Central Records System, as maintained in the Oklahoma City Office, located material responsive request [sic] to your request. This material is being withheld in its entirety pursuant to the following subsection of Title 5, United States Code, Section 552: (b) (7) (A)

When Jones finally filed a motion for disclosure after prosecutors refused to hand over the tapes, he was given 400 hours of footage. According to defense attorney Amber McGlaughlin, the tapes did not reveal the presence of Timothy McVeigh.[583]

Of course, who knows what the FBI actually turned over to the defense. In the Kennedy case, the most revealing evidence was the Zapruder film—home-made footage showing Presidents Kennedy's head being blasted towards the right-rear—indicating the fatal shot came from the Grassy Knoll, not the Book Depository as the government claimed. Yet the FBI confiscated Zapruder's film and altered the sequence of the incriminating frames, reversing them to give the impression that Kennedy's head had lurched forward. It was only later that experts revealed the tampering.

The FBI said it was a "mistake."

The Zapruder film was finally released in 1968, the result of District Attorney Jim Garrison's courageous efforts to reveal the truth. The question is, when will the American public get to see the video footage of the Oklahoma City bombing? (The author was involved in a Freedom of Information Act lawsuit against the FBI for the tapes when this book went to press.)

While the FBI did their best to keep key evidence from the Grand Jury, as in the Kennedy case, they even went so far as to convince several witnesses that their former statements were false, and to retract them in lieu of statements more favorable to the prosecution. A primary example is Michael Fortier, who originally told investigators, "I do not believe that Tim [McVeigh] blew up any building in

Oklahoma. There's nothing for me to look back upon and say, yeah, that might have been, I should have seen it back then—there's nothing like that.... I know my friend. Tim McVeigh is not the face of terror as reported on *Time* magazine."

But after the FBI raided his home, Fortier reversed his statement, saying that he and McVeigh "cased" the federal building, in response to an offer of a plea bargain. Fortier was then transferred to the Federal Medical Facility at Fort Worth, Texas. It is not known why.[584]

According to Heidelberg, the FBI brought 24-hour-a-day pressure on Fortier for months before he was arrested. Consequently, Fortier did not retain a lawyer, didn't know he needed one, and was subsequently bullied by the Bureau. By the time he managed to retain a lawyer, Fortier had already been broken.

Lori Fortier testified that McVeigh tried to solicit Nichols' help in building the bomb, but that Nichols wanted out. He then allegedly tried to solicit her husband. According to her testimony, McVeigh got down on the floor of their trailer and, using soup cans to represent 55-gallon drums, demonstrated how to make a bomb.*

Were the Fortiers relaying accurate testimony? Like the testimony of Eldon Elliott about McVeigh's height, or that of Thomas Manning regarding McVeigh's phone call to Elliott's, none of this information was contained in prior statements made by the Fortiers to the FBI.

As will be seen with prior incidents of government witness tampering and fabricated testimony, their testimony is highly circumspect.

The Fortiers' testimony is also somewhat questionable due to their drug use. According to co-worker Deborah Brown, who testified at McVeigh's trial, Lori Fortier used crystal methamphetamine almost daily. Methamphetamine is widely known for its ability to induce delusional or even psychotic states over time.[585]

Fortier eventually confessed to transporting and selling stolen firearms, drug possession, foreknowledge of the bombing plot, and failing to inform federal authorities.** Said juror Hoppy Heidelberg, "The FBI relied on a man, Fortier, who really couldn't provide anything important to them. You need to remember that. That's important."[586]

Lori Fortier also testified that "I still believed he [McVeigh] couldn't really do it." Jones then asked her, "Ms. Fortier, you said you thought McVeigh really

---

* The assertion was that McVeigh was demonstrating how to make a "shaped charge," which would have been impossible to make using 55-gallon barrels of ANFO.

** Fortier was intent during testimony to impress the jury that the guns from the Moore "robbery" were stolen. Responding to Jones' cross-examination, Fortier shouted, "No, no! I'm convinced those guns were stolen!" Fortier's successful plea-bargain was no doubt dependent on carrying that fact forward.

wouldn't carry out his plans, then you said you 'wanted out.' How can you 'want out' if there was nothing to 'be in'?"

On cross-examination, he assiduously questioned Michael Fortier's motivations:

Jones: Now, in addition, in your conversation you had with your brother on April the 25th, 1995—that's your brother John?

Fortier: Yes, sir.

Jones: Did you make the following statement: "I've been thinking about trying to do those talk-show circuits for a long time, come up with some asinine story and get my friends to go in on it?"

Fortier: Yes, sir, I made that statement.

Jones: And in the same conversation, did your brother say to you: "Whether the story is true or not, if you want to sit here and listen to a fable, that's all it was at the time is a fable?" And then did you say: "I found my career, 'cause I can tell a fable?" And then did you burst out laughing and say, "I could tell stories all day?"

Fortier: Yes, sir.

Jones: Then do you know an individual named Glynn?

Fortier: Yes.

Jones: And his last name, sir?

Fortier: I think you're referring to Glynn Bringle.

Jones: Did you have a conversation with him by telephone on April the 30th?

Fortier: Yes.

Jones: And did you say, "I want to wait 'til after the trial and do book and movie rights. I can just make up something juicy?" And then did you laugh?

Fortier: I'm not sure if I laughed or not, but I did make that statement.

Jones: "Something that's worth *The Enquirer*, you know." You made those statements.

Fortier: Yes, sir.

As Jones pointed out during his closing argument, the terms of Fortier's plea agreement provided that leniency would be contingent upon his performance in court.

Not true, according to the FBI, which spent over 175 hours soliciting statements from the Fortiers; and Joseph Hartzler, who met with his "star witness" between seven and 10 times to "make sure he told the truth." *

In fact, during McVeigh's trial, Lori Fortier testified on cross-examination

---

* Even Judge Matsch was forced to tell the jury: "You should bear in mind that a witness who has entered into such an agreement has an interest in this case different from any ordinary witness. A witness who realizes that he may be able to obtain his own freedom or receive a lighter sentence by giving testimony favorable to the prosecution has a

that she arrived in Denver five days before she was scheduled for trial. She testi-fied that she spent the better part of Friday, Saturday, Sunday, and Monday prac-ticing her testimony with federal prosecutors.

Philadelphia prosecutors spent a lot of time with Veronica Jones to "make sure she told the truth" implicating journalist Mumia Abu-Jamal, accused of shooting police officer Daniel Faulkner. Jones, who was facing unrelated felony charges at the time, originally told police she saw two other men flee the scene. After threats and promises from police, she changed her story, testifying to the government's version of events. Her felony charges were subsequently dropped.[587]

Fortier, whose speech and appearance were magically transformed for his day in court, reportedly received a reduced sentence of three years in exchange for his tes-timony. His wife Lori was granted complete immunity from prosecution for her's.

Jones also accused the FBI of harassing Jennifer McVeigh and her friends in the days after the bombing, hoping to obtain derogatory information about her brother. He said the FBI scared people "beyond belief with threats of prosecution" if they didn't talk.[588]

On the fifth day of Jennifer McVeigh's interrogation, the FBI ushered her into a room with huge blown-up pictures of her and her brother (taken off her refrig-erator door), and babies who died in the bombing. Interspersed between the pho-tos were statutes from the U.S. Code pertaining to treason, with phrases such as "Treason is punishable by death," and "The penalty for treason is *DEATH*." (Government's emphasis.)

Under cross-examination, Jennifer was asked if she was aware treason is pun-ishable only in times of war. Stunned by this revelation, she answered, "No."

The FBI tricked Jennifer into testifying by promising immunity if she coop-erated. During a break in the trial, a reporter asked prosecutor Vicky Behenna why Jennifer needed immunity. "She didn't," Behenna replied," but she wouldn't testify without it, so we gave it to her."[589]

The FBI also tricked Marife Nichols into signing a consent form before they searched her house. When she was asked if the agents advised her of her right to retain a lawyer or refuse to answer questions, the 23-year-old Filipino answered, "I don't remember. I don't think so." Marife said that FBI agents discouraged her when she asked whether she needed a lawyer during interrogation. "They told me, 'You're okay as long as you are telling the truth. You don't need a lawyer."[590]

James Nichols believes the ATF, which raided his house, set him up to be murdered, either as an act of revenge or to prevent him from testifying at trial. He told *Dateline's* Chris Hansen that after the agents entered his home, they asked him to retrieve a gun he kept in his bedroom. Nichols responded, "No, I won't go

---

motive to testify falsely. Therefore, you must examine his testimony with caution and weigh it with great care."

get it. I told you, send an agent or two in there to go do it.' 'Aw, go ahead. Go and do it,' the agent responded, and they all turned their backs, real nonchalantly. I said, 'Whoa, wait a minute ...' They'd a shot me, because they would have just said 'He pulled a gun on us.' The fate of Terry and Tim would have been signed, sealed and delivered. Dead people don't testify." [591]

For his part, Terry Nichols believed that he was not in custody after he walked into the Herrington, Kansas police station on April 21 to see why his name was being broadcast on television. Apparently, the agents were hoping to get more out of Nichols by leading him to believe they had no intention to arrest him.

"Mr. Nichols was coerced, deceived, and subjected to psychological ploys designed to overcome his will and make him confess," his attorney stated in a legal brief. Defense attorneys also contend Nichols was falsely promised he could review agents' notes on his statements for accuracy, and was falsely told he or his wife could be present at searches.

Prosecutors countered that federal agents acted "with remarkable diligence and in a manner that honored the Constitution."

Sure.

FRANK KEATING: DAMAGE CONTROL INC.

"The business of the New York journalist is to destroy the truth, to lie outright, to pervert, to vilify, to fawn at the feet of Mammon, and to sell his race and his country for his daily bread."
—John Swinton, CEO, *New York Times*, New York Press Club, April 12, 1953

"The Central Intelligence Agency owns everyone of any significance in the major media."
—William Colby, former CIA Director

Eight months after the bombing, Oklahoma State Representative Charles Key, dissatisfied with the "official" investigation, attempted to form a state oversight committee. House Speaker Glen Johnson ridiculed Key's efforts, stating his satisfaction with the Justice Department's official tale. Anyone who challenged the government's official line was publicly discredited by Governor Keating, sneered at by Attorney General Drew Edmondson, and laughed at by the mainstream press.*

---

* Most noticeably horse-laughs emerged from *Tulsa World*, which earned the nickname *The Tulsa Pravda.*" *The Daily Oklahoman* has been called the *"Daily Joke-la-homan"* by locals.

The local media provided a convenient platform for Governor Keating to dismiss critics of the government, including Edye Smith, Hoppy Heidelberg and Representative Key. In an attempt to discredit Heidelberg, Keating headed a carefully orchestrated chorus of media pundits, stating that Heidelberg was "off the reservation."

Keating also joined KWTV in attacking KFOR's coverage of the Middle Eastern connection, stating they lacked integrity.

He labeled Jim Levine, an attorney who represented several victims *pro bono* in an attempt to release money from the Governor and Mayor's Victims Relief Funds, a "bottom-feeding" lawyer.*

For his efforts to uncover the truth, Keating said Representative Key was "baying at the moon."**

Along with bombing victim Glenn Wilburn, Key attempted to impanel a County Grand Jury. Such a jury, operating outside the scope of the federal investigation, would not only have the power to investigate facts ignored by the Federal Grand Jury, but have the power to level criminal obstruction of justice charges against anybody whom they believed might have impeded the investigation.

Given the allegations of wrongdoing in the federal investigation, such charges could conceivably be leveled against everybody from the ATF to the Justice Department.

In an interview in the *McCurtain Gazette*, Key explained, "Indisputable proof exists now that the Federal Grand Jury was purposely shielded from witnesses who saw Timothy McVeigh with other suspects, both prior to and immediately after the bombing assault.... They may have a good motive for this, but thus far it escapes me—and, I might add, several members of the Federal Grand Jury who witnessed this farce."

Keating's response, quoted in the *Daily Oklahoman* was: "I don't think a legislative committee would contribute one whit of intelligence to this process." [592]

The Daily Oklahoman and the *Tulsa World*, the state's two largest dailies, which should have led the pack in ferreting out the truth of this terrible tragedy, instead led the local media chorus with editorials such as one in the *Daily Oklahoman* entitled, "Drop It, Mr. Key."

---

* Levine graciously represented Representative Key and several investigators, including the author, who set up a charitable trust to investigate the bombing, for free, and brought homemade chicken soup to the author when he was sick.

** Keating told Gary Harper during one of his weekly citizen chat sessions that Key was sleeping with a judge's wife. Keating unsuccessfully tried to find a political candidate to run against the popular five-term Representative.

The Daily Oklahoman has opposed Key's mission from the beginning.... State Rep. Charles Key's quest to prove that a government conspiracy played some role in the Murrah Building bombing is a weird and misguided exercise.... Oklahoma County District Attorney Bob Macy is correct in appealing a court ruling that allows Key a free hand to seek a County Grand Jury probe of his conspiracy theories....[593]

The *Tulsa World* chimed in with editorials such as "Making Tragedy Pay," labeling Key as a "dedicated hustler" peddling "goofy theories" to right-wing crank audiences." They also accused the representative of profit-making from the sale of his bombing videos. Unmentioned by *Tulsa World* was the recent loss of Key's insurance business due to his ceaseless efforts to investigate the bombing and his attempts to support his wife and three children in a ramshackle house on a $33,000-a-year salary.

The local media eagerly focused on the efforts of Drew Edmondson, who accused Key of proposing a "wasteful witch hunt" and of engaging in "the worst kind of paranoid conspiracy pandering."

One article reported how Edmondson convinced the State District Attorney's Council to oppose Key's investigative funding bill. "This is unprecedented, as far as I know, for the Attorney General to go to such lengths with the District Attorneys Council and to use such intemperate language," the soft-spoken Key told *The New American*.

While the *Tulsa World* and the *Daily Oklahoman* went to extremes to label Key a "conspiracy nut," they never mentioned that radio polls revealed an overwhelming majority of Oklahomans supported Key's efforts.

Key's Grand Jury petition was quashed on November 6th, 1995 by District Judge Daniel Owens on the grounds that it would be "re-inventing the wheel." *

Key appealed. As his attorney, Mark Sanford stated, "Legally [Owens] didn't have the right to quash the petition. But because he's a judge he has the power, whether it's legal or not."[594]

Beverly Palmer from Bob Macy's office argued at the appeals hearing in defense of Owens, claiming that the petition was "insufficient on its face," and the request was duplicitous of the Federal Grand Jury's efforts.

Yet, as Appeals Judge Ronald Stubblefield pointed out, nowhere did Judge Owens state why the petition was insufficient. "I question whether Judge Owens has the discretion," said Stubblefield. "He's just operating on what he knows about the bombing. Do you think it's right to make a judgment based on what he reads in the newspaper?"[595]

The same could be said about DA Bob Macy. At the time I interviewed him,

---

* Shortly after Key and Wilburn drew up their petition to impanel the Grand Jury, a bill was introduced in the State Legislature to change the Grand Jury petitioning process.

he was collecting information on the case by reading Morris Dees' *The Gathering Storm*, and *The Turner Diaries*. This was a year-and-a-half after the bombing—a bombing that occurred right outside his window. He didn't know about John Doe 2. He had no idea about the Middle Eastern connection. He had done absolutely no investigation.

"I have not seen these things you are talking about right now," Macy told me. "When I see the evidence … I haven't been presented with the evidence." Macy subsequently claimed he wanted me to work with his so-called "task force" that was "investigating" the bombing, then never called me back.

His attitude was reflected by his Assistant DA, Beverly Palmer. Visibly nervous, Palmer grasped at straws during the appeals hearing, arguing that the Grand Jury shouldn't be convened because of the need for "judicial economy," and that it contravened "public policy concerns."

"What policy concerns?" Judge Daniel Boudreau asked.*

In spite of the efforts of a group of good ol' boy politicians to sabotage justice, Judge Stubblefield remained firm: "The people have the right to circulate a petition if the people find that things aren't going the way they ought to be," he said. "Is it not the right, by the sanctified right of the Grand Jury in Oklahoma, to inquire whether a crime is committed? Don't they have the right to investigate people who they think are involved? This is a highly protected right."

The Appeals Court upheld Key's right to petition for a County Grand Jury by a unanimous vote.

Just two months before the hearing, DA Macy told this author he intended to prosecute McVeigh and Nichols in a state trial on 161 counts of First Degree Murder. "I don't like taking a second seat to the [federal] prosecution," Macy stated. "The bombing killed 10 of my friends."

In a May 24, 1995 letter to Senator Orrin Hatch, one of the original drafters of the Anti-Terrorism Bill, Macy wrote:

First, immediately following the trial or trials in Federal Court, I shall, working in conjunction with the United Sates Department of Justice and the federal law-enforcement agencies investigating the bombing of the Alfred P. Murrah Building, prosecute the cowards responsible for murdering innocent people in the area sur-

---

* The County didn't possess the resources and funds, Palmer replied, to pursue such a big case. Besides, she pleaded, the "investigation" was already "complete," being a "thorough investigation" from "several different federal agencies." Palmer claimed a County Grand Jury would "jeopardize the federal case." The federal gag order prevents interviewing prospective witnesses, she claimed. Sanford countered that there would be no interference with the federal case as long as they were interviewing witnesses and suspects that federal prosecutors ignored, which seem to be in abundance.

rounding the Federal Building....

The State of Oklahoma has an overwhelming, compelling interest to seek and obtain the maximum penalty allowable by law for the senseless and cowardly killings. Not only is it in the interest of the State, it is my sworn duty to seek those sanctions, and I intend to fully carry out my responsibilities....

Every day of delay represents a victory for these cowardly cold-blooded killers and another day of defeat and suffering for the victims and all other Americans who cry out for justice.[596]

Macy impressed upon the author: "I'm prepared to do what ever it takes to get to the truth. My sole intent is in learning the truth!"

Yet when asked if he intended to conduct an investigation independent of the Feds', he said, "I don't want to be a party to anything that will interfere with the Feds' prosecution. I don't want to open up a new can of worms."[597]

After Macy lost the appeals hearing, he met with Wilburn and Key, explaining that he actually wished to cooperate with their investigation. Three days later, the two men discovered that Macy had decided to contest the Appeals Court's decision.

When a furious Key confronted Macy, all the DA told him was, "*They won't let me.*" When Key demanded to know who "they" were, Macy just lowered his eyes to the floor and repeated, "They won't let me."[598]

Key later learned from a source at ABC News that Macy had received a conference call from Janet Reno's Deputy Jamie Gorelick, and the government's lead prosecutor, Joseph Hartzler, along with Governor Keating, Oklahoma City Fire Chief Gary Marrs, and Judge Daniel Owens.

When the Grand Jury was finally impaneled, federal prosecutors quickly attempted to block the testimony of federal employees.

Key also accused [Chief Assistant DA Pat] Morgan and others in Oklahoma District Attorney Bob Macy's office of influencing and intimidating witnesses. "I am very upset about it," Key said. "Everyone should be outraged because of this."[599]

Interestingly, during a debate with Representative Key, Keating stated, "Nobody could get away with a cover-up; it would not be tolerated by civilized Oklahoma City.... Nobody's afraid of the truth."[600]

KFOR's Jayna Davis shed some light on the "truth-seeking" efforts of Bob Macy. Two years earlier, after an eight-year-old boy was raped, both Davis and the Public Defender demanded to know why Macy hadn't done anything. When Macy thought the camera was off, he whipped around and sternly admonished the reporter: "Lady, I don't know who you are or where you came from, but this isn't how we do business in Oklahoma!"[601]

Representative Key eventually took the case to the Oklahoma Supreme

Court. In his opposing brief, DA Macy again argued that it would be "a waste of the taxpayers' time and money to convene an Oklahoma County Grand Jury when one was already in session or when a Federal Grand Jury had already heard all available evidence."

The Supreme Court did not agree with Macy. They unanimously upheld Key's right to impanel the Grand Jury, which was seated in June, '97, and is hearing evidence as of this writing.

The Daily Oklahoman quickly pumped out a piece titled "Conspiracy Theories," stating that the County Grand Jury exacerbates the "agony" of victims, who are apparently more concerned with "closure" than learning the truth:

> Whatever the cause, the delay adds to the agony of those bombing victims who believe the investigation is a waste of time.
>
> *The Oklahoman* shares that belief, but we are optimistic the probe may satisfy many who are suspicious about events before the bombing. Yet, we wonder if the more conspiratorial-minded will ever be satisfied....
>
> Conflicting conspiracy theories and an olio of circumstantial evidence abound here. Jurors in Denver sorted through testimony and found McVeigh guilty. Frustrating as it may be to some, there is little more to this crime than meets the eye. The rest is the stuff of fiction.[602]

By the *Daily Oklahoman's* account, the numerous credible witnesses who saw Timothy McVeigh with other suspects on the morning of the crime adds up to little more than "circumstantial evidence," while irrelevant emotional tales from bombing victims and McVeigh's political views—are not.*

Given the local media's connection to the political good ol' boy network via the Washington-connected Frank Keating, their position is hardly surprising. Famed Watergate journalist Carl Bernstein put some perspective on the matter when he revealed in a 1977 *Rolling Stone* article that over 400 U.S. journalists were employed by the CIA.

> These ranged from freelancers who were paid for regular debriefings, to actual CIA officers who worked under deep cover. Nearly every major U.S. news organization has had spooks on the payroll, usually with the cooperation of top management.
>
> The three most valuable assets the CIA could count on were William

---

* "They're coming up with a substitute for proof," said Denver defense attorney Larry Pozner. "They're softening the jury up with emotional testimony about the bombing and McVeigh's politics. They're saying, 'We'll give you every reason in the world to hate Tim McVeigh.'" (Kevin Flynn, "Softening the Jury," *Rocky Mountain News*, 5/8/97.)

Paley's CBS, Arthur Sulzberger's *New York Times* and Henry Luce's *Time/Life* empire. All three bent over backwards promoting the picture of Oswald as a lone nut in the JFK assassination.[603]

The good ol' boy network wasn't finished trying to stop the efforts of Representative Key. On May 7, 1997, Oklahoma Attorney General Drew Edmondson subpoenaed Key before a Multi-County Grand Jury, alleging that he violated procedures in raising money for the bombing investigation. The *Daily Oklahoman* proclaimed how it helped bring about the state's legal action:

> The Attorney General's action is a result of an inquiry by *The Oklahoman* about Key's seven-page solicitation letter on the Internet. The letter asks for money to "secure copies of the voluminous (federal) government documents and to pay independent investigators" and other expenses for the County Grand Jury investigation.

Bill Graves, an attorney who represented Key at the Grand Jury inquest, stated: "The law is pretty clear that you are not required to register before you hit the ten thousand dollar threshold, and Charles [Key] had not hit that limit so was not required to register. Edmondson knows that. They're just trying to slow Charles down or stop him through harassment."[604]

"This is all about stopping us and making us shut up," said Key. "If I would just quit the Grand Jury deal, this would all go away."[605]

Says V.Z. Lawton, a HUD worker who survived the bombing, "You don't have to be that bright or look that hard to see the fraud and hypocrisy in these charges. For over a year and a half, they've been doing everything imaginable and employing the most absurd arguments to prevent Charles from impaneling a Grand Jury to investigate one of the worst crimes in our country's history. Now, after he's overcome all of their legal challenges in the courts and is close to getting a County Grand Jury investigation going, they drag him before a Multi-County Grand Jury for what amounts to jaywalking, while the bombing and other genuine, serious crimes go uninvestigated."[606]

Lawton also brought to the attention of bombing investigators a February 5th fax transmission to federal employees on the official letterhead of Attorney General Drew Edmondson. The letter sought signatures from survivors to go with letters that were to be sent to various news organizations. The cover sheet said it came from Richard M. Wintory, Chief Deputy Attorney General of the Criminal Division.

The letter, entitled, "A Plea to the Media from Oklahoma City: Don't O.J. Us!!!" purports to be a spontaneous response from victims asking the media not to "manipulate" and "exploit" them "for no purpose other than to enhance their ratings on the air and in publications."

This obvious propaganda counteroffensive was in response to ABC 20/20's January, 1996 show about prior knowledge. It referred to the "so-called report" by ABC as "tabloid journalism" filled with "unsubstantiated and baseless claims that have been repeatedly debunked."

"We are appalled at the lack of interest in the truth and the underhanded method utilized by 20/20," stated the letter, which claimed that ABC had wrongfully implied that certain victims agreed with the "paranoid delusion" of the "ridiculous theory of government conspiracy in this crime." It added that "reporters are sometime tempted to forget the truth." Ultimately, it stated, "It is PEOPLE that matter in this life, either money nor possession nor a Pulitzer Prize."

This classic Psyop piece launched by Edmondson (which he angrily denied in a letter to the author) was signed, "Many Survivors and Family Members, Oklahoma City Bombing."

HUD employees V.Z. Lawton and Jane Graham were two survivors who angrily denounced the letter. "Since the communication was loaded with lies and half-truths, I certainly could not sign it," said Lawton, "and I felt like a State Attorney General could better spend his time supporting an effort to find the truth rather than this transparent effort at helping to hide it."

"I am angry," stated Graham in a typed response to the letter, "that the Attorney General's office would play on the emotions of this office at HUD under the guise of keeping us posted on how they are proceeding and planning the case, causing further emotional turmoil in this office between employees." [607]

In a June 13, 1997 television interview, Edmondson was asked why those witnesses who saw McVeigh with other suspects were never called to testify at McVeigh's trial. Edmondson replied that prosecutors usually don't present witnesses whose testimony isn't "credible" or conflicts with other witnesses. Rodney Johnson, who saw McVeigh with another man in front of the Murrah Building moments before it exploded, called Edmondson's statement "misguided." "I took those comments to be rather personal," said Johnson. [608]

Edmondson's attempt to coerce victims so they pander to the official government line is similar to a letter from a group of victims suggesting passage of the Anti-Terrorism Bill, enacted shortly after the OKC bombing. Recipients were urged to call Edmondson if they were interested in participating.

Interestingly, several months after the scandalous smear campaign against Representative Key, Governor Keating was accused by the Oklahoma Ethics Commission of 32 violations of using state-owned vehicles for political fund-raising, including the state's $2.9 million airplane. Conveniently forgetting his own dishonest smear attacks against Representative Key, Keating sanctimoniously whined about how the allegations were "irresponsible, silly and completely unjustified." No doubt the Ethics Commission was "off the reservation," and "baying at the moon."

In spite of his unsuccessful attempts to smear honest men like Representative Key, Keating and his cronies wasted no time in discrediting Edye Smith, calling her allegations "hysterical." Smith was the mother of two young boys who perished in the bombing—Chase and Colton. Smith immediately gained the attention of concerned citizens all across America. Hundreds of thousands of letters and checks began pouring in, and relief agencies used Chase's photo on a poster memorializing the disaster.

On May 23, the day the Federal Building was demolished, Edye Smith stated in a live interview on CNN, "There's a lot of questions that have been left unanswered. We're being told to keep our mouths shut, not to talk about it, don't ask those questions." *

CNN's Gary Truchmann asked Smith to describe the nature of the questions: "We, along with hundreds of thousands of other people want to know, where was the ATF the morning of April 19th? All of their employees survived. They were supposed to be the target of this explosion and where were they? Did they have a warning sign? I mean, did they think it might be a bad day to go in the office? **

"They had an option to not go to work that day," Smith continued, "and my kids didn't get that option, nobody else in the building got that option. And we're just asking questions, we're not making accusations. We just want to know why and they're telling us, 'Keep your mouth shut, don't talk about it.'" †

Truchmann quickly ended the interview.

Kathy Wilburn was the Grandmother of Chase and Colton. Wilburn was

---

* The building was demolished because officials claimed it was eerie reminder of that tragic day. Yet authorities made no effort to remove the charred remains of the Athenian Restaurant directly across the street, which to this day stands as a shocking monument to the brutality of the bombing.

** According to a 1988 GAO (General Accounting Office) report, the Federal Building was not a "safe" place to install a day care center. Allegedly based on the 1983 plot by white supremacist Richard Wayne Snell (CSA member and friend of Robert Millar) to bomb the facility, the report concluded that a day care center should not be placed inside the Murrah Building. "No federal law enforcement agents who worked in the building, including the BATF, Secret Service, and the DEA, ever had any of their children in the Murrah's day care center … ever," said Smith.

† Smith complained that when she appears on local radio shows, it seems to her that "more people around here now hate me than like me. People that don't want to think that the government would do such a thing."

among the first to arrive at the scene of the bombing, and she and Smith, who both worked at the nearby I.R.S. office, had witnessed the carnage first-hand. Now, as she watched the building come down, an eerie silence came over her. Later that afternoon, Kathy Wilburn walked into the empty room where the little boys had lived, picked up their stuffed animals, and began to cry.

Wilburn's husband Glenn had been a vocal opponent of the government's investigation, and their explanation of the bombing did not sit well with him. The Grandfather felt the loss of the two boys keenly. Wilburn had taken it on his own to investigate the bombing, and the facts he was coming up with did not make him happy.

The afternoon the building was demolished, Wilburn received a call from U.S. Attorney Patrick Ryan. Ryan wanted to meet with him and speak with the family. "They wanted to set our minds at ease our minds that there wasn't anything sinister going on," said Wilburn. Two days later, Edye Smith and Wilburn were visited by an entourage of federal agents including Ryan, ATF Agents Chris Cuyler and Luke Franey, an IRS Criminal investigator, and a member of Louis Jolyon West's victims assistance team.

"They all came in and sat down and said 'We want to answer your questions and make you feel good.' I said 'fine.' Then I looked them right in the eye and said, 'You guys had no indication that April 19th could be a dangerous day down there?' They both answered, 'no sir.'"

"Well, two hours later I turned on the TV, and CNN is interviewing ATF Director John Magaw. The interview starts out, "Mr. Magaw, based on the significance of April 19th, did you take any precautions?'"

"Clearly there was an interest all over the country to do that," replied Magaw. "And I was very concerned about that. We did some things here in headquarters and in all of our field offices throughout the country to try to be more observant."

"Well, if there was ever a point that I was hooked into this thing, and there was nothing that was gonna' stop me," recalls Wilburn, "that was it, because, by God, somebody lied that morning."

Ryan's conciliatory meeting with the family did not last long. The federal prosecutor became nervous after Wilburn mentioned that he talked to a family lawyer. Ryan quickly got up and left.

While Edye Smith was quoted as saying that she was "satisfied" the agents had explained their whereabouts, she later told me, "I believe they sat their and lied to us."

Unmarked cars soon began showing up at Glenn Wilburn's house. When Wilburn went out to confront them, they sped off.[609]

Two months later, Edye Smith and Kathy Wilburn had their Worker's Compensation checks cut off. Out of 462 federal employees affected by the blast, they were the only two employees who were mysteriously "denied."

Out of thousands of checks sent to Smith through the Red Cross, none were ever received. All the letters had been opened, the checks missing, including some sent via the Governor's and Mayor's office. "All the mail that the Red Cross delivered to my house, probably thousands of pieces of mail, every single piece was opened before I got it. And it all had my name on it," said Smith.

"We started noticing that the mail that came to the house had money in it," said Kathy Wilburn, "but the majority of the mail that came to us through the Red Cross … it was all opened and there was never a thin dime in any of it."

When Smith called the Red Cross to complain, she was told that her mail wasn't being opened, and that no money was being taken. When Wilburn confronted the head of the local Red Cross, she was told their letters were being opened to check for "hate mail." Wilburn told her that the explanation was "ridiculous."

"A mother sent me a little card that her little boy drew," said Smith, "She said 'my little boy saved this three dollars and wanted you to have it.' And the three dollars was gone." [610]

Keating's answer to the missing funds? Interning college students were responsible for the thefts.

Leaning on government critics are not unusual tactics for a man who worked as an FBI agent during COINTELPRO (the FBI's Counter Intelligence Program of the late-60s to mid-70s), where he personally infiltrated anti-government activists like the Weathermen, the Black Panthers, and the SDS (Students For A Democratic Society). Keating stated he sees little difference between leftist protest and militias. [611]

Keating also served as Assistant Attorney General under Edwin Meese. Meese was Attorney General during the 1985 fire-bombing of MOVE headquarters. MOVE was a group of black housing activists living in a squatted building in Philadelphia. The satchel charge, dropped from a helicopter by Philadelphia's finest (with a little help from the FBI), resulted in the deaths of over 11 people, including five children, destroying numerous square blocks of the city.

Instead of launching proper investigation into the matter, Meese's response was, "consider it an eviction notice."

Meese would later be implicated in the October Surprise scandal, which propelled Ronald Reagan into the White House via a secret deal to release the hostages in Iran after the defeat of Jimmy Carter. As his reward, Meese was appointed Attorney General, where he would go on to commit, then cover-up other crimes, the two most notorious being Iran-Contra and the Inslaw affair.

Keating served in the Bush administration as Assistant Treasury Secretary during the Iran-Contra investigations. Former Tulsa police officer and Army CID investigator Gene Wheaton, who worked for the Christic Institute, observes that Bush personally selected Keating as Assistant Treasury Secretary in 1985, where he supervised INTERPOL, the Customs Service, the Secret Service, and the ATF.

As Wheaton writes:

The word in Tulsa is that Bush is his "political godfather" that Keating got his job in the Treasury Department through Bush's good offices and that Bush "loves Keating." The connection appears to be an old-boy connection through the Southern Hills Country Club in Tulsa, Oklahoma.[612]

"In his position, Keating could control both the investigative and prosecutorial side of any scandal that came his way," adds *Portland Free Press* publisher Ace Hayes. "1985-88 had guns, drugs, and illegal money moving all over the globe. Was the ATF, who couldn't find its ass with both hands, really as incompetent as it appeared, or was Frank Keating there to make sure they did not?"[613]

While Keating served as Assistant Treasury Secretary, IRS investigator Bill Duncan—who was investigating Iran-Contra drug-running activities at Mena—was instructed to perjure himself. As Duncan stated in a deposition before a joint Congressional/Arkansas Attorney General investigative committee:

Duncan: In late December of 1987, I was contacted by [the] Chief Counsel for the House Judiciary Subcommittee on Crime … who told me that they were looking into the reason why no one was indicted in connection with the Mena investigations. The Internal Revenue Service assigned to me disclosure litigation attorneys, which gave me instructions which would have caused me to withhold information from Congress during my testimony and to also perjure myself.

Committee: And how did you respond to the Treasury Department?

Duncan: Well, I exhibited to them that I was going to tell the truth in my testimony. And the perjury, subornation of perjury resulted because of an allegation that I had received, that Attorney General Edwin Meese received a several hundred thousand dollar bribe from Barry Seal directly. And they told me to tell the Subcommittee on Crime that I had no information about that.[614]

Arkansas State Police investigator Russell Welch, who provided the information to Duncan, was subsequently poisoned. Two months later, Keating was appointed Associate Attorney General.

It seems that Frank Keating has served as a point-man, weaving a twisted trail through some of America's most notorious crimes, including Iran-Contra, BCCI, Iraqgate, the S&L crisis, and … Oklahoma City. Keating has always been at the nexus bridging the agendas of good ol' boys like George Bush, with their elitist agendas, and the subsequent covert-operations subcultures they spawned. In an article in the *Portland Free Press* entitled "Another Bush Boy," Wheaton writes:

The covert-operations "lunatic fringe" in Washington, which took over key operations at the national security level, [and] still controls them today, was Bush's 1981 agenda, and Keating is the next generation to carry it on.*

The Oklahoma City bombing occurred just three months after Keating's inauguration as Governor. Given his background and grooming, Keating was in a perfect position to direct "damage control." As Wheaton notes:

> Keating is an a perfect position to control the direction and scope of any state investigation which might not correspond to the official federal inquiry.

It appears Keating did just that. As Governor, Keating could have halted the hurried demolition of the Murrah building, ordered by federal authorities under the guise of "safety." Bob Ricks, the FBI PR flack who spoon-fed a daily dose of fibs to the press during the Waco siege, was appointed Oklahoma Director of Public Safety by Keating after the demolition. Keating and Ricks were good friends from college.

The demolition was ordered under the pseudo-psychological premise of providing "closure" to the festering wound hanging over the city. The demolition also effectively prevented any independent foresnsic investigation of the bomb site.**

Said a victim whose spouse was killed in the explosion, "I was upset right from the start when there was the big rush to destroy the crime scene, to take the building down. A lot of important evidence was destroyed that could have helped solve this." [615]

The Feds' decision to destroy crucial forensic evidence has an eerie parallel to the demolition of Mt. Carmel. Destroying the Branch Davidian church prevented independent examiners from determining the ATF had fired into the roofs of the building during the early part of the raid, and that FBI snipers deliberately shot people trying to escape.

The destruction of the Murrah Building is also akin to the Secret Service's hasty (or carefully planned) decision to illegally remove President Kennedy's body from Parkland Memorial Hospital. Once under control of military officials, including Generals who were likely involved in the assassination plot, Kennedy's autopsy could proceed under carefully controlled parameters. While observing

---

* Wheaton suggests that Keating is being groomed for the 2000 presidential [or vice-presidential] candidacy.

** The same reason for demolishing the Federal Building was given for demolishing the buildings at Waco: "Safety concerns." Yet the Waco buildings were miles from anywhere. Furthermore, an architect who inspected the Federal Building soon after the bombing said there was no immediate danger. But, according to David Hall, owner of KPOC-TV in Ponca City, Oklahoma, this architect was later "persuaded" to change his opinion.

the autopsy, these military officials prevented a thorough examination of the body, which would have revealed the presence of multiple entry wounds. Back in Dallas, Secret Service agents carefully washed Kennedy's limousine to remove all traces of bullet fragments, and had Governor Connolly's clothes, bulletholes and all, cleaned and pressed.

Said Jannie Coverdale, who lost her grandsons Aaron and Elijah in the bombing, "Everyone I talk to has the same questions: What happened? What is going on? We don't want this to be another John F. Kennedy deal, where 32 years later the real story is still unknown."

THE FEDERAL BUREAU OF INTIMIDATION

"There is no place on earth where you will be safe from the most powerful forces of justice."

—FBI Director Louis Freeh.

In a motion filed by Stephen Jones, affidavits show that numerous witnesses were instructed by the FBI to "keep quiet" so the facts of the case "wouldn't get distorted." This aura of secrecy quickly turned into obstruction of justice, as FBI agents routinely instructed witnesses not to talk to defense team investigators or journalists.

When defense investigator Marty Reed attempted to interview Oklahoma Highway Patrolman Charlie Hanger (the patrolman who arrested McVeigh), he was told by OHP chief legal counsel John Lindsey, "The FBI has requested that no one interview Trooper Charlie Hanger."

Mitchell Whitmire, who knew McVeigh when they were both in the Army, was contacted by defense investigator Neil Hartley. Whitmire told Hartley he was instructed by the FBI not to talk to anyone about the case unless he obtained permission from the FBI.[616]

When this author tried to interview two members of the Sheriff's Bomb Squad, they became visibly nervous. They claimed that no other bombs were pulled out of the building, clearly contradicting news accounts showing additional bombs that were taken away and detonated.

As discussed previously, FBI agents put up a protective perimeter around Eldon Elliott, preventing him from talking to journalists and defense investigators.

KFOR-TV, who took the lead in investigating the case, found it almost impossible to interview witnesses. "We get there and all of a sudden they've been told to shut up," said Melissa Klinzing, KFOR's former News Director.[617]

A Tulsa Fire Captain told investigator Craig Roberts he saw machine-gun toting black-clad agents with no markings removing boxes of files from the post office ten days after the bombing. When he was subsequently interviewed by this author, he denied seeing anything.

Ann Domin, who originally told a Tulsa police officer she had seen two Middle Eastern males loitering near the front of the Murrah Building just before the blast, later denied saying that.[618]

According to a conversation Jon Rappaport had with *Daily Oklahoman* reporter Ann Defrange, witness Peter Schaffer told Defrange he had seen the Murrah Building collapse in on itself, suggesting that cutting charges were used. When Rappaport questioned Schaffer, he denied seeing the building falling down at all. When Rappaport got back to Defrange, she remained adamant about what Schaffer told her. "She didn't budge at all," said Rappaport.[619]

"The FBI must have gotten to him," said Heidelberg. "You know, the FBI has been able to get witnesses to shut up about important things they know. We've talked to some of these people. In certain instances the witnesses believe that concealing evidence is the right thing to do. They really believe it. The FBI has sold them a bill of goods about national security or something like that. In other cases the FBI has used straight-out intimidation on witnesses. They size up people. On one witness they'll use something like national security. On another, they'll go for intimidation." [620]

Heidelberg's own brush with the government didn't end with his dismissal from the Grand Jury. Several minutes after agreeing to do an interview with Jayna Davis, he received a call from U.S. Attorney Joseph Hartzler telling him that a reporter was on her way and that he was not to talk to her, or he would be arrested. Obviously, Heidelberg's phone was tapped.*

"They tried everything to shut me up," said Heidelberg. "They have said they were going to throw me in jail. When that didn't work, they got down on their hands and knees and begged. I mean … they have tried everything to keep me from talking to the press about this."

On July 19, FBI agents Jon Hersley and William Teater appeared at Heidelberg's home, just hours after Judge Russell called him and discovered he had taken his Grand Jury notes home. Apparently Teater wasn't too pleased with Heidelberg's casual attitude. At one point, he pulled back his jacket, revealing his gun, which he had conspicuously stuck in his waistbelt.

"They were trying to give me the message that this is big time, that this is heavyweight," said Heidelberg, "and I was supposed to be frightened … Guns mean business … I was supposed to behave and be a good boy and not give them any trouble. The implication was that they were gonna' shoot me, but I knew better than that," Heidelberg said.**

---

* In fact, many times when I have spoken to Heidelberg, I could hear the distinctive clicks of a tapped phone.

** "They sent another team out on October 20," added Heidelberg. "Agents Marry Judd

Heidelberg doesn't feel he will serve any jail time for his actions. "They don't want me exonerated or indicted," said Heidelberg. "They want me twisting in the wind." [621]

In February of '97, ABC planned a follow-up to their 20/20 "Prior Knowledge" piece, which included an interview with ATF informant Carol Howe. Hours before the piece was to air on World News Tonight, it was killed.

According to former ABC producer Roger Charles: "They were uncomfortable with it after a series of phone calls from high-level Justice Department and ATF people, saying that well, yes, the story is right, but you're going to draw the wrong conclusions unless we can explain it." According to an interview with ABC conducted by McVeigh's defense team, the conversation went something like this:

Justice Dept: "We have to admit now Strassmeir has been investigated."
ABC: "But you have denied over and over that he was ever the subject of an investigation."
Justice Dept: "Well, we're undenying that now. He has been investigated, but we could not involve him specifically in the bombing of the building.... [Regarding Howe's reports of others involved, we] "could not find anyone who bought fertilizer, could not find anyone who rented a truck, so therefore we could not charge them with anything. [Besides], we're not sure the information was credible."
ABC: "But did you or did you not send her back out?"
Justice Dept: "Yes, she was sent back out."
ABC: "Well, what in the hell does that mean?"
Justice Dept: "She did go back out, but she was unable to develop any evidence that these people had participated, [although] essentially your information is correct."

ABC then said the Justice Department press spokesman attempted to downplay the credibility of Howe by stating that the government hears these types of statements all the time from "White Supremacist compounds."

ABC: "Yeah, but there's one difference here."
Justice Dept: "What is that?"
ABC: "The goddamn building blew up, that's what." [622]

Cheryl Wood, an employee at Love's convenience store, who saw Timothy McVeigh and John Doe 2 on April 17, told FBI agents their security camera had

---

and Dave Swanson. "They said 'do you know how much trouble you're in?,' and I said 'well, apparently not,' and I just laughed at them like I'm laughing now [bursts out laughing]. And they don't know what the hell to do with that. What do you do with a guy that just laughs at you?"

captured images of the two men. The FBI didn't take the tapes and didn't want to use Wood's story. "They tried to convince Wood that she was crazy—that she hadn't really seen them," said a *Newsweek* reporter who interviewed Wood. "They rattled her real good." When the store manager decided to take the video home himself, the FBI changed their minds, and confiscated the tape.

McVeigh and his friends also stopped at another convenience store about 45 minutes from Love's. As a *Newsweek* reporter who interviewed the employees told me, the FBI didn't use the statements of those witnesses either, because it didn't fit the FBI's official timeline.[623]

Mike Moroz, the Johnny's Tire Shop employee who gave McVeigh and John Doe 2 directions to the Murrah Building on the morning of the blast, was interviewed by the FBI several times. On the last interview they told him that he had seen McVeigh drive in a different direction than he originally stated. The FBI then claimed to the press that Moroz had made a mistake and was confused.

Danny Wilkerson, the Regency Towers employee who sold McVeigh two soft drinks and a pack of cigarettes 10 minutes before the bombing, claims FBI agents tried very hard to get him to change his story. Wilkerson saw McVeigh and another man in an older, shorter Ryder truck with a cab overhang. FBI agents showed Wilkerson a catalog of different Ryder models, trying to coerce him into stating that the truck he saw was bigger and newer than the one actually seen. Wilkerson refused to change his story.

As previously discussed, Catina Lawson knew McVeigh when he was stationed in Kansas, and saw him at parties with Andreas Strassmeir and Michael Brescia. When Lawson saw the artist's sketch of John Doe 2, she said, "That's Mike [Brescia]. Lawson repeatedly called the FBI to tell them it was Brescia, but they didn't want to listen, and stopped returning her calls.

"I kept telling them that the man in the [John Doe 2] sketch was that Mike guy, a nice-looking guy, dark-skinned. But the FBI made me feel guilty, then ignorant, as if I didn't know what I was saying. Then, later, I tried to call in with more information and they wouldn't even talk to me."

Debra Burdick had seen the yellow Mercury, the brown pick-up, and the blue Chevy Cavalier at 10th and Robinson on the morning of the blast. Burdick called the FBI and the OSBI, and "they blew me off. They said they didn't have time to get over there…. They told me, 'you didn't see anything.' And that's when I thought I was going crazy…."[624]

Jane Graham, along with three other women, had seen a trio of suspicious-looking men in the Murrah Building's underground garage the Friday before the bombing. The men were working with wire and a small, putty-colored block which appeared to be C-4 plastic explosives.

FBI Agent Joe Schwecke made two appointments to interview Graham, but kept neither of them. "He never showed up," said Graham. "I again called and set up another appointment for the following week and that was never kept."

When Schwecke finally spoke to her, he "only wanted to know if I could identify McVeigh or Nichols. Apparently the FBI was not interested in any time other than the Monday or Tuesday—the week of the bombing!" exclaimed Graham, "and only if the responses pointed directly to McVeigh!" [625]

The manager of the Great Western Inn in Junction City was certain the Middle Eastern man who had stayed in room 107 on April 17 was a dead ringer for John Doe 2. Yet the FBI tried to discredit him, saying that the inquiry there had been a waste of time. If that is true, why did the FBI confiscate the hotel's register? [626]

Barbara Whittenberg at the Sante Fe Trail Diner told Bill Jasper the FBI tried to get her to change her story. [627]

Jeff Davis, who delivered Chinese food to a man in room 25 at the Dreamland Motel, had been interviewed numerous times by the FBI. They appeared interested in trying to get Davis to say that McVeigh was the man he saw.

During McVeigh's trial, prosecutor Larry Mackey attacked Davis' credibility, noting that two days after the bombing, he told FBI agents that the man was a white male, 28 or 29, about six feet tall, about 180 pounds with short, sandy hair, clean-cut with no mustache.[*]

Yet Davis originally told the FBI, "The man to whom I delivered that bag of Chinese food is not Tim McVeigh." [628]

Still, Mackey tried to shake Davis' confidence in his memory, suggesting Davis had told a bartender and an ABC sketch artist that he saw McVeigh.

> **Mackey:** "You deny that?"
> **Davis:** "Yes sir, I do,"

In fact, the person Davis saw had "unkempt" hair, a regional accent, possibly from Oklahoma, Kansas or Missouri, and an overbite. McVeigh possesses none of these characteristics. [629]

"I was frustrated quite a bit because they just didn't seem to want to say 'Okay, there's somebody we may not have.' A lot of it seemed 'Damn! I just wish he'd say it was McVeigh so we could be done with it.'" [**]

---

[*] Mackey also accused Davis of telling a bartender in Denver that McVeigh was in the room. Davis denied it.

[**] During the Pan Am 103 investigation, authorities attempted to coerce a civilian searcher into signing a statement that he had discovered a piece of microchip on which the government's theory hinged. In fact, the searcher was brought a bag of various unidentified components and asked to sign the statement, even though he wasn't sure he had found the items.

Davis told *The Denver Post* that the FBI never even bothered making a composite sketch of the man he saw. A TV network finally hired an artist to do one.

Daina Bradley had seen only one man—olive-skinned, dark-haired, wearing jeans, jacket, and baseball cap—get out of the passenger side of the Ryder truck in front of the Federal Building moments before it blew up. Yet when she testified for the defense during McVeigh's trial, she switched tracks, saying she saw two suspects.

In numerous interviews with the media, prosecutors, and the defense team, Bradley maintained that she had seen only one suspect—John Doe 2. Weeks before her testimony, Bradley again told U.S. Attorney Patrick Ryan and defense attorney Cheryl Ramsey she was certain the man she saw wasn't Timothy McVeigh.

Yet shortly after the start of McVeigh's trial—after meeting with federal prosecutors—Bradley suddenly "changed her mind." FBI agents were conveniently waiting at the airport to intercept some of McVeigh's defense witnesses, who would be "persuaded" to change their testimony.[630]

Under cross-examination by Ryan, Bradley—who had maintained a rock-solid story of John Doe 2 since the day of the bombing—now claimed she saw a second man. Yet during trial she was nervous and faltering, her testimony wavering constantly. At one point, she covered her face with her hands and quietly said, "I want to talk to my lawyer."

Ryan eventually got Bradley to say she wasn't sure whether the second suspect was McVeigh, but that there was "nothing different" between McVeigh's features and those of the second man.

In addition, Bradley told the jury she thought the truck was parked against the flow of traffic on the one-way street—a ludicrous proposition, but convenient for a government intent on convincing a jury that Bradley saw the suspect—who was not John Doe 2, but possibly McVeigh—get out of the driver's side.[631]

Gary Lewis, the *Journal Record* pressman almost run over by McVeigh and two of his associates in the yellow Mercury shortly before the blast, suddenly denied seeing them at all. Just before he was subpoenaed to testify before the County Grand Jury, Lewis told reporters, "What I seen wasn't a fact, it wasn't true."

Claiming the FBI "cleared up his confusion" more than a year ago, Lewis said the FBI showed him a photograph of McVeigh's distinctive battered yellow Mercury, and convinced him it wasn't the same car he spotted on April 19. "It was real similar to it," Lewis said. "It was real close but it wasn't it."

Lewis then claimed his eyewitness account, which had already been published in striking detail, had been exaggerated by Representative Key and Glenn Wilburn. "I don't care for [Wilburn] or Charles Key," Lewis told *The Daily Oklahoman*. "They kind of pushed it along for reasons I don't know why. That is about all I have got to say." [632]

This was quite a change from the nervous witness who checked the underside of his car every morning for bombs, afraid he was targeted for assassination by either bombing suspects or the Feds.[633]

As previously mentioned, Dr. Paul Heath, the VA psychologist, had spoken to McVeigh and two of his associates at his office several weeks before the blast when they approached him looking for "jobs."

Heath was interviewed by the FBI no less than 10 times. On the last visit, "[The FBI agent] confronted me saying he did not want me telling the story any longer. He said it was a false story, that I had made it up, that it was a figment of my imagination, and that if I pursued it, he would publicly discredit me.

"I said to him, 'that is the most despicable, uncalled-for attitude I've ever seen, and I don't know why you said that to me, but I can tell you, you're not going to change my reality with it.'" Heath, already upset by what he witnessed the day of the bombing, is now uncertain what will happen to him.[634]

Lea Moore, a woman badly injured in the blast, was contacted by a reporter from the *Los Angeles Times*. While he was en-route to interview her, she received a mysterious phone call telling her not to talk to him. Moore, a diminutive woman in her 50s, was frightened. When the reporter showed up at her door 15 minutes later, Moore didn't answer.

Melba, the Albertson's worker who made sandwiches for McVeigh and John Doe 2, was hostile and frightened when questioned by the author—too scared to talk.

Connie Hood, who saw John Doe 2 at the Dreamland Motel shortly after midnight on April 16, then again the next morning, was interviewed numerous times by the FBI. They even went so far as to administer several polygraph tests. Hood told the agents exactly what she saw. On the last test, the FBI agent "turned around and got in her face," recalled her friend David Keen, "and said, 'You've never seen John Doe! He never existed!'"

The experience of Hood and Keen is reminiscent of the interrogation of JFK witnesses in Dallas on November 22, when FBI agents pointedly told them they did not see any shooters on the Grassy Knoll.

"This big old dude [FBI agent] right out told me, 'You did not see that!'" recalled Hood. "It got to the point where I was saying, 'Excuse me, excuse me, there was someone in that room next to us. I know for a fact there was someone in that room next to us. I did not imagine someone coming out of that fricking room!'"

Hood is sure of what she saw, and is furious about the games the FBI played with her. "I'm angry," said Hood. "It made my blood boil."[635]

Nor were journalists investigating Oklahoma City immune from harassment. Jayna Davis, the courageous KFOR reporter who tracked down Hussaini and Khalid, received a warning from the FBI that she was getting "too close" to the truth, and should drop her investigation.

Journalists and investigators attempting to interview rescue workers, including firemen, police and other city officials, were denied interviews. Most workers say they've been told not to talk by their superiors or the FBI. "They're afraid of losing their jobs or being subjected to abuse if they say something," said Jane Graham.

Nurse Toni Garret was one of many people who had volunteered to help tag dead victims that terrible morning. Garret and her husband Earl had just taken a break when they noticed federal agents arriving to set up a command post. "They acted like it was just a drill, like it was no big deal, said Garret. "They were kind of joking around and all that kind of stuff."

Approximately 20 minutes later, when the Garrets re-entered the makeshift triage center, they found many of the doctors and nurses gone, and a completely different atmosphere prevailed. "There was nobody helping anymore," said Earl. "Before, there were people bringing in food and medical supplies—just everything. When we came back in, there was a cold, callous atmosphere. I found out later that the FBI had taken over."

But what really upset Toni Garret was the fact that the FBI and the Medical Examiner were suppressing the body count, which they claimed as only 22 dead. Garret, who had personally tagged over 120 dead bodies that day, was shocked. "I was being interviewed by a lady from TBN [Trinity Broadcasting Network]. I told her that I was highly upset because the news media and the information they were being given was not accurate information. There were many more bodies than what they were saying on the news media and releasing at the time."

"[The FBI] didn't like that Toni was being interviewed by the media," said Earl. "An agent came [up] to me and said, 'Do you know her?' pointing to Toni. I said, 'Yes, she's my wife.' He said, "What is she?' I said, 'Well, she's been down here all day trying to get people out of this building and help people.' He turned around to his friends and said, 'Well, we need to get her out of here.' Toni then told me that the agents had told her that the FBI was taking over and all of us could get out. They told us to keep our mouths shut."

Said Toni, "When they came over to me, one of the agents was very pompous and arrogant about asking me who I was, what I was doing there, if I was a civilian, where I worked, and what my name was. I didn't feel like any of that pertained to what was going on that day or what had happened that day, and he wanted to know everything about me.

"He said, 'Well, we're down here now, and we're taking over the building. It would be advisable and recommendable that you keep your mouth shut."[636]

Norma Smith, who worked at the Federal Courthouse across from the Murrah building saw, with numerous others, the Sheriff's Bomb Squad congregated in the parking lot at 7:30 that morning. Shortly after Smith's story appeared in a local newspaper, her house was broken into—twice. Smith, frightened, took early retirement and moved out of state. She is currently too afraid to talk to anyone.

The Bomb Squad, incidentally, denied being there.

New American editor William Jasper learned from an OCPD officer that during a mandatory daily security briefing at the Murrah Building, he and other assembled police/rescue/recovery personnel were told "in no uncertain terms" by one of the lead federal officials that it was necessary for "security" reasons to provide the public with "misinformation" regarding certain aspects of the case, and that this "official line" was not to be contradicted by any of those in attendance.[637]

"There's a lot that's being covered up, for some reason," charged a federal employee who narrowly escaped death but who lost many friends in the terrorist attack.

Said a man who lost his father, "I'm angry because I know I'm being lied to."

"Many of us are going to come forward and challenge what's going on as soon as we get some more of the pieces figured out," pledged a law enforcement officer.[638]

This same police officer later told me he was called into the offices of OCPD Chief Sam Gonzales and U.S. Attorney Pat Ryan and told to "cease and desist." *

Another officer told to "cease and desist" was Sergeant Terrance Yeakey. On May 8, 1996, only three days before Sergeant Yeakey was to receive the Oklahoma Police Department's Medal of Valor, he "committed suicide." The 30 year-old cop was found in a field near El Reno, not far from where El Reno Prison guard Joey Gladden "committed suicide." Yeakey's wrists were slashed in numerous places, as was his neck and throat. Apparently not satisfied with this initial attempt to take his life, he got out of his car, walked a mile-and-a-half over rough terrain, then pulled out his gun shot himself in the head.

The media claimed Officer Yeakey "was wracked with guilt" over his inability to help more people that fateful morning. They also claimed he led a "troubled family life," having been recently divorced from his wife Tonia, and separated from his two daughters, aged two and four, whom the *Daily Oklahoman* claimed he was not permitted to see due to a restraining order.

Other accounts suggest that Yeakey was reluctant to receive the Medal of Valor due to his "guilt" over being injured in the Murrah Building. "He didn't like it," said his supervisor Lt. Jo Ann Randall. "There are some people that like to be heroes and some that don't. He was not one that wanted that."

"He had a lot of guilt because he got hurt," added fellow officer Jim Ramsey.[639]

Apparently, there was much more behind Officer Yeakey's reluctance to be honored as a hero.

"He kept telling me it wasn't what I thought it was," said his ex-wife, Tonia Rivera, "that they were only choosing officers who were not even at the site, you know—who

---

* He said they made up a bogus complaint about him threatening a reporter. I spoke to that reporter and discovered the complaint was false.

didn't see anything—to take public rewards, recognition, that sort of stuff.

"They started pressuring them into taking [the rewards]," added Rivera. "There came a time about mid-year, where they were forcing him into going to these award ceremonies. As in, 'Yes, you could not go, but we'll make your life hell.'"

The story of the reluctant hero, she added, was nothing more than a "real thin veil of truth" which covered up a "mountain of deceit."

"[T]erry wanted no part of it."*

His sister, Vicki Jones, agreed. "Terry hated that stuff. 'I'm no hero,' he would say. 'Nobody that had anything to do with helping those people in that bombing are heroes.'"

Why would the Medal of Valor recipient make such a bizarre-sounding statement? In a letter he wrote to bombing victim and friend Ramona McDonald, the officer tells the real reason for his reluctance to be honored as a hero:

Dear Ramona,

I hope that whatever you hear now and in the future will not change your opinions about myself or others with the Oklahoma City Police Department, although some of the things I am about to tell you about is [sic] very disturbing.

I don't know if you recall everything that happened that morning or not, so I am not sure if you know what I am referring to.

The man that you and I were talking about in the pictures I have made the mistake of asking too many questions as to his role in the bombing, and was told to back off.

I was told by several officers he was an ATF agent who was overseeing the bombing plot and at the time the photos were taken he was calling in his report of what had just went down!

I think my days as a police officer are numbered because of the way my supervisors are acting and there is [sic] a lot of secrets floating around now about my mental state of mind. I think they are going to write me up because of my ex-wife and a VPO.

I told you about talking to Chaplain Poe, well the bastard wrote up in a report stating I should be relieved of my duties! I made the mistake of thinking that a person's conversation with a chaplain was private, which by the way might have cost me my job as a police officer! A friend at headquarters told me that Poe sent out letters to everyone in the department! That BITCH [Jo Ann Randall] I told you about is up to something and I think it has something to do with Poe. If she gets her way, they will tar and feather me!

I was told that Jack Poe has written up a report on every single officer that has

---

* According to Rivera, the recalcitrant police officer was forced into making a public service announcement with Governor Keating. "He was told he'd make that or he was fired," said Rivera. The officer they sent to Washington to accept an award on behalf of the OCPD, he told Rivera, wasn't even at the site!

been in to see him, including Gordon Martin and John Avery.

Knowing what I know now, and understanding fully just what went down that morning, makes me ashamed to wear a badge from Oklahoma City's Police Department. I took and oath to uphold the Law and to enforce the Law to the best of my ability. This is something I cannot honestly do and hold my head up proud any longer if I keep my silence as I am ordered to do.

There are several others out there who was [sic] what we saw and even some who played a role in what happened that day.

[Two Pages Missing]

My guess is the more time an officer has to think about the screw up the more he is going to question what happened.... Can you imagine what would be coming down now if that had been our officers' who had let this happen? Because it was the Feds that did this and not the locals, is the reason it's okay. You were right all along and I am truly sorry I doubted you and your motives about recording history. You should know that it is going to one-hell-of-a-fight.

Everyone was behind you until you started asking questions as I did, as to how so many federal agents arrived at the scene at the same time.

Luke Franey [an ATF agent who claimed he was in the building] was not in the building at the time of the blast, I know this for a fact, I saw him! I also saw full riot gear worn with rifles in hand, why? Don't make the mistake as I did and ask the wrong people.

I worry about you and your young family because of some of the statements that have been made towards me, a police officer! Whatever you do don't confront McPhearson with the Bomb Squad about what I told you. His actions and defensiveness towards the bombing would make any normal person think he was defending himself as if he drove the damn truck up to the building himself. I am not worried for myself, but for you and your group. I would not be afraid to say at this time that you and your family could be harmed if you get any closer to the truth. At this time I think for your well being it is best for you to distance yourself and others from those of us who have stirred up to many questions about the altering and falsifying of the federal investigation's reports.

I truly believe there are other officers like me out there who would not settle for anything but the truth, it is just a matter of finding them. The only true problem as I see it is, who do we turn to then?

It is vital that people like you, Edye Smith, and others keep asking questions and demanding answers for the actions of our Federal Government and law enforcement agencies that knew beforehand and participated in the cover-up.

The sad truth of the matter is that they have so many police officers convinced that by covering up the truth about the operation gone wrong, that they are actually doing our citizens a favor. What I want to know is how many other operations have they had that blew up in their faces? Makes you stop and take another look at Waco.

I would consider it to be an insult to my profession as a police officer and to the citizens of Oklahoma for ANY of the City, State or Federal agents that stood by and let this happen to be recognized as any thing other than their part in participation in letting this happen. For those who ran from the scene to change their attire to hide the fact that they were there, should be judged as cowards.

If our history books and records are ever truly corrected about that day it will show this and maybe even some lame excuse as to why it happened, but I truly don't believe it will from what I now know to be the truth.

Even if I tried to explain it to you the way it was explained to me, and the ridiculous reason for having out own police departments falsify reports to their fellow officers, to the citizens of the city and to our country, you would understand why I feel the way I do about all of this.

I believe that a lot of the problems the officers are having right now are because some of them know what really happened and can't deal with it, and others like myself made the mistake of trusting the one person we were supposed to be able to turn to [Chaplain Poe] only to be stabbed in the back.

I am sad to say that I believe my days as a police officer are numbered because of all of this....

Officer Terrance Yeakey was not the type of person to easily show his feelings. He didn't want to tell his family anything that might get them hurt.

"He told me enough to let me know that it was not what they were making it out to be," said Rivera, "and that he was disgusted and didn't want any part of it, but he never went into detail. It scared me."*

According to a sympathetic government source who has spoken to Rivera, Yeakey began receiving death threats within days of the bombing. He was at his ex-wife's apartment when the calls came. Afraid for his family, he got up and left.

"When he came to my apartment two weeks prior, trying to give me these insurance policies," said Rivera, "he sat on my living room couch and cried and told me how he had a fight with [his supervisors] Lt. Randall and Maj. Upchurch. He did not tell me what that entailed, but he was scared—he was crying so badly he was shaking.

"He wouldn't totally voice whatever it was," recalled Rivera. "It was like he'd be just about to tell me—he'd want to spill his guts—and then he stopped, and he just cried. And that's when he kept insisting that I take the insurance policy."

Although Yeakey was concerned for his family, the marriage was not without abuse. Rivera had filed a VPO (Victim's Protective Order) against him slightly

---

* Yeakey was also angry because he couldn't get access to his own report about the bombing (which numbered between 9-10 pages). "He was in a full-fledged rampage over the report," said Rivera, whom he wouldn't even show it to.

over two years ago. In a fit of temper, Yeakey had once threatened to take his life and those of his wife and children.

"I think it was said in the haste of, well, he's going to kill all of us kind of thing—cop under pressure," said Rivera. But that was over a year and-a-half ago. Yeakey spent considerable time with his wife and children since then, taking them on family outings and so forth.

Nevertheless, the Oklahoma City Police Department (OCPD) attempted to use the incident to claim that Yeakey was suicidal. It was on the day of his death, around 1:30 P.M., that they called Rivera, trying to get her to file a VPO Violation based on the two-year-old report. "They wanted me to come down and make some statements against him," Rivera said.

On the same afternoon, in-between messages on his answering machine from his sister, Vicki Jones and Lt. Jo Ann Randall, Yeakey had a message from Tonia. "The message was like at 5:30 in the afternoon," recalled Rivera. "I sound like I'm whispering, and I'm apologizing for waking him up—at 5:30 in the afternoon—on Wednesday."

It seems the intent behind this cleverly-crafted deception was to convince the family and potential investigators that Rivera was an "evil person," who was sleeping with him the night before, but "went down and filed a VPO the next day."

"That tape was planted," said Rivera. "I never called his house."

It seemed the OCPD was playing an elaborate game to sow confusion and mistrust to create the appearance that Rivera was responsible for her ex-husband's death.

"So it comes out in paper after paper how he's having problems with his ex-wife, how he's not allowed to see his children. They're trying to play up the story of the bitch-ass wife whose trying to get him fired."

Yet Rivera claimed she never filed a VPO violation. "The OCPD wanted to file one," said Rivera. "But I never signed it." Rivera claimed she had gone to the police station, but simply out of concern for her ex-husband, who had been acting strangely.

"Nobody ever said, 'Mrs. Yeakey, Terry's missing. Do you know anyplace he might have gone to? They never told me that they weren't able to locate him, that they were concerned, you know—nothing. I never knew he was missing."

If Officer Yeakey's death was anything more than a suicide, the OCPD didn't go to any great lengths to find out. While Yeakey's death occurred in El Reno, the OCPD took over the crime scene, squeezing the El Reno Police Department out of the picture. The OCPD's Media Relations officer, Cpt. Ted Carlton, explained, "It was our police officer who was killed. It's not uncommon [to take over the investigation] in the case of a smaller police agency." [640]

Although forensics are also standard procedure in the event of a violent or suspicious death, especially that of a police officer, Yeakey's car was never dusted for prints. "And the next day, they gave us the damn car!" said Mrs. Jarrahi. "It was full of blood."

When Yeakey's brother-in-law, Glenn Jones, inspected the dead man's car, he discovered a bloody knife stashed underneath the glove compartment. Yet according to the responding officer, Yeakey used a razor blade. Where did the knife come from? Since no forensic investigation was conducted, this remains unclear.

No autopsy was ever conducted.

"There were common sense things that were wrong about the whole thing, that makes it so weird," added Mrs. Jarrahi. "It just doesn't seem right. Why would policemen and the authorities make such common mistakes that would leave questions? It's just really weird."

If Yeakey's death was suicide, he left no note. Although he was upset over his divorce, according to the family, he was *not* suicidal. It is also unlikely that he abused drugs, as he was an instructor at DARE, a program designed to keep children *off* drugs.

Former Canadian County Sheriff Clint Boehler, who claims to have known Yeakey, doesn't concur with this analysis. Boehler said that Yeakey showed up at his house in El Reno on the afternoon of his death, his car stopped at an angle in the middle of the road. When Boehler and his girlfriend Kate Allen, a paramedic, ran outside, they found the police officer virtually passed out.

"He couldn't tell us his name initially," said Allen. "He was ill, and he was very anxious. His heart rate was rapid; he was sweaty.... He told us he had been having concentration problems, he hadn't slept. He had all the appearances, my first guess would be, of someone who was having emotional problems. And my second guess would be, of some kind of substance abuse problem. But that's a pure guess."

Boehler added that Yeakey said he hadn't eaten, and was throwing up, taking medication, and incoherent. "He was taking medications for his back," said Boehler. "He had four or five medications in the car."

Boehler and Allen didn't know that Yeakey had Sickle-Cell Anemia—a blood-sugar-related condition that caused seizures. It was these seizures, Rivera explained, that would occasionally cause her ex-husband to act "out-of-sorts," or even to slip into unconsciousness.

According to Canadian County Sheriff Deputy Mike Ransey (no relation to OCPD Officer Jim Rasey), who drove Yeakey home, Yeakey was not suicidal. "He didn't give me any indications that he was out to do harm to himself," said Ramsey. "He seemed more disoriented, tired."

Many things about Officer Yeakey's death remain a mystery. While Boehler described a man on drugs, the Medical Examiner claims they didn't bother to conduct a drug test because it "costs too much." [641]

The ME's field investigator, Jeffrey Legg, also reported that Yeakey "had been drinking heavily" the day before, based on statements made by OCPD Homicide

Detectives Dicus and Mullinex. Yet Terrance Yeakey didn't drink, and their own report concluded that there was no alcohol in the body at the time of death.

Canadian County Sheriffs discovered the abandoned car, filled with blood, about two and-a-half miles from the old El Reno reformatory. The OCPD was notified, and Police Chief Sam Gonazles flew out by chopper. Using dogs, they followed a trail of blood, and found the body in a ditch, about a mile and-a-half from the car. (Legg reported the body was one-half mile south of the car, when in fact it was one-and-a-half miles northeast of the car.)

Apparently Yeakey tried to cut himself in the wrists, neck, and throat, then, after losing approximately two pints of blood, got out of his car (conscientiously remembering to lock the doors), walking a mile-and-a-half over rough terrain, crawling under a barbed-wire fence, wading through a culvert, then laying down in a ditch to shoot himself in the head.*

As is this weren't strange enough, Yeakey's diet-related condition would have made him too weak to walk the mile and-a-half from his car to where his body was found—especially after losing two to three pints of blood.

Nevertheless, the OCPD ruled suicide on the spot. Their investigation remains sealed. This reporter was unable to obtain it, and not even the family was allowed to see it.

Right before Yeakey's murder, the couple's Ford Explorer began getting mysterious flats. "When I'd roll it into a shop," said Rivera, "they'd pull out like six or seven nails." This occurred between eight and ten times, she claims. On April 24, two weeks before Yeakey was found dead, the Explorer began acting strangely. When Rivera pulled it into the local Aamco Transmission Center, she found that it had been tampered with. "Somebody who knew what they were doing pulled hoses from your car," said Todd Taylor, the chief mechanic. "I'm sorry to tell this ma'am, but this is not just something you can pull randomly...." Taylor also said he though Rivera's brakes had been tampered with.[642]

About two weeks before this story went to press, the Ford's brakes went out suddenly while Rivera was traveling at 40 mph. "I went to brake," said Rivera, "and guess what? No brakes!" The large 4×4 slammed into the back of smaller car, damaging it badly. "The message is 'we can get to you if we want to,'" she concluded.

After Yeakey's death, the OCPD began conducting surveillance on the dead man's family. Harassment against Officer Yeakey's family wasn't limited to mere

---

* Several Medical Examiners explained that it is not uncommon for an individual to attempt suicide by one method, then continue to take additional measures until they are dead. San Francisco's ME told me about a man who, upon discovering he had AIDS, tried to hang himself, then threw himself off the balcony. Perhaps Terrance Yeakey was not satisfied with his alleged attempts to slash himself. As Dr. Fred Jordan, Oklahoma's Chief Medical Examiner explained, "It hurts, and nothing much is happening."

surveillance. After Rivera met with State Representative Charles Key, her car was broken into. Her house was broken into twice.

If Terrance Yeakey had friends in the Police Department, they were among the beat patrolmen, not the upper echelon. According to Rivera, the brass "hated his guts." "Him and [Maj.] Upchurch had a hate-hate relationship," she said.

For his part, detective Mullinex claims he was "totally unaware" of any problems Yeakey was having in regards to what he knew about the bombing. "It is my opinion as a 14-year homicide veteran that it was a suicide," said Mullinex.... If we thought it was anything [other than a suicide] we would have pursued it to the ends of the earth. We're not hiding anything." [643]

According to Rivera, three government sources, including a U.S. Attorney and a U.S. Marshal, hold a slightly different view. As relayed by Rivera, Officer Yeakey's death transpired as follows:

At 9 A.M., Officer Yeakey was seen exiting his Oklahoma City apartment with nine boxes of videos and files. He then drove to the police station where he had a fight with his supervisors.

He was told to "drop it" or he'd "wind up dead."

Yeakey was also due for a meeting with the heads of several federal agencies that morning. He apparently decided to skip the meetings, instead, driving straight to a storage locker he maintained in Kingfisher.

What he didn't realize was that the FBI had him under surveillance, and began pursuit. The six-year OCPD veteran and former Sheriff's Deputy easily eluded his pursuers. Once at his storage facility, he secured his files.

What were in the files? According to one of Rivera's sources, incriminating photos and videos of the bombed-out building. Perhaps more.

On the way back, the Feds caught up with him just outside of El Reno. "He had nothing on him," at that point, said Rivera, "just copies of copies."

While it is not precisely known what transpired next, Rivera's confidential source "described in intimate detail" the state of the dead man's car. The seats were completely unbolted, the floorboards ripped up, and the side panels removed, all in an apparent effort to find the incriminating documents.

There were also burn marks on the floor. Apparently, the killers used Yeakey's car to destroy what little evidence they discovered. [644]

The report released from the Medical Examiner described numerous "superficial" lacerations on the wrists, arms, throat, and neck, and a single bullet wound to the right temple, which entered just above and in front of the right ear, and had exited towards the bottom of the left ear. A person shooting themself would tend to hold the gun at an upward angle, or at the most, level. It would rather difficult for a large, muscle-bound man like Yeakey to hold a heavy service revolver or other large caliber weapon at a downward angle to their head.

While Dr. Larry Balding, Oklahoma City's Chief Medical Examiner, quickly ruled the death a "suicide," another Medical Examiner's report would, according to Rivera, surface like an eerie, prescient message from the grave. This other report, redacted and hidden from public view, showed a face that was bruised and swollen; blood on the body and clothes that was not the dead man's blood type; and multiple deep lacerations filled with grass and dirt, as though the body had been dragged a distance.

While attending a social function, Rivera claims her sister had a chance encounter with the mortician who worked on Yeakey's body. She was discussing the strange inconsistencies of his death with someone at the party, when the mortician, not knowing the woman was Rivera's sister, spoke up. "That sounds just like a police officer we worked on in Oklahoma City," he said. When asked if that man happened to be Terrance Yeakey, the mortician "freaked."

When pressed, he told the shocked relative that the dead man's wrists contained rope burns and handcuff marks. The mortician said that Yeakey's lacerations were already sewn up when the body arrived from the Medical Examiner's office. Dr. Balding's response was that the marks were merely "skin slippage" resulting from the natural decomposition.

While the family was at Police Headquarters, an officer who Rivera described as Yeakey's "only true friend," pulled them off to the side, and whispered, "They killed him." [645]

Like Terrance Yeakey, the press claimed Dr. Don Chumley was saddened and disturbed he hadn't helped more people the terrible day. Chumley, who ran the Broadway Medical Clinic about half a mile from the Federal Building, was one of the first to arrive at the bombing site on April 19. Shaun Jones, Chumley's stepson, was assisting him. Jones recalled the scene:

"They had sent us around to the underground parking garage, where some people were trapped. Suddenly, three guys come running out of the basement yelling, 'There's a bomb! A bomb! It's gonna blow!' Everybody panicked and ran screaming away from the building as fast as they could."

Chumley, who was working with Dr. Ross Harris, was one of the few doctors who actually went into the Federal Building, while the others waited outside. He had helped many people, including seven babies, whom he later pronounced dead.

Chumley was killed five months later when his Cessna 210 crashed near Amarillo, Texas in what Stephen Jones calls "mysterious circumstances."

"It's a pretty mysterious circumstance," said McVeigh's attorney. "There's no apparent reason—there's nothing we can think of."

Jones added that Chumley had been in a minor wreck during a landing a year earlier when his plane became trapped in a vortex caused by a large jet landing nearby. The small plane was forced into a snow bank causing some damage to its left wing tip. The damage had been repaired.

Would this contradict Jones' hypothesis?

"Well, from talking to pilots I that know, they say that can't cause a plane to crash. I mean, as good a pilot as he is, that's not going to cause his plane to go straight down into the ground. Another pilot said, 'That's just like a car that's out of alignment—it happens all the time—it's just something you learn to fly with.' The plane had been flown several times since that."

According to reports in *The Daily Oklahoman*, Chumley, who was on a hunting trip that weekend, had twice landed earlier—on Friday, due to bad weather conditions. The crash occurred three days later, on a Monday.

"The thing that's odd to me is that Don was perfectly healthy," said Jones. "He was talking to the tower, and from one minute to the next he just went straight smack down into the ground."[646]

Investigators said they could find no evidence of an explosion at the macabre scene. Chumley's throttle was still set at cruise, and his gear and flaps were up. The FAA inspector stated there were "no anomalies with the engine or the airframe," and "pathological examination of the pilot did not show any preexisting condition that could have contributed to the accident."[647]

"To me it's unusual because I know he was a good pilot," added Jones. "Everything was fine, he was in the air for 15 minutes, he was climbing, he had just asked permission to go from six to seven thousand feet. They tracked him on the screen at 6,900 feet, and the radar technician said he saw him on the radar, then he looked back and he was gone, and the plane came straight, straight down. I mean, no attempt to land ... nothing, just straight down."

Mike Evett, a Federal Public Defender, had known Don Chumley for over twenty years. "I would never get into an airplane with anybody I didn't know," said Evett, "and I would never be afraid to fly with Don. For the life of me, this doesn't sit right with me."[648]

Did Dr. Chumley crash on the evening of September 25th due to bad weather? Did he commit suicide due to his grief over what he saw on the morning of April 19th? Or was Don Chumley murdered?

It was rumored that Chumley was about to go public with some damning information. According to a local journalist who has investigated the bombing, Chumley was asked to bandage two federal agents who falsely claimed to have been trapped in the building morning. Since the pair was obviously not hurt, Chumley refused. When the agents petitioned another doctor at the scene, Chumley intervened, threatening to report them.

Don Chumley evidently learned of the government's hastily planned cover-up surrounding the Oklahoma City bombing.

Had he, like so many others, made the decision to go public?

Glenn Wilburn, who lost his grandsons Chase and Colton in the bombing, was one of the very first to go public. A staunch opponent of the government's case, Wilburn teamed up with reporter J.D. Cash and State Representative

Charles Key to investigate the crime. His evidence was proving more and more embarrassing to authorities.

About a year after he began his investigation, Wilburn, 46, came down with a sudden case of pancreatic cancer. Initially recovering after surgery, he died on July 15, 1997, the day after the County Grand Jury which he convened began hearing evidence.

Three weeks later, on August 5, Assistant U.S. Attorney Ted Richardson was found in a church parking lot with a shotgun wound to the chest. The Medical Examiner's report stated: "No powder residue is apparent, either on the external aspect of the wound or in the shirt." An interesting observation considering Richardson had allegedly pushed a shotgun up to his chest and pulled the trigger.[649]

The death was ruled a "suicide." *

Yet the circumstances seemed to concur. Richardson had been depressed. He had been seeing a psychiatrist and was on Prozac. He once told a hunting buddy he "felt like ending it all."[650]

One sunny morning, Richardson rose, fed his two dogs, got in his car, drove to a church near his house, pulled out a shotgun and shot himself through the heart.

He left no note.

Was Ted Richardson depressed enough to kill himself? And if so, why? The 49-year-old father of two had a happy marriage, and adored his 8-year-old son.

The two weeks he took off of work due to unexplained "pressures" may provide a clue. Richardson was the bombing and arson specialist for the Western District of Oklahoma. He was inexplicably transferred to the bank robbery detail after the bombing—an area in which he had no expertise. As his brother Dan explained, "Ted should have gotten the bombing case." **

Instead, the case was given to Joseph Hartzler.

Friends described Richardson as "one of the few good guys," and a man with a "strong sense of conscience."[651] It is uncertain if the same can be said of Hartzler. Given the Federal Government's conduct in this case, such labels might tend to render a man such as Richardson a piranha.

Interestingly, Richardson was the U.S. Attorney who prosecuted Sam Khalid in 1990 for insurance fraud. It was rumored that he was looking into Khalid's suspicious activities subsequent to the bombing, and was about to bring charges.

He decided to kill himself instead.

Is it a coincidence these individuals, who witnessed events on April 19, or had been vocal opponents of the government's case, died?

---

* He was wearing a t-shirt inscribed: "Nameless Saints We Give Our Thanks—The hundreds of people that give it their all without personal individual acknowledgment, April 19, 1995, Oklahoma City, OK."

** His partner was ATF agent Harry Eberhardt.

"Out of roughly 5,000 of us who were originally involved in Iran-Contra," said journalist Al Martin, "approximately 400, since 1986, have committed suicide, died accidentally or died of natural causes. In over half those deaths, official death certificates were never issued. In 187 circumstances, the bodies were cremated before the families were notified." [652]

Craig Roberts and John Armstrong, who investigated a similar spate of suspicious deaths in their book, *JFK: The Dead Witnesses,* revealed that most of the deaths peaked in the months leading up to one of the investigations, with deaths often coming days or even hours before the person was supposed to testify.

In the three years following the Kennedy assassination, 18 material witnesses perished. In the time period leading up to 1979, when the last of the Kennedy investigations ended, over 100 witnesses died. Most of the deaths coincided with one of the four main investigations: Warren Commission (1964–65); Jim Garrison investigation (1965–69); Senate Committee investigation (1974–76); and the House Committee on Assassinations investigation (1976–79).

Naturally, the CIA had an answer for these mysterious deaths. In a 1967 departmental memo, a CIA officer wrote:

Such vague accusations as that more than 10 people have died mysteriously can always be explained in some rational way: e.g., the individuals concerned have for the most part died of natural causes; the [Warren] Commission staff questioned 418 witnesses—the FBI interviewed far more people, conducting 25,000 interviews and re interviews—and in such a large group, a certain number of deaths are to be expected.

Yet Roberts and Armstrong note that if the CIA were not involved in any of the deaths, why was such a memo disseminated?

Then, to add further fuel to the fire, CIA technicians testified before the Senate Committee (Church Committee) in 1975 that a variety of Termination with Extreme Prejudice (TWEP) weapons had been used throughout the years, and many were chosen because they left no postmortem residue.

In one particular memo, the author states:

You will recall that I mentioned that the local circumstances under which a given means might be used might suggest the technique to be used in that case. I think the gross divisions in presenting this subject might be:

1. bodies left with no hope of the cause of death being determined by the most complete autopsy and chemical examination;
2. bodies left in such circumstances as to simulate accidental death;
3. bodies left in such circumstances as to simulate accidental death;
4. bodies left with residue that simulate those caused by natural death.

Regarding deaths that could be simulated to appear as "natural causes," the various assassination experts within the intelligence communities of the world knew quite well of the effects of such chemical agents as sodium morphate, which caused heart attacks; thyon phosphate, which is a solution that can suspend sodium morphate and provide a vehicle to penetrate the surface of the skin with the chemical (which is used to coat something the victim might touch); and beryllium, which is an extremely toxic element that causes cancer and fibrotic tumors.[653]

The daughter of a CIA contract agent who worked with Oliver North told me: "They eliminated my father, and I know what they do in the Agency. I know how they work as far as the Mafia goes. They have no scruples. And they don't go by any law but their own. There is no conscious to these people; the end justifies the means. They will shut anybody up that they possibly can. They're amazing. And they will go through anything to make you look crazy, to make you appear to be a liar....

"And they go into these operations, and they run amok. They run amok. And then when it gets carried away or there's a leak, here comes the damage control, and you have to make everybody else appear like they're crazy. I mean people out there drop like flies. How many people can commit suicide for God's sake. How many people can be handcuffed behind their back, and they can call it suicide because they were shot in the head?"[654]

TIP OF THE ICEBERG

"Justice can kill or thwart any investigation at will, and it does so on a regular basis."
—Former U.S. Senate investigator

"[Justice] has been engaged in sharp practices since the earliest days and remains a fecund source of oppression and corruption today. It is hard to recall an administration in which it was not the center of grave scandal."
—H.L. Mencken

As an experienced investigator once said, "A cover-up often proves the crime, and lifts the identities of the perpetrators into relief."

In this case, those covering up the Oklahoma City bombing appear to be the Federal Government itself. Law-enforcement officials, including those at the local level, lied about their foreknowledge of the attack. They rushed to destroy all forensic evidence of the site. They ignored dozens of credible witnesses and intimidated others. And they organized a media smear campaign against anyone who threatened to reveal the truth.*

Ironically, the letters "FBI" stand for "Fidelity, Bravery, and Integrity." A more appropriate definition might be "Federal Bureau of Intimidation."

It might be interesting to note that the FBI's current director, Louis Freeh, rose to his position on the victory of the Leroy Moody case. (Moody was convicted of killing Federal Judge Robert Vance with a letter-bomb.) Freeh's chief witness, Ted Banks, later told an appeals court that Freeh threatened him into testifying against Moody. Banks was subsequently sentenced to 44 months in prison for "perjury."

For his part, Freeh was promoted to FBI Director, where he drew around him such figures as Tom Thurman, Roger Martz, and Larry Potts, who led the murderous debacles at Waco and Ruby Ridge.

Freeh placed Potts in charge of the "investigation" in Oklahoma City.**

Overseeing the FBI is the Department of Justice, undoubtedly the most misnamed federal agency ever created. While purporting to be a law-enforcement body independent of the legislative and executive branches, in reality it is little more than a political tool utilized by corrupt leaders to cover up high crimes and intimidate and imprison whistle-blowers.

Janet Reno, the current Attorney General, rose to her position on a wave of highly dubious child abuse cases, where the only abuse, it appeared, was fostered by Reno herself.

In 1984, Reno, then Dade County District Attorney, prosecuted Ileana Fuster, a 17-year-old newlywed who helped her husband Frank by operating a day-care out of their home. To illicit the required confession from Ileana, Reno had her locked away in a solitary confinment. Stephen Dinerstein, a private investigator employed by the Fuster's attorneys wrote in his report that the formerly bright, attractive 17-year-old:

> Appeared as if she was 50 years old. Her skin was drawn from a large loss of weight.... She had sores and infections on her skin and states that no sanitary conditions exist or are provided, that the shower, when received, is a hosing down in the cell. That she is in a cell with nothing in it but a light in the ceiling and that she is often kept nude and in view of everybody and anybody." [Dinerstein also noted that Ileana had become] a constantly crying, shaking, tormented person who under-

---

* The only mainstream media who have made some effort to report the truth have been CNN, *Dallas Morning News, Denver Post,* FOX News, and ABC 20/20. Unfortunately, the information 20/20 presented only covered limited aspects of prior knowledge by the government. KFOR, the only station that has covered the Middle Eastern connection, ceased their reporting when they were bought out by the New York Times Broadcasting Company.

** Potts was later taken off the case due to heat from the Ruby Ridge incident.

stands little if anything about the whole process and is now being threatened and promised and is totally in a state of confusion to the point of not having the slightest idea as to month and date.... Mrs. Fuster's condition has deteriorated so badly she could hardly move and was very slow to respond to any questions. When asked if Mr. Van Zamft (her attorney) was present, she could not even recall, but said simply that the woman State Attorney (Reno) was very big and very scary and made suggestions as to problems that would arise if she didn't cooperate.

After almost a year kept in this deplorable condition, including visits by Reno to coerce her, and visits by psychiatrists to get her to confess, Ileana cracked, "confessing" to a whole legion of imaginary acts.

After serving three out of a 10-year sentence, she was deported to Honduras, where her mind now clear, she immediately recanted her confession.

Only days before she was scheduled to retestify via satellite (the DA's office threatened to charge her with "perjury" if she returned), she retracted her retraction in a letter to the *Miami Herald*. her attorney believes she was threatened.[655]*

Several weeks after Reno was sworn in as Attorney General, she authorized a plan to flood the church at Waco (containing women and children) with CS tear gas and ram it with battle tanks, based on allegations of "child abuse." A 1988 Amnesty International report claimed that "CS gas contributed to or caused the deaths of more than 40 Palestinians—including 18 babies under six months of age—who had been exposed to tear gas in enclosed spaces."* Reno's attempt to

---

* In 1984, Reno prosecuted Grant Snowden, Miami's 1983 Police Officer of the Year, whose wife ran a day-care center. Snowden had threatened to report a father whose son showed up with bruises. The man retaliated by accusing Snowden of the abuse. The case was finally dropped when the psychiatrist examining the boy revealed that the father had coerced the child into perjury. Reno pervservered, however, bringing in two self-styled child-abuse experts—Joseph and Laurie Braga—to elicit the required testimony from the latest victim that Reno's office had turned up. Snowden was acquitted. Making good on her promise to try Snowden on one child at a time until there was a conviction, Reno pushed ahead. While the latest child was not even able to identify Snowden in court, the judge allowed the testimony from the previous two children (even though Snowden was found to be innocent), excluded testimony of Snowden's flawless record, and sentenced him to secure five consecutive life sentences. These cases, although highly manipulated by government prosecutors, should not be taken as an inference that child abuse, including ritual child abuse, does not occur, as some media pundits have tried to suggest.

** Reno had previously displayed her concern for children when several days earlier, two men who had driven all day and all night from Indiana to bring baby food to the children at Waco were arrested.

"save the children" in Waco resulted in the deaths of 86 people, including 25 children.

As for the allegations of child abuse, both the County Sheriff and the Texas Welfare Department, who were two of the first to interview Davidian children, indicated there was no signs of abuse. The FBI later acknowledged their own reports to be false.[656]

Representative James Traficant (D-OH) summed up the situation at "Justice" when he wrote to members of Congress on April 15, 1997:

> There have been numerous cases of prosecutorial misconduct, fraud and outright murder on the part of Justice Department personnel that have gone largely unpunished. The American people expect the Justice Department, more than any other federal agency, to be beyond reproach when it comes to ethics and responsible behavior. Something is seriously wrong in our democracy if criminal and unethical behavior at the nation's top law enforcement agency goes unpunished.*

The crimes Traficant speaks of are legion. The scandals covered up by corrupt DoJ officials are endless. The cases of individuals who have been singled out for prosecution by the Justice Department would fill volumes.

Perhaps the most infamous case of DoJ corruption in modern history is the Inslaw affair, where DoJ officials conspired to steal software from the small computer company, defraud them out of payments, then force them into bankruptcy. The Inslaw case provides a perfect example of how the DoJ regularly lies, destroys evidence, selectively prosecutes people, obstructs Congressional investigations, and murders those who threaten to reveal their wrongdoing.

In 1982, the DoJ signed a $10 million contract with Inslaw to install an enhanced version of their PROMIS (Prosecutors Management Information System) software in 42 U.S. Attorneys offices. Inslaw completed the project, but was never paid for their services. Heavily in debt, they had no choice but to file for bankruptcy.

It seemed that a rival firm named Hadron, attempted to purchase PROMIS from Inslaw. "We have ways of making you sell," said CEO Dominic Laiti, who warned Inslaw owner Bill Hamilton that Hadron was connected to Attorney General Edwin Meese. Both Meese and his close friend, Earl Brian, had financial interests in Hadron.

After the DoJ refused to pay Inslaw, Meese handed the software over to his crony Brian, who had CIA contract agent Michael Riconosciuto reconfigure the program with a special "trap door," allowing U.S. intelligence agencies to monitor and manipulate accounts of banks and intelligence agencies who subse-

---

* Letter from Rep. James Traficant to members of Congress, 4/15/97. Traficant introduced a bill (H.R. 692) that seeks the appointment of an independent counsel to investigate cases of DOJ misconduct. Traficant is also pushing for OK bomb hearings.

quently purchased the program. The profits, of course, went to Brian and his cronies at the DoJ.*

When Inslaw attempted to sue the DoJ, their attorney was threatened and dismissed from his firm.[657] In spite of the stonewalling and harassment, Inslaw eventually won their case. Judge George Bason, ruling in favor of the company, wrote:

> [DoJ officials] took, converted, stole [the plaintiff's property] by trickery, fraud and deceit. [They made] an institutional decision ... at the highest level simply to ignore serious questions of ethical impropriety, made repeatedly by persons of unquestioned probity and integrity, and this failure constitutes bad faith, vexatiousness, [a] fraudulent game of cat and mouse, demonstrating contempt for both the law and any principle of fair dealing.[658]

After Judge Bason ordered the DoJ to pay Inslaw $6.8 million in licensing fees and roughly another $1 million in legal fees, he suddenly discovered that he was not being reappointed to the bench.[659]

The Senate Permanent Subcommittee on Investigations, chaired by Senator Sam Nunn, agreed wholeheartedly with Judge Bason. Yet the committee's efforts to probe the Inslaw scandal were blocked by the DoJ, who refused to allow their personnel to testify under oath. The Senate report stated that it had found employees "who desired to speak to the subcommittee, but who chose not to, out of fear for their jobs."[660]

Said a former Congressional investigator who dealt with the Justice Department for 15 years, "I've got to tell you, the bottom line is that the DoJ as presently constituted is a totally dishonest organization, riddled with political fixes. They know how to write the memo, how to make the phone call, how to deny access to Congress. The game over there is fixed."

The stonewalling by the DoJ during the Inslaw investigations paralleled that of the Oklahoma City bombing, where defense attorneys encountered continuous denials in their requests for discovery. The stonewalling of the Inslaw investigation, stated the Congressional report, included, "restrictions, delays, and outright denials to requests for information ... obstructed access to records and witnesses, [and] the illegal shredding of documents."

Yet the committee did nothing to punish those responsible, merely recommending that the DoJ request the Court of Appeals to appoint an "independent"

---

* As the Congressional committee probing the Inslaw affair later wrote: "The enhanced PROMIS software was stolen by high level Justice officials and distributed internationally in order to provide financial gain to Dr. Brian and to further intelligence and foreign policy objectives of the United States."

prosecutor. While Attorney General William Barr initially refused, he eventually succumbed to media pressure, appointing one of his old DoJ cronies, Nicholas Bua, to "investigate" the matter. Bua impaneled a Federal Grand Jury. But, as in the Oklahoma City case, the prosecuting attorney, Bua's law partner Charles Knight, manipulated and controlled the witnesses. When the jury started giving credence to the allegations against the DoJ, Bua quickly dismissed the jury and impaneled another one.*

Not surprisingly, one of Bua's chief investigators was none other than Joseph Hartzler. In a letter Hartzler wrote to Assistant Associate Attorney General John Dwire in October of 1994, the noble government prosecutor states:

> I applaud your efforts and especially your conclusions. To paraphrase Theodore Roosevelt, we spent ourselves on a worthy cause.

Hartzler's next "worthy cause" would be to serve as lead prosecutor in the Oklahoma City bombing case, assisting the DoJ in one of the largest cover-ups of the 20th Century.

> "I don't understand where they found him or why they chose him," says Michael Deutsch, who as an attorney in Chicago defended a Puerto Rican terrorist in a 1985 bombing case prosecuted by Hartzler, a successful prosecution that is often cited as one of the reasons Hartzler got the Oklahoma City job.[660]

Deutsch is referring to the prosecution of four Las Fuerzas Armadas de Liberacion National Puertorriqueo (FALN) members, a Puerto Rican nationalist group the government claimed was responsible for more than 100 bombings or attempted bombings since 1970. The defense of the FALN paralleled that of the Oklahoma City bombing defendants, with crucial evidence being withheld—evidence that would have implicated the FBI and ATF in COINTELPRO-style illegal activites directed against the Chicano and Puerto Rican Movements. The judge in the FALN case, Federal District Judge George Leighton, has reported connections to the CIA.**

Yet Hartzler claimed he volunteered for the role of lead prosecutor. Whether or not that is true, Hartzler, a wheelchair-bound multiple sclerosis victim, is the

---

* Sherman Skolnick and Mark Sato of Chicago's Citizens Committee to Clean Up the Courts filed a lawsuit against Bua and Knight, charging them with obstruction of Justice. They informed Bua that they were going to circumvent the special prosecutor and present evidence to the Grand Jury themselves. Bua replied that he would hold them in contempt. "I do not intend to prosecute anyone," he told them.

** Leighton was reportedly the secret attorney for Lee Harvey Oswald.

perfect choice—a man able to pander to the sympathies of a jury already over-whelmed by images of dead and handicapped victims. This astute observation was made by none other than *Newsweek,* which wrote: "Some suggested that a wheelchair-bound prosecutor would appeal to a jury in a case with so many maimed victims." [662]

As the *Legal Times* observed:

Having a lead prosecutor who maneuvers around the courtroom in a motorized scooter, some say, is a good tactic for gaining sympathy with a jury—especially in a case where more than 500 people were injured. [663]

"Others saw a malleable personality easily micromanaged by superiors in Washington," added *Newsweek.* A rather candid observation in a case where "micromanaging" is key.

"I don't think that Joe is in charge of the prosecution team," said Stephen Jones. "The shots are called by [Deputy Attorney General] Jamie Gorelick and [her top aide] Merrick Garland."

Justice Department officials scoff at such a notion, pointing out that they are too far away and too busy to micro-manage the trial team. Hartzler, they say, is firmly in charge…. [664]

Interestingly, Hartzler was chief of both the civil and criminal division of the Chicago U.S. Attorney's office during his 10-year term, a jurisdiction not unknown for its share of corruption-ridden scandals.

His assistant, Scott Mendeloff, was accused by Sherman Skolnick of the Chicago-based Citizens' Committee to Clean Up the Courts of covering up the murder of Wallace Lieberman, a Chicago Federal Bankruptcy Court official ready to finger several judges for bribery. "The assassination of Lieberman, as Mendeloff knew, was tied to the corrupt activities of First National Bank of Cicero, a Mafia/CIA laundry," writes Skolnick. [665]

Naturally, Hartzler doesn't see any corruption in Oklahoma. "I am 100 percent confident that when this case is resolved, everyone will think that complete and fair due process was obtained by the defendants," Hartlzer told the *American Bar Association Journal.*

To facilitate this "complete and fair due process," the DoJ transferred Assistant U.S. Attorney Ted Richardson from his position as chief bombing and arson pros-ecutor for the Western District of Oklahoma to the bank robbery detail. As pre-viously noted, Richardson was the U.S. Attorney who prosecuted Sam Khalid for insurance fraud. It was rumored that Richardson, who friends claim had a "very strong sense of conscience," was looking into Khalid's subsequent activities. On

August 5, 1997, Richardson "committed suicide."

On August 10, 1991 reporter Danny Casolaro, who had been investigating the Inslaw scandal and a related web of corruption he called "The Octopus" was found dead in his Martinsburg, West Virginia hotel room. Casolaro was there to meet with a witness who was supposed to provide the key link between the DoJ and Inslaw.

Like Sergeant Yeakey, Casolaro's wrists were slashed numerous times. Like Yeakey, his notes and briefcase were missing. And like Yeakey, the death was immediately ruled a suicide by police, who made no attempt to contact Casolaro's family before ordering an immediate and unprecedented embalming of the body. A team of contract cleaners was brought in to scour clean the hotel room from top to bottom, eliminating all forensic evidence.*

The death of Casolaro led to an investigation by the Congressional Subcommittee on Economic and Commercial Law, headed by Representative Jack Brooks (D-Texas). The report stated:

Instead of conducting an investigation into Inslaw's claims that criminal wrongdoing by high level government officials had occurred, Attorney Generals Meese and Thornbugh blocked or restricted Congressional inquires into the matter, ignored the findings of two courts and refused to ask for the appointment of an independent counsel. These actions were taken in the face of a growing body of evidence that serious wrongdoing had occurred which reached to the highest levels of the Department. The evidence received by the committee during its investigation clearly raises serious concerns about the possibility that a high level conspiracy against Inslaw did exist and that great efforts have been expended by the Department to block any outside investigation into the matter.

The DoJ also prosecuted a key witness in the Inslaw case, Michael Riconosciuto, who was set up on phony drug charges to prevent him from testifying. The Congressional committee probing the matter noted:

---

* Those within the DoJ who had an interest in covering up reporter Danny Casolaro's death were quick to point out that the investigative reporter suffered from Multiple Sclerosis, and was therefore despondent. Interestingly, Hartzler also suffers from Multiple Sclerosis. In his letter to Dwire, he adds: "The more the implicit connection between Mr. Casolaro's Multiple Sclerosis and his suicide may create too dire a picture of Multiple Sclerosis. That linkage invites readers to cluck with pity and nod knowingly about the presumably devastating effect of Multiple Sclerosis. I trust that if Ms. Reno, Ms. Gorelick and Mr. Smith are not already familiar with MS, you will offer them this note of balance and assure them that Multiple Sclerosis flourishes even in the Justice Department and expects no pity."

[A DEA agent] reassignment in 1990 to a DEA intelligence position in the State of Washington, prior to Michael Riconosciuto's March 1991 arrest there on drug charges, was more than coincidental. The agent was assigned to Riconosciuto's home state to manufacture a case against him. Mr. Coleman stated he believes this was done to prevent Mr. Riconosciuto from becoming a credible witness concerning the U.S. Government's covert sale of PROMIS to foreign governments.[666]

Another example of selective prosecution on behalf of DoJ is Juval Aviv, owner of the investigative firm Interfor. A former Israeli intelligence agent, Aviv was hired to look into the 1988 bombing of Pan Am flight 103 over Lockerbie, Scotland. His report was directly at odds with the government's "official" conclusions—that two Libyan terrorists were responsible for the bombing. Aviv discovered that not only had U.S. officials been specifically warned of the ensuing attack, but may have had direct complicity in the murder of 270 people.

For his embarrassing disclosures, Aviv was targeted for prosecution, and investigated by the very same FBI agents who "investigated" the Pan Am case. To punish Aviv, the DoJ fabricated evidence that Interfor defrauded G.E. Capital Corporation, a client who was completely satisfied with Interfor's work, and hadn't even filed a complaint against the firm.

Nevertheless, in 1995, the DoJ indicted Aviv on three counts of defrauding G.E.—charges for which he was unanimously acquitted. In his ruling opinion, the judge wrote:

The chronology of the investigation, the fact that it is resulting from no external complaint whatsoever but simply internally within the FBI as far as any witness has testified, leads to an inference that it was generated from some other sources, and the only source in the record so far for which any such purpose could be ascribed is the report in the other case, in the Lockerbie case.

Yet DoJ wasn't finished with Aviv. They canceled their contract with Interfor and began a systematic campaign to intimidate his clients. Interfor was financially devastated. The U.S. Government, through the DoJ, believed that by intimidating people such as Juval Aviv, they could prevent public knowledge of their complicity in the murder of 270 innocent people.

As in Oklahoma City, witnesses who knew too much about Pan Am 103, or those who possessed politically inconvenient facts, were intimidated. Five years on, volunteers and policemen who participated in the search remained recalcitrant—most so those who had searched the area where the heroin was found. The Justice Department also attempted to sanction Pan Am's lawyers with huge fines for daring to challenge the government's case.

The government also went after Allan Francovitch, producer of the award-winning documentary on Pan Am 103, *The Maltese Double Cross*, which was due to premiere at the 1994 London Film Festival. For the first time in its 38 year history, the festival pulled the film at the last minute.[667] A few weeks after the film previewed at London's alternative Angle Gallery, it suffered a major fire. One day before the film was to air on Channel 4, both the Scottish Crown Office and the U.S. Embassy sent every national and Scottish newspaper a press pack smearing four of the film's interviewers.[668]

Within days of film being broadcast, Juval Aviv was indicted on fraud charges. His attorney, Gerald Shargel, applied for a dismissal on the grounds of selective prosecution. Even the judge was forced to condemn the prosecution's arguments as "pathetic" and "dishonest."[669]

Allan Francovitch wasn't so lucky. Within minutes of arriving in the United States to testify at Aviv's trial, he was detained by Customs agents in a private interrogation room, and dropped dead on the spot. All evidence and documents in Francovitch's brief case were found "missing" from the scene. Francovitch had been working on three other documentaries at the time, including a devastating exposé of U.S. atrocities in Panama.

In Oklahoma, ATF informant Carol Howe would be arrested on trumped up charges and forced to take refuge inside a jail cell, her testimony of the bombing blocked from even her own trial.[670]

For his role in revealing the truth about Pan Am 103, former DIA agent Lester Coleman would be arrested on fabricated passport charges and forced to seek asylum with his family in Sweden.

While reporter Danny Casolaro was murdered investigating matters related to Inslaw and BCCI, he was also checking on a lead provided to him by Coleman.

Curiously, Pan Am has never been able to review those documents which the government claims would merely show its "innocence." Like so many other heinous crimes, the government sought to hide its wrongdoing under the catch-all of "national security." The government, claiming it had nothing to hide, conspired with Federal Judge Thomas Platt to deny Pan Am's discovery requests on the grounds of "national security." As Pan Am's lawyer, James Shaughnessy, wrote in opposition to the government's motion to dismiss the company's third party liability suit:

> The government has fought strenuously and successfully for three years to prevent any discovery of it.... Now, the government seeks millions of dollars of sanctions to punish and bankrupt my firm and me for having the temerity not only to assert claims against the government but also for even seeking discovery from the government.
>
> The government condemns as sanctionable any view of the facts that differs from its own. In effect, what the government condemns is defendants' refusal to blindly adopt its version of the facts despite the government's refusal to produce the

evidence from which defendants could have determined whether the government's version of the facts was correct....

The government expects this blind trust even though we had information from multiple sources that conflicted with the government's sweeping assertions and that suggested the government was responsible for the failure to prevent the bombing.

Seven years later, the DoJ and FBI would ask the victims in Oklahoma City for this same blind trust—lying about their prior knowledge of the attack. Lying about the number of bombs found. Lying about the APB put out on the brown pick-up. Lying about the presence of other suspects. Ignoring witnesses who saw those suspects and trying to get them to change their stories. Tapping people's phones and exhorting them into not talking to the press and defense investigators. And intimidating several witnesses into silence.

In their attempt to frame Carol Howe on phony explosives charges, the government was unsuccessful. In his closing argument, Howe's attorney Clark Brewster passionately announced to the jury, "There was no bomb threat here, the only threat here is what the government can do to people when they don't like what you say or what you might say."

Howe was acquitted.

Many others wouldn't be so fortunate.

"It's a total conspiracy. It has government written all over it."

—Tom Posey, Civilian Military Assistance Group/Iran-Contra Player, in reference to the Oklahoma City bombing

April 19, 1995 was, like November 22, 1963, a day that devastated America. Stunned citizens everywhere watched anxiously as another painful drama unfolded before them.

Within minutes of the brutal attack on Oklahoma City, an army of agencies leapt into action. In the White House Situation Room the atmosphere was tense as officials from the National Security Council, the Secret Service, the FBI, ATF, NSA, and CIA assembled to brief the President.

This crisis team, led by the Justice Department, linked up to command centers around the globe, monitored by a plethora of intelligence agencies on extra-high alert. The FBI, the CIA's Directorate of Operations and their domestic arm, the National Resources Division, sent agents hither and yonder in a frantic and desperate search for information concerning the catastrophic attack.

In a quiet Maryland suburb, one former CIA official sat back and calmly monitored the ensuing chaos. He picked up his pipe, casually adjusted the volume on his television, and leaned back in his comfortable leather chair.

Two thousand miles away in Albuquerque, D'Ferdinand Carone, the daughter of former police detective, CIA operative, and Mafia bag-man, "Big Al" Carone, picked up the telephone and dialed a very private number.

Half a continent away, the former CIA Deputy Director of Covert Operations tapped the contents of his pipe into an ashtray, hit the mute button on his remote control, and answered the phone.

Carone had been trying to reach Theodore Shackley for over two weeks. As they talked, her attention was suddenly diverted by a horrible scene. What appeared to be an office building lay smoldering in ruins. People and sirens were screaming in the background as bodies were carted away by ambulance.

"I said, 'Oh my God, they bombed Oklahoma!'"

"This was about the time they were talking about the plane they stopped in Heathrow [with Abraham Ahmed], and I said, 'here we go again.'"

Carone was referring to the World Trade Center bombing by a group of Middle East terrorists. She assumed this was more of the same.

"And Ted said, 'Now wouldn't you find it interesting if you found out it was terrorists from here?'

"I said, 'Excuse me?'

"And he said, 'Just what I said.'

"Then it hit me like a ton of bricks. I got the distinct feeling that he knew who it was, and that it actually had something to do with the Agency."*

While scores of intelligence and law-enforcement agencies scoured the globe for clues as to who had bombed the Alfred P. Murrah Building, one man in a small office in Maryland seemed to have the answer.[671]

How did he know?

---

* "My thought was that it was our government," said Carone. "I honestly believe that." According to one account of the conversation, Shackley was elated.

> "The covert operators that I ran with would blow up a 747 with 300 people to kill one person. They are total sociopaths with no conscience whatsoever."
>
> —Former Pentagon CID Investigator Gene Wheaton

Chapter Eight

LOCKERBIE — A PARALLEL

On December 21, 1988, in the tiny town of Lockerbie, Scotland, 270 lives came to a traumatic and fiery end when Pan Am flight 103 was blown out of the skies. Two hundred and fifty-nine people plunged to their deaths, and 11 more died on the ground.

Several minutes before flight 103 took off from London's Heathrow airport, FBI Assistant Director Oliver "Buck" Revell rushed out to the tarmac and pulled his son and daughter-in-law off the plane.[672]

How did he know?

Perhaps Revell's intimate knowledge derived from his relationship with Oliver North. In March of 1986, North advised Attorney General Edwin Meese to head off the FBI's ensuing investigation into Iran-Contra. Meese informed Revell. Consequently, North managed to keep abreast of the FBI's investigation by conveniently receiving copies of all FBI files.*

Widely known for his inestimable and illegal support of the Contras, North (along with General Richard Secord and Iranian Albert Hakim) was a business associate of Syrian arms and drug runner Monzer al-Kassar. For his role in shipping Polish arms to North's mercenary army, al-Kassar became the recipient of North's undying gratitude [and laundered drug proceeds].**

---

* North contacted Meese through Admiral Poindexter. Meese informed Revell, who called Deputy Assistant Attorney General for the Criminal Division Mark Richard, and told him: "Please get on top of this; Jensen is giving a heads-up to the NSC." Deposition of Mark M. Richard before the Joint Congressional Committees, 8/19/87. Jensen is Deputy Attorney General Lowell Jensen; Kellner is Attorney General Leon Kellner. The rest of the conversation went as follows: "Call Kellner, find out what is up, and advise him that decision should be run by you."

** As investigative journalist Joel Bainerman writes: "Officials said that al-Kassar maintained offices in Warsaw and was a major broker of the Polish-owned weapons compa-

Like so many criminals, drug-dealers, and mass-murderers the CIA had cozied up to over the years, al-Kassar enjoyed the highly-valued status of CIA "asset."

Al-Kassar was also closely aligned with Rifat Assad, brother of Syrian dictator Hafez Assad. Assad's daughter Raja was Kassar's mistress, and had once been married to Abu Abbas, colleague of the notorious terrorist Abu Nidal. Rifat himself was married to the sister of Ali Issa Dubah, chief of Syrian intelligence, who, along with the Syrian army, controlled most of the opium production in Lebanon's Bekka Valley. The drug profits financed various terrorist groups, including the Popular Front for the Liberation of Palestine-General Command (PFLP-GC), run by former Syrian army officer Ahmed Jibril.[673]

Al-Kassar also acted as middleman in the ransom paid by the French to effect the release of two hostages held in Beirut. Given his assistance in securing the release of those hostages, the CIA believed al-Kassar would prove invaluable in negotiating the release of the six American hostages then being held in Lebanon.

In return for this favor, al-Kassar's drug pipeline to the United States would be protected by the CIA. This would not prove difficult, as the DEA was already using Pan Am flights out of Frankfurt, Germany for "controlled delivery" shipments of heroin. Realizing they couldn't halt the flow of drugs coming out of Lebanon, the DEA utilized the controlled shipments, escorted through customs by DEA couriers, as part of a sting operation, with the intention of catching the dealers in the U.S.[674]

Negotiation with individuals like Monzer al-Kassar had only one drawback: al-Kassar was closely linked, not only with the terrorist-sponsoring Syrian government, but with groups such Ahmed Jibril's PFLP-GC. Jibril was also aligned with the Iranian-backed Hezbollah, which had a somewhat different agenda than al-Kassar.

On July 3, 1988, less than six months before the Pan Am 103 bombing, the U.S.S. Vincennes shot down an Iranian airliner over the Straits of Hormuz, killing all 290 people on board. Assuming the plane was a hostile craft, the captain of the Vincennes, Will Rodgers III, gave the command to fire.

While the people of Iran grieved, the officer responsible for the fatal mistake

---

ny, Cenzin. The first arms purchase by North from al-Kassar totaling $1 million was sent by boat to an unidentified Caribbean port in the Fall of 1985 and was later distributed to the Contra fighters. In April of that year, a second shipment of Polish arms was sold to the CIA as part of this transaction." (*Los Angeles Times*, 7/17/87, quoted in Joel Bainerman, "Bush Administration's Involvement in Bombing Pan Am 103," *Portland Free Press*, May/June, 1997. See Bainerman's book, *The Crimes of a President*, SPI Books, 1992, regarding the illegal deals of George Bush).

was awarded a medal.*

Under Islamic law, the crime had to be avenged. As Juval Aviv of Interfor stated in his report, "It was known at the time that the contract was out to down an American airliner."

That contract—$10 million dollars—was given to Ahmed Jibril.** Jibril had already established a base of operations in Neuss, Germany, not far from Frankfurt. Central to his cell was one Marwan Abdel Razzack Khreeshat. Khreeshat's specialty was in building small, sophisticated bombs incorporating timing mechanisms capable of detonating at predetermined altitudes.

By mid-October 1988, Jibril was ready. Khreeshat had assembled five bombs, built into Toshiba radio-cassette players. However, the German police were watching him. On October 26, Khreesat and 14 other PFLP-GC suspects were rounded up in the operation code-named "Autumn Leaves." One of the bombs was seized. Four more remained at large.

While in custody, Khreesat demanded to make a phone call, then refused to answer any questions. Within hours, he was mysteriously released.[675]

The incident is strikingly similar to the arrest of Andreas Strassmeir on traffic charges in February, 1992. "Boy, we caught hell over that one," recalled tow-truck driver, Kenny Pence. "The phone calls came in from the State Department, the Governor's office, and someone called and said he had diplomatic immunity."[676]

Similar calls were made on behalf of Khreesat. Former CIA agent Oswald Le Winter, who investigated the case, stated, "Pressure had come from Bonn ... from the U.S. Embassy in Bonn ... to release Khreesat."

It seems that both Strassmeir and Khreesat were operatives of U.S. intelligence. "I had spoken to a German reporter who refuses to go on camera," adds Le Winter, "but who is very close to federal intelligence sources in Germany, who assured me that Khreesat was an agent of the Jordanian service, and an asset of the Central Intelligence Agency."†

Given the close relationship between the Jordanians and the CIA, this is not surprising. Yet it appeared Khreesat wasn't only reporting to the Jordanians and

---

* As former Iranian president Abulhassan Bani Sadr observed, "The people of Iran saw this as a crime ... shooting down an airplane, killing almost 300 people is a crime. Had it involved another country, there would have been legal proceedings. A lot of fuss would have been made all around the world. But here they destroyed the aircraft, and then congratulated themselves." (Allan Francovich, *The Maltese Double-Cross,* 1992.)

** U.S. investigators traced a wire transfer of several million dollars from Teheran to a bank account in Vienna controlled by the PFLP-GC. (*U.S. News & World Report,* 11/25/91.)

† This also raises the issue of whether Abraham Ahmed, who was released from custody after his mysteriously-timed departure from the U.S. after the Oklahoma City bombing, was an operative of the U.S. Government.

the Americans; he was also reporting to Ahmed Jibril.

Two months before the bombing, Jibril and al-Kassar were spotted by a Mossad agent dining at a Lebanese restaurant in Paris. Jibril was hoping to use al-Kassar's controlled drug shipments through Frankfurt to effect the delivery of a bomb. The problem: how to protect the drug shipments while at the same time extract revenge on the Americans? Al-Kassar preferred the former option, but, due to political pressure, he grudgingly agreed to the latter.

While a CIA team in Wiesbaden, code-named "COREA," was negotiating its secret deal with al-Kassar for release of the hostages (and protecting his drug route), a second team, led by Major Charles McKee of the Defense Intelligence Agency (DIA), and Matthew Gannon, the CIA's Deputy Station Chief in Beirut, traveled to Lebanon to assess the odds for a military-style rescue operation.[677]

According to Aviv's report, McKee's team had stumbled onto the first team's illegal drug operation while reconnoitering for release of the hostages. McKee refused to participate. When he and Gannon contacted their control in Washington, they received no reply. Against orders, they decided to fly home to blow the whistle. According to Aviv:

> They had communicated back to Langley the facts and names, and reported their film of the hostage locations. CIA did nothing. No reply. The team was outraged, believing that its rescue and their lives would be endangered by the double dealing.
>
> By mid-December the team became frustrated and angry and made plans to return to the U.S. with their photos and evidence to inform the government, and to publicize their findings if the government covered up.

They never arrived. That night, Pan Am flight 103 was blown out of the skies.

Was the death of McKee, Gannon, and five others on their team an unfortunate coincidence, or did someone want to ensure that they didn't reveal the carefully guarded secrets of the Octopus?[678]* Given the ample and specific warnings received by the U.S. Government from the BKA, the Mossad, and a Palestinian informant named Samra Mahayoun, it would seem the latter.

Whatever the case, it is indisputable that U.S. authorities were warned of the attack, and failed to stop it.

Was their failure deliberate?

"Do I think the CIA was involved?" asked a government Mideast intelligence specialist quoted in the financial weekly, *Barron's*. "Of course they were involved. And they screwed up. Was the operation planned by the top? Probably not. I doubt they sanctioned heroin importation—that came about at the more zealous

---

* PBS Frontline investigators believe that the intelligence officers were "a strong secondary target."

lower levels. But they knew what was going on and didn't care." The expert added that his agency has "things that support Aviv's allegation, but we can't prove it. We have no smoking gun. And until the other agencies of the government open their doors, we will have no smoking gun."

The Lockerbie bombing was not the first time authorities were warned in advance of a pending terrorist attack. The situation would repeat itself five years later in New York City, and seven years later in Oklahoma. It was an all-too-eerie coincidence.

U.S. authorities disingenuously denied receiving any warnings for Lockerbie, as they would later do in New York and Oklahoma. Yet, as in those cases, evidence of prior knowledge would eventually become known. "It subsequently came to me on further inquiries that they hadn't ignored [the warnings]," said a Pan Am security officer. "A number of VIPs were pulled off that plane. A number of intelligence operatives were pulled off that plane."

Due to the warnings posted in U.S. embassies by the State Department (but not forwarded to Pan Am), many government employees avoided the flight. In fact, the large 747 was only two-thirds full that busy holiday evening. South African president Peter Botha and several high-ranking officials were advised by state security forces to change their reservations at the last hour. The South African State Security forces have a close relationship with the CIA.*

Just as they would do in Oklahoma, government officials promised a complete and thorough investigation. Stated Oliver "Buck" Revell, who headed the Bureau's investigation: "All of us working on the case made it a very, very personal priority of the first order."

Fronting for the CIA, Vince Cannistraro chimed in: "I had personal friends on that plane who died. And I assure you that I wanted to find the perpetrators of that disaster as much as anyone wanted to."

As in Oklahoma City, this would become the catch-all phrase that would set everything right and prove the government had no involvement. Of course, this would be somewhat difficult in Revell's case, since he pulled his son and daughter-in-law off the plane minutes before it took off. (This was suspiciously reminiscent of the ATF agents who were paged not to come into work on April 19.)

Interestingly, Revell was the FBI's lead investigator in the crash of an Arrow Air DC-8 which exploded on December 12, 1985 in Gander, Newfoundland, with the loss of all 248 personnel. As in Oklahoma City, that site was quickly bulldozed, destroying crucial forensic evidence, with an Army official maintaining a watchful eye at all times.[679]

---

* Also aboard flight 103 was Bernt Carlsson, the Swedish UN diplomat who just completed negotiating the Namibian independence agreement with South Africa. He was due in New York the next day to sign the agreement.

Hiding behind the cover-up was the same cast of characters—Oliver North, Duane "Dewy" Clarridge, and Vince Cannistraro—who was North's deputy at the NSC during Iran-Contra, and would later appear in Lockerbie. The same cast of characters that lurked behind the scandals in Nicaragua and Iran, and would appear like ghostly apparitions in the smoldering ruins of Oklahoma City.

It was also an act that the U.S. shadow government, responsible for precipitating, was anxious to cover up. Had the true cause of the crash—North's double-dealing with the Iranians—been revealed, the Iran-Contra scandal would have surfaced two years before it had.

"Buck" Revell would be on hand to make sure it didn't.

Three years later, in Lockerbie, the government was still claiming its hands were clean. Yet it vigorously protested Pan Am's attempts to subpoena warning memos and other documents that would have revealed the government's fore-knowledge, just as it did in Oklahoma.

Simply stated, the attack on Pan Am 103 was in retaliation for the downing of the Iranian airbus. The reason for targeting Pan Am was simple: the airline was regularly used by al-Kassar's operatives to ferry drugs. It would be a simple matter to switch a suitcase containing drugs for one containing a bomb.

That appears to be just what happened. According to Lester Knox Coleman III, a former DIA agent in Cyprus seconded to the DEA: "I knew from the conversations around me in '88, that he [Lebanese drug courier Khalid Jaffar] was involved in the controlled deliveries. There's no doubt in my mind about that at all. When I found he was on 103 and was killed, and there was a controlled delivery going through at the time, and I knew the security problems the DEA had, and the relationships they had with the people in Lebanon, with the issues involving security, it was very simple for me to put one and one together and get the big two—that the DEA's operation had a role in all this."

According to Juval Aviv, the drug suitcase was switched at Frankfurt, where Turkish baggage handlers working for al-Kassar had been regularly switching bags for those containing heroin. As the Interfor report stated:

> On December 21, 1988, a BKA surveillance agent watching the Pan Am flight's loading noticed that the "drug" suitcase substituted was different in make, shape, material and color from that used for all previous drug shipments. This one was a brown Samsonite case. He, like the other BKA agents on the scene, had been extra alert due to all the bomb tips. Within an hour or so before takeoff he phoned in a report as to what he had seen, saying something was very wrong.[680]

The BKA reported this to the CIA team in Wiesbaden, who, strangely, did not reply. According to Aviv, "[The CIA unit] reported to its control. CONTROL REPLIED: DON'T WORRY ABOUT IT, DON'T STOP IT, LET IT GO."

Apparently, the CIA team "did not want to blow its surveillance operation and undercover penetration or to risk the al-Kassar hostage release operation," wrote Aviv. It seemed the CIA figured the BKA would intercept the terrorists, keeping the CIA out of the picture, thereby maintaining its cover.

Yet this explanation hardly seems credible. The BKA had informed the CIA about the threat—a threat to one of its own planes. They also knew the Americans were running a sensitive undercover operation, and must have assumed the Americans would want to handle the situation themselves.

Moreover, there is no indication that the CIA instructed the BKA or any other German authorities to stop the bombing. The question is: why not? Certainly the CIA wouldn't blow its cover by asking the BKA to intercede, as they were already aware of the CIA/DEA operation.

This raises even more disturbing questions. Had the CIA "control" in Washington, monitoring the situation, purposely allowed the bombing to occur? Was the McKee team, about to blow the whistle on the Octopus, specifically targeted for elimination? Had Middle Eastern terrorists knowingly or unknowingly conspired with the Octopus in eliminating a group of pesky whistle blowers?

Strangely, after the crash, large numbers of American "rescue" personnel began showing up rather quickly. As one searcher, a member of a mountain rescue team recalled: "We arrived within two hours [of the crash]. We found Americans already there."*

The first to appear was an FBI agent. According to George Stobbs, a Lockerbie police inspector, "[I] started to set up a control room, and [between] eleven o'clock and midnight, there was a member of the FBI in the office who came in, introduced herself to me, and sat down—and just sat there the rest of the night. That was it." **

---

* As British journalist David Ben-Aryeah reported: "Very strange people were at work very early on. Within a matter of three hours there were American accents heard in the town. Over that night there were large numbers, by which I mean 20, 25, 30 people arrived." (Franckovich, *Op Cit.*)

** As investigator and former law-enforcement officer Craig Roberts points out in *The Medusa File:* "The unusual activity of this alleged "FBI" agent is striking, but not quite as odd as the fact that Lockerbie is over 350 miles from London, which is the nearest point an American FBI agent might be. To reach Lockerbie that night from London, even if traveling by air, would have taken far more than one hour considering the sequence of events that would have had to occur. Assuming a timely notification, an American agent in London would have had to have been tracked down considering the late hour, notified to pack up for an investigation, rush to Heathrow, board a waiting airplane, fly immediately to the nearest airport that could land a jet transport, obtain ground transportation from there to Lockerbie, then locate the command center. An effort that would require four to six hours at the minimum."

Was this so-called FBI agent there to observe the Scottish police's investigation, and report any conflicting findings back to her superiors?

Tom Dalyell, a member of British Parliament, remarked: "Absolutely swarms of Americans [were] fiddling with the bodies, and shall we say tampering with those things the police were carefully checking themselves. They weren't pretending, saying they were from the FBI or CIA, they were just 'Americans' who seemed to arrive very quickly on the scene."

The scenario was eerily similar to that in Oklahoma City, where rescue workers and Bomb Squad technicians seemingly appeared out of thin air.

Recall that Oklahoma City eyewitness Debra Burdick, who was near ground zero when the bomb went off, said: "And right after that, here comes the Bomb Squad, before the ambulances and the Fire Department."

"They would have had to have had some kind of warning to respond that quick, said Burdick's husband, "because they would have had to get in their gear and everything." [681] Burdick wasn't the only one who saw federal agents and rescue personnel arrive a bit too quickly. J.D. Reed, who was in the County Office Building when the bomb went off, later wrote: "The paramedics and firemen were already at work. How could they move so quickly? They were there by the time we got down to the street!" [682]

Then there was Sergeant Yeakey's ominous letter to his friend Ramona McDonald, which stated: "Everyone was behind you until you started asking questions as I did, as to how so many federal agents arrived at the scene at the same time...."

In Lockerbie, a number of American agents—some wearing Pan Am jumpsuits—were desperately searching for something. As Dalyell recalled: "It was ... odd and strange that so many people should be involved in moving bodies, looking at luggage, who were not members of the investigating force. What were they looking for so carefully? You know, this was not just searching carefully for loved ones. It was far more than that. It was careful examination of luggage and indeed bodies." [683]

Dr. David Fieldhouse, the local police surgeon, identified Major McKee early on. "I knew that [the identification of] McKee was absolutely correct because of the clothing which correlated closely with the other reports and statements, and the computers that were linked up to Washington." [684] This would subsume that Washington knew exactly what McKee—who hadn't told Control he was coming—was wearing. In other words, it means he was under surveillance by the Octopus.

Fieldhouse tagged over 58 bodies. "I later learned that when the bodies were taken to the mortuary, all the labels which had been put on them had been removed with the exception of two," said Fieldhouse, "but all the rest had been removed and discarded." [685]

A similar incident would occur in Oklahoma City. After nurse Toni Garret took a break from tagging dead bodies, she walked back to the makeshift morgue that had been set up in a nearby church. "When we came back in, there was a cold, callous atmosphere," said Garret. "I found out later that the FBI had taken over."[686]

In Lockerbie, police officers and military personnel were prohibited under the Official Secrets Act from talking about what they had witnessed. What had they seen that was so sensitive?

Jim Wilson knows. A local farmer, Wilson told relatives of Pan Am victims that he was present "when the drugs were found." The Tundergarth farmer had discovered a suitcase packed with heroin in one of his fields. Worried that it might harm his sheep, he informed local police, who notified the Americans, who then raced to the scene in an all-terrain vehicle. Wilson noted that the Americans seemed extremely angry that the drugs had not been discovered earlier by their own personnel.

One Scottish police officer who did speak out said that his department had been told to keep an eye out for the drugs early on. He also overheard American personnel say that there was a drug courier on the plane—Khalid Jaffar—one of the Lebanese informants used by the DEA.[687]

Had the heroin belonged to Jaffar? Since the drug suitcase had been switched at Frankfurt, it would seem unlikely. A more probable explanation is that it belonged to Gannon or McKee—evidence of the illegal operation being run by the Octopus.

It would certainly explain why U.S. officials were so desperate to find the suitcase before the Scottish authorities did. Once located, the heroin was removed, and the bag placed back in its original position like nothing had happened.

In Oklahoma City, 10 hours after the blast(s), federal agents halted rescue efforts to remove files from the building. While limited numbers of rescue workers were constrained to the lower right side of the building, between 40 and 50 federal agents began carting away boxes of files from the ATF and DEA offices.

"You'd think they would have let their evidence and files sit at least until the last survivor was pulled out," one angry rescue worker told the *New York Daily News*.[688]

Approximately 10 days after the blast, two white trucks pulled up to the postal annex across from the Murrah Building that was being used to store emergency supplies. A dozen men in black unmarked uniforms, wearing ski masks and carrying submachine guns, jumped out and formed a protective corridor to the building. Others, wearing blue nylon windbreakers and carrying hand-held radios, formed an outer perimeter. As a witness watched, he observed "box after box of what appeared to be files or documents in boxes [that] were loaded on the unmarked trucks that looked like Ryder rental trucks, but were white."[689]

The witness, a Tulsa Fire Captain who was filming the site of the explosion, was told by one of the agents to put down his camera. His film was later confiscated.

What were in the boxes—boxes that were originally stored in the Federal

Building—that over a dozen mysteriously anonymous federal agents armed with submachine guns were so anxious to secrete into hiding? Were they files that were being taken away to be destroyed … or to be protected? And by whom?

The public would never learn of this bizarre incident, just as they would never learn of the Middle East connection, the numerous John Does, the prior warnings of Cary Gagan and Carol Howe, and the elaborate cover-up. The government had convicted their man—Timothy James McVeigh—just as they had done with Lee Harvey Oswald 34 years ago. The victims who subscribed to the government's version of the case could now begin to experience a sense of "closure," whether they had learned the truth or not.

Five years before, the government had attempted to provide "closure" to the Pan Am bombing by announcing its newly discovered "evidence"—a tiny piece of microchip allegedly linked to the bomb. This new evidence, discovered in a remote field 10 months after the crash, would conclusively prove, the government claimed, that Libyan terrorists had destroyed the plane.

Like the evidence of McVeigh's racing fuel purchases which suddenly came to light 18 months after the bombing, or the startling new "revelations" of Eldon Elliott, Thomas Manning, and Daina Bradley, this "new evidence" would help the government divert attention from the true perpetrators of the crime.

Tom Thurman, the FBI lab technician who matched the chip—a tiny charred fragment that had miraculously survived two Scottish Winters—would later be accused of perjury in unrelated cases.

Nevertheless, the discovery was hailed as a major find. Vince Cannistraro, the CIA counter-terrorism Chief on the National Security Council, was the frontman for new "Libyan" theory.

"The principle avenues that led to identification of a foreign role in an act of terrorism," Cannistraro quipped with mock assurance, "was forensic evidence recovered by the Scottish police at Lockerbie themselves. Investigators and townspeople on their hands and knees, crawling along the countryside, picking up minute bits of debris. And one of those bits of debris turned out to be a microchip, which was analyzed microscopically that led to the Libyan connection."

Like the Ryder truck axle in Oklahoma City that allegedly discovered by several different people, the microchip had a confusing and contradictory bevy of claimants. "Three of his people [FBI agents] sworn that they had found this piece in a piece of a coat and had signed a paper to this effect," stated Bollier. "I later heard that it was the Scottish police who had found the piece in a shirt that came from Malta." Yet in spite of this, the Scots would attempt to have a townsperson sign a statement that he had found the chip.

Yet the townsperson whom the FBI claimed had discovered the chip could not even recall finding it. The man, named "Bobby," said "I got a call from a policeman asking if he could come down to my home, and would I sign to say that I picked those [items] up. He brought with him three small bags about the size of an eight-by-five piece of paper, one of which contained an item of cloth, one of which contained a brown piece which looked very much like a piece of plastic, the third piece I couldn't tell what it was."

Had the chip been planted by the FBI? The Bureau admitted that it already possessed two such timers, confiscated from two Libyans in Dakar and Senegal in 1986. The incident was remarkably similar to the Oklahoma City bombing witnesses who were coerced into signing statements that differed from what they actually saw.

Yet British authorities would willingly cooperate with the U.S. as the result of a phone call made by President Bush to Prime Minister Margaret Thatcher. According to syndicated columnist Jack Anderson, the two heads of state agreed that the investigation should be "limited" in order to avoid compromising the two nations' intelligence communities.*

For his part, Cannistraro had developed, along with NSC staffers Howard Teicher and Oliver North, the Reagan-inspired propaganda policy of destroying the Libyan regime of Colonel Muammar al-Qaddafi. As Bob Woodward wrote in the *Washington Post:*

> Vincent M. Cannistraro, a veteran CIA operations officer and director of intelligence on the National Security Council staff, and Howard R. Teicher, the director of the office of political military affairs in the NSC, supported the disinformation and deception plan.

"I developed the policy toward Libya," said Cannistraro. "In fact, I even wrote the draft paper that was later adopted by the President." **

In spite of the obvious propaganda ploy, the evidence against Libya was dubious at best. Even more dubious was the government's theory of how the bomb got on board. According to "Buck" Revell, the bomb, built by two Libyan intelligence agents—Abdel Basset al-Megrahi and Lamin Khalifah Fhima—was placed inside a suitcase and smuggled into the airport at Malta, and tagged for its final destination to JFK airport in New York. It then flew, unaccompanied, to Frankfurt, where it changed planes, also unaccompanied, then flew to London, where it managed to change planes again, only to explode over Lockerbie.

---

* Although Thatcher acknowledged the conversation took place, she denied that she and Bush sought to interfere with the investigation.

** Interestingly, some of these same players worked with CIA Director Bill Casey and Vice President George Bush to build Iraq (whose president, Saddam Hussein, Bush called "worse than Hitler") into a major military power. This policy perfectly illustrated the Reagan/Bush administration's propensity to cuddle up to whatever dictator or terrorist was in favor at the time.

Like the specter of two lone amateurs with a fertilizer bomb, the government expects the public to believe that a sensitive altitude-triggered time-bomb managed to pass through three countries unaccompanied, pass through security and customs checks, change planes twice, then detonate at precisely the right moment over its target destination.

Such a suggestion, even to the uninitiated, is ridiculous.

And there was no evidence to support it. According to Dennis Phipps, former head of security for British Airways: "The records of handling of that fight were made available for me to see. There was no evidence of any unaccompanied bags. All of the bags that were carried as passenger baggage on that flight, had to be checked in by a passenger who actually traveled on the flight."

Said Michael Jones, Pan Am's London Security Chief: "I've never seen any documentation whatsoever, produced by Pan Am or anybody else, showing there was any interlying baggage to Pan Am from the Air Malta flight."

Even the FBI's own telex, dated October 23, 1989, stated:

> To Director, FBI, Priority—Records there is no concrete indication that any piece of luggage was unloaded from Air Malta 100 sent through the luggage routing at Frankfurt airport then loaded on board Pan Am 103.

In fact, it is absurd to suggest that trained intelligence agents or even clever terrorists would opt for such a far-fetched and risky plan. Especially given the security measures regarding unaccompanied bags, which would have surely aroused suspicion. This premise becomes even more ludicrous considering the unexpected delays inherent in winter holiday flights. How had the bomb, after passing through three countries, managed to arm itself and detonate at precisely the right moment?

Miraculously, eight months after the bombing, a baggage print-out was obtained by the BKA showing an unaccompanied bag that had been transferred from Air Malta.

The government finally had its "evidence." *

---

* Yet they were still left with the problem of proving how the microchip had been traced to al-Megrahi and Fhima. The FBI claimed it had traced the chip to Mebo, a Swiss manufacturing firm in Zurich run by Edwin Bollier. Agents showed Bollier a photograph of the chip, and asked if it was from their MST-13 O-series. "I immediately recognized from the photo that the fragment found in Lockerbie was without a doubt from a timer that we ourselves had made," stated Bollier. Yet they still hadn't proven how the timer had come to be in the possession of Fhima and al-Megrahi. Stasi (East German secret police) files showed that Bollier had not only sold timers to the Libyans, but to the Palestinians, the Red Army Faction, and Arabs in both Germanies. The Stasi concluded that Bollier was a triple agent, probably working for the CIA as well, since

Just as they had suddenly dropped the Mid East lead in Oklahoma, the government was now switching tracks and blaming the Libyans for the Pan Am bombing. But why? Why, after two years of solid evidence pointing to Syrian and Iranian involvement, was the government now blaming Libya—and on such flimsy pretenses?

Naturally, like the theory of McVeigh's "revenge for Waco," the government had a handy explanation: Libya's motive for the attack stemmed from the April, 1986 U.S. air-raid on Tripoli and Benghazi, in which over 37 civilians, including Qaddafi's infant daughter, were killed. *That* raid was in retaliation for the bombing of the La Belle Discotheque in Berlin a year earlier, in which two U.S. servicemen and a Turkish woman were killed.

In fact, the involvement of Libya in the disco bombing was highly questionable. It is also curious why Qaddafi would wait two-and-a-half years to extract his revenge on the Americans for the Benghazi attack.

The government's desire to implicate Libya for the bombing of Pan Am 103 was no different than its desire to implicate the militia for the bombing in Oklahoma City. In that case, they claimed, the motive was revenge for the government's atrocities at Waco.*

President Bush knew perfectly well who bombed flight 103. Six months after the bombing, Secretary of State James Baker visited Syrian Foreign Intelligence Minister Farouk al-Sharaa. Baker asked:

"What are you doing about the GLC group?"

"What are you talking about," asked al-Sharaa.

"Jibril," answered Baker. "We know they are responsible for Lockerbie. What are you doing about them?"

"How do you know that?"

"We have the evidence," Baker replied. "And the evidence is irrefutable."[690]

Nevertheless, the government lied to the American people.** The investigation turned political. In July of 1990, Iraq invaded Kuwait. President Bush began

---

he seemed to easily be able to get very special American equipment for them. Yet when Bollier asked the FBI to see the actual fragment, they said they didn't have it; the Scottish police had it. When Bollier approached the Scottish police, they refused to show it to him. Nor was he was given a satisfactory explanation of how either the FBI or the Scotts managed to trace it to the Libyans.

* U.S. officials also tried to blame the murder of three IBEX executives in August of 1976 on "Libyan-trained Islamic Marxist guerrillas."

** U.S. Attorney General Robert Mueller told the public, "We have no evidence to implicate another country (other than Libya) in this disaster." Gene Wheaton described it as "OPSEC" (operation security), providing layers of deniability and disinformation, false leads and stories.

forming his Gulf War coalition. Syria, formerly viewed as a terrorist state, was now seen as a necessary ally.

Bush had been quietly making overtures to Syrian President Assad for years. Assad was a bitter enemy of President Saddam Hussein of Iraq. In order to bring Syria into the coalition, all evidence pointing to them was dropped. And, in November of 1991, the Libyan theory became the "official" version of the bombing.[691]

The real story appears somewhat different.

On December 20, an intercept of a call made to the Iranian embassy in Beirut confirmed that an American operative named David Lovejoy (aka Michael Franks, Michael Schafer) had spoken to Iranian Chargé d'Affaires Hussein Niknam, and advised him that the McKee team had changed its travel plans and booked passage on flight 103. The next day, Niknam called the Interior Ministry in Teheran and passed on Frank's information.[692]

The DEA was also monitoring McKee, and separately informed the CIA in Washington, British MI6, and the CIA team in Wiesbaden.[693]

Al-Kassar's operatives had also observed Gannon making travel arrangements in Nicosia, and reported this to their CIA handlers in Wiesbaden. This wasn't difficult, as the DEA's "controlled delivery" operation, run by DEA Station Chief Michael T. Hurley in Cyprus, utilized Arab informants, some of whom, according to Coleman, were reporting back to Ahmed Jibril.[694]

As one source familiar with the case said, "Every spook in Europe knew that McKee and Gannon were flying home on flight 103."

Yet while the McKee team was obviously compromised, the question begging to be answered is, who is Michael Franks? And why did Franks inform the Iranian embassy, a bitter enemy of the U.S., of McKee's travel plans?

An associate of Oliver North, Franks worked for Overseas Press Service (OPS) a television consultancy firm run by W. Dennis Suit. A former CIA operative in Central America, Suit was an associate of Oliver North, William Casey, John Singlaub, Jack Terrell, and Contra leaders Adolfo and Mario Calero. Lester Coleman aptly described him as a representative of North's "Georgia Mafia."

In other words, Franks worked for the Octopus.

Sent to Cyprus by OPS as a "cameraman," Franks was in a perfect position to monitor the activities of the DEA.

The other question begging to be answered is: who at CIA Control in Washington (not their headquarters in Langley) told the CIA team in

---

* U.S. Attorney General Robert Mueller told the public, "We have no evidence to implicate another country (other than Libya) in this disaster." Gene Wheaton described it as "OPSEC" (operation security), providing layers of deniability and disinformation, false leads and stories.

Wiesbaden: "DON'T WORRY ABOUT IT, DON'T STOP IT, LET IT GO"?*

It has been argued by apologists for the CIA that the Agency didn't stop the bombing because it didn't want to compromise its hostage-rescue mission—an operation being run by the Octopus in collusion with Monzer al-Kassar. Essentially, we are asked to accept the idea that the CIA was ready to sacrifice the lives of 270 people so as not to risk the opportunity to free six people.

A more plausible explanation is that the Octopus didn't want to compromise its profitable drug and gun-running operation—an operation that traces its roots from the Corsican Mafia, through the Hmong tribesman in Laos, to the Mujahadeen in Pakistan and Afghanistan, and finally to the cartels in Columbia and Mexico. It is an enterprise run by many of the same spooks that ran the Cold War, channeling billions of taxpayer dollars into the military/industrial establishment, while funneling thousands of tons of heroin and cocaine into our cities' streets.

As intelligence analyst Dave Emory notes, "When federal intelligence agencies in the United States decide to move in a particular direction—or when a faction of them decides to move in a particular direction—they do so when to move in that direction would scratch a number of different itches at different levels simultaneously." [695]

By passing on the travel plans of the McKee team to the Iranians, Franks allowed Ahmed Jibril to bomb the plane, eliminating McKee and Gannon in the process, and preventing exposure of the Octopus. At the same time, the Iranians got revenge for the shootdown of their airliner, and the drug dealers kept their operation relatively intact.

Using the Iranians as proxies permitted the Octopus to maintain "plausible deniability."

Describing how proxies or "cut-outs" are used in assassination work, 25-year DEA veteran Mike Levine said, "When you say 'they wouldn't do it,' surely you don't think that the Sicilian Mafia (to use an example) sends out a couple of Italians to do a hit on a U.S. Attorney that they could link directly back? No, absolutely not. What they might do is use what's left of [August] Ricord's organization [a drug dealer in South America], they might talk to an Italian who lives in Paraguay or Monte Madeo, he then talks to the son of a German who lives in Paraguay. An arrangement is made. They want them hurt. This organization finds out that this guy's wife is flying on a plane. Not that that's happened. I'm giving you a scenario … that's the way it's done. We're living in a world where murder has become very, very high-tech, very convoluted, with cut-outs.…

"TWA, Pan Am 103—this is the perfect M.O. of this organization," adds

---

* One person familiar with the case believes it was Ted Shackley himself.

Levine. "Not that they [Ricord] did it, but when they did things, there was no way it would ever go back to them, because they would do it for someone else." [696]

In the case of Pan Am 103, it appeared that the Octopus was more interested in covering up its involvement with drug smugglers than in securing the release of American hostages. And it was willing to sacrifice 270 lives to do so.

"There were people in a position of authority that knew something was going to come down, and they didn't do anything about it ... and people got killed."

—Tom G., 22-year CIA/DIA veteran, regarding Oklahoma City

The logistical apparatus that allowed the PFLP-GC to bomb flight 103 was a controlled drug delivery at Frankfurt airport—a sting operation run with the full knowledge of American, German, and Israeli intelligence. It was a sting operation that had been penetrated by Mid East terrorists intent on wreaking havoc.

In Oklahoma City, another sting operation was underway. Like the DEA's controlled delivery of drugs through Frankfurt, the ATF and FBI would seek to utilize a "controlled delivery" of a bomb in Oklahoma.

As previously discussed, the FBI, ATF, and U.S. Marshals, all had ample prior warning. Not only had the Marshals Service been warned of a *fatwa* against American installations as a result of the World Trade Center convictions, but the FBI received warnings from the Israelis, the Saudis, the Kuwaitis, and their own informant, Cary Gagan, concerning threats against federal buildings in Phoenix, Denver, and Oklahoma City.

Additionally, ATF informant Carol Howe specifically warned authorities about a neo-Nazi plan to blow up a federal building in either Tulsa or Oklahoma City as far back as November, '94.

As the fateful day drew closer, warnings began pouring in. Judge Wayne Alley, whose office sits across from the Murrah Building, was told several weeks prior to the blast by "security officials" to take "extra precautions." The federal judge, who was not in his office at the time, but whose clerks were injured in the blast, told the *Oregonian*, "Of all the days for this to happen, it's absolutely an amazing coincidence." When asked to discuss the nature of the warnings, Alley said, "Let me just say that within the past two or three weeks, information has been disseminated ... that indicated concerns on the part of people who ought to be a little bit more careful."

This is not surprising. Gagan had warned the FBI as far back as September that federal agents and judges were targeted for assassination. As previously noted, Gagan had been deep inside the Middle Eastern cell involved in the bombing. Gagan informed the Feds on September 21, 1994 that his Arab comrades had been cruising Denver in a white Mercury photographing federal agents. Gagan told the author that he was instructed to assassinate Judge Lewis Babcock.*

Had the Feds warned Judge Alley? "My subjective impression," said Alley, "was there was a reason for the dissemination of these concerns, strongly suggesting an impending proximate event." [697]

The Oklahoma City Fire Department, unlike Judge Alley, had the benefit of more specific warnings. On Friday, April 14, the FBI placed a call to Assistant Chief Charles Gaines to warn him of a potential terrorist threat within the next few days.

When Glenn Wilburn confronted Gaines, he was met with a blanket of denial. Wilburn then walked down the hall and confronted Chief Dispatcher Harvey Weathers, who unhesitatingly replied that they had in fact received a warning. Wilburn told him, "Well, you're going to be surprised to learn that Chief Gaines' memory is failing. He says it never happened." Weathers replied, "Well, you asked me and I told you. I'm not going to lie for anybody. A lot of people don't want to get involved in this." [689]

When Assistant Chief Jon Hansen was later interviewed by KFOR's Jayna Davis, he said he could no longer recall exactly who had called the Department, but convincingly reassured skeptics, "The FBI came in yesterday and told me it wasn't them."

Yet two reserve Sheriff's deputies on duty at the Murrah building the night of the bombing, Don Hammons and David Kachendofer, signed sworn affidavits that Representative Ernest Istook (R-OK) told them of the government's prior knowledge—a waring they received on April 9. Kachendofer was guarding the northwest corner of the building when Istook approached and chatted with him. "[Istook] made the comment to me, he says, 'Yeah, we knew this was going to happen.'

"And I said, 'Excuse me?'

"And he says, 'Yeah, we knew this was going to happen. We got word through our sources that there is a radical fundamentalist Islamic group in Oklahoma City and that they were going to bomb the Federal Building.'"

The day after the bombing, FBI SAC Bob Ricks managed to keep a straight face while announcing to reporters: "The FBI and Oklahoma City has not received any threats that indicated that a bombing was about to take place."

Like the fox assuring the farmer he hadn't made off with any chickens, the FBI's claims proved of little solace. Fortunately for the FBI, the audio logs of the Fire Department's incoming calls were mysteriously "erased." [699]

---

* I managed to partially confirm this by speaking to Judge Babcock, and his neighbor, both of whom said that extra security was provided the judge at that time.

As *The Daily Oklahoman* reported on August 14, 1997:

Vance DeWoody, owner of Opal's Answering Service, and his employee, Pat Houser ... received an anonymous telephone call saying that a bomb was going to go off in the office of the U.S. Secret Service on the ninth floor of the Murrah Building.

Through Opal's, this particular call for the Secret Service came four days *before* the bombing. Then, on the morning of April 19, the Executive Secretariat's Office of the Justice Department received a mysterious call from someone claiming the Murrah Building had just been blown up ... 24 minutes *before* the blast. ABC 20/20 quoted the official government document:

The Department of Justice ... received a telephone call ... twenty-four minutes prior to the bombing.... The caller said, "The Federal Building in Oklahoma City has just been bombed."[700]

ABC anchor Tom Jarriel noted that "no action was apparently taken" by the Justice Department in response to the emergency call minutes before the blast.[701]

Not long after Bob Rick's announcement, Carol Howe and Cary Gagan would make their presence known—informing the public that the government did indeed have prior knowledge of the attack. To cover themselves, the government only admitted that they had vague, unspecified warnings of the impending plot. As Stephen Jones wrote in his brief of March 25, 1997:

Soon the government's position will revert to the ridiculous and it will only deny any knowledge that the Murrah Building was specifically targeted at 9:02 A.M. on April 19, 1995, to be destroyed by a bomb delivered in a Ryder rental truck by Timothy McVeigh.... That is the Federal Government playing word games in order to avoid what is potentially the single most embarrassing and humiliating situation since the public found out that the FBI had an informant inside the terrorist group that bombed the World Trade Center in New York—an informant that actually helped make the bomb—but they bungled the entire situation and did not prevent that tragedy.

Nevertheless, it wouldn't be long before a significant percentage of the population would learn about the suspicious activites in Oklahoma City the morning of April 19. Attorney Daniel J. Adomitis was driving downtown around 7:30 A.M. that morning when he noticed a white Bomb Squad truck parked on the west side of the courthouse, close to the Murrah Building. Adomitis told the *Fort Worth Star/Telegram*, "I remember thinking as I passed that, 'Gee, I wonder if they had a bomb threat at the County Courthouse?'"

Norma Smith, who worked at the Federal Courthouse across from the Murrah Building, saw, along with numerous others, the Bomb Squad congregated in the parking lot. Smith recounted her story for her hometown Texas newspaper, the *Panola Watchman:*

> The day was fine, everything was normal when I arrived at 7:45 to begin my day at 8 A.M., but as I walked through my building's parking lot, I remember seeing a Bomb Squad. I really did not think about it—especially when we did not hear more about it....
>
> There was some talk about the Bomb Squad among employees in our office. We did wonder what it was doing in our parking lot. Jokingly, I said, "Well I guess we'll find out soon."[702]

Renee Cooper, whose infant son was killed in the day-care center, was driving down Robinson Street when she saw several men in dark jackets standing in front of the Federal Courthouse. The men's jackets were inscribed with the words "Bomb Squad."

Reporter J.D. Cash spoke with a woman whose brother worked in the Federal Building. "Frantic with worry, Jackie Stiles said she talked to an FBI agent at the scene who told her there had been a bomb threat made against the Murrah Building the previous week."

This fact was also confirmed by Michael Hinton, a former police officer who was staying across the street at the YMCA. Hinton witnessed what appeared to be a bomb threat evacuation of the Murrah Building two weeks earlier.[703]

Naturally, the Bomb Squad denied being there. In an interview with Jayna Davis, Sheriff J.D. Sharp claimed that the Bomb Squad truck was ten miles away at the time. "I can assure you from the testimony of witnesses and the bomb commander that our bomb unit was not anywhere near the Murrah Building the morning of the blast."

When the author attempted to interview two members of the Bomb Squad, one of them became visibly nervous, and demanded I speak to his superior. He denied removing additional bombs, or being at the Federal Building early that morning.

The Sheriff's Department later told NBC Extra's Brad Goode that the Bomb Squad was in fact deployed downtown for "training purposes," but claimed they were not in bomb attire. At the same time, the OCPD told Extra the Bomb Squad was not there *at all.*[704]

Reporter J.D. Cash received a similar response from Bomb Squad Captain Robert Heady. When confronted with the fact that at least two eyewitnesses saw the Bomb Squad members in their black t-shirts with the words "BOMB SQUAD" emblazoned across their chests in silver-white letters, the captain said, "We don't wear those type shirts."

Interestingly, a videotape made by Deputy Sheriff Melvin Sumter at the scene of the blast shows the Bomb Squad members, along with the captain, in t-shirts with words "BOMB SQUAD" in large silver-white letters written across their chests.

Still, the Bomb Squad would attempt to maintain this duplicitous charade. When he was summoned before the County Grand Jury reinvestigating the blast, Deputy Bill Grimsley claimed that the Bomb Squad was indeed downtown that morning. Grimsley claimed that he had left the county jail at 7:00 A.M., stopped at the nearby courthouse for a few minutes to take care of an errand, went to McDonald's for breakfast, then drove to the bomb training site 10miles away.

Yet Norma Smith saw the Bomb Squad truck downtown at 7:45 A.M. Renee Cooper saw it five minutes after eight—hardly in keeping with Grimsley's story.

Others, like Oklahoma Private investigator Claude Criss and County Appraiser J.D. Reed saw the Bomb Squad in full gear. "The presence of law enforcement was in the air," said Criss. "It was everywhere downtown that morning."

As previously discussed, Debra Burdick was sitting at a red light at 10th and Robinson, five blocks from the Murrah Building. "As the light changed, we started through the intersection," recalled Burdick, "and [that's when] the bomb went off ... and right after that, here comes the Bomb Squad, before the ambulances and the Fire Department."

J.D. Reed, who rushed out of the County Office Building when the bomb went off, later wrote in a company newsletter: "The paramedics and firemen were already at work. How could they move so quickly? They were there by the time we got down to the street!" [705]

The testimony of Burdick and Reed dovetails with that of Criss, who arrived at his office at 8:58 A.M. "I heard a lot of sirens at that time," he said. "A lot of sirens, coming from the west, approaching downtown. There was approximately seven trucks that were traveling at a high rate of speed. When they reached the top of that hill right there, the explosion went off." [706]

When ABC Extra contacted the Oklahoma City Fire Department to inquire about Criss's claim, they replied, "We can't really confirm or deny that claim." [707]

As Sergeant Yeakey, one of the first rescue workers at the scene later wrote to bombing survivor Ramona McDonald:

Everyone was behind you until you started asking questions as I did, as to how so many federal agents arrived at the scene at the same time.... For those who ran from the scene to change their attire to hide the fact that they were there, should be judged as cowards.

Associated Press photographer Pat Carter, who was at the scene within one hour of the blast, said that ATF agents were wearing full combat gear. Had they been preparing for a bust? [708]

HUD worker V.Z. Lawton was on the eighth floor of the Murrah Building when the bomb(s) went off. Lawton described four men who gave him a ride home that afternoon. They told him they were General Services Administration (GSA) employees out of Fort Worth, and were there doing a "routine" security check on the Federal Building. The men told Lawton this "security check" was conducted in the wee hours of the morning.*

Two of the men, Dude Goodun and Brent Mossbarger, later told the *Daily Oklahoman* they did not take Lawton home that day.[710]

As previously mentioned, HUD worker Jane Graham also recalled seeing two maintenance men in the building whom she had never seen before, on April 18, the day before the blast. Graham thought the men were GSA employees. She was later told that the men were Danny Paine and Harvey Norris—two maintenance workers for the Journal Record building who had been cleared by the FBI. But employees of the maintenance company that Paine and Norris worked for said they were definitely not the same individuals Graham had seen. The descriptions of the men were completely different.[709]

Even more interestingly, it was alleged that no ATF agents (as opposed to clerical workers) were in the Murrah Building at the time of the blast. Word of this quickly spread when Bruce Shaw, whose wife worked in the third-floor credit union, ran up to an ATF agent anxiously asking of her whereabouts. Shaw told KFOR's Brad Edwards that the agent "started getting a little bit nervous. He tried reaching someone on a two-way radio. [But] couldn't get anybody. I told him I wanted an answer right then. He said they were in debriefing, that none of the agents had been in there. They'd been tipped by their pagers not to come to work that day. Plain as day out of his mouth. Those were the words he said."[71]

The second witness, Shaw's boss Tony Brasier, was present when the agent made those comments, and confirmed to KFOR the accuracy of Shaw's testimony.[712]

The third witness was Tiffany Bible, a paramedic. When she asked an ATF agent on the scene if any of his fellow agents were still in the building, she was told they "weren't here" at the office that morning.

"It's clear to me that the ATF knew in advance something was about to happen," says a man whose wife was seriously injured that morning.[713]

In an attempt to steer suspicious eyes away from ATF culpability, Lester Martz, regional head of the ATF, put out a press release stating that several agents—Vernon Buster, Luke Franey, and Alex McCauley—had been trapped inside the building during the bombing:

---

* As previously mentioned, Guy Rubsamen, the Federal Protective Services guard on duty that night, said that nobody had entered the building. Yet Rubsamen took off at 2:00 A.M., and claimed that nobody was guarding the building from 2:00 A.M. to 6:00 A.M.

ATF's Resident Agent in Charge Alex McCauley was with a DEA agent (David Schickedanz) in the elevator when the bomb exploded. The elevator dropped in a free fall from the eighth floor to the third. The two men were trapped in the smoke-filled elevator. The emergency buttons and the phone were inoperable. On their fourth attempt they managed to break through the doors and escape from the elevator.[714]

Yet according to elevator repairman Duane James, who, along with several co-workers was checking equipment across the street that morning, Martz's statement is "pure fantasy." James, who was interviewed by J.D. Cash and ABC's 20/20, said five of the building's six elevators had frozen in place when the blast occurred, their doors blown inward. "Once that occurs, the doors cannot be opened—period," said James. "What I and some others did was kick in the ceilings on each of those elevators and determined that no one was in them."

James claims the remaining elevator was sitting at the third or fourth floor level and had no one in it. "Certainly it had not 'free fallen,' nor had any of the others." James explained that modern elevators cannot free fall due to counterbalancing weights on them which prevent such occurrences. The elevators are also equipped with automatic safety switches that cut speed and power if the elevator starts accelerating too fast.*

"None of those switches were tripped on any of the elevators in that building," said James. "I, along with other men with our company, checked the equipment several times. Absolutely no elevators dropped that morning."

Oscar Johnson, James' boss, told the *Daily Oklahoman* that when the elevator was found, a wall was pushed against the top of it "and there is no way you could have gotten the doors open. Our guys were the first ones there to open the top emergency access, and there was no one in it."[715]

Federal elevator inspector Dude Goodun told the *Daily Oklahoman* that he agreed with Johnson.[716]

So does former ATF agent Rick Sherrow. "This elevator business was garbage—about Franey being trapped in the elevator—because it didn't happen" said Sherrow. "Franey I pretty much believe was there, [but] this free-fall business, it just didn't happen."[717]

Naturally, Martz insisted five ATF employees were inside the Murrah Building. Valerie Rowden, the office manager, was cut all over. Jim Staggs was hospitalized with head wounds. Vernon Buster, they claimed, had a nail driven through his arm, and his name showed up on a list of the injured. But according to David Hall, owner and manager of KPOC-TV in Ponca City, who checked

---

* The author confirmed the story with Oscar Johnson, owner of the elevator company. According to Johnson, the freight elevator's doors were blown outward. If the sole blast had come from outside the building, how could this be?

with local hospitals, both Buster and Martz are lying.[718]

According to a reporter who interviewed Joe Gordon, an ATF agent from Colorado Springs, there was at least one ATF agent from out-of-town (believed to have been Dallas) injured in the blast that the ATF hadn't admitted to. While Buster's name showed up on the list of the injured, his name didn't.[719]

Another reporter from New York developed information that the Dallas ATF office—Martz's office—was also suspiciously vacant that morning. Was the ATF running a combined operation out of Dallas and Oklahoma City? This would make sense, since Martz is the regional director.[720]

DEA Assistant Agent in Charge Don Webb called the allegations against the ATF "bullshit." Webb told the author that McCauley and Schickedanz were indeed in the elevator when the bomb went off. He also said that "Luke Franey was on the phone" at the time of the bombing (although Webb admitted to me that he himself was at a golf tournament that morning).[721]

According to Sergeant Yeakey, Franey was not in the building:

Luke Franey was not in the building at the time of the blast, I know this for a fact,
I saw him! I also saw full riot gear worn with rifles in hand, why?[722]

Yeakey also wrote that Franey ran *into* the building. While news footage showed Franey standing in a blown-out window on the 9th floor shortly after the blast, he appeared surprisingly neat and clean. His appearance contrasted sharply with other survivors who were covered in dust and debris. In the photos, Franey is holding a box in one hand, and a walkie-talkie in the other.

Interestingly, he later showed up at Glenn Wilburn's house with a bandaged arm. Was Franey one of the agents who Dr. Chumley refused to bandage? According to a federal law-enforcement supervisor who works in the Federal Protective Services, Franey "was a bloody mess. He had a big gash on his forehead."[723]

Whatever the true story, it is generally agreed that the Federal Building was suspiciously empty that morning. Wendy Greer, the sister-in-law of senior FBI Agent Jim Volz (retired), told me her brother said that the FBI's offices at 50 Penn Place (several miles from the Murrah Building) also appeared to be suspiciously vacant the morning of the blast.

If these agents weren't in their offices, where were they? Some FBI agents, it appeared, were at a Special Olympics golf tournament in Shawnee (Webb told me he saw no ATF agents at the tournament). Yet this still wouldn't account for the strange activities that morning.[724]

In the early morning of April 19, Bob Flanders and his wife were driving east on I-44 at approximately 3:30 A.M., when they saw a strange team of men near the State Fairgrounds. The men, dressed in government black and driving black cars, were in the grass alongside the road, operating "hoops"—circular-shaped, radio beacon directional finders. Flanders recalled that the devices were about the size of a car steering wheel, and the men held them over their heads, slowly rotating them in a circular pattern.*

Around 4:00 A.M., a man who was driving home after work saw another team operating these unusual looking devices, this time by the Alfred P. Murrah Building. As he approached 5th Street, he was directed to one lane. The person directing traffic was not a police officer, and was standing next to a white vehicle with a yellow stripe. As the man drove by, he saw several men on the sidewalk holding these hoop-like devices above their heads, slowly turning them in different directions. As the man passed through, a roadblock was set up behind him, and all traffic was diverted from the area.

The equipment these witnesses describe matches that of RDF direction finding antennas that are used to home in on electronic transmitters. Was there a concealed radio transmitter on the one of the Ryder trucks, sending out a signal to these teams? It is likely, given the requirements of a successful sting operation, that they were electronically tracking the truck. The location of the team at the fairgrounds, high on a hill overlooking the city, is a clue to its intended mission.

Why were they tracking the truck? Had their quarry eluded them? Is it possible that one of the bombers, perhaps one of their own trusted undercover agents, turned off the transmitter, resulting in the loss of the signal? If so, it seems that the agents would have had what's known in law-enforcement parlance as a "loose tail," and, it appeared, they were frantically trying to find the truck.

Andreas Strassmeir, McVeigh's friend and alleged government operative, admitted that much in an interview with the *London Sunday Telegraph's* Ambrose Evans-Pritchard:

> The truck had a transmitter, so they could track it with a radio receiving device. I don't know how they could have lost contact. I think there was misinformation that the operation had been canceled.

According to KPOC's David Hall, the plan was to arrest the bombers at 3:30 in the morning. Given the ATF's past publicity stunts, it is likely that they were

---

* In kind of a bizarre twist to the story, they said that at one point one of the men rolled a hoop across the road to the team on the other side. A witness who saw the black-garbed team operating hoops by the Murrah building called the FBI's special 800 number to report what he saw. Afterwards he began noticing that his phone clicked constantly, and a mysterious black car began appearing outside his house. By the time Representative Key and I drove to Dallas to interview him, he was too afraid to talk, and we had to get the information through a friend.

hoping to arrest the suspects at or near the Murrah Building to ensure a highly publicized bust. As Strassmeir told Evans-Pritchard:

"It's obvious that it was a government 'op' that went wrong, isn't it? The ATF had something going with McVeigh. They were watching him—of course they were," he asserted, without qualification. "What they should have done is make an arrest while the bomb was still being made instead of waiting till the last moment for a publicity stunt. They had everything they needed to make the bust, and they screwed it up."[725]*

Strassmeir added that the ATF thought that the bomb was set to go off at 2 or 3 A.M., but somehow the plan was changed. "McVeigh made some changes in the plan," said Strassmeir. "He is a very undisciplined soldier, you know ... In retrospect, the ATF should have made the bust when the bomb was being built in Junction City."[726]

The bombers, according to the former Elohim City security chief, were to be captured "during the night, when no one was there—that's why the ATF had the building staked out from midnight until 6:00 A.M. Later, the informant believed that the bombing was off for the day and reported that ... the ATF lost control of the situation, and McVeigh and the others were able to bomb the building."[727]

While Strassmeir heaps most of the blame on the ATF, he does task the FBI for its failure:

The different agencies weren't cooperating. In fact, they were working *against* each other. You even had a situation where one branch of the FBI was investigating and not sharing anything with another branch of the FBI.... Whoever thought this thing up is an idiot, in my opinion.[728]

While Strassmeir continually protested that he himself was not involved in the plot, as either a suspect or a provocateur, he did say that the plotters consisted of "four [men], plus the informant and McVeigh."

"They probably were going to entrap whoever was coming in," said Sherrow. "They had enough intelligence that they were going to set up an operation to pop this guy, whether it was McVeigh or whoever else, and something fell through the cracks....

"Talking from the perspective of a former ATF man, say they're going to buy

---

* Strassmeir told the author in an interview from his home in Berlin that Pritchard misquoted him—that Strassmeir relayed the preceding statement from another ATF agent. Pritchard disagrees, and stands by his story.

explosives, or let somebody plant a bomb … they will let the deal go until the last second, before making the arrest."

Somehow, the deal went wrong.

While this startling evidence would soon make itself known to investigators, bombing victims, and a limited segment of the public—the Justice Department, federal prosecutors, and the ATF all rushed to refute the evidence.

"Can you imagine if we had known that … and let that happen?" said ATF agent Harry Eberhardt. "I had a lot of friends in that building—a lot of friends.... We never would have let that happen." [729]

Dewy Webb, the current ATF RAC (Resident Agent in Charge), concurred. "They had so many friends they lost in the bombing—they had to pick which funeral they could go to." [730]

Though Eberhardt's reasoning sounds valid, it is likely his concern is overrated. While it is doubtful the ATF, FBI, or local officials would purposely allow such a catastrophic event to occur, it is likely—highly probable in fact—that through their stupidity and negligence, such an event did occur.

Said Sherrow, "I've got agents in their court testimony saying that they don't care about the public's safety. They don't consider it. They arranged to meet with a guy here in Phoenix who allegedly had hundreds of pounds of explosives, and they chose a crowded shopping center parking lot, running around with MP-5s [sub-machineguns] and handguns and everything else.

"This happened before Oklahoma, and it continues to happen. We had a case in Pennsylvania where a guy wanted to sell a small amount of explosives. He wanted to meet [the agents] way out in the country. Instead they decided to meet him on an Interstate rest stop that was jammed with people, and brought the media. They endanger the public right and left and they don't care about it." [731]

Sherrow's analysis is based on more than historical precedent and informed opinion. While ATF agents refused to admit their involvement in the bungled operation, Martz met with local TV producers behind closed doors shortly after the bombing. Martz's intent was to convince the journalists that what was underway was a sensitive undercover operation, and that they should take pains not to reveal it.*

---

* As for Eberhardt, his name showed up on an ATF report concerning Carol Howe's activities at Elohim City. The report indicated that an "irate" Eberhardt expressed his concern that Howe's cover had been "severely compromised" due to the release of a report by FBI agent James R. Blanchard III. Although the report was prepared almost a year after the bombing, the fact that Eberhardt's name appeared prominently on the report suggests that his office was involved, along with the Tulsa office, on the Elohim City investigation.

This is most interesting considering that ATF agent Angela Finley-Graham's report of August 30 stated that their investigation of Elohim City was classified as "SENSITIVE" and "SIGNIFICANT" (as opposed to routine), and the investigation concerned "terrorist/extremist" organizations.

According to former ATF official Robert Sanders, such classifications mean that all reports would automatically be sent to Washington, as well as being routinely routed to Martz at the Dallas Field Office, which in fact, they were.

Sanders, who held every possible supervisory position including that of ATF Assistant Director, told *The New American* magazine that the activities cited in the ATF reports have "such a high potential for affecting national security" that they would have most likely been sent to the heads of the Treasury and Justice Departments as well as the White House and National Security Council.[732]

Martz admitted to incredulous reporters was that there was indeed a sting operation underway on the night of the 18th that was called off at 0600 hours (6:00 A.M.). When reporters asked Martz if the operation involved Timothy McVeigh, he replied "I can neither confirm or deny that."[733]*

David Hall attended the closed-door meeting with Martz. "I don't believe that the ATF wired the building and blew it up. I do believe that they knew that there was going to be a possible bomb threat to the building, because they had set it up themselves, with their informants and different people they were working with. And somebody really slipped it to 'em."[734]

Hall had also been long-time friends with Harry Eberhardt, and was one of the first to develop inside information regarding the ATF's activities that morning. While Martz held fast to his claim that three ATF agents were in the Murrah Building at the time of the blast, Hall insists, "that's an outright lie."**

The seasoned investigative journalist contends that at least eight of the ATF's regular compliment of 13 agents were on assignment away from the Federal Building that morning. "Three agents [Don Gillispie, Delbert Canopp and Tim Kelly] were in federal court in Newkirk, on an arson case that occurred in Ponca City.... Two agents [Karen Simpson and Harry Eberhardt] were in federal court in Oklahoma City. Three more were in Garfield County at a hearing. The other five were out on surveillance."[735]

Just who were they surveilling?

"As far as can be determined," said Sherrow, "they had an undercover sting operation. They had a sting operation going that night, with about six agents

---

* Luke Franey claimed the only sting they were working involved a narcotics case with the Norman Police Department.

** Franey claims that agent Darrell Edwards was at home, talking on the phone to him. Bruce Anderson was on his way to a compliance inspection, and agent Mark Michalic, who had worked late with Franey the night before, was on his way to the office.

involved, and they terminated it at six in the morning. Martz has admitted to this, then since backed off.... Given the circumstances, it's reasonable to assume that the person they were surveilling was McVeigh."

Hall concurs. "We developed from our sources inside the ATF that five agents were up on surveillance all night long. We have to assume at that point, basically probably surveilling either McVeigh—and let me say this about McVeigh—there's a good chance that McVeigh could be an informant in this operation."

According to Glenn Wilburn, the ATF's plans changed at the last minute, and they stood down at 6:30 A.M. Then the Bomb Squad came on the scene at 6:30, checked the building for bombs, then stood down at 8:30. When the building blew up at 9:02 A.M., all the agents and police, who were already on the scene or nearby, quickly responded.

Yet it appears there is more to the story. Hall claims that on the night before the bombing, several witnesses saw McVeigh meet with ATF agent Alex McCauley and two other individuals of Middle Eastern descent in an Oklahoma City McDonalds at approximately 9:30 P.M. "He was a known ATF agent," said Hall. "[And] money changed hands."

Could this money have been the $2,000 that was discovered on McVeigh at the time of his arrest?

Terry Nichols was interviewed by Hall early on, and was told that McVeigh met with men who provided him a $2,000 payoff. Nichols left the restaurant at approximately 9:45 P.M. and drove back to his home in Herrington, Kansas. Hall interviewed Nichols' neighbors who claimed he arrived early that morning.[736]

Another witness, an unidentified homeless man, contacted KTOK reporter Jerry Bonnen, and told him McVeigh drove past the McDonalds and yelled "Hey, want to have a few beers?" McVeigh then gave the man some cash, whereupon he purchased two quarts at the Total convenience store across the street. A Total employee, Ron Williams, reported that a Ryder truck was parked at the McDonalds.[737]

An anonymous informant who contacted Representative Key, claiming to be a friend of those involved in the bombing, said that McVeigh had indeed met federal agents at an unnamed restaurant in Oklahoma City, and had rendezvoused with at least four of them prior to the bombing. Key taped the conversation:

"This guy here, he has a recording—a video recording—a camcorder recording that shows this same DEA agent and McVeigh in the parking lot of a restaurant. And this is was shot about dusk. And two people in suits go over to the car, McVeigh and this DEA agent get out and they're standing back by the trunk. And the DEA agent's patting McVeigh on the shoulder, and then one of the two men in suits passes McVeigh a white envelope and then they leave, And he has this on tape."[738]

While Representative Key never did get the videotape, another source close to the investigation told him that McVeigh was indeed an informant.

What he didn't explain was the reason for the presence of the DEA.

KFOR's Brad Edwards developed similar information," said Hall, "from totally different sources. "So we have four different sources telling us this. He also has the same name of the agent (McCauley). "I think that when this is all said and done, that we're going to find out—and this is what I've said from the beginning—that this was a sting operation gone sour."

But do you really need two tons of explosive in order to set up a sting? Yes, according to Hall. Ammonium-nitrate isn't illegal in Oklahoma, and a few hundred pounds won't convince prosecutors there was a serious bomb threat in the works. "I think the intent there was to show that it was going to do some damage, rather than, you know, a pipe bomb. It wouldn't bring the intention here in Oklahoma." [739]

Strassmeir agrees. "I am told they thought it would be better to put a bigger bomb in there. The bigger the better. It would make them more guilty." [740]

While Martz would not confirm who the actual target of the sting was, one person who did confirm it was a man who spoke with bombing survivor and activist Ramona McDonald. McDonald had formed a group called Heroes of the Heart. Through her numerous meetings with paramedics and police, firefighters and federal agents, McDonald began learning the sickening truth about what really happened that day.

As the meetings wore on, a consensus was reached that the truth needed to be told. The question was how. As McVeigh's trial approached, McDonald and her group were gearing up for a trial of their own. McDonald had contacted former Pentagon counter-terrorism analyst Jesse Clear, and Clear had contacted a young firebrand attorney named Joseph Camerata. Camerata's intent was to sue the government for negligence.

In August of 1996, about a month before Camerata came to Oklahoma to interview his prospective clients, McDonald received a mysterious phone call. Although the caller didn't identify himself by name, McDonald thought she recognized the voice of as that of Representative Ernest Istook (R-OK). The caller asked McDonald, "What do we have to do to get you to drop this?"

Although he didn't realize it, McDonald was taping the conversation. The scenario the caller lays out is, to the uninitiated, both startling and frightening. He describes in almost precise detail how the operation was a sting gone bad; how federal agents allowed a truck with a powerful bomb to be driven through a crowded city and parked next to a building containing hundreds of people. And, revealing the mystery of the elusive John Doe 2, he explains how he was an undercover agent, supposed to defuse the bomb at the last minute … and failed to do so.*

---

* Notice how the caller depicts McVeigh as the sole target of the sting, and attempts to distance himself from the operation by talking of it in the third tense.

Caller: "I don't think they expected the truck to blow up. I believe, and I've believed this for a long time … I believe that number two—John Doe #2—was a federal agent working undercover. And I believe that he helped McVeigh steal the goods and helped buy the equipment, and I believe that he helped McVeigh make the bomb, and I believe that his whole task in this whole thing … his only real task was to render the device safe so that the federal agents could pretend to remove it and move in. They did not want to move in until he was cleared of the scene so that they wouldn't tip their hands. See what I'm saying? And the odds are pretty good that whole reason behind this is because they were after someone bigger than McVeigh, which means they probably think he was linked to somebody in the Militia movement or something like that.

"So I think what you're saying … you know I understand what you're saying … but I don't think you see the big picture. I don't think that, you know, I'd only divulge a look at the big picture if that's the actual scenario. If that's the actual scenario, which I believe it to be, I think there really is no claim that the agent, that was John Doe #2, did not render the bomb safe. Which he very well may have rendered the bomb safe, and then McVeigh may have put in a second fail-safe which he didn't know about. Which is probably what's happened….

"I would bet money on that's, in fact, the way this whole thing came down. Yes, they stood out in front of the building. Yes, they followed him directly to the building. Yes, they watched him get out of the building … get out of the truck. Yes, they watched him drive off. That's not … that was their plan. I don't believe they ever planned to apprehend him anywhere near the building. I believe that John Doe #2 was a federal witness. His job was to render the device safe. Therefore, the only thing sitting out in front of that building was a bomb … a truck loaded with a bomb that would not go off. And I think that's the situation. In fact I know it is."

McDonald: "Okay … so … so why didn't they just come out and explain that to everybody?"

Caller: "The public doesn't have to know that. When it comes to the national security and things like this, the public does not have to know … the public is not required to know. First of all, by doing that, they would've, uh, put their witness, which is the federal agent John Doe #2, they would have blown his cover, first of all. Which possibly he's involved in something right now that you have no idea about. You know, there very well may have been numerous plots involving numerous buildings. See what I'm saying? You don't have the whole picture … without full knowledge … what you may do may cost them their lives. You should be very aware of that."

McDonald: "Okay. Well, that's what I've been trying to be very careful of. I don't want to see anyone else get hurt. At the same time …"

Caller: "Well, if that guy's cover's been blown, he'd dead already."

McDonald: "Do you think so?"

Caller: "Sure … I'm sure. Once you have gone up to this point, it has gotten out, which I'm sure it has, because there are moles everywhere … the chances are good that he's been terminated already and this whole thing has blown up in their face. I don't believe that, out of an act of negligence, these highly trained professionals would have allowed that man to leave that truck out in front of that building with its live bomb in it."

McDonald: "No, no, no. It stood out there for the whole time, from the time it pulled up until it went off."

Caller: "That's what I'm saying. They would not have allowed it. The only reason they allowed the truck to sit there so long, is because in my opinion they were under the impression that that bomb was rendered safe. And I'd say that there was no rush … there was no reason … to evacuate the building. There was no rush to make an arrest. The truck was just going to sit out there until they went and towed it off. So I don't think they thought it was an emergency and I think either that John Doe #2 made a mistake in rendering the bomb safe, or McVeigh was smart enough to plant a second fail-safe. Which most bomb makers do."

McDonald: "Do you think that's why they didn't tell anybody?"

Caller: "No. The bomb was safe as far as they knew."

McDonald: "Okay. Well, that explains why there was so many of them [federal agents] there so fast."

Caller: "Exactly. They followed him to the building, their agent was in the truck with him when they followed him to the building, everything was under control, as far as they thought, all they had was the man who built the bomb that was not going to go off, because their agent had rendered it safe. And their whole thing was not a problem. Let him drive his truck right in front of his target, then they allowed him to drive off.

"Once he drives off, he renders the truck safe, and then we can have the trooper arrest him on the interstate for bogus charges. Which they did, and this was all planned out 100 percent. I … I … I don't believe they allowed that truck."

McDonald: "You don't think they intentionally let the bomb go off?"

Caller: "No, that's right. I'll never believe that."

McDonald: "Well, I mean, that's the only thing about this that I found so hard to believe."

Caller: "They thought the bomb was safe. They thought that their agent, who was in the truck and who helped prepare the bomb, would set it so it would not go off. Now, whether McVeigh went back to the truck … where the agent did not know … and put a second fail-safe … or the agent made a mistake and did not actually render the bomb safe like he was supposed to … that's what's going on here."

McDonald: "Well, see, that's it then. I wanted someone that would be able to tell us for a fact if this was, like, deliberate or not. You know what I'm saying?"

Caller: "I'm not gong to tell you that. Let me tell you something. I'm sure they had … everything was under surveillance there. So I'm sure they *do* have pictures of the building blowing up, and I'm sure they *do* have pictures of federal agents, and I'm sure they *do* have audio tapes of them saying: 'Let 'em go, let 'em go … Wait, wait, wait.…' There was no rush in their mind. In their mind, there was no rush to get that truck away from that building … that bomb … was not supposed to go off.

"Therefore, everything they did, fits, if you think about it. They followed it, they allowed it to drive up there knowing that there was a bomb in the truck. Their idea was to let John Doe #2—their federal agent—they would be able to use him in further investigations of these bombings of these groups that are in militia groups. And this was a perfect entry in, because he could have went through there.

"After McVeigh was arrested, John Doe #2 would have become a hero to the cause of the militias. And the militias would have taken him in and hid him, which would have made him part of the infrastructure of the militias. Which is what their goal was for this whole thing … was to bust the militias. If you take the big picture, and look at the big picture, there were very few mistakes made on this sting operation. [Except blowing up a building and killing 169 people.] With the exception that John Doe #2, the federal agent, did not render the bomb safe. Just think of it this way, Ramona."

McDonald: "I've always been a big fan of the United States and that, but then … I've always been … this was the one thing that bothered me."

Caller: "They didn't let the building fall intentionally. Their opinion was that this bomb was rendered safe and this bomb would not go off. And their whole thing on this thing … if you think about it … it makes sense from a tactical standpoint. You would follow the truck to the building. You allow your lead suspect to get away from the building because it didn't blow up, because it's not supposed to. You take John Doe #2 … he gets away, which is your federal agent. John Doe #1—McVeigh—is arrested on a bogus charge and then later proven that he's the one who planted the bomb that did not go off."

McDonald: "But you honestly don't think that they really intended."

Caller: "Not at all. Not at all. They would not have to. No.… Basically, what happened is, this was a mistake. Someone screwed up and the only one that screwed up … The agents on the scene? They didn't screw up. They did exactly what their orders were: Wait … allow the suspect to leave the scene. Once the suspect had left the scene, then render the truck safe, which is already safe. All they have to do is get in, give it a hot-wire, and drive it off to a safe location and then open up the back and disarm the bomb. Which was supposedly rendered safe to begin with. Okay?

"And then, from there they charge in … See, this plan was put in motion before the bomb ever went off. Their intent was to allow McVeigh to be arrested later on … John Doe #2 to get away … and then, John Doe #2, the Federal Government would have released a sketch or picture. And then, that man would have had to go underground and hide. Where would he hide? He would have hid with the militias.

The militias would take him in as a hero. The militias would give him hero status in the Militia movement, which would allow him to be privy to information that the government could use later on....

"They did not want that building to blow up. I guarantee you this ... their whole intent was that that bomb was rendered safe before it was ever parked in front of that building ... otherwise, they would have quietly."

McDonald: "Got everybody out of the building?"

Caller: "Got everybody out of the building, before the bomb ever even pulled up in front of the building. There was no reason for them to do that, because according to their plan, the bomb was safe now. There was no reason to evacuate the building and the panic ... because there was a truck loaded with a bomb that was not going to blow up."

McDonald: "Okay."

Caller: "See what I'm saying? And John Doe #2 ... By going this far with it ... Let me explain something to you. Your actions have consequences. There are a lot of witnesses. There are a lot of agents right now in the hills that are infiltrating these militia groups, and ... all these people will get killed. Their blood will be on your hands. I understand that you want ... If I really thought that the government allowed the building to blow up, I would be with you 100 percent. But I know ... and I believe ... they were horrified when the bomb went off ... really horrified."

McDonald: "Yeah, they all looked like they were in shock."

Caller: "They figured, as soon as McVeigh got free, as soon as he got ... drove off in his car ... and I'll tell you something they did. Do you know what they did?"

McDonald: "What?"

Caller: "They stole his license plate off that car. You know why? So they'd have probable cause to stop him on the interstate.... They stole his plate. Why do you think the plate was never found? His plate was stolen from the vehicle and the Federal Government stole the plate from the vehicle, so that he would be arrested ... John Doe #2 would go free, they would put a sketch out that would make him America's Most Wanted. The only place that a man that would be wanted by the government can hide would be to be hid by the militia groups inside their infrastructure.

"But once he infiltrates the infrastructure ... and he's in ... all of a sudden he's a hero. And right now, you know, these groups probably believe that they have John Doe #2 and that they're hiding him from the government and they're doing the patriotic thing ... and they believe that the building should have blown up. So they're holding him. Now, this man's privy to all kinds of information about future bombings, which we don't even know how many bombs they have stopped because the agents ... how many lives have been saved because that agent's now in the militia. And if this comes to light ... this operation ..."

What the caller does is attempt to instill guilt in McDonald over her efforts to reveal the truth. Yet McDonald did not allow 169 innocent people to be killed through her negligence and stupidity. The government did.

This ridiculous and immoral rationale is similar to that used by Winston Churchill during WWII. Churchill knew the German Luftwaffe were going to bomb the city of Coventry, because the British had cracked the German code using a device called the "Enigma" machine. Churchill feared that by evacuating Coventry on the night in question, the Germans would realize their codes had been broken and change them, thus hampering British intelligence efforts. Churchill, having knowledge of the forthcoming raid, let it proceed, at the cost of thousands of lives and millions in property damage, in order not to compromise their source—in this case—the Enigma machine.

In a similar vein, the Feds would cover up the truth about Oklahoma City so as not to compromise their undercover agent—John Doe 2—and ultimately, reveal their own negligence.

Nevertheless, McDonald's caller makes the case that she should respect these agents, who he terms "highly trained professionals," conducting an operation that has already resulted in the criminally negligent deaths of 169 people, and allow it to continue unabated, when it was undoubtedly government agents who acted as provocateurs and goaded the suspects into carrying out the bombing in the first place.

These are the same "highly trained, dedicated professionals" who murdered 86 innocent men, women and children at Waco, who murdered most of an innocent family at Ruby Ridge, who dropped a bomb on the MOVE housing activists in Philadelphia, killing 11 people, including five children, and who bungled the World Trade Center sting operation, resulting in the deaths of six people and the injury of over 1,000.

What nitwit is supposed to buy the story that "highly trained, dedicated professionals" would drive a truck laden with explosives around a busy city—a bomb that could explode at any minute? More likely, the caller is using the "federal agent in danger" line with McDonald as a ruse to cover up the fact that these "highly trained, dedicated professionals" are nothing more than a bunch of highly dangerous, out-of-control, self-serving lunatics.

"The government must, and I say must, take responsibility for their sting operation going sour," said HUD worker Jane Graham. "We are not expendable for their cause." [741]

As of this writing, the McDonald's tape is being analyzed by an audio forensics expert. Oklahomans who have listened to the tape strongly believe that it is Representative Ernest Istook. Istook sits on the Subcommittee on National Security, which would tend to explain his rationale that "the public doesn't have to know ... when it comes to the national security and things like this, the public does not have to know."

Istook voted for the 1995 Crime and Anti-Terrorism bills, and is reportedly very friendly with Senator Orrin Hatch, one of the original drafters of the latter. Istook is also on close terms with the FBI, which would go a long way towards explaining his apologetic tone. He also lives in the same Congressional district and neighborhood (Warr Acres) as McDonald.*

This scenario is also reinforced by a second individual—a police officer named Bob Cancemi. He told McDonald he knows "for a fact" that authorities knew in advance specifically when and how the Ryder truck-bomb was to arrive at the Federal Building. But, he says, something went "very wrong"—the bomb was supposed to have been disarmed. "I feel pretty confident that they knew exactly what was going on," he said, "and … things didn't go according to plan." [742]

Cancemi's information, and that of McDonald's caller, is backed up by Daina Bradley. Peering out the window of the Social Security office minutes before the blast, Bradley caught a glimpse of a stocky, dark-skinned man exiting the passenger side of the Ryder truck. She said the man walked to the back of the truck to open the door, then spun around, looking "very nervous, almost confused." He then ran down 5th Street in the opposite direction and jumped into a brown pickup which sped away. Could the man's confused expression have been the result of an unexpected occurrence? Perhaps when he lifted the rear gate he saw a second timing device attached to the bomb that he didn't know how to disarm? And not knowing what to do, he fled.

Yet while the caller admits the government's involvement in the bombing, he fails to take into account the additional bombs *inside* the building. He fails to explain why the government quickly demolished the bomb site, destroying all forensic evidence. And his story does not account for Middle Eastern and numerous other suspects.

The caller's explanation also goes a long way towards explaining a statement made by Terry Nichols after his arrest. When Lana Padilla asked her ex-husband during a prison visit about John Doe 2, he said, "If they want to find John Doe 2, they should look in their own backyard." [743]

What is clear is that the government could take no chances in allowing any of their undercover operatives and informants—Strassmeir, Brescia, Howe, Gagan, Hussaini, and others—to testify at trial. To cover their butts, federal law enforcement agencies ignored, discredited, and even killed those who attempted to reveal the truth. As Officer Terrance Yeakey wrote before he was murdered:

---

* Recall that Sheriff's Deputies Don Hammons and David Kachendofer signed sworn affidavits that Rep. Istook told them of the government's prior knowledge of the attack. Istook also told bombing investigator Pat Briley that he was very close to the FBI's investigation of the bombing, and made it his business to know the details. "There is nothing you can tell me and the FBI about the bombing that we don't already know," Istook said.

I took an oath to uphold the Law and to enforce the Law to the best of my ability. This is something I cannot honestly do and hold my head up proud any longer if I keep my silence as I am ordered to do.

My guess is the more time an officer has to think about the screw up the more he is going to question what happened ... Can you imagine what would be coming down now if that had been our officers' who had let this happen? Because it was the Feds that did this and not the locals, is the reason it's okay.

The sad truth of the matter is that they have so many police officers convinced that by covering up the truth about the operation gone wrong, that they are actually doing our citizens a favor. What I want to know is how many other operations have they had that blew up in their faces? Makes you stop and take another look at Waco.

I would consider it to be an insult to my profession as a police officer and to the citizens of Oklahoma for ANY of the City, State or Federal agents that stood by and let this happen to be recognized as any thing other than their part in participation in letting this happen....

Those who said the bombing was an excuse to destroy the militias were dismissed as paranoiacs, but McDonald's caller admits the entire operation was to ensnare the movement. McDonald's caller makes no distinction between militias and neo-Nazi groups. Militia groups angrily denounced the bombing.

If the bombing of the Alfred P. Murrah Building was merely a failed sting operation, where did it go wrong? Those who remember the World Trade Center bombing, may recall that it, too, was a fouled sting operation.

In that case, the FBI's original plan to entrap the Al-Gama'a al-Islamiya group was to have their undercover operative, Emad Eli Salem, substitute a harmless powder for the real explosive, which he would help them build. Instead, due to a disagreement, the FBI pulled Salem off the case.

Like Cary Gagan, who tried to warn the FBI of the Oklahoma City bombing, and Samra Mahayoun, who tried to warn officials of the Pan Am 103 attack, Salem, they insisted, was just not credible. Several weeks later, a truck-bomb detonated under the World Trade Center, killing six people and injuring 1,000 more.

Unbeknownst to the FBI, Salem, a former Egyptian Army colonel, had secretly recorded his conversations with his FBI handlers.* Portions of the tapes were made public and reprinted in the *Wall Street Journal* and the *New York Times*. In broken English, Salem talks with the unnamed FBI supervisor who pulled him off the case: "We'll be going building the bomb with a phony powder, and grabbing the people who was involved in it. But since you, we didn't do that."

---

* According to former CID investigator Gene Wheaton, Salem worked for the TRD— Egypt's version of the CIA, controlled by the CIA. Salem admitted to being a double-agent for the U.S. and Egypt.

When Salem decided to complain to FBI headquarters, FBI supervisor John Anticev dissuaded him: "He said, I don't think that the New York people would like the things out of the New York Office to go to Washington, D.C."

Salem's immediate handler, agent Nancy Floyd, is heard on the tapes agreeing with the Egyptian's account, saying, "Well, of course not, because they don't want to get their butts chewed."

In one conversation, Salem tells Floyd:

"Since the bomb went off, I feel terrible. I feel bad. I feel here is people who don't listen."

Ms. Floyd seems to commiserate, saying: "Hey, I mean it wasn't like you didn't try, and I didn't try."

Salem recounts another point in the conversation he said he had with Anticev, saying:

"I said, 'Guys, now you saw this bomb went off, and you both know that we could avoid that.'"

Salem talks of the plan to substitute harmless powder for explosives during another conversation with Agent Floyd. In that conversation, he recalls a previous discussion with Anticev. Mr. Salem says he told the other agent:

"Do you deny that your supervisor is the main reason of bombing the World Trade Center?"

Mr. Salem said that Anticev did not deny it.[744]

It's interesting to note that not only did the FBI "foul up" the operation, but had Salem act as a provocateur, recommending potential targets, teaching the terrorists how to build the bomb, then teaching them how to drive the truck used in the bombing.

As the *Wall Street Journal* reported in regards to Salem's activities inside the Sheik's group immediately following the World Trade Center bombing:

Mr. Salem helped organize the "battle plan" that the government alleged included plots to bomb the United Nations and FBI buildings in New York, and the Holland and Lincoln tunnels beneath the Hudson River. Working with a charismatic Sudanese man named Siddig Ali, a follower of Sheik Omar, Mr. Salem recruited seven local Muslims to scout targets, plan tactics and obtain chemicals and electrical parts for bombs, the government alleged. The FBI supplied a safehouse in Queens.[745]

As Floyd later explained to her superior, "Emad had the information about the bombs and where they wanted to have them placed. If we had done what we were supposed to have done, we would have known about it ... we would have used our heads and come up with the solution of trying to neutralize the situation."[746]

When Salem was pulled off the case, the bombers contacted Ramzi Yousef, a reported Iraqi agent and expert bomb maker. Mujahadeen veteran and World Trade Center bomber Mamud Abouhalima met Yousef in Afghanistan in 1988, and brought him and co-conspirator Ahmed Ajaj to the U.S. in September of 1992. Far from building a harmless device, Yousef constructed a sophisticated, powerful bomb, capable of causing extensive damage. Had patsy driver Mohammed Salemeh parked the truck next to a key column, they might have toppled the 110 story Twin Towers, killing as many as 20,000 people.

As William Norman Grigg writes in the February 19, 1997 issue of the *New American:*

> Shortly after Yousef's arrival, the FBI subpoenaed two dozen of Sheik Omar's followers and questioned them about the sheik, Nosair, and Abouhalima. However, no arrests were made, no Grand Jury investigation was launched, and the FBI chose to downgrade its scrutiny of Omar's network—just as plans were being finalized for the Trade Center bombing. This curious decision is even more peculiar in light of the fact that the FBI had obtained intelligence on the network's capabilities and intentions from Emad A. Salem, a former Egyptian Army officer and FBI informant who served as Omar's security guard.

The FBI defended themselves by alleging that Salem refused to cooperate with FBI guidelines and procedures. He didn't want to wear a body-wire they claimed, and refused to testify against his so-called terrorist comrades in court. Salem was summarily dismissed. When these "highly-trained, dedicated professionals" pulled Salem off the case, they lost control of the situation, and the bombers made their move.

The FBI claimed the exact same thing about one of their informants in the Oklahoma City case—Cary Gagan. Although the Justice Department granted Gagan a Letter of Immunity, they and the FBI failed to follow up on the informant's apparently credible information. Gagan hadn't just contacted the FBI and the Marshals Service once or twice, but informed them on numerous occasions of the terrorists' plans. To the Gagan's knowledge, none of this information was followed up.

After the bombing, the Justice Department tried to maintain that Gagan wasn't credible. The U.S. Attorney's Office revoked his Letter of Immunity, ignored his information, and apparently tried to assassinate him. In order to prove their bogus allegations, they removed reports from his informant file that showed Gagan assisted the DEA in recovering critical information.

The government's conduct with Gagan paralleled their treatment of Carol

Howe. As previously discussed, Tulsa ATF Agent Angela Finley-Graham placed Howe inside Elohim City, where she reported on the activities of Mahon, Strassmeir, and others allegedly involved in the plot. It was recently learned that Howe secretly taped conversations with her ATF handler as Salem had. Those tapes have not been made public as of this writing.

Still, the government would try to cover its tracks by claiming that Howe's information was unspecific, and that she was emotionally unstable. Yet two days after the bombing, the ATF renewed its contract with her, and sent her back to Elohim City to collect additional information. In the aftermath of the World Trade Center bombing, the FBI renewed its association with Emad Salem, paying him a reported $1 million to infiltrate Sheik Omar's group once again.

Given the Tulsa ATF's interest in Strassmeir and Elohim City, it is highly likely that they were the initial target of the sting. ATF agent Angela Finley-Graham conferred with her superiors about raiding the compound in February, '95 and arresting Strassmeir, but FBI and DoJ officials advised against it.[747]

The ATF's actions at Elohim City were a curious parallel to those of the FBI's in New York. As the *London Sunday Telegraph's* Ambrose Evans-Pritchard stated, "It appears that the local BATF had stumbled on a bigger operation being run by the grown-ups at the Justice Department." *

If the Arabs plotted with neo-Nazis to blow up the Federal Building, it is a foregone conclusion that they were under surveillance by the ATF and FBI.

Recall that Timothy McVeigh and Sam Khalid were both investigated by the FBI. McVeigh in 1993, and Khalid in 1990. Since Mike Khalid was investigated for espionage by Army CID, it is reasonable to assume that attention was focused on his brother as well.

Said David Hall, "I felt like ... that probably the agencies involved in this, their intent was to tie together some Patriot groups and to tie in some other terrorist groups. I think the intent here was to say—go to Congress and say—that we have domestic and foreign terrorist groups, Mideast or foreign, working together and trying to blow up buildings here in the United States."

It is likely that the FBI became aware of collusion between the two groups—neo-Nazis and Arabs—as early as 1994, when Gagan reported that Terry Nichols met

---

* Craig Roberts, a 20-year Tulsa police officer, concurs: "[The Tulsa ATF office] did surveillance, took photos, used informants (Howe) and yet no matter what they did, they couldn't get any cooperation out of D.C. They knew something was wrong, but couldn't get a handle on it. I think it's because Strassmeir was working as an infiltrator at the D.C. level, and they were protecting him without tipping off the local office—which they obviously didn't trust to keep a secret from the local police. This is not unusual. In fact, the field agents with the ATF and FBI often do not get along well with the D.C. officials—and vice/versa."

with "Iranians" in Henderson, Nevada. With the involvement of the Arabs, and the white supremacists at Elohim City, the sting became a joint ATF/FBI operation.

Interestingly, Hall learned that the FBI and the ATF got into a shouting match while debriefing Janet Reno. According to Hall, when Reno left the room, the FBI and ATF began yelling at each other, angrily accusing each other for the tragedy.

Somewhere along the line in Oklahoma City, the FBI and ATF lost control of the situation, and the bombers were able to make their move. As in the World Trade Center case, someone who had infiltrated the operation in Oklahoma had substituted a real bomb for a phony one, or had placed a redundant timer on the bomb, or simply provided false information to the agents in charge, preventing them from stopping the attack.

Were the FBI and ATF double-crossed by one of their own informants? Or, as in the Pan Am case, did someone in a position of authority look at the situation and say, "Don't stop it, let it go?"

If the FBI and ATF were double-crossed, it may have been by one of their own agents. Recall that Michael Franks, a rogue American agent with connections to the Octopus, had provided the key information that allowed Ahmed Jibril to target Pan Am 103.

Former FBI SAC Ted Gunderson described to me what he called a "unilateral transfer" of CIA agents into various federal law-enforcement agencies in the early 1980s. The purpose of this Reagan/Bush covert policy was to permit the CIA to head off any inconvenient investigations that such agencies might be undertaking. If so, it would go a long way towards explaining the FBI's curiously-timed fit of incompetence.

There are precedents. In 1971, Louis Tackwood, an agent provocateur working out of the LAPD's Criminal Conspiracy Section (CCS), charged that the CCS "had been set up on the same basis as the CIA." Tackwood disclosed that CCS agents—approximately 125 of whom were agent provocateurs—were sponsored by federal intelligence agencies. As researcher Alex Constantine notes in his book, *Blood, Carnage, and the Agent Provocateur*, the CCS was directly linked to the Washington, D.C.-based Inter-Agency Group on Domestic Intelligence and Internal Security, a little-known covert operations unit made up of right-wing agents from the FBI, CIA, DIA, NSC, Army, Air Force, and local police departments.[748]

The CCS's spying activities came to a head in 1973 with the publication of Tackwood's *The Glass House Tapes*, and the unit was summarily disbanded. In its place evolved the Organized Crime Intelligence Division (OCID), which, interestingly enough, maintains no files on organized crime, but plenty on local citizens and politicians.

The OCID also still maintains its ties with the federal intelligence apparatus. According to Pasadena City Council member Michael Zinzin, who won a $3.8 million dollar lawsuit against the LAPD's Anti-Terrorist Division, that apparatus is the same secret cabal involved in the Iran-Contra imbroglio. In other words, the Octopus.

Mike Rothmiller, a former OCID detective, stumbled upon the connections and subsequently fell prey to an assassin's bullet. At the time, Rothmiller had been investigating one Robert Terry, an arms and drug smuggler with links to the CIA.[749]

Gunderson's "unilateral transfer" could explain how intelligence operatives were able to manipulate the sting operation in Oklahoma City. If there were duplicitous agents inside the ATF and FBI, they would have known when and where the bomb was to be delivered. They would have known how [one of] the FBI's undercover agent(s)—John Doe 2—was to disable the bomb. They would have had full and detailed knowledge of the plot.

Like Michael Franks, they could have easily informed those who had an interest in changing that plot—those who had an interest in seeing that the building, and possibly some of those inside it—was destroyed.

Chapter   Ten

THE COVERT COWBOYS

The nomenclature of the Lockerbie and World Trade Center bombings provide a unique and unparalleled insight into the dynamics of the Oklahoma City bombing. Each event gives the reader a glimpse of how the Shadow Government operates, utilizing drug dealers, criminals, and terrorists to do its bidding.

The use of former enemy soldiers, criminals, and terrorists for their dirty work is also a time-honored tradition among intelligence agencies, who stand to gain the "plausible deniability" so coveted in the world of covert operations.*

At the close of WWII, the U.S. Government helped thousands of Nazi war criminals escape justice, integrating them into its scientific/military/intelligence establishment. Reinhard Gehlen, Hitler's senior intelligence officer on the Eastern Front, and other high-ranking Nazis, were spirited out of Germany with the aid of the OSS and the Vatican, then installed in top-secret, sensitive posts in the U.S. and abroad.

Gehlen's SS officers had been instrumental in the mass extermination of Gypsies and Jews, and Gehlen was personally responsible for the torture, interrogation, and murder by starvation of some four million Soviet prisoners of war.

Gehlen later boasted of teaching the newly-formed CIA everything it knew.

Many of the world's deadliest terrorists were in fact trained by agencies such as the CIA and KGB, who went on to commit mayhem and murder on an unprecedented scale. A prime example is Ted Shackley's JM/WAVE anti-Casto campaign of the mid-1960s, which trained Cuban exiles in techniques of assassination and terror, then unleashed them on their native country. The most infamous of these "Cuban Cowboys," Luis Posada Carriles (aka Ramon Medina), a member of the anti-Casto group CORU (also a member of the CIA's ZR/RIFLE assassination team under the command of E. Howard Hunt), killed 78 people in October of 1976 by bombing a Cuban airliner.

Carriles said he planned the bombing at the CIA's instigation.

---

* As former high-ranking CIA official Victor Marchetti explained, "They're smart enough always to work through other parties. Generally, the dirtier the work is, the more likely it is to be farmed out."

As one of CORU's members explained in a CBS interview, "We use the tactics that we learned from the CIA because we—we were trained to do everything. We are trained to set off a bomb, we were trained to kill ... we were trained to do everything."[751]

The mastermind of the bombing, Orlando Bosch, responsible for more than 50 anti-Castro bombings in Cuba and elsewhere, was released from prison at the behest of George Bush's son Jeb, who has strong ties to both the Cuban expatriate community and the Contras.

As Vice-President, Bush also headed the Task Force on Combating Terrorism. Proudly displaying his condemnation of terrorism, Bush pardoned Bosch, giving him special permission to live in Miami.[752]*

The CIA's support of the Afghani Mujahadeen between 1979 and 1989 resulted in a huge wave of well-armed and trained Muslim extremists bent on venting their political and ideological rage against the U.S. At the same time, the overflow from the Afghani operation resulted in one of the largest pools of potential recruits for covert operations.

One of the main operatives the CIA had utilized in its war against the Soviets was Sheik Abdel Omar Rahman. The CIA utilized Rahman because of his influence over the Mujahadeen, then brought him into the U.S. on a CIA-sponsored visa. While the Sheik was eventually convicted for conspiracy to bomb targets in the U.S., prosecutors encountered resistance in pursuing him and other World Trade Center bombing suspects because of their ties to the Mujahadeen, and *their* ties to U.S. intelligence.

As Jack Blum, investigator for the Senate Foreign Relations Subcommittee, put it: "One of the big problems here is that many suspects in the World Trade Center bombing were associated with the Mujahadeen. And there are components of our government that are absolutely disinterested in following that path because it leads back to people we supported in the Afghan war."[753]

A staunch anti-Western crusader, Rahman became a shining light for thousands of Muslim extremists after the war in their crusade for the holy Jihad. Nearby Peshawar, Pakistan became the staging area for tens of thousands of radicals, many of whom went on to form smaller cells around the world, including the U.S. The groups that flocked to Pakistan's terrorist training centers included the Egyptian Al-Gama'a al-Islamiya, the Palestinian Hammers, the Algerian Al-Jihad, and the Filipino Moro Liberation Front.

World Trade Center mastermind Ramzi Yousef also spent considerable time in Pakistan. As one Western diplomat noted: "The United States created a

---

* This is not surprising, as it has been alleged by former CIA agents that Bush allowed the Agency to use his offshore oil drilling company, Zapata Oil, as a front for numerous CIA operations, including the Bay of Pigs invasion.

Moscow Central in Peshawar for these groups, and the consequences for all of us are astronomical." [754]

As Mary Ann Weaver writes in the May, 1996 issue of *The Atlantic Monthly:* "The CIA helped to train and fund what eventually became an international network of highly disciplined and effective Islamic militants—and a new breed of terrorist as well."

> To the CIA, which pumped more than $2 billion into the fourteen-year Afghani resistance effort, Sheik Omar was what intelligence officials call "a valuable asset." [755] *

El Sayyid Nosair, a core member of the Al Salaam Mosque run by Rahman, shot and killed the right-wing Rabbi Meir Kahane in November of 1990. During a conversation between a 20-year veteran FBI agent and one of his top undercover operatives, the operative asked:

> "Why aren't we going after the Sheik [Adbel Rahman]?" demanded the undercover man.
>
> "It's hands off," answered the agent.
>
> "Why?" asked the operative.
>
> "It was no accident that the Sheik got a visa and that he's still in the country," replied the agent, visibly upset. "He's here under the banner of national security, the State Department, the NSA, and the CIA."
>
> The agent pointed out that the Sheik had been granted a tourist visa, and later a green card, despite the fact that he was on a State Department terrorist watch-list that should have barred him from the country. He's an untouchable, concluded the agent." [756] **

It was also revealed during the Sheik's conspiracy trial that in 1989 the U.S. Army had sent Special Forces Sergeant Ali A. Mohammed to Jersey City to provide training for Mujahadeen recruits, including Nosair and Mahmud Abouhalima, a convicted World Trade Center bomber. Interestingly, this was at the same time the pair were under surveillance by the FBI as suspected terrorists. [757]

The experiences of the CIA's expatriated Nazis, Anti-Castro Cubans, and Mujahadeen veterans were strikingly similar to that of the Ku Klux Klan, which

---

* Recall that another one of the CIA's "valuable assets," Mir Aimal Kansi, opened fire with an AK-47 outside of CIA headquarters in January, 1993, killing two Agency employees. Like World Trade Center bomber Ramzi Yousef, he fled to Pakistan.

** Egyptian President Hosani Mubarak claimed that Sheik Rahman was connected to the CIA. (*Las Vegas Sun*, 8/1/93.)

for decades remained on the end of a long leash controlled by J. Edgar Hoover.

One of the most infamous examples of FBI-orchestrated terror-murder were the brutal 1963 KKK attacks on civil rights workers in Birmingham, Alabama, led by FBI informant Gary Rowe.

It seems that Rowe was no mere informant. As Curt Gentry writes in *J. Edgar Hoover: The Man and the Secrets:* "Klan members stated he had veto power over any violent activity contemplated by the Eastview 13 Klavern." [758]*

Rowe also participated in the 1965 murder of civil rights marcher Viola Liuzzo. As the *National Review* reported, "The 1978 investigation implicated [Rowe] as an agent provocateur.... Three other Klansmen testified that it was Rowe who had actually shot Viola." While Rowe was indicted for first degree murder, a federal judge blocked Rowe's extradition, claiming that a federal agent has rights that protect him when "placed in a compromising position because of his undercover work." A Federal Appeals Court upheld the ruling.

The FBI informant was also accused of helping plant the bomb that killed four black girls in a Birmingham church. Although Gary Rowe failed lie-detector tests regarding his complicity in that and the Viola murder, he was never prosecuted, and instead was given a $20,000 "reward" by the FBI. [759]

A similar case of government-orchestrated terror-murder would come about in 1979 in Greensboro, North Carolina with the murder of five Communist Workers Party members by KKK and Nazi Party goons—led by FBI operative Edward Dawson and ATF informant Bernard Butkovich. Both the *Washington Post* and the *New York Times* reported that Butkovich "offered to procure explosives," and "offered to train them in activities such as making pipe bombs and fire bombs." [760]

Even more suspiciously, the tactical squad assigned to monitor the march was reportedly "out to lunch" at the time, and a patrol car that happened to be in the area, was told to "clear the area as soon as possible." [761]

The incident is suspiciously similar to the ATF agents in Oklahoma who were paged not to come into work the morning of the blast.

Echoing the factitious rants of ATF chief Lester Martz, Governor Frank Keating, and other federal officials in Oklahoma, FBI Director William Webster called the charges of federal complicity "utterly absurd." Although the killers had been recruited, organized and led on their murderous rampage by ATF and FBI operatives, none ever served a day of jail-time. [762]

Like the FBI's KKK mules, or the ATF's pet Nazis at Elohim City, the Pakistani/Afghani Mujahadeen and Iraqi veterans resettled into the U.S. represent the next wave of "covert cowboys"—ready and willing to do the CIA/FBI's dirty work.

---

* Not only was Rowe never prosecuted, the FBI paid his medical bills and gave him a $125 bonus for "services rendered."

As Gene Wheaton observes: "Every major Middle-Eastern terrorist organization is under surveillance and control of the intelligence agencies in the U.S. None of these guys move around as freely as they'd like you to think."[763]

Ali Hassan Salameh, leader of the PLO splinter group Black September, which carried out the 1972 Munich Olympics massacre, was put on the CIA's payroll. That is, until the Mossad caught up with him in 1979. Even so, the Israelis checked with the CIA before killing him.

A Pakistani named Ali Ahmand was standing directly behind Senator Robert Kennedy when he was shot. Former CIA contract agent Robert Morrow saw Ahmand holding a Nikon camera, and recalled seeing Nikon cameras that fired bullets while at the CIA.

Another "valuable asset," Mir Aimal Kansi, had been recruited by the CIA to assist in the smuggling of weapons to the Mujahadeen. Kansi, who had a "financial misunderstanding" with the Agency, resolved the issue by opening fire with an AK-47 outside of CIA headquarters in January of 1993, killing two Agency employees. Like World Trade Center bomber Ramzi Yousef, he fled to Pakistan.[764]*

Curiously, Hussain al-Hussaini—who had been seen speeding away from the bombing in a brown pick-up—would make no similar attempt to flee. Was he part of a government-sanctioned operation? As Professor Bruce Hoffman at The Center for the Study of Terrorism and Political Violence at St. Andrew's University in England noted, there have been various attempts to infiltrate Islamic terrorist teams in Oklahoma.[765]

Could this be why FBI Agent Jeffrey Jenkins "cringed" when he saw KFOR's televised report on Hussaini?**

Did Hussaini and "Khalid," like Timothy McVeigh casually pulling over for Patrolman Hanger, believe they were protected?

The FBI's refusal to arrest or detain "Khalid" strongly points to such a possibility. "Khalid's" ability to monitor the activities of a group of Middle Eastern immigrants (through giving them jobs and renting them homes), and his status as a former felon, make him a likely candidate as an operative or informant.

And why did McVeigh meet Hussaini in the first place? Like Carol Howe and Andreas Strassmeir, were they both acting as undercover operatives without each other's knowledge? †

---

* Kansi's original target was believed to have been CIA Director Robert Gates.

** Curiously, Robert Jerlow, KFOR's private investigator, spotted the FBI watching al-Hussaini at the same time he was.

† It is also curious why one prominent alternative investigator ignored the Middle Eastern lead altogether, focusing solely on Elohim City. What this alleged reporter consistently missed is the dismembered military leg found in the rubble, the numerous wit-

Readers will recall that Timothy McVeigh was still in the Army when he wrote his sister telling her that he was picked for a Special Forces Covert Tactical Unit (CTU) involved in illegal activities. These activities included "protecting drug shipments, eliminating the competiton, and population control." This is exactly what Ted Shackley, Tom Clines and Richard Secord did in Laos—assassinating and bombing Vang Pao's opium competition out of existence.

When rogue CIA agents Ed Wilson and Frank Terpil were selling arms and explosives to Libya, they were reporting to no one other than Ted Shackley. Reporter Jonathan Kwitny notes that Wilson and Terpil were hiring anti-Castro Cubans from Shackley's old JM/WAVE program to assassinate President Qaddafi's political opponents abroad:

> Some U.S. Army men were literally lured away from the doorway of Fort Bragg, their North Carolina training post. The GIs were given every reason to believe that the operation summoning them was being carried out with the full backing of the CIA....[766]

Could this CTU McVeigh claims he was recruited for be a latter-day version of Shackley's assassins? Former federal grand juror Hoppy Heidelberg said McVeigh's letter indicates that he turned them down, while former FBI SAC Ted Gundersen claims McVeigh actually worked for the group for a while, then became disenchanted.[767]

If McVeigh had actually been recruited for such a group, a question arises. What cover story he was given? Told that he was on an important mission—to infiltrate a terrorist organization and prevent a bombing? Considering McVeigh's background and character, he seems an unlikely terrorist who murdered 169 innocent people.

Recall that McVeigh was seen with Hussain al-Hussaini. The Iraqis would provide a convincing and plausible excuse if McVeigh was let to believe he

---

nesses who saw Middle Eastern suspects, and the APB on the brown pick-up driven by al-Hussaini. This reporter even went so far as to suggest that the men in the pick-up were Dennis Mahon and his comrades dressed up as Arabs. Given the scenario of a "second-level damage-control" operation steering critics of the government's case solely onto Elohim City, it can be surmised that at least some of the real bombers were part of the Middle Eastern contingent, and were CIA/FBI controlled, supplied and activated. This would explain why Gagan's involvement in the Middle Eastern cell was apparently ignored by the FBI. It would explain why Gagan was asked by an covert operative to deliver a Lely mixer to Junction City. And it would explain why the FBI cleared Hussain al-Hussaini, and why "Sam Khalid" acted so non-chalant when confronted with evidence of his involvement.

was part of a sting operation.

It is possible that McVeigh was sheep-dipped as a disgruntled ex-GI for infiltrating a neo-Nazi community, which would provide a doorway into the bombing conspiracy through places like Elohim City.

Or perhaps, as a result of his becoming disenchanted and leaving the CTU, he became targeted for "termination," and was setup as a fall guy. Such is standard operating procedure for those who attempt to leave the world of covert operations.

Either way, there appears to be two "Timothy McVeighs," just as there were two Oswalds, suggesting a sophisticated intelligence operation, one designed to put McVeigh in the wrong place at the wrong time.

Like Oswald, McVeight may have believed himself to be a government agent, part of a secret project. This may explain why an armed McVeigh didn't shoot and kill officer Hanger when he was stopped on the Interstate after the bombing. Why would a man who had just killed 169 men, women and children balk at killing a cop on a lonely stretch of highway? Perhaps McVeigh believed he was part of a sting operation—a government asset—and would be protected.

Like McVeigh, Hussaini was likely recruited into a covert intelligence unit after his resettlement into the U.S. Believing he was working for the government, he was given a cover story that he was preventing a bombing.

Given the necessary compartmentalization of covert operations, it's likely that each was on a "need-to-know" basis. While McVeigh, Hussaini, and their pals parked the Ryder truck in front of the Murrah Building, the *real* bombers were the third component of the compartmentalized operation.

Recall that five days before the bombing, HUD worker Jane Graham saw three men in the garage who she thought were telephone repairmen. They had plans of the building, and were holding what appeared to be C-4 plastic explosive. "It was a putty color," said Graham, "a solid piece of block … they had that and they had this wiring.

"The man in the brown shirt obviously knew what he was doing and was in charge," said Graham. "He reminded me of a surveyor or construction foreman except that I doubt that they would have been in that good of shape. These men were definitely physically well-trained." [768]

The men looked "uncomfortable" when they saw Graham, and quickly put the items into a paper bag and hid it in their car—which was clearly not a utility company vehicle. [769]*

Another witness saw several men working on the pillars in the garage, in the dark, without lights. When they were questioned by this visitor, they said, "We're just putting things right again."

---

* As previously mentioned, representatives of the electric, telephone and gas companies all denied having workmen who fit the men's description at that location.

Were they, or were they placing explosive charges to be activated later?

This bizarre activity was seen by at least two other witnesses—IRS worker Kathy Wilburn, and a HUD worker named Joan. None of the "repairmen" matched the description of Timothy McVeigh, Terry Nichols, or Hussain al-Hussaini.*

Twenty minutes before the blast, Michael Linehan saw McVeigh's yellow Mercury run a red light and slip quickly into the building's garage. Why did "McVeigh" need to enter the building moments before the blast? To place secondary charges or activate remote detonators, perhaps?**

Several minutes later, a woman riding the elevator saw a young Arab man with a backpack frantically pushing the lobby button, trying to exit the building.

After the blast, Kay H. was almost run over by a brown pick-up driven by Hussain al-Hussaini. There were three suspects in the truck. At least two of them were Arabs.

Seconds later, Gary Lewis ran outside to see a Middle Eastern man grinning from ear to ear.

Approximately 15 minutes later, HUD employee Germaine Johnston came across McVeigh and John Doe 2 in an alley near the Murrah Building. "They were just standing there watching," she said. McVeigh then asked Johnston if anyone had been killed, and both men looked sad when she told them that children had died.[770]

If McVeigh had blown up the building—a building he knew to contain a day-care center—as an act of revenge, why would he appear sad? And if Hussain al-Hussaini had conspired with McVeigh for similar motives, why did he cry upon learning that children had been killed?

And why would he casually hang around the scene of the crime? "I ask you, does that sound like a man who was running?" asked Johnston's friend and co-worker Jane Graham. "I don't think so. It sounds like a plan that went awry or something he did not know was going to happen."[771]

And those federal agents who had been surveilling the building all night long … why did they appear so shocked when the bomb(s) went off? Because they didn't *expect* them to go off. As Representative Istook reportedly remarked, John Doe 2, one of the government's undercover agents, did not know how to dis-

---

* Also recall that on the same day or the following Monday, VA employees Dennis Jackson and Craig Freeman saw a suspicious group of Arabs inside the building after hours. One of them closely matched the description of the suspect seen with "McVeigh" by Phyliss Kingsley at the Hi-Way Grill that Sunday. They exited, said Freeman, towards the underground parking garage.

** Why would McVeigh enter the federal building so conspicuously, running a red light, attracting the attention of the police?

arm the truck-bomb, which contained a redundant timing device.

And the Army leg who helped place the shaped C-4 charges on the building's columns was not advised that he had a zero-time-delay detonator and was going to be vaporized. The leg was on the wrong side of the column when the detonator was activated.

Fortunately for the conspirators, the crime scene was leveled to preclude any independent forensic analysis. Federal agents and local officials quickly scrambled to initiate their damage-control operation.*

Those who threatened to reveal the "sting gone bad" were told to keep quiet for "the good of the country." Yes, it was a terrible tragedy. But brave undercover agents like John Doe 2 were safely on the job, just waiting to prevent more "militiamen" like Timothy James McVeigh from blowing up more babies.

Honest law-enforcement personnel like Sergeant Terrance Yeakey, who didn't go along with the cover-up "committed suicide."

And the American public, was fed a completely different lie. A disgruntled racist and latent neo-Nazi and his anti-government friend, angry over Waco, using a homemade bomb, had vented their rage in a brutal and vicious act of revenge.

---

* It has been well-documented that the FBI and ATF illegally leveled the crime scene at Waco, which was supposed to be under the jurisdiction of Texas Rangers, destroyed evidence that ATF helicopters had indiscriminately fired into the roofs of the building at the beginning of the raid killing several people; had fired at the front door well before any shots had been fired in return, and had set explosive charges on top of a concrete vault in which women and children were hiding to escape the fire. The front door (a metal door) which would have proved the second allegation was later found to be mysteriously "missing."

Chapter Eleven

THE MOTIVE

> *"Governments, in order to perpetuate themselves, will sacrifice 400-500 people without a second thought."*
>
> —Fourteen-year DEA
> veteran Basil Abbott

To understand the motive behind the Oklahoma City bombing, one must understand the political situation in the country at the time.

In 1989, with the fall of the Berlin Wall, the Cold War was officially over. The intelligence community was in danger of losing its appropriations; it needed a new mission.[772]

In 1963, the Kennedy administration was said to have commissioned a group of analysts and scholars to evaluate the problems inherent in a post-Cold War society. Entitled *Report from Iron Mountain on the Possibility and Desirability of Peace,* its conclusions and validity have been hotly debated since its "unauthorized" publication in 1967.

Although featured on the front page of the *New York Times* and subsequently translated into 15 different languages, many establishment icons and media pundits would only acknowledge the work as a "clever satire."

The *Times,* which received a "no comment" response from the LBJ White House while attempting to verify its authenticity, wrote that "the possible hoax was a possibly suppressed report."*

Others, such as Colonel L. Fletcher Prouty (Ret.), former Chief of the Special Operations Division for the Joint Chiefs of Staff, quoted from the document in his book, *The Secret Team.* And renowned economist, author, and professor John Kenneth Galbraith stated that he would "put [his] personal repute behind the authenticity of this document." As late as 1995, *The Nation* was still denigrating the report as a "hoax" while the *Wall Street Journal* was seriously debating its merits.[773] As Robert Tomsho wrote in the May 9, 1995 edition of the *Journal:*

Given the tumultuous times when the document surfaced and the air of respectabil-

---

* Iron Mountain is a nuclear hideout in Hudson, NY, similar to Mt. Weather in Virginia.

ity surrounding those involved with it, few readers were willing to dismiss the mysterious headline-grabbing book as a hoax.[774]

Whether *Report from Iron Mountain* was in fact a hoax, its conclusions lend a somewhat prescient and frightening measure of truth to the contemporary reality of the 20th century. Written in cold, empirical think-tank language, the report postulates that war is the fundamental basis for all political, social, and economic unity.

In somewhat Machiavellian fashion the report suggests initiating "ritual blood games," renewing "slavery" and creating an "omnipotent" international police force as mitigating substitutes for the alleged socio-economic void created by a post-Cold War society. The report defined the sociological implications thusly:

> War, through the medium of military institutions, has uniquely served societies, throughout the course of known history, as an indispensable controller of dangerous social dissidence and destructive antisocial tendencies.... No modern political ruling group has successfully controlled its constituency after failing to sustain the continuing credibility of an external threat of war.
>
> The war system makes the stable government of societies possible. It does this essentially by providing an external necessity for a society to accept political rule.... An effective substitute for war would require "alternate enemies."

A national security establishment no longer focused on the "external necessity" of an outward military threat (e.g., the Soviet Union), can turn its attention towards the ever-present specter of an internal threat—the "alternate enemy." As the report states:

> The motivational function of war requires the existence of a genuinely menacing social enemy.... The "alternate enemy" must imply a more immediate, tangible, and directly felt threat of destruction.

The Oklahoma City bombing, occurring as it did in the "heartland" of America, served as no other "terrorist" act has in the history of the United States in channeling the attention of the American people towards the "immediate, tangible, and directly felt threat of destruction."

More significantly, it did so by directing the attention of the public towards an "alternate enemy"—in this case—an "internal" one.

This mode of sychological manipulation by the ruling elite is simply the war spirit refocused. This ubiquitously American quality, so effectively used against the Germans in the 1940s, the Communists in the 1950s, and the Iraqis in the 1990s, would now be directed inward—against the Patriot/Militia movement.

By linking Timothy McVeigh to the Militia movement through a massive media campaign, the Militia movement is seen as the primary motivational force behind the bombing. The movement, becomes, by proxy, the new "alternate enemy."

By substituting what it terms a "fictive model" for war, the Plutocracy engages the false sentiments of the masses, creating, as it states, "a sociomoral conflict of equally compelling force and scope." From the perspective of the ruling elite, this sociomoral conflict must:

> Justify the need for taking and paying a "blood price" in wide areas of human concern.... The fictive models would have to carry the weight of extraordinary conviction, underscored with a not inconsiderable actual sacrifice of life.

That shocking revelation was written in 1963. Thirty-three years later, former presidential advisor Arthur Schlesinger, Jr. would write in *Foreign Affairs*, the journal of the Council on Foreign Relations, that mouthpiece of the plutocratic establishment:

> We are not going to achieve a new world order without paying for it in blood as well as in words and money.[775]

Quite a profound statement, coming as it did less than two months after the Oklahoma City bombing.

Was this "blood price" carried out on April 19, 1995?

Barbaric acts of mass-terror by governments to manipulate political objectives is hardly new. Deliberately manipulated outrage-incidents, such as the sinking of the Lusitania, the burning of the Reischtag, and the attack on Pearl Harbor—asl precursors to military campaigns, have held several functions: triggering nationalistic war spirit, channeling wrath toward the nominated enemy, and concentrating power in the executive branch, where elite control is unhampered by popular influence.

President Franklin D. Roosevelt, who allowed 2,403 servicemen to be slaughtered at Pearl Harbor to initiate America's entry into WWII, said: "In politics, nothing happens by accident. If it happens, you can bet it was planned that way."

The American public, brainwashed by the conventional wisdom of history, with an attention span as long as the latest sitcom, is oblivious to this fact. A public consumed by materialism and stultified by television poses no serious threat to the ruling plutocracy. A savvy populace, intimately aware of the corruption in government, and threatening to expose or even depose the powers behind it, poses a very serious threat to the ruling elite.

The primary group standing in the way of plans of the transnational corporate cabal today is a group of Americans who call themselves Patriots. These

Patriots—numbering roughly five million men and women—are comprised of approximately 400,000 individuals who belong to a militant arm: the Militia.

These individuals are increasingly opting out of the federal system. They are establishing precedents for their own governance, with names like Sovereign Citizenship, States' Rights and County Rule.

Some are relinquishing their Social Security cards. Others refuse to pay income tax, which they insist are in direct contravention of the Constitution, and an illegal outgrowth of the privately-owned Federal Reserve. Many are buying gold and silver. Some are even issuing their own currencies.

They point out the importance our founding fathers attributed to the Second Amendment—the right to bear arms—as the first and final bastion against a tyrannical government. Ultimately, they are willing to defend themselves against a increasingly oppressive federal system.

To the government, such a movement must not be allowed to grow teeth, as did the Anti-War movement of the 1960s, or the anti-corporate labor movement of the 1930s. Distrusting the Federal Reserve, believed by many to have engineered the Great Depression, many of these communities began issuing their own money—as many as 1,500 different currencies. As journalist Jon Rappaport notes:

> These events created anxiety for the wealthy one percent of the country. Things might have gotten out of hand. There was a danger of mass rebellion, decentralization, a power shift downward, and so on. World War Two not only solved a job crises, it reunified the nation around an external threat. It temporarily eliminated the possibility of the disintegration of the body politic.[776]

Like the aforementioned outrage-incidents, the Plutocracy required a tragedy to manipulate public opinion. The Oklahoma City bombing served this purpose in the most sublime fashion. In the aftermath of that tragedy, the ruling elite sought to unify the nation around an internal threat—dressed up and repackaged in the form of the Patriot/Militia movement.

Many so-called liberal intellectuals and media pundits have dismissed the notion of the Oklahoma City bombing as a deliberately engineered act to discredit the militia as preposterous paranoia. Yet as former CIA Director William Colby stated to his friend, Nebraska State Senator John DeCamp, literally days before the bombing:

> "I watched as the Anti-War movement rendered it impossible for this country to conduct or win the Vietnam War. I tell you, dear friend, that this Militia and Patriot movement in which, as an attorney, you have become one of the centerpieces, is far more significant and far more dangerous for America than the Anti-War movement ever was, if it is not intelligently dealt with. And I really mean this."[777]

In the absence of war, when "motivational forces governing human behavior" no longer translate "into binding social allegiance," the ruling elite required a substitute. By demonizing the Patriot/Militia movement, the Plutocracy seeks to divide and conquer and to distract the population. Professor and dissident intellectual Noam Chomsky writes:

> Over the last ten years, every year or two, some major monster is constructed that we have to defend ourselves against. There used to be one that was always available: the Russians. But they're losing their attractiveness as an enemy, and it's getting harder and harder to use that one, so some new ones have to be conjured up. They've got to keep coming up, one after another. You frighten the population, terrorize them, intimidate them.... That's one of the ways in which you can keep the bewildered herd from paying attention to what's really going on around them, keep them diverted and controlled.[778]

FBI Director Louis Freeh stated before the Senate Judiciary Committee two days after McVeigh's conviction: "Most of the militia organizations around the country are not, in our view, threatening or dangerous."[779]

Yet Freeh stated before the Senate Appropriations Committee that the focus of the government's domestic anti-terrorism efforts are "various individuals, as well as organizations, some having an ideology which suspects government of world-order conspiracies—individuals who, for various reasons, have organized themselves against the United States." The chief domestic "enemy," said Freeh, consists of "individuals who espouse ideologies inconsistent with principles of Federal Government."[780]

Freeh's alarmist comments impart the genuine concern which the ruling elite have for the growth of the Patriot/Militia movement. As Colby told DeCamp:

> "It is not because these people are armed, that America need be concerned," Bill explained to my surprise. "It is not that these people stockpile weapons and have para-military training sessions, that they are dangerous," Colby continued.
>
> "They are dangerous, John, because there are so many of them. It is one thing to have a few nuts or dissidents. They can be dealt with, justly or otherwise, so that they do not pose a danger to the system. It is quite another situation when you have a true movement—millions of citizens—believing something, particularly when the movement is made up of society's average, successful citizens."[781]

While the so-called Justice Department was busy covering up evidence of the bombing, President Clinton ardently sought to smear those of the far-right— "The purveyors of hatred and division, the promoters of paranoia," as he put it. "They do practice and they do preach violence against those who are of a different color, a different background, or who worship a different God. They do feed on fear and uncertainty. They do promote paranoia."

Challenging the American people to follow him in a campaign of divide and conquer, Clinton charged: "These people attack our government and the citizens who work for it who actually guarantee the freedoms they abuse.... They can certainly snuff out innocent lives and sow fear in our hearts. They are indifferent to the slaughter of children. They threaten our freedoms and our way of life, and we must stop them."

Echoing and amplifying Clinton's defamations were the mainstream media, which, all but ignoring the relevant evidence, launched vitriolic attacks against the Patriot/Militia community. Leading the charge were the ADL and the SPLC, whose connections to the Mossad, U.S. law enforcement, and infiltration of the Patriot/Militia community have been well documented. The ADL's ties to the FBI, in fact, had been forged long ago.*

At the same time, all legitimate expressions and concerns are ignored. Militia members are portrayed as gun-crazed racists with overly conspiratorial views. As *Relevance* magazine notes:

> If anyone dares to make a suggestion that serious crimes by high-ranking federal officials or an agency of government have been committed, that suggestion instantly becomes, almost by definition, a conspiracy theory, which is itself (almost by definition) beyond the pale of responsible discussion.[782]

Attempts by the left and right to join together are explained away by establishment intellectuals as a strange aberration. In a June 19, 1995 *New Yorker* article entitled "The Road to Paranoia," author Michael Kelly describes "views that have long been shared by both the far right and the far left, and that in recent years have come together, in a weird meeting of the minds, to become one, and

---

* George Mintzer, the director of criminal investigations of the U.S. Southern District Attorney's Office from 1926 to 1931, maintained files on over 32,000 "subversive" Americans at the behest of his boss, Treasury Secretary Henry Morgenthau, a man who had close links with the ADL. Mintzer's files were made available to the Office of Naval Intelligence, the State Department, and to the FBI. In the mid-1950s, New York publisher Lyle Stuart exposed how the ADL was actually financing a rag-tag "neo-Nazi" group which would engage in loud demonstrations outside synagogues at precisely the same time that the ADL was engaging in anti-Nazi fund-raising efforts. What is also interesting is that the ADL played a large role in protecting Mob figures such as Meyer Lansky, smearing potential law enforcement opponents as "Anti-Semitic." (*Dope, Inc.: The Book That Drove Kissinger Crazy, Executive Intelligence Review*, 1992, p. 582; *The Spotlight*, 5/26/97.)

to permeate the mainstream of American politics and popular culture. You could call it fusion paranoia."[783]

Contrary to popular opinion, the Patriot/Militia movement is more than just a fringe element of right-wing conspiracy nuts. While it contains individuals who are myopic concerning social welfare issues and environmental concerns, increasingly, this group represents a broad spectrum of Americans concerned about governmental corruption and loss of Constitutional rights. Far from being impotent, as Louis Freeh asserts, the Patriot/Militia movement represents a threat to an establishment seeking to maintain corrupt control over its citizenry at all costs.*

While it cannot be said for certain that the Alfred P. Murrah Building was destroyed as part of a preconceived plan to create the illusion of a domestic terrorist threat within America—as a foundation for destroying political dissent—it is clear that the investigation was crafted for just that purpose.

In March, 1995, Congressman Steve Stockman (R-TX) learned that a nationwide, early-morning paramilitary raid against militia groups was planned for March 25. It seemed that a couple of concerned ATF agents had informed the National Rifle Association (NRA) about the plan, code-named Operation ROLLING THUNDER. Stockman immediately fired off a letter to Attorney General Janet Reno:

> It has come to my attention through a number of reliable sources that an impending raid, by several Federal agencies, against the "citizen's militias" groups, is scheduled for March 25 or 26 at 4:00 A.M. A paramilitary style attack against Americans who pose no risk to others, even if violations of criminal law might be imputed to them, would run the risk of an irreparable breach between the Federal Government and the public, especially if it turned out to be an ill considered, poorly planned, but bloody fiasco like Waco.[784]

---

* A recent Scripps Howard News Service and Scripps School of Journalism poll of "conspiracy fears" revealed that 40% of Americans think it is very likely or somewhat likely that the FBI deliberately set the fires at Waco; 51% believe federal officials were responsible for the Kennedy assassination; 52% believe that it is very or somewhat likely that the CIA pushes drugs in the inner-cities; 39% believe it is very likely the U.S. Navy accidentally or purposefully shot down TWA Flight 800. 80% believe that the military is withholding evidence of Iraqi use of nerve gas or germ warfare during the Gulf War. Yet in the wake of the Oklahoma City bombing, 58% of Americans surveyed by the *Los Angeles Times* indicated they would trade some civil liberties if it would help thwart terrorism. Another poll, taken after the bombing by the Associated Press, revealed that 54% of Americans were willing to trade off some of their rights to prevent more Oklahoma City-style attacks. A poll taken during the Bush administration revealed that 60% of the population said that they would give up their rights to win the drug war.

Stockman's letter went unanswered, and two Senators who confronted the Assistant Secretary of Defense were thrown out of his office.

It is interesting to note that the raid was scheduled just one month prior to the Oklahoma City bombing, an incident that launched the largest anti-militia media campaign ever witnessed.[785]

The tension surrounding the Militia movement wasn't the only pressure boiling the political pot. On April 17, a Special Federal Grand Jury handed down a sealed indictment charging Hillary Clinton with bank fraud—misappropriating or embezzling $47 million from a federally insured S&L, and benefitting from secret offshore accounts payable to Vincent Foster, Jr.

That same evening, April 17, a military C-21 Lear Jet carrying several high-ranking military officials, including a supervisor to the NSA, crashed near Alexander City, Alabama. The disaster, which occured on a clear day, appeared more than a simple accident. The highly experienced crew reported "fuel management" problems, a classic sabotage technique. Witnesses Miranda Wyckoff and Jimmy Keel claim they heard multiple explosions while the plane was airborne.*

The plane crashed not far from a Delta Force base in Alabama. It has been rumored that elements of the 20th Special Operations Group (SOG) guarded Mena airport during the Iran-Contra drug-running. A Special Federal Grand Jury in Alabama was blocked from investigating the crash.**

---

* The C-21 Lear Jet is a highly reliable craft. This particular plane was part of the presidential fleet based at Andrews Air Force base. According to military sources, the pilots who fly them are "the best of the best." ("Rescuers Find Recorders in Military Crash," *Washington Post* (Reuters), 4/18/95; "The Eight Who died in Ala. Crash," *Air Forces Monthly*, date unknown; *Alexander City Outlook*, 4/18/95; Joe L. Jordan, National Vietnam P.O.W. Strike Force; other information from confidential sources.)

** The downing was suspiciously similar to the U.S. Air Force plane carrying Commerce Secretary Ron Brown, that crashed in Bosnia on April 3, 1996, killing all 35 people onboard. While the major news media attributed the crash to foul weather, the Air Force investigation report concluded that "the weather was not a substantially contributing factor to this mishap."

The Air Force skipped the first phase of its standard investigative process, known as a safety board, in which all crashes are treated as suspicious, proceeding immediately to the second phase, an accident investigation. Nevertheless, two military pathologists at the Armed Forces Institute of Pathology (AFIP)—Air Force Lt. Col. Steve Cogswell and Army Lt. Col. David Hause—were quoted in the [Pittsburg] Tribune-Review as saying that Brown suffered a head wound that could have been caused by a gunshot. No autopsy was conducted, and all of the original head X-rays of Brown are now missing from Brown's case file at the AFIP.

The Mena drug-running, intimately connected with the activities of the Iran-Contra Octopus, was also on the Congressional investigative agenda, as were the activities of the ATF and FBI at Waco. The investigations were scheduled to start in May.

Yet on April 19, two days after the crash, the Oklahoma City Federal Building was bombed. The bombing conveniently shifted attention from Clinton's activities at Whitewater, the ATF and FBI's murderous actions at Waco, and the Octopus' drug-running at Mena onto Oklahoma City, and "the new enemy in our midst."

Was it just a coincidence that two weeks after the bombing, a group of anonymous, black-hooded, machinegun-toting federal agents began loading files removed from the Murrah Building onto two unmarked trucks?

What were in the files that a over dozen heavily-armed agents were so anxious to hide? Were the files records incriminating the Octopus for its drug-running at Mena, or records incriminating the ATF for their actions at Waco? It may be more than a coincidence that the ATF agents who raided Waco wore black uniforms with no identifying badges.

On the May 14, 1995 edition of Face the Nation, White House Chief of Staff Leon Panetta denounced those chairing the Waco hearings as "despicable," claiming they "wanted to take attention away from the tragedy of Oklahoma City."

Republican legislators complained bitterly about the Executive Branch's tardy and disorganized production of documents regarding Waco. Representatives could not find in their 48,000 documents a copy of any April 19 Waco operation plan.[786]

It has been suggested that the files removed from the Murrah Building were records implicating George Bush and company for their role in selling Iraq biological weapons that have infected large numbers of American troops and their families. Peter Kawaja, who served as Louis Champon's chief of security at his

---

The sole survivor, stewardess Shelly Kelly, who had only minor cuts and bruises, mysteriously bled to death from a neat 3" incision above her femoral artery upon arrival at the hospital. Brown's law partner at Patton, Boggs and Blow died in a mysterious car wreck within one hour of the crash. Three days later, Niko Jerkuic, the maintenance chief at the Tulsa airport, who guided the plane to its fatal rendezvous through misplaced ground navigation beacons, "committed suicide."

Ron Brown, under investigation for bribery linked to DNC fundraising and the mysterious Lippo Group, in turn linked to President Clinton, reportedly possessed sensitive information that could have implicated Clinton in a long list of criminal acts. Congresswoman Maxine Waters called for an investigation into Ron Brown's death. (Christopher Ruddy and Hugh Sprunt, "Questions linger about Ron Brown plane crash," 11/24/97; Christopher Ruddy, "Experts differ on Ron Brown's head wound," Tribune-Review, 12/3/97; "Ron Brown conspiracy protest today," UPI, 12/24/97.)

Product Ingredient Technologies in Boca Raton, FL—secretly being used by his business partner Ishan Barbouti, an Iraqi arms dealer, to produce Cyanide shipped to Iraq—claims that documents implicating Bush, Secretary of State James Baker, and others involved in the "Iraqgate" scandal were moved to the Alfred P. Murrah Building.[787]

Whatever the case, someone was obviously concerned about some files in the Federal Building—concerned enough to send a team of hooded, heavily-armed agents to whisk them away.

Several days after the bombing, President Clinton sent his Anti-Terrorism Bill to Congress. The legislation, originally introduced after the World Trade Center bombing, had been languishing on the Congressional shelf. On June 7, the Senate passed the sweeping measure by a vote of 91 to 8.*

Concurrent with the new legislation was a massive smear campaign against the militias, trumpeted by President Clinton. As the *Sunday Telegraph's* Washington correspondent, Ambrose Evans-Pritchard, noted:

> The momentum of Republican "revolution" drained away overnight, as people drew back from the anti-government rhetoric of the right, unleashing the startling decline in its fortunes. President Clinton told reporters that he owed his political comeback to that bomb. "It broke the spell," he said.[788]

---

* Secretary of State Warren Christopher had unveiled a similar plan four months earlier: "International terrorists, criminals and drug traffickers pose direct threats to our people and to our nation's interests."

Chapter Twelve

THE POLITICS OF TERROR

"Power concedes nothing without a demand ... it never did, and it never will. Find out just what the people will submit to, and you have found out the exact amount of injustice and wrong which will be imposed upon them."
—Frederick Douglas, August 4, 1857

Ten years after *Report from Iron Mountain* was published, Theodore Shackley published *The Third Option: An Expert's Provocative Report on an American View of Counterinsurgency Operations.*

Shackley was one of the original proponents of "low intensity conflict," which manifested itself as the Phoenix Program in Vietnam, and as death squads in South and Central America. Shackley euphemistically describes this concept as "the third option."

> Senior intelligence officers like myself, who had experience in paramilitary operations, have always insisted that the United States should also consider the third option: the use of guerrilla warfare, counter-insurgency techniques and covert action to achieve policy goals.... Political warfare is very often the stitch in time that eliminates bloodier and more costly alternatives.[789]

Gene Wheaton calls Shackley's *Third Option* the "operational manual" for the covert intelligence "lunatic fringe." This same lunatic intelligence crowd, states Wheaton, "as far back as the early 1980s, wanted to create a domestic terrorist threat in America so the people would become so frightened that they would give up some civil liberties and Constitutional rights, and give the CIA and Pentagon covert operators major domestic counter-terrorism powers."

As Wheaton writes:

> The Third Option is not to have peace in the world, and not to have a full-scale world war. Instead, they wanted to cause worldwide instability, chaos and civil unrest in order to manipulate and control people and governments, including the United States; thus the creation of the domestic terrorist threat.[790]

Otherwise known as the "Hegelian Principle," this is the technique by which a normally repugnant idea (in this case a totalitarian police state) is offered as the only viable solution to a intractable problem (in this case domestic terrorism), deliberately engineered by the state itself. As *New American* editor William Jasper notes:

> History is replete with examples of ruthless and corrupt politicians who have shamelessly exploited and manipulated tragic events and the criminal acts of a few to advance their own lust for power. In cases too numerous to mention, tyrants and aspiring despots have gone even further, engaging agents provocateurs to carry out assassinations, foment riots and rebellion, precipitate financial panics, attempt palace coups, feign foreign invasion, initiate acts of terrorism, and perform other infamous acts—all for the purpose of establishing a mass psychology of fear, a sense of "crisis," of imminent danger requiring the government to suspend normal liberties and seize vast new powers to deal with the "emergency."

Hitler came to power in precisely this manner, by burning down the German Parliament, the Reichstag, then blaming it on his enemies—in this case, the Communists. He then passed the Enabling Act (a form of anti-terrorism bill) for the "protection of the people and the state."

History is now repeating itself. As Adam Parfrey writes in *Cult Rapture:*

> By definition, a terrorist must take credit for his violence, or else there is no compelling reason to commit a crime. The specific purpose of terrorism is gaining leverage on a specific political objective through the ability of threatening future terrorist acts. No one has claimed credit for the Oklahoma City bombing. Militia groups produced particularly vehement public statements condemning the crime.

"If the bombing was not terrorism," asks *Portland Free Press* editor Ace Hayes, "then what was it? It was pseudo-terrorism, perpetrated by compartmentalized covert operators for the purposes of state police power." [791]

> "*The Portland Free Press* editor has studied the secret state for decades and can say that the OKC crime has all the characteristics of state-planned and-executed propaganda. It is not different from the bogus Viet Cong units that were sent out to rape and murder Vietnamese to discredit the National Liberation Front. It is not different from the bogus 'finds' of Commie weapons in El Salvador. It is not different from the bogus Symbionese Liberation Army created by the CIA/FBI to discredit the real revolutionaries."

Probably the most well-known case was the Reichstag fire, which led to the rise of Nazi Germany through the implementation of sweeping legislative powers. On February 27, 1933, a fire tore through the German parliament building, the Reichstag. The Nazis immediately accused a Dutch Communist named Marinus van der Lubbe of the crime, and subsequently executed him.

The parallels between the Reichstag fire and the Oklahoma City bombing are eerily similar, both in the likeness of the crime, and in their political ramifications. As author William Shirer writes in his epic, *The Rise and Fall of the Third Reich:*

The idea for the fire almost certainly originated with Goebbels and Göering. Hans Gisevius, an official in the Prussian Ministry of the Interior at the time, testified at Nuremberg that "it was Goebbels who first thought of setting the Reichstag on fire," and Rudolf Diels, the Gestapo chief, added in an affidavit that "Göering knew exactly how the fire was to be started" and had ordered him "to prepare, prior to the fire, a list of people who were to be arrested immediately after it." General Franz Haider, Chief of the German General Staff during the early part of World War II, recalled at Nuremberg how on one occasion Göering had boasted of his deed:

"At a luncheon on the birthday of the Fuehrer in 1942 the conversation turned to the topic of the Reichstag building and its artistic value. I heard with my own ears when Göering interrupted the conversation and shouted: 'The only one who really knows about the Reichstag is I, because I set it on fire!' With that he slapped his thigh with the flat of his hand."

[Marinus] Van der Lubbe, it seems clear, was a dupe of the Nazis. He was encouraged to try to set the Reichstag on fire. But the main job was to be done— without his knowledge, of course—by the storm troopers. Indeed, it was established at the subsequent trial at Leipzig that the Dutch half-wit did not possess the means to set so vast a building on fire so quickly. Two and a half minutes after he entered, the great central hall was fiercely burning. He had only his shirt for tinder.

The main fires, according to the testimony of experts at the trial, had been set with considerable quantities of chemicals and gasoline. It was obvious that one man could not have carried them into the building, nor would it have been possible for him to start so many fires in so many scattered places in so short a time. Van der Lubbe was arrested on the spot and Göering, as he afterward told the court, wanted to hang him at once.[792]

Shirer may just as well have been describing the bombing in Oklahoma City. Timothy McVeigh appears as a modern-day Van der Lubbe—a dupe who could not possibly destroy the Murrah Building with s crude, homemade fertilizer bomb. Yet he was set up in exactly the same manner as the Dutch Communist, arrested instantly, and proclaimed the ultimate societal enemy—representing a group that threatened the continuity of the state—just as Clinton did with the militias in the aftermath of the Oklahoma City bombing.

Although Göering didn't admit at Nuremberg that his agents set the fire, the Nazis seized on the event, claiming Lubbe's act was the precursor of a Communist invasion. Chancellor Hitler persuaded President Hindenburg to sign an emergency decree—Article 48 of the Weimar Constitution, "for the Protection of the People and the State"—which immediately abrogated most of the German people's constitutional protections.

A supplemental decree created the SA (Storm Troops) and SS (Special Security) federal police agencies. These decrees (similar to executive orders of the President of the United States), gave Hitler and his goons the ability to ruthlessly suppress all opposition in the upcoming elections. As a result, the Nazis gained a 44 percent plurality in the Parliament, and [soon-to-be] Luftwaffe General Herman Göering declared that there was no further need for state governments.

The Nazis were successful in eliminating the state's authority in the same manner—instigating disorder, then quelling it by replacing local governments with Nazi-appointed Reich Commissioners.

This precedent was officially established on March 23 when the "Enabling Act" transferred the power of the states to the central Nazi-run government—making the federal government responsible for all law-enforcement, and conferring on Hitler the legal status of dictator.

Hitler immediately appointed Joseph Goebbels as Minster of Propaganda, and as Interior Minister—the top police post—Hitler appointed Herman Göering. Göering immediately filled the ranks of the Prussian police with loyal SA and SS members. As Suzanne Harris of the *The Law Loft* notes:

> All of the key strategic moves were made by Göering in setting the stage for a take-over. Why? Because in order to take over a government, you have to eliminate your political enemies before they strike, not after. This means that you have to transform the police from a crime-detecting and punishing apparatus to a crime preventing apparatus. You have to expand the definition of key crimes so that you can identify and incarcerate your enemies before they strike. You have to transform the attitudes of the police so that they view the public as the enemy and not as citizens with rights. You have to have tactical police units in place that will execute your orders rapidly without question.[793]

Soon Nazi storm troopers were roaring through the streets at all hours, rounding up suspected dissidents, including politicians, who were then hauled off to makeshift concentration camps and tortured or killed. As Shirer writes:

> Just to make sure the job would be ruthlessly done, Göering on February 22 established an auxiliary police force of 50,000 men, of whom 40,000 were drawn from the ranks of the S.A. and the S.S.... Police power in Prussia was thus largely car-

ried out by Nazi thugs. It was a rash German who appealed to such a "police" for protection against the Nazi terrorists.[794]

Hitler's promises that "the government will make use of these powers only insofar as they are essential for carrying out vitally necessary measures" were belied by the ruthless tally of history.[795]

In a manner faintly reminiscent of Hitler's assurances concerning the 1933 "Enabling laws," FBI Director Louis Freeh recently sought, and won, tentative agreement on a package of anti-terrorism measures that would expand wiretapping authority. Freeh assured legislators that the proposals would not give the government "expansive powers."[796]

Like the CIA's announcement to investigate itself for its own drug-running, the wolf now seeks to reassure the public that it has no intention of invading the hen house.

One year to the day after the Oklahoma City bombing, President Clinton signed his Anti-Terrorism Bill, "for the protection of the people and the state."

"We can't be so fixated on our desire to preserve the rights of ordinary Americans," Clinton was quoted in *USA Today* in March, 1993.[797]

"A lot of people say there's too much personal freedom," Clinton stated on MTV in March, '94. "When personal freedom's being abused, you have to move to limit it."[798]

Clinton's Anti-Terrorism Bill includes plans to establish a new FBI counterterrorism center with 1,000 new "anti-terrorist" agents. One proposal, harking back to the days of COINTELPRO, would add 25 intelligence analysts, 190 surveillance specialists with 143 support personnel, 31 engineers and mathematicians for intercepting digital communications, and various other experts and analysts. The bill also includes a $66 million windfall for the ATF for "anti-terrorism" efforts.[799]

Now the FBI has now unveiled its "Critical Incident Response Group." Divided into five units, the "Undercover Safeguard Unit" selects recruits for even more undercover agents to be sent amongst the American people; the "Aviation and Special Operations Unit" creates an FBI Air Force for both logistics and spying; the "Investigative Support Unit," permits the FBI's crime lab to become available for every law-enforcement agency in the country; and the "Crisis Management Unit" which assists the Bureau cover up unfriendly mishaps or intentsion. Then there is the "SWAT Training Unit," and the "Tactical Support" Division, which includes the infamous "Hostage Rescue Team," which rescued a nursing mother at Ruby Ridge by shooting her in the face, and rescued 86 men, women and children at Waco by gassing, shooting, and burning them alive.[800]

One recent manifestation of America's drift toward a national police force is the final report of the National Performance Review (NPR) headed by Vice President Al Gore. Said to be a blueprint for "reinventing government," this report recommends "the designation of the Attorney General as the Director of

Law Enforcement to coordinate federal law enforcement efforts." This was the same Attorney General who, along with Deputy Attorney General Webster Hubbell and President Bill Clinton, gave the final solution order at Waco.

Now, under H.R. 97 (the "Rapid Deployment Strike Force Act"), Clinton, Reno and Freeh are calling for a 2,500-man "Rapid-Deployment" force composed of FBI and other federal agents, all under the supervision of the Attorney General.[801] The bill states:

> On application of the Governor of a State and the chief executive officer of the affected local government or governments ... and upon finding that the occurrence of criminal activity in a particular jurisdiction is being exacerbated by the interstate flow of drugs, guns, and criminals, the Deputy Assistant Director may deploy on a temporary basis a unit of the Rapid Deployment Force.

Judiciary Committee spokesmen interviewed by *Relevance* magazine said the Rapid-Deployment Strike Force "would also serve as a model unit for local officers to emulate." Joe Hendricks, Chief of Police of Windsor, Missouri, expressed his concern over this trend in the June, 1997 issue of the *Idaho Observer:*

> Unfortunately, at the present time, an agent of the FBI could walk into my office and commandeer this police department. If you don't believe that, read the Crime Bill that Clinton signed into law in 1995. There is talk of the Feds taking over the Washington, D.C. Police Department. To me this sets a dangerous precedent.[802]*

Said Joseph McNamara, former police chief in San Jose and Kansas City, now at the Hoover Institute at Stanford University: "Despite the conventional wisdom that community policing is sweeping the nation, the exact opposite is happening.... It's a very dangerous thing, when you're telling cops they're soldiers and there's an enemy out there. I don't like it at all."[803]

Charles "Bud" Meeks, executive director of the National Sheriff's Association, adds, "By passing statutes in an effort to make [the crime situation] better," he observed, "we're getting closer to a federal police state."[804]

"In SWAT units formed since 1980, their use has increased by 538 percent," said police researcher Peter Kraska. Originally designed to control armed, barricaded suspects, SWAT teams are now being routinely used in the so-called "War on Drugs," and in places like Fresno, CA., are being deployed full-time as roaming patrols.

---

* Recent rules in certain counties in Wyoming have changed this policy, and legislation is pending as of this writing in Montana to require federal agents to seek authorization of the local sheriff before conducting a raid.

"The drug war created the atmosphere for this kind of pro-active policing," Kraska said. "We have never seen this kind of policing, where SWAT teams routinely break through a door, subdue all the occupants and search the premises for drugs, cash and weapons."

One increasing manifestation of this trend are Multi-Jurisdictional Task Forces (MJTF) training for urban guerrilla warfare (UGW). As numerous newspaper articles have noted over the past few years, sweeps by Army helicopters in towns and cities across America in conjunction with paramilitary police raids and training exercises have been increasing. The following incident was reported by Jim Keith and verified by the author:

During the Summer of 1993, residents of Midtown, Atlanta, Georgia were shocked in the early hours of the morning as three military helicopters came churning through their high-rise condo canyons as part of military Special Operations Command practice raids. In the same area in July of 1994, automatic weapons fire and explosions echoed off an abandoned state office building on Peachtree Street. Employees of a Kinko's copy center at 793 Peachtree Street saw men in battle gear atop the building. An employees remember a bullet shattering the store's window during the exercise.

During January of 1994, troops from the U.S. Army Special Operations Command, which includes the Green Berets, Rangers, and psychological warfare specialists, were seen rappelling off the empty 11-story St Moritz Hotel in Miami, firing paint pellets in mock assault exercises.[805] In Fort Lauderdale during November, 1996, troops from the 160th Special Operations Aviation Regiment from Fort Campbell, Kentucky, along with Special Forces, Rangers, Navy SEALSs, and psychological warfare specialists, practiced "night urban navigation training."

In Houston, the crash of an Army helicopter alerted citizens to troops practicing UGW copter exercises, small arms fire and explosives in vacant buildings.[806]

Similar exercises were practiced near Detroit during the summer of 1994. In Van Buren township, citizens were treated to the sound of explosions and automatic gunfire. When residents complained, they were told by police, "Don't worry about it. The MJTF and Van Buren PD SWAT teams were practicing."

Resident Bridget Tuohey wasn't reassured. "I have two little kids here who are semi-hysterical," Tuohey told the *Detroit News*. When Van Buren resident Mark Spencer went to investigate, he saw men in Ninja-style black uniforms with no markings practicing mock assaults on abandoned houses.

As Spencer recalls, "Never in 25 years of living in this area have I ever heard automatic weapons fire. Never have I heard explosives training being done here. Never have I seen men dressed in black battle dress roaming the wooded areas of my home." [807]

On June 6, 1996, the *Washington Times* reported:

> Nine Army helicopters swooped into Pittsburgh in the middle of the night this week and turned parts of the city into war zones, complete with sounds of explosions and gunfire that frightened residents and sent one pregnant woman into labor.

What are these troops training for? According to a report in the March, 1995 issue of *Soldier of Fortune*, about 40 Army and Air Force legal and other personnel attended a secret "research symposium" at XVIII Airborne Corps between December 6th and 8th, 1994, to strategize and study for the deployment of U.S. personnel and resources to aid civilian authorities in "the suppression of domestic civil unrest." Army lawyers repeatedly brushed aside Airborne officers concerns that such deployment would violate the Posse Comitatus Act. One lawyer, responding somewhat cryptically said, "Not anymore, it doesn't." *

In early March, '66, dozens of defense industry leaders, government policy makers, and military analysts met with federal law enforcement officials at the Ritz-Carlton in McLean, Virginia. Their purpose was to strategize the "Operations Other Than War/Law Enforcement" (OOTW/LE) initiative, designed to increase coordination between law-enforcement and the military—a trend which has been accelerating in recent years. As *Sources Ejournal* reported:

> In hearings on the joint Pentagon/law enforcement OOTW program in June, 1994, Dr. Anita K. Jones, director of defense research and engineering, told the House Armed Services Committee that she foresees the military increasingly being called upon to respond to "rising violence on our city streets" and to deal with the "widespread availability of increasingly powerful weapons." [808]

One particularly frightening aspect of this trend is the transfer of new high-tech weapons and surveillance gear to domestic law enforcement. The *Orange County Register* of March 19, 1993 reported that Camp Pendleton Marine base in southern California recently added an $8.4 million facility to train for urban warfare. [809]

---

* It seems that President Clinton suspended the law restricting the use of military force within U.S. borders in a little-known codicil of PDD-25, a Presidential Decision Directive that is an "open secret" in the military and Congress, but is largely unknown to the American citizens.

While the DoD claims these exercises are training for "overseas" commitments, Major General Max Baratz dropped the ball when he wrote in the Summer, 1994 issue of *Army Reserve Magazine:*

> In addition to providing fully ready units for our international missions, we'll have an enhanced capability to support domestic actions, [including] regional planning related to Military Support to Civilian Authorities and FEMA (Federal Emergency Management Agency) activities.[810]

As William Jasper reported in the October 31, 1994 issue of *The New American,* soldiers are currently undergoing training in disarming civilian militias at the $12 million Military Operations on Urban Terrain (MOUT) complex at Ft. Polk, Georgia.[811]

This plan came to fruition in February, 1995, when a source inside the Nevada National Guard said the FBI had asked for 400 National Guardsmen to help "put down" the Nevada State's Rights Movement. When the Guard refused, the FBI threatened to bring in federal troops.

One National Guardsman who had participated in "Desert Massacre" told an observer his outfit was being trained to "attack urban buildings." When asked for clarification, he said, "If they told us there were guns or drugs in a house, we know how to take it down."

Oliver North and "Buck" Revell helped develop the policy of militarizing our law-enforcement. One example is the FBI, which is now being given sniper training by the military. That training helped the Bureau massacre 86 people at Waco, the first time in recent history that the government violated the Posse Comitatus Act by using federal troops on American citizens.

To put some perspective on FEMA's connections to the lunatic fringe, note that Oliver North served on the Reagan-created Emergency Mobilization Preparedness Board, which oversaw FEMA's planning and operations.

Raymond "Buddy" Young, President Clinton's former Director of Security, was appointed director of FEMA's Region IV post. Young reportedly participated in and covered-up the Octopus's various illegal activities at Mena, Arkansas. He later showed up in the aftermath of the Oklahoma City bombing, directing FEMA traffic and holding press conferences.

North himself proposed a suspension of the Constitution upon the planned U.S. invasion of Nicaragua. In fact, North testified during the Iran-Contra hearings that they were prepared "to suspend the Constitution in the event of mass immigration and domestic political unrest."

The plan was called Operation Rex-84-Alpha (Readiness Exercise 1984, Exercise Plan). Rex-84, which ran concurrently with the first annual show of U.S. force in Honduras in April 1984, was designed to test FEMA's ability to round

up 400,000 undocumented Central American immigrants and domestic protesters in the event of an invasion by U.S. forces, and its ability to distribute hundreds
of tons of small arms to State Defense Forces (SDF). Reagan and North planned
to utilize the SDFs to control and imprison American citizens and Central
American refugees.

General Frank Salcedo, Chief of FEMA's Civil Security Division, stated in
1982 that at least 100,000 U.S. citizens, from survivalists to tax protesters, pose
serious threats to civil security.[812]

Rex-84 (along with other joint-mobilization exercises as "Proud Saber/Rex-
82," "Operation Garden Plot," and "Operation Night Train") was practiced with
34 other agencies such as the CIA, FBI and the Secret Service. Ben Bradlee, in
his book, *The Rise And Fall of Oliver North,* writes that the Rex exercise was
designed to test FEMA's readiness to assume authority over the DoD, the
National Guard, and "a number of state defense forces to be established by state
legislatures." The military would then be "deputized," making an end run around
the Posse Comitatus Act, the same Posse Comitatus Act breached at Waco and
the L.A. riots.

Detainment camps (concentration camps) were set up on U.S. soil to deal with
the expected flood of refugees and political dissenters. Informed sources say they
still exist. Such operations represent a frightening precedent for the Shadow
Government to suspend Constitutional rights (or what little we have left) in the
case of political dissent. This probability was raised by a CIA agent in conversation with DEA veteran Mike Levine. Levine recalls the discussion in his book,
Triangle of Death:

"Don't you realize that there are factions in your government that want this to happen—an emergency situation too hot for a constitutional government to handle."

"To what end?" I asked

"A suspension of the Constitution, of course. The legislation is already in place.
All perfectly legal. Check it out for yourself. It's called FEMA, Federal Emergency
Management Agency. 'Turn in your guns, you bloody bastards, from here on out,
we're watching you, you anti-government rabble rousers.' And who would be king,
Michael?"

"CIA," I said.[813]

While Levine supposedly had this conversation with the Argentine CIA
Station Chief in 1991, he told me the actual discussion took place with a drunk
CIA agent in Buenos Aries twelve years earlier. As Levine recalls: "He told me
America should be more like Argentina. That Americans have more rights than
they should have. He said, 'Give Americans a car, a TV set, a home, and they're
happy.' He told me all you had to do was create a situation of fear and anarchy so

that Americans will give up their rights.... I believe this is part of what's happening now."[830]

A prime example was the 1992 L.A. riots. While the beating of black motorist Rodney King was not part of a preconceived plan, many insist that the riots were allowed to rage out of control to test the government's plans for martial law, and provide an excuse for further erosion of our civil rights. It was widely reported that Police Chief Daryl Gates deliberately held back his officers, some of whom literally cried as they watched the ensuing chaos.*

Even that bastion of the establishment, the *New York Times*, reported:

Emerging evidence from the first crucial hours ... provides the strong indication that top police officials did little to plan for the possibility of violence and did not follow standard procedures to contain the rioting once it began....

The police ... violated the basic police procedure for riot-control by failing to cordon off the area around one of the first trouble spots and not returning to that area for hours.

Police 911 dispatchers attempted to send squad cars to the scene of the first violent outbreaks, but were repeatedly ignored or overruled.[815]

One Deputy Chief, commenting on the hundreds of officers (and National Guardsmen) who were deliberately held back, told the *Los Angeles Times*, "This is alien to everything we're supposed to do in a situation like this."[816] Compton Councilwoman Patricia Moore publicly stated that the police themselves started the riots. Backing up Moore was CIA operative Frederick George Celani (aka Fred Sebastian), who insisted that the riots were "fomented by federal agents."**

Should a situation such as Levine refers to actually take place, the first to be "detained" would be those who oppose the current system—dissidents, radicals, and primarily, those in the Patriot/Militia movement. The movement represents a threat to the existing power structure in the same way that the Anti-War movement represented a threat to the military-industrial establishment, or the Sandinistas and the FMLN represented a threat to their U.S.-backed fascist dictators.

Used to viewing challenges to its authority on counterinsurgency model, the ruling elite regard the Patriot/Militia movement along the same lines.

Such counterinsurgency training originated in Vietnam under the infamous Phoenix Program of CIA officials William Colby and Ted Shackley. Not surpris-

---

* The Los Angeles riots resulted in 11,113 fires, 2,383 injuries, and 54 deaths. There were 13,212 arrests. The damage was estimated at $717 million.

** Alex Constantine *(Blood, Carnage, and the Agent Provocateur)*, who interviewed local residents, discovered that some of the arsonists were clearly not locals.

ingly, Shackley uses examples such as Phoenix and the latter-day death squads of
Latin America as splendid examples of how to curb an "insurgency." Shackley
refers to the poor, common people of these countries as little more than sinister
insurgents out to destroy all vestiges of democracy, when in fact, any semblage of
democracy, if it ever existed, would be quickly extinguished to protect the interests of U.S. industrial cartels.

Now our own democracy, largely a sham to begin with, is beginning to follow
the model of these third-world countries. Shackley's "Third Option" has become
the model for the counter-insurgency program now being waged against the
American people. As Ace Hayes writes:

> The Imperial State is planning for war with the American people. It is planning to
> win that war. There is no other possible explanation for the frenzied framing of a
> fascist police state.[817]

The Shadow Government's willingness to kill large numbers of foreigners in
its bloody wars and covert operations is now being extended to the American
people, as its goals shift from controlling third-world populations to controlling
American citizens. The same techniques of propaganda, torture, and other coercion that was field-tested by the CIA against "Communists" and other insurgents
in South and Central America could ultimately be used on American citizens as
the U.S. moves closer and closer politically and economically to its third-world
cousins.

A Special Forces combat veteran who coached desert warfare exercises said,
very matter-of-factly, that such training would be used on American citizens. "I
don't know [when]," he said, "but sooner or later, it's inevitable."

As nationalism becomes less and less the defining factor, the ethical and moral
equation shifts with it. It is a short leap from rationalizing the killing of hundreds
of thousands or even millions of foreigners to killing a few hundred or a few thousand Americans, if the policy objectives deem it necessary. These deaths are simply viewed as "collateral damage" by the ruling elite.

While this may sound like a drastic concept, the basic idea underlying it is
the same. Governments need to control their people. In Latin America, Red
China, Turkey, and Indonesia, control is maintained through repressive laws,
incarceration, torture, and death squads. In "civilized" countries such as the
United States, the techniques are the same, they only differ in the degree that
they are used.

Ted Shackley's "Third Option," originally a model for counterinsurgency
against the third-world, is now being put to the test in the U.S.—a program of
counterinsurgency against the American people.

While the U.S. escalates its use of repressive laws, imprisonment, torture, and murder, the main tool has always been propaganda, in the form of the corporate-controlled press.* As Shackley writes:

> There are cases in which a cause supported, a newspaper campaign initiated, or a particular candidate encouraged in an election could mean (and in the past has meant) that the crisis in which our vital interests might be at stake never arises.[818]

Hitler expressed similar sentiments in *Mein Kampf:* "The task of propaganda lies … in directing the masses towards certain facts, events, necessities, etc., the purpose being to move their importance into the masses' field of vision."

Lt. Col. Michael Aquino—a U.S. Army mind control expert—certainly has no aversion to practicing Nazi ritual. The self-avowed leader of the Temple of Set once performed Satanic ritual in the Hall of the Dead at Germany's Westphalian castle, an occult sanctuary for Heinrich Himmler's SS elite. As the *San Francisco Examiner* reported:

> Aquino once urged the Pentagon, in a controversial psychological warfare study entitled "Mind War," to overwhelm enemies by mobilizing every means of domestic and foreign propaganda, including brainwashing the U.S. public.

The Anti-Terrorism and Crime Bills permit the Federal Government to maintain an unprecedented level of control over the American people.

Ensconced in the Anti-Terrorism Bill's cryptic language are provisions that allow the President and the Justice Department to define which groups are subject to the increasingly broad definition of "terrorist." It allows expanded use of wiretaps and illegally-seized evidence to be used in court. It permits federal and local police agencies to trace financial information without obtaining evidence of a crime. It expands use of current laws prohibiting fund-raising for terrorist organizations, denial of visas, increased cooperation with other governments on money laundering and asset seizures. It permits "no-knock" searches. And it allows the military to intervene in domestic situations deemed a national security threat.

In short, it guts the First, Fourth, Fifth, Sixth, and Eighth Amendments to the Constitution, lays the framework for an entrenched police state, and gives the Federal Government full power to target anybody deemed a threat to its authority.

While the final version rammed through Congress was watered down some-

---

* PBS Frontline did a piece in 1995 showing victims of torture occurring in one Chicago police district. It was claimed that torture was often used on suspects in that district to obtain confessions.

what, it was the beginning of a wave of "anti-militia" legislation introduced in the wake of the bombing.

On November 2, Representative Charles Schumer (D-NY) introduced H.R. 2580, his attempt to "cleanse the illness of violent extremism" from America's political culture by outlawing militias.[819]

H.R. 2580 followed on the heels of its sister bill, H.R. 1544, the "Domestic Insurgency Act," introduced by Representative Gerald Nadler (D-NY). The Domestic Insurgency Act purports to prevent two or more individuals from possessing "any weapons capable of causing death or injury with the intention to unlawfully oppose the authority of the United States." Such a paramilitary group could conceivably include a pair of senior citizens with Swiss Army knives at a church picnic discussing their unhappiness with the Social Security Administration.

Not surprisingly, it was Theodore Shackley who first recommended the concept of an Anti-Terrorism Bill:

> *Guide governments in the preparation of anti-terrorist laws.* When the cadre phase begins to unfold, many countries find they do not have laws on the books to deal with the threat.... it is better to be able to arrest and convict subversives on the basis of a *law* then on an executive *order.* If such laws cannot be passed expeditiously, the party in power should mount an education campaign to rally public opinion on behalf of their enactment.*

Since Shackley was the first to come up with the concept of an Anti-Terrorism Bill, and since he was also one of the first to run a major CIA-sanctioned drug-running operation, one could effectively argue that the controls offered by the Anti-Terrorism Bill will go a long way towards assisting these bands of covert operators and international criminals in their illegal enterprises.

The General Services Administration noted that the Digital Telephony Bill would "make it easier for criminals, terrorists, foreign intelligence and computer hackers to electronically penetrate the public network and pry into areas previously not open to snooping."

President Reagan's Executive Order 12333 assisted in this development by "privatizing" intelligence gathering. Not surprisingly, Shackley, Casey, and Bush attended the December 5, 1980 meeting to draft E.O. 12333, which states:

> Agencies within the Intelligence Community are authorized to enter into contracts or arrangements for the provision of goods or services with private companies or institutions in the United States and need not reveal the sponsorship of such contracts or arrangements for authorized intelligence purposes....

---

* Emphasis in original.

Not that the government needed a new law to conduct its criminal activities—it simply codified what had already been established. By privatizing covert operations, the government gets to maintain "plausible deniability."

Intelligence agency front companies such as EATSCO, Stanford Technologies, Intercontental Industries, E-Systems, Southern Air Transport, and a bewildering array of others, allow the Octopus to make large amounts of money while providing the Plutocracy with an "off the shelf" capability to conduct covert operations while skirting Congressional oversight. As former CIA agent Marchetti writes:

> With the cooperation of an acquiescent, ill-informed Congress, and the encouragement and assistance of a series of Presidents, the cult has built a wall of laws and executive orders around the CIA and itself, a wall that has blocked effective public scrutiny.[820]

The goals of these "Secret Teams" naturally overlap with the agendas of the corporate-financial elite. "[Roy] Godson estimates that international crime groups outperform most Fortune 500 companies. They deliver drugs, illegal aliens, and laundered money, and provide services like violence and extortion—all with organizations that resemble General Motors more than they resemble the traditional Sicilian Mafia." Godson should know. As a member of the National Strategy Information Center, founded by former CIA Director William Casey, Godson helped Oliver North raise funds for the drug-running Contras.[820]

Another example of the symbiotic relationship between the private sector and the covert community is Peregrine International in Dallas, Texas. Founded by Guy S. Howard and Ronald R. Tucker, Peregrine was most recently run by George Petrie, a veteran the Army's secret Delta-Force. Petrie told the *Dallas Morning News* that his company "consults" with foreign governments on terrorism. Petrie displays pictures of him with George Bush and other prominent politicians.*

As reported in the *Philadelphia Inquirer*, Peregrine conducted covert ops with Defense Department approval from 1981 until 1984, when the company folded (although Texas Secretary of State records indicate the company was still active as of 1996). As the *Inquirer* wrote:

---

* Interestingly, William Northrop is a good friend of George Petrie's, and acted as a middle-man between the CIA, the Israelis, and the Contras in illegal arms deals. He was prosecuted by former U.S. Attorney for the Southern District of New York (now Mayor) Rudolph Giuliani, who described him as one of the "Merchants of Death."

The company hired both retired and active duty military personnel on leave to act as "guns"—guys who had no qualms about blowing people away. Their assassination targets included planning to kill drug smugglers in Peru, Honduras, Belize, and Caribbean nations; arm and train Contras, and arm and train official military commando units in El Salvador, Honduras and Peru.[822]

Was Peregrine's plan to kill drug smugglers part of a program to clean up the drug trade? Or was it an extension of Shackley's program to eliminate the CIA's heroin competition, as it had in Laos?

Perhaps that is what Timothy McVeigh's letter (about being recruited for a Covert Tactical Unit) meant about "eliminating the competition."

Navy SEAL Commander Robert Hunt, who used to teach assassination teams for the CIA, described the activities of ANV, which served as an umbrella for Peregrine. As Rodney Stich writes in *Defrauding America:*

Shareholders in the company were present and former CIA personnel, reportedly involved in some aspect of CIA-related drug trafficking. They included, for instance, Theodore Shackley, who was heavily involved in the CIA Far East drug trafficking and then in the drug trafficking from Central and South America.... Hunt stated there were numerous ties between the groups and the Richard Secord-Theodore Shackley-and Thomas Clines Associates, all of whom were reportedly associated with the opium trade and assassination program in Laos.

ANV is the "action arm" of Continental Shelf Associates (formerly Perry Submarines/Perry Off-Shore) of Jupiter, Florida. A former CIA proprietary, it was operated by Robert "Stretch" Stevens, who had served as Shackley's Maritime Operations Chief from the Bay of Pigs to South East Asia (Shackley sits on the board of CSA). In this regard, the activities of organizations like ANV and Peregrine are no different than those of groups like the CIA's old ZR/RIFLE, set up to assassinate Fidel Castro and Che Guevera.

ANV (also known as the "Fish Farm") specializes in training foreign nationals for commando-type mercenary operations and assassinations—rented to various groups and governments around the world. On the board of ANV is Bill Hamilton, former Director of Navy Special Operations who attempted to establish the "Phoenix Battalion," a privately-funded, covert group that would launch "preemptive strikes" against organizations it defined as "terrorist."[823]

Could Hussain al-Hussaini and his associates have been some of the foreign nationals trained by ANV?

According to Wheaton, this same group of covert operators controls a secret base on Andros Island in the Bahamas operated by the super-secret NRO

(National Reconnaissance Office), the USMC, and the Navy. Named AUTEC, it is an underground/underwater computerized facility for tracking both friendly and enemy ships and subs. Wheaton claims that an "illegal secret operation buried within the complex is a covert intelligence project, database and operation directed against the civilian population of the United States...."

Wheaton claims the facility "is central control for Ted Shackley's 'Third Option' and the project to create domestic unrest, chaos, and the illusion of a domestic terrorist threat within America." [824]

While operations from super-secret high-tech bases may sound like the stuff of Ian Fleming novels, Shackley allegedly directed the overthrow of Australia's Prime Minister Gough Whitlam—the first Labor Prime Minister in over two decades—from the super-secret Pine Gap facility run by the CIA. As the Sheehan Affidavit states:

> On November 2, 1975, Whitlam publicly accused the CIA of subsidizing his opposition, and named National Country Party chief Doug Anthony as a collaborator. The next day, the *Australian Financial Review* reported that the super-secret U.S.-Australian "space study station" in Australia, known as Pine Gap, was actually a CIA electronic intelligence facility. The article also identified Richard Stallings, former director of Pine Gap and friend of Anthony, as a CIA agent. Pine Gap's true function shocked not only the Australian public, but also top government officials, including the Prime Minister.... [825]

The corollary between the situation in the U.S. and that in Australia may be significant, since that country is now undergoing wholesale gun confiscation of its citizenry under "Operation Cabin Thrust"—the first step to total control of its population.

In the Philippines, "anti-terrorism" legislation has already been passed, further restricting peoples' rights. In England, laws mandating wholesale handgun confiscation have recently been implemented.

Primarily targeted is America, "land of the free," as new restrictions on privacy, free speech, and self-defense are invoked in the wake of the World Trade Center and Oklahoma City bombings.

Zbigniew Brezinsky, Executive Director of the Trilateral Commission and National Security Advisor to Jimmy Carter [and four other presidents], explained it best: "The technotronic era involves the gradual appearance of a more controlled society. Such a society would be dominated by an elite, unrestrained by traditional values."

The reader has already been given a glimpse of this "elite" and their so-called "values." Dominating society will be a Plutocracy controlling everything from politics and media, education, commerce and industry, even private property.

Such plans calls for more governmental programs, more governmental controls, and more government-imposed order.

Caroll J. Quigley, former Professor of International Affairs at Georgetown University and Bill Clinton's mentor, grasped the Orwellian implications of this over 30 years ago. As Quigley observes in *Tragedy and Hope:* "[The individual's] freedom and choice will be controlled within very narrow alternatives by the fact that he will be numbered from birth and followed, as a number, through his educational training, his required military or other public service, his tax contributions, his health and medical requirements, and his final retirement and death benefits."

Utilizing their minions in the media and the alphabet soup of federal agencies—the FBI, ATF, DEA, CIA, NSA, IRS, INS, FDA, BLM, FINCEN, and FEMA—the elite seek total control over our family, our health, our finances, our education, our thoughts, and ultimately, our lives. What is sought is nothing less than a global plantation run by the transnational corporate elite—a modern day form of world-wide fascism.

"*The Chickens*

are coming

home to roost."

C h a p t e r   T h i r t e e n

A STRATEGY OF TENSION   —Malcolm X

Like the Reischtag fire, the Oklahoma City bombing served as the catalyst to impose a new wave of draconian legislation on the American people.

The bombing also dovetailed perfectly with the policy of blaming pre-arranged groups, developed in the early 1980s by the CIA's Vince Cannistraro, to divert attention to Libya in the Lockerbie bombing.

The CIA established a precedent for such policies more than 40 years ago in Italy and Greece when the OSS intervened in those countries' elections by supporting fascist collaborators who would attack the population and disrupt political proceedings. Through Operation SHEEPSKIN, the CIA worked with former Nazi collaborators in Greece to institute a campaign of black propaganda, terrorist bombings and other provocations to be blamed on the left, resulting in a fascist coup and the murder and repression of thousands.

The CIA helped create a "Strategy of Tension" in Italy through collaboration with the Mafia, corrupt Italian secret services, and fascists working through Masonic Mafia-linked societies such as Licio Gelli's Propaganda Due (P2 Lodge). Gelli (aka the "Puppet Master") had been friends with fascists such as Benito Mussolini, Croatia's Dr. Pavlic, and Juan Peron of Argentina, and had also fought with the Italian Blackshirts during the Spanish Civil War.

Gelli's P2 and elements within the Vatican (such as Father Krujoslav Dragonovic, a Croatian Catholic priest—one of many who helped the CIA export Nazi war criminals out of Germany through its Rat Lines), worked in conjunction with the CIA by aligning with criminals, corrupt police, and high government officials to discredit the emerging left. "The Vatican's fear was clear: Communism posed a threat to its religious, political, and economic strength." [826]

On behalf of democracy, the Mafia enlisted as their agent Salvatore Giuliano. He and his cousin Gaspere Pisciotta led their men into Portella della Ginestra. Without prejudice, they shot and killed a dozen people and wounded more than fifty others. New elections were held, and the Christian Democratic party won a resounding victory. Later, at the orders of the Mafia, Pisciotta murdered Salvatore Giuliano. At his trial, Gaspere Pisciotta said of the massacre, "We were a single body: bandits, police, and Mafia, like the Father, the Son, and the Holy Ghost." [827]

P2—essentially a right-wing parallel government aligned with a super-secret Italian organization called Il Gladio—was set up in 1956 with the help of British Intelligence and the CIA. Gladio was part and parcel of MI5 and the CIA's 1948 efforts to establish a European "Stay Behind" network of guerrilla fighters who would conduct covert operations after a Soviet invasion—using arms and explosives that had been previously cached.

This network was conceived by the U.S. Joint Chiefs of Staff, and organized by the NSC, which set up the Office of Policy Coordination to run it, staffed and funded by the CIA. Like Operation SHEEPSKIN, most of the so-called "freedom fighters" it recruited were little more than fascist collaborators from WWII. Like the Nazi organization ODESSA, its tentacles extended throughout Europe and Latin America, and even the United States.[828]

While the main focus of Il Gladio was to resist a Soviet invasion, its fascist roots and violent history indicate it served largely as a policy instrument to resist *internal* subversion—through terrorist means. This goal was revealed in a briefing minute of June 1, 1959, which stated Gladio's concern with "internal subversion" and its determination to play a role in the "politics of emergency." This emergency would come about during the 1960s and 1970s with the emergence of the anti-Capitalist movement, and the shift from the center to the left by the ruling Christian Democratic Party.

The covert objectives of Gladio were to spread panic and unrest by implementing "terrorist outrages," and directly attacking the left in an attempt to provoke them into armed response. The purpose of this strategy was to demonize the left and isolate them from popular support, while providing an excuse to curtail civil liberties. As a 1969 memo from Aginter Press, a fascist front group, explained:

> Our belief is that the first phase of political activity ought to be to create the conditions favouring the installation of chaos in all of the regime's structures. This should necessarily begin with the undermining of the state economy so as to arrive at confusion throughout the whole legal apparatus. This leads on to a situation of strong political tension, fear in the world of industry and hostility towards the government and the political parties…. In our view the first move we should make is to destroy the structure of the democratic state, under the cover of Communist and pro-Chinese activities. Moreover, we have people who have infiltrated these groups and obviously we will have to tailor our actions to the ethos of the milieu—propaganda and action of a sort which will seem to have emanated from our Communist

adversaries and pressure brought to bear on people in whom power is invested at every level. That will create a feeling of hostility towards those who threaten the people of each and every nation, and at the same time we must raise up a defender of the citizenry against the disintegration brought about by terrorism and subversion.[829]

General Gerardo Serravalle, head of "Office R" from 1971-1974 (the secret service office that controlled Gladio), revealed that at a Gladio meeting in 1972, at least half of the upper echelons "had the idea of attacking the Communists before an invasion. They were preparing for civil war."[830] As the 1969 dispatch added:

The introduction of provocateur elements into the circles of the revolutionary left is merely a reflection of the wish to push this unstable situation to breaking point and create a climate of chaos.[831]

One early Gladio-precipitated incident was the December, 1969 bombing of the Banca Nazionale del' Agricoltura in Milan's Piazza Fontana. The attack killed 16 people and wounded 88. Police immediately arrested and blamed anarchists. One anarchist leader, Giuseppe Pinelli, took the fall for the bombing, literally, when police tossed him out the window of the local precinct headquarters.

In addition to this, the Procurator General of the Republic, De Peppo, ordered the one unexploded bomb found in the wreckage to be detonated immediately. As in Oklahoma, the destruction of this evidence destroyed the single best chance at uncovering the true perpetrators of the deadly attack.

Nevertheless, police eventually discovered the real perpetrators—two fascists: Franco Freda and Giovanni Ventura. Ventura was in close contact with Colonel Guido Giannettinni of the SID (part of the secret services), a fervent supporter of MSI. The trial of Ventura and Freda was delayed for 12 years, when they were finally given life sentences, only to be cleared on appeal.[832]

Former Gladio agents also attributed the 1969 Piazza Fontana bombing and the 1974 [and subsequent 1980] Bologna bombings, which resulted in over 113 deaths and 185 injured, to P2. These attacks include the Mafia's involvement in the Red Brigade's kidnap and murder of Italian Prime Minister Aldo Moro in 1978. The P2 organization was also suspected of the 1976 assassination of Italian magistrate Vittoria Occorsio. Occorsio was investigating P2 links to neo-Nazi organizations at the time. His death conveniently terminated any further investigation.[833]

This "Strategy of Tension," organized around a brutal campaign of terror and murder, resulted in the deaths of hundreds of people during the decades of the

1970s and '80s. The wave of terror led to the severe restriction of civil rights, with a 1975 law restricting popular campaigning and radical political discussion. Many people were locked up under "anti-terrorist" legislation—sound familiar?—or expelled from the country.

When the Red Brigades resorted to armed struggle, it only strengthened Gladio/P2's position. Systematically infiltrated by the secret services, the Red Brigades were repeatedly blamed for the attacks, all the while unknowingly serving the agenda of the P2 establishment.

One unforgettable example of this wave of terror was the Bologna railway bombing in 1980 that killed 80 people and injured over 160. While reportedly masterminded by P2 members Stefano Delli Chiare and Licio Gelli, the attack was blamed on the Red Brigades to discredit the Italian Communist party.

This covertly-orchestrated strategy of tension would repeat itself in Belgium in the mid-'80s in a bizarre series of killings called the "Supermarket Massacres," in which hooded gunmen walked into crowded supermarkets and began firing away. The massacres, orchestrated by a group calling itself the "Killers of Brabant," were later discovered to be linked to Belgium's Gladio unit.

The Supermarket Massacres occurred during the period when the U.S. was pushing a plan to base the Euro-Missiles (nuclear-tipped Cruise missiles) in different European countries. The plan led to huge demonstrations in Europe, with certain countries threatening to break ranks with NATO. Belgium was one such country. The Belgian Parliament, which investigated the incidents, felt that they were another attempt to sow confusion and fear among the populace, thereby generating public outcries for a law-and-order government which would be amenable to the Euro-Missiles.[834]

Proof surfaced when a former *gendarme*, Madani Bouhouche, who worked for state security and was a member of the neo-Nazi paramilitary group Westland New Post (WNP), was arrested with one of the murder weapons. The next day, Bouhouche's friend and fellow right-wing militant Jean Bultot fled to Paraguay (a popular respite for Nazis). While in Paraguay, Bultot admitted to Belgian journalist René Haquin that the killings were a state security destabilization operation with government participation "at every level."

On January 25, 1988, another former *gendarme*, Robert Beyer, who police caught with a file of state security agents and addresses of garages filled with stolen arms, stated on Belgian television that state security had provided the weapons used by the killers.[835]

One of the attacks, the 1982 bombing of a Synagogue on the Rue de la Régence in Brussels, was linked to a security guard for the Wackenhut Corporation—Marcel Barbier. An ardent anti-Semite and member of the WNP, Barbier had been guarding the synagogue when it was attacked. In August, 1993, police discovered plans of the synagogue in Barbier's home, with detailed points of access. The Belgian director of Wackenhut at the time was Jean-Francis Calmette, a member of the WNP.*

The European "Strategy of Tension" is strikingly similar to the Oklahoma City bombing. The U.S. establishment, seeking to demonize the Patriot/Militia movement in the aftermath of the attack, followed a similar path that Gladio/P2 followed a decade earlier. Their links and associations to P2 make the parallel all the more ominous.

In 1994, a car-bomb blew up a Jewish community center in Buenos Aires, killing 87 people. Police blamed the attack on unnamed Arab militants. Yet in July, 1996, Argentine authorities arrested 17 police officers in connection with the attack.[836]

On October 3, 1980 the Paris synagogue on rue Copernic was bombed, killing four people and injuring 24 others. In media reports suspiciously similar to the Oklahoma City bombing, it was announced that "right-wing" extremists were involved. Yet French intelligence pointed fingers at the Mossad. A French Intelligence report stated:

> On April 6, 1979, the same Mossad terror unit now suspected of the Copernicus carnage blew up the heavily guarded plant of CNIM industries at La Seyne-sur-Mer, near Toulon, in southeast France, where a consortium of French firms was building a nuclear reactor for Iraq.... The Mossad salted the site of the CNIM bomb blast with "clues" followed up with anonymous phone calls to police—suggesting that the sabotage was the work of a conservative environmentalist group.

Two years later, six people were killed and 22 injured when terrorists attacked Goldenberger's Deli in Paris. Again, "right-wing extremists" were blamed. Implicated in the attack was one Jean-Marc Rouillan, leader of a mysterious left-wing group called Direct Action. While the real facts were covered up by the government, angry French intelligence officers—some who had quit in disgust—decided to leak the story to the Algerian National News Service. Rouillan, it turns out, had been operating in the Mediterranean under the cover name of "Sebas" and had been linked to the Mossad.[837]

Illustrating the concept of trained killers who work on a "need-to-know" basis, former Mossad Agent Ari Ben-Menashe describes how Abu Abbas launched an attack on the Greek Cruise ship *Achille Lauro* in 1985. According to Ben-Menashe, Rafi Eitan, the director of *Lakam*, a super-secret agency in the Israeli Ministry of Defense, gave orders to former Jordanian Army Colonel Mohammed Radi Abdullah, who passed on instructions to Abu'l Abbas, leader of the Tunis-

---

* It was also discovered by the Belgian press that Wackenhut guards had been luring immigrant children into basements and beating them.

based PLF, who in turn was receiving millions from Israeli intelligence officers posing as Sicilian dons. Abbas' orders were to "make it look bad," and to show what a deadly, cutthroat bunch the Palestinians were. The "terrorists" complied by killing Leon Klinghoffer, an elderly Jewish man in a wheelchair, then throwing his body overboard. As Ben-Menashe states, the entire operation was nothing more than an "Israeli 'black' propaganda operation." [838]

Abu Nidal, blamed for the Klinghoffer murder, began his long and bloody career in the PLO, only to become a bitter rival of Yasser Arafat. It was a situation that the Israeli Mossad, in a manner similar to their CIA cousins, would seek to exploit. As Middle East expert Patrick Seale writes:

> Israeli penetration of Palestinian organizations was common, but it was clearly not the whole story. Most intelligence sources I consulted agreed that it was standard practice to use penetration agents not simply to neutralize or destroy the enemy but to try to manipulate him so that he did one's bidding without always being aware of doing so....
>
> Whatever jobs [Abu Nidal] might have done for Arab sponsors, and they had been numerous and nasty, he had done many other jobs from which Israel alone appeared to benefit." [839]

Confirming Seale's theory are top Middle East terrorism experts, including intelligence officers in Arab countries, and even within Abu Nidal's own organization. One French terrorism expert stated: "If Abu Nidal himself is not an Israeli agent, then two or three of his senior people most certainly are. Nothing else can explain some of his operations."

A former senior Jordanian intelligence officer said: "Scratch around inside Abu Nidal's organization and you will find Mossad."

Abu Iyad, former chief of PLO Intelligence, added, "Every Palestinian who works in intelligence is convinced that Israel has a big hand in Abu Nidal's affairs." [840]

Nidal's organization has been responsible for some of the most brutal acts of terrorism in the world. According to the State Department, Abu Nidal has carried out more than 100 acts or terrorism that have resulted in the deaths of over 280 people. Some of these attacks include the 1986 grenade and machine-gun assaults on El Al counters at the Rome and Vienna airports, attacks on synagogues, and assassinations of Palestinian moderates.

Abu Nidal's most well-known attack was on a Greek cruise ship in 1988 that left nine people dead and 80 wounded. As Seale points out regarding the attack on the vessel City of Poros, "no conceivable Palestinian or Arab interest was served by such random savagery." In fact, Greece was the European country most sympathetic to the Palestinian cause, and its prime minister, Andreas

Papandreou, often defended Arabs against Israel's charges of terrorism. After the attack, Greece was furious with the Palestinians, who had damaged Greek tourist trade and hastened the fall of the Papandreou regime. The motive, as in the *Achille Lauro* attack, was apparently to cast the Palestinians as heartless murderers. Several sources that Seale consulted were convinced the attack was a typical Mossad operation.[841]

It's curious that Israel never punished Abu Nidal's organization. Israel has a long-standing policy of launching immediate and massive retaliation against any terrorist attack. While Israeli forces have bombed, shelled and raided Palestinian and Shi'ite positions in Lebanon, and have sent hit teams to kill Palestinian guerrilla leaders in other countries, they have never attacked Abu Nidal. Given Israel's unrelenting policy of retribution against terrorist attacks, this seems bizarre. As Seale concludes:

> Abu Nidal is a professional killer who has sold his deadly services certainly to the Arabs and perhaps to the Israelis as well. His genius has been to understand that states will commit any crime in the name of national interest. A criminal like Abu Nidal can flourish doing their dirty work.*

One of the most recent examples of the use of "false flags" (scapegoats) was the November 4, 1995 assassination of Israeli Prime Minister Yitzhak Rabin. In a classic case of political demonizing strikingly similar to the Oklahoma City bombing, the gunman, Yigal Amir, was held out to be a "right-wing fanatic." As William Jasper writes:

> The alleged gunman, Yigal Amir, was said to be a "fanatic Jewish fundamentalist." What's more, we were told repeatedly, he was part of a conspiracy of "religious extremists"—a conspiracy so nefarious and immense, mind you, that it had achieved meteorological significance, creating a "climate of hate" and an "atmosphere of violence." According to *Time* magazine, Rabin's opponents had created climatologically "the equivalent of the right-wing milieu that led to the Oklahoma City bombing." In fact, said *Time*, even if Amir had acted alone, "he had many ideational conspirators."[842]

But unlike the massive cover-up obsfucating the Oklahoma City bombing, it didn't take long for investigators to discover that Amir was actually a paid infor-

---

* Abu Nidal did business at the Bank of Credit and Commerce International (BCCI), a CIA proprietary which laundered drug proceeds for the North/Secord "Enterprise," the Mujahadeen, and catered to the likes of Manuel Noriega, Saddam Hussein, and Ferdinand Marcos.

mant for the Israeli security service, the Shabak. Before the "assassination," Amir was inexplicably allowed to wander through Rabin's protective security perimeter. Amir's accomplice—leader of the right-wing extremist group Eyal, Avishai Raviv, turned out to be a Shin Bet operative (General Security Service, the Israeli equivalent to the FBI).

The irony was that the Shin Bet was controlled by Rabin himself, who had personally selected its head, and served as its supreme chief. In a policy suspiciously similar to the Oklahoma City situation, instead of employing the Shin Bet to protect Israelis from Arab terrorists—its primary task—Rabin employed them to infiltrate and smear his right-wing opponents. Politicizing the Shin Bet for his own purposes, Rabin began orchestrating an Israeli version of COINTELPRO. This included setting up phony right-wing militant groups such as Raviv's Eyal.

As Rabin's popularity ratings dropped to a mere 32 percent, he escalated his dirty-tricks campaign, using agents provocateur to attack and smear the Prime Minister, who would then publicly criticize them for planning public disorder. Raviv's job was to distribute fervid anti-government literature which contributed to the "climate of hate" that allegedly motivated Amir. The *coup d'etat* in this covert campaign would come in the form of a phony assassination attempt on Rabin himself. The Shin Bet would foil the gunman at the last moment, and all the world would see first-hand evidence of the crazy right-wing conspirators.

But like the disastrous sting attempt in Oklahoma City, this covert operation went horribly wrong. Certain that the boastful and talkative Amir would inform his trusted mentor of the moment of his attack (as the FBI assumed with Emad Salem in the World Trade Center bombing), the Shin Bet dropped their guard, and Rabin paid the price for his mendacity.

At least that is what seems obvious. But it doesn't seem obvious why the Shin Bet, who had ample notice of the threat on the Prime Minister's life, failed to prevent the assassination. As authors Uri Dan and Dennis Eisenberg note: "No human shield was formed around Rabin, surveillance of the crowd was lax, Rabin wasn't wearing a bulletproof vest, and an [apparently] unknown 25-year-old was able to gain unobstructed access to Rabin." [843] The parallels to the Oklahoma City bombing are all too familiar.

Prime Minister Shimon Peres, like President Clinton in regards to Oklahoma, promoted the idea that Rabin was killed by a disgruntled "right-winger." And like his American counterpart, Peres promised to crack down on "political dissent." [844]

On his August 19, 1995 radio address, President Clinton complained that Congress still had not passed the Anti-Terrorism Bill. "It's hard to imagine what more must happen to convince Congress to pass that bill," warned Clinton.

Just two months later, on October 9, the nation witnessed its first attack on a passenger train, when Amtrak's "Sunset Limited" was derailed while enroute from Phoenix to San Diego. The derailment, caused by sabotage, resulted in over 100 injuries, including one death.

The terrorists left behind a cryptic note, calling themselves the "Sons of the Gestapo." The mainstream press quickly jumped on this latest "terrorist" attack, coming only six months after the Oklahoma City bombing. While no one, including law-enforcement officials, had ever heard of the "Sons of the Gestapo," the incident was immediately played up as the obvious work of a "right-wing" militia group. Exhaustive searches through numerous databases revealed no group called "Sons of the Gestapo."

In the aftermath of the Oklahoma City bombing, any such attack on American citizens would be excuse enough to push the Anti-Terrorism Bill through Congress. And the press and anti-militia activists such as the ADL and the SPLC were eager to jump on the militia connection. "Sons of the Gestapo," asserted the ADL, could only be the pseudonym for a right-wing hate-group.

Yet law enforcement officials had only an enigmatic message to guide them. The note left behind by the saboteurs railed against the ATF and FBI for their actions at Waco and Ruby Ridge, and stated, "This is not Nazi Germany."

Why anyone would attack a passenger train to exact revenge on government officials for killing innocent civilians (or blow up babies as revenge for killing children) is beyond credulity. Yet, as in the Oklahoma City case, this was the message that the saboteurs—and the government-controlled press—wanted us to believe. America was filled with hateful right-wing extremists who would do anything— kill women and children—to pursue their violent anti-government agenda.

While the FBI swarmed through Maricopa County, interrogating local residents and harassing the few isolated "desert rats" who inhabited the surrounding countryside, a real investigation was being conducted by a lone Maricopa County Sheriff. With the assistance of Craig Roberts, a retired Tulsa police officer with military intelligence experience who worked on the Oklahoma City investigation, the Sheriff was able to uncover some amazing evidence.

Other than rescue vehicles, they found no vehicle tracks entering or exiting the crash site. The site itself was extremely remote, being near the summit of the rugged Gila Bend Mountains, which surrounded the site to the east, north, and west. It was there, along a sharp S-curve, that the perpetrators had pulled 29 spikes from the tracks, causing the fatal crash.

Why had the perpetrators chosen such a remote location, Roberts wondered? Had they picked a more accessible spot, he reasoned, it would have surely lessened their chances of being caught, since all they would have had to do was drive to the nearest highway. In this case, the nearest road was Highway 8, 38 miles away, necessitating a difficult drive over rugged terrain at the same time law-enforcement officers would be on heightened alert.

Roberts and his sheriff partner also discovered that 90 minutes away by air, in Pinal County, was a mysterious airbase known as Marana. The locked-down facility was owned by Evergreen, Inc., a government contractor reportedly involved in drug smuggling during the Iran-Contra period. The base, located off of Highway 10 between Phoenix and Tucson, was the site of strange night-time training maneuvers involving black and unmarked military-type helicopters. Passersby had also witnessed black-clad troops dropping into the desert en mass, using steerable black "Paracommander" parachutes.

This began to raise interesting possibilities. Had the perpetrators been dropped into the remote site by air, then picked up by chopper? Both Roberts and his colleague at the Sheriff's Department were experienced military pilots. They observed that it would have been easy for a helicopter to fly low through the mountain passes, avoiding radar, and insert and extract a team. As Roberts noted, "A full moon, wind out of the south at eight knots, and a clear sky would be an ideal night for air operations." [845]

The possibility of a covert paramilitary commando team being responsible for the attack raised more than a few eyebrows at the Maricopa County Sheriff's Department, until they began investigating a lead provided by a sympathetic FBI agent that several hikers had seen a small group of parachuters drop into the desert that night. They also discovered the following information:

A VFR target squawking 1200 that left Tri-City airfield in Albuquerque on a southwest course, climbed to 10,500 feet, then, when it was exactly due east of the Amtrak site, turn due west and flew a course line that took it one mile south of the site. But just before arriving over the site, it dropped to 8,500 feet. After crossing the target zone, it turned on a southwesterly course towards California at 8,500 feet. Albuquerque contacted the Los Angeles Center which tracked the aircraft to a landing at Montgomery Field in San Diego.... It crossed the valley south of the bridge at 1940 hours (7:40 P.M.).

Since the winds that night were at eight knots out of the south, a drop one mile from the target site would compensate for wind drift. Moreover, such a flight is not required to file a flight plan listing its passengers. It wouldn't look suspicious.

When they checked with the refueler at Montgomery Field, records indicated that the "N" number checked to a Beechcraft, registered to Raytheon. Raytheon owns E-Systems. Like Evergreen, E-Systems, based in Greenville, Texas, is a covert government contractor, reportedly involved in drug-running. The NSA contractor allegedly developed sophisticated systems to create electronic "holes" which would allow planes to cross the border without tripping the NORAD

Early Warning Systems. E-Systems, reputed to have "wet-teams" (assassination teams), was directed by former NSA Director and CIA Deputy Director Bobby Ray Inman.

While it is possible a jump was made from the twin-engine Beechcraft, a plane commonly used for such purposes, it still left the problem of the team's extraction. With the radar track information, the Maricopa Sheriff then went to the Air Force at Yuma, who monitor the Aerostat radar drug balloons. The DEA balloons have "look-down" capability for detecting low-flying aircraft. The Master Sergeant at Yuma agreed to help out. A short time later he called back.

"Sorry," he said. "We can't help you out."

"What? Why?" asked Jack.

"The plug's been pulled."

"What does that mean?"

The sergeant sounded very uncomfortable when he replied. "We really wanted to check this out, but all I can say is the balloons were down that night."

"Why?" asked Jack.

"Maintenance."

"All of them?" asked Jack, incredulously.

"Yes, sir." The sergeant sounded very nervous.

"Why?"

"All I can tell you is that they were ordered down for maintenance. It came from above my pay grade."

Why would all the balloons be ordered down for maintenance? Obviously, a cover-up was in progress. Only the government—or shadow elements within the government—had the capability of pulling that off. No "lone nut" could order such last-minute changes, or orchestrate such a massive and well-executed cover-up. Moreover, no militia group could order all the radar balloons down on the night of the attack.

What about the "Sons of the Gestapo?" As Roberts wrote: "As an old Southeast Asia hand[a marine sniper during Vietnam], I remember that one of the terms used by Phoenix Program assassins working under MACV-SOG (Military Advisory Command, Studies and Observations Group) was a twisted barroom version of the last acronym. "Yeah," a drunk trooper would mention. "I'm SOG ... a son of the Gestapo." [846]

Apparently, the "Sons of the Gestapo" note left behind was a "false flag"—a distraction designed to serve a political purpose. In this case, the purpose, like the Oklahoma bombing that preceded it, was to connect the Amtrak attack with the Patriot/Militia movement. Considering the reaction of the mainstream press, it appears they largely succeeded.

In September, 1997, a confidential FBI memo intended for the U.S. Attorney's Office in Phoenix was accidentally faxed to the *Arizona Republic*, the Associated Press, and other news media. The memo states that the FBI's prime suspect is "a man with law enforcement and firefighting experience who recently moved out of Arizona." [847]

The same year as the Oklahoma City bombing, a grenade exploded near the Citibank building in Manila. Another hit the Shell Petroleum building. Four people were injured. The military claimed the blasts were political statements from the leftist Alex Boncayao Brigade (ABB). Yet five Philippine Congressmen accused the military of carrying out the attack to justify the passage of anti-terrorism legislation.

> The strongest accusation came from Makati Congressman Joker Arroyo, who said the bombings could not have been staged by the insurrectionary group, the Alex Boncayao Brigade or bank robbers.
>
> "I don't think it is the ABB nor a bank robbery group as what the police investigators said. Only the military has the capability of using grenade launchers," Arroyo commented. [848]

The U.S. certainly had its own share of manufactured incidents, ranging from the sinking of the Lusitania to the Gulf of Tonkin incident. Yet in the recent annals of CIA-connected provocations, probably no better example exists than the 1985 bombing of the La Belle Discotheque. The April 5th attack in Berlin killed two U.S. servicemen and a Turkish woman, and left 200 others injured, including 50 G.I.s.

Libya was quickly blamed by the U.S. for the attack. Propagandized by the American press as the preeminent sponsor of terrorism, Libya had early on incurred the wrath of the U.S. by nationalizing oil production and shutting down U.S. military bases. Libyan President Muammar al-Qaddafi began using the wealth formerly exported to multinational corporations to improve the living standards of his own people. Huge strides were made in education, housing, medicine and agriculture in a county in which the literacy rate had increased tenfold since 1969. Qaddafi made the mistake of supporting national liberation and social justice movements—assisting such groups as the Sandinistas, the Basques, the Kurds, and the Palestinians. [849] This, unfortunately, also included such terrorists as Abu Nidal.

In 1980, Ronald Reagan came to power on a pledge to restore U.S. military might and prestige around the world—also making a deal with the Iranians to hold the hostages until after his election. This little scandal was known as "October Surprise."

One of Reagan's first acts was to order the CIA to destabilize, overthrow, and assassinate Qaddafi. The attempts not only failed, but resulted in a covert battle of nerves and dead bodies scattered across Europe. After Abu Nidal's attacks on the Rome and Vienna airports in December of 1986, Reagan imposed sanctions and asset freezes on Libya.[850]

Angry over the recent terrorist bombings, frustrated by the CIA's failure to eliminate Qaddafi, and still smarting from Israeli rumors of a Libyan hit-squad sent to assassinate him, the President opted for a military-style assault. All the White House needed was an excuse, and this came in the form of an attack on the La Belle Discotheque. Nine days later, Reagan ordered U.S. planes to attack the Libyan cities of Tripoli and Benghazi, which resulted in over 37 dead, including Qaddafi's infant daughter. Unfortunately for Reagan, Qaddafi survived the attack.[851]

But had Libya actually bombed the disco? The White House was adamant. The National Security Agency (NSA) had intercepted coded exchanges between Tripoli and the East Berlin Libyan Peoples Bureau that purportedly said, "We have something that will make you happy." A second cable, hours after the bombing read, "An event occurred. You will be pleased with the result."[852] Under orders from the NSC, the raw coded intercepts were sent straight to the White House, bypassing normal NSA analysis channels, drawing criticism from at least one NSA officer. A West German intelligence official who later saw the cables said he was very critical and skeptical of U.S. intelligence blaming the Libyans.[853]

The U.S.'s evidence hinged on reports in Stasi (East German police) files passed on to West German officials. The Stasi reports, based on three separate informants, indicated the attack was planned by the Popular Front for the Liberation of Palestine-General Command (PFLP-GC), which had met in Tripoli a month earlier. A member of that group, living in Berlin, Youddeff Chraidi (code-named "Nuri"), had carried out the attack.

Yet the "Libya did it" theory quickly fell apart during the trial of Imad Mahmoud, another member of Nuri's group (Nuri could not be found), as the Stasi informants' contradictions and inconsistencies cast doubts on the case. One informant, Mahmoud Abu-Jabber (code named "Faysal") was, according to KGB files, a CIA informer. One KGB report indicated that "Faysal" had met with his CIA contact two days prior to the attack, and told them the price of the bombing would be $30,000, and not $80,000 as previously agreed.[854]

Stasi defector Colonel Frank Weigand concluded that Nuri was an agent for the West German police. While Nuri was wanted for the murder of a Libyan CIA informer, he managed to repeatedly cross Checkpoint Charlie (the East-West Berlin border crossing), one of the most tightly-guarded border crossings in the world. When German authorities finally located Nuri in Lebanon in 1994,

U.S. officials failed to provide the evidence needed to extradite him, despite repeated pleas by West German officials.[855]

Ultimately, West German officials concluded that the CIA was responsible for the bombing.

> Weigand recalled one phone conversation intercept where a high-ranking West German intelligence officer spoke with the Berlin official responsible for the La Belle investigation. According to Weigand, the investigator, when pressed for his conclusion, told the West German spook, "Well, when I add it all up, I think the Yanks did this thing themselves."[856]

A similar government-orchestrated outrage-incident was the 1985 plot to bomb the American embassy and presidential offices in Costa Rica as a pretext for a full-scale U.S. invasion of Nicaragua. The plan was an offshoot of Operation Pegasus, the CIA's program of political assassinations, similar to the Phoenix Program.

The conspiracy was akin to the many American-engineered provocations of the past. The U.S.—through the skullduggery of the CIA—would bomb their own embassy, blaming it on the Sandinistas.

Civilian Military Assistance (CMA) leader Tom Posey and his band of mercenaries—Steven Carr, Robert Thompson, Rene Corvo, and Costa Rican-American land-owners John Hull and Bruce Jones—arranged for a patriotic Cuban-American, Jesus Garcia, to take part in the plot. According to Leslie Cockburn in *Out of Control*, Posey showed Garcia blueprints of the embassy. "They came to me with a plan to hit the American embassy in Costa Rica," recalls Garcia. "They had an idea this would start a war between Nicaragua and the United States."

In addition to bombing the embassy, they were to "take out" the American ambassador, Lewis Tambs, a vocal opponent of Colombian/Contra cocaine trade, and collect the $1 million reward that the Ochoa clan placed on his head. The CIA-led group, which had been funding their covert operations through arms and drug trafficking, would solve the problem of an American official who had dared interfere with their profitable business, while at the same time, serving the lofty goals of U.S. foreign policy.*

According to CMA mercenary Jack Terrell, the plan was to place C-4 plastic explosive in a light-box outside the embassy and detonate it. When Tambs ran outside, he would be shot. A Nicaraguan would then be killed and fake documents placed on his person to incriminate the Sandinistas.[857]

While Garcia refused to participate in the plot, he recalled, "The embassy plan

---

* Posey denied the allegations in an interview with the author. Federal Public Defender John Mattes told me he felt the plot wasn't being seriously considered.

was blessed from the White House. There were too many big people involved in this. In order to hit a U.S. embassy even us Cubans who are here in Miami would normally out of courtesy notify the CIA." Considering the players involved, it appeared the CIA knew fully well of the plot, drawing members from Brigade 2506, Ted Shackley's old anti-Castro mercenary group.*

A second plot involved the bombing of Los Chiles, a small town along the border of Costa Rica. The plan was to use a plane painted to look like a Sandinista craft to drop bombs on unarmed townspeople. Terrell described it as a "continuous undercurrent of … terrorist activity to try to draw the United States Government into direct conflict with the Nicaraguans because they were to be made to look like they were committing overt acts against a neutral and unarmed country, Costa Rica." [858]

Garcia later learned that another hit was planned, this time on the Cuban and Soviet embassies in Nicaragua. The plan was proposed to Garcia by Major Alan Saum, a confederate of Posey's, and General Vernon Walters, U.S. ambassador to the UN and former Deputy Director of the CIA. As Garcia later testified in court, "Saum had come from the White House." Saum told Garcia the plan was "Vice-President Bush's baby."

While neither plot was carried out, the Octopus did manage to murder eight people, mostly reporters, at La Penca, Costa Rica on May 30, 1984. The target was Eden Pastora, a Contra leader who wasn't going along with the plan, and was about to announce his misgivings at a press conference. CIA Deputy Director Dewy Clarridge recently relayed a message to Pastora through Alfonso Robelo (who previously met with Bud McFarlane at the White House) that his story would be "stopped" if he did not acquiesce.**

The bombing was carried out by Amac Galil, who posed as a photographer, carrying a bomb inside a camera case. CIA "hit-man" Felipe Vidal told Terrell that Galil was a Mossad agent. He allegedly received his explosives training from John Harper, and his C-4 courtesy of John Hull. Vidal also told Terrell, "We put a bomb under him and it didn't work because of bad timing."

As Terrell later stated: "If anything happens to these people, whether they were carrying out directly or indirectly any plan of our government, it's easy to be at

---

* Statements of Jesus Garcia to Federal Public Defender John Mattes. The plot is briefly mentioned in Jack Terrell's book, *Disposable Patriot* (National Press Books, 1992), p. 321; Terrell also confirmed the plot in an interview on NBC nightly news; Peter Glibbery, a mercenary operating in Contra camps near Hull's ranch, recalled attempting to transport explosives from the ranch to Jones' ranch, and being told it was needed "for the embassy job."

** According to Jack Terrell, Contra leader Adolfo Calero complained that Pastora had described the FDN (Contras) as "homicidal, Somicista sons of bitches."

arm's length and have this great big beautiful deniability factor." [859]

The *Washington Post* and *New York Times* blamed the bombing on the Sandinistas.[860]*

Garcia knew better. "There are people here who are above the Constitution," recalled Garcia. "I didn't know the federal system was like this. I never dreamed." [861]

Garcia was eventually set up by Saum on a federal gun charge, he figured, either because he refused to go along with the first plot, or simply because of his knowledge of it.**

John Mattes, Garcia's defense lawyer, while investigating his client's story, uncovered North and Casey's twisted web of gun and drug smuggling. While Mattes was eager to present the evidence in court, he never got the chance. The Justice Department, which initially started a probe, suddenly switched tracks. They "weren't interested" in going any further with it, Mattes said. He and his investigator were later called into the U.S. Attorney's office in Miami and told, "Get out. You're out. Stay out. You've crossed the line. You've gone too far." [862]

Terrell would eventually express his misgivings to the press. As he writes in *Disposable Patriot:*

> During an operation, the gravity of what you are doing is obscured by the determination to do whatever it is you have been programmed to do. If you whack a bunch of people, blow up cars or hotels, or murder children, it doesn't make any difference. Something in your character sets you apart from normal people, and once it's trained and propagandized to where you start believing what people are telling you, you lose your sense of right and wrong, and in some cases, your sense of morality. In the end, when the veil of perceived sanction is lifted and you no longer have the protection of the invisible barrier that justifies all your actions, then those unspeakable acts committed in the name of freedom and democracy, come back in a more objective retrospect. Finally, you understand the impact. You say to yourself, did I do that? Usually, you did.[863]

Former CIA officer Victor Marchetti discovered this unfortunate truth long ago. As Marchetti writes in *The CIA and the Cult of Intelligence:*

> The "clandestine mentality" is a mind-set that thrives on secrecy and deception. It encourages professional amorality—the belief that righteous goals can be achieved

---

* On June 22, 1984, Pastora met with Dewy Clarridge and Vince Cannistraro, who offered to help Pastora find the killers. (Sure.) Harper's explosives training was allegedly courtesy of John Singlaub and Robert K. Brown (publisher of *Soldier of Fortune*).

** Garcia and his family were later threatened with a live 105mm mortar round placed on their front lawn.

through the use of unprincipled and normally unacceptable means. Thus, the cult's leaders must tenaciously guard their official actions from public view. To do otherwise would restrict their ability to act independently; it would permit the American people to pass judgment on not only the utility of their policies, but the ethics of those policies as well.

Finally, there is the uninhibited statement by former OSS Colonel George White, one of the founders of the CIA.

I toiled wholeheartedly in the vineyards because it was fun, fun, fun. Where else could a red-blooded American boy lie, kill, cheat, rape and pillage with the blessings of all the highest?[864]

Chapter Fourteen

LET THEM EAT O.J.

McVeigh is sentenced to death. We are all saved.

Anyone who believes this is brain-dead and deserves the consequences. Lies beget new lies. Crimes beget new crimes. Murder begets new murder. Nothing has changed in people's thinking in five thousand years. If there is a blood sacrifice for the gods, all is well. The rule of ritual blood sacrifice supplants due process and constitutional rights under the rubric of "victims rights.'" The regression to social barbarism is matched by individual regression to infantile magical thinking and the Lord of the Flies *is the ultimate destination.*

—Ace Hayes, *Portland Free Press,* July–October, 1997.

On June 2, 1997, Timothy McVeigh was convicted of all 11 counts in the federal indictment: eight counts of murdering federal agents, and one count each of possessing a weapon of mass destruction; of conspiring to use a weapon of mass destruction; and of destroying federal property with a weapon of mass destruction. The sentence was death by lethal injection.

In the trial, hailed as "brilliant," "textbook," and "close to perfect" by legal pundits, prosecutors presented largely circumstantial evidence combined with emotional tales from bombing victims, winning an immediate conviction.

In the last murder "trial of the century," prosecutors displayed an impressive array of hard, solid evidence against O.J. Simpson and were met with acquittal.*

Federal prosecutors introduced no witnesses who could have placed McVeigh in Oklahoma City on April 19 because McVeigh was always seen in the company of other suspects—a can of worms the government, and the defense, could not afford to open. Yet while prosecutors interspersed relatively circumstantial evidence with heart-wrenching, irrelevant tales from tearful bombing victims, the defense wasn't allowed to present any expert witnesses debunking the government's "single bomb" theory, or any evidence linking other suspects to the crime.

---

* "The prosecutors must pare down their case so that it does not bore the jury," legal analyst Kenneth Stern recommended in the American Jewish Committee's recent white paper on the trial. "In cases such as these, prosecutors too often present a 'Cadillac' when a 'Chevrolet' would do much better." (Associated Press, 04/18/97.)

Just one month before the start of McVeigh's trial, the *Dallas Morning News* "leaked" alleged documentation that McVeigh had "admitted" to defense team member Richard Reyna that he alone drove the Ryder truck to the Alfred P. Murrah Building. Like the startling revelations of McVeigh's racing fuel purchases a year-and-a-half after the fact, this well-timed ruse was engineered to resuscitate the government's rapidly deteriorating case.

While Stephen Jones' superbly crafted and highly revealing Writ of Mandamus barely registered a blip on the official radar screen of the mainstream press, McVeigh's dubious "confession" became the immediate focus of tabloid attention.

In documents recently discovered by the *National Globe*, it was learned that Lee Harvey Oswald made a "confession" to Dallas Police on November 22, in which he states that he, a) Acted alone, b) Had no ties with any mob or intelligence organizations, and c) Was mad at the President and wanted to make a political statement.

"That should put this controversy to rest for all time," said former president and Warren Commission member Gerald Ford.

Lee Harvey Oswald didn't live to tell the truth. Timothy McVeigh chose not to speak it. Yet, as Stephen Jones noted, if McVeigh dies, the truth may die with him.

While Judge Richard Matsch eliminated relevant evidence pertaining to the case, he permitted numerous victims' completely irrelevant testimony about their personal trauma, obviously designed to sway the emotions of an ignorant and confused jury.

Matsch also barred ATF informant Carol Howe's testimony from McVeigh's trial as "irrelevant," saying that it "would confuse or mislead the jury." Howe's attorney, Clark Brewster, said his client could have given "compelling testimony in support of a potential conspiracy theory."

The trial was also one of the most secretive ever held. According to the Associated Press, a "review of 1,000 documents filed between Feb. 20 and Sept. 5 found 75 percent of the records have been at least partially sealed." [865]

Given the mainstream media's largely acquiescent attitude towards the government's fairy tale, such revelations would have hardly mattered. One of the most important documents in the case, McVeigh's Writ of Mandamus, was dismissed as a concoction of conspiracy theories designed to cast doubt on McVeigh's guilt. Judge Matsch would have no part of "conspiracy theories." He ordered all the important exhibits of McVeigh's Writ sealed.

While Jones and the government both decided that McVeigh couldn't receive a fair trial in Oklahoma, critics argued that the case was moved to Denver to put it under the careful control of federal lapdog Richard Matsch. In one of the most controversial environmental cases ever, Matsch used a one-sided hearing to brush aside charges that radioactive contamination from the Rocky Flats nuclear weapons plant near Denver was adversely undermining the health of area residents.

Matsch, a Nixon appointee, also presided over the Silverado Savings and Loan case involving George Bush's son Neil—a case thick with dirty covert operatives and shady criminals linked to the CIA and the Iran-Contra operation. Bush walked.

McVeigh's defense lasted little more than a week—little different than the trial of the surviving Branch Davidians, who were not allowed to introduce evidence that they had acted in self-defense. The superficial two day Branch Davidian defense came about when Judge Smith did not allow the defense to "put the government on trial." Several jurors expressed the opinions that the government should have been on trial—not the surviving Branch Davidians.

While he wasn't allowed to introduce evidence of a broader conspiracy, Jones did spend considerable time focusing on the disembodied leg clothed in military garb found amid the rubble of the Federal Building.

Jones introduced expert testimony that such a leg could be left intact from a blast that disintegrated the remaining body. It was this leg, which wasn't matched to any other victim, Jones suggested, that belonged to the real bomber.

Judge Matsch wasn't about to allow Jones reveal his knowledge of a wider plot, as was portrayed in his Writ:

> The theory of the prosecution in this case, not the Grand Jury's theory, is that the two named Defendants constructed a simple device capable of toppling a nine-story building at a public fishing lake and that one of them transported this device over two hundred miles without blowing himself up. That is the heart of the prosecution's case. Any evidence concerning the participation of others, the complexity of the device, or foreign involvement takes away the heart of the government's case and there is therefore an institutional interest on the part of the government in keeping such evidence shielded from the defense and the public.

Some critics argued that Jones' decision to wait until one week before the start of his client's trial to file the important and revealing document ensured that the higher court would reject the motion.

Prominent "Patriot" attorney Nancy Lord insisted that Jones "should have violated the judge's order, presented evidence of a larger conspiracy to the jury, and gone to jail for contempt. If I would have been the defense attorney, some things are important enough to go to jail for," said Lord. "I am shocked at Stephen Jones' conduct in this case."

As Jones solemnly stated in November, 1995, "Some day, when you know what I know and what I have learned, and that day will come, you will never again think of the United States of America in the same way."

The American public never learned what Stephen Jones knows. Yet on the day of his sentencing, Timothy McVeigh finally spoke out, though enigmatically: "Our government is the potent and omnipresent teacher for good or for ill. It teaches the whole people by its example. That's all I have to say." *

Naturally, the government and many of the bombing victims took this as a sign of McVeigh's confession. The rest of the quote may shed some light on meaning:

"Crime is contagious. If the government becomes a lawbreaker, it breeds contempt for the law; it invites every man to become a law unto himself; it invites anarchy. To declare that in the administration of the criminal law the end justifies the means— to declare that the government may commit crimes in order to secure the conviction of a private criminal—would bring terrible retribution."

McVeigh also accused Jones of lying and screwing up. "The truth is this guy only succeeded in getting [me] the death sentence," said McVeigh, "and now he doesn't want to let go."

Asked what lies Jones told him, McVeigh was not specific: "It's for Congress, the bar, and the judiciary to investigate and discover. You would not believe some of the things that have occurred in this case. The man has repeatedly lied to me in the past." [866]

Obviously, Timothy McVeigh is holding his cards close to his vest. As Jones stated during his closing argument: "Two people share a terrible secret. One will not talk, the other is bound by law and can not talk."

The public still hasn't learned what that terrible secret is.

Other rumors abound that Jones—who stands to make millions in legal fees from the government and from book sales—purposely threw the case.

"He is the most dishonest person I've ever met, including all the criminals I've defended," says his onetime law partner Alec McNaughton, who nevertheless describes Jones as "brilliant." [867]

As a young attorney in 1964, Jones began his career working for a lawyer named Richard Milhous Nixon. His clients have run the gamut from '60s radicals such as Abbie Hoffman to establishment politicians such as Governor Frank Keating.

Jones and Terry Nichols' attorney Michael Tigar share a common bond through the late Edward Bennett Williams, senior partner of Williams &

---

* As McVeigh later explained to his hometown newspaper: "In the instant context, you could take [the statement] to reflect on the death penalty and the charges leveled against me. I was accused and convicted of killing—they say that's wrong, and now they're going to kill me."

Connolly (later Williams, Wadden & Stein). Williams' client roster included Senator Joseph McCarthy, Mafia don Frank Costello, Teamster Jimmy Hoffa, industrialist Armand Hammer, and Texas Governor John Connally.

A man on intimate terms with the CIA, Williams was offered the post of CIA director by two presidents, a job which he declined, probably because he was already a de facto CIA official.*

While Jones openly admires Williams, Tigar was actually employed by him in the late 60s and mid 70s. Williams often referred to Tigar as his "most brilliant protégé."

A University of Texas Law School professor, Tigar himself claims an interesting bevy of clients, ranging from "Chicago Seven" member Angela Davis, who was tried for conspiracy to incite riots at the 1968 Democratic Convention, to John Demjanjuk, accused of being the notorious Nazi concentration camp guard "Ivan the Terrible."

Jones and Tigar have collaborated before, defending a controversial Oklahoma City psychotherapist.[868]

"Tigar is a passionate defender of people who have been oppressed by the government," said 24-year Oklahoma City attorney Jim Bellingham, who thinks the possibility of Jones and Tigar running "damage control" for the government is "hogwash."

"I can't imagine the man selling out, and nobody's going to tell him how to run his defense," said Bellingham.[869]

But Former Nebraska State Senator John DeCamp, who investigated a child abuse ring run by high government officials, doesn't put much faith in Stephen Jones. DeCamp believes Jones actually made a deal with the Feds. DeCamp represented a bombing victim in an early action against the Federal Government and was just about to file a motion to preserve the building as evidence. As he wrote in his book, *The Franklin Cover-Up:*

Only hours before I was to file the legal papers for a civil action to keep the building standing, I was contacted by Timothy McVeigh's attorneys, who presented me with two major requests.

First, they asked that I allow them to file the motions to keep the building standing so that the investigation could be conducted. They had cogent legal arguments for this request: because McVeigh was/is under federal criminal charges, he had the definite legal right to keep the building standing under the federal rules of evidence which grant criminal defendants the right to preserve evidence that would significantly impact their defense. It was clear that if McVeigh's attorneys believed, or even

---

* Senior partner Brendon Sullivan represented Oliver North during the Iran-Contra hearings.

suspected government cover-up, they would definitely want the building examined.

Their second request was that I release from retainer the bomb investigation team I had assembled—John A. Kennedy and Associates—which, they claimed, they wanted to hire.

I granted these requests to McVeigh's attorneys.

A few hours later, I watched in horror as CNN and all the national news channels reported that McVeigh's attorneys had no intent to file any motions to keep the Federal Building standing. They had "just reached agreement with the government," the reporters explained, to permit the building to be destroyed almost immediately.

Angry beyond belief, I called McVeigh's attorney and asked what they were doing. Since this all occurred on a weekend, I could take no legal action to stop the building's destruction. McVeigh's attorney told me, "Oh yes, we are going to allow the building to be destroyed." "Why?" I demanded. "Because we could not afford to pay the retainer fee that the Kennedy and Associates firm wanted," he answered.

Shocked by this feeble explanation, I asked, "Well, just how much do they want?" McVeigh's attorney floored me: "$30,000," he said, "and we have no resources to pay it, because we are a court-appointed attorney and there are no funds for this purpose."

"For God's sake!" I screamed at him. "I will raise the money! I will pay the fee! There's too much at stake for America. "How," I demanded, "can McVeigh go along with wanting that building destroyed, when that building is the one thing that can tell America the story of what really happened? I will get you the money, somehow, but don't refuse to keep the building up for that reason!"

My protests were futile. Within hours of my call, by mutual agreement between McVeigh's attorneys and the government prosecutors, the building was destroyed, and any evidence was destroyed with it.[870]

Jones disputed this in a letter to the author:

If anyone took the trouble to check the public filings in the case of *United States v. McVeigh* they will find that one of the very first Motions that I filed was to stop the implosion of the Murrah Building until the Defense could go in and take films and moving video pictures. The Court sustained my Motion and we were able, together with an architect and an explosives expert, to tour the building. Any claim that we made a "deal" with the Federal authorities to permit the demolition of the Murrah Building before the Defense could inspect if is absurd and contradicted by the public record.[871]

A source within the defense team told me that Jones' team actually did go into the building to conduct forensic analysis. The group consisted of a videographer, a still photographer, and one bomb expert, who were accompanied by several FBI and ATF agents. The source said that the bomb expert walked around with only a jeweler's loupe, no forensic kit, and did not take any samples for analysis. The agents restricted their passage through the building, and by the time they arrived, the bomb crater had already been filled.

Jones also made no mention of the amazing letter McVeigh sent to his sister, describing his recruitment into a secret government team involved in illegal activities, which she had read before the Federal Grand Jury.

What he did do was show a film about Waco, further reinforcing the allegations that his client murdered innocent children in Oklahoma to avenge the murder of 25 innocent children at Waco.

Did Jones have a *quid pro quo* with the government not to reveal any evidence that his client was a government agent? Did he purposely throw the case? His highly incriminating Writ of Mandamus and impressive opening statement tend to belie that theory. As Jones said in his opening statement:

"I know who bombed the Alfred P. Murrah building. It was NOT Tim McVeigh.

"Even more important, the government knows who bombed the Alfred P. Murrah building. The government knows it was NOT Tim McVeigh.

"The government also knows that its case against Tim McVeigh is corrupt. At its core, it's rotten. I will show you in what way, and why.

"The most important difference between us, is that the government won't tell you who bombed the Alfred P. Murrah building.

"I will."

Jones never got the chance. The exclusion of ATF informant Carol Howe sounded the death knell for other defense witnesses such as bomb expert General Benton Partin, seismologist Dr. Ray Brown, and the many witnesses who saw additional suspects. While the government solicited the testimony of British explosives expert Linda Jones, McVeigh's attorney curiously did not call Partin, who could have blown the lid off the government's single bomb theory.

"The judge would not permit … in his ruling he would not permit anything except one man, one bomb," said Partin. "They structured the whole case—the whole prosecution—completely eliminating the building and anything to do with it because they couldn't afford to get into that."

Referring to Jones, Partin added, "I didn't be expect to be called by these guys. I had absolutely no confidence in them. I didn't expect it—not from Jones." [872]

In response, Jones said, "I did not put Partin on the stand because my experts do not credit his theory." [873]

Yet the question still remains: why didn't Jones take the issue of Judge Matsch's illegal decisions before the Appellate or Supreme Courts? Jones replied by stating that the appellate court "refused to accept jurisdiction of the case and said [it] would review the issues on appeal, if there was a conviction." [874]

Some have speculated that the millions Jones stands to make in legal fees from the government played a part in his apparently poor defense.

Those who expected a similarly poor defense from Michael Tigar were shocked to find him introducing evidence of other suspects, and putting ATF informant Carol Howe on the witness stand.*

No doubt Nichols' conviction of conspiracy and involuntary manslaughter stemmed from the critical opinions jurors had of the prosecution's "limited hang-out."

"I do not believe that the government gave us the whole case," said Linda Morgan, one of the jurors who decided Nichols only had a minor role in the bomb plot. McVeigh, she said, "was seen with too many other people. Who were these other people?"

"I think that the government perhaps really dropped the ball," said jury fore-woman Niki Deutchman, who critized the FBI for halting its investigation after arresting Nichols and McVeigh.

"I think there are other people out there," she said, recalling defense witnesses who saw others with McVeigh before the bombing. "I think this was a horrible thing to have done … and I doubt two people were able to bring it off."

Deutchman also criticized the FBI's sloppy crime lab procedures, and claimed agents were "arrogant" for failing to tape record Nichols' initial nine-hour inter-rogation. "It seems arrogant to me on the part of the FBI to say, you know, 'We have good recall and you can take what we have said.'"

Nor could jurors agree on the scope of Nichols' involvement. While most believed he played a major role, others questioned if he did much at all or had backed out completely or been coerced.

"Some people felt he wasn't involved at all in building the bomb," Deutchman said before echoing an oft-repeated mantra from the defense: "I think he was building a life."

Juror Holly Hanlin, too, felt the government failed to fully prove its case. "We couldn't find enough evidence to convince at least all of us that he intended, that he was involved from the very beginning, that he built the bomb. We felt that evidence was shaky at best."

Others, like juror Keith Brookshier, said, "[I] know that Terry Nichols was into it up to his eyeballs, and that's the only thing I had to decide. We're not trying

---

* "[Howe] said she saw McVeigh walking with Elohim City security chief Andreas Strassmeir, who had advocated violence against the government. One juror didn't at first even recall Howe's testimony. Another, [juror Chris] Seib, said, "I don't know. We felt there was something there. You know, we kind of skimmed through that pretty quick."

John Doe 2, or or 3 or 4 or whatever." U.S. Attorney Beth Wilkinson naturally added her voice to the ensemble, stating that "sightings of John Doe 2 were about as common and about as credible as sightings of Elvis."

By the time this book is published, a few select facts may be brought to light. They will first be revealed by a few victims' families, angrily demanding justice; by the few public officials courageous enough to risk their careers. And finally, they will be echoed in the courts by the inevitable specter of civil litigation.

Then the powers that be will hasten to construct a new layer of damage control, and the cover-up will begin anew. Like the crime scene quickly demolished, and the John Does that never existed, these few "startling revelations" will no doubt be used as a dam to hold back the onrushing tide of truth.

Will Timothy McVeigh ever choose to reveal that truth—what he knows of it—or will it go with him to the grave, or die with him in a prison "suicide?"

As Fletcher Prouty states: "The whole story of the power of the cover-up comes down to a few points. There has never been a Grand Jury and trial in Texas [referring to Lee Harvey Oswald]. Without a trial there can be nothing. Without a trial it does no good for researchers to dig up data. It has no place to go and what the researchers reveal just helps make the cover-up tighter, or they eliminate that evidence and the researcher."

The government illegally prevented a state trial in Dallas in 1963, as they tried to do in Oklahoma City in 1995. It came down to one courageous District Attorney in New Orleans to open up a can of worms.

As this book went to press, a County Grand Jury, convened at the behest of two courageous men in Oklahoma, began hearing evidence.

Will these jurors will more objective and effective than the highly manipulated Federal Grand Jury? One County Grand Juror, Ben Baker, was quoted in *The Daily Oklahoman* as saying: "Everyone I've talked to believes this is a waste of time and taxpayers' money. I believe the same thing."

Another County Grand Juror, Kenneth Rickenbrode, is a lieutenant with OCPD Internal Affairs, which should serve rather nicely to hamstring any serious inquiry into the murder of OCPD Officer Terrance Yeakey.

Finally, there is the County Grand Jury forewoman, Gwendolyn Sloan, the manager of the Oklahoma Employment Security Commission—and a Frank Keating appointee.

Bob Macy's Chief Assistant DA, Pat Morgan and Assistant DA Suzanne Lister-Gump are on hand to "advise" the jurors and "pre-screen" the evidence.

Charming.

Representative Key had little choice but to work with Macy's people, the alternative being a special prosecutor being appointed by political hacks Attorney General Drew Edmondson or Governor Frank Keating. Although Key could have objected to both Edmondson and Keating based on their obvious prejudice, he felt the Supreme Court would have sat on the issue, perhaps not appointing a special prosecutor for over a year. After waiting two years, he was anxious to get the process started. The choice was "deciding between bad, worse, and worse," said Key, who now believes that Macy is "on our side." [875]*

Bob Macy—a man who "investigated" the case by thumbing through an old copy of *The Turner Diaries*—now insists he intends to uncover the truth. "I'm prepared to do what ever it takes to get to the truth!" Macy declared. "My sole intent is in learning the truth," Macy stated to the author five months before kowtowing to Justice Department wishes in opposing the Grand Jury.

Macy's most telling statement came when he was asked if he intended to pursue an investigation independent of the Feds. "I don't want to be a party to anything that will interfere with the Feds' prosecution," said Macy. "I don't want to open up a new can of worms." [876]

This is not surprising, coming from a man who refused to prosecute eight felony indictments against a sitting governor who was a campaign manager for President Clinton.

Consequently, Key petitioned the Oklahoma Supreme Court to order Macy to do his job. In reply, Macy stated, "I *am* going to do my job. This action by him won't have any effect one way or another. I am still going to do it the way it is supposed to be done."

Former Congressman George Hansen (R-ID) thinks Macy, whom he says was "straddling the fence," has now turned around. "Look, "he's obligated to do the will of the establishment," said Hansen. "He went along … with defending the establishment."

An old friend of Macy's from Washington, D.C., Hansen learned the hard way what it's like to suffer at the hands of a corrupt and vindictive Justice Department. Not one to easily trust the Federal Government, Hansen genuinely believes his old friend from the Department of Agriculture is now honestly going to challenge that government. "Give the guy a chance to turn around," said Hansen. "He honestly wants that Grand Jury to come out with as much of the truth as possible." [877]

If true, perhaps Macy should imbue a sence of open-mindedness in his so-called investigators. In an affidavit filed by Richard Sinnett, the eyewitness claims that one of Macy's investigators made sarcastic comments to him about the Grand Jury investigation shortly before he was subpoenaed.

> Sinnett could not identify the person. However, he said in the signed affidavit, the man who called him said "he did not know why he was having to do this, that

---

* Key's attorney Mark Sanford said the Supreme Court was willing to back Key by forcing Macy to do his job properly.

Charles Key was pushing this and that nothing would come of it and that was a waste of time."

Naturally, Macy's office denied the charge.

Perhaps the Supreme Court should order Judge Burkett, presiding over the County Grand Jury, to do *his* job. Burkett attempted to disallow hearsay evidence to be presented to the Grand Jury—a clear violation of Oklahoma Grand Jury procedures.*

"Do not accept hearsay," Burkett said in his opening instructions to the Grand Jurors. "Hear only those witnesses who would present facts, which if true, would substantiate an indictable offense and not needlessly delay the courts in their other functions by listening to radical persons or facts about which you could do nothing if it were true." **

Judge Burkett's subtle signal is suspiciously reminiscent of the 1976 House Select Committee on Assassinations investigation of the Kennedy assassination, which admitted that the evidence led to a probable conspiracy. No indicments were ever handed down.

KFOR's Jayna Davis, who testified before the Grand Jury, didn't miss this subtle signal. She told *The Daily Oklahoman* she expects prosecutors "to express a legitimate interest" in pursuing indictments against the suspects her witnesses identified.[878]

Even if Macy and Burkett are eventually forced to do their jobs, the FBI can undoubtedly be counted on to intimidate key witnesses, as they did in the federal trial. Kay H., who saw Hussain al-Hussaini speed away in the brown pick-up, is reportedly afraid to testify before the Grand Jury, after publicly stating—twice—that Hussaini was the man she saw. Gary Lewis, the *Journal Record* pressman who was almost run over by McVeigh and John Doe 2, has now recanted his story. After his testimony before the County Grand Jury, Professor Ray Brown of

---

* According to Oklahoma Statutes, Title 22, Section 331 (General powers and duties of Grand Jury), Notes of Decisions: "Grand jury functions as an inquisitorial body; once it is convoked by the court, its duty is to investigate law violations [Tweedy v. Oklahoma Bar Ass'n, Okl. 624 P.2d 1049 (1981)]. Investigation by Grand Jury or a preliminatry examination by magistrate is not a trial, and the rules of evidence are not to be applied as rigidly as in trial of case before court." [Magill v. Miller, Okl. Cr., 455 P.2d 715 (1969).]

** In a letter hand-delivered to the Grand Jury, Representative Key asked to testify a second time to present evidence that the DA's office refused to allow a video of "contemporaneous news accounts" because it was considered to be hearsay. As Mike Johnston, Key's attorney, stated in the letter, "The objection or contention that a Grand Jury cannot use hearsay evidence is not well founded." Morgan responded by thereafter refusing to communicate with Key except through his attorney. So much for cooperation.

the University of Oklahoma had a change of heart: "There's no evidence in the [seismographic] bomb signals for any additional charges," Brown told reporters.[879]

The federal agents who might be subpoenaed will no doubt attempt to quash them on the grounds of "national security."

It is rumored that no County Grand Jury indictments will ever be returned.

Said Stephen Jones, "A living nightmare for the Department of Justice is an Oklahoma state criminal trial, not only a nightmare for them, but a nightmare for the intelligence community, for the ATF. There isn't going to be any Oklahoma trial."

"If I thought the State of Oklahoma was really interested in the truth as opposed to just some political side show," added Jones, "I would insist that Mr. McVeigh have a state trial and demand that he be released to the state authorities. But this is all politics."[880]

"What [Judge Hartzler] is trying to do is not have people learn," said McVeigh in an interview from his prison cell. "He wants to have them put their heads in the sand."

What McVeigh states may be an unfortunate axiom. Many Americans aren't interested in knowing the truth. They don't want to open up a new can of worms. Many people, even those in Oklahoma, don't want to believe that the government, or elements within the government, could or would, do, or cover-up, such an evil act.

However, "very few will cover-up the violent deaths of their sons and daughters, or the children of a close family friend, no matter what the price," argued a poster to an Internet newsgroup called OKBOMB.[881]

Surprisingly, many of these people—including a significant number of bombing victims—are naive, intellectually lazy, and unreasonably indignant. Like this poster, these people haven't done their homework regarding the corruption in this country, so they don't have any basis for understanding or challenging it. Driven solely by instinct and emotion, and speaking from a place of ignorance, they react angrily to those attempting to expose the truth, whatever that truth might be.

As another OKBOMB poster observed, "They want their lives to go on as easily as possible, without being harassed by the government, but without admitting to themselves that they sold their souls for a continued paycheck and a good credit rating."[882]

Two hundred years ago, Samuel Adams said: "If ye love wealth better than liberty, the tranquility of servitude better than the animating contest of freedom, go home from us in peace. We ask not your counsels or arms. Crouch down and lick the hands which feed you."

Fortunately, there are enough people who want to know the truth. Approximately 500 bombing victims and their relatives are beginning to seek answers. They have brought two civil suits against the Federal Government. The suits seek to prove beyond a shadow of a doubt that the government had advance knowledge of the plot but failed to stop it, in what amounted, at least on one level, to a sting operation gone wrong.[882]

As Stephen Jones said in his opening statement, "Outrageously, the government shares part of the blame. Its hands have blood on them as surely as the hands of the man who lit the fuse. Horrifically, the government knew what was coming, but failed to stop it. Then it covered up its role for fear of being held accountable for its inexcusable conduct."

The acquittal of ATF informant Carol Howe and the resulting publicity surrounding Elohim City will no doubt affect the balance of evidence. Yet given the fact that no Middle Eastern witnesses have been called (at least as of this writing), the revelations of Howe will only serve to highlight the role that neo-Nazi elements played in the bombing—to the exclusion of the Arab faction.

This is nothing more than a "limited hang-out." Given the government/mass-media propaganda effort aimed at linking McVeigh and Nichols to the Militia movement, and the Militia movement to the neo-Nazi community, the end result differs little from the government's original premise—that the militias, being essentially neo-Nazis, are in effect, responsible for the bombing.

Should Howe's testimony reveal the government's prior knowledge, perhaps the ATF, FBI, and the Justice Department will eventually be forced to admit a minor role in their "tragic blunder," and those starved for a little truth will be, at last, temporarily satisfied.

Then the hearings will begin. Like the Warren Commission, the Watergate hearings, or the Iran-Contra hearings, it will eventually be revealed that a few bad apples, acting alone and outside the realm of official responsibility, were "negligent." Inevitable wrists will be slapped.

Then, as the hearings draw to a close, the deeper and more pressing questions will be swept under the rug, as the shock and tragedy of the moment gradually fades in the wake of next year's TV sitcoms. Those who orchestrated the conspiracy will disappear into the invisable cracks of time, protected by the same malignant forces that nurtured them into being.

A Congressman who allegedly displayed an interest in alternative bombing evidence was Senator Arlen Specter. As a young assistant prosecutor on the Warren Commission, Specter propounded the "magic bullet" theory. Now, on the same day as the bombing, Specter's foregone conclusions could be heard on McNeil-Lehrer, propounding the "magic bomb" theory.

Soon after, Specter, who is head of the Senate Intelligence Committee, asked KFOR for all the evidence they'd collected on John Doe 2. No doubt the good Senator's collecting this information for the next Warren Commission report.

One American's foregone conclusion of the Oklahoma City bombing may be more revealing however. It is from a letter sent to the hospitalized survivors by a third grade boy. It reads:

> Hello, I hope you feel better from the explosion in Oklahoma. I wish it never happened. I felt sad when it happened. I felt bad for the people who died and the people who got hurt. That's only the beginning of what's going to happen to America. Hope you feel better.

ENDNOTES

1. Detective Jay Einhorn, interview with author.
2. Nancy Gibbs, "The Blood of Innocents," *Time*, 5/1/95.
3. *Ibid.*
4. According to Lawence Myers of *Media Bypass*, McVeigh exited his vehicle and met officer Hanger between the two cars. Hanger asked McVeigh for his license. He then informed the cop that he was moving from Arkansas, at which point Hanger walked back to his vehicle and ran McVeigh's license. Hanger's video camera was on, as well as his microphone. As he walked back to McVeigh, he noticed a bulge under his jacket, and as he handed McVeigh his license, he quietly flipped the snap on his holster. He asked McVeigh if he was carrying a gun, and McVeigh informed him he was, at which point Hanger drew his weapon, shoved McVeigh against the car and spread his legs, McVeigh told Hanger that he had a concealed carry permit and showed him his old Burns Security badge. McVeigh sat in the passenger side of the patrol car and talked about the bombing as it flashed over the radio. When he arrived at the jailhouse, he asked, "When's chow?"
5. Sam Cohen's letter to Representative Key, 6/29/95.
6. William Jasper, "Explosive Evidence of a Cover-Up," *The New American*, 8/7/95.
7. *Ibid.*
8. Christine Gorman, "Bomb Lurking in the Garden Shed," *Time*, 5/1/95.
9. Rick Sherrow, interview with author.
10. Linda Jones, trial transcript, *U.S. vs. McVeigh.*
11. *Sacramento Bee*, 4/30/95.
12. Brian Ford, "McVeigh Placed at Kansas Store," *Tulsa World*, 9/12/97.
13. *Military Explosives, TM 9-1910/TO 11A-1-34,* Dept. of the Army and the Air Force, 4/14/55, p. 121.
14. Michele Marie Moore, *Oklahoma City: Day One* (Harvest Trust, 1996), p. 122.
15. KFOR-TV, 4/19/95.
16. *USA Today*, 4/28/95.
17. *New York Times*, 10/19/95.
18. Memorandum to all U.S. Attorneys from Acting Assistant Attorney General John C. Keeney, 1/4/96.
19. "Outside Experts to Review FBI Crime Lab," *Wall Street Journal*, 9/19/95.
20. The Gunderson Report on the Bombing of the Alfred P. Murrah Building, Oklahoma City, April 19, 1995, 11/1/96.
21. *Ibid.*
22. Richard Sherrow, "Bombast, Bomb Blasts & Baloney," *Soldier of Fortune*, 6/95.
23. Rabauch's letter to Partin, dated 7/18/95.
24. CNN World News, 6/26/96.
25. Jim Loftis, interview with author.
26. Lou Kilzer and Kevin Flynn, "Were Feds Warned Before OKC Bomb Built?" *Rocky Mountain News*, 2/6/97. The fuel dealer reported the purchasing attempt to the ATF, but the agency did not follow up.
27. Gronning's letter to Key, dated 6/27/95.

28. James L. Pate, "Bloody April: Waco Anniversary Triggers Oklahoma City Atrocity," *Soldier of Fortune*, August, 1995.

29. Larens Imanyuel, interview with author.

30. *Engineering News*, May 1, 1995, page 10-11.

31. The Gunderson Report on the Bombing of the Alfred P. Murrah Building, Oklahoma City, April 19, 1995, 11/1/96.

32. Larens Imanyuel, "The Bombing of the Oklahoma City Federal Building: Was a Cruise Missile Warhead Design Used?" *Veritas*, 12/18/95.

33. Timothy McVeigh's Petition for Writ of Mandamus, 3/25/97, p. 35.

34. Ramona McDonald, interview with author.

35. "The Worst Terrorist Attack on U.S. Soil: April 19, 1995," CNN, 12/20/95.

36. Sam Cohen, interview with author.

37. Gene Wheaton, "The Covert Culture," *Portland Free Press,* May/June 1996.

38. David Noble, "Professors of Terror," *Third World Resurgence* , February-March, 1992, p. 34, quoted in Ramsey Clark, *The Fire This Time* (Thunder's Mouth Press, 1992), p. 44.

39. Adel Darwick and Gregory Alexander, *Unholy Babylon* (St. Martin's Press, 1991), p. 104.

40. Harry M., confidential letter to author.

41. "Iraq Also Worked on Hydrogen Bomb," Associated Press, quoted in *The Nashville Tennessean*, 10/9/91, as quoted in Charles T. Harrison, "Hell in a Hand Basket: The Threat of Portable Nuclear Weapons," *Military Review*, May, 1993.

42. E-Mail message to Tony Sgarlatti; interview with author.

43. Harrison, *Op Cit.*

44. Edward Zehr, "Turning Point: Resolving The Enigma of Oklahoma City," *Washington Weekly, 11/18/96.*

45. Sam Cohen, *Journal of Civil Defense*, Fall, 1995, quoted by F.R. Suplantier in *Behind the Headlines.*

46. "A classified Pentagon study determines Oklahoma bombing was caused by more than one bomb," *Strategic Investment Newsletter,* 3/20/96.

47. William Jasper, "Multiple Blasts: More Evidence," *The New American.*

48. "The Oklahoma City Bombing: Improved building performance through multi-hazard mitigation," FEMA, quoted in *Relevance* magazine, April, 1997.

49. General Benton K. Partin, interview with author.

50. *New American,* date unknown.

51. Sam Cohen, interview with author.

52. Jeff Bruccelari, Oklahoma Radio Network, interview with Dr. Ray Brown, 2/18/97.

53. Jerry Longspaugh, *Cover-Up in Oklahoma City* video, 1996.

54. Ramona McDonald, interview with author.

55. William Jasper, "Seismic Support," *The New American,* 8/7/95, 1995.

56. Nolan Clay, "Scientists Debate Meaning of Bombing Seismograms," *The Daily Oklahoman,* 11/21/95.

57. Moore, *Op Cit.,* p. 223.

58. William Jasper, "Seismic Support," *The New American,* 8/7/95. Brown later added that the one-fourth of the building collapsing on 4/19 could have created a larger pulse if it had help, say, from high-explosives, "so you wouldn't need quite as much building to be collapsing to cause the same sized pulse that we observed on the day of the explosion."

59. William Jasper, "Were There Two Explosions?" *The New American,* 6/12/95.

60. *Washington Post, 4/23/95.*

61. Moore, *Op Cit.,* p. 223.

62. Hassan Muhammad, interview with author.

63. "William Jasper," OKC Investigator Under Attack," *The New American*, 6/23/97; video deposition of Jane C. Graham, 7/20/97.

64. "Oklahoma City: What Really Happened?" video by Chuck Allen, 1995.

65. *Media Bypass,* June, 1995.

66. Jasper, *Op Cit.*, 6/12/95.

67. Guy Rubsamen, interview with author.

68. Dr. Paul Heath, interview with author.

69. "Witness Accounts Vary in Oklahoma City Bombing," *Dallas Morning News*, 10/8/95; Associated Press, 8/27/95; Associated Press, 9/9/95.

70. Statement of unidentified witness talking to Rep. Charles Key.

71. Graham, *Op Cit.* One of the men was tall, late '30s, nice-looking, very dark hair, mustache, black cowboy hat, jeans. The others were slightly older; wearing khakis, short sleeves, all Caucasians. The FBI agent who interviewed Graham was Joe Schwecke.

72. Interviews with Paul Renfroe, OG&E; Thom Hunter, Southwestern Bell; Don Sherry, Oklahoma Natural Gas. Interviews with approximately 20 construction companies involved with a renovation bid by GSA. Contractor list supplied by GSA to author.

73. David Hall, interview with author.

74. J. D. Cash & Jeff Holladay, "Secondary Explosion Revealed in Murrah Blast," *McCurtain Daily Gazette*, 5/4/95.

75. Allen, *Op Cit.*

76. Jon Rappaport, *Oklahoma City Bombing—The Suppressed Truth* (Blue Press, 1995).

77. *Veritas*, 10/9/95.

78. Craig Roberts, "The Bombing of the Murrah Federal Building: An Investigative Report," (prepared for the Tulsa Office of the FBI), 6/4/95.

79. General Benton K. Partin, interview with author.

80. KFOR-TV.

81. Jim Keith, *OKBOMB—Conspiracy and Cover-Up* (Illuminet Press, 1996).

82. Edward Comeau, "Fire Investigation Report: Oklahoma City Bombing and Rescue Operation," National Fire Protection Association, 11/12/95.

83. Allen, *Op Cit.*

84. Moore, *Op Cit.*, p. 221. Ricks made this statement the day of the bombing.

85. General Benton K. Partin, interview with author.

86. Rick Sherrow, interview with author.

87. BATF RAC Dewy Webb, interview with author; OCPD Officer Don Browning, interview with author.

88. J.D. Cash & Jeff Holladay, "Worker Helped Remove Munitions, Missile from Murrah Building," *McCurtain Daily Gazette*, 7/7/95.

89. *Ibid.*

90. *Relevance* magazine, 7/95.

91. Moore, *Op Cit.*, p. 107.

92. *Ibid.*

93. Allen, *Op Cit.;* Moore, *Op Cit.*

94. *Ibid.*, p. 116.

95. Richard L. Sherrow, "Aftershocks and Subterfuge: Cloud of Doubt Lingers Over Government Cover-up," *Soldier of Fortune*, April, 1996; Moore, p. 106.

96. Lawrence W. Myers, "Bureau of ANFO Truck-Bomb Fabrication," *Media Bypass*, November, 1996.

97. "Who Are They? The Oklahoma Blast Reveals The Paranoid Life and Times of Accused Bomber Timothy McVeigh and His Right-Wing Associates." *Time*, 5/1/95.

98. Dale Russakock & Serge Kovaleski, "An Ordinary Boy's Extraordinary Rage; After a Long Search For Order, Timothy McVeigh Finally Found a World He Could Fit Into," *Washington Post*, 7/2/95.

99. John Kifner, "Oklahoma Bombing Suspect: Unraveling a Frayed Life," *New York Times*, 12/31/95.

100. "An Ordinary Boy's Extraordinary Rage," *Washington Post*, 7/2/95.

101. Robert D. McFadden, "Terror in Oklahoma: The Suspect—One Man's Complex Path to Extremism," *New York Times*, 4/23/95.

102. Sheffield Anderson, interview with author.

103. Prime Time Live, 5/10/95.

104. "Biography: McVeigh, Part II," *Media Bypass*, May, 1996. Myers would later rescind this statement to me, saying he thought McVeigh was the "most maniacal terrorist in U.S. history."

105. "An Ordinary Boy's Extraordinary Rage," *Washington Post*, 7/2/95.

106. *Media Bypass*, May, 1996.

107. "An Ordinary Boy's Extraordinary Rage," *Washington Post*, 7/2/95.

108. *Media Bypass*, 5/96.

109. *Washington Post*, 7/2/95.

110. *Media Bypass*, May, 1996.

111. Robert D. McFadden, "Terror in Oklahoma: A Special Report—John Doe No. 1, A Life of Solitude and Obsessions," *New York Times*, 5/4/95.

112. *Washington Post*, 7/2/95.

113. *Media Bypass*, May, 1996.

114. Lana Padilla and Ron Delpit, *By Blood Betrayed* (Harper Collins, 1995), p. 63.

115. David Hackworth & Peter Annin, "The Suspect Speaks Out," *Newsweek*, 7/3/95.

116. *Newsweek*, 5/15/95.

117. John Kifner, "The Gun Network: McVeigh's World—A Special Report; Bomb Suspect Felt at Home Riding the Gun-Show Circuit," *New York Times*, 7/5/95.

118. FBI 302 Statement of Carl. E. Lebron, Jr., 4/22/95.

119. *Washington Post*, 7/2/95.

120. *New York Times*, 5/4/95.

121. *Media Bypass*, March, 1995.

122. *New York Times*, 5/4/95.

123. *Media Bypass*, March, 1995.

124. *New York Times*, 5/4/95.

125. *Ibid.*

126. *Media Bypass*, March, 1995.

127. "Oklahoma Bombing Suspect: Unraveling a Frayed Life," *New York Times*, 12/31/95.

128. Padilla, Delpit, *Op Cit.*, p. 153.

129. Keith, *Op Cit.*, p. 41.

130. "McVeigh's Army Pals Join Bid to Save His Life," CNN, 6/9/97.

131. Kenneth Stern, *A Force Upon the Plain: The American Militia Movement and the Politics of Hate* (Simon and Schuster, 1996), p. 190; *New York Times*, 5/4/95.

132. "Inside the Mind of McVeigh," *Media Bypass*, April, 1996.

133. "Biography: McVeigh, Part II," *Media Bypass*, May, 1996.

134. *New York Times*, 12/31/95.

135. *Washington Post*, 7/2/95.

136. *New York Times*, 12/31/95.

137. *New York Times*, 5/4/95.

138. *New York Times,* 7/5/95.

139. *Washington Post,* 7/2/95.

140. "The Suspect Speaks Out," *Newsweek,* 7/3/95.

141. Released by McVeigh's attorney Stephen Jones to the *Washington Post.*

142. *Newsweek,* 7/3/95.

143. *Washington Post,* 7/2/95.

144. *Media Bypass,* March, 1995.

145. Report of Investigation, David B. Fechheimer, 12/13/96, addressed to Stephen Jones.

146. Released by Stephen Jones to the *Washington Post.*

147. *New York Times,* 5/4/95.

148. *Washington Post,* 7/2/95, 4/23/95.

149. Glenn Krawczk, "Mind Control and the New World Order," *Nexus* magazine, February-March, 1993, quoted in Keith.

150. *Ibid.,* p. 196.

151. Constantine, "The Nazification of the Citizen's Militias and the Transformation of Timothy McVeigh from Hyper-Military 'Robot' to Mad Bomber," 12/9/95.

152. *Nexus,* February-March, 1993, quoted in Keith.

153. The U.S. General Accounting Office issued a report on September 28, 1994, stating that between 1940 and 1974, DOD and other national security agencies studied hundreds of thousands of human subjects in tests and experiments involving hazardous substances. Medical testing of nerve agents, nerve agent antidotes, psychochemicals, and irritants were classified. The CIA has not released the names of 15 out of approximately 80 organizations that conducted experiments under the MKULTRA program, which gave psychochemical drugs to an undetermined number of people without their knowledge or consent. According to the GAO report, the CIA has not released this information because the organizations do not want to be identified. ("Is Military Research Hazardous To Veterans' Health? Lessons Spanning Half A Century," The Rockefeller Report, Senator Jay Rockefeller, 12/8/94.)

154. "A By the Book Officer, 'Suspicious By Nature,' Spots Trouble and acts fast," *New York Times,* 4/23/95.

155. Dick Russell, *The Man Who Knew Too Much* (Carroll & Graf), 1992, p. 679.

156. Project MKULTRA, The CIA's Program of Research in Behavioral Modification, Joint Hearing Before the, Senate Committee on Intelligence, 8/3/77. U.S. Government Printing Office, 1977.

157. Thomas, *Op Cit.,* p. 116.

158. Russell, *Op Cit.,* p. 673.

159. William M. Turner and Jonn G. Christian, *The Assassination of Robert F. Kennedy: A Searching Look at the Conspiracy and Cover-Up 1968-1978* (Random House, p. 197), Quoted in Constantine, p. 12.

160. Russell, *Op Cit.,* p. 681.

161. *Ibid.,* p. 675.

162. *Ibid.,* p. 673. (Warren Commission Report, Vol. 5, p. 105.)

163. *Ibid.,* p. 19.

164. Art Ford & Lincoln Lawrence, *Were We Controlled?* (University Books), 1967, quoted in Russell.

165. Robert O. Becker, M.D. and Gary Selden, *The Body Electric: Electromagnetism and the Foundation of Life* (William Morrow & Co.), p. 1085, quoted in "Bioeffects of Microwave Radiation," *Unclassified,* Vol. IV, No. 3, June/July, 1992, National Association of Security Alumni.

166. Turner and Christian, *Op Cit*, Anthony Sampson, *The Arms Bazaar: From Lebanon to Lockheed* (Viking Press, 1977), p. 276, quoted in Constantine, p. 12.

167. Ted Gunderson, interview with author.

168. Tim Kelsey, "The Oklahoma Suspect Awaits Day of Reckoning," *London Sunday Times*, date unknown.

169. Sherman Skolnick, *Conspiracy Nation*, June, 1996.

170. Constantine, "The Good Soldier," 1995.

171. Brandon Stickney, *All American Monster: The Unauthorized Biography of Timothy McVeigh* (Prometheus Books, 1996), p. 226.

172. Scott Anderson, "*Globe* publishers' Viet tour in mind warfare," *Now Magazine*, 5/26/94, Quoted in Keith, p. 179.

173. Gene Wheaton, memo, copy in author's possession; interview with author.

174. Jay Wrolstad, "Smoking Gun: Does Dan Marvin Have Evidence of a Kennedy Assassination Conspiracy?" *The Ithaca Times*, 8/22/96; Franklin Crawford, "Local Man Tells JFK Story," *The Ithaca Journal*, 11/16/95; Daniel Marvin, "Bits & Pieces: A Green Beret on the Periphery of the JFK Assassination," *The Fourth Decade*, May, 1995; Colonel Daniel Marvin, interview on Tex Marrs' World of Prophecy, WWCR shortwave, 4/20/96. Marvin's authenticity and credibility have been established by professor L. Pearce Williams of Cornell University, and Jacqueline Powers, former managing editor of the *Ithaca Journal*, who said, "[Col. Marvin] had evidence to back up what he was claiming. I believe him. Everything he has said to me has been true; he's willing to tell what he knows, which can't be easy for him."

175. Jonathan Kwitny, *The Crimes of Patriots* (Simon & Schuster, 1987), p. 103; Affidavit of Colonel Edward P. Cutolo, commander of the 10th Special Forces Group (Airborne), 1st Special Forces, 3/11/80.

176. Hoppy Heidelberg, interview with author.

177. "The Gunderson Report on the Bombing of the Alfred P. Murrah Federal Building, Oklahoma City, Oklahoma, April 19, 1995."

178. Russell, *Op Cit.*

179. "Something Big is Going to Happen," *Time*, 5/8/95.

180. *Washington Post*, 5/4/95.

181. *New York Times*, 4/23/95.

182. "Terror in Oklahoma: The Suspect; Arizona Neighbors Recall a Man's Love of Weaponry and 'Poor Attitude,'" *New York Times*, 4/23/95.

183. *Washington Post*, 7/2/95.

184. Marylin Hart, interview with author, 1/15/96 & 4/1/96.

185. Rob Rangin, interview with author, 4/1/96.

186. Marylin Hart, interview with author, 1/15/96.

187. *New York Times*, 4/23/95.

188. Steve Wilmsen and Mark Eddy, "Who bombed the Murrah Building?" *Denver Post*, date unknown.

189. FBI 302 of Lebron, *Op Cit.*

190. Patrick E. Cole, "I'm Just Like Anyone Else," *Time*, 4/15/96.

191. "An Ordinary Boy's Extraordinary Rage," *Washington Post*, 7/2/95.

192. *New York Times*, 4/24/95.

193. Mark Schaffer, "Gun Class Sheds New Light On McVeigh," *Arizona Republic*, 5/28/95, quoted in Keith.

194. *New York Times*, 12/31/95.

195. Kevin Flynn and Lou Kilzer, "John Doe 2 Remains a Mystery: OKC Bombing Case's Unknown Suspect Could be More Than One Man, Investigators Believe," *Rocky Mountain News*, 3/3/97.

196. *New York Times,* 4/24/95.

197. *Media Bypass,* March, 1995.

198. *New York Times,* 7/5/95.

199. Tim Kelsey, "The Oklahoma Suspect Awaits Day of Reckoning," *London Sunday Times,* 4/21/96.

200. Robert Vito, "Three Soldiers," CNN News, 8/9/95.

201. Trial of Timothy McVeigh.

202. Opening statement of lead prosecutor Joseph Hartzler at Timothy McVeigh's trial.

203. Howard Pankartz and George Lane, "Sister Testifies Against Brother," *Denver Post,* 5/6/97.

204. George Lane, "Letters Provide Damaging Evidence," *Denver Post, 5/6/97;* "Sister's Role Seen as Pivitol," *Denver Post,* 5/6/97.

205. *Time,* 5/1/95.

206. *New York Times,* 5/4/95.

207. "Oklahoma Bombing Plotted for Months, Officials Say, but Suspect Is Not Talking," *New York Times,* 4/25/95, quoted in Keith, p. 28.

208. Emma Gilbey, "Brothers in Arms with a Destructive Hobby," *London Sunday Telegraph,* 3/24/95.

209. Affidavit of FBI Agent Patrick W. Wease.

210. *Newsweek,* 5/15/95.

211. Robert Jerlow, interview with author.

212. *New York Times,* 7/5/95.

213. Dateline, NBC, 2/13/96.

214. *Washington Post,* 7/2/95.

215. *New York Times,* 7/5/95.

216. *Ibid.; Washington Post,* 7/5/95.

217. *The Spotlight,* 5/26/97.

218. Jim Garrison, *On the Trail of the Assassins* (Warner Books, 1988), p. 157.

219. *Media Bypass,* 3/95; *New York Times,* 7/5/95.

220. Beth Hawkins, "The Michigan Militia Greet the Media Circus," *Detroit Metro Times,* 3/26/95.

221. David Van Biema, *Time,* 6/26/95.

222. *Washington Post,* 7/2/95.

223. Ken Armstrong, *No Amateur Did This* (Blackeye Press, 1996), p. 17.

224. J.D. Cash, "McVeigh's Sister Laundered Bank Robbery Proceeds: ATF Surveillance Confirmed by Informant," *McCurtain Daily Gazette,* 1/28/97.

225. Arnold Hamilton, "Bombing Accounts are Varied," *Dallas Morning News,* 10/8/95.

226. Connie Smith, interview with author. These accounts appeared in the *McCurtain Gazette, The New American,* and the *Denver Post,* among other places.

227. Dr. Paul Heath, interview with author.

228. Hoppy Heidelberg, interview with author.

229. Trish Wood, The Fifth Estate, Canadian Broadcasting Corporation; J.D. Cash, "Is a Videotape From a Tulsa Topless Bar the 'Smoking Gun' in Oklahoma City Bombing?" *McCurtain Daily Gazette,* 9/25/96.

230. Tony Boller, Assistant Project Manager, Goodwill Industries, interview with author.

231. Jane Graham, interview with author. Graham is a friend and co-worker of Joan's.

232. J.D. Cash, *McCurtain Daily Gazette,* 7/14/96.

233. Sherie, confidential interview with author.

234. Dan Parker, "McVeigh Defense Questions Co-Defendant's Claim," *Daily Oklahoman,* date unknown; Steve Wilmsen and Mark Eddy, "Who bombed the Murrah Building?" *Denver Post,* date unknown; Timothy McVeigh's Petition for Writ of Mandamus, 3/25/97, p. 36.

235. Linda Kuhlman and Phyliss Kingsley, interviews with author.
236. Mark Eddy, "Witnesses tell a different story," *Denver Post*, 6/16/96.
237. Chuck Allen, interview with author.
238. *Ibid.*
239. Jane Graham, interview with author. Graham is a friend and co-worker of Johnston's.
240. "Feds Charge Terry Nichols in Bombing," *Los Angeles Times*, 5/10/95, quoted in Keith, p. 185.
241. FBI FD-383 (FBI Facial Identification Fact Sheet) of Tom Kessinger, dated 4/20/95, copy in author's possession.
242. *London Sunday Times*, 4/21/96.
243. Affidavit of FBI Special Agent Henry C. Gibbons, 4/21/95, copy in author's possession.
244. Garrison, *Op Cit.*, p. 65, p.77.
245. *Ibid,* p. 66.
246. *Ibid.,* p. 79.
247. Julie DelCour, "Informant Says Tulsan Talked About Local, OC Bombings," *Tulsa World*, 2/9/97.
248. "TNT, $5 a stick. Need more. Call after 1 May, see if I can get some more."
249. William Pepper, *Orders to Kill: The Truth Behind the Murder of Dr. Martin Luther King* (Carroll & Graf), 1995, p.156.
250. *London Sunday Times,* 4/21/96.
251. Kevin Johnson, "McVeigh Lawyer Says FBI Agents Using Trickery," *USA Today*, 8/14/95, quoted in Keith, *Op Cit*, p. 57.
252. Lana Padilla, interview with author.
253. Bob Papovich, interview with author.
254. "A Look at Terry Nichols," Associated Press, 4/5/96.
255. Lana Padilla, interview with author, Diane Sawyer, ABC News Prime Time Live, 5/10/95.
256. Padilla and Delpit, *Op Cit.*, p. 36.
257. Associated Press, 4/5/96.
258. Steve Wilmsen and Mark Eddy, "Who bombed the Murrah Building?" *Denver Post*, date unknown.
259. Serge F. Kovaleski, "In a Mirror, Nichols Saw a Victim," *Washington Post*, 7/3/95.
260. "A look at Terry Nichols," Associated Press, 4/5/96.
261. *Media Bypass.*
262. *Ibid.*
263. Kovaleski, *Op Cit.*
264. Padilla and Delpit, *Op Cit.*, p. 168.
265. Keith, *Op Cit.*, p. 179.
266. Kovaleski, *Op Cit.*
267. Associated Press, 4/5/96.
268. Kovaleski, *Op Cit.*
269. Lana Padilla, interview with author.
270. Elizabeth Gleick, "Who Are They? The Oklahoma Blast Reveals the Paranoid Life and Times of Accused Bomber Timothy McVeigh and His Right-wing Associates," *Time*, 5/1/95.
271. *Ibid.*
272. Barbara Whittenberg, interview with author.
273. *Washington Post*, 7/3/95.
274. *Denver Post*, date unknown.
275. Kovaleski, *Op Cit.*

276. Padilla and Delpit, *Op Cit.*, p. 3.

277. Lana Padilla, interview with author.

278. Padilla and Delpit, *Op Cit.*, p. 6; interview with author.

279. KFOR interview with Lana Padilla; Interview with author.

280. Padilla, *Op Cit.*, p. 5, p. 9.

281. Lana Padilla, interview with author.

282. Padilla, *Op Cit.*, p. 12.

283. Lana Padilla, interview with author.

284. Lou Kilzer and Kevin Floyd, "McVeigh Team Tries Again for Delay," *Rocky Mountain News*, 3/26/97; Timothy McVeigh's Petition for Writ of Mandamus, 3/25/97.

285. Telephone records of Terry Nichols, copy in author's possession.

286. David Jackson, Linnet Myers, Flynn McRoberts, *Chicago Tribune*, 5/11/95.

287. Padilla and Delpit, *Op Cit.*, p. 201.

288. J.D. Cash, *McCurtain Gazette*, date unknown.

289. Barbara Whittenberg, interview with author.

290. Nolan Clay, Robby Trammell, Diana Baldwin and Randy Ellis, "Nichols, Bomb Materials Linked," *Daily Oklahoman*, date unknown.

291. Jerri-Lynn Backhous, interview with author.

292. Dorinda J. "Wendy" Hermes, interview with author.

293. *New York Times*, 5/20/95.

294. Edward Zehr, "Oklahoma City Cover-up Exposed: But the Mainstream Media are Still in Denial," *Washington Weekly*, 2/17/97.

295. "The Company They Keep," Transcript of the Canadian Broadcasting Company "Fifth Estate" piece on Oklahoma City, originally broadcast on October 22, 1996, Host, Bob Oxley, Voice-Over Announcer, Trish Wood, Francine Pelletier; Guest, Robert Millar, Leader, Elohim City; Kerry Noble, Formerly Of CSA; Steven Jones, Timothy McVeigh's Lawyer; Joe Adams, Bailiff; Ross Mcleod, Security Agency Owner.

296. Warren Gotcher, interview with author.

297. Anthony Thornton, "Bomb Plans Found in Defendant's Home, FBI Agent Testifies," *The Daily Oklahoman*, 4/3/96. "Anthony Thornton, "Three Defendants Found Guilty in Bomb Plot, *The Daily Oklahoman*. date unknown.

298. Judy Thomas, "We Are Not Dangerous, Leader of Separatists Says," *Kansas City Star*, 3/17/96.

299. Mark Fazlollah, Michael Matza, Maureen Graham and Larry King, "FBI: Heist Trail Led to White Supremacists," *Philadelphia Inquirer*, 6/30/96.

300. "Bank Bandits Tied to Rightists," Associated Press, 1/21/96; J.D. Cash with Jeff Holladay, "Rebels With a Cause, Part 3: The Aryan Republican Army, *McCurtain Daily Gazette*, 12/29/96.

301. Bill Morlin, "Devoted to Making Nation 'Ungovernable': Group Patterns its Organization After Irish Republican Army," *Spokesman-Review*, 12/29/96.

302. J.D. Cash, "The Spy Who Came in From the Cold," *McCurtain Daily Gazette*, 2/11/97.

303. J.D. Cash with Jeff Holladay, "Rebels With a Cause, Part Four: An Ex-Wife's Suspicions In The OKBOMB Case," *McCurtain Daily Gazette*, 12/31/96.

304. Andreas Strassmeir, interview with author.

305. Judy L. Thomas, "Man Target of Bank Robbery Inquiry," *Kansas City Star*, 1/29/97.

306. Ambrose Evans-Pritchard, *The Secret Life of Bill Clinton: The Unreported Stories* (Regnery), p.80.

307. Pritchard, *Op Cit.*; William Jasper, "More Pieces to the OKC Puzzle," *The New American*, 6/24/96.

308. February, 1996 press release from the Cause Foundation, quoted in *The New American*.

309. Laura Frank, "Oklahoma City Probe May Touch Tennessee," *The Tennessean*, 6/30/96.

310. J.D. Cash, "Is a Videotape From a Tulsa Topless Bar the 'Smoking Gun' in Oklahoma City Bombing?" *McCurtain Daily Gazette*, 9/25/96.

311. Judy Thomas, *Kansas City Star*, 3/17/96.

312. Dennis Mahon, interview with William Jasper.

313. Timothy McVeigh's Petition for Writ of Mandamus, 3/25/97, pp. 44-45.

314. Jeff Steinberg, interview with author.

315. The members, Gene Schroder, Alvin Jenkins, and Ed Petruski, met with Iraqi Ambassador Mohammed Mashat before the start of Desert Storm. The Iraqis took notice of the group's patriotic activities, and invited them to Washington. "They were hoping to open up negotiations with America," explained Schroder, a farmer and veterinarian from Campo, Colorado. "They knew that we'd meet with them and push the issue some with our Representatives and Congressmen." The entire affair was completely legitimate and well-publicized, having been reported in at least one local newspaper in Colorado. The Constitutionalists and anti-war activists also had the support of Senators Hank Brown and Bob Dole. "We called the State Department and everything was cleared," they explained. Yet it seemed Jones was trying to portray the meeting as part of a broader conspiracy between Iraqis and American dissidents. The attorney referred to the three men as Posse Comitatus members—a tax-protest organization of the mid-'80s with anti-Semitic overtones and connections to white supremacist groups. All three denied belonging to the group. Jones then mentioned that Petruski lived an hour's drive from bombing defendant Terry Nichols' house. Petruski denied knowing Nichols. (Eugene Schroder, Alvin Jenkins, and Ed Petruskie, interviews with author; Timothy McVeigh's Petition for Writ of Mandamus, 3/25/97.)

316. Pritchard, *Op Cit.*, 3/30/97.

317. Ingo Hasselbach with Tom Reiss, *Fuhrer-Ex: Memoirs of a Former Neo-Nazi* (Random House, 1996), p. 215; John Michael Johnston, "Investigative Report Concerning Fact-Finding Trip to Germany," 5/15/96, copy in author's possession.

318. "Black History and the Class Struggle," *The Separatist League*, No. 11, August, 1994. In a letter to his followers concerning his strange alliance with the NOI, Rockwell wrote: "I was amazed to learn how much they and I agree on things: they think that blacks should get out of this country and go back to Africa or to some other place and so do we. They want to get black men to leave white women alone, and white men to leave black women alone, and so do we. The Honorable Elijah Muhammad and I have worked out an agreement of mutual assistance in which they will help us on some things and we will help them on others."

319. *Washington Times*, 9/30/85.

320. Ambrose Evans-Pritchard, "IRA supplied detonator for Oklahoma terror bomb," *London Sunday Telegraph*, 3/30/97.

321. Tom Conlon and Helen Curtin, *Dublin Sunday Times*, 7/13/97, quoted in *McCurtain Daily Gazette*, 7/15/97.

322. Rita Cosby reporting, KOKH, FOX, 4/2/97; Andreas Strassmeir, interview with author.

323. "Strassmeir, OKC, And The CIA," *The New American*, 7/22/96.

324. Phil Bacharach, "Casting Doubts: Were Others Involved in the Federal Building Bombing?" *Oklahoma Gazette*, 2/13/97.

325. J.D. Cash, with Jeff Holladay "Weeks Before OKC Bombing, ATF Had 'Wanted' Posters On Strassmeir," *McCurtain County Gazette*, 7/28/96.

326. J.D. Cash, "Agents Probe OKC Bombing Links To Bank Robberies," *McCurtain Daily Gazette*, 7/16/96.

327. Tulsa Police Intelligence, confidential interview with author.

328. Cash, *Op Cit.*

329. Pritchard, *Op Cit.*

330. J.D. Cash, *McCurtain Daily Gazette*, 7/14/96. Dennis Mahon also admitted that Strassmeir worked for the GSG-9.

331. J.D. Cash and Jeff Holliday, "Weeks Before Bombing, ATF Had Out 'Wanted' Posters," *McCurtain Gazette*, 7/29/96, quoted in *American Freedom*, September, 1996.

332. J.D. Cash, "Controversy Over Howe's True Loyalties Become Focus of Her Trial," *McCurtain Daily Gazette*, 7/30/97.

333. J.D. Cash, *McCurtain Gazette*, 7/14/96. The source claimed that classified computer records of the ATF contained evidence that Strassmeir was indeed a key component in the agency's espionage operation at Elohim City, and numerous neo-Nazi groups throughout the country.

334. *London Sunday Telegraph*, date unknown.

335. "Hate and the Law: Kirk Lyons, Esq." Anti-Defamation League, *Special Edition*, June, 1991.

336. Lyons had this to say about Mahon in an interview with *Volkstreue*, a German neo-Nazi magazine: "I have great respect for the Klan historically but sadly, the Klan today is ineffective and sometimes even destructive. There are many spies in it and most of its best leaders have left the Klan to do more effective work within the movement. It would be good if the Klan followed the advice of former Klansman Robert Miles: 'Become invisible. Hang the robes and hoods in the cupboard and become an underground organization.' This would make the Klan stronger than ever before."

337. Ambrose Evans-Pritchard & Andrew Gimson, "Did Agents Bungle U.S. Terror Bomb?" Some of the dialogue was added from Pritchard's *The Secret Life of Bill Clinton*, p. 90.

338. Andreas Strassmeir, interview with author.

339. Alex Constantine, *Op Cit.*

340. Petition for Writ of Mandamus of Timothy McVeigh, 3/25/97, p. 44.

341. Constantine, *Op Cit.*

342. *Ibid.*

343. William Jasper, "Elohim, Terror, and Truth," *New American*, 3/31/97.

344. James Ridgeway, "Lone Assassins?: A Series of Arrests May Link the Oklahoma City Bombing Suspects to a Larger Plot," *Village Voice*, 2/5/97; Mark Eddy, "Others Eyed in Bomb Probe?" *Denver Post*, 1/29/97.

345. Cash, *Op Cit.*

346. Zehr, *Op Cit.*

347. Letter read into testimony at Howe's trial.

348. Frank Donner, *Protectors of Privilege: Red Squads and Police Repression in America* (University of California Press, 1990), p. 360; Michael Novick, "Blue by Day, White by Night: Organized White Supremacist Groups in Law Enforcement Agencies," People Against Racist Terror, 2/3/93, p. 3.

348. Ivo Dawnay, "Informant Accuses FBI Over Oklahoma Bomb," *Electronic Telegraph*, 7/20/97.

349. Kay Clarke, interview with author.

350. Diana Baldwin and Ed Godfrey, "Separatist Asks for Immunity—Witness Takes the Fifth Before Grand Jury," *Daily Oklahoman*, 7/17/97.

351. Ambrose Evans-Pritchard, "'Master of Disguise' Ready to Run," *London Sunday Telegraph*, 3/30/97.

352. Cash, *Op Cit.*

353. "Ex-Informant Indicted on Charges," Associated Press, 3/13/97, Indictment No. 97-CR-05-C, Northern District of Oklahoma, 3/11/97.

354. Richard Leiby, "How a Wheaton Kid Became a Neo-Nazi Bank Robber, and One Confused Human," *Washington Post*, 2/13/97.

355. James Ridgeway, *Village Voice*, 7/23/96; Cash, *Op Cit.*

356. Fazlollah, et al., *Op Cit.*

357. *Ibid.*

358. Leiby, *Op Cit.*

359. Morlin, *Op Cit.*

360. Leiby, *Op Cit.*

361. Paul Queary, "Bombing Informant Ruffles Case," Associate Press, 2/23/97.

362. Robert Heibel, interview with author.

363. Walter Goodman, "Terror in Oklahoma City: TV Critics' Notebook;" "Wary Network Anchors Battle Dubious Scoops," *New York Times*, 4/20/95.

364. Craig Roberts, interview with author.

365. Arnold Hamiltion, "Oklahoma City Car Bomb Kills at Least 31; Scores Missing in Rubble of Office Building," *Dallas Morning News*, 4/20/95.

366. Hugh Davies, "Rental Car is Key Clue on Trail of Terrorists," *London Sunday Telegraph*, 4/21/95. Abdul Yasin, another Iraqi, was released and returned to Iraq. Abdul Basit is Yousef's real name.

367. Patrick Cockburn, "Defector Exposes Saddam's Lies on Chemical Weapons," *The Independent*, 5/7/96. "General Sammara'i says that the committee in charge of sabotage on which he served, and which uses a special 600-strong military unit called 888 to carry out operations, still exists and he suspects it was involved in giving support to the bombers."

368. Paul Anderson, Metro Correspondent Chicago, "Threat of Terrorism Further Increases," *Net News Service*, 07/07/93.

369. *Ibid.*, Center for National Security Policy, No. 95-D23 11 April 1995 Decision Brief.

370. William Carley, "A Trail of Terror," *Wall Street Journal*, 6/16/93, quoted in James Phillips, "The Changing Face Of Middle Eastern Terrorism," Heritage Foundation Report, 10/6/94.

371. Jack Anderson, Dale Van Atta, "Iraq Reported to Send Terrorists to U.S.," *Washington Post*, 1/28/91.

372. The bombings included a Jewish community center in Buenos Aires and the Israeli embassy, the downing of a commuter plane in Panama, and a Jewish charity organization in London. It is assumed that the July, 1994 attacks by Hizbollah—which coincided with King Hussein's peace-making trip to Washington—were primarily to disrupt the Israeli/PLO peace talks.

373. According to James Phillips: "Islamic radicals also often have a different audience in mind than Palestinian nationalists. Instead of using terrorism to influence Western powers to change their policies, they often use terrorism to punish Western powers and inspire other Muslims to rise up against the West. This focus on the Muslim audience rather than an American audience helps explain how the bombers of the World Trade Center could rationalize their bloody actions. The bombing was meant to demonstrate the power of Islamic radicals and the vulnerability of the U.S., not to lead the U.S. to rethink its Middle East policy."

374. Confidential report of William Northrop to KFOR, 5/10/96.

375. Phillips, *Op Cit.* "Between 1980 and 1989 over 400 terrorist actions spilled over from the Middle East to other regions, with 87 percent of these actions occurring in Western

Europe." Paul Wilkinson, "Terrorism, Iran and the Gulf Region," *Jane's Intelligence Review*, May 1992, p. 222.

376. "Jihad in America," PBS documentary, 11/21/94.

377. Yehizkel Zadok, "The FBI is Conducting a Search for 'Three Middle Easterners,'" *Yediot Arhonot*, 4/20/95.

378. Report of William Northrop, and interview with author.

379. Timothy McVeigh's Petition for Writ of Mandamus, 3/25/97, p. 81. Jones points out, given the issue of the credibility of the information, that the head of Saudi Intelligence is the King's own son.

380. Cary Gagan, interview with author.

381. Deposition of Cary James Gagan, 7/14/95. Copy in author's possession.

382. Mike Levine, interview with author.

383. Report of Craig Roberts, 5/8/95. Roberts is the author's partner on the Oklahoma City bombing investigation.

384. Gagan contacted Dave Floyd at the U.S. Marshals Office. He said, 'We've got to get moving on this right away.' I said, 'Well, I've got to have immunity.'"

385. FBI Agent Mark Holtslaw, interview with author.

386. Hand-written letter from Gagan to Tina Rowe.

387. Kevin Flynn, "Romer, Norton get Bomb Threats: CBI Informant's Reliability in Question; He Also Warned of Federal Building Blast," *Rocky Mountain News*, 8/12/95. Gagan was worried about what had happened in Mexico with the Soviets, and didn't want to accept a plea bargain.

388. Federal Public Defender, confidential interview with author.

389. Letter of Immunity from U.S. Justice Dept. signed by Henry Solano, to Gary James Gagan.

390. "FBI Furor," *Unclassified*, Summer, 1997.

391. Gail Gibson, "The Strange Murder-For-Hire Trial of Chuck Hayes Got Even Stranger Yesterday," *Lexington Herald-Leader*, 1/16/97. Myers claimed that Hayes, a former CIA operative, had tried to hire a hit-man with a mere $5,000, using an open phone line.

392. Former Army C.I.D. investigator, confidential interview with author.

393. Dick Russell, "Spook Wars In Cyberspace: Is the FBI Railroading Charles Hayes?" *High Times*, June, 1997.

394. Florida police detective, confidential interview with author.

395. OCPD Dispatch of 4/19/95.

396. David Harper, "Just Who is Carol Howe? Jurors Will Have To Decide Who the Real Woman Is," *Tulsa World*, 7/28/97. "Howe said she heard a 'powerful murmur' in the fall of 1995 that Tulsa could be the target of a major bombing in the spring of 1996. Howe said Thursday she left messages in 1995 but that her calls weren't returned."

397. Robert Rudolph, "Lawmen Get Warning of Plot on U.S. Targets," *Newark Star Ledger*, 3/22/95.

398. Wendy Holden and David Millward, "Oklahoma Bomb Suspect Seized at Heathrow," *London Sunday Telegraph*, date unknown.

399. *Ibid.*

400. *Ibid.*

401. Steven Emerson and Brian Duffy, *The Fall of Pan Am 103* (G.P. Putnam), 1990, p. 176; also see "The Maltese Double Cross," a British TV documentary on Pan Am 103 by Allan Frankovich.

402. Police Report of arrest of Hussain Al-Hussaini. Sharon Twilley also stated she believed she had seen McVeigh in a bar on NW 10th Street, and had seen Hussaini in the same bar at different times.

403. Craig Freeman and Dennis Jackson, interviews with author.

404. Sharon Cohen, Associated Press, 4/26/95.

405. Ruby Foos, interview with author; Davies, *Op Cit.,* 4/21/95.

406. Jim Polk, CNN, 4/20/95; Sharon Cohen, Associated Press, 4/21/95.

407. William Jasper, "The Trial of John Doe No. 2," *The New American,* 5/13/96.

408. J.D. Cash, "Lose Your Illusion," *Media Bypass,* February, 1996.

409. Margaret Hohmann and Ann Domin, interviews with author.

410. Debra Burdick, interview with author.

411. Jayna Davis, KFOR, shadow interview with Kay H., 6/17/95.

412. David Snider, interview with author.

413. OKPD Dispatch of 4/19/95.

414. David Hall, interview with author. Hall said the APB was canceled by an FBI agent named Webster. According to OCPD officer Don Browning, the FBI later "admitted" to "fabricating" the APB.

415. "Ernie Cranford," interview with author.

416. OCPD D.U.I. report.

417. George Lang, "Out on a Limb," date unknown.

418. Dave Balut reporting, KWTV, 10:00 p.m. newscast, 6/16/95.

419. "Sam Khalid," interview with author.

420. Yousef arrived in New York on September 1, 1992. Many New York law enforcement officials reportedly believe that Iraq was involved in the Trade Center bombing, although they can not prove it. (Laurie Mylroie, "World Trade Center Bombing —The Case of Secret Cyanide," *The Wall Street Journal,* July 26, 1994), quoted in James Phillips, "The Changing Face of Middle Eastern Terrorism," *The Heritage Foundation, Backgrounder,* #1005, 10/6/94.

421. Louis Champon, interview with author. According to Champon, who is suing the federal government, Peter Kawaja, who was head of security for Champon's plant, hired Wackenhut. Kawaja was later given immunity to act as an informant. Said Robert Bickel, a Customs informant and investigator familiar with the case: "Hell, Barbouti was treated more like a damn state bird than a terrorist."

422. Mike Johnston, interview with author. John Conally, "Inside the Shadow CIA," *Spy* magazine, September, 1992; Said Louis Champon, "They are so well-protected by an entity in our own government, that they have put up a wall...."

423. TK-7 is a chemical company in Oklahoma City owned by Moshe Tal, an Israeli. Barbouti had attempted to purchase a formula from them that could extend the range of rocket fuel for the Iraqi SCUD missiles.

424. Clark, *Op Cit,*

425. *Ibid.,* pp. 70-72, Quoted in William Blum, *Killing Hope: U.S. Military and CIA Interventions Since World War II* (Common Courage Press, 1996), p. 335; "The Gulf War and its Aftermath," *The 1992 Information Please Almanac,* p. 974, Quoted in Blum, p. 335.

426. Laurie Garrett (medical writer for *Newsday*), "The Dead," *Columbia Journalism Review,* May/June, 1991, p. 32, quoted in Blum, p. 335.

427. *Needless Deaths, Op. Cit.,* p. 135, quoted in Blum, p.335.

428. *Ibid.,* pp. 201-24; Clark, pp. 72-4; *Los Angeles Times,* 1/31/91; 2/3/91, quoted in Blum, p. 336.

429. Bill Moyers, PBS Special Report: After the War, Spring, 1991, quoted in Clark, p. 53.

430. "Biography: McVeigh, Part Two," *Media Bypass,* March, 1995.

431. Yossef Bodansky, *Terror: The Inside Story of the Terrorist Conspiracy in America* (SPI Books, 1994), quoted in Keith, *Op Cit.,* p. 154.

432. *Ibid.,* p. 153.

433. Indeed, a major terrorism summit sponsored by Teheran in June of 1996 saw delegates from Afghanistan, Pakistan, Iraq, Saudi Arabia, and other Mid-East and African states, as well as Bosnia-Herzegovina, Germany, France, Britain, Canada, and the U.S. come together to form a joint working committee under the command of the new HizbAllah International—transforming that group into "the vanguard of the revolution" of the Muslim world.

434. *Defense & Foreign Affairs, Op Cit.*

435. *Ibid.*

436. Ronald W. Lewis, "Uncivil Air War (The Shootdown of TWA Flight 800)," *Air Forces Monthly,* No. 104, November 1996, posted by *S.A.F.A.N. Internet Newsletter,* No. 213, December 21, 1996.

437. Dr. Laurie Mylroie, Ph.D., "Terrorism in Our Face," *American Spectator,* April, 1997.

438. Phillips, *Op Cit.* It is reported that hundreds of them are also being trained by Iranian Revolutionary Guards in Sudanese training camps.

439. See Edward Gargan, "Where Arab Militants Train and Wait," *New York Times,* 8/11/93; Tim Weiner, "Blowback From the Afghan Battlefield," *New York Times* Magazine, 3/13/94; Daniel Klaidman and Gregory L. Vistica, "In Search of a Killer," *Newsweek,* 8/11/97.

440. "The New Era of Global Terrorism," *MSA News,* date unknown, posted on Internet. The leaders of Abu Sayyaf are: Abdurajak Abubakr Janjalani, Amilhussin Jumaani, Edwin Angeles, Asmad Abdul.

441. "U.S. Forces in Gulf on High Security Alert," Reuters, 4/7/97.

442. Patrick Cockburn, "Defector exposes Saddam's Lies on Chemical Weapons," *The Independent,* 5/7/96. "General Sammara'i says that the committee in charge of sabotage on which he served, and which uses a special 600-strong military unit called 888 to carry out operations, still exists and he suspects it was involved in giving support to the bombers.

443. Charles Wallace, "Weaving a Wide Web of Terror," *Los Angeles Times,* 5/28/95; Robert D. McFadden, "Nine Suspected of Terrorism are Arrested in Manila," *New York Times,* 12/30/96.

444. *Ibid.,* p. 3.

445. Lana Padilla, interview with author.

447. Lou Kilzer and Kevin Floyd, "McVeigh Team Tries Again for Delay," *Rocky Mountain News,* 3/26/97; Timothy McVeigh's Petition for Writ of Mandamus, 3/25/97.

447. Lana Padilla, interview with author.

448. "Petition For Writ of Mandamus of Petitioner-Defendant, Timothy James McVeigh and Brief in Support," Case No. 96-CR-68-M, 3/25/97.

449. "Omar Khalif was one of the aliases listed on "Khalid's" 1990 federal indictment.

450. Melissa Klinzing, former KFOR news director, interview with author.

451. Gordon Novel, interview with author.

452. "Ernie Cranford," interview with author.

453. Keith, *Op Cit,* p. 148.

454. Joe Royer, interview with author. The FBI agent who interviewed the couple told them that one VIN number was left intact, and fingerprints were found.

455. Rex Carmichael, interview with author.

456. Tom's is now run by an individual described by Carmichael as "bad news."

457. Bob Jerlow, interview with author.

458. OCPD detective, confidential interview with author.

459. U.S. vs. "Sam Khalid," Response to Presentence Report; "Sam Khalid," interview with author.

460. FBI spokesman Charles Steinmetz said the information he gave Burnes came from former FBI Deputy Assistant Director Bob Ricks.

461. Karen Burnes, "Palestinians: Dirty Business," CBS West 57 Street News magazine, 5/2/89, Cited in Howard Rosenberg, "'Palestinian Network': A Full Report?," *Los Angeles Times*, 6/1/89.

462. Northrop, *Op Cit.*

463. In federal court filings, WISE was described as "a front used to bring international terrorists to the United States."

464. Retired U.S. Army CID investigator, interview with author.

465. General Robert L. Moore (Ret.), interview with author.

466. "FBI Finds Possible Evidence in OKC Bombing, CNN, 7/20/95.

467. Hugh Dellios, "Federal Marshals Arrest Chemist," *Chicago Tribune*, 5/13/95; Mark Schaffer, "Probe Nets 2nd Man in Oatman," *Arizona Republic*, 5/14/95, quoted in Keith, p. 52; Katherine Mauro, Oatman Mining Co., interview with author; Records of the Federal Bureau of Prisons.

468. Diane Sawyer, "Prime Time Live," 4/25/95.

469. Mike Johnston, "Investigative Fact Finding Trip to Germany," 1995; Jonathan Vankin, *Conspiracies, Cover-Ups & Crimes: From Dallas to Waco*, (Illuminet Press, 1996), p. 211.

470. Johnston, *Op. Cit.;* Vankin, *Op Cit.*, p. 226; Martin A. Lee and Kevin Coogan, "Killers on the Right: Inside Europe's Fascist Underground," *Mother Jones*, May, 1987.

471. *Der Speigel* writer Martin Killian, interview with author. Libya also reportedly funded the Irish Republican Army.

472. Johnston, *Op. Cit.*

473. Mike Levine, interview with author.

474. Tom Jarriel, ABC 20/20, January 19, 1996.

475. Jeffrey A. Builta, "Extremist Groups," Office of International Criminal Justice, Chicago, date unknown. The connection is reportedly through Pakistani Brigadier General Imtiaz.

476. Terrorist Group Profiles, Dudley Knox Library, Naval Postgraduate School, date unknown.

477. Builta, *Op Cit.*

478. Kevin Flynn, "Romer, Norton Get Bomb Threats: CBI Informant's Reliability in Question; He Also Warned of Federal Building Blast," *Rocky Mountain News*, 08/12/95. Gagan said he met with Al Fuqra members on different occasions between October, 1995 and February 1996.

479. Judge Lewis Babcock and John Strader, interviews with author. Gagan said he met with U.S. Marshal Jake Warner at Brooklyn's restaurant on October 27, 1995. "In all the years that I've known [Gagan], he's never met with a pair of people in suits," said the manager in an interview with the author.

480. Hampton's alias was Abd al-Rashid Abdallah, and Gant's was Abd Rashid.

481. Jim Killackey, "Leg Confirmed as 169th Victim's," *Daily Oklahoman*, date unknown; "Leg Lost in Blast Still a Mystery," *Dallas Morning News*, 10/19/95; "Oklahoma Bomb Victim Exhumed," 3/15/96, Associated Press; Gary Tuchman, "Does severed leg prove McVeigh's innocence?," CNN, 8/7/95.

482. William Jasper, interview with author. Mahon stated this to Jasper on October 1, 1996,

483. "Rise of HizbAllah International," *Defense & Foreign Affairs*, 8/31/96.

484. FBI 302 statement of Mohammad Abdul Haggag, quoted in Mylroie, *Op Cit.*

485. Timothy McVeigh's Writ of Mandamus, 3/25/96.

486. Phillips, *Op Cit.*

487. She said that her father had also met Yasser Arafat, and had his photograph on his wall.

488. Keith, *Op Cit.*, p. 151.

489. There were no purges in the Communist intelligence services in the former Soviet Union [FSU]. Documents and records, as General Sejna points out, were transferred from Eastern Europe to Moscow. Those who ran the KGB still run the SVR, and a dozen other services in Russia and the FSU.

490. Michael Hedges, "Senate Resolution Asks Clinton to Block Resettlement of Iraqis," *Washington Times*, 9/14/93; "Iraq: Admission of Refugees into the United States," Congressional Research Service Report for Congress, Library of Congress, 10/28/93; Letter from Senator David Boren to Craig Roberts, 3/14/94, copy in author's possession; Denmark, Norway, Sweden, the U.K., Australia, Pakistan, and Syria absorbed the remaining refugees.

491. *Ibid.*

492. McVeigh was indicted on 11 counts: conspiracy to use a bomb to destroy the Federal Building, detonating the bomb, destroying a federal building, and murdering eight federal law enforcement agents.

493. Brandon M. Stickney, *Op. Cit.*, p. 177; Richard Serrano, "Clues Sought in Details from McVeigh's Arrest," *Los Angeles Times*, 9/10/95, quoted in Armstrong, *Op Cit.* p. 118.

494. Col. David Hackworth and Peter Anninn, "And We're Going to Go to Trial," *Newsweek*, 7/3/95.

495. Richard A. Serrano, "Clues Sought in Details from McVeigh's Arrest," *Los Angeles Times* 9/10/95, quoted in *Ibid.*

496. Application and Affidavit FBI Special Agent Henry C. Gibbons.

497. Elizabeth Gleick, "Who Are They?" *Time*, 5/1/95.

498. *New York Times*, 4/22/95.

499. United States v. Timothy James McVeigh, direct testimony of FBI Agent James Elliott, 4/28/97. The complete confidential vehicle identification number was 1FDNF72 J4PVA26077.

500. FBI FD-383 (FBI Facial Identification Fact Sheet) of Tom Kessinger, dated 4/20/95. Tim Kelsey, "The Oklahoma Suspect Awaits Day of Reckoning," *London Sunday Times*, 4/21/96.

501. Cash, *Op Cit.*

502. Edward Zehr, "The McVeigh Trial Gets Underway: Mainstream Media Miss The Real Story," *Washington Weekly*, 5/5/97.

503. Affidavit of Richard Renya, July 5, 1995

504. *Newsweek* reporter, confidential interview with author.

505. "Phone Records Link Suspects Before Blast," *Daily Oklahoman*, 5/3/96.

506. Testimony of OPUS Telecom expert John Kane, U.S. v. McVeigh.

507. Kevin Flynn, "Computer Records Show Calls Made But Aren't Clear Who Made Them," *Rocky Mountain News*, date unknown. "Prosecutors have pressured OPUS representatives not to discuss this issue with the News, even asking them not to verify how their computer systems work, the employees said."

508. Steve Wilmsen, "Records Point to John Doe 2," *Denver Post*, date unknown; Steven K. Paulson, Associated Press, 2/15/97. In a later ruling, Judge Matsch stated that Manning denied prosecutors did anything wrong to elicit his testimony.

509. J.D. Cash, interview with James Sargeant, *Media Bypass*, July, 1996.

510. Barbara Whittenberg, interview with author.

511. Investigation on 5/7/95 at Junction City, Kansas File # 174A-OC-56120-D-815 by SA Mark M. Bouton-WSA, date dictated 5/8/95.

512. Robert Vito, "Oklahoma Bombing Investigators Hit Troublesome Snags," CNN, 11/24/95.

513. *Newsweek* reporter, confidential interview with author.

514. Hoppy Heidelberg, interview with author.

515. Joseph Vinduska and Dennis Euwer are two witnesses who saw the truck at the lake on the 18th.

516. Steve Wilmsen and Mark Eddy, "Who bombed the Murrah Building?" *Denver Post*, date unknown.

517. Jack Douglas Jr. "Bomb link to lake reportedly scrapped," *Fort Worth Star-Telegram*, 3/25/97.

518. Evan Thomas, "This Doesn't Happen Here," *Newsweek*, 5/1/95; U.S. v. McVeigh.

519. U.S. v. James Douglas Nichols and Terry Nichols, Criminal Complaint, statements of FBI Special Agent Patrick Wease.

520. "Some Witnesses Leery Of Bombing Grand Jury," *Daily Oklahoman*, 8/10/97; Gary Antene, interview with author.

521. U.S. v. McVeigh, testimony of Richard Chambers.

522. "FBI Investigates Possible McVeigh Link to Fuel Buy," *Rocky Mountain News*, 4/11/97.

523. Ed Hueske, interview with author.

524. Frank Shiller and Max Courtney, interviews with author.

525. Lou Kilzer and Kevin Flynn, "Were Feds Warned Before OKC Bomb Built?" *Rocky Mountain News*, 2/6/97.

526. Testimony of Kevin Nicholas, U.S. v. McVeigh.

527. Padilla and Delpit, *Op Cit.*, p. 209; David Johnson, "Agents in Kansas Hunt for Bomb Factory as Sense of Frustration Begins to Build," *New York Times*, 4/30/95, quoted in Keith, p. 37.

528. "McVeigh's Fingerprints Not on Key Items," CNN, 5/15/97.

529. Whitehurst contended the problems in the FBI's lab had been occurring since at least 1989.

530. David Johnston and Andrew C. Revkin, "Report Finds FBI Lab Slipping From Pinnacle of Crime Fighting," *New York Times*, 1/29/97.

531. "Report: FBI Lab Botched Oklahoma Bombing Evidence," CNN, 3/22/97.

532. John Kelly, "FBI: McVeigh Contradictions," *Unclassified*, date unknown; Memorandum to all U.S. Attorneys from John Keeney, Acting Assistant Attorney General, 1/4/96. "Outside Experts to Review FBI Crime Lab," *Wall Street Journal*, 9/19/95; "Team to Investigate FBI Chemist's Bias Claims," Associated Press, date unknown; Pierre Thomas, "FBI Lab Audit Finds Some Discrepancies," *Washington Post*, 9/15/95.

533. Memorandum to Scientific Analysis Chief James Kearny.

534. "FBI Furor," *Unclassified*, Summer, 1997.

535. Garrison, *Op Cit.*, P. 116.

536. Ryan Ross, "Blasting the FBI," *Digital City Denver*, 1997.

537. Nolan Clay, "McVeigh Items Seized From Home, Brief Says," *Daily Oklahoman*, 6/11/96; U.S. v. McVeigh, testimony of Special Agent Steven Burmeister.

538. Karen Abbott, "Defense Says FBI Tainted Residue: Evidence Questioned; British Expert Testifies; "The Tables Turn Today," *Rocky Mountain News*, 5/21/97. Burmeister said he photographed the crystals before they disappeared.

539. Deputy Sheriff Clint Boehler, interview with author.

540. Ryan Ross, *Digital City Denver*, 1997. Reno would later comment, "It is unfair, it is unreasonable, it is a lie to spread the poison that the government was responsible at Waco for the murder of innocents. That kind of language is unacceptable in a society that values truth."

541. U.S. v. McVeigh.

542. Hoppy Heidelberg, interview with author.

543. David Maranise, Pierre Thomas, "Officials See Conspiracy of at Least Four in Blast; Probe Focuses on Suspect's Right-Wing Ties," *Washington Post*, 4/23/95.

544. *Ibid.*

545. *Dallas Morning News*, 6/15/95.

546. Peter Carlson, *Washington Post*, 3/23/97.

547. Nolan Clay and John Parker, "John Doe 2 Still Sought, Letter Says Prosecutors Doubt Witnesses Mistaken," *The Daily Oklahoman*, date unknown.

548. William Jasper, *New American*, date unknown.

549. Nolan Clay and Penny Owen, "'Wacky Theories' Unfair, McVeigh Attorney Says," *Daily Oklahoman*, 10/29/96. "We have an obligation to investigate everything," Hartzler told a group of bombing victims. "And if we find some rumor or whatever it is, it makes it into an FBI report."

550. John Gibson, interview with Charles Key and V.Z. Lawton, MSNBC, 4/25/97; V.Z. Lawton, interviews with author.

551. *New York Times*, 12/3/95.

552. Harry Wallace, CBS This Morning, 10/16/95.

553. Jon Rappaport, *The Oklahoma Bombing: The Suppressed Truth* (Blue Press, 1995).

554. Hoppy Heidelberg, interview with author.

555. J.D. Cash, "New Investigation Into Oklahoma City Bombing Demanded," *Jubilee*, Nov/Dec, 1995. "In the Whitewater affair, a special federal judge panel, by statute, appointed an Independent Counsel, Kenneth Starr, supposed to be separate and apart from the Justice Department. Under the law, this was supposed to assure the public that there would be an 'independent' investigation of possible high-level criminality, not a whitewash. Miguel Rodriguez was reportedly blocked by Starr and others from probing and calling independent witnesses, not necessarily FBI nor forensic experts beholden to a political agenda. All this, in respect to suspicions that White House deputy counsel Vincent Foster, Jr. was not really a suicide but murdered." "Whitewater And The 'Runaway' Federal Grand Jury," Sherman H. Skolnick. *Conspiracy Nation*, Vol. 5, No. 30.

556. Reddy and Wilmsen, *Op Cit.*

557. Dr. Paul Heath, interview with author.

558. Sharon Cohen, Associated Press, 4/27/95, quoted in Armstrong, *Op Cit*, p. 27.

559. Barbara Whittenberg, interview with author.

560. Jayna Davis, interview with author.

561. Linda Kuhlman and Phyliss Kingsley, interviews with author.

562. Connie Hood, interview by Glenn Wilburn and J.D. Cash; Keith, *Op Cit.*, p. 147.

563. *Ibid.*

564. Tony Boller, Assistant Project Manager, Goodwill Industries, interview with author.

565. Jerri-Lynn Backhous and Dorinda Hermes, interviews with author.

566. Kevin Flynn, "Guard Saw 2nd Truck At Building: Story Mirrors Bombing Trial Witness' Account of Blast Day," *Rocky Mountain News*, 5/24/97.

567. Arnold Hamilton, *Dallas Morning News*, 11/27/95.

568. Brian Ford, "McVeigh Placed at Kansas Store," *Tulsa World*, 9/12/97.

569. Hamilton, *Op Cit.*

570. Mark Eddy, "Witnesses Tell a Different Story," *Denver Post*, 6/16/96.

571. Rodney Johnson, interview with author.

572. "Some Witnesses Leery Of Bombing Grand Jury," *Daily Oklahoman*, 8/10/97.

573. *Monterey County Herald*, 4/29/95, quoted in Armstrong, *Op Cit.*, p. 8.

574. Judy Kuhlman and Diana Baldwin, "Witnesses Say McVeigh Not Alone—Testimony Places John Doe 2, Another Man With Bomber," *Daily Oklahoman*, 9/11/97.

575. "FBI Searching for Third Man in Oklahoma City Bombing," CNN, 3/10/97.

576. Cash, *Media Bypass,* February, 1996, *Op Cit.*

577. Foreign Policy Institute expert, confidential interview with author.

578. U.S. v. McVeigh, Timothy McVeigh's Petition for Writ of Mandamus, 3/25/97.

579. Ambrose Evans-Pritchard, "Victims Sue in Oklahoma: Fight for Truth," *London Sunday Telegraph,* 3/23/97.

580. J.D. Cash and Jeff Holladay, "Day of Blast 'An Amazing Coincidence,'" *McCurtain Gazette,* 12/1/95.

581. Pat Briley, interview with author.

582. Ken Armstrong, interview with Oklahoma Highway Patrol, August 30, 1995.

583. Amber McGlaughlin, interview with author.

584. Ken Armstrong, *No Amateur Did This,* 1996.

585. Testimony of Deborah Brown, U.S. v. McVeigh.

586. Hoppy Heidelberg, interview with Jon Rappaport.

587. *The Fifth Estate,* Fall, 1996, Vol. 31, #2.

588. *Denver Post,* 5/6/97.

589. "Juror's Emotions With Crying Witnesses," *The Spotlight,* 5/26/97.

590. "Nichols' Wife Says She Didn't Understand FBI Consent Form," CNN, 6/28/96.

591. Chris Hansen, "His Brother's Keeper," Dateline, 1995, quoted in Keith, p. 36; Bob Papovich, interview with author.

592. Robby Trammel and Randy Ellis, "Call For Bomb Investigation Debated," *Daily Oklahoman,* 6/29/95.

593. "As we argued when Key first set out on this course, the Legislature and its staff had no business investigating the bombing. It was, and is, poorly equipped to do so. The same can be said of a panel of local citizens who would be asked to investigate one of the most complicated cases ever to come before the courts." Yet as *The New American* pointed out, state legislatures are regularly tasked on important and sensitive investigations. And the County Grand jury? Is that not "a panel of local citizens," the same as the Federal Grand jury that originally "investigated" the bombing?

594. Mark Sanford, interview with author.

595. Even Palmer admitted that the statutes were limited as to what Judge Owens could do or how he could interpret the law.

596. Moore, *Op Cit.,* p. 140.

597. District Attorney Bob Macy, interview with author.

598. Rep. Charles Key, interviews with author.

599. Diana Baldwin and Judy Kuhlman, "Court Filings Stop Bombing Testimony of Postal Worker," *Daily Oklahoman,* 9/9/97.

600. Rita Cosby, FOX News, 4/4/97.

601. Interview with Jayna Davis. Macy's Assistant DAs who handled the boy rape case were John Farely and Jane Brown.

602. *Daily Oklahoman,* 8/14/97.

603. "The CIA & The Media," *Rolling Stone,* 10/20/77, cited in Mark Zepezauer, *The CIA's Greatest Hits* (Odionian Press), 1994.

604. Mark Sanford, interview with author; William Jasper, "OKC Investigator Under Attack," *New American,* 6/23/97.

605. Brian Ford, "Fund-Rasing Probed: Jury Looks into Efforts of Rep. Charles Key," *Tulsa World,* 5/6/97.

606. Jasper, *Op Cit.*

607. *Ibid.*

608. Brian Ford, "McVeigh Placed at Kansas Store," *Tulsa World,* 9/12/97.

609. Glenn Wilburn, interview with author.

610. Kathy Wilburn and Edye Smith, interviews with author.

611. "Tested by Fire," *People* magazine, date unknown, quoted in, Gene Wheaton, "Another Bush Boy," *Portland Free Press,* July 1995. Keating stated, "The leftists I dealt with would never consider themselves patriots, and they had contempt for the government. The right-wing crowd has contempt for the government, and yet see themselves as patriots. It's a curious anomaly, but both of them are very similar."

612. Gene Wheaton, "Another Bush Boy," *Portland Free Press,* July, 1995.

613. Ace Hayes, letter to author.

614. Deposition of William C. Duncan.

615. William Jasper, *New American,* date unknown.

616. Affidavit of Neil Hartley.

617. Melissa Klinzing, interview with author.

618. Ann Domin, interview with author.

619. Rappaport, *Op Cit.*

620. Hoppy Heidelberg, interview with Jon Rappaport.

621. Hoppy Heidelberg, interview with author.

622. Timothy McVeigh's Petition for Writ of Mandamus, 3/25/97, pp. 71-72.

623. *Newsweek* reporter, confidential interview with author.

624. Debra Burdick, interview with author.

625. Deposition of Jane C. Graham, 7/20/97; Statement of Jane Graham, 11/15/96.

626. Sharon Cohen, Associated Press, 4/26/95; Brian Duffy, "The Manhunt: Twisting Trail," *U.S. News & World Report,* 5/8/95.

627. Bill Jasper, interview with author.

628. Testimony of John Jeffrey Davis, U.S. v. McVeigh.

629. Timothy McVeigh's Petition for Writ of Mandamus, 3/25/96, p. 36.

630. J.D. Cash, *McCurtain Gazette,* quoted in B.C. Specht, "Ministry of 'Slick Justice' Scores Big Coup," posted on Internet, 5/26/97.

631. Ryan Ross, "Final Witness Before Explosion—Two Men in Truck, Neither was McVeigh?" *Digital City Denver News,* 5/23/97; Adrian Croft, "Oklahoma City Bombing Trial Takes Dramatic Twist," Reuters, 5/23/97.

632. Diana Baldwin and Ed Godfrey, "Sighting Accounts Differ—Grand Jury Witnesses Put Bomber in 2 Places," *Daily Oklahoman,* 7/15/97.

633. Rep. Charles Key, interview with author, account of interview with Gary Lewis.

634. Dr. Paul Heath, interview with author.

635. David Keen and Connie Hood, interview by J.D. Cash, tape transcribed by author.

636. Allen, *Op Cit.*

637. William Jasper, *New American,* date unknown.

638. *Ibid.*

639. Paul Queary "Oklahoma Hero Commits Suicide," Associated Press, 5/13/96.

640. Cpt. Ted Carlton, interview with author.

641. Oklahoma City Medical Examiner's Report, copy in author's possession; Dr. Larry Balding and Dr. Fred Jordan, interview with author. They said the drug test costs between $400 and $500 dollars.

642. Taylor recalled the incident for this author. "There's only a few times in my life that I remember that somebody had done something weird like that, and that's why I wrote it down."

643. OCPD Detective Mullinex, interview with author.

644. Regarding Rivera's source, she claimed he knew things about her that no one could have known. "He sat there and told me about stuff I hadn't told anybody," which included break-ins at her apartment.

645. The author knows the name of this individual, but cannot release it at this time.

646. Shaun Jones, interview with author.

647. FAA report, copy in author's possession. Investigators and pilots I've talked to indicated various ways a plane can be rigged to crash, including tampering with the fuel gauge so it reads full when empty, and putting a corrosive acid on the control cables.

648. Mike Evett, interview with author.

649. Medical Examiner's report, 8/5/97, by Dr. Fred Jordan.

650. Dan Richardson, interview with author.

651. John Michael Johnston, interview with author.

652. Al Martin on the Tom Valentine show, date unknown. The author has interviewed Martin extensively.

653. Craig Roberts and John Armstrong, *JFK: The Dead Witnesses* (Consolidated Press Int'l, 1995), pp. iii-vii, 173-76.

654. D'Ferdinand Carone, interview with author. Carone was subsequently threatened by anonymous telegram after I interviewed her on my radio show, KHNC, Denver, American Freedom Network.

655. Rael Jean Isaac, "Abusive Justice: Janet Reno's Dirty Secret," *National Review*, 6/30/97.

656. Thompson, *Op Cit.*

657. Rariner was then paid $120,000 over the next five years on the condition that he not practice law during that time. Former Mossad agent Ari Ben-Menashe claimed he personally saw a cable from Israel's Joint Committee to the U.S., requesting that $600,000 be transferred from the CIA-Israeli slush fund to Hadron to pay Rariner. Former National Security Advisor Robert "Bud" McFarlane had sold PROMIS to the Israelis.

658. Rodney Stich, *Defrauding America* (Diablo Western Press, 1994), pp. 371-97.

659. *Barron's*, 3/21/88. As Judge Bason wrote, "I have come to believe that my non-reappointement as bankruptcy judge was the result of improper influence from within the Justice Department which the current appointment process failed to prevent."

660. Stich, *Op Cit.*, pp. 377-78.

661. Robert Schmidt, "Low Key, High Pressure," *Legal Times*, 9/2/96.

662. "An Irresistible Case," *Newsweek*, 8/14/95.

663. Schmidt, *Op Cit.*.

664. *Ibid.*

665. Sherman Skolnick, *Conspiracy Nation*, date unknown.

666. The committee noted: "Riconosciuto stated that a tape recording of the telephone threat was confiscated by DEA agents at the time of Riconosciuto's arrest.... the timing of the arrest, coupled with Mr. Riconosciuto's allegations that tapes of a telephone conversation he had with Mr. Videnieks were confiscated by DEA agents, raises serious questions concerning whether the Department's prosecution of Mr. Riconosciuto was related to his cooperation with the committee."

667. The government also attempted to destroy William Chasey, author of *The Lockerbie Cover-Up*.

668. *Ibid.*

669. John Ashton, "US Government Still on Ropes Over Lockerbie," *The Mail on Sunday*, 6/9/96.

670. Kevin Flynn, "Testimony Blocked at Trial of McVeigh," *Rocky Mountain News*, 7/14/97.

671. D'Ferdinand Carone, interview with author.

672. Paul Hudson, head of U.S. Pan Am survivors group, interview with author.

673. Administration officials who discussed these deals said al-Kassar had clear business links with Abu Nidal's organization. *Los Angeles Times*, 7/17/87.

674. Jim Berwick, a Pan Am security consultant in London, told Francovich, "An HM Customs officer involved in the investigation of narcotics, left a message for me. I subsequently contacted him and met with him and he advised me that he had been in Frankfurt and had been at a meeting of drug enforcement agents in Germany, America and Britain, and that it was well known and discussed at that meeting that Pan Am was the airline that was being used as a drug conduit."

675. One interesting piece of evidence was a call to Damascus, Syria, intercepted by authorities, in which Khreesat stated: "I have made some changes to the medicine. It is better and stronger."

676. Pritchard, *Op Cit.*

677. According to a special report in *Time* (April 27, 1992), COREA used the following front companies for its overseas operations: Sevens Mantra Corp., AMA Industries, Wilderwood Video and Condor Television Ltd. The report revealed that Condor did its banking through the First American Bank, a subsidiary of BCCI. (Bainerman, *Op Cit.*)

678. Donald Goddard and Lester Coleman, *On the Trail of the Octopus* (Bloomsbury Publishing, 1993), pp. 143, 201.

679. Two separate eyewitnesses remember General Crosby ordering the "immediate bulldozing of the crash site."

680. Interfor report; PBS Frontline believes the suitcase belonging to Gannon was switched in London. According to their investigators, Gannon's was the only piece of luggage not accounted for from the flight.

681. Debra Burdick, interview with author.

682. J.D. Reed, "Wednesday, April 19, 1995: A Black Day for All of Us," *Workin' Interest*, Vol. 96, Issue No. 3.

683. *Ibid.*

684. *Ibid.*

685. *Ibid.*

686. Allen, *Op Cit.*

687. The Jaffar clan had been at the center of the opium production in the Bekka Valley for years.

688. "Files Before Victims," *New York Daily News*, 5/1/95.

689. Tulsa Fire Captain, confidential interview with Craig Roberts.

690. Jeffrey Steinberg, "CIA Man: Iran, Syria Bombed Pan Am 103," *New Federalist*, 7/2/93.

691. In August 1991, Larry Cohler, a writer for *Washington Jewish Week*, reported on a set of secret negotiations which took place between Syria and the U.S. over the release of the hostages and which led to a number of covert trips by Bush to Damascus; Regarding the announcement of the Libyan theory, see: *New York Times*, 11/15/91; *Time*, 4/27/92.

692. Coleman/Goddard, *Op Cit.*, pp. 201, 256, 275; James Shaughnessy said that he "had also been advised separately by four investigative journalists" that they had evidence of these intercepts, one having claimed to have actually heard the tapes. "Finally, I was told that Mr. Lovejoy used a number of aliases, including Michael Franks."

693. This wasn't difficult, as the McKee team (via Gannon) had made its travel arrangements through the DEA's travel agent in Nicosia.

694. A May, 1989 report in the Arabic newspaper *Al-Dustur* reported on the situation involving Lovejoy/Franks/Schafer. Lester Coleman, a trained DIA agent, claims he warned Hurley repeatedly about the compromised situation. Hurley would later seek to dismiss Coleman's claims as unsubstantiated, and seek to discredit Coleman.

695. Dave Emory, Pacifica Radio Network, WBAI-FM, date unknown.

696. Mike Levine, interview with author.

697. Dave Hogan, "If He'd Been at Work … Former Portlander Says," *Portland Oregonian*, 4/20/95.

698. Glenn Wilburn, interview with author.

699. J.D. Cash and Jeff Holladay, "Day of Blast an Amazing Coincidence,'" *McCurtain Gazette*, 12/1/95.

700. Tom Jarriel, ABC 20/20, 1/17/97.

701. Ian Williams Goddard, "Federal Government Prior Knowledge of the Oklahoma City Bombing," 5/26/97, posted on Internet.

702. Sherry Koonce, *Panola Watchman*, 4/23/97.

703. Allen, *Op Cit.*

704. KFOR, Jayna Davis reporting, 11/21/96; WNBC Extra, Brad Goode reporting, 3/19/97.

705. J.D. Reed, "Wednesday, April 19, 1995: A Black Day for All of Us," *Workin' Interest*, Vol. 96, Issue No. 3.

706. *Ibid.*

707. ABC Extra: Prior Knowledge, 11/20/96.

708. "Indictment: Inside the Oklahoma City Grand Jury, The Hoppy Heidelberg Story," Equilibrium Entertainment, 1996.

709. V.Z. Lawton, interview with author; "Diana Baldwin and Judy Kuhlman, "Elevator Accounts Questioned—Inspector Talks of Bomb's Effect," *Daily Oklahoman*, 7/16/97.

710. Deposition of Jane C. Graham, 7/20/97; interview with author.

711. William Jasper, "Prior Knowledge: Powerful Evidence Exists that Federal Agents were not Surprised by OKC Blast," *New American*, 12/11/95.

712. "Since his story was made public, Shaw said he and his wife have taken a lot of flak over it, and it has created a hardship for them. 'There's us that knows the truth and those who hate us. The ones that hate us are the ones trying to cover it up,' Shaw said." ("Some Witnesses Leery Of Bombing Grand Jury," *Daily Oklahoman*, 8/10/97.)

713. William Jasper, *New American*, date unknown.

714. J.D. Cash, "ATF's Explanation Disputed," *McCurtain Sunday Gazette and Broken Bow News*, 7/30/95. Schickedanz won the National Policeman of the Year Award for his "heroic" role.

715. Ed Godfrey and Diana Baldwin, "Bombing Grand Jury Calling 6 Witnesses This Week, " *Daily Oklahoman*, 7/13/97.

716. "Diana Baldwin and Judy Kuhlman, "Elevator Accounts Questioned—Inspector Talks of Bomb's Effect," *Daily Oklahoman*, 7/16/97.

717. Rick Sherrow, interview with author.

718. David Hall, interview with author.

719. Gordon would not return the author's calls. The interview conducted by the other reporter was early on, before the cover-up got into high gear.

720. Ames Yates, interview with author.

721. Rick Sherrow, interview with author; Don Webb, interview with author.

722. Letter of Terrance Yeakey to Ramona McDonald.

723. Federal agent, confidential interview with author.

724. List of attendees of Sheriff's golf tournament.

725. Pritchard, *Op Cit.*, p. 90.

726. Edward Zehr, "Turning Point: Resolving The Enigma of Oklahoma City," *Washington Weekly, 11/18/96.*

727. J.D. Cash, "Agents Probe OKC Bombing Links To Bank Robberies," *McCurtain Daily Gazette,* 7/16/96.

728. Pritchard, *Op Cit.*, p. 90.

729. Harry Eberhart interviewed by Tom Jarriel, ABC 20/20, 1/18/97.

730. Dewy Webb, interview with author.

731. Richard Sherrow, interview with author.

732. Charles, *Op Cit.;* William F. Jasper, "Undercover: The Howe Revelations," *The New American,* 9/15/97.

733. David Hall, interview with author; Rick Sherrow, interview with author.

734. David Hall, interview with Tom Valentine.

735. David Hall, interview with author.

736. David Hall, interview with author.

737. Jon Rappoport, *Oklahoma City Bombing: The Supressed Truth*, pp. 75-76.

738. Conversation between informant and Rep. Charles Key, copy in author's possession. A voice stress analysis we ran on this individual's interview tape indicated he was being truthful.

739. David Hall, interview with author.

740. Pritchard, *Op Cit,* p. 90.

741. Statement of Jane Graham, 11/15/96.

742. Bill Jasper, *New American.* The author also heard one of the Cancemi tapes, but with a slightly different account.

743. Lana Padilla, interview with author.

744. Ralph Blumenthal, "Tapes Depict Proposal to Thraw Bomb Used in Trade Center Blast," *New York Times,* 10/28/93. The transcripts, which are stamped "draft" and compiled from 70 tapes recorded secretly during the last two years by Salem, were turned over to defense lawyers, in the second bombing case, by the government under a judge's order barring lawyers from disseminating them. A large portion of the material was made available to the *New York Times.*

745. Waldman and McMorris, *Op Cit.*

746. Jim Dwyer, David Kocieniewski, Deidre Murphy, and Peg Tyre, *Two Seconds Under the World,* 1994, quoted in William Jasper, "Evidence of Prior Knowledge," *New American,* 5/13/96.

747. J.D. Cash, "The Rev. Robert Millar Identified As FBI Informant," *McCurtain Daily Gazette,* 7/1/97.

748. Citizens Research and Investigations Committee and Louis Tackwood, *The Glass House Tapes* (Avon Press, 1973), p. 5, quoted in Alex Constantine, *Blood, Carnage, and the Agent Provocateur,* 1993, p. 13; "King Aftermath Rekindles Police Spying Controversy, *Los Angeles Times,* 6/18/91, quoted in *Ibid.*, pp. 16-18.

749. *Ibid.*

750. Hoppy Heidelberg and Ted Gunderson, interviews with author. Recall that Heidelberg heard McVeigh's sister Jennifer read the letter into testimony.

751. Scott and Marshall, *Op Cit.,* p. 16.

752. Deirdre Griswold "Cuba Defended Itself, Washington Is The Terrorist," *Workers World,* 3/7/96; Jack Calhoun, "The Family that Prays Together," *Covert Action Quarterly,* Summer, 1992; also see Thomas & Keith.

753. Friedman, *Op Cit.*

754. *Ibid.*

755. Mary Ann Weaver, "Blowback," *Atlantic Monthly,* May, 1996.

756. Friedman, *Op Cit.*

757. Peter Waldman and Frances A. McMorris, "The Other Trial: As Sheik Omar Case Nears End, Neither Side Looks Like a Winner," *Wall Street Journal,* 9/22/95.

758. *National Review,* 7/10/95, quoted in *Ibid.;* Curt Gentry, *J. Edgar Hoover: The Man and the Secrets* (W.W. Norton, 1991), p. 484.

759. Rowe failed lie-detector tests regarding his complicity in the church bombing and the Viola murder.

760. Donner, *Op Cit.,* p. 365

761. Frank Donner, *Protectors of Privilege: Red Squads and Police Repression in America,* (University of California Press, 1990), p. 360

762. Ward and Churchill, *Op Cit.,* p. 181; *Washington Post,* 7/15/80; *New York Times'* 5/15/80, quoted in *Ibid.*

763. Gene Wheaton, interview with author.

764. *Intelligence Newsletter* (France), April 1993; *Unclassified,* National Association of Security Alumni, date unknown.

765. Ben MacIntrye, *London Times,* 4/21/95, quoted in Keith, *Op Cit.,* p. 154.

766. Kwitny, *Op Cit.,* p. 103.

767. Hoppy Heidelberg and Ted Gunderson, interviews with author. Recall that Heidelberg heard McVeigh's sister Jennifer read the letter into testimony.

768. Statement of Jane Graham, 11/15/96.

769. Jane Graham, video deposition of 8/20/97 and interview with author.

770. Jane Graham, interview with author.

771. Statement of Jane Graham, 11/15/96.

772. Tim Weiner, "Aging Shop of Horrors: The C.I.A. Limps to 50," *New York Times,* 7/20/97. As Milt Bearden, the Agency's last chief of Soviet operations, said, "The collapse of our enemy ensured our own demise." "We're a confused group, dying for stability," the Agency's Inspector General, Fred Hitz, said in a May speech.

773. Victor Navasky, "Anatomy of a Hoax," *The Nation,* 6/12/95; Robert Tomsho, "A Cause for Fear; Though Called a Hoax, 'Iron Mountain' Report Guides Some Militias," *Wall Street Journal,* 5/9/95, quoted in "Report from Iron Mountain: A Fraud?" *Conspiracy Nation,* Vol. 5. No. 8.

774. Leonard C. Lewin, *Report from Iron Mountain on the Possibility and Desirability of Peace,* (Simon & Schuster/Free Press, 1996); Victor Navasky, "Anatomy of a Hoax," *The Nation,* 6/12/95; Robert Tomsho, "A Cause for Fear; Though Called a Hoax, 'Iron Mountain' Report Guides Some Militias," *Wall Street Journal,* 5/9/95, quoted in "Report from Iron Mountain: A Fraud?" *Conspiracy Nation,* Vol. 5. No. 8.

775. *Foreign Affairs,* June/July, 1995.

776. Rappaport, *Op Cit.*

777. DeCamp, *Op Cit.,* p. 380.

778. Noam Chomsky, *Alternative Press Review,* Fall, 1993.

779. The majority of militia members are nonviolent and some have assisted the bureau in its investigations, he said.

780. William Jasper, "Enemies of World Order," *The New American,* 6/23/97.

781. DeCamp, *Op Cit.,* p. 382.

782. "The Truth Steps Out: End of Blind Trust in the Media," *Relevance,* April, 1997.

783. Daniel Brandt, "The 1960s and COINTELPRO: In Defense of Paranoia," *NameBase NewsLine,* No. 10, July-September 1995.

784. Rep. Steve Stockman, letter to Attorney General Janet Reno, 3/22/95.

785. *Ibid.*

786. Carol Moore, "Report on 1995 House Waco Hearings," revised, May, 1996.

787. Peter Kawaja, interview with author.

788. Ambrose Evans-Pritchard, "IRA 'supplied detonator for Oklahoma terror bomb,'" *London Sunday Telegraph,* 3/30/97.

789. Theodore Shackley, *The Third Option: An Expert's Provocative Report on an American View of Counterinsurgency Operations* (Dell Publishing, 1981), p.17.

790. Gene Wheaton, "CIA: The Companies They Keep," *Portland Free Press*, July-October, 1996.

791. *Portland Free Press*, June/July, 1997.

792. William Shirer, *The Rise and Fall of the Third Reich.*

793. Suzanne Harris, J.D., "From Terrorism to Tyranny: How Governments Use Domestic Terrorism to Promote Totalitarian Change," *The Law Loft*, Los Angeles, CA, 1995.

794. Shirer, *Op Cit.*

795. Orville R. Weyrich, Jr., "Reichstag Fire," Weyrich Computer Consulting, 1995; William Jasper, "A Post-Oklahoma Kristallnacht," *The New American*, 5/129/95.

796. Jonas Bernstein, "U.S., Russia Sign Anti-Gangster Pact," *Washington Times*, 7/6/94; quoted in *Namebase Newsline*, "Organized Crime Threatens the New World Order," Jan-March, 1995; "FBI Chief: U.S. 'Under Attack' by Terrorists," *U.S. News & World Report*, 8/1/96.

797. *USA Today*, 3/11/93.

798. MTV, 3/22/94.

799. The Bill appropriates $114 million dollars for the FBI for fiscal year 1997 and $166 million for 1998. The White House, Press Briefing By Under Secretary of the Treasury For Enforcement Ron Noble, Deputy Attorney General Jamie Gorelick, and Deputy Assistant to the President for Domestic Policy Bruce Reed, 4/26/95.

800. Ace R. Hayes, "G-Men Cop Plea on Ruby Ridge," *Portland Free Press*, September/October, 1995. "The third sub-unit of this division is the "Special Detail Unit" which is designated to keep Gen. Reno from harm."

801. HR 97's sponsor is Rep. Barbara Kennelly (D-CT). The Senate's version is S. 1581, introduced in 1993 by Senator Joseph Lieberman (D-MA). Page five of the bill states: "Members of the Rapid Deployment Force who are deployed to a jurisdiction shall be deputized in accordance with State law so as to empower such officers to make arrests and participate in the prosecution of criminal offenses under State law." "On The Fast-track To Fascism," *Relevance* , February, 1995.

802. Joe Hendricks, Chief of Police, Windsor, Missouri, "Police Chief Rejects Trend Toward National Police," *The Idaho Observer*, June, 1997.

803. William Booth, *Washington Post*, 6/17/97.

804. *Soldier of Fortune*, August, 1995.

805. Associated Press, 12/24/94.

806. "Hard Landing by Army Copter Hurts Two," *Houston Chronicle*, 10/29/96.

807. Lori-Anne Miller, "Bombing Sounds Rattle Neighborhood," *The Detroit News*, 10/2/94; Mark Spencer, posted on AEN Newsgroup, 10/02/94.

808. "The Pentagon Brings its Wars Home," *Sources Ejournal*, Volume 2, Issue 1, January, 1997. Army Lt. Gen. J.H. Binford Peay points out in an Army publication titled *Tomorrow's Missions*, that "military forces [today] are required to provide domestic national assistance, such as internal peace-keeping and anti-drug operations and support of civil authorities to maintain stability in a rapidly changing America."

809. Jonathan Volzke, "Urban Combat Training: Marines Hit the Rooftops," *Orange County Register*, 3/19/93, quoted in Terry Cook, *The Mark of the New World Order* (Whitacker House, 1996), p. 81.

810. Major General Max Baratz, "New shape of Army Reserve Supports New Missions," *Army Reserve*, Summer, 1994.

811. William F. Jasper, "Fact and Fiction: Sifting Reality from Alarmist Rumors," *New American,* 10/31/94.

812. Keenen Peck, "The Take-Charge Gang," *The Progressive,* May, 1985; Reynolds, *Op Cit.*

813. Michael Levine with Laura Kavanau, *Triangle of Death* (Delacorte Press, 1996), p. 353.

814. Mike Levine, interview with author.

815. "Police May Have Ignored Basic Riot Plan," *New York Times,* 5/7/92.

816. "Riot Found Police in Disarray—Officers Kept from Flash Point Despite Pleas," *Los Angeles Times,* 5/6/92, quoted in Constantine, p. 33.

817. Ace Hayes, "G-Men Cop Plea on Ruby Ridge," *Portland Free Press,* September/October, 1995.

818. Shackley, *Op Cit.,* p. 13.

819. *The New American,* 3/18/96. Apparently, Schumer felt that Militia hearings were more important than an investigation of the murder of 86 innocent people by the Federal Government at Waco. Fortunately, most of his fellow Congressmen did not agree.

820. Marchetti, *Op Cit.*

821. Daniel Brandt, "Organized Crime Threatens the New World Order," *NameBase NewsLine,* No. 8, January-March 1995.

822. Frank Greve, Matthew Purdy, and Mark Fazlollah, "Firm Says U.S. Urged Covert Plots," *Philadelphia Inquirer,* 4/26/87, quoted in Christic, *Op Cit.,* and Rodney Stich, *Defrauding America* (Diablo Western Press, 1994), p. 604. "Richard Meadows served for a time as Peregrine's president. Charles Odorizzo and William Patton, worked for the group. Peregrine's key contacts were retired Army Lt. Gen. Samuel Wilson (former Director of the DIA) and Lt. Col. Wayne E. Long, who as of April 1987 worked as a senior officer in the Foreign Operations Group, which is a part of the Army's intelligence support activity office."

823. Stich, *Op Cit.,* p. 604; ANV had a contract with U.S. Military Central Command, the influential connection coming through USMC Major General Wesley Rice of the Pentagon Joint Special Operations Agency. Rice was a close friend of Bush, Helms, and Shackley, Wheaton, *Op Cit.;* Deposition of Sam Hall, 9/9/87, quoted in Christic, *Op Cit.*

824. Gene Wheaton, "Secret Island Spy Base," *Portland Free Press,* July-October, 1996. Wheaton and Hunt both claim that an ABC news helicopter was shot down over the island in 1985, killing a female reporter. The incident was covered up for reasons of "national security."

825. Declaration of Plaintiff's Counsel, U.S. District Court, Southern District of Florida, Tony Avirgan and Martha Honey v. John Hull, et al., Civil Case No. 86-1146-CIV-KING, filed 3/31/88 by the Christic Institute; It seems Whitlam was about to announce the truth of Pine Gap at a press conference. By November 7, 1975, the covers of three more CIA agents had been blown in the press.

826. Luigi DiFonzo, *St. Peter's Banker* (Franklin Watts, 1983); *NameBase NewsLine,* No. 5, April-June 1994. According to *Conspiracy Nation* publisher Brian Redman, Gelli attended Ronald Reagan's inauguration and the accompanying ball in 1981; Mark Aarons and John Loftons, *Ratlines* (London, Heinemann, 1991), p. 89, quoted in *Nexus,* February/March, 1996.

827. *Ibid.*

828. "Staying Behind: NATO's Terror Network," *Arm The Spirit,* October, 1995, (Source: *Fighting Talk* - Issue 11 - May 1995; Thomas & Keith, *Op Cit.,* p. 77. According to Jonathan Vankin, Italian Journalist Mino Percorelli claimed the CIA pulled P2's strings. He was killed after publishing the article.

829. Stuart Christie, *Stefano Delle Chiaie: Portrait of a Black Terrorist* (Dark Horse Press, 1984), p. 32.

830. *Ibid.*

831. Christie, *Op Cit.*

832. *Ibid.*

833. David Yallop, *In God's Name* (Corgi Books, 1985), p. 172; "Il Gladio," BBC exposé, June, 1995, quoted in *Ibid.*

834. Stuart Christie, "Stefano Delle Chiaie: Portrait of a Black Terrorist," *Anarchy Magazine,* Refract Publications, 1984.

835. Edward S. Herman, *The Terrorism Industry* (Pantheon, 1989), p. 226.

836. Reuters, 7/14/96.

837. *New American, Op Cit.*

838. Ari Ben-Menashe, *Profits of War: Inside the Secret U.S.-Israeli Arms Network* (Sheridan Square Press, 1992), p. 122. Eitan was responsible for collecting scientific and intelligence information from other countries through espionage. (Art Kunkin: "The Octopus Conspiracy.")

839. Patrick Seale, *Abu Nidal: A Gun for Hire,* (Random House, 1992), p. 158.

840. *Ibid.,* p. 153, 214.

841. *Ibid.,* pp. 265-66.

842. William Jasper, "The Price of Peace," The *New American,* 2/5/96.

843. Uri Dan and Dennis Eisenberg, *A State Crime: The Assassination of Rabin* (Belfond, 1996), quoted in *Conspiracy Nation,* Vol. 8, Number. 2.

844. *New American,* 12/25/95.

845. *Ibid.,* p. 369.

846. *Ibid.,* p. 402.

847. "FBI accidentally faxes memo on Amtrak suspect," Associated Press, 9/4/97.

848. "Grenade blast Rocks Makati—4 Wounded: Rep. Arroyo Accuses Military of Bombing to Justify Anti-Terrorist Bill," source: Manila dailies.

849. Husayn Al-Kurdi, "Libya: The Perpetual Target," *News International Press Service,* date unknown. Regarding America's reaction to Libyan independence, Kurdi notes: "The idea that emancipation from want, ignorance and injustice was to be actually implemented somewhere is unacceptable to an entity that foments poverty and dependence everywhere."

850. Under the authority of the 1977 International Emergency Economic Powers Act.

851. John Goetz, "Ten Years Later: La Belle Disco Bombing," *Covert Action Quarterly,* Spring, 1996. (Author's note: the *Los Angeles Times* reported that "Israeli intelligence, not the Reagan administration, was a major source of some of the most dramatic published reports about a Libyan assassination team allegedly sent to kill President Reagan and other top U.S. officials ... Israel, which informed sources said has wanted an excuse to go in and bash Libya for a long time, may be trying to build American public support for a strike against Qaddafi.")

852. Seymour Hersh, "Target Qaddafi," *New York Times Magazine,* 2/22/87, quoted in *Covert Action Quarterly,* date unknown.

853. *Ibid.*

854. Goetz, *Op Cit.* Faysal testified, saying: "I am not of the opinion that the attack against La Belle was done by those Libyans whom I know [the Nuri group], but rather by a different group Many of the Libyans behaved suspiciously. That was to hide the group that in reality did the attack."

855. Rick Atkinson, "US Delays Underlined As Disco Bombing Suspect Freed in Lebanon," *Washington Post,* 8/3/94; quoted in *Ibid.*

856. Goetz, *Op Cit.* "A week after the bombing, Manfred Ganschow, chief of the anti-terrorist police in Berlin, "rejected the assumption that suspicion is concentrated on Libyan culprits."

857. Christic, *Op Cit.;* Jack Terrell, interview with author. (Also see the *Village Voice,* 9/29/87, and 13/30/86.)

858. Jack Terrell, NBC transcript, quoted in Christic, *Op Cit.* The Octopus would attempt to silence Terrell by informing the FBI that he had threatened the life of the President.

859. Cockburn, *Op Cit.*

860. Deposition of Gene Wheaton; Deposition of Eden Pastora; testimony of Jack Terrell, quoted in Christic, *Op Cit.*

861. Cockburn, *Op Cit.,* pp. 56-57; Christic, *Op Cit.*

862. *Ibid.,* John Mattes, interview with author.

863. Jack Terrell, *Disposable Patriot* (National Press Book, 1992).

864. As Col. Dan Marvin notes, that statement, written by White in a letter to a friend, was broadcast on ABC TV in 1979 in a documentary produced by John Marks.

865. Steven K. Paulson, "Media Object to Sealed Documents in Oklahoma City Bombing Case," Associated Press, 12/13/96.

866. Associated Press & The Hays Daily News, 8/14/97.

867. Bill Hewitt and Nickie Bane, "Humble? Forget It," *People,* 3/31/97.

868. Janet Elliott, Mark Ballard, Robert Elder Jr., Gordon Hunter, "Nichols' Lawyers: The Odd Couple," *Texas Lawyer,* 3/22/96; Robert Schmidt, "Representing the Accused Bomber," *Legal Times,* 5/22/95; Constantine, "The Good Soldier," *Op Cit.*

869. Jim Bellingham, interview with author.

870. John DeCamp, *The Franklin Cover-Up* (AWT, Inc., 1996), pp. 345-46.

871. Letter from Stephen Jones to author, 4/21/97.

872. General Benton K. Partin, interview with author.

873. Stephen Jones, letter to author, 9/9/97.

874. *Ibid.*

875. John Greiner, "Court Asked to Ensure Macy Explores All Bombing Angles," *Daily Oklahoman,* 6/28/97.

876. District Attorney Bob Macy, interview with author.

877. George Hansen, interview with author.

878. "Grand Jury Told Seismic Readings Unclear in Bombing," *Daily Oklahoman,* 9/19/97.

879. *Ibid.*

880. KWTV Channel 9 broadcast, 06/16/97.

881. Lynn Wallace, posted on OKBOMB mailing list.

882. Michael Rivero, posted on OKBOMB mailing list.

883. Edye Ann Smith, Individually and on Behalf of Her Minor Children, Chase Smith, Deceased, and Colton Smith, Deceased, Plaintiffs, vs. Timothy James McVeigh, Michael Brescia, Michael Fortier and Andreas Carl Strassmeir and other unknown individuals, Case No. CJ-96-18.

Clockwise from top-left: "The Face of Terror." The *real* face of terror—unidentified ATF agent. McVeigh being led away like Lee Harvey Oswald without requested bulletproof vest. More faces of terror: Tim in school, and with young Jason Torres.

Clockwise from top: The Alfred P. Murrah Building. Khobar Towers, Saudia Arabia. A trailer packed with plastic explosives did less damage to a far smaller and weaker building. Notice the size of the crater compared to the one in Oklahoma (opposite page); Army Math Lab at the University of Wisconsin. A similar 2,000 pound ANFO bomb parked right up against the building only blew a small hole in the wall.

Clockwise from top: The Federal building quickly demolished and buried; photo of crater, showing it as approximately 16 feet. *Time* magazine's version, claiming it was 30 feet. The bomb scares, which authorities claimed were false. The Athenian restaurant, 150 feet north of the Murrah Building. Extreme level of damage possibly indicative of a fuel-air bomb or a backpack nuke.

Clockwise from top: Grandstanding Chief; inset: Baylee Almon and firefighter. Generalissimo Janet Reno. FBI Director Louis Freeh.

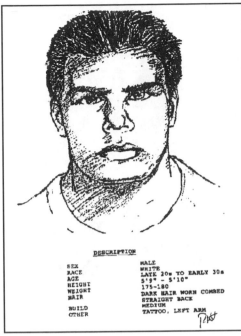

DESCRIPTION

SEX	MALE
RACE	WHITE
AGE	LATE 20s TO EARLY 30s
HEIGHT	5'9" – 5'10"
WEIGHT	175–180
HAIR	DARK HAIR WORN COMBED STRAIGHT BACK
BUILD	MEDIUM
OTHER	TATTOO, LEFT ARM

The infamous John Doe 2.

John Doe 3, seen by David Snider in the second Ryder truck. Dennis Mahon in disguise?

Sketch of Peter Ward—the man who actually rented the Ryder truck?

Hussain al-Hussaini, seen in the brown pick-up speeding away from the scene of the bombing.

The mysterious Omar: possible Middle Eastern cell leader.

Andreas "Andy the German" Strassmeir, government agent provocateur?

Michael Brescia: the actual John Doe 2?

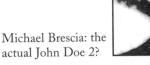

458

ROGUES GALLERY 2

ATF Director John Magaw.

OKC FBI SAC Bob Ricks, who presided over the FBI massacre at Waco.

Judge Richard Matsch, who refused to allow evidence of a broader conspiracy.

Oklahoma Governor Frank Keating, another Bush boy.

OCPD Chief Sam Gonzales.

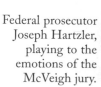

Federal prosecutor Joseph Hartzler, playing to the emotions of the McVeigh jury.

Michael Fortier. The prosecution worked on him for months to get his story straight.

Terry Nichols with son Josh and baby deer.

Edye Smith, husband and father-in-law Glenn Wilburn. "Where was the ATF?" asked Smith, who lost two children. Wilburn was surveilled and bugged by the FBI for publicly expressing his concerns. He died of cancer soon afterwards.

Jennifer McVeigh

Officer Terrance Yeakey. He spoke to the wrong people about his concerns, and paid the ultimate price. Yeakey, shown with ex-wife Tonia and daughter.

ATF agents take aim.

Not all militia members fit the typical stereotype.

Steve Stockman, who discovered plan, for nationwide raid against militia groups one month before bombing.

ALL IN FAVOR OF "GUN CONTROL" RAISE YOUR RIGHT HAND

Political prisoners and Death Camps can't exist without "Gun Control". Some Americans still feel "Gun Control" is a good idea. To prevent a "Schindler's List" in America, we must destroy "Gun Control"!!

Jews for the Preservation of Firearms

FALSE PATRIOTS

THE THREAT OF ANTIGOVERNMENT EXTREMISTS

SPLC's propaganda.

George Bush: a New World Order of death.

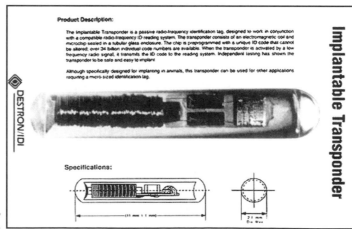

Implantable Transponder

Product Description:

The Implantable Transponder is a passive radio-frequency identification tag, designed to work in conjunction with a compatible radio-frequency ID reading system. The transponder consists of an electromagnetic coil and microchip sealed in a tubular glass enclosure. The chip is preprogrammed with a unique ID code that cannot be altered; over 34 billion individual code numbers are available. When the transponder is activated by a low frequency radio signal, it transmits the ID code to the reading system. Independent testing has shown the transponder to be safe and easy to implant.

Although specifically designed for implanting in animals, this transponder can be used for other applications requiring a micro-sized identification tag.

DESTRON/IDI

Specifications:

Bio-chip, the real McCoy.

Bomb Damage Analysis Of
Alfred P. Murrah Federal Building
Oklahoma City, Oklahoma

Benton K. Partin
Brigadier Gen. USAF (Ret.)

On April 19, 1995, the Alfred P. Murrah Federal Building, Oklahoma City, Oklahoma was bombed, causing extensive damage to the structure, the loss of 168 innocent lives, the victimization of the families of those who lost loved ones, hundreds of non-fatal injuries, and substantial property damage in the vicinity.

The media and the Executive branch reported that the sole source of the devastation was a single truck bomb consisting of 4,800 pounds of ammonium nitrate, transported to the location in a Ryder Truck and parked in front of the building. It is impossible that the destruction to the building could have resulted from such a bomb alone.

To cause the damage pattern that occurred to the Murrah building, there would have to have been demolition charges at several supporting column bases, at locations not accessible from the street, to supplement the truck bomb damage. Indeed, a careful examination of photographs showing the collapsed column bases reveals a failure mode produced by demolition charges and not by a blast from the truck bomb.

To understand what caused the damage to the Murrah Building, one needs to understand some basics about the use and nature of explosives.

First, blast through air is a very inefficient energy coupling mechanism against heavily reinforced concrete beams and columns.

Second, blast damage potential initially falls off more rapidly than an inverse function of the distance cubed. That is why in conventional weapons development, one seeks accuracy over yield for hard targets. That is also why in the World Trade Center bombing (where the only source of blast damage was a truck bomb) the column in the middle of the bombed-out cavity was relatively untouched, although reinforced concrete floors were completely stripped away for several floors above and below the point of the bomb's detonation (see *Time Magazine*, 3-8-93, page 35).

By contrast, heavily reinforced concrete structures can be destroyed effectively through detonation of explosives in contact with the reinforced concrete beams and

Partin's bomb damage analysis continues to page 485.

columns. For example, the entire building remains in Oklahoma City were collapsed with 100-plus relatively small charges inserted into drilled holes in the columns. The total weight of all charges was on the order of 200 pounds.

The detonation wave pressure (1,000,000 to 1,500,000 pounds per square inch) from a high detonation velocity contact explosive sweeps into the column as a wave of compressive deformation. Since the pressure in the wave of deformation far exceeds the yield strength of the concrete (about 3,500 pounds per square inch) by a factor of approximately 300, the concrete is turned into granular sand and dust until the wave dissipates to below the yield strength of the concrete. This leaves a relatively smooth but granular surface, with protruding, bare reinforcement rods —a distinctive signature of damage by contact explosives. The effect of the contact explosive on the reinforcement rods themselves can only be seen under microscopic metallurgical examination. (The rods are inertially confined during the explosion and survive basically in tact because of their much higher yield strength and plasticity.)

When a reinforced concrete structure is damaged through air shock coupling and the pressure is below the compressive yield strength of the concrete, the failure mode is generally compressive structural fracture on one side and tensile fracture on the other — both characterized by cracks and rough fracture surfaces. Such a surface texture is very different from the relatively smooth granular surface resulting from contact explosives.

Analysis of Graphic Evidence

Tab 2 is a cross section view of the building looking from the west. The very large header or cross beam is shown at the north edge of the third floor. A large but smaller header is seen at the recessed north edge of the second floor with a brace beam extending out to the large columns in Row A. The front of the whole building is glass.

Tab 3 shows the architectural layout of the first floor of the Murrah Building and the location of the truck bomb with superimposed circles of roughly equal levels of damage potential. The explosive force drops rapidly (initially proportional to one over the distance cubed) as the shock front travels farther and farther away from the truck bomb. After the release wave, the shock front will propagate proportional to one over the distance squared.

The maximum possible yield from 4800 pounds of ammonium nitrate would be obtained if it were in a compressed sphere and detonated from the center. That would produce a 4.4 foot diameter sphere of detonation products at about 500,000 pounds per square inch. By the time the blast wave hits the closest column, the pressure would have fallen off to about 375 pounds per square inch. That would be far below the 3500 pound compressive yield strength of the concrete. Any column or beam failure from the truck bomb would therefore have been from blast wave structural loading and not from any wave of deformation in the concrete.

The basic building structure consists of three rows of columns (35 feet apart) with eleven columns in each row (20 feet apart). The four corner columns have an external clamshell-like structure for air ducts, etc. If we label the column rows A, B, and C from front to back, and number the columns 1 through 11 from left to right, then columns A_2, A_3, A_4, A_5, A_6, A_7, A_8, and B_3 collapsed, essentially vertically. Tab 2 shows a very large reinforced concrete header at the floor level of the third floor of column row A. Much larger columns extend from the header down for the odd-numbered columns, i.e., A_3, A_5, A_7, and A_9. The even- and odd-numbered columns extended from the top of the building down to the header. The foundation of the building is a heavy, reinforced concrete slab with no sub-levels.

From the potential damage contours on Tab 3, and assuming the single truck bomb, the pressure and impulse for collapsed columns B_4, B_5 and A_7 are all in the 25 to 35 pounds per square inch region. However, the much smaller and closer columns, B_4 and B_5, are still standing, while the much larger column A_7 is down. Column B_3 is down with 42 percent less pressure and impulse than columns B_4. These facts are sufficient reason to know that columns B_3 and A_7 had demolition charges on them. Moreover, there is not sufficient blast impulse at that range to collapse any of the three. In fact, columns B_2, B_4 and B_5 all have the sheet rock and furring strip finish still intact on the second and third floors except where damaged by falling debris.

The large header across the front of the building at the third floor of Row A was not blown back into the building as one may expect from such a large bomb. The header came straight down but rolled backward 90 degrees because the columns above the header rested off center toward the back.

Analysis of Photographic Evidence

A careful examination of photos showing the "A" row columns and the large header from the third floor reveals absolutely no air blast shock wave fracture, which is consistent with the pressure fall-off with distance from the truck bomb. The cleaned-up building structure (Tab 4) shows that the failure line across the roof goes all the way to the

3

ground except around columns B4 and B5 at the second and third floor levels. Reinforcement rods stripped out of beams and floors extend straight down on all floors. Columns A3, A5, A7, and B3 collapsed straight down as the apparent result of demolition charges at the column juncture with the third floor for column B3 and with the third floor level header for columns A3, A5, and A7. The even numbered columns (A2, A4, A6, and A8) in Row A collapsed straight down because they were supported at the third floor by the header, which necessarily failed with the demolition of its conjunctions with columns A3, A5, and A7. When columns A2 through A8 collapsed straight down, the roof and floor fracture lines at all floors acted as an instant hinge line, which would have given all floors collapsing down a slight tug toward column row B. Because of the collapse of column B3, the floors were cropped closer to the north side of columns B4, B5, which resulted in damage by falling debris to sheet rock on columns B4 and B5 at the third floor level.

The so-called "pit" area behind columns B4 and B5 was caused either by the blast from the truck bomb pushing out the ceilings of the first and second floors or from the demolition charge on column B3. From the third floor it would look like a "pit" into which much debris fell. The blast pressure in this area would have been sufficient to exceed the ultimate yield design strength of the floor. There were large areas at this pressure being held only by the floor-thick, reinforced concrete around the 20-inch reinforced concrete columns in the B row. The floor of the first floor could not be blown downward, because it was a heavy concrete slab on compacted earth. The ceilings of the first and second floors nearer the truck between the A and B column rows could also have been blown upward initially.

Although the truck bomb had insufficient power to destroy columns, the bomb was clearly responsible for ripping out some floors at the second and third floor levels.

Photographic Evidence of Demolition Charges

Turning next to the demolition charges in the building, refer to the picture at Tab 5. Here you see column A9 with no spalling as one would expect with the blast pressures involved and the decorative indents are unmarred. Note also the grooves at the top of the column and across the header. When the demolition charge on column A7 went off, the charge instantly left a 40 foot cantilevered header supporting column A8. Cascading columns and beams from above probably snapped off the end with a clear structural fracture, including rugged cracks and rough surfaces. There is a large unseen beam extending from behind the column, between the decorative groves, back to the first floor header. This beam adds considerable rigidity to the lower odd-numbered columns in Row A.

Turning next to Tab 6, the stub of column B3 has been cleared, showing the bare reinforcement rods at the third floor level. The large header from the third floor level has fallen almost straight down with what appears to be demolition charge damage clearly evident to the right of column A3. The exposed reinforcement rods are clearly seen at the header end to the right of column A3. It appears that the demolition charge pulverized the header and columns out to about two feet from the juncture. Column A3 is standing there with the clean reinforcement rods clearly extended. Also, the architectural decorative band is clearly evident without blemish (indicating no blast damage in excess of yield strength). In this picture, the failure of the header at column A5 is still covered with rubble, and is not visible. However, the discontinuity in the slope of the header on either side of the column A5 location clearly shows that it failed in the region of its juncture with column A5.

Tab 7 shows the localized damage to the header at the position of column A5, the closest column to the truck bomb crater. The end of the beam on which the men are standing shows evidence of a demolition charge at its juncture with column A5. Several feet of the beam juncture appear to have been pulverized away by a demolition charge and the ends jammed together in the collapse. The blast pressure from the truck bomb would have been in the 400 pounds per square inch region — a factor of 10 below the yield strength of concrete.

Tab 8 shows the localized demolition damage at the juncture of column A7 and the header. The same telltale demolition charge evidence is clear. The straight edge of the decorative grove at the juncture can be seen on both the column and the header.

In my discussions with the building architect, who was on the scene as an advisor throughout much of the cleanup, he told me that the residual building was structurally sound and that the Murrah Building could have been rebuilt. This is totally consistent with the collapse of columns with demolition charges because the inflicted structural damage is more localized.

Discussions above have been limited to the reinforced concrete structure of the Murrah Building. Reinforced concrete columns are hard targets for high-explosive bombs. Structures that have large areas for blast loading and low mass can be destroyed at considerable range from a large blast. That is why glass, plaster, and light structures were destroyed at considerable distance from the Murrah Building, but not reinforced concrete columns. Five pounds of blast pressure will flatten most frame houses.

Seismograph Readings

Much has been said about seismograph readings. Was there more than one explosion? Most people I talked to in Oklahoma City heard two explosions relatively close together. Some close by said they didn't even hear an explosion. That is not unreasonable, when you consider that getting walloped by an intense shock wave is about like being hit across the ear by a 2" x 4". One would expect the demolition charges to have had an electrical or primacord interconnect. If so, it would be difficult to separate them on a seismograph. If delays were used, they would be discrete. If a sensitivity switch was used inside the building, the explosions would have been distinct. Bomb initiations could have been easily designed to go off either simultaneously or with separation.

Conclusion

The Murrah Federal Building was not destroyed by one sole truck bomb. The major factor in its destruction appears to have been detonation of explosives carefully placed at four critical junctures on supporting columns within the building.

The only possible reinforced concrete structural failure solely attributable to the truck bomb was the stripping out of the ceilings of the first and second floors in the "pit" area behind columns B4 and B5. Even this may have been caused by a demolition charge at column B3.

It is truly unfortunate that a separate and independent bomb damage assessment was not made during the cleanup — before the building was demolished on May 23 and hundreds of truck loads of debris were hauled away, smashed down, and covered with dirt behind a security fence.

When the picture at Tab 4 was made, all evidence of demolition charges had been removed from the building site (i.e., the stubs of columns B3, A3, A5, A7 and the demolished junctures at the header with columns A3, A5 and A7.

All ambiguity with respect to the use of supplementing demolition charges and the type of truck used could be quickly resolved if the FBI were required to release the surveillance camera coverage of this terribly tragic event.

BENTON K. PARTIN

Biographical Notes

Thirty one years active duty in the Air Force. Progressively responsible
executive, scientific and technical assignments directing organizations
engaged in research, development, testing, analysis, requirements generation
and acquisition management of weapons systems. Assignments from laboratory
to the Office of the Secretary of Defense.

Personal contributions made in the fields of research and development
management, weapon system concepts, guided weapons technology, target
acquisition aids, focused energy weapons, operations research and joint
service harmonization of requirements. Retired as a Brigadier General.

White House appointed Special Assistant to the Administrator, Federal
Aviation Administration. Personally designated to prepare the White Paper on
the Federal Aviation Administration for the 1989 Presidential Transition
Team. This included development of policy initiatives on FAA/USAF joint use
of the Global Positioning System (GPS), operational life for commercial
aircraft, anti-terrorism, airport and airway capacity, requirements in the
FAA acquisition process and FAA leadership and management development.

Military Command Pilot and Command Missleman with 4000 hours (37 combat.)

Education: B.S. Chemical Engineering; M.S. Aeronautical Engineering; Ph.D.
Candidate, Operations Research & Statistics (Academics Completed.)

Publications/TV

    Sino-Soviet Conflict, Competition and Cooperation:
    Risks in Force Structure Planning.
    A Reduced Upper Limit for Sequential Test Truncation Error.
    Frequent TV Talk Shows on the Voice of Freedom.

Honors: Distinguished Service Medal, Legion of Merit thrice, Distinguished
Graduate - Air War College

Community Affairs:

    Chairman, United States Defense Committee
    Member of the Board, In Touch Missions International
    Member of the Board, Front Line Fellowship
    Founding Chairman of the School Board, Engleside Christian School
    Washington Representative for the Association of Christian Schools
    International (1981-1983)
    Chairman Fairfax County Republican Party (1982-1986)

Lifelong Professional Challenge: Continuing studies and analyses to
anticipate and forecast the future course of world
military/political/economic transforming processes.

Tab 1

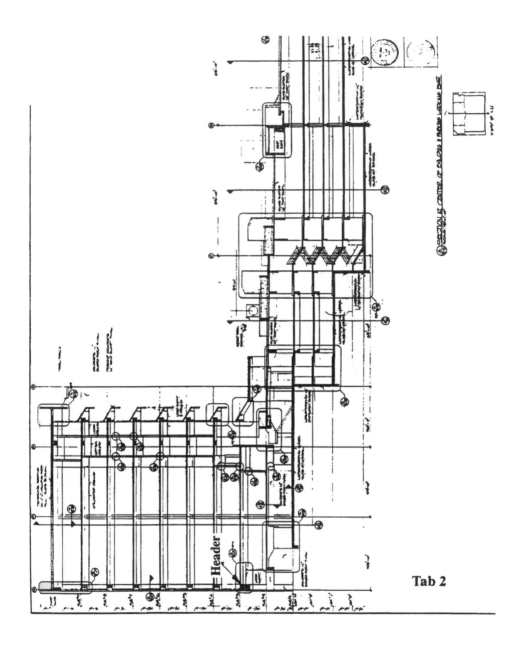

Header

Tab 2

469

A P MURRAH BUILDING

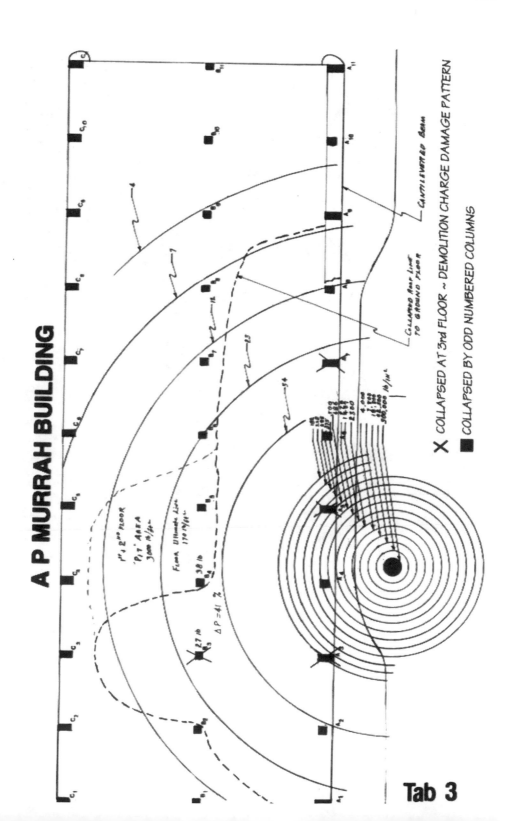

X COLLAPSED AT 3rd FLOOR ~ DEMOLITION CHARGE DAMAGE PATTERN

■ COLLAPSED BY ODD NUMBERED COLUMNS

Tab 3

Fracture at
Column A1 & Header

Sheet Rock Surface

3rd Floor

The Pit

Tab 4

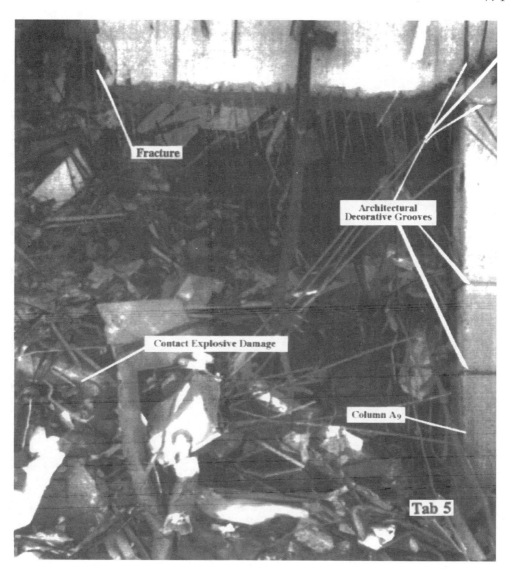

Fracture

Architectural
Decorative Grooves

Contact Explosive Damage

Column A9

Tab 5

Crater

Header at Column A$_5$ Juncture

Tab 7

Column A₇
3rd Floor Level End

Header at Column A₇

Tab 8

Rodger A. Raubach Ph.D

18 July 1995

Brigadier Gen. Benton K. Partin

Dear Gen. Partin;

Earlier today I received a copy of your report on the bombing in Oklahoma City, entitled "Bomb Damage Analysis of the Alfred P. Murrah Federal Building,Oklahoma City". This report was dated July 13,1995.

I read this report carefully and examined the exhibits appended to the text. Your observations and photographic analysis are meticulous in the extreme , and you are to be commended for your insights regarding the effects of blast vs. distance from the detonation.

The major points of the report which I believe need to be emphasized are: (1) the fact that rebar reinforcing rods were broken but appear to be embedded in concrete;(2) very little concrete appears to have been crushed by the blast. These observations alone are at extreme variance with the hypothesis of a single large truck bomb containing ANFO. For the large (4800 lb.) ammonium nitrate bomb to have caused the damage, there would be huge amounts of sand generated from the crushed concrete around the columns wherein the rebar was fractured.

I took the liberty of checking with the leading concrete supplier in my area in order to confirm the compressive yield figure that you used,that being 3500 psi. What I was told about concrete was very interesting. A 3500 psi figure is extremely low for structural concrete. A properly mixed and cured structure of the type dealt with in your report would probably have a yield strength of 5600 psi.

In conclusion,General,I find myself in awe of the technical achievement that your report represents. I can find no scientific flaws in either your observations or your conclusions. I am,therefore,in full agreement with the conclusion of strategically placed small explosive charges being responsible for the destruction of the building.

We can only hope and pray that a few good men and women in our Congress will heed your report and take action that results in the punishment of the real guilty parties responsible for this heinous crime against the American people,and that these same few good people are able to stem the abrogation of any more of our Constitutional rights.

Please keep up the good work that you are doing for your countrymen.It is an honor to be able to correspond with you on this matter and perhaps to be of some small service to our country,the Constitutional Republic,to which many of us have sworn to defend to the best of our abilities.

If I may be of any further assistance,please contact me at any time. Looking forward to your response,I remain

Very Truly Yours,

Rodger A. Raubach Ph.D.

Tab 9

476

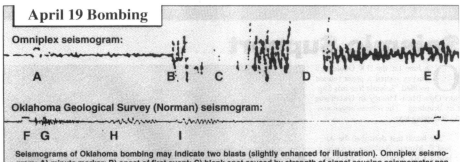

April 19 Bombing

Omniplex seismogram:

A   B   C   D   E

Oklahoma Geological Survey (Norman) seismogram:

F G   H   I   J

Seismograms of Oklahoma bombing may indicate two blasts (slightly enhanced for illustration). Omniplex seismogram: A) minute marker; B) onset of first event; C) blank spot caused by strength of signal causing seismometer pen to move too fast to register. C is composed of two five-second segments, thought to represent two explosions; D) airwave from events in C causes repeat of hyper pen action; E) minute marker. OGS seismogram: F) minute marker; G) traffic noise; H) onset of first event (explosion); I) onset of second event; J) minute marker.

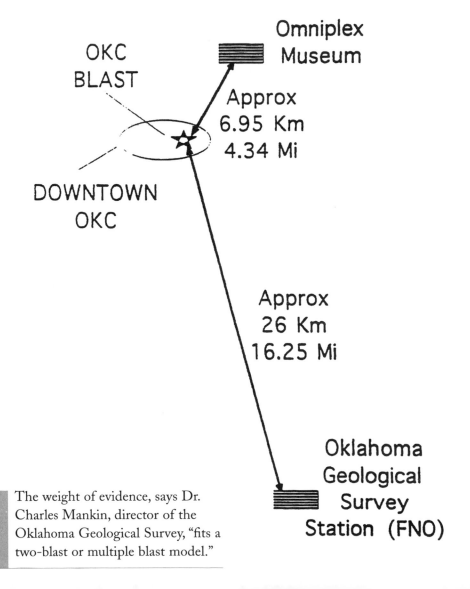

OKC BLAST

Omniplex Museum

Approx
6.95 Km
4.34 Mi

DOWNTOWN OKC

Approx
26 Km
16.25 Mi

Oklahoma Geological Survey Station (FNO)

The weight of evidence, says Dr. Charles Mankin, director of the Oklahoma Geological Survey, "fits a two-blast or multiple blast model."

OKLAHOMA HIGHWAY PATROL
Okla
RADIO DIVISION

Cpl
Call

RADIO LOG

DATE __4-19-95__ SHIFT __day__ OPERATOR_____ DISPATCHER_____ SHEET __1__

No.	TIME	FROM	TO	MESSAGE, DISPATCH, AS TRANSMITTED
001.	1027	NOTE		AT REQ OF #36, CONT ||ADE WITH THE TRAINING CENTER TO GET #366, 668, 61 AND #154 10-8 TO ASST WITH TRAFF CONTROL ON THE CROSSTOWN/
002.	1029			RONNIE THO|PSON ON RADIO
				RANDY ||OSS ON RADIO LOG
003.	1030	CO||CTR		ANOTHER BO||B FOUND ON THE S. SIDE OF THE BUILDING/
004.	1035	UNIT		TRIAG HAS BEEN ||OVED TO 5TH AND BROADWAY AT THIS TI||E/OK
005.	1037	368		OC FIRE DEPT CONFIR|IS THEY DID FIND A SECOND DEVICE IN THE BLDG/OK
006.	1040	12		CONT ALL TROOPERS AND HAVE THE| ||OVE ALL CIVILIAN PERSONNEL BACK 1 ||OR BLOCK/
007.	1045	H108		ALL ||EDICAL PERSONNEL ARE ||OVING TO 10THAAND HARVEY/RT
008	1049	CO||C|NT WILL BE ||OVING CP-1 TO 8TH AND HARVE|| VERY SHORTLY/OK		
009	I||1100		gb	tt
010	0|0|6|111|5	0KC		NEED A RESCUE UNIT AT NW th AND ROBIN$ON/ok
011	0|s125			WHERE IS THE TRAGE SET UP/THE INFOR||ATION WE HAVE IS 6TH AND HARVEY/OK
012	1-120	R1208		HAVE A ||ASSTRANS BUS AT 5HT AND DEWEY OFFIRING ASSISTANCE/OK TRIAGE IS SET UP AT 6TH AND HARVEY/OK
013	1125		NOTE	CO||AND POST ||OVED TO 8TH AND ||ARVEY IN THE PARKING LO|| OF SW||ELL/RT
014	1142	V30		THE FIRE DEPART||ENT ADVISED IT WOULD BE BEST TO SET UP TRIAGE HERE/OK
015	1142	HQ116		SET UP TRIAGE ON THE S SIDE OF THE FE||ERAL BUILDING
016	1155	hq65		have 10 TROOPERS AT THE SCENE THAT WE DON'T HAVE CHECKED I||/OK H106 ADVISED HE HAS THE|| CHECKED IN/OK
17	1155	HQ65		HAVE A STRONG GAS ODO|| AT THE Y||CA 5TH AND ROBINSON/AFFIR||ATIVE
18	1155	66		HAVE THE GAS CO||A|ANY WILL BE SHUTTING THAT DOWN ||O||ENTARILY/OK
19	1159	A837		||.E. WANTS FATALITIES LEFT THERE WHERE THEY ARE THEY WANT IT TREATED A| A CRI||E SCENE/OK
20	1203	HQ48	FIR	FIRE DPT NOTIFIED/OK
21	1209	OKC		HAVE P4210-21 CO|| CENTER/OK
22	1209		GB	SUBFLEET ASSIGN||ENTS/OK
23	1224		V780	NO SIGNALS/OK
24	1226	V30		WE WILL BE ||BLOCKING OFF ROBINSON BETWEEN NW 5TH AND NW 6TH FOR EVIDENCE/OK
25	1233		CC	||/THE FAX AT THE CO||AND POST IS NOW 10-8/OK
26	1235	A603		CAN YOU ADV WHERE TRIAGE IS SET UP/THERE IS A FIELD HOSP AT 5TH AND HARISON/OK
27	1247	I800		WILL BE BRINGING VICTI||S OUT THE BACKSIDE OF THE BLDG AT 4TH AND HARVEY
28	1248	S125		HAVE A GENE WHITSET WITH ABS SECURITY AT NW 6TH AND ROBINSON, WANTS TO KNOW WHEN HE CAN GET TO HIS BLDG TO GET SO||E EQUIP||ENT OUT/ADV HI|| TO CO||E TO THE CP AND CHECK WITH THE CO||AND PERSONNEL HERE/OK
29	1300		GB	TT
30	1304		PS	ADV HQ48 VIA PS AUTH CTP ||EADOWS TO GET ALL OHP PERSONNEL OUT OF THE BLDG AND REPORT TO THE OCFD AT THE NORTH END OF THE BLDG WHERE THE LADDERS ARE/HQ48 OK
31	1318	A603		WERE AT 6TH AND ROBINSON, 508 AND ||YSLEF, THE AIR FORCE IS HERE TO TAKE OVER THIS, WHERE DO WE NEED TO GO/STANDBY WILL CHECK
32	1319		A603	CO||E TO THE CP FOR REASSIGN||ENT/OK, ENRT
33	1322	CK137		ADV 48 I A|| AT THE SCENE, ADV WHERE HE WANT ||E/GO TO THE NORTH SIDE OF THE BLDG WHERE OCFD IS, WILL BE WHERE THE LADDERS ARE
34	1335	R1207		HAVE A 10-12 THAT NEEDS TO DELIVER SO||ETHING, 10-20 OF CP/ADV/OK
35	1349		GB	EVACUATE THE I|||EDIATE AREA, UNCONFIR||ED REPORT OF ANOTHER DEVICE LOCATED IN THE BLDG/GB
36	1400		GB	TT
37	1433	V30		AT 8TH AND WALKER THERE IS #441 AND #541, THEY NEED RAIN GEAR
38	1434	V30		7TH AND WALKER, THERE IS A CAPITOL PATROL UNIT, NO ONE ON ASSIGN||ENT

Oklahoma Highway Patrol Radio Log confirms concern of multiple bomb devices inside the Murrah Building on the morning of the explosion.

478

Byron G. Rogers Federal Building
Twelfth Floor, Drawer 3615
1961 Stout Street
Denver, Colorado 80294

(303) 844-2081

FAX 844-6725

September 14, 1994

Cary James Gagan

Re: Letter of Immunity

Dear Mr. Gagan:

This letter is to memorialize the agreement between you and the United States of America, by the undersigned Assistant United States Attorney. The terms of this agreement are as follows:

1. You have contacted the U.S. Marshals Service on today's date indicating that you have information concerning a conspiracy and/or attempt to destroy United States court facilities in Denver and possibly other cities.

2. The United States agrees that any statement and/or information that you provide relevant to this conspiracy/conspiracies or attempts will not be used against you in any criminal proceeding. Further, the United States agrees that no evidence derived from the information or statements provided by you will be used in any way against you.

3. In return for this grant of use/derivative use immunity, you agree to fully and completely cooperate with all federal law enforcement authorities in the District of Colorado regarding your knowledge of and participation in any crimes and/or related activities. All statements and any testimony you give pursuant to this agreement will be protected by use/derivative use immunity as stated in paragraph 2 above.

4. If you make or give any false statements or testimony at any time, this agreement becomes null and void. The decision as to whether a violation of this agreement has occurred remains solely in the discretionary judgment of the Office of the United States Attorney for the District of Colorado.

5. If this agreement is violated, any statement made or testimony given by you during the course of this investigation and agreement will no longer be protected by any kind of immunity and you may be prosecuted for any crime of which the United States has knowledge, including knowledge obtained by your own

statements and/or testimony. Additionally, the information you provide may also be used to impeach your testimony during and future court proceedings related to this investigation, should there be any.

If you agree to accept the terms of this agreement as set forth in the above paragraphs, you should acknowledge your acceptance by signing below. By signing this agreement you are not only accepting this agreement but are also stating that you have carefully read and fully understood this agreement and voluntarily accept all of its terms and provisions. By signing this document you further agree that no additional promises or conditions have been entered into by either party and only the specific terms of this document are the subject of this agreement.

Sincerely,

HENRY L. SOLANO
United States Attorney

By: JAMES R. ALLISON
Assistant United States Attorney

Date SEPT. 14, 1994

READ AND ACCEPTED:

9/14/94
Date

Letter of Immunity agreement for federal informant Cary Gagan.

LINDA ROWE, U.S. MARSHALL

APRIL 6, 1995

DEAR MS ROWE:

AFTER LEAVING DENVER FOR WHAT I THOUGHT WOULD BE FOR A LONG TIME, I RETURNED HERE LAST NIGHT BECAUSE I HAVE SPECIFIC INFORMATION THAT WITHIN TWO WEEKS A FEDERAL BUILDING (S) IS TO BE BOMBED IN THIS AREA OR NEARBY.

THE PREVIOUS REQUESTS I MADE FOR YOU TO CONTACT ME 27TH + 28TH OF APRIL '95 WERE IGNORED BY YOU, MR. ALLISON AND MY FRIENDS AT THE FBI.

I WOULD NOT IGNORE THIS SPECIFIC REQUEST FOR YOU PERSONALLY TO CONTACT ME IMMEDIATELY REGARDING A PLOT TO BLOW-UP A FEDERAL BLDG. IF THE INFORMATION IS FALSE REQUEST MR. ALLISON TO CHARGE ME ACCORDINGLY.

IF YOU AND/OR YOUR OFFICE DOES NOT CONTACT ME AS I SO REQUEST HEREIN, I WILL NEVER AGAIN CONTACT ANY LAW ENFORCEMENT AGENCY FEDERAL OR STATE, REGARDING THOSE MATTERS SET OUT IN THE LETTER OF IMMUNITY.

CALL 832-4091 (NOW)

Federal informant Cary Gagan warns U.S. Marshal Service of federal building explosion two weeks prior to the Murrah Building tragedy.

INFORMANT AGREEMENT

This confirms the agreement entered into between the Bureau of Alcohol, Tobacco and Firearms (ATF) and

Carol Elizabeth Howe .

1. ATF has asked me to assist in an official investigation. In furtherance of this investigation, I agree to (describe activity informant or cooperating witness/subject will be doing for ATF).

   undercover contacts, undercover telephone, purchase of firearms and/or explosives

2. ATF has assigned Special Agent _Angela Finley_ to serve as my supervisor in this investigation. It is imperative that I maintain contact with S/A _Finley_ and advise him/her of my activities and abide by his/her instructions.

3. I will not participate in any unlawful activities except insofar as ATF determines that such participation is necessary to this investigation and ATF expressly authorizes such acts in advance. I understand that any violation of the law, not expressly authorized by ATF, may result in my prosecution.

4. Under no circumstances will I participate, or be permitted to participate, in acts of violence. If I am asked to participate in any act of violence, or learn of such plans, I will attempt to discourage those plans or acts and will promptly notify ATF.

5. I will not initiate any plans to commit criminal acts. Further, I understand that I will not induce any individual to commit a crime that he or she has no predisposition to commit.

6. I will not attempt to be present during conversations between individuals under criminal indictment and their attorney. If I am inadvertently present and learn of defense plans or strategy, I am not permitted to report such conversations without prior approval from the United States Attorney's Office.

DEFENDANT'S EXHIBIT

Carol Howe's informant agreement signed prior to the Oklahoma City bombing, page 1.

am not ⋅ law enforcement officer, an employee, or agent oₓ ATF, and that I will not ₕold myself out to be such.

8. I understand that information that I provide to ATF may be used in a criminal proceeding. All legal means available will be used to maintain the confidentiality of my identity but I may be required to testify before a grand jury and at any subsequent hearing and trial. I understand that I have an obligation to provide truthful information and testimony, and that any deliberate false statement or testimony will subject me to criminal prosecution.

9. If, as a result of being a cooperating witness, it is determined by ATF that my life (or that of any member of my immediate family) may be in danger, ATF will, with my permission, apply to the Department of Justice to admit me to the Witness Protection Program. I understand that the final decision is made solely by, and at the discretion of the Department of Justice, and not ATF.

10. I will in no way reveal the confidential and sensitive nature of this investigation. Further, I will not undertake any publication or dissemination of any information or material that results from this investigation without the prior express authorization of ATF.

11. ATF will reimburse me for expenses incurred which are deemed by ATF to be reasonable and in furtherance of this investigation.

12. I understand that any monetary or other type of rewards given to me by ATF, either for services rendered or information provided, must be declared as other income on any income tax return I may be required to file.

Carol E. Howe 8/25/94
signature/date

Angela Finley 8/25/94
Special agent   witness/date

Carol Howe's informant agreement signed prior to the Oklahoma City bombing, page 2.

INFORMANT AGREEMENT

This confirms the agreement entered into between the Bureau of Alcohol, Tobacco and Firearms (ATF) and

Carol Elizabeth Howe   .

1. ATF has asked me to assist in an official investigation. In furtherance of this investigation, I agree to (describe activity informant or cooperating witness/subject will be doing for ATF).

    undercover contacts, undercover purchases

2. ATF has assigned Special Agent _Angela Finley_ to serve as my supervisor in this investigation. It is imperative that I maintain contact with S/A _Angela Finley_ and advise him/her of my activities and abide by his/her instructions.

3. I will not participate in any unlawful activities except insofar as ATF determines that such participation is necessary to this investigation and ATF expressly authorizes such acts in advance. I understand that any violation of the law, not expressly authorized by ATF, may result in my prosecution.

4. Under no circumstances will I participate, or be permitted to participate, in acts of violence. If I am asked to participate in any act of violence, or learn of such plans, I will attempt to discourage those plans or acts and will promptly notify ATF.

5. I will not initiate any plans to commit criminal acts. Further, I understand that I will not induce any individual to commit a crime that he or she has no predisposition to commit.

6. I will not attempt to be present during conversations between individuals under criminal indictment and their attorney. If I am inadvertently present and learn of defense plans or strategy, I am not permitted to report such conversations without prior approval from the United States Attorney's Office.

DEFENDANT'S
EXHIBIT

Carol Howe's informant agreement signed
after the Oklahoma City bombing, page 1.

7.   While I will be working closely with ATF for purposes of this investigation, I understand that I am not a law enforcement officer, an employee, or agent of ATF, and that I will not hold myself out to be such.

8.   I understand that information that I provide to ATF may be used in a criminal proceeding. All legal means available will be used to maintain the confidentiality of my identity but I may be required to testify before a grand jury and at any subsequent hearing and trial. I understand that I have an obligation to provide truthful information and testimony, and that any deliberate false statement or testimony will subject me to criminal prosecution.

9.   If, as a result of being a cooperating witness, it is determined by ATF that my life (or that of any member of my immediate family) may be in danger, ATF will, with my permission, apply to the Department of Justice to admit me to the Witness Protection Program. I understand that the final decision is made solely by, and at the discretion of the Department of Justice, and not ATF.

10. I will in no way reveal the confidential and sensitive nature of this investigation. Further, I will not undertake any publication or dissemination of any information or material that results from this investigation without the prior express authorization of ATF.

11. ATF will reimburse me for expenses incurred which are deemed by ATF to be reasonable and in furtherance of this investigation.

12. I understand that any monetary or other type of rewards given to me by ATF, either for services rendered or information provided, must be declared as other income on any income tax return I may be required to file.

Carol E. Howe 5/18/95
signature/date

Angela Finley
special agent

witness/date

Carol Howe's informant agreement signed *after* the Oklahoma City bombing, page 2.

DEPARTMENT OF THE TREASURY - BUREAU ALCOHOL TOBACCO AND FIREARMS

REPORT OF INVESTIGATION (Law Enforcement)

		1. LOCATIONS	Page 1 of
		ROUTINE	
		X SENSITIVE ☐ SIGNIFICANT	5 pages

2. TO:
Special Agent in Charge
Dallas Field Division

3. MONITORED INVESTIGATION INFORMATION (Number and Branch)
CIP: DALLAS FY-95
FIREARMS VIOLATIONS
REPORT 004

4. TITLE OF INVESTIGATION
White Aryan Resistance, W.A.R.

5. INVESTIGATION No. (Include Suspect No.)
53270-94-0124-B

6. TYPE OF REPORT (Check applicable boxes)

	PRELIMINARY		COLLATERAL (Request)
X	STATUS		COLLATERAL (Reply)
	FINAL		INTELLIGENCE
	SUPPLEMENTAL		REFERRAL (Internal)

7. BUREAU PROGRAM

	TITLE I	
X	TITLE II	FIREARMS
	TITLE VII	
X	TITLE II	EXPLOSIVES
	TITLE XI	
	TOBACCO	
	ALCOHOL	

8. PROJECT(S)

	TARGETED OFFENDER
X	TERRORIST/EXTREMIST
	OCD
	ITAR
	SHAR
	OMO
	OTHER (Specify)

9. DETAILS:

This is a 30 day status report in the investigation of the White Aryan Resistance and the violation of federal firearms and conspiracy laws in various counties in the Northern Judicial District of Oklahoma.

On October 27, 1994 CI-183 met with Mahon to discuss an upcoming trip to Elohim City.

On October 28, 1994 this field office received a fax from Mahon. The fax was generic and no action was taken by this agent.

On October 31, this agent met with CI-183 and received two cassette tapes.

On November 2, this agent and TOO Pat McKinley rewired CI-183's residence for better video and audio.

On November 3, CI-183 traveled to Elohim City with Mahon. When they arrived at EC, they were met at the gate with six firearms pointed at them due to the fact that they did not initially recognize their vehicle. All six men were dressed in full camouflage.

During this visit, Mahon discussed Syntex and said that it costs $100.00 per pound. He said he knows where to get it and that there's a lot of it around.

Mahon wants to set a pipe bomb off at the door of a Mexican owned video store in Tulsa.

Mahon and Andy discussed shooting M-1's and they agreed how fun they were

10. SUBMITTED BY (Name) Angela Finley	**11. TITLE AND OFFICE** S/A, Tulsa, Oklahoma	**12. DATE** 11/29/94
13. REVIEWED BY (Name) David E. Roberts	**14. TITLE AND OFFICE** RAC, Tulsa, Oklahoma	**15. DATE** 11 30 94
16. APPROVED BY (Name) Lester D. Martz	**17. TITLE AND OFFICE** Special Agent in Charge	**18. DATE** / /

ATF EF 3170.1 (5-90)

AFT report regarding Carol Howe's information on Dennis Mahon and Andreas Strassmeir's interest in explosives to destroy the U.S. government, page 1.

DEPARTMENT OF THE TREASURY
BUREAU OF ALCOHOL, TOBACCO AND FIREARMS

REPORT OF INVESTIGATION - CONTINUATION SHEET
(Law Enforcement)

PAGE 2
OF 5 PAGES

TITLE OF INVESTIGATION	INVESTIGATION NO.
White Aryan Resistance, W.A.R.	53270-94-0124-B

DETAILS (Continued)

to shoot.

██████ took CI-183 to his trailer, now set up on the property, and ██████ It is suspected that he did the ████████ drilling etc., at his residence in Tulsa. It was a ████████████ ██████████ and CI-183 hiked about half a mile from the homes at EC. ████ placed the grenade under a bucket he had with him and secured the bucket with a large rock. Mahon stated that this would be a good shrapnel test. The ████████████ and CI-183 retrieved one piece of shrapnel and the bolt from the grenade itself. They were later given to this agent.

Mahon and Andy also discussed using pressure sensitive pads under the dirt road to sound an alarm. Andy said they already have an alarm system.

On November 4, Mahon gave CI-183 the name of a man in Lawton, Oklahoma who was also involved with W.A.R. and allegedly provided funding for Tom Metzger's trip to Oklahoma. The man from Lawton is Peter Lipron, a South African neurosurgeon. CI-183 was told to contact him and arrange a meeting between Lipron and Metzger.

On November 6, 1994 CI-183 met with Tom Metzger, the national leader of W.A.R., for approximately two hours. This meeting was video taped. Metzger and CI-183 discussed the White Aryan Resistance in detail. Metzger had also visited Mahon, Lipron and the people at Elohim City. This agent later retrieved the video tape.

On November 11, CI-183 received a call from Rachael Patterson at EC. Patterson offered to take care of CI-183 for a week while he/she was recovering from surgery. Patterson stated that all the people at Friday's service prayed for CI-183.

On November 12, Mahon went to CI-183's residence to further promote doing an action at the Mexican owned video store in Tulsa.

From November 14 to November 19, CI-183 stayed at Elohim City in Rachael Patterson's home. The following information was retrieved:

CI-183 has become close to the head of security, Andy LNU, and has received various information. Andy described a proper combat load as being 200 to 280 rounds per person, usually worn on a chest pouch. The women usually carry 180 to 200 rounds in the same way. During "patrol" the amount is halved. Andy stated that he deals with a Class III dealer in Ft. Smith, Arkansas and would give CI-183 the address at some point. All the men who are 17 and-older always wear weapons either handguns holstered at the hip, rifles strapped across the shoulder or they may wear both. Most of the rifles are Mini-14's, AR-15's and SKS. It is not known at this time if any of these firearms are full auto. Andy is still refusing to let CI-183 fire any of the weapons owned by the members. Andy stated that he

AFT report regarding Carol Howe's information on Dennis Mahon and Andreas Strassmeir's interest in explosives to destroy the U.S. government, page 2.

DEPARTMENT OF THE TREASURY
BUREAU OF ALCOHOL, TOBACCO AND FIREARMS

REPORT OF INVESTIGATION - CONTINUATION SHEET
(Law Enforcement)

PAGE 3
OF 5 PAGES

TITLE OF INVESTIGATION	INVESTIGATION NO.
White Aryan Resistance, W.A.R.	53270-94-0124-B

DETAILS *(Continued)*

could convert an SKS to full auto using a piece from a food can. Andy leads the young adults in guerrilla warfare and tactical maneuvers training on Sunday afternoons. This training is done discreetly and CI-183 is excluded from participating. Andy said that he spends 96% of his money on weapons and military supplies. He helps to outfit others with firearms and equipment.

The security uniforms are a dark blue t-shirt with "SECURITY OFFICER" in yellow on the back and a shield or badge on the left breast. They also wear black jeans or fatigues and combat boots.

Andy stated that he was involved with CSA, the Covenant, Sword and Arm of the Lord. He was born in 1959 and served in the West German military starting in 1979. He was an infantry officer. His plans are to forcibly act to destroy the U.S. Government with direct actions and operations such as assassinations, bombings and mass shootings. He believes the biggest enemy to be the United States Government (ZOG).

Andy stated that when someone comes to EC and does not work out, fit in or is found to be a snitch, he and his security team have the capability of making their lives hell on the outside. They will beat people, sabotage them financially, ruin their reputation or do whatever they can unless they get the word from Millar to cease action.

Andy stated that he is in charge of all applicant background checks and has connections all over the world. He would not check 183 due to the fact that he/she had already been screened by Mahon.

Most of the weapons are stored at Andy's house. There are approximately 25-30 ammo cans full of ammo and grenade casings on shelves. It is not known the type of ammunition or if the grenades are destructive devices.

Every Saturday is the "Sabbath" and the people have worship for approximately four hours. During this time, Andy walks in and out of the church building searching for people who have left the meeting then he brings them back to the meeting.

There is a curfew every night at 9:00p.m. for all the people in school and 10:00p.m. for everyone else. The curfew is enforced and people must be in their homes by this time. This is the time that Andy closes and locks the gates. Around 12:00a.m. he and the other security officers patrol the perimeter.

People arise each day, except Saturday around 4:00a.m.. Men begin working around 6:00a.m. and children start school at 5:45a.m.. School ends at 4:30p.m.. Everyday the people have a meeting and worship at 11:30am and it lasts from one hour and a half to two hours. Most people attend the meeting, even if they work away from EC.

AFT report regarding Carol Howe's information on Dennis Mahon and Andreas Strassmeir's interest in explosives to destroy the U.S. government, page 3.

RCS ATF R 3270.1

DEPARTMENT OF THE TREASURY- BUREAU ALCOHOL, TOBACCO AND FIREARMS	1. [...]IGATION IS	Page 1 of
REPORT OF INVESTIGATION (Law Enforcement)	☐ ROUTINE ☒ SENSITIVE ☐ SIGNIFICANT	__2__ pages

2. TO: Special Agent in Charge Dallas Field Division	3. MONITORED INVESTIGATION INFORMATION(*Number and Branch*) CIP: DALLAS FY-95 FIREARMS VIOLATIONS REPORT 007

4. TITLE OF INVESTIGATION White Aryan Resistance, W.A.R.	5. INVESTIGATION No. (*Include Suspect No.*) 53270-94-0124-B

6. TYPE OF REPORT(*Check applicable boxes*)

				7. BUREAU PROGRAM		8. PROJECT(S)	
	PRELIMINARY		COLLATERAL *(Request)*.	X	TITLE I		TARGETED OFFENDER
				X	TITLE II	FIREARMS	X TERRORIST/EXTREMIST
			COLLATERAL *(Reply)*		TITLE VII		OCD
X	STATUS			X	TITLE II	EXPLOSIVES	ITAR
	FINAL		INTELLIGENCE		TITLE XI		SEAR
					TOBACCO		OMO
	SUPPLEMENTAL		REFERRAL *(Internal)*		ALCOHOL		OTHER *(Spec)*

9. DETAILS:

This is a 30 day status report in the investigation of the White Aryan Resistance and the violations of federal firearm, explosive and conspiracy laws in both the Northern and Eastern Judicial Districts of Oklahoma

On April 20, 1995 this agent was contacted by CI-53270-183 in regard to the bombing in Oklahoma City, Oklahoma. CI-183 stated that he/she believed suspect #2 resembled one of the residents of Elohim City, Tony Ward.

On April 21, 1995 this agent, along with Special Agent John Risenhoover, traveled to Tulsa to pick up CI-183 and transport him/her to Oklahoma City. CI-183 was debriefed by Special Agents from ATF and FBI. A lead sheet was then completed. It was then determined that CI-183 would be sent to Elohim City to obtain any intelligence relating to the bombing.

On April 29, 1995 CI-183 met with area W.A.R. leader, Dennis Mahon, and obtained several video tapes regarding the movement. CI-183 stated that they discussed alibi's for April 19, 1995 and the components of the explosive. CI-183 stated that Mahon mentioned the name of a man familiar in explosives who lives in Illinois. Mahon used the name, Pierson, however, he was not sure. CI-183 stated that Mahon could have been referring to Paulson because he cannot remember people's names.

On May 1, 1995 CI-183 traveled to Elohim City and stayed for three days.

On May 3, 1995 this agent met with CI-183 and debriefed him/her. This agent then took CI-183 to Oklahoma City to meet with ATF and FBI agents for further debriefing. CI-183 stated that while he/she was inside, a news crew was also there doing a story and that he/she was asked to stay out of

10. SUBMITTED BY (*Name*) Angela Finley	11. TITLE AND OFFICE S/A Tulsa, Oklahoma	12. DATE 05/22/9
13. REVIEWED BY (*Name*) David E. Roberts	14. TITLE AND OFFICE RAC Tulsa, Oklahoma	15. DATE 5 B1 K
16. APPROVED BY (*Name*) Lester D. Martz	17. TITLE AND OFFICE Special Agent in Charge	18. DATE / /

ATF EF 3270.2 (5-90)

489

DEPARTMENT OF THE TREASURY
BUREAU OF ALCOHOL, TOBACCO AND FIREARMS

REPORT OF INVESTIGATION - CONTINUATION SHEET
(Law Enforcement)

PAGE **2**
OF **2** PAGES

TITLE OF INVESTIGATION	INVESTIGATION NO.
White Aryan Resistance, W.A.R.	53270-94-0124-B

DETAILS (Continued)

sight. CI-183 was excluded from the daily worship meetings due to the media attention. CI-183 did speak to an individual who stated, "There is a big secret out here." CI-183 also was informed by Zara Patterson IV that James Ellison was now residing at Elohim City, however, CI-183 did not see him. Ellison was the former leader of the Covenant, Sword and Arm of the Lord in Arkansas. CI-183 stated that he/she viewed the freshly dug grave of Snell, the man executed in Arkansas on April 19, 1995 for the slaying of an Arkansas trooper. CI-183 was informed that Robert Millar had attended the execution and transported the body to his compound for burial. CI-183 stated that individuals spoken with were supportive of the bombing of the building in Oklahoma City.

On May 18, 1995 this agent met with CI-183 to discuss returning to Elohim City in order to determine what the "big secret" is and to attempt to identify suspect #2.

On May 22, 1995 this agent was contacted by CI-183 who stated that he/she had been contacted the previous day and informed that he/she had better not go to Elohim City. CI-183 stated that the person called again on this day and gave him/her the same warning. CI-183 did not reveal the source at this time. CI-183 then stated that he/she had seen the numerous television broadcasts about Elohim City and was too frightened to go.

On May 24, 1995 this agent was informed by RAC, David Roberts that Robert Millar suspected CI-183 of being a confidential informant. It was determined that CI-183 would not be sent to Elohim City at this time or in the future.

This investigation to remain open.

AFT report from Carol Howe showing the approval of the Oklahoma City bomb in Elohim City, and her knowledge of a "big secret."

DEPARTMENT OF THE TREASURY
BUREAU OF ALCOHOL, TOBACCO AND FIREARMS

125 West 15th Street, Suite 500
Tulsa, Oklahoma 74119-3822

April 22, 1996

Refer to

MEMORANDUM TO: Special Agent in Charge
Dallas Field Division

THRU: David E. Roberts, Resident Agent
Tulsa Field Office

FROM: Special Agent Angela Graham
Tulsa Field Office

SUBJECT: Threat Assessment for CI 53270-183

This informant is involved with the OKC bomb case which is pending prosecution in Denver and was the key in identifying individuals at Elohim City, which is tied to the OKC bomb case. The majority of the associates of CI 52705-183 are militia members.

CI 53270-183 has no criminal record.

The threat to CI 5270-183 comes from the release of his/her identity by the FBI to Timothy McVeigh's defense attorney. CI 53270-183 told this agent that s/he has been receiving suspicious phone calls; has been followed on numerous occasions; and has had frequent unidentified visitors. CI 53270-183 stated that Dennis Mahon, area leader of White Aryan Nation has stated that he knew there was a snitch he had been dealing with in the past. This CI thought he was referring to him/her.

The FBI is the lead agency on this case, however, many other federal state and local agencies are involved. Individuals who pose immediate danger to CI 53270-183 are: (1) Dennis Mahon, (2) members of Elohim City, and (3) any sympathizer to McVeigh, i.e., militias.

CI 5270-183 has expressed a great deal of concern for his/her safety, although s/he is in fear because of serious threats made by former and current associates regarding the discovery of a "snitch".

This agent has known CI 53270-183 for approximately two years and can assert that this informant has not been overly paranoid or fearful during undercover operations. This agent believes that s/he could be in serious danger when associates discover his/her identity.

Angela S. Graham

AFT memo regarding threats to informant Carol Howe.

From Feral House

Virtual Government
CIA Mind Control Operations in America
Alex Constantine

Mind control dwells in a twilit zone of so-called "alien invasions," "zombie killers," "cult murder/suicides," "remote viewing," and "lone nut assassinations." Remarkable researcher Alex Constantine connects the dots on such crimes as CIA experiments on children, the infestation of American media by intelligence operatives, the mob/drug connection to the murder of Nicole Simpson, and the integration of Nazis into U.S. government operations. "Alex Constatine is the foremost journalist and contemporary historian of the murky worlds of vice and vice-squads." — Donald Freed
301 pages • $14.95 • ISBN: 0-922915-45-8

The Octopus
Secret Government and the Death of Danny Casolaro
Kenn Thomas and Jim Keith

Casolaro was murdered by sinister forces as he was researching his unfinished book, *The Octopus*. This volume picks up Casolaro's existing notes, retracing his fatal steps, from investigating stolen police software to bizarre murders in tribal lands to dirty tricks accomplished through the notorious Wackenhut security firm.
181 pages • photos • hardcover • $19.95 • ISBN: 0-922915-39-3

Cult Rapture
Adam Parfrey

"From cults and conspiracies to isolated loons, from fakes and grifters to the painfully sincere and the seriously terrifying, Parfrey lucidly exploresthe nation's rarely acknowledged subcultures." —Katherine Dunn. "Plumb loco from start to finish and wonderfully entertaining, *Cult Rapture* is some kind of instant classic." — *Loaded* magazine. Editor's Pick: Utne Reader.
371 pages • photos • $14.95 • ISBN: 0-922915-22-9

The titles above may be ordered from Feral House for check or money order plus $2 each book for shipping. For a free catalogue, send an SASE. Credit card orders: call Atomic Books (800) 778-6246.

Feral House • 2532 Lincoln Blvd. #359 • Venice • CA • 90291